Policy Analysis in
National Security Affairs

Policy Analysis in National Security Affairs
New Methods for a New Era

by Richard L. Kugler

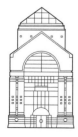

PUBLISHED FOR THE
CENTER FOR TECHNOLOGY AND SECURITY POLICY
BY NATIONAL DEFENSE UNIVERSITY PRESS
WASHINGTON, D.C.
2006

This is the official U.S. Government edition of this publication and is herein identified to certify its authenticity. Use of ISBN 1-57906-070-6 is for U.S. Government Printing Office Official Editions only. The Superintendent of Documents of the U.S. Government Printing Office requests that any reprinted edition clearly be labeled as a copy of the authentic work with a new ISBN.

Library of Congress Cataloging-in-Publication Data

Kugler, Richard L.
    Policy analysis in national security affairs : new methods for a new era / by Richard L. Kugler.
        p. cm.
    Includes bibliographical references and index.
    ISBN 1–57906–070–6
        1. National security—Methodology. 2. National security—United States—Methodology.
    I. Title.
    UA10.5.K84 2006
    355'.03—dc22

                                        2006044405

First Printing, June 2006

For sale by the Superintendent of Documents, U.S. Government Printing Office
Internet: bookstore.gpo.gov Phone: toll free (866) 512-1800; Washington, DC area (202) 512-1800
Fax: (202) 512-2250 Mail: Stop SSOP, Washington, DC 20402-0001
ISBN 1-57906-070-6

Contents

Illustrations

Tables

Figures

Dedicated to Leo A. Stapleton, MD:
father-in-law, friend, and counselor.

Preface

This book is intended to help fill a void in the literature while making a contribution to public awareness. Most books on national security affairs focus on
substantive issues, such as nuclear proliferation, arguing in favor of one policy or
another. This book addresses something more basic: how to conduct policy analysis in the field of national security, including foreign policy and defense strategy. It illuminates how key methods of analysis can be employed, by experts and
nonexperts, to focus widely, address small details, or do both at the same time.
To my knowledge, there is no other book quite like it.

This is not a recipe book for measuring and calculating or for otherwise employing
techniques and procedures. Along the way, it covers these facets of policy analysis, but
it is not mainly about them. Instead, it is a philosophical and conceptual book for
helping people think deeply, clearly, and insightfully about complex policy issues. It
is anchored in the premise that knowing how to think enhances the odds of reaching
sound judgments. Thus, it is a thinking person's book because thinking is the well-
spring of good policy analysis. While this book is written to be reader-friendly,
it aspires to in-depth scholarship. It takes its subject and its readers seriously by
endeavoring to put forth material that captures the full richness of policy analysis in
this important field.

If this book has to be placed on the political spectrum, it should be seen at the bipar-
tisan center of opinion. As such, it will provide little ammunition to those who portray
the debate over national security policy and defense strategy as a polarized clash between
competing ideologies: between liberals and conservatives, or between idealists and
realists. This book reflects the viewpoint that the best policies normally come from
efforts to synthesize competing camps by drawing upon the best from each of them
and by combining them to forge a sensible whole. Its pages offer new-era methods for
pursuing visionary goals in ways that are coherent, balanced, effective, and efficient.
These are the hallmarks of policies that can actually achieve their aims rather than dissolve into failure.

To a degree, this book reflects my personal experience: over three decades in the
national security field, principally at the Department of Defense and RAND, and as an
adjunct professor of international affairs at two major universities. Along the way, I have
written many studies, published books and articles, advised senior officials of six administrations, supervised analytical staffs, participated in policy reviews, directed major
research projects, helped create new strategic concepts, and taught hundreds of graduate
students and government employees.

From this experience, I have come away with three conclusions. The first is that
the U.S. Government will continue to face many difficult decisions in the national

security arena because the future is hard to see, and the consequences of alternative policies are hard to predict. Second, systematic analysis can help improve the quality of these decisions—sometimes only marginally, but sometimes hugely. In particular, it can help the Government think clearly at times of uncertainty and during noisy debates about policy and strategy. But it can do so only if it responds to the changing times and if its diverse analytical methods are used together. Third, there has long been a crying need for a book of this sort. Virtually all academic disciplines have many books on analytical methods, but national security policy does not. Time and again, a forward-looking, multidiscipline book on methods could have helped to educate practitioners and contribute to important policy studies.

This book is written in the hope that it will result in better trained people, sounder analyses, and wiser policies. The Cold War generation has, by now, the benefit of years in this field, but a new generation of young Americans is arriving that lacks such experience. They will need all the help they can get. Perhaps this book can help them.

Three or four decades ago, this field was the subject of considerable intellectual ferment and publishing, but this has not been the case since the 1970s. Perhaps the reason was a general feeling that enough had already been said about analytical methods for the Cold War. But the Cold War has passed into history, and an entirely new era has arrived that will demand analytical methods of its own, many of them different from those of the past. If this book helps trigger interest in others to write books on this topic, so much the better.

I am grateful for the support provided by Hans Binnendijk and the Center for Technology and National Security Policy at the National Defense University. I want to thank Paul K. Davis, Christopher Lamb, and Stuart Johnson for helpful reviews of the entire book, and others for comments on various aspects of it. I want to thank Teresa Lawson for her superb editing. I also want to thank National Defense University Press for its help in bringing this book to publication. My wife, Sharon Stapleton, has my gratitude both for technical help and for her support throughout. I am hugely indebted to the many government professionals, scholars, and students who have helped sharpen my thinking in countless ways over the years. William Kaufmann and Robert Komer deserve special mention because they were mentors early in my career, when help was especially needed. I extend my thanks to them and to everybody else. I remain solely responsible for this book's contents.

– Richard L. Kugler
Washington, DC

Policy Analysis in
National Security Affairs

Chapter 1
Why This Book is Necessary

In November 2004, President George W. Bush was reelected, defeating his Demo-cratic rival, Senator John F. Kerry. In sharp contrast to the three previous campaigns since 1992, which focused on domestic policy, the 2004 campaign focused on na-tional security affairs. Future Presidential campaigns are likely to do the same, and in the years between elections, national security will be a daily preoccupation of the U.S. Government and a constant concern of citizens everywhere.

In today's world, the challenges facing U.S. national policy are truly daunting because so much is demanded and expected. Success is essential, and mistakes can be fatal. Because the United States is a global superpower acting in a world that is often dangerous, it needs sound national security policies. But how will it know when its policies are sound? It cannot risk failure by trying them out in order to see whether they work. It must figure out beforehand, as much as possible, whether its policies are wise and likely to succeed. This is the role of policy analysis.

U.S. national security policy is the subject of voluminous books, journal articles, and newspaper columns. Surprisingly, however, few recent publications address how policy analysis in this field is best carried out. There is even less material on the meth-odologies that can be used during a policy analysis to evaluate the important choices facing the United States and other countries. This book takes a step toward remedying that deficiency. In providing guidance on how to perform policy analysis today, this book identifies a spectrum of relevant analytical methods from three different academic dis-ciplines: strategic evaluation, systems analysis, and operations research. It portrays their key features, assets, and liabilities in some depth so that readers, from college students to professionals, can become aware of the large menu of analytical tools available and how these tools can be used. Its purpose thus is educational, rather than to advocate any particular method, much less to endorse specific policies.

The Importance of Policy Analysis

The U.S.-led invasion of Iraq in early 2003 cast a spotlight on the importance of policy analysis because forging a strategy for it illuminated the demanding intellectual challenges of national security policy. The invasion was an assertive exercise in strategic conduct: the United States, acting in the face of great complexity, was trying to gain con-trol over a deteriorating situation in the Middle East. This demanded use of analytical tools to craft a complex strategy for the invasion, for the diplomacy that preceded it, and for the continuing presence that followed it, as well as for an accompanying long-term effort to bring democracy and peace to the Middle East.

Because the United States sought to mold events rather than merely react to them, most aspects of its demanding strategy had to be devised before the main actions got under way. Although considerable analytical effort was devoted to developing this strategy and its multiple components, decisions had to be made in the face of considerable uncertainty. Once taken, they set irreversibly into motion a widespread chain reaction that the United States could only partly control. The United States thus entered the crisis both empowered and constrained by its strategy. It knew that it stood a good chance of succeeding if it had calculated correctly, but that it might face trouble if it had judged incorrectly.

The military phase of the invasion was swift and successful. Afterward, however, troubles arose during the continued U.S. presence in Iraq owing not only to insurgent opposition, but also to the serious political, economic, and social problems existing there, all of which posed tough obstacles to the installation of democracy. The United States found itself making frequent adjustments to its strategy, often shifting directions in response to the sheer dynamism and difficulty of the situation, while spending more time, blood, and treasure than originally anticipated.

Events as difficult and controversial as the invasion of Iraq may not be common in the years ahead, but there will nevertheless be a continuing need for complex, prearranged strategies in peace, crisis, and war. Such strategies will need to be formed without the convenient certitudes of the Cold War. Uncertainty about many things will often be a dominant theme, and the situation abroad will seldom make the best policy and strategy obvious. Thus, the United States will need to make tough strategic choices, and it will find itself the beneficiary or victim of its own thinking and planning, much of which will need to be done beforehand in the face of fluidity and confusion, or during difficult involvements that resist easy solutions.

The need to get such thinking right is a core reason why policy analysis is so important in the early 21st century. No amount of analysis can wipe away uncertainty, nor can analysis prevent controversy about policy choices or alter the reality that hindsight will always be better than foresight. But policy analysis can help the U.S. Government make the wisest and most effective national security decisions possible. This is its promise and its potential.

Purposes of this Book

In today's globalizing world of accelerating change and mounting complexity, the United States is compelled to think and react faster than ever before and to take actions that rapidly have far-reaching consequences. It often faces great pressure to commit itself quickly to a course of action in situations where the room for trial and error is rapidly narrowing. As a result, its need for sophisticated policy analysis in national security affairs is growing, yet awareness of how to practice this demanding art and science at high levels of government and for big-time policies is not widespread. Few universities teach the subject in-depth. Many government officials wish they knew more about it, but the experienced practitioners of the Cold War generation are headed toward retirement. Years ago, literature on the subject was published, but it is now old, rusty, and covered with barnacles. There is also another cause for concern. When U.S. national security policy is criticized today, the common reason is not that its values and visions are lacking, but that its analyses are flawed and its actions are unwise. The U.S. Government may do a better job of evaluating its policies and strategies than most other governments, but it could undoubtedly do better.

This book is written in the hope of helping improve upon today's situation and filling a cavernous gap in the professional literature. It provides an appraisal of methods that can be employed to analyze issues ranging from the lofty abstractions of national security policy and strategy to the concrete specifics of plans, programs, and budgets. It is not a book on theoretical methods in the abstract, but rather a book on applied methods: real-world tools for studying contemporary policy issues and options and helping to resolve debates about them. It suggests ways to make policy analyses not only insightful but relevant as well. It is written for anybody who wants to learn about this important field, including youngsters and graybeards.

Why does this book focus on something as forbidding-sounding as analytical methods? The answer goes beyond the fact that these methods are not as forbidding as they sound. A good national security study advances not just conclusions and recommendations, but also the reasons for them. But where do these reasons come from, and why are they valid? Often they are generated by methodologies, which are intellectual engines for thinking in orderly, productive, and creative ways. The better the methodology and its associated thought-tools, the better the ideas flowing from a study will be. Mastering methodology means acquiring powerful tools for preparing sound and influential analyses.

The business of forging national security policy has two main components: first, determining how the United States should use its powers abroad to pursue its goals, and second, determining how the United States should spend money in order to build its military posture, defense strategy, and other related assets. Both of these components and their interrelationships are addressed in this book. It thus touches upon many important issues that are constantly being debated at high levels within the U.S. Government as well as on the front pages of newspapers, among them:

- How can the United States best create a national security strategy to guide its conduct in world affairs in the coming years?

- How can it best blend its political diplomacy, military power, and foreign economic policies to carry out this national security strategy?

- How can it craft policies for encouraging reform of its alliances in Europe and Asia?

- What are its best policies for dealing with Russia and China, and for handling tyrants and terrorists in the Middle East and elsewhere?

- How can it promote economic progress and democracy in poor regions?

- How can it shape its military posture to carry out national defense strategy most effectively?

- How should it transform its military forces for the information age?

- How can it reorganize its ground forces to prepare them for joint expeditionary warfare?

- How can it afford the expensive but necessary procurement effort required to modernize its air and naval forces?

- How can it determine its priorities for national missile defense?

- How can it design an overseas military presence for the future?

- How can it best develop plans for conducting military interventions in distant crisis spots?

As the book describes these issues, it puts forth ideas for new policies from time to time. But its agenda is not to recast U.S. foreign policy and defense strategy in some particular way. Instead, its focus on methods provides something more enduring: insights on how to analyze these questions, how to forge sensible answers to them, and how to evaluate policy options for responding to them. It offers a set of tools that can be used to analyze a wide range of issues, including those that lie in the distant and indistinct future.

Policy analysis and its methods are aids to wise judgment, not a replacement for it. They are only as good as the people who use them and the information given to them. Because world politics and military affairs are changing rapidly, policy analysis and its methods must change as well. They will need to grapple with the issues ahead, not merely perpetuate the practices of the past. The task of determining how to make these changes makes this field interesting and exciting.

Three Methods for Multidisciplinary Analysis

This book surveys three categories of methods for national security analysis: strategic evaluation, systems analysis, and operations research. Arrayed across a wide spectrum of purposes and degrees of formality, these methods are equipped with differing conceptual lenses, research languages, and analytical models.

Strategic evaluation uses political analysis to identify policies that can achieve national goals. Strategic evaluation methods are commonly used by political analysts to appraise basic choices facing U.S. foreign policy and national security strategy. An example is an analysis of how the United States might best forge an overall global national security strategy aimed at reforming its democratic alliances for new security missions, preserving stable relations with Russia and China, containing new threats in the greater Middle East, and promoting progress in Latin America.

Systems analysis uses economic analysis to show how policies can be translated into plans and programs. Systems analysis methods are commonly used by managers, economists, and others to address macroeconomic choices in the formation of defense plans and programs. An example is how the United States might best pursue the transformation of its military forces in order to modernize its air forces while making its ground forces more mobile and agile.

Operations research uses mathematical analysis to derive, from plans and programs, specific implementation steps and resource allocation priorities. Operations research methods are commonly used by mathematicians and others to examine defense resource allocation issues when details about cost and performance are critical. An example is how the United States could best deploy limited ballistic missile defenses through a combination of midcourse interceptors and boost-phase interceptors.

This book describes a family of subordinate analytical methods in each category. It portrays their contents, discusses where they can be applied effectively, identifies their assets and limits, and shows how they can be used by experts and nonexperts alike. This book thereby offers readers an opportunity to become familiar with the tools of this important discipline, both individually and as a whole. It is intended to be the kind of book that professionals choose to keep handy, but it also offers an opportunity for the general reader to learn about these analytical methods and the modern-day policy issues that they confront.

As the book shows, these three methods are not completely different disciplines. Rather, they often overlap in important ways, and they share many things in common. It can sometimes be difficult to specify where strategic evaluation leaves off and systems analysis begins, or where systems analysis becomes an exercise in operations research. In fact, some of the best studies in national security policy employ elements of all three methods. Even so, the methods are sufficiently distinct in their core perspectives and techniques to justify viewing them separately. The act of seeing them as separate and distinct is a good way to begin learning about them, to appreciate their individual strengths and limits, and to grasp how they can be blended together when the situation warrants.

The days are gone in which foreign policy, defense strategy, military forces, technologies, and budgets could be treated as separate domains. In order to bring them together to form a composite whole, multidisciplinary analysis is needed. Therefore, in addition to urging reform of these three methods individually, this book argues that, rather than viewing them as separate disciplines to be applied to separate problems, they now must be fused so that they can collaborate to address the complex policy challenges ahead.

The idea of such integrated thinking and analysis is not new, but it has mostly been neglected. Too often, the consequence has been stovepiped analysis and fragmented policy responses. By bringing these three methods together where they can be seen in relation to each other, this book is intended to help readers see how to use them together.

The Role of Policy Analysis and Its Methods

This book reflects the premise that systematic policy analysis truly matters in the real world of government decisionmaking. National security policies can seldom be explained solely in terms of rational calculations; many other factors enter the equation, including a country's geopolitical setting, its resources, and its internal politics. Yet within this framework, the U.S. Government and other countries normally try to weigh rationally the policy alternatives open to them and to select the options that will best advance national interests and goals. Policy analyses can and often do play influential roles in the decisionmaking process, which can be improved by subjecting alternative options to inquiry about their aims and expectations. Participants in the process spend much time analyzing key issues and options, and in their debates, the winners often are those who marshal the most convincing arguments. For all these reasons, careful attention to how policy analysis is best conducted makes sense.

The purpose of analytical methods is to improve the quality of policy analysis. To some, the term *analytical methods* suggests forbidding scientific tools usable only by the cognoscenti. To others, it means a frivolous academic exercise in arcane rituals that has no relevance in the real world. These impressions are understandable, but they are wrong. When the man in the street thinks about government policies, he employs a methodology of some sort—that is, a pattern of thinking intended to bring order to the subject. Whether simple or complex, methodologies are cut from the same cloth. They are neither arcane nor unapproachable. Indeed, they can be learned with modest effort, and they can be applied by people who have a solid grasp of the policy issues at hand, even if they are not steeped in the philosophy of science.

Within the academic community, the study of national security affairs often takes the form of empirical research aimed at developing theories regarding how nations and other actors behave in this arena. Political scientists, for example, are often preoccupied by such issues as whether an old-era alliance tends to fall apart when a new era dissolves the threats that formerly menaced it. Another prominent question is whether multipolar international systems eventually become bipolar and do so in ways that explode into war. Empirical-minded economists address such issues as whether, and how, the emergence of a hotly competitive world economy can bring prosperity to poor regions and thereby enhance chances for peace. In both disciplines, scholars hope that their research will not only help build theories of international politics and economics, but also prove relevant to government policymaking by answering questions of critical importance. The policy advice that they offer tends to be general, not specific. The analytical methods employed by them are intended to facilitate their kind of research, and properly so.[1]

Such empirical research can be both relevant and immensely helpful. Indeed, such research can be a key input to policy analysis by defining the strategic situation facing the United States. The U.S. Intelligence Community engages in considerable research of this kind when it produces estimates of trends abroad.

Yet empirical research is different from policy analysis, which aspires to help guide specific choices about concrete policies. Not surprisingly, the methods of policy analysis differ appreciably from those of empirical scholarship. Whereas the latter are designed to investigate cause-and-effect relationships between variables, the methods of policy analysis are designed to weigh the relationship between actions and consequences, as well as the comparative values of alternative policy options. Policy analysis often employs empirical scholarship to help sharpen its judgments, but its unique features make it a wholly separate discipline unto itself. Books providing empirical analyses of national security issues are common. So are books providing substantive evaluations of U.S. policies. But a book on methods for policy analysis for national security is rare.

This book is unique for another reason. In public policy fields other than national security, books on methods typically cover only one discipline. This book, by contrast, discusses the analytical methods of three quite different disciplines. It thus offers broader coverage than usual. The three methods discussed here—strategic evaluation, systems analysis with economic models of choice, and mathematical operations research—come from different disciplines, but they are complementary. They allow the analyst to focus widely or narrowly, to measure just as precisely as necessary, and to present findings and conclusions with appropriate degrees of formality. Within their domains, each offers multiple techniques that can be used for the study at hand. Together, these methods cover the full spectrum of how most policy analyses are conducted.

Knowledge of these methods can help seasoned professionals as well as aspiring beginners to perform better. Many practitioners have received little, if any, formal training in the methods of policy analysis. Even most of those who have received training were educated in only one discipline; most people from the fields of political science, managerial economics, or operations research tend to know only the methods of their own field, not those of the others. Knowing the methods of all three disciplines greatly expands the range of issues that analysts can address and strengthens their capacity to probe deeply. These are key skills in this field, and they also are keys to forging sound policies.

Why Thinking in Multidisciplinary Terms Makes Sense

U.S. Government agencies that handle national security affairs unquestionably face a compelling need for multidisciplinary analyses and for trained people capable of performing such analyses. Owing to globalization and other dynamics, the time has long gone when national security issues could be broken into separate bailiwicks—political, economic, military, or budgetary—and their work parceled out to stovepiped bureaucracies that seldom deal with one another, much less collaborate together. In today's world of overlapping policies, such isolation and lack of integrated analysis are a ticket to failure. Many policy issues start out as political and strategic, but once their broad parameters are established, they become managerial and economic. Thereafter they become budgetary, technical, and quantitative. This three-stage evolution cannot be successfully guided if separate bureaucracies, each trained in handling only one stage, lack the skills to coordinate the transition from that stage to the next. The result too often is strategic policies of one sort, economic and managerial policies of a different sort, and budgetary policies of yet another sort. As a result, the U.S. Government may wind up committing major resources to a strategic problem and yet not achieve its goals because the three stages of its policy operate in separate domains toward inconsistent purposes.[2]

For similar reasons, think tanks and consulting firms in national security need cross-disciplinary talents. Inside the Beltway, organizations perform political-strategic analysis, or economic and managerial analysis, or mathematical operations research, but only a small number of firms aspire to perform all three functions skillfully. The resulting lack of intellectual cross-fertilization weakens the quality of analytical advice flowing into the government, leaving it with fragmented views of policy issues.

Even within the establishments that do perform all three functions—RAND is one example—practical problems arise in forming multidiscipline teams. Such teams are often composed of people who each grasp only one discipline or another and thus have not learned how to work together effectively in collaborative ways. Corporate financial flows can also make it hard to keep talented staffs in all three areas. Such firms draw most of their money from external sponsorship of research projects, often by the Department of Defense (DOD). In any single year, these projects typically ebb and flow in response to ongoing policy debates and the need for timely analyses of them. In one year, ample money can be available for strategic evaluations, but not for economic analysis or operations research. The next year, funds for strategic evaluations may dry up, while funds for economic analysis and operations research surge. It can be hard to keep talented people employed when their talents are not in immediate demand. The result can be fast staff turnover, damaging the firm's continuity and analytical resources. The solution is to employ analysts who can move skillfully from one intellectual discipline to the next, but such people are rare. For practical business reasons, training them makes sense.

Making Use of This Book in an Era of Change

This book responds to the growing need for multidisciplinary talent in national security affairs. While it does not cover all analytical methodologies worth addressing, it does cover a robust spectrum of those that are relevant and potent. It is written for a professional audience, but its contents are intended to be understood by graduate students, undergraduates, and the interested citizen.

The next chapter provides a brief overview of policy analysis and its methods. The main part of the book is then organized into three major sections. The first examines how strategic evaluation methods can be used to analyze issues and options facing U.S. national security policy and strategy. The second addresses how the methods of systems analysis can be used to address defense plans and programs. The third and final main section examines the methods of operations research and how they can be used to address defense resource allocation issues. Each section has some chapters that explain the relevant method as a stand-alone technique, while others are decidedly multidisciplinary, showing how all three methods can be blended and used to illuminate the issues and options. The book concludes with a chapter that sketches ideas for how the teaching and practice of policy analysis can be strengthened within the academic community and the U.S. Government.

Together, the book's chapters address both foreign policy and defense strategy, showing how analytical methods can be used in both domains. Some chapters examine the theory of the three analytical methods under discussion, and others show how these methods can be applied to examine key trends, issues, and options in multiple arenas of contemporary U.S. national security policy. Some chapters contain ideas for new policies, strategies, and programs; these appear not as an exercise in advocacy, but rather to help illuminate the choices, priorities, and uses of analysis ahead.

A dominant theme underlies and animates all of this book's pages. Although many analytical methods from the past will remain relevant, the winds of change are blowing over this profession as well as over U.S. national security policy as a whole. If the United States is to remain secure in a future of great dangers and opportunities, knowledge and wisdom are required because physical resources alone will not be enough. New forms of analysis and new methods are needed. The analytical profession must rise to this challenge. Without pretending to exhaust the subject, this book tries to outline both old and new methods. In calling for new methods, it does not throw out the baby with the bathwater. In many cases, the basic foundations of old methods should be preserved, but in order to update them, they should be configured with new superstructures of concepts, thought-tools, and measuring sticks. To the extent this book succeeds in articulating an agenda of change while educating readers, it will have served its purpose.

Notes

[1] See Stephen Van Evera, *Guide to Methods for Students of Political Science* (Ithaca, NY: Cornell University Press, 1997). For analysis of contemporary debates, see Fareed Zakaria, ed., *Foreign Affairs Agenda: The New Shape of World Politics* (New York: Foreign Affairs Books/Norton, 1997). See also Robert O. Keohane, ed., *Neorealism and Its Critics* (New York: Columbia University Press, 1986). For a recent theoretical effort, see John J. Mearsheimer, *The Tragedy of Great Power Politics* (New York: W.W. Norton, 2001).

[2] For analysis of the need for interdepartmental coordination in national security affairs, see Stephen J. Flanagan, Ellen L. Frost, and Richard L. Kugler, *Challenges of the Global Century: Report of the Project on Globalization* (Washington, DC: National Defense University Press, 2001). See also *The National Security Strategy of the United States of America* (Washington, DC: The White House, 2002).

Chapter 2

Policy Analysis and Methodology: A Necessary Discipline for the Future

E xactly what is the discipline of policy analysis, and how do its methodologies contribute to its products? To answer these questions, this chapter begins by discussing how the strategic setting of today's world shapes the agenda facing policy analysis. Then, it examines the essence of policy analysis in national security affairs, as well as its uses and abuses. Finally, it discusses the methods of strategic evaluation, systems analysis, and operations research, including their features and contributions.

The Strategic Setting

A century ago, most Americans would have dismissed the notion that their country needed a vigorous national security policy in order to assert control of events far beyond its borders. Although President Theodore Roosevelt was trying to establish the United States as a global power, his vision was not widely shared. Most of his countrymen accepted George Washington's admonition that the country should stand aloof from foreign entanglements.

By the middle of the 20th century, most Americans had acquired a different view. They accepted the need for a strong national security policy. The experiences of World War I, World War II, and the early Cold War taught them to reject isolationism and to recognize that their physical security, economic prosperity, and democratic freedoms were vulnerable to events aboard. Still, however, they viewed national security in traditional terms of protecting America's shores and overseas commercial relationships and of helping defend close allies in Europe and Asia. The general view defined national security policy in terms of limited geographic zones beyond which the United States did not have much at stake. The Middle East, South Asia, and Central Asia were seen as well beyond America's national interests and outside its strategic perimeter.

Another half-century later, the difference is profound: the United States still has traditional interests, but beginning in the last two decades of the 20th century, new interests appeared beyond the old strategic perimeter. Testimony to this staggering change is the fact that U.S. forces recently invaded and are still present in Afghanistan, a country once thought to be as remote from U.S. interests as any place in the world. Today, as the United States pursues safety, prosperity, peace, and the spread of democratic values, it does so in many new places. Efforts to set limits on U.S. strategic interests and involvements have been rendered obsolete by world affairs, almost before the ink had dried.

Like it or not, the United States is now truly a global power. Its foreign policy and diplomacy are carried out worldwide, and it has acquired national security stakes in multiple regions. Although some of these interests are less vital than others, many are now deemed important enough for the United States to spend blood and treasure in their defense. Distant places often involve derivative interests, that is, interests that may not themselves be vital but that are critical to prevent threats from arising to truly vital interests. For example, the United States had a vital interest in removing the Taliban regime not because Afghanistan was vital, but because al Qaeda operatives there threatened the U.S. homeland. Globalization has made such distant interests important, as it brings the entire world closer together and washes away the illusion of distance. Because the United States has become vulnerable to events in so many new places, it has little choice but to be involved across a broad landscape. This profound transformation in interests and involvement has greatly magnified the agenda for U.S. national security policy and strategy for the early 21st century. The United States must now carry out a vast array of national security policies. All of them require not only physical resources but also expert knowledge. This demand for knowledge drives today's growing need for sophisticated policy analysis in this arena. Simply stated, the agenda facing policy analysis is larger, more complex, and more demanding than ever confronted before.

The Essence of Policy Analysis

A national security policy is an organized action or an integrated set of actions—from making public declarations to waging war—intended to bring about favorable consequences that will help achieve articulated national goals. Such goals can range from protecting a country's borders to conquering its enemies. Policy analysis is a concerted effort to investigate the core properties of alternative policies. It can be conducted within the government or outside it, by advocates or by critics who want to get new policies adopted. Good policy analysis probes intently into policies: not only their goals and activities, but their rationales and results as well.[1]

One of the most important functions of policy analysis is often to help identify new goals to be pursued abroad or old goals that need fresh efforts. Policy analysis may call attention to emerging threats and challenges to key U.S. goals or to opportunities emerging in the near term, the midterm, or the distant future. Another main function of policy analysis is to determine how key goals can be pursued in the most effective and efficient manner possible. Policy analysis can compare alternative approaches and options, and discern how they perform in relation to each other. It can help determine how new technologies can be developed and applied to national purposes. It can be helpful in determining how multiple programmatic efforts in different arenas can be blended together to serve a common purpose. It can help monitor policies as they are being implemented, provide midcourse guidance on how to correct them, and determine when they should be terminated.

The Purpose of Policy Analysis

Policy analysis seeks answers to key questions, such as those outlined in table 2–1. A serious policy analysis aimed at answering such questions takes time and labor. Its preparatory steps include surveying relevant literature and opinions, posing explicit questions, gathering data and information, and mobilizing help from colleagues as well as other sources. In the middle phase comes a focused process of investigation and reasoning that employs analytical methods, including those described in this book, to produce insightful,

Table 2–1. **Key Questions in Policy Analysis**

What goals does a particular policy seek to achieve, and why?

What activities will this policy carry out, what resources will it need, and what will they cost?

What are the reasons for believing that the policy's proposed actions will attain its goals?

What are the potential consequences of this policy, intended and otherwise?

To what degree is the policy likely to be effective?

What will be its cost-effectiveness—the balance between resources expended and goals attained?

What is the risk that the policy will fail or even make the situation worse?

What are the risks that, even if it achieves its own aims, the policy will damage other goals in other arenas, and perhaps do more harm than good?

All things considered, will this policy yield a satisfactory achievement of its goals at an acceptable price?

How does it compare to other policy options that seek the same goals with different activities and costs?

Would another policy be equally effective and cost less, or cost the same and achieve more?

If no clear winner emerges among several options, how can their tradeoffs be assessed?

On balance, which option makes best sense?

reliable results. At the end comes the effort to disseminate the results, which can have a lengthy dynamic of its own.

Knowledge of the methods of the profession is not enough; the best policy analysis cannot normally be carried out by "hired guns" not steeped in the substantive issues at hand. Experts on the substantive issues, however, can profit hugely by practicing this tradecraft. Especially when the policy issues are complex and demanding, the techniques of policy analysis can be indispensable. Scholars in the academic community know that when they write and speak about national security policy choices, their work is best prepared, and is best received, when it is anchored in systematic analysis. For similar reasons, important national security studies in the government are seldom simply tossed together; normally they are conducted as organized analyses.

Even when a good policy analysis has been produced and has identified a strong option, senior officials must set their own priorities and must often consider matters that go beyond the scope of the analysis. The President or Cabinet members, for example, must fit a particular policy into the overall goals and priorities of the administration. After a policy option has been embraced, it must then be implemented, a process that can be lengthy and complicated. A new departure in foreign policy might require prolonged activities by the State Department and overseas Embassies, including complex negotiations with allies and adversaries. A new departure in defense policy might require procurement of new forces, new weapons, new logistic support systems, and new bases at home and abroad, an effort that could take years. Good policy analysis thus is not synonymous with good decisions or with effective execution. However, it helps set the stage for both.

Serious policy analysis in national security affairs first entered the U.S. Government in the early 1960s, under Secretary of Defense Robert McNamara. Since then, it has experienced ups and downs. It is no longer viewed as a miracle worker, but its contributions are sought and welcomed. Multiple staffs in the Department of Defense—assigned to the Office of the Secretary of Defense, the Joint Staff, and the services—perform studies and analyses full-time, as do similar staffs at the State Department, the intelligence agencies, the National Security Council staff, and Congress. Outside the government, many consulting firms provide analytical services for hire, and such think tanks as the Brookings Institution and the Heritage Foundation publish a regular stream of books and papers. This field of inquiry and its professional practices are not going away any time soon. Indeed, in today's topsy-turvy world, modern-day policy analysis is more necessary than ever.

Policy analysis is both an art and a science. In contrast with scholarly inquiry, which normally is empirical and aims to describe and explain phenomena and to contemplate the future, policy analysis is normative and prescriptive. Unlike academic disciplines that may prize their detachment from public affairs, policy analysis seeks engagement and policy relevance. It evaluates the policy choices facing the United States, and it often recommends a course of action. Indeed, some of the best policy analyses have proposed innovative strategic departures that break sharply from the status quo. But even when innovation is being sought, good policy analysis is not an exercise in arm-waving or one-sided advocacy. Instead, it is reasoned, disciplined, and fair to all sides. A policy analysis may confirm the status quo, or modify it slightly, or overthrow it entirely, or urge nothing at all. What matters is not what an analysis recommends, but the enlightenment that it offers. Above all, it must be honest and objective in its treatment of issues and options; these are characteristics it shares with good scholarship. Good analysis aims to enhance understanding, not to replace the need for sensible instincts and reasoned decisions by senior officials. While it may favor one policy, it should be explicit about its own assumptions and biases, and it should acknowledge the conditions under which other options might be better choices. When analysis embraces these virtues, it can be helpful in guiding the selection and pursuit of national security policies.

Because of its quest for relevance, policy analysis is judged by a different standard than academic research. The core purpose of scholarly research within the academic community is to contribute to the search for truth and to improve mankind's understanding of the world. In its ethics, policy analysis shares this commitment to truth and enlightenment. But in terms of its functional role, its ultimate purpose is to help the government conduct its foreign policy more wisely and use its strategic power more effectively.

Few seasoned observers would question the proposition that in the United States, policy analysis performs this function reasonably well, or at least better than in most other countries. Foreigners often remark how the U.S. Government has a much larger analytical community at its disposal than do their governments. They believe that this community makes a difference in the quality of U.S. policy, and they are right. In today's world, foreign policy and national security strategy are knowledge-based. More than ever before, knowledge is essential for a country to use its physical resources effectively abroad. Technology, money, and military power are not enough. Policy analysis, when it does its job well, helps provide knowledge for using such resources to maximum advantage. This is the reason why so much emphasis is placed on policy analysis by the United States today, and why foreign governments often wish that they had better analytical resources at their disposal. It is also the reason why policy analysis in the U.S. Government, and in other governments, needs to be strengthened. Good analysis does not guarantee an effective policy any more than it guarantees peace. But it can improve the odds for success. It can help ensure that if a country goes to war, for example, it does so for good reasons, with good prospects for success.

Policy analysis is often thought to be applicable mainly in defense affairs and military strategy. Defense issues do tend to provide the combination of concrete technologies, specific goals, and measurable results that lend themselves to investigation and assessment. Policy analysis, however, can also be applied to issues that lie mainly in the political realm, including such important foreign policy areas as big-power diplomacy, regional security affairs, alliance reform, global economics, and crisis management. Many such political issues present the basic ingredients—goals, actions, and consequences—that are amenable to careful policy analysis. Although these ingredients may be harder to define and measure than in the defense realm, they can still be subjected to scrutiny that is rigorous enough to distinguish good ideas from bad. Indeed, contemporary U.S. foreign policy might benefit if it were subjected more often to the kinds of searching inquiry that has been the norm in the defense arena.

Policy analysis can come in different forms. In its simplest form, a policy analysis can investigate the properties of a single option, probing into it as deeply as the situation merits. In doing so, it might accept that option's main features at face value and examine its performance as a whole, or it might probe deeper by examining that option's internal components and subcomponents, questioning whether each of them makes sense on its own merits and whether a better internal mix can be found. When an analysis probes this deeply, it becomes a program evaluation: an effort to determine how the parts of an option can best be assembled. Normally, however, policy analysis focuses on a single option and its program components only after that option has already been adopted and thus the thorny details of implementation must be decided.

When the issue is whether to adopt a particular option at all, most policy analyses are comparative; they compare and contrast a menu of options, searching for the best candidate. An analysis might assess the performance of an existing policy, examine a single new candidate to replace it, and compare the results. Or it might compare and contrast a bigger set of alternative options, perhaps three, five, or even more. It can examine how these options achieve a single goal, or how they achieve several goals. It might focus on multiple goals, develop a separate policy for each of them, and assess how these separate policies could be blended together to make a coherent whole. It might then assess how to coordinate and synchronize the execution of these policies. When it gets this ambitious, policy analysis becomes an exercise in strategy development. The most comprehensive policy analyses are those that perform both strategy development and program evaluation. These are rare but often pathbreaking. Regardless of its focus, a policy analysis needs intellectual tools applied in systematic ways so that it produces credible results.

Uses and Abuses of Policy Analysis

Policy analysis sometimes gives rise to bad policies. During the 1960s, the decision to enter the unwinnable Vietnam War with a bad strategy and the efforts to wage it for several frustrating years, with little progress toward victory or peace, were reinforced by a torrent of policy analyses that, in retrospect, seem wrongheaded. In the eyes of critics, the Vietnam War shows that even well-trained policy analysts and strategic thinkers can err badly when they wear blinders and that an entire government can fall victim to "group-think." At its worst, policy analysis can be little more than a rationalization for preordained assumptions without examination of their validity or whether other ideas are better. Such policy analysis cannot turn mush into pudding. If analysts' heads are filled with wrong ideas to which they stubbornly cling in the face of contrary evidence, their work is likely to say unwise things even if they employ a sophisticated methodology. But if the analyst has sound ideas from the onset and uses sound analytical methods to help refine them, the resulting work is likely to say wise and helpful things. The Vietnam experience was an aberration, not the norm. It occurred not only because flawed analyses were put forth, but also because senior officials chose to discount better analyses that also were in abundance at the time.

Policy analysis can also be a malign tool in the hands of hucksters and con men who use it to obscure the truth rather than to reveal it. A saving grace is that, unlike other sales pitches, the arguments of such an analysis are often sufficiently visible that they can be scrutinized. Analysis should be anchored in ethics that begin with the honorable intentions of those practicing it. Analysis should not be viewed as a way of turning big decisions over to technocrats. Policy analysis works best when its results are placed in the hands of policymakers who have an independent capacity to sort out the good, the bad, and the ugly. It works best when it is embedded in the pluralist practices of democracy, where there is a competitive marketplace for ideas, plus plenty of people able to ferret out flawed or phony arguments.

Policy analysis thus does not always lead to the correct answers, and even when its intentions are pure, it cannot guarantee results or be sure of rising above normal human frailties. But when it is done well and the surrounding political conditions are right, it can be a powerful tool for good. A famous example is the U.S. Government's efforts to improve the North Atlantic Treaty Organization (NATO)–Warsaw Pact military balance during the Cold War. During the early 1960s, the U.S.–NATO military strategy in Central Europe was one of "massive retaliation," which called for a wholesale nuclear response in the face of a Soviet attack, nuclear or nonnuclear.[2] Inside and outside the government, activists used thorough analysis to question this risky strategy and to make the case for a different strategy—that of flexible response backed up by a strong conventional defense.[3] The debate that they triggered was ferocious on both sides of the Atlantic, but ultimately their view prevailed.

When the new strategy was adopted in 1967, many people questioned whether NATO could muster the resources to build a conventional posture that could not be swept easily from the battlefield by the Warsaw Pact. Analysts examined the widely accepted assumption of Warsaw Pact force superiority. They used their craft to show that NATO was stronger than commonly believed and that it could achieve a viable defense simply by doing a better job with the resources at its disposal. This realization gave rise to a succession of NATO force improvement efforts during the 1970s and 1980s, guided by analyses that addressed the programmatic aspects of building better forces and devising a more agile battlefield strategy. By the time the Cold War ended in the late 1980s, NATO was pursuing a position of near equality or better in the conventional force balance, a development that may well have played a role in the Soviet Union's decision to end the contest and withdraw its military forces from Eastern Europe. This succession of wise strategic decisions unquestionably owed a great deal to policy analysis that acted as a powerful engine of reform and renewal.[4]

Insightful analyses of national security policies will continue to be needed far into the future. Only a few years ago, it was claimed that this field was going out of business because "history had ended" and the human race was headed toward an enduring era of peace. Events since then have shown that, even with the emergence of a larger democratic community, the world is still a dangerous and violent place. Boiling chaos stretches along the vast southern arc from the Balkans and Caucasus, through the greater Middle East and Persian Gulf, to the East Asian littoral. There and elsewhere, new threats menace not only the overseas interests of the United States, but even its homeland, as well as the safety of close allies. History has not come to an end; for this discipline, the demands are greater then ever before.

Globalization, along with other dynamics, is reshaping how national security studies are defined and conducted. U.S. interests are extending into unfamiliar new places, and the world itself is drawing closer together as the flow of information, trade, and technology accelerates. Regions that once seemed separated by time and space are becoming more enmeshed, to the point where a financial crisis in Thailand can trigger a worldwide economic slowdown, or a country as isolated as Afghanistan can become a launching pad for global terrorism. U.S. national security policy, which earlier had focused on regions as separate entities, must now think in global terms, seeing the world as a whole as well as its component parts. It also must think in functional terms, responding to emerging transnational dynamics such as terrorists, tyrants, the spread of weapons of mass destruction (WMD), and cross-regional alliances based on ideology or geopolitics. The era is ending when military, diplomatic, and economic policies could operate in their own domains, largely apart from one another. In the information age, plans for military activities will need to take into account their political impact. Diplomacy will need to address security management and economic integration. All of these trends add up to a challenging future for national security policy studies.

What types of people will be needed to perform future policy analyses, blending the old and the new? This tradecraft does not require a genius intellect, but rather a working knowledge of changes in the world and in the national security field. As in the past, it will require a capacity to think boldly and systematically, a searching eye that sees both the big picture and its details, a willingness to be reflective about one's own assumptions, and a talent for assessing the relationship between means and ends. When analysis is guided by these characteristics, it can produce valuable insights. When it is received by political leaders willing to act upon its messages, it can have considerable influence.

A Spectrum of Methods: Telescopes and Microscopes

Policy analysis involves dissection and integration: tearing a policy apart in order to see its component parts and then putting them back together to see how they add up. Analytical methods can help make this task easier. This book surveys three major categories of methods. They come from three different academic disciplines—political science, managerial economics, and operations research—each of which has unique ways of pursuing its craft. While all of these methods are applicable to analyzing U.S. national security policies—the main focus here—they also can be employed to analyze policies for other governments, multinational institutions, or transnational actors.

Policy analyses range across a wide spectrum, from those that cover very broad issues and require sweeping strategic appraisals to those that are narrow and mandate tightly circumscribed appraisals. Some analyses are like a wide-angle telescopic lens aimed at seeing a big picture, some like a microscope aimed at revealing otherwise invisible things, and others a bit of both. Regardless of its scope, any policy analysis requires a methodology so it can be conducted in a disciplined, thorough manner to maximize its value.

The term *analytical methods* is often misinterpreted to mean scientific techniques for gathering and interpreting data. But methodology is far more than this narrow function. For example, Einstein said that he relied on "thought experiments" (*gedankenexperimenten*), not laboratory testing, to create his theory of relativity.[5] Creative and disciplined thinking, not measuring, was the heart of his methodology for theoretical physics. Such thinking is, similarly, at the heart of policy analysis. Data measurement and appraisal can matter, but policy analysis is more than simply assembling information in the hope that it will produce sound conclusions. The most important role of analytical methods is to help people conceptualize better, assess issues and options better, and produce better advice.

The idea that conceptual thinking plays a big role in research—sometimes bigger than the examination of data—will come as no surprise to those familiar with the philosophy of science. Textbooks in this field commonly stress the importance of the human mind in determining how reality is perceived and knowledge is built. History bears out this judgment. In the 1960s, Thomas Kuhn's widely discussed book, *The Structure of Scientific Revolutions*, distinguished between "normal science" and "revolutionary science." Kuhn acknowledged that normal science—the act of building upon existing theories—typically unfolds through a patient, laborious process of gathering and arranging data. But, he asserted, revolutionary science—the act of creating entirely new theories and paradigms—is typically a product of original conceptual thinking.[6]

At the time, Kuhn's argument was controversial. Indeed, it rocked to its foundations logical positivism, the school of thought that emphasizes theory-building through empirical research. Yet Kuhn was mostly right about cases in which big scientific break-throughs require the wholesale dismissal of existing, widely supported theories in order to allow new theories to be erected. Einstein's success at creating relativity, overthrowing Newtonian physics in the process, certainly falls into the category of revolutionary science. So did Copernicus' assertion that the earth revolves around the sun, which grew out of conceptual insight, not painstaking measurements or tinkering at the margins of existing theories. The same applies to many other great scientific breakthroughs, such as Darwin's theory of evolution, Maxwell's theory of electromagnetism, and Harvey's theory of blood circulation. All were fundamentally products of conceptual insight, although field research and laboratory work played important roles too.[7]

What applies to natural science applies also to policy analysis. While there is a role for empirical research in policy analysis, the major requirement is for original, clear thinking. Especially when big changes are being considered, policy analysis often in-volves far more than gathering and interpreting data; when analysis begins, the slate may be blank. Whereas scholarly studies often are conducted amidst plentiful data, warring hypotheses, and a prior published literature, policy analysis typically confronts much uncertainty. It may face questions whose answers are inherently unknowable. There may be no existing hypotheses or arguments to test, and initially there may be no way of knowing what data should be gathered or how to interpret it. Consequently, the analyst must think about how to create the conceptual edifice necessary to bring intellec-tual order to the issues at hand, just as Einstein first created post-Newtonian relativity in his mind; only later was it submitted to measurements to test its validity. This espe-cially holds true in areas where there is as yet no strategic paradigm about international trends and U.S. responses. In such cases, often the norm in today's fast-changing world, innovative conceptual thinking is essential, and data interpretation is merely a means to help determine its correctness and relevance.[8]

The Cold War period offers an illustration of the importance of conceptual think-ing in creating strategic theories. The two principal theories of the Cold War concerned bipolarity and alliance development. Bipolarity theory portrayed the adversarial relation-ship between the Communist powers led by the Soviet Union and the Western democratic powers led by the United States. Alliance theory portrayed how those democratic pow-ers organized themselves in order to deal with the Soviet threat in Europe and Northeast Asia. Neither theory existed when the Cold War began gaining force in the late 1940s and early 1950s. Because there was no lengthy modern experience in dealing peacefully with a bipolar world, initial theorizing about bipolarity was almost entirely conceptual and was driven by logic and inference rather than analysis of data. Similarly, conceptual thinking initially led the way during the creation of the NATO alliance in Europe and U.S. alliances with Japan and South Korea in Asia. Among the products of this concep-tual thinking were the concepts of containment, deterrence, and flexible response. When experience was gained with these theories and data became available, key hypotheses were developed and modified through empirical research. As the Cold War dragged on, policy research and analysis came to be dominated by a combination of conceptual thinking and data interpretation, further modifying and enriching the two core theories.

Something similar is happening in the post–Cold War world, although no comparable strategic theories have yet emerged to match those of the Cold War. The theory of globalization is one candidate that may ultimately prove to have considerable analytical power. A decade or more ago, globalization was a term familiar only to a narrow band of specialists, and it possessed no powerful theory to portray its main features or its policy implications. But as the 1990s drew to a close, the term began spreading: several books about it appeared, and U.S. strategy documents began to point to its importance. Again, there was no lengthy experience to draw upon; the globalization dynamic of the information age was mostly new. As a result, initial analytical work on the subject was mostly conceptual and largely speculative. As experience is gained and more information has become available, researchers have begun testing empirical theories and policy theories.[9]

For these reasons, the term *methodology*, as used here, means the entire intellectual process by which analytical products are created, from start to finish. This definition reflects three postulates about how thinking begets purposeful knowledge: it proceeds phenomenologically, in that rigorous thinking in abstract conceptual terms—of the sort that creates awareness where none previously existed—can greatly strengthen the capacity of policy analysts to assess the issues facing them; it creates knowledge epistemologically, in that such thinking is best enhanced when it employs disciplined analytical procedures in order to sharpen its judgments; and it proceeds teleologically, in that the ultimate goal of such thinking is to impart an organized sense of design and purpose to how it portrays the policy domain.

This definition of methodology thus includes not only the collection and examination of data, but also the dynamics of reasoned creativity and deliberate scrutiny. This definition, with its emphasis on original thinking, rather than simply gathering information that is left to speak for itself, presumes that policy analyses seek to create two types of relevant knowledge: empirical knowledge—attitudes and beliefs that define the world around us—and directive knowledge—judgments that create guidance for how we should act in particular situations. Policy analysis seeks empirical knowledge as an input and is focused on developing directive knowledge as its main output. Methodologies are the thought-tools by which fresh knowledge of both types can be added to the existing storehouse of knowledge.

In the field of national security policy, the process of employing analytical methods to develop and enhance thought-derived knowledge begins by creating new abstract concepts and generalized theories about security affairs, assessing how strategic trends affect U.S. interests and goals, posing issues and options, and choosing subject areas for scrutiny. Once a conceptual framework of these elements is developed, the analytical process next relies upon such traditional instruments as deductive logic, inductive reasoning, and inference to generate hypotheses and conduct initial appraisals of how policy actions may produce strategic consequences. Then such technical tools as evaluation criteria, performance metrics, data analysis procedures, standards for verification and falsification, formal models, and mathematical equations are employed to transform tentative hypotheses into solid propositions and thence into firm conclusions. Finally, the process includes the important step of presenting the analytical results comprehensively, making them clear even to readers and listeners who are not well versed in the subject.

The three categories of analytical methods surveyed in this book can all readily provide essential ingredients for this process, but they differ from one another in how they investigate policies and in what they try to produce. In examining these categories, the book begins with the methods that facilitate a broad telescopic focus on big-picture subjects. It then moves to methods that are mainly designed to perform like microscopes that give a close-up view of finer details. Telescopes and microscopes have something in common: they magnify their subjects, thereby making them easier to see. But there is a big difference between using a wide-angle telescope to study a solar system and a microscope to study a molecule. Taken together, these three methods provide a capacity to do both.

- Strategic evaluation methods are typically used for big-picture subjects. Often employed by political scientists, these methods, although rigorous, tend to be verbal and qualitative rather than quantitative. They are aimed at making broad-gauged judgments rather than fine-grained assessments.

- Systems analysis methods using economic models of choice typically have a somewhat narrower focus. Used particularly by managerial economists, these methods are more formal and quantitative than strategic evaluation. They make frequent use of graphical curves and related calculations to help focus on the cost-effectiveness of tradeoffs among different policies and programs, especially those that consume large quantities of resources, such as weapons systems. They aspire to get the numbers for costs and effectiveness basically right, but not to an extreme degree of precision.

- Operations research methods are normally employed by mathematicians and others for issues that are more narrowly construed or more tightly bounded than those addressed by strategic evaluation and systems analysis. The most formal and number-laden of the three methodologies, operations research methods use mathematical models, equations, and quantitative data to make detailed calculations about how alternative policies and programs perform. They aspire to get the numbers as precise as possible.[10]

Although strategic evaluation methods are most common in national security studies, none of these three categories is a preferred research tool for all issues. Each has its uses, and all have considerable analytical power. They do not always settle policy debates, but when used properly, they can enhance the quality of those debates.

In choosing among methods, much depends upon the relative need for linguistic rigor and numerical precision. Strategic evaluation is easiest to use but generates less precise results. Systems analysis and operations research are more demanding of detailed calculations while offering greater precision. In any single study, methods from all three categories might be used. For example, strategic evaluation might first be used to generate and compare alternative policy options; systems analysis might then evaluate composite plans and programs for implementing the best policy; finally, operations research might examine the detailed features of individual programs. Analysts should select the method, or combination of methods, that seems best suited to the issues at hand.

The proper role of these analytical methods is to inform policy deliberations as well as possible. Ideally, their use should lead even readers who disagree with a study's judgments and recommendations to respect the study's rigor and to be better educated on the core issues. These methods should be judged not by whether they generate lengthy calculations or create the surface impression of sophistication, but by their ability to produce accurate and relevant insights. Sometimes simple "back-of-the-envelope" techniques are more appropriate analytical tools than elaborate computer models, especially if the former do a better job of reflecting reality, or if the computer models are filled with wrong-headed assumptions and contrived data. As someone once said, "It is better to be approximately right than precisely wrong."

All of these methods should be viewed as instruments for enhancing analytical inquiry, but not as substitutes for rigorous thinking. Indeed, they are only as powerful as the intellectual frameworks in which they are employed. Any good policy analysis must start with a rich conceptualization of the key variables and their relationships. For example, a computer simulation of a military battle must be anchored in assumptions and data that portray the key features of that battle, not some other battle under different conditions. The best policy analyses are those performed by knowledgeable individuals who master their material, create strong conceptual order, develop innovative perspectives, and generate insightful inferences.

Methodologies are not prefabricated magic wands that can be taken off the shelf and waved at an issue in the hope of getting instant analysis. During a study, the analyst may bend, mold, and shape the methodology to perform the tasks at hand. Before a methodology is chosen and tailored, some basics about the study must first be addressed. What is to be the study's structure? What is to be its conceptual framework? How formal should its language be for conducting its investigation and reporting its results? Asking these questions, and getting the answers right, is critical to choosing a methodology correctly and to tailoring and employing it effectively. Before selecting a methodology, the practitioner should establish a clear sense of what an analysis is supposed to accomplish and how it is to be conducted. Choosing the methodology first, and only then figuring out how the study is to unfold, is a recipe for trouble.

Because policy analysis is not only a science but an art, it can profit from employing the methodology of art. Landscape painters, for example, know that setting up the structure of a painting is crucial to its success. Before they put paint on canvas, they identify the guiding concept of the painting: its subject and what it is trying to convey. They think about the painting's composition: how to use shapes, colors, perspective, and light to convey its message. Only then do they begin drawing and using their brushes. They block out the basic composition first; details, highlights, and finishing touches are added last. The same artful approach applies to conducting a policy analysis and to producing a written product. The first imperative is to get the structure right, for a sound structure is what determines a study's success.

A key structural feature of any policy analysis is a careful appraisal of the relationship between actions and consequences. What matters is whether, and to what degree, the policy under review will actually achieve its goals in affordable ways and whether it performs better or worse than other candidates. Providing insights on this subject to make decisionmaking easier is the core challenge of policy analysis. To the extent a policy analysis performs this critical task, it will be judged a success. If it does not do so, it will be a failure regardless of how many detailed calculations or fancy graphics it offers.

In order to perform this task, the foundation of a strong conceptual framework should be laid as the methodology is chosen and developed. When fully developed, this framework must identify in clear language the key issues at stake and the main factors at work. It must accurately identify the goals being pursued and specify criteria for gauging their achievement. It must identify the policy options that should be considered. It must provide a credible theory of how these options are intended to perform in pursuing goals, showing how these options would influence the strategic environment so as to help achieve the goals. The framework must specify performance measures for gauging effectiveness, resource commitments, and costs, financial and otherwise. It should also provide for an assessment of key uncertainties, sensitivities, and unintended second-order consequences.

The methodology that is chosen should be a logical extension of the study's structure and conceptual foundation to provide the suitably narrow focus or breadth of view. It should permit the study to conduct and communicate its analyses in an appropriate language. Analytical language can be verbal, formal, or mathematical. A verbal statement, for example, might posit a cause-and-effect relationship between two factors, but it would not normally be specific about the exact nature of that relationship. An example of such a statement might be, "The spread of democracy will help bring peace to turbulent regions, with varying success in different regions." A formal statement will seek greater specificity to portray the relationship: "The spread of democracy will enhance prospects for peace in regions that are becoming wealthy and have a stable balance of power, but will have only a modest impact on poor regions that are destabilized by major imbalances." A mathematical statement will seek to attach exact numbers to the formal estimate, as for example, "the spread of democracy will produce a 75 percent chance of enduring peace in the former regions, but only a 40 percent chance for peace in the latter."[11]

By and large, strategic evaluation methods rely on verbal language, or language that is only modestly formal, while systems analysis methods use formal or somewhat mathematical language, and operations research uses language that is predominantly mathematical. Yet this portrayal oversimplifies reality; these three languages are arrayed across a continuum, with verbal language at one end, mathematical language at the other end, and formal language in the middle. Verbal language can be general and colloquial or fairly rigorous. Formal language can be a great deal more formal than the example mentioned above. For example, it might group variables into separate blocks, posit interactions among these blocks, and employ multiple feedback loops. These are all techniques for directing attention to the flow of causal dynamics. Mathematical language can range from inferential statistics and simple algebraic equations to the elaborate systems of differential equations that often drive computer simulations.

The choice of what place along this continuum a study should occupy is for the practitioner to make. Greater precision in language has obvious advantages because it helps provide enhanced clarity to judgments and lessens the risk that vague formulations will lead to misunderstandings. For example, one might simply say that two new policy options will both cost more but perform better than now. Alternately one might, more precisely, say that option A will increase costs from $10 billion to $50 billion while elevating the odds for success from 40 percent to 50 percent, while option B will increase costs from $10 billion to $20 billion while doubling the odds for success from 40 percent to 80 percent. Whereas the first statement says nothing about how the two options compare, the second and more precise statement shows that option B is the better one by a wide margin.

Yet precision is not always the dominant value. While verbal language may lack some precision, it permits a breadth of expression and accessibility that cannot be matched by formal language and mathematics. The latter two languages can often be understood only by the initiated, and even studies that have employed them to conduct research must often express their results in verbal terms. Thus, no single one of these languages is always better or more appropriate than the others. What matters is what the situation requires, what works best, and what can be usefully communicated to senior officials who will be employing the study in order to make policy decisions.

The bottom line is that these three methods should be seen as instruments for helping people think clearly and deeply; they are far more than merely techniques for calculating and measuring. When used properly, they can shed a great deal of light on complex policy issues that otherwise would be indecipherable. Whether used individually or in combination, each of them is a powerful thought-tool that can help bring the profession of policy analysis to life.

Notes

[1] Standard textbooks on public policy analysis in general (not specifically about national security policy analysis) include Edith Stokey and Richard Zeckhauser, *A Primer for Policy Analysis* (New York: Norton, 1978); Frederick S. Hillier and Gerald J. Liberman, *Introduction to Operations Research* (Oakland, CA: Holden-Day Inc., 1980); Ralph L. Keeney and Howard Raiffa, *Decisions with Multiple Objectives: Preferences and Value Tradeoffs* (New York: John Wiley and Sons, 1976); David L. Weiner and Aidan R. Vining, *Policy Analysis: Concepts and Practice* (Upper Saddle River, NJ: Prentice Hall, 1999); Robert D. Behn and James W. Vaupel, *Quick Analysis for Busy Decision Makers* (New York: Basic Books, 1982); Lee S. Friedman, *Microeconomic Policy Analysis* (New York: McGraw-Hill, 1984); Duncan Macrae, Jr., and Dale Whittington, *Expert Advice for Policy Choice: Analysis and Discourse* (Washington, DC: Georgetown University Press, 1997); and Eugene Bardach, *A Practical Guide to Policy Analysis: The Eightfold Path to More Effective Problem Solving* (New York: Chatham Publishers, 2000).

[2] William W. Kaufmann, *The McNamara Strategy* (New York: Harper and Row, 1964).

[3] See Alain Enthoven and K. Wayne Smith, *How Much Is Enough? Shaping the Defense Program, 1961–1969* (New York: Harper and Row, 1971).

[4] See Richard L. Kugler, *Commitment to Purpose: How Alliance Partnership Won the Cold War* (Santa Monica, CA: RAND, 1993).

[5] Lloyd Motz and Jefferson Hane Weaver, *The Story of Physics* (New York: Avon Books, 1989). See also David Greene, *The Fabric of the Cosmos: Space, Time, and the Texture of Reality* (New York: Vintage Books, 2004).

[6] Thomas S. Kuhn, *The Structure of Scientific Revolutions*, 2d ed. (Chicago: University of Chicago Press, 1970). As Kuhn himself points out, a revolutionary scientific breakthrough seldom results simply from a fresh idea that

suddenly pops into the mind of an independent-spirited scientist. Rather, it tends to occur as a result of lengthy, painstaking effort that begins with recognition that existing theories cannot resolve newly appearing dilemmas and puzzles. Initially, efforts are made to amend the existing theory, and only after this effort fails, leaving anomalies too big to ignore, does attention shift toward creating a new theory. The act of crafting this new theory is where creative thinking comes to the fore.

[7] See Bernard I. Cohen, *Revolution in Science* (Cambridge: Belknap Press, 1985).

[8] Policy analysis draws upon three schools from the philosophy of science: cognitive rationalism, which emphasizes the role of abstract conceptual thinking in creating theories; empirical logical positivism, which emphasizes the role of measurement as a means to test theories; and linguistic pragmatism, which emphasizes the role of language as a tool for building and interpreting theories. While all three schools of thought are important and should be used to help guide policy analysis, the first of these, abstract conceptual thinking, plays the lead role when new strategic phenomena are being encountered and new policy theories must be created. For analysis of these three schools and associated issues, see Marx W. Wartofsky, *Conceptual Foundations of Scientific Thought: An Introduction to the Philosophy of Science* (London: Macmillan, 1968).

[9] See Richard L. Kugler and Ellen L. Frost, *The Global Century: Globalization and National Security*, vol. I and II (Washington, DC: National Defense University Press, 2001).

[10] In practice, these disciplines are applied by people from diverse academic backgrounds. At the Department of Defense and RAND, for example, physicists work on studies that employ strategic evaluation, and historians work on studies that employ operations research. Often there is little correlation between a person's field of initial academic training and his or her analytical expertise. However, all analysts must learn each of these methodologies before employing them. There is a need for multidisciplinary training. People who can move comfortably among these three methods are scarce; more of them are needed.

[11] See Hubert Blalock, *Causal Models in the Social Sciences* (Chicago: University of Chicago Press, 1972).

Part I—Strategic Evaluation

Chapter 3
Overview

Strategic evaluation is a methodology for analyzing U.S. national security policies and strategies. It is employed to help analyze how the United States can best shape its strategic conduct for managing the high politics of global security affairs and defense preparedness. As such, it has a more macroscopic focus than systems analysis or operations research. Strategic evaluation can be employed as a stand-alone methodology or in concert with the other two methods. When it is used with other methods, a sequential approach is used. Strategic evaluation typically comes first because it helps shape the broad framework of U.S. policies and strategies, including their goals, associated activities, and resource requirements. Then, systems analysis may help design plans and programs for determining, in more focused and specific ways, how these activities are to be carried out and the amount of effort to employ for each of them. Finally, operations research can help determine, in even more detailed ways, how budgetary resources are to be allocated among these plans and programs. These three methods thus can be employed together in ways that allow an analysis to start out as macroscopic and goal-oriented, and then to become increasingly microscopic and resource-oriented as it moves toward completion.

This section examines strategic evaluation, its components, and how it can be carried out. Strategic evaluations may deal with political issues, such as U.S. policies for enlarging NATO while also promoting collaborative relations with Russia. They may deal with political-military issues, such as reforming NATO's military forces and command structure in order to perform new missions outside Europe. While they are not often used to fine-tune the equipping of U.S. military forces, they are frequently used to help design new U.S. defense strategies and the force postures to support them. In a war, strategic evaluation may be employed to help ensure that U.S. combat operations attain not only their military goals, but their political goals as well. Strategic evaluation may also be used to help design U.S. foreign economic policy and to coordinate it with diplomacy and military strategy in order to advance national interests in a specific region, such as the Middle East. Issues such as these go to the heart of how the United States conducts itself in strategic terms around the world today, the goals it seeks, and the actions it takes to attain them.

Strategic evaluation thus has a big responsibility. Not surprisingly, it also plays a big role in U.S. policymaking. When a new Presidential administration takes power, it normally conducts an interagency review of national security policy and strategy, which typically takes the form of a strategic evaluation. When a new administration announces a big change in policy, such as switching from diplomacy to military confrontation in order to deal with a rogue country poised to commit aggression, that change typically is a product of a strategic evaluation. Most administrations will conduct dozens such evaluations and will use them to help define stewardship over national security.

From the Kennedy era onward, every administration has bequeathed a lengthy history of strategic evaluations that guided interagency policymaking. DOD has a similar record. Since 1996, Congress has mandated a Quadrennial Defense Review at the start of each new administration in order to make public the new administration's thinking on defense strategy and forces. The State Department is less known for publishing its strategic evaluations, but behind the scenes, it too employs this method for some analyses. Such think tanks as Brookings and RAND also publish strategic evaluations when major goals and priorities are at stake in national security. Academic scholars often publish their evaluations in the form of books and journal articles.

Preparing a strategic evaluation can be difficult, and even when the final result is well done, it may be controversial. Fortunately, the methods of strategic evaluation are well suited for contentious issues. While these methods normally employ a language that is less formal than systems analysis or operations research, it can have a conceptual rigor of its own, and it can be capable of getting the job done effectively. Many high-level policy issues deal in so many abstractions and intangibles that they do not lend themselves to highly formal language, mathematical equations, or masses of quantitative data. Fine-grained precision may not be required in order to analyze the issues and options adequately. Indeed, false precision and meaningless number-crunching damage a study's credibility. A more general, more qualitative treatment may be best where that is what the situation requires and what the consumers want.

The disciplined use of ordinary English language can sometimes be the best tool for a comprehensive, in-depth analysis of complex issues and for communicating the results to senior officials. For example, an assessment of U.S. national security policy in Asia might best be conducted verbally, with an appropriate level of conceptual and linguistic rigor. In such cases, strategic evaluation methods are not only suitable for the inquiry, but may be essential or even unavoidable. Thus, these methods are normally the preferred choice for studies that wrestle with the big issues and policy options that animate national security debates. Many superb studies have relied upon these methods, such as the path-setting National Security Study Memorandum-3 study of 1969.[1] Because these methods will be important arrows in their quivers, policy analysts should master them.

Where do the data and information for strategic evaluations come from? For existing strategic situations, valuable information can be gleaned from official documents that articulate the policies and behavior patterns of the United States and other governments. Helpful empirical data can be gathered by scouring reference books on relevant issues, such as military forces or economic trade. For situations that do not already exist, but may arise in the future, data and information may not be plentiful. Indeed, a core purpose of a study may be to help define a potential future situation so that new U.S. policies can be crafted; in such a case, the analyst may have to design and initiate appropriate empirical studies. Valuable insights might be gained from brainstorming with colleagues or from academic conferences that bring experts together. More formally, intellectual capital can be gained from political-military simulation exercises, of the sort that RAND employed in its "Day After" studies of potential crises involving WMD.[2] Policy analysts must often develop the necessary intellectual architecture, with supporting information, forecasts, and conjectured relationships. Thus, strategic evaluations often require research and analysis that is highly original and can result in entirely new creations. Such studies are thought-pieces, not exercises in data-crunching.

Strategic evaluation methods are indispensable for examining big strategic issues where political, military, and economic assessments must form a composite evaluation of options that span a wide range of choices that are not easily decided. These methods, while not a substitute for wise judgments by senior officials, can help improve the quality of those judgments and the decisions flowing from them.

These methods are a thinking person's tool. Their purpose is not to help analysts gather reams of empirical data to plug into statistical equations or computer models to generate optimum policy choices automatically. Strategic evaluation is normally more theory-driven than data-driven. Typically it relies upon general theories of actions and consequences, in order to see the forest rather than be distracted by the trees. As a result, the main role of its methods is conceptual. They can help analysts to bring intellectual order to complex issues that might otherwise defy orderly appraisal, to get the issues and options right, to weigh and balance the options effectively, to portray their features and tradeoffs, and to show the conditions under which one or more of them make sense.

The first two chapters in this section on strategic evaluation present theoretical material. Chapter 4 examines how to analyze a menu of policy options for pursuing a single goal. It emphasizes comparative analysis: the process of weighing and balancing alternative policy options in relation to each other. It discusses the steps that must be carried out in preparing this type of strategic evaluation (and most other types as well), with particular attention to developing a rich conceptual framework and to employing the tools of reasoning as a basis to make comparative judgments about multiple options under review. Using the methods of chapter 4, chapter 5 then focuses on the analysis of strategies—action agendas composed of multiple policies in pursuit of multiple goals—a comprehensive and particularly demanding form of strategic evaluation.

Chapters 6 through 9 are applied rather than theoretical. By way of illustration, they examine new challenges and opportunities facing strategic evaluation in major substantive areas of contemporary U.S. national security policy and strategy. Each chapter discusses critical issues, goals, and options facing the United States in a specific area and shows how the methods of strategic analysis can be employed to evaluate the tradeoffs and priorities ahead. In particular, they assess how strategic evaluation will need to change by adopting new methods and techniques to deal with emerging challenges and opportunities. They articulate the theme that strategic evaluation faces a future of major change and innovation.

Chapter 6, the first of these applied chapters, shows how to analyze the manner in which policy instruments—political diplomacy, military power, and economic instruments—are brought together to help the United States perform strategic functions on the world stage in order to forge an overall national security strategy. It highlights three key U.S. functions: leader of the democratic community and of bilateral and multilateral alliances; architect of global and regional security affairs; and global promoter of the world's economy, including its poorer regions. The three chapters that follow employ this framework of functions—along with associated instruments and goals—to

analyze issue areas of critical importance. Chapter 7 deals with U.S. approaches for leading and shaping alliances, especially NATO. Chapter 8 addresses U.S. relations with
other big powers and the existing challenges to the creation of stable security affairs
along the southern arc from the Middle East to East Asia. Chapter 9 addresses the task
of analyzing U.S. policy and strategy for promoting worldwide economic development,
including economic progress in poor regions and democratization.

Strategic evaluation can be used as a stand-alone method when the issues and options at stake require only a general appraisal. But when the need arises for attention to
details and for judgments about programs and budgets, strategic evaluation often must
be augmented by systems analysis and operations research. In this spirit, chapters 6 and
7 discuss some of the details that arise in strategic evaluations, including the design and
use of military forces for attaining political goals. Owing to space limitations, chapters
8 and 9 pay less attention to such details, confining themselves to broader matters.
The intent of these chapters is to impart a sense of strategic orientation rather than to
develop the specificity and concreteness that often must accompany strategic evaluations. The issues raised by these four chapters can be addressed through strategic evaluation alone, but they could also profit from treatment by all three methods, including
systems analysis and operations research.

The purpose of these four applied chapters is not to advocate particular conclusions
or policy recommendations, nor do they present fully detailed cost-benefit analyses of all
the options that are mentioned. Instead, their purpose is to erect a conceptual framework
of issues, goals, and options that can be employed in order to conduct such analyses.
They thereby help illuminate how policy analyses using strategic evaluation methods can
be used to assist governmental decisionmaking. The result is a tour of the contemporary
U.S. strategic terrain that explores the policy and strategy agenda ahead and that can help
equip readers with the intellectual tools to conduct strategic evaluations in these areas.

This section thus emphasizes the increasing need for new forms of strategic evaluation in the coming era in order to equip U.S. national security policy and strategy with
necessary new knowledge. Globalization and other sweeping changes of the information
age have ended any hope that the United States could remain secure and prosperous by
focusing mainly on the defense of Europe and Northeast Asia. The United States must
now think in truly global terms and act firmly in many regions—indeed, in virtually all
regions, especially those that are turbulent and poverty-stricken. It must also think and
act in terms that extend beyond a narrow focus on military and security affairs. Globally and regionally, its strategic thinking will need to synthesize and harmonize the
military, economic, diplomatic, and political dimensions of national security policy.
Above all, its thinking will need to be attuned to the continuing reality that fast-paced
changes can overturn established theories of policy and strategy almost overnight.

This threefold challenge of global awareness, synthetic thinking, and fast innovative
responses spells the intellectual agenda facing strategic evaluation in the coming years.
Can the analytical community respond with the necessary agility and insight? The challenge is demanding. Whether it is met will have major bearing on how the United States
fares in the future international era.

Notes

[1] National Security Study Memorandum-3 was a national security and defense study conducted by the Nixon administration during 1969–1970 to identify a spectrum of strategic options as the United States was withdrawing from Vietnam and turning to meet a growing Soviet challenge in Europe and elsewhere. See Henry Kissinger, *Years of Upheaval* (Boston: Little, Brown, 1982).

[2] See David Mussington, "The 'Day After' Methodology and National Security Analysis," in Stuart E. Johnson et al., *New Challenges and New Tools for Defense Decisionmaking* (Santa Monica, CA: RAND, 2003).

Chapter 4
Analyzing Policy Options for Single Goals

Now that the bipolarity of the Cold War has been replaced by a fluid and unpredictable international system, strategic issues that challenge the fundamentals of U.S. national security policy are arising with growing frequency. These issues will demand appraisals of the options facing the United States, for which the strategic evaluation method can be well suited.

The simplest form of strategic evaluation takes place when an analysis examines a small handful of policy options to determine which option can best achieve a single goal. Even this form of strategic analysis demands attention to the methods employed and the examination of competing policy options comparatively, rather than in isolation from one another. Analyzing whether one policy option will adequately achieve a single goal sounds simple, but it can be a demanding enterprise. Comparing multiple policy options in terms of their ability to achieve that goal is more demanding yet and never something to be treated lightly.

An example will help illustrate the sorts of issues that require this form of analysis. During the mid-1990s, the United States confronted the question whether to carry out NATO enlargement into Eastern Europe. The answer was anything but obvious. Practically all participants in the stormy debate agreed on the strategic goal: making Europe as stable, peaceful, and democratic as possible. But they disagreed strongly on the best policy for achieving that goal. One faction favored NATO enlargement coupled with a diplomatic effort to preserve stable relations with Russia. Another faction opposed enlargement and argued instead for preserving NATO's Cold War borders and building ties with Eastern Europe through NATO's Partnership for Peace and enlargement of the European Union (EU), while refraining from any steps that might menace Russia's borders. Both sides had clear, cogent arguments, but they embraced different strategic theories about how best to handle modern European security affairs. Those favoring NATO enlargement argued that it would be an effective way to help unite Europe under the mantle of democracy and would strengthen NATO and that the Russians could be persuaded to accept it. Those opposing NATO enlargement argued that it would overextend the alliance, add little to Eastern Europe's stability, and trigger a new Cold War with Russia. The debate between these two factions swirled for 5 years and ended only when NATO offered admission to Poland, Hungary, and the Czech Republic in 1999.[1]

For all its passions, the debate was not an exercise in blind advocacy. The contending strategic theories advanced by both sides were anchored in explicit propositions about geopolitical dynamics in Europe and about how policy actions would produce strategic consequences. These propositions could be subjected to inquiry using strategic evaluation methods, and indeed, several studies were written that employed those methods. These studies neither fully validated nor fully refuted the claims of either side. But they produced valuable material that elevated the quality of the debate, illuminated the tradeoffs, and helped educate policymakers on both sides of the Atlantic. They thus contributed to an improved policy. When NATO chose to enlarge, it did so in a manner designed to pre-serve its cohesion as a collective defense alliance, to enhance its ability to act firmly in Eastern Europe so that stability was advanced, and to maintain cooperative relations with Russia through new consultative forums. The advocates of NATO enlargement won the de-bate, but the opponents, too, succeeded in that their concerns were reflected in the careful ways in which enlargement was pursued.

Strategic issues that pit two or more policies against one another in support of the same goal arise frequently in national security affairs. One contemporary example is whether the United States can best keep Asia stable by trying to contain and deter China or rather by trying to draw China into the world economy and the Western security system. The strategic evaluation method offers tools for analyzing such issues.

Strategic evaluations aimed at comparing multiple policy options in order that one may be selected can come in many different forms: short or long, simple or elaborate. All are best conducted through a process whose three main steps are the subject of the rest of this chapter.

The first step is to develop a conceptual framework. This involves defining the prob-lem, identifying interests, goals, and options, and choosing substantive areas of analysis. Twenty-five such areas are listed in this chapter. The second step is to perform the analy-sis: the chapter outlines essential elements of the reasoning process and useful analyti-cal procedures. The third and final step is disseminating the final product, whether by oral briefing or written publication.

Step 1: Develop a Conceptual Framework

The first step in a strategic evaluation of any size and scope is to develop a conceptual framework, which will have enormous bearing on how the analyst perceives reality and evaluates options. Constructing such a framework best begins by taking stock of the in-ternational situation that has triggered the issue now facing U.S. national security policy. Normally, policy issues do not come from the blue; they tend to arise when some crit-ical event has taken place, a new danger or opportunity has appeared, or a new trend has gained strength. Developments of this sort raise questions about whether an exist-ing policy should be retained or instead replaced by a new policy. This is especially the case when the existing policy shows signs of no longer working well enough or even of failing entirely. This situation invites an appraisal of the policy's continued usefulness and a serious examination of other candidates.

There are three essential steps in developing a conceptual framework: defining the problem; identifying interests, goals, and options; and choosing the crucial subject areas to be analyzed.

Defining the Problem

Strategic evaluation requires that the problem or challenge to be addressed is first carefully identified. While this observation may seem obvious, it often is not adequately heeded. In the past, many strategic evaluations have suffered from a lack of focus owing to failure to crystallize the problem or challenge. (In this, strategic evaluation is unlike systems analysis and operations research, which both come with built-in analytical techniques to perform this vital function.)

In order to set the stage for a focused analysis of the international situation, care should be taken to define the exact trend, development, or threat being addressed. Within the U.S. Government, the overall task of assessing the international scene is handled by the Intelligence Community. Chief among its products are the National Intelligence Estimates. While such studies can be an invaluable source of basic information, often they are of limited applicability to policy analyses. Typically they are so focused on examining the conduct and motives of foreign actors that they do not provide much insight on how U.S. activities may be influencing the situation. Nor do they always present their evaluations in terms that facilitate the appraisal of policy options facing the U.S. Government. For these reasons, a policy study often cannot rely upon an existing intelligence appraisal. Instead, it must appraise the relevant intelligence itself and make judgments about its implications for policy choices. What holds true within the U.S. Government applies even more forcefully to policy studies performed outside it by scholars, consultants, or others.

Preparing an assessment of the international situation that is policy-relevant is likely to become increasingly difficult. During the Cold War, the international security structure was so frozen that most intelligence issues had been studied for years; new developments were seldom encountered. Today's world, by contrast, is dominated by great uncertainty about why new global trends are emerging and where they are headed. In recent years, the U.S. Government has often been caught by surprise by events that seemed to come out of nowhere, or at least were not expected. A good example is the outbreak of savage ethnic fighting in the Balkans during the early 1990s, which may not have caught seasoned Balkan experts by surprise, but surprised many senior policymakers who had grown accustomed to years of relative stability there. Uncertainty, surprise, and unexpected developments have become the rule rather than the exception. Before a policy analysis gets under way, therefore, it must be preceded by a thoughtful and thorough intelligence analysis.

The difficulty of gaining and assessing intelligence is showcased by many events of past years. During the early 1970s, for example, the U.S. Government was slow to recognize the scope and intentions of the Soviet Union's military buildup, which came at the same time that the Soviet government also started pursuing détente. As the Cold War was ending, the U.S. Government failed to foresee Saddam Hussein's invasion of Kuwait. During the 1990s, it was slow to grasp the mounting threat posed by global terrorism. During 2002 and 2003, it misjudged whether the Saddam Hussein regime still held large quantities of WMD systems. Such failures must be judged in a larger context: for the most part, the U.S. Intelligence Community has produced accurate estimates about many difficult issues. But periodic errors can have bad consequences on policy, and when they have occurred in the past, they were often a product of faulty analytical thinking rather than a lack of hard data.

A full dissection of intelligence estimating lies beyond the scope of this book,[2] but past experience shows that accurate intelligence will not be automatically available for policy analysis. The problem is not that intelligence staffs are necessarily prone to imag-ining threats where they do not exist or failing to perceive them when they do exist. Rather, the problem is that although modern technical intelligence collection systems can provide many types of valuable information, they cannot always discern the politi-cal intentions of governments that are intent on keeping actions secret. Coming to grips with many other modern trends is equally difficult where they, too, are enshrouded in fog and uncertainty.

Gaining accurate current intelligence about ongoing trends can be difficult enough. Developing accurate estimates about their larger consequences and implications—where these trends are headed and what they may produce in several years—is even harder. There is a clear need to develop better intelligence. Until this difficult goal is achieved, the need for a policy analysis to prepare its own appraisal of key intelligence judgments is paramount.

An intelligence appraisal must be specific and concrete, avoiding abstractions un-less they are truly descriptive of the matter at hand. For example, there is a difference between dealing with global poverty everywhere and dealing with it in sub-Saharan Africa. Similarly, transnational threats such as organized crime, drug trafficking, and terrorism are not all the same and are likely to call for different policy responses. Care must be taken to define explicitly the central issues that are posed for U.S. policy: the is-sue of dealing with global WMD proliferation in general is different from confronting a rogue country that is rapidly deploying nuclear weapons and missiles in order to commit aggression. Likewise, saying the issue is "ways for the United States to promote Europe's future unification" is different from saying that the issue is "ways for the United States to support the next stage of NATO and EU enlargement." The former is general; the latter is specific. If the issue is truly general, the analysis should say so, but if the issue is specific, the analysis should be explicit about it.

In addition to defining an international problem explicitly, the analysis should pro-vide information about its magnitude and the pace at which it is unfolding. Emerging threats, often a preoccupation of national security analyses, can come in different sizes. Some threats are immediate, others arise in the midterm, and others will peak only in the long term. For those that already exist, a forecast of their future is important. This forecast should address whether the threat will lessen, remain the same, increase within its own domain, or metastasize into other regions and problem areas. Similarly, oppor-tunities abroad can come in different sizes, shapes, and future horizons. Regardless of whether an overseas trend poses a threat or an opportunity, portraying it in accurate and focused ways is important to developing a sensible policy response. Getting the magnitude of the trend right is important because it influences how the United States should respond; getting the time horizon right is important because it affects when the United States should respond.

Effective policy analysis requires not only a description of the problem at hand, but also a sophisticated explanation of its causes, including the role played by U.S. activities. The analysis should tell not only what is happening abroad, but also why it is happening. De-scription might be easy, but explanation can be challenging. Few international problems are caused by one single factor; many are a product of multiple causal factors. Some of these factors may be direct, while others may lie in the background, yet exert influence in powerful ways. Some causal mechanics may already be well understood; others may be new in ways that catch even seasoned observers by surprise. Some causes may lie on the surface; others may be deep-seated. For example, an ethnic conflict that has been directly triggered by disputes over territory and governing authority may also reflect underlying cultural antagonisms and differing economic fortunes. Likewise, an adversary country may be acting in a particular way for reasons that differ from its public statements. An entire region may be drifting in a particular direction for reasons that are different from, and more complex than, surface appearances suggest.

An effort to explain developments is doubly important in today's world because often old explanations no longer apply, and new explanations are anything but obvious. For example, when the end of the Cold War diminished the fear of global nuclear war, the new era was widely heralded as a time of enduring peace. Yet the United States was compelled to wage war four times between 1991 and 2003, and the war against terrorism will not end any time soon. Why so many wars? Why their growing frequency? Is it because rogue countries and other actors have been freed from the shackles of bipolarity to commit aggression? Is it because multiple regions are experiencing greater turbulence in their politics, economics, and security affairs? Are both explanations partly correct? The answers can make a difference in deciding how the United States tries to prevent wars and how it wages them when they occur. Likewise, the world economy is showing greater volatility, with short periods of progress suddenly giving way to brief downturns. Why is this happening? Is it because exports, imports, and investments have made international commerce more important for many countries? Is it because global finances move so quickly from place to place? Is it because too many countries lack capable governments, stable currencies, and sound banks? Do all of these explanations apply? Here again, the answer can have a big impact on U.S. policies and how they are evaluated.

An example from defense management will help illuminate why getting the causes of a problem right can affect how policies should be developed and analyzed. A few years ago, DOD officials grew concerned by a recent rise in their department's spending on operations and maintenance (O&M). The annual O&M budget of about $100 billion for 2000 was about $20 billion higher than historical norms. Initial appearances suggested that the rise was due to three factors: a recent surge in overseas peacekeeping missions, rising expenses on spare parts and repairs for aging weapons, and the failure to consolidate excess basing capacity fast enough. Closer inspection, however, showed that these three factors accounted for only one-fifth of the spending increase. Analysts came to conclude that nearly all of the O&M budget's 30 different components were responsible to some degree. For example, health care expenses had soared due to rising costs for modern medical treatment; aging buildings and plants required upkeep more often; and DOD was now hiring a larger number of outside contractors for administrative services. Whereas the initial explanation mandated new policies in only 3 areas, the latter explanation called for new policies in fully 30 areas—a big difference.[3]

As a general rule, the better the causal explanation, the better the policy analysis and the decisions that flow from it—not only for defense management, but for strategic evaluations as well. The importance of accurately describing the problem abroad, explaining its causes, and predicting its future cannot be overemphasized. A medical doctor must correctly diagnose a disease, determine the extent it has invaded the body, and gauge its future growth before prescribing a cure. Otherwise the patient might not get better or even die. The same applies to policy analysis. The historical record shows many cases in which the United States succeeded because it diagnosed problems accurately or failed because it diagnosed improperly. The stark difference between the two underscores the value of hard work in this area.

Identifying Interests, Goals, and Options

Once the international challenge and the issue raised by it have crystallized, the strategic evaluation method next identifies how U.S. interests and values are affected, for good or ill, and whether their importance is vital, major, or peripheral. For example, a solemn treaty commitment to a longstanding ally ranks higher than a normal diplomatic relationship with a country whose ties to the United States have not been as close. Similarly, the United States is typically willing to pay a higher cost, or even use military force, to protect vital interests and values, whereas for lesser interests and values, it typically applies a stringent cost-effectiveness calculus and may rely upon less expensive and less risky instruments, such as diplomacy and economic aid. Normally, analysis will be expected to give particular scrutiny to ambitious, expensive policies that fall into the former category, but policies of the latter type should also be examined; for example, they might make the resort to force unnecessary.

Next, the evaluation should determine the strategic goal—the desired end-state—that is to be pursued in order to defend or advance those interests and values. This goal should be defined carefully because haziness at the outset can cause the analysis to lose rigor as it unfolds. For example, there can be a big difference between containing a new threat and deterring it; the former might mandate strong diplomacy, while the latter may require a strong military presence.

For simplicity's sake, this chapter considers situations where only one strategic goal is being pursued. In other situations (for example, those examined in the next chapter as well as other chapters) strategic evaluations may need to consider multiple goals. Although this complicates the analysis, it does not alter the fundamentals of how strategic evaluations are conducted. The main task is to determine how the various policy options produce consequences in several goal areas and then to calculate the overall result. For example, an option might perform well at achieving one goal and poorly at achieving another; depending upon how the two goals are prioritized, the option might be given an overall medium evaluation. Even when only one goal is being considered, however, it should not be treated simplistically. The core purpose of a policy is to achieve a strategic goal. If the goal is not clearly specified, policy options cannot be compared because their performance cannot be measured.

Goal identification should be accompanied by an assessment of the existing situation: whether the goal is in deep trouble, or modestly strained, or on the verge of soaring success. The analysis should also specify criteria for judging when the goal has been attained. Attaining it in minimally acceptable ways might mandate one type of policy, while fully achieving it might demand a completely different policy. Some policies might be capable of achieving only modest goals, while others have greater potential. Ideally, these criteria should include measuring sticks, or metrics, for determining when the goals have been met.

The need for clarity also applies to subsidiary objectives whose attainment might be important in achieving the goal. For example, the analysis might conclude that the goal of achieving 10 percent annual growth rates for a poor economy might require a 20 percent increase of foreign investments on its soil, a 30 percent increase in its internal investments, and a reduction in its inflation rate to 5 percent. Such details are important to judging how policies can best be designed and evaluated. Whereas one option might not appear capable of attaining its goal when such subsidiary objectives are examined, another option might be able to withstand such scrutiny. In the above example, perhaps option A offers a 100 percent increase in foreign investments, but fails because it produces nothing toward the other two objectives, whereas option B might succeed because it does, not perfectly, but well enough on all three objectives.

Once the goal has been defined and criteria have been articulated, the analysis should then state the policy options to be examined. Each option should provide a clear sense of scope and purpose and a basis for determining how its instruments are to perform functional activities that create consequences that achieve the goal being pursued. The number of options examined should be dictated by the situation, but normally should be no more than five. Readers can have trouble absorbing more than five options, and this number should usually be sufficient to cover the spectrum. Sometimes the policy options to be studied are dictated by policymakers; other times, the analyst determines them. Regardless, the options chosen should illuminate the key issues and range of choices. Many analyses have failed because, in their efforts to put forth several options, they neglected to include the option that was the best performer or stood the greatest chance of being adopted. Such mistakes can happen when attention is given only to those options that enjoy widespread support. Often creative thinking is needed to identify the best policy or the most promising one.

Gauging the needs and inclinations of policymakers can be important in ensuring that the analysis includes the options that are wanted and the one most likely to be chosen. Sometimes senior officials prefer merely to tinker with the status quo, but other times, they are willing to make big changes. Studies have flopped because they failed to give policymakers creative new options, or failed to articulate the specific policy that most interested those officials. Analyses have often succeeded at high levels when they rose above the ingrained, status quo thinking of the bureaucracy. Indeed, senior leaders often commission policy reviews precisely for the purpose of shaking up the bureaucracy and generating fresh ideas. In-depth analysis is not the enemy of creative, relevant thought; done properly, analysis and creativity can fuel each other. When multiple options are portrayed, they should be arrayed along a spectrum whose logic is simple and clear, such as a spectrum stretching from options that are most peace-preserving to those that are most warlike, or one that stretches from unilateral to multilateral options, or from the least ambitious to the most ambitious. The middle options are not always the best, and the extreme options are not always throwaways; all options along a spectrum should be well developed. In selecting the options, the analyst should have a clear grasp of the core choice to be made and the main purpose of the study: is it to identify the policy that does the best job of achieving the goal at a given cost, or the one that adequately achieves the goal at the least cost? Is the purpose to array a spectrum of policies that perform increasingly well at ascending costs? If the purpose is to challenge the status quo, the spectrum might move from policies that preserve the status quo, to those that rearrange it or shake it up, to those that wholly abandon it in favor of radical change. Success at designing the options and making clear how they relate to each other is essential for a successful analysis.

Choosing Subject Areas for Analysis

The next step in crafting a conceptual framework is to develop subject areas for guiding the analysis. These subject areas help pose the critical questions to be asked and define the types of information and judgments needed to evaluate the options. Their purpose is to tell policymakers and other readers what they need to know about the options. They focus on such critical issues as the nature of the policy options, their performance characteristics, whether they are likely to succeed or fail, the broader considerations that influence evaluation of them, and their overall merits. Selection of subject areas will have a big impact on the quality and relevance of the analysis. Past policy analyses that have succeeded often have done so because they performed well in this area. Other analyses have failed because they neglected to include subject areas and associated questions that were crucial to the evaluation process. Policymakers cannot evaluate options if they are told only about actions and potential benefits, but not about costs and risks. Their choice may depend on such issues.

Subject areas will vary from study to study. Table 4–1 is a list of 25 potential subject areas. They are examined in the remainder of this section, with key questions each poses. Not all of the questions need be covered in every study, and in some studies, different subject areas may be appropriate. But a study that includes this list is likely to be on the path to solid coverage. This list can be used to assess each policy option individually and then to compare them. The discussion here talks in terms of assessing a single option, but the same procedure would be applied to all the options in a study. When multiple policy options are being considered, the analyst must select and employ subject areas that will facilitate a comparative evaluation. What must be avoided is a scheme of subject areas that stacks the deck, improperly favoring one option at the expense of others. The choice of subject areas thus must be guided by both comprehensiveness and objectivity. The 25 subject areas for study that are discussed in this chapter present a good start.

Visions, Values, and Ambitions. An early subject of study should generate an outline of the visions, values, and ambitions of the policy. What is this option's heart and soul? What is it trying to achieve, and what underlying values and calculations does it represent? Does it provide for a sufficiently strong assertion of U.S. power and resolve to get the job done? Does it have a vision that is bold and clear, rather than cautious and muddled? Is it wise and mature, rather than impulsive and foolhardy? Does this option carry forth existing policy, or reflect a linear extrapolation of it, or overturn it by crafting an entirely new policy and strategic rationale? How ambitious is this policy? Are its aims modest, or does it aim high? How realistic are its aspirations, and do they reflect the best traditions of American values? Does this option propose to achieve the U.S. goal fully or only partly? Is it based on a sensible reading of events and U.S. priorities, rather than stretching credibility in both areas?

Main Actions, Instruments, and Other Characteristics. What does this option propose that the United States should do in terms of concrete actions, and what instruments does it intend to use? Does it create a simple agenda, or does it require multiple activities and

Table 4–1. **Subject Areas for Analysis: A Preliminary List**

1. Visions, values, and ambitions

2. Main actions, instruments, and other characteristics

3. Theory of actions and consequences

4. Expected effectiveness, benefits, and losses

5. Level of effort, resource requirements, and costs

6. Cost-effectiveness

7. Implementation strategy

8. Time horizons

9. Constraints, difficulties, and roadblocks

10. Confidence levels: U.S. ability to make policy succeed

11. Consistency with other policies

12. Unilateral or multilateral

13. Feasibility and prerequisites for success

14. Encouraging signs and warning signals

15. Robustness and flexibility

16. Vulnerability to opposition

17. Externalities, wider consequences, and implications

18. Persuasion and public support

19. Assumptions, uncertainties, and biases

20. Sensitivities and risks

21. Contentious issues and key judgments

22. "Gold badges" and "red flags"

23. Tradeoffs

24. Adaptability to other ideas

25. Bottom-line appraisal

instruments? Do these activities and instruments easily blend together into a coherent whole, or are they not natural partners of each other? Does blending them require a great strategic labor? What other characteristics mark this option?

Theory of Actions and Consequences. What is this option's theory of actions and consequences, or its core rationale for an expectation that it will succeed? Exactly how are its actions abroad supposed to bring about favorable consequences to achieve national goals? What cause-and-effect mechanisms does it rely upon to produce these consequences? Does the option put forth a credible interpretation of these action-and-consequence dynamics? Are these dynamics simple or complex? Can success be achieved through a single change in strategic affairs, or is a chain of successes required? Do these successes promise to be readily accomplished, or will they be hard to bring about? Overall, is this theory of actions and consequences based on credible logic, instead of representing a mere hope, or someone's flawed reading of the matter at hand?

Expected Effectiveness, Benefits, and Losses. Judged in relation to the U.S. goal and its own ideal aims, how effective is this option likely to be, and what are the benefits and payoffs likely to flow from it? To what degree will it not only achieve its aims, but also set the stage for additional progress in other domains? What negative consequences and losses might it produce in its own domain or elsewhere? Overall, will this option be highly effective or only marginally so? Will its gains exceed its losses? By how much will it produce net benefits on the balance sheet, by a lot or only a little? What are the odds of it succeeding: does it offer a 75 percent chance of attaining 90 percent of its aims, or only a 50 percent chance of attaining 50 percent of its aims?

Level of Effort, Resource Requirements, and Costs. How much effort will the United States have to exert in order to pursue this option, a little or a lot? What resources will this option require in political, economic, military, and technological terms? What will be its budgetary costs, direct and indirect, for personnel, or investment in technologies, or daily operations? Are these budget costs readily affordable, or barely affordable, or too expensive to contemplate? What other costs must be paid, including time, attention, and resources diverted away from other priorities? What are its opportunity costs in terms of inability to pursue other endeavors? Are its sacrifices easily bearable, or will the United States give up too much elsewhere in order to pursue this option? If only a portion of the necessary resources can be mobilized, is the option still a viable proposition or not?

Cost-effectiveness. How do the expected effectiveness and benefits stack up in relation to the costs that must be paid, budgetary and otherwise? Do the gains of this option exceed its costs by a wide margin, or only barely, or do its costs instead seem higher than its benefits? Does this option offer a wise and profitable way to spend money and resources, or could the same assets be allocated elsewhere for substantially better returns? If only two-thirds of the required funds are committed, would the option yield two-thirds of its expected benefits, or one-third, or less? Surveying the balance sheet, does this option add up to a sensible investment, or does it waste resources?

Implementation Strategy. How will the United States go about implementing this option? Can one executive department implement it, or will a large interagency effort be needed? Will Presidential support be required? Is congressional approval required, and in what ways? What key constituencies would have to be mobilized? Should all of its activities at home and abroad be launched at once, or should they be phased to unfold sequentially and to achieve their aims in cascading fashion? What steps have to be achieved in order to make others possible? Does this implementation strategy promise to be easily carried out, or is it quite demanding?

Time Horizons. How will this option and its consequences unfold over the coming years: do its actions start fast and peak within 2 or 3 years, or do they start slowly, reach maturity within a few years, and continue for a full decade or more? What is its benefit stream: does it achieve its goals and provide other benefits in the near term, the mid-term, or the long term? What is its cost stream: do its costs peak early, or are they spread out over the entire course of the policy? How do its benefit stream and cost stream compare? Do its major benefits come early and its costs later, or the converse? Should the distant future be discounted, and if so, what discount rate should be applied: 5 percent? 50 percent? Does the discount rate alter the appraisal by elevating the benefits in relation to the costs, or the other way around?

Constraints, Difficulties, and Roadblocks. What constraints could impede the adoption or execution of this option? What difficulties could be encountered? What roadblocks to success might be encountered along the way? How strong are these impediments? Can they be overcome? How could they be lessened?

Confidence Levels: U.S. Ability to Make Policy Succeed. How confident can the United States be that this option will succeed in doing what it is supposed to do? Should the government be highly confident, moderately confident, or not confident at all? What is the path of events, including actions by the United States and reactions by allies and adversaries, by which this policy can succeed? What is the path by which it could fail? If it is adopted, how will the United States be able to tell—early enough to make a difference—whether it is on the path of success or failure? What is the main scenario for this policy succeeding? What is the main scenario for it failing? Which scenario is the more likely to unfold? To what degree does the United States have the strength and influence to channel events in directions that foster the favorable scenario and prevent the unfavorable scenario? Does the United States possess the power to make this policy succeed even in the face of problems and opposition?

Consistency with Other Policies. Is this option consistent with overall U.S. national security strategy and with other policies that might be operating in the same region? Does it reinforce these other policies, making them easier to carry out and succeed, or rather work at cross-purposes with them, or even threaten to damage them fatally? If there are inconsistencies, how does the importance of this option compare to that of other policies? Is it so important that other policies should be subordinated or sacrificed to it, or do the other policies weigh larger in U.S. priorities? How can this policy be adjusted to minimize any interference elsewhere?

Unilateral or Multilateral. Is this option to be pursued by the United States alone, or will it require cooperation from friends, allies, partners, and international bodies? If it is multilateral, how large a team of contributors must be assembled: a small coalition, or all of NATO, or a majority in the United Nations? What are the prospects for assembling such a team: good or problematic? Will the United States be obligated to make concessions—within the policy or elsewhere—in order to gain the necessary multilateral cooperation? What are these concessions, and how do they affect this policy's drawbacks? Are the prices worth paying?

Feasibility and Prerequisites for Success. What is the feasibility of launching this option and pursuing it to completion? Can the necessary domestic consensus and resources be mobilized? Can key policy instruments, such as the U.S. military, be diverted from other tasks at acceptable levels of risk? To what degree does cooperation from other countries influence feasibility? Is it likely to be forthcoming? If there are multiple prerequisites for success in these areas, what do they suggest about feasibility? Can these prerequisites be met if the necessary efforts are made, or are they beyond the realm of the possible?

Encouraging Signs and Warning Signals. What signs at home and abroad provide encouragement for this option? Is the smell of success in the air? What warning signals are coming from at home and abroad? What is the net balance of encouraging signs and warning signals: does one dominate the other?

Robustness and Flexibility. Is this option robust or brittle? Will it make sense even in the eyes of people who hold somewhat different views and priorities? Can it encounter unanticipated problems and absorb reversals, yet still march onward to success? Or will it fall apart if only a few things go wrong? How flexible is this option? Does its implementation permit only a single narrow game plan, or can it be pursued in different ways? Can the United States shift gears along the way and pursue other paths that still enable the option to achieve its goal, or is the option so rigid that it cannot tolerate changes of direction even if they are necessary?

Vulnerability to Opposition. If this option seeks success at the expense of adversaries, how vulnerable is it to countervailing strategies that these adversaries might adopt? Can it withstand challenges and active opposition, or will it fall short of success if an opponent develops ways to undermine and dilute it? Can this policy emerge victorious in a tough competitive setting, or might it result in defeat in ways that damage and embarrass the United States?

Externalities, Wider Consequences, and Implications. What external considerations should be taken into account in evaluating this option? What could be this policy's unintended consequences and spin-offs? What impact will this policy have on international affairs outside its immediate domain and on U.S. interests and goals there? Is it mostly self-contained, or will it produce major ripple effects—good or bad—that must be taken into account in evaluating it? What precedents will it set around the world? Do these potential secondary effects make the option look better or worse?

Persuasion and Public Support. Is this option easy to sell to others, or will it be hard? How is it likely to be perceived and accepted at home and abroad? Will it be understood and accepted, or misperceived and widely criticized? Can a public relations campaign be mounted to counter criticisms and lessen negative reactions? Can such a campaign succeed? How and why will it succeed?

Assumptions, Uncertainties, and Biases. What key assumptions does this option make about the problem or opportunity being addressed and about its own performance? Are any assumptions hidden but deserving of close scrutiny? What uncertainties does this option face, and how important are they to evaluating its likely performance? Does this option contain biases and blinders that might compromise the ability of policymakers and those who implement it to think and act clearly?

Sensitivities and Risks. How sensitive is this option to its own calculations and presumptions? Are its expectations for success vulnerable to minor changes in key factors, or do they remain valid in the face of substantial variations? What risks does this option entail? Are they small or large? What wildcards or unpleasant surprises could plunge the United States into deep trouble? Could the option backfire if it were to suffer bad luck that made the existing situation worse or created some new and unwelcome situation?

Contentious Issues and Key Judgments. Does the wisdom of this option turn on a few contentious issues about which difficult judgments must be made? What are these special issues, and what judgments must be made about them? How confident can the United States be that its judgments in these areas will be accurate?

"Gold Badges" and "Red Flags." Are there features of this option that make it highly attractive, or necessary, or unavoidable—what might be called "gold badges"? Is it the only viable way to attain high-priority goals and protect vital interests? Is it a sure-fire success, or at least far more likely to succeed than its competitors, and substantially cheaper as well? Or, instead, are its costs transparently unaffordable, its difficulties insurmountable, its payoffs too small, or its risks too big? In other words, are there "red flags"? Should this option be adopted or rejected for these reasons alone, irrespective of its other strengths and weaknesses?

Tradeoffs. Does this option pose important tradeoffs—something lost in exchange for gain—that must be considered? What are they? Does it offer high payoffs in exchange for heavy costs and big risks? Or does it call for modest efforts and resources in exchange for modest performance and achievements? Does it offer strong implementation in exchange for less flexibility and adaptability? Does it offer the independence and other benefits of unilateral conduct in exchange for the loss of support from allies? Does it confront adversaries firmly at the expense of the disapproval of countries who resent U.S. superpower status? On balance, how do these tradeoffs add up? Are the gains worth the losses and sacrifices?

Adaptability to Other Ideas. Can this option be broadened to include good ideas contained in other options? If it is embraced by the President but encounters resistance in the Congress, can it be broadened to include changes and amendments during legislative review and remain coherent? Can it be used as a basis for negotiations with allies and adjusted to their views? Can it accommodate concessions to opponents or allies?

Bottom-line Appraisal. All things considered, is this option clearly a good idea or a bad idea? Or, instead, is the appraisal foggy, ambiguous, and full of tradeoffs, some of which argue in favor of the policy while others argue against it? How does this option compare with other alternatives? Is it a clear winner, a clear loser, or an equal competitor? Under what conditions or judgments does this option make more sense than others? Under what conditions does it make less sense, or no sense at all?

Once a conceptual framework has been established and its critical questions answered, the strategic evaluation proceeds to the actual analysis.

Step 2: Performing the Analysis

If the study is being done by a single person, he or she enjoys considerable latitude in choosing the procedures by which the analysis is conducted. In theory, an analysis should be conducted sequentially, with the first step completed before the next step is begun, and so forth. In reality, many studies unfold in a less orderly fashion, with the analyst moving back and forth among all the steps, shaping and modifying them in an iterative manner. This more helter-skelter process can succeed if the study retains its orderly logic and the results come together at the end. Sometimes, the analyst will have a good sense at the outset of where the study is headed and what it is likely to produce. In this event, the process of conducting a study becomes easier. When this is not the case, the analyst must formulate a clear sense of direction as soon as possible, and then go back into the earlier material in order to bring it into line with the study's direction. Regardless of the procedure and the expertise of the analyst, it is a good idea to make the material available to others for feedback as it emerges. Colleagues can provide invaluable advice and help prevent the study from wandering off course.

When a study is done by a group, the process may differ. The best small group studies typically include three analysts, enough to provide a range of talents and synergy without having too many cooks to spoil the broth. Even with only three analysts, care must be taken to ensure that they share common aims and styles and that their orientations can be coordinated, rather than tearing the group apart. Studies by a small group can typically be flexible in their authority structure and procedures. A study conducted by a large group is an entirely different story. In the government, study teams composed of 20 or even 50 analysts are common. Large group efforts require an executive leader with the authority to set the agenda, a frame of reference for all to follow, and a formal schedule of how the study is to move from outlines to rough drafts, then to final drafts and on to review. The study director may require a small team of deputies and administrative aides. If each of the options is being analyzed by a team with a vested interest in promoting that option, the study's leaders will need to exert firm quality control over all of the teams and ensure that the teams have a full opportunity to critique each others' work.

The Reasoning Process

Regardless of who conducts the study and how it is structured, the intellectual process of analysis will determine the study's success. Because policy issues normally do not arise in a vacuum, analysis normally does not take place in a vacuum either. Indeed, a well-elaborated intellectual paradigm may already exist regarding current U.S. policy in the area being examined. This paradigm might provide ready-made answers to the questions raised in many of the subject areas. In this event, the analytical task may be minor—that of tinkering with the paradigm in a few places and applying it to new options. A different situation arises, however, when such a paradigm does not already exist or when it must be discarded in favor of fresh concepts. In this event, analysis must plow entirely new ground in all subject areas, and it may have to entertain options that were unthinkable when the old paradigm ruled. Pathbreaking analysis of this sort can be difficult and contentious, but it also can establish a new way of thinking—a change of paradigm.

Paradigm change is not the norm, but it does happen frequently. During the Cold War, the analyses that created the doctrines of containment and deterrence were products of new paradigms. After the Cold War, the idea of NATO enlargement was also a product of a new paradigm, which had to be understood by proponents and opponents alike if its good and bad features were to be appraised. Since then, other new issues have required new policy paradigms, among them globalization, terrorism, accelerating nuclear proliferation, multinational coalition-building, and defense transformation. In the coming decades, the creation of new paradigms, as well as new policies, may become common. Physicists and chemists, as well as social scientists, know that there is a big difference between normal research and paradigm-changing research in their fields. The same applies to policy analysis. Creating a new paradigm may require not only a fresh analysis of the strategic situation but also a reinterpretation of U.S. and allied interests, common goals, and available options for policies, strategies, and programs. It thus involves a wholesale rethinking of what the United States is trying to achieve as well as of underlying strategic calculations.

Especially when fresh paradigms are being created and major policy departures are under review, the analysis should aim to evaluate the options by comparing them, not just assessing each of them individually in its own "stovepipe." While the individual merits of each option are important, what matters is how they rate in relation to each other. This is especially important to policymakers when the options differ appreciably both from existing policy and each other. Studies that provide a comparative appraisal will be far more successful and influential than those that do not. A penetrating analysis is needed in each of the subject areas because the options might differ significantly from each other, thus widening the distance separating them and making the task of judging them more complex. As each subject area is evaluated, the best practice is to treat initial judgments as tentative hypotheses, and then to subject them to increasingly demanding scrutiny so as to transform them gradually into propositions that are validated as firmly as possible. Initial hypotheses often have a way of evolving as they are improved and may mutate into final propositions that say different things than originally conceived. This is a sign that the analytical process has done its work.

All studies should aim to generate the information in each subject area that is necessary to evaluation. The more effort that is exerted in gathering such information, the better will be the results. Studies can rise and fall on their ability to grasp thorny details and to fill in all the boxes of a matrix. Yet in strategic evaluations, data-gathering normally is not the essence of the analytical process. The main challenge is that of evaluating available information, even when it is incomplete, in order to generate an assessment of what it means in relation to the issues and options at stake. The analysis should aim to provide well-reasoned assessments that can be subjected to critical scrutiny. Strict scientific standards of verification and falsification may not be feasible, or even desirable. After all, the purpose of a strategic evaluation is not to create enduring scientific theory for the ages, but instead to facilitate informed policymaking. Yet, there is a big difference between assessments that rest on hasty conjecture and those that reflect careful thought and systematic research.

The intellectual process of moving from initial conjecture to solid conclusions is demanding. Here, systems analysis and operations research have the advantage of being able to employ mathematical models, graphical curves, quantitative data, and numerical criteria for guiding how they translate hypotheses into propositions and then into validated claims. Strategic evaluation methods, however, usually lack such concreteness; they are more dependent upon disciplined reason to guide this process. Disciplined reason does employ data, quantitative or qualitative, but it mainly advances through deductive logic, inductive reasoning, inference, analogy, and other forms of rigorous thought. These are aimed not only at generating assessments but also at steadily improving them and ultimately validating them. In other words, strategic evaluation methods employ the thought-tools of producing reasoned judgments about policy options in the face of uncertainty.[4]

Deductive logic moves from premises to conclusions that are logically true because they are subordinate to the premises. A simple mathematical equation illustrates the point: If $A + B = 9$, and if $A = 5$, then $B = 4$. In this equation, B necessarily equals 4 if the two preceding statements are true; it cannot possibly be any other value.

Inductive reasoning, by contrast, is a form of logic that uses inference to generate conclusions that, while not necessarily true, are probably true. As the inductive process unfolds, inference (the act of moving from one judgment to another) is used to build a growing number of reliable conclusions. Typically, inductive reasoning moves from parts to a whole, or from the particular to the general. It can combine separate pieces of information in order to create holistic generalizations that may not be apparent when such pieces are examined apart from each other. It involves the careful weighing of direct evidence and circumstantial evidence to generate credible conclusions. As Sherlock Holmes said, the best explanation for a puzzling issue is one that is fully consistent with all the relevant facts and that passes tests of close scrutiny better than all other explanations. Credible conclusions need not, at first glance, seem highly probable. As Holmes further said, "When you have excluded the impossible, whatever remains, however improbable, must be the truth." Credible conclusions and persuasive judgments are not necessarily true as a matter of irrefutable deductive logic, but ideally they pass tests of close scrutiny and are substantially more believable than any other explanations.

In addition to moving from the particular to the general, inductive reasoning can move from the general to the particular. An example of a general statement is that big geopolitical powers seek to dominate a zone of safety around their borders. A particular inference is that China can be expected to do so because it is such a power. Inductive inference may also reason by analogy. For example, because policy A worked well in the past, it can be expected to work well again if circumstances are similar. The various techniques of inductive reasoning can be used singly or together to create causal models that can be applied to policy analysis in order to assess the relationship between actions and consequences.

Although deductive logic can sometimes be employed in strategic evaluations, more often the assessments are built through inductive reasoning and inference. Because this form of reasoning is subject to error, care should be taken in determining how it is employed. The subtle pitfalls of fallacious reasoning—for example, non sequiturs caused by errors in induction and inference, not just wrong data—should be avoided.[5] Collection of a few supporting facts does not automatically make a generalization true. Merely because one country is similar to others in some respects does not guarantee that it will behave like them in all respects. A policy that succeeded in one case will not necessarily succeed again. Inductive reasoning and inference should be guided by demanding standards. Judgments made through inductive reasoning should rest on a solid foundation or the preponderance of evidence, not a loose collection of a few facts that leaves out equally compelling facts that pull in the opposite direction. Judgments reached by inference should rest on explicitly stated and convincing reasons why they are likely to be true in the specific cases being examined, not just on unexamined comparisons.[6]

Ideally, strategic evaluation methods should aspire to create new knowledge of such analytical power that it meets the extremely demanding standards of mathematics and theoretical physics, or at least fulfills the courtroom standard of proof beyond a reasonable doubt. More often, however, irreducible uncertainties and looming imponderables make these standards impossible to achieve. Then, strategic evaluations should aspire to create solid "best estimates": judgments that are as well refined as analysis can make them and that inspire sufficient confidence that they provide a justifiable basis for decisive action. When a complex issue is being examined, a good strategic evaluation typically will rest on an edifice of such best estimates. It may not be able to pass strict scientific tests of reliability because to one degree or another, its estimates are uncertain constructs. But it will be solid enough to qualify as an analytical foundation for evaluating options and choosing a policy to be implemented.

The act of making such evaluations and conveying them to readers can be aided by employing metrics for gauging not only whether the goal is achieved but the implications in each subject area as well. In an operations research analysis, mathematicians often try to rank performance on a numerical scale, such as 0 to 10, in each subject area. Precision of this sort often is impossible in a strategic evaluation, but even the use of such qualitative terms as high, medium, and low can be valid and enormously helpful. For example, policy A may be appraised as having a high expectation of success and low negative implications elsewhere, while policy B is appraised as having low likelihood of success while being highly likely to cause big troubles elsewhere. This distinction will greatly facilitate the clarity of the comparison. Employing metrics intensifies pressure on the analysis to perform well in all subject areas because its conclusions must be fine-tuned enough to be ranked.

As the analysis confronts the task of forging estimates in multiple subject areas, it should not be so reluctant to make strong claims in the face of uncertainty that it deteriorates into a muddle of caveats and cautions aimed at fending off criticism. If the weight of evidence suggests a particular interpretation, even a controversial one, the study should say so clearly. For example, it is probably useful to acknowledge that two different interpretations have an equal chance of being right. It is not useful to take an interpretation that has a 90 percent chance of being right and to water it down to where it seems too uncertain to be used as a basis for decisionmaking. Whereas the former is intellectual honesty, the latter is obfuscation or cowardice. The proper way to handle uncertainty is to conduct sensitivity analysis—by showing how policy evaluations can vary if alternative interpretations are embraced—not to sweep the entire subject under the rug. In particular, sensitivity analysis can show whether the various options still withstand scrutiny if their key assumptions are altered significantly, or instead fall apart when such assumptions are altered only slightly. The result can be insights that separate robust options from brittle, fragile ones.

Strong interpretations sometimes leap into the hands of policy analysts by virtue of the data and information itself. For example, if intelligence sources provide indisputable evidence that one country is preparing to invade another, this may be reason enough for reaching the conclusion that war is around the corner. But on big strategic issues befogged by uncertainty and complexity, strong interpretations will often rest on the informed judgments of the analysts themselves. How can such interpretations be made and justified? In a scientific laboratory, interpretations normally are left to rigorous tests and experiments performed with precise tools in ways that minimize the need for subjective human judgment. In most strategic evaluations, however, disciplined human reflection is the main tool for reaching conclusions and for determining when interpretations should be accepted as valid. In other words, policy analysts must use their brainpower in order to generate powerful insights that matter. Sometimes, they must also use their creative instincts and imaginations in order to create the new explanatory and prescriptive formulations required by fresh situations. To skeptics, reliance on human reflection and creativity to evaluate policies may seem like an invitation to disaster. But it should be remembered that Einstein relied on his mind and his creative imagination, not a laboratory, to create the new theories that revolutionized physics. While few people have Einstein's brainpower, most trained and knowledgeable analysts have ample capacity to generate sound interpretations and prescriptions by applying thought and care.

The act of applying one's analytical talents requires hard work, intellectual rigor, and deep thinking, all of which take time and effort. Inductive reasoning and inference are reliable tools for making interpretations, but the rigor with which they are applied can have a big impact on whether judgments are sound or shaky. In order to produce reliable and meaningful results, use of these tools for reasoning must be tightly disciplined. Care should be taken to define concepts clearly, to generate explicit propositions that are sound logically, to assess the available data thoroughly, and to reach conclusions that not only make the most sense but can also withstand critical scrutiny. All key interpretations should be subjected to demanding tests of reliability, including the test of whether the opposite interpretation also has merit.

When interpretations are forged on the basis of disciplined reasoning and can withstand such tests, they are likely to be on target even if there is lingering uncertainty. What should be remembered is that in the past, the best strategic evaluations and the wisest policies have often been products of human judgments made in the face of major uncertainty by using incisive thinking. In contrast, failed policies have often come from flawed judgments derived from weak reasoning in the face of ample information that would have permitted a correct judgment. The difference was in the quality and rigor of the thinking.

Analytical Procedures

The analysis normally should begin by describing each option, including its rationale, aims, actions, and implementation strategy. The heart and soul of an analysis, however, is not description but rather evaluation of how each option likely will perform. A searching appraisal of each option's theory of actions and consequences is critical, yet often is overlooked in many analyses. This theory serves as a fundamental basis for verifying whether the option's credibility and its claim to effectiveness are valid. If the theory is correct, then the option is likely to deliver what it promises. If it is not, the option may be an exercise in self-delusion. The theory for each option should be presented clearly, along with a justification of its underlying rationale.

In some options, this theory may be straightforward because it is anchored in physical mechanisms that can be readily measured. An example is waging war against an adversary military in order to conquer its territory, an act whose postulated features can be studied in depth. Another example is the employment of investments, grants, and loans to accelerate a poor country's economic growth; this is also subject to modeling of physical phenomena. A less measurable task arises when the policy options seek to influence the political choices of a government. Exactly how and why could each option motivate a foreign government to act in a particular way that may be different from how it might otherwise behave? Does the option have a high probability of succeeding, or do its actions seem to require a stretch? Questions such as these require clear answers that seem plausible, even if they are hard to measure and prove.

Even more nebulous is the act of appraising how policy options aim to influence multiple governments in ways that produce a cascading chain of events. An example is a policy that aims to influence country A, with an outcome that will then influence countries B and C, whose actions are presumed to influence countries D, E, and F. In this era of complex geopolitics, strategic policies often have such complex action-reaction dynamics in mind. An example is the strategic task of trying to mold a stable Asian security system, which requires influencing the foreign policies of multiple nations, all of which may have different aims and interests than those of the United States. In cases like these, an option's theory of actions and consequences must be evaluated carefully, for unless the option gets this calculation right, it might not succeed and could even backfire.

After examining the theory of actions and consequences for each and every option, the analysis should then appraise the likely effectiveness of each at achieving the goal and providing other benefits. Care should be taken not to exaggerate or underestimate effectiveness. Here, use of metrics—quantitative or qualitative—is especially important. Often individual options do not promise to achieve their goal fully. But determining how close each option comes to the goal, or how far it falls short, may matter a great deal. Other things being equal, an option that gets 75 percent of the job done is lots better than an option that achieves only a 50 percent rating. Costs must also be included, and estimates of cost-effectiveness offered. A good study will also include a sense of time horizons: how costs and benefits unfold in the near term, midterm, and long term. Whereas some options may be costly in the near term and provide their benefits only over the long haul, other options (which might, for this reason, be more attractive) may start delivering early and accrue their costs only in the distant future.

In studies examining options whose activities turn on diplomacy and political affairs, budget costs may not be an issue, or at least not big enough to make a difference. (Even in such a case, however, the overall level of political effort required of a government can matter; policymakers often favor reasonably effective options that are not terribly demanding.) By contrast, in studies involving military forces, economic assistance, or any other expensive activity, costs can be highly influential in determining which option is judged best. An option that performs as well as the others but is less expensive will score ahead in the competition, while high costs can drag the most effective option down from its top perch. For example, senior officials might discard an option that achieves 80 percent of the goal at a cost of $20 billion in favor an option that achieves 70 percent at half the cost. They might feel satisfied with a 70 percent performance and unwilling to pay an extra $10 billion for an additional 10 percent performance.

The analysis also should devote attention to the many factors that can help options to succeed or can impede them. These considerations can shape the evaluation in subtle ways that go beyond a mechanical accounting of costs and benefits. Some options might look good on paper, yet be unacceptable owing to a lack of domestic consensus or support from other countries. An option facing few roadblocks will look more attractive than one that must leap over multiple barriers. If an option requires multilateral support and will attract help from allies, this argues in its favor. If the option is intended to coerce an adversary, but the adversary might foil it with a clever response, this argues against it. If the option provides a flexible capacity to adapt to surprises, this argues in its favor over options rigidly tied to a single plan. The same applies to other subject areas that might reinforce the case for one option over the others, such as consequences and spinoffs, or core assumptions and sensitivity to unexpected developments, either of which could alter the appraisal.

At the end, after analyzing the individual subject areas for each option, the next task is that of synthesizing the material and presenting an overall evaluation of how the options compare as a whole. If one option stands out as clearly best, the analysis should say so and explain why. If the analysis can rank the options from best to worst, this is also good. If the options instead present complex tradeoffs, in ways leaving none of them clearly superior to the others, the analysis should admit this and not try to point to a winner.

A simple criterion of evaluation normally offers a good weathervane for an initial comparison of the options—an option will stand out as better than the others if it offers greater benefits at equal costs, or if it offers the same benefits at lower costs. This simple formula must then be supplemented by a host of additional considerations to determine whether they alter the calculus. The attractiveness of the most cost-effective option might be dragged down by multiple constraints such as the imponderables accompanying it, the risks it entails, the difficulty of mustering support for it, the problems of implementing it, its vulnerability to being thrown off course by unexpected setbacks, or the prospect of negative second-order consequences. A second- or even third-place option might be elevated to front-runner status because it suffers from fewer such impediments.

Such considerations may often push the boldest and most promising options to one side in favor of more conservative options that entail fewer uncertainties and worries. When this is clearly the case, the analysis should say so, but not with unwarranted caution when the consequence is sacrifice of potentially successful policies. The best practice is that of clearly and objectively delineating the full set of considerations and tradeoffs accompanying each option, so that decisionmakers are informed of all that must be taken into account. If this is done, the study is likely to be well received regardless of whether the option ultimately chosen is the one suggested by the study or favored by the analyst.

An analysis should offer a recommendation when this step is appropriate. But strategic evaluations typically are not valued for high-pressure sales tactics; these could taint them with charges of zealous advocacy and bias. Instead, the best-received strategic evaluations make clear the conditions under which specific options might be chosen. They thus entrust to policymakers the task of judging which conditions apply. When they take this step, one of two good things can happen. Users might be led to prefer the option suggested by the study because it comes across as the best choice to them as well. Or they might prefer a different option and feel grateful for the study because, instead of loading the dice, it had the honesty to show them why their chosen option made sense in their own eyes. Many studies that have been celebrated for their achievements actually paved the way for policies that their authors believed to be second-best. Success can be achieved in more ways than one.

Step 3: Disseminating the Final Product

The final step—presenting the results—should not be treated as an afterthought. The mode of production and dissemination can have a big impact on determining who the study reaches and how they appraise it. In the consulting industry and private business, the packaging of studies is often an obsessive preoccupation, and it typically results in glossy publications and showy briefings. In the academic community and government, greater emphasis normally is placed on substance, but style can matter too. Consumers are more likely to absorb a study if its material can be readily grasped and if it provides them clearly with what they need to know. User-friendly studies tend to make a bigger impact.

Should a study be written and published, or instead be presented as an oral briefing? Each mode has its advantages and disadvantages, but often the best practice is to do both. In the academic community, studies are usually published first, to be disseminated to the public with an editorial imprimatur as evidence of prior peer review. Occasionally, scholars do hit the lecture circuit first, with presentations not yet anchored in written publications. In the government, either mode may be appropriate. The natural temptation is just to prepare a briefing because it is easier to assemble and can reach a large audience of senior officials. However, even though a written analysis can require lots of time and effort, it offers major advantages. Chief among these is that the act of writing imposes an intellectual discipline of its own. Typically, writing results in a sharper, better product with improved arguments and insights. Analyses of controversial and complex subjects may lack credibility unless they are written in ways that expose their arguments to careful scrutiny. Although senior officials may not be willing to peruse lengthy documents, they typically ask their staffs to do so and to prepare a critique. Some senior officials do read voraciously. Secretary of Defense Harold Brown, for example, had a reputation for reading 400-page documents in a single night and offering hand-written comments from the first page to the last. A trained scientist, he was not impressed by oral briefings because they often seemed too superficial.

Written Presentations

The process of writing should be carried out carefully, with attention to both structure and style. The document should be written in a manner that accords with its mode of publication. Academic publications typically require a structure that includes footnotes, citations, and literature reviews. By contrast, government studies place less emphasis on footnotes and citations; literature reviews often are not wanted, or are treated suspiciously if they suggest that the study is trying to argue from authority rather than from explicitly presented fact and logic. Government studies tend to emphasize not what other people have said, but what this particular study uniquely has to offer.

Both academic publications and government studies have in common that they are not mystery novels; they should not try to entice the reader with hints of surprises in the first pages, gradually develop a plot as their chapters unfold, and unveil the results only at the end. Instead, they should express their main judgments at the beginning and then present supporting arguments and information in a logical manner that explicates these judgments. That way, the reader is quickly made aware of the main thesis and is better able to evaluate it as the study unfolds.

How long should a written study be? Academic publications typically come in three forms: journal articles of perhaps 15 to 20 pages, book chapters of 20 to 35 pages, and entire books that can range from 150 pages to 1,000 pages. Government studies place more emphasis on brevity, but length can vary as a function of the study's scope and purpose. Harried senior officials often have time to read only 1 to 3 pages and will not look at anything more. Memoranda to staff typically run 10 to 15 pages. For longer studies, a common practice is to write a short executive summary of 1 to 2 pages to accompany a text of 20 to 30 pages, with additional argumentation and data placed in appendices. That way, readers can select how much detail they want to absorb; senior officials can quickly read the executive summary, their top aides can read the text, and their staffs can prowl though the appendices.

Regardless of their length, studies in both the academic community and government should be written clearly. Good writing is focused and articulate, not an exercise in impressionism with thoughts blurred around the edges. Such writing takes time and effort. Perhaps a few superb writers can craft polished text in one sitting, but for most mortals, good writing often requires a process of successively closer approximations. Writers should avoid saying too much or too little, and should trim redundancy and extraneous material. Their prose should be pleasing and appropriate to the subject—not pretentious or ponderous yet not frivolous. While the language should have a rhythm and a melody, this is not the place to mimic famous authors renowned for their soaring prose. Analytical writing should be simple, straightforward, and, above all, clear. A main goal should be to attract interest by motivating readers and to convey a sense of gravitas and credibility, indicating that the writers know what they are talking about. The writing should be guided by a sense of the audience to whom the study is speaking. Writing for the President and Cabinet members is different from writing for a group of scientists or other specialists. Normally the tone should be that of equals speaking to equals, not upward or downward. The tone should be respectful of the right of readers to make their own judgments about the study's contents.

The normal rules of English composition apply. Clarity usually benefits when sentences and words are kept short. Short words are better than long words. Sentences should be as simple as possible, and even compound or complex sentences should not run more than three lines. Paragraphs should contain a single theme, not a hodgepodge of multiple unrelated ideas. Paragraphs should have at least three sentences, but normally their length should be no longer than one-half or one-third of a page, in order to provide readers with regular breathing space. A lengthy study should be broken into sections and subsections that help the reader discern the overall structure. Pretentious and phony jargon should be avoided. Key words or phrases that are not widely understood should be defined. Writing should speak in the active voice, not passive. It should use nouns and verbs to compose sentences, with adjectives and adverbs kept to a minimum because these parts of speech are discursive and can suggest bias or dice-loading. Writing should be understandable and credible.

A well-written study almost always has a single, clear thesis. The study's title is a good place to convey this thesis and rewards careful thought. A title such as "U.S. and European Policies in the Middle East" reveals the topic, but not a thesis. "Allies at Odds: U.S. and European Policies in the Middle East" does a better job of making clear what the study says. The title "U.S. Foreign Policy in Asia" is a mere label; the title "Balancing Multiple Imperatives: Setting U.S. Priorities in Asia" reveals much more.

The authors should answer a key question before the writing begins. If readers come away from this study remembering only one thing about its contents, what should it be? The authors should be able to crystallize this message in a single clear sentence, and they should put it prominently on display in their publication. This main message should be stated at the start of the study and at the end, and it should also permeate the entire product as it unfolds. The written product should not provide a mélange of disassociated, unsynthesized data and interpretations. One that does so is unlikely to be published, read, or remembered. One of the most difficult tasks in writing a policy analysis is that of articulating its message in a way that does not create bias toward one option or another. This requires careful, honest writing. While there is no simple formula for achieving success in this area, many successful studies have struck the right balance in conveying a powerful message while acknowledging the complexity of the topic and not loading the dice.

Who should do the writing? The answer is obvious if the study was prepared by only one person. But if the study is a group effort, one approach is to parcel out the various sections to the analysts who led the work in each section; this can work if the various analysts write in the same style. A better approach may be for the entire study to be drafted by the person who has the best command of the whole subject, or the best understanding of the writing style most appropriate to the audience being addressed. The draft should then be reviewed and commented upon by the entire team and sometimes by outside experts. The process of forming a consensus among them should be handled carefully. They should not "wordsmith" so as to obscure differences or sand away controversial issues. The best consensus-building efforts are those that further sharpen the analysis, deepen its judgments, and bolster its recommendations. The same standards apply to studies that are written by multiple government offices whose agendas may differ from one another. Strong efforts to find common ground are always necessary, but if the product is bland homogenization or a five-humped camel, the study is unlikely to accomplish its purpose and may be met with disfavor by senior officials. One reason for presenting multiple options with different rationales is to allow differences in opinion to surface, not conceal them.

Virtually all written analyses emerge initially as first drafts and must go through a process of editing and revising. First drafts, however, should be done as well as possible because this will lessen the need for editing and allow editors to focus their efforts. Initial editing is typically done by colleagues or supervisors and usually focuses on improving substantive content. When the revision is ready, it is often sent to a professional editor to improve the clarity of the presentation. To authors, the editing process can be difficult and prolonged and tends to come at a time when their energies have already been spent. Yet authors should participate in this process wholeheartedly because, even if their initial draft is good, editing can improve its quality and thus its impact. The final product is almost always considerably better than the first draft.

Briefings

Briefings have an art and science too. Because they are normally short, they can hit only the main highlights of the study. This is another reason why issuing a written study to accompany the briefing may be important. By providing the necessary backup material, it allows a briefing to address big points and avoid being bogged down in details. Preparing good briefings takes time and effort, including multiple reviews and editing.

The structure should be guided by the purpose and scope of the presentation. Even when offering its own judgments, the briefing should endeavor to give listeners the material they need to know in order to form their own opinions. When a briefing intends to convey substance, this is normally not the time to deliver a complex explanation of methodology. Unless the methodology itself is new and controversial, it should be mentioned only briefly. A briefing that evaluates policy options should focus mostly on how they compare and contrast. If the main purpose is to address implications of a single option and to develop an implementation strategy and supporting program for it, the briefing should focus on these matters. Focus is necessary because if a briefing tries to address multiple subjects, it is unlikely to treat any of them well.

The person giving the briefing should decide whether the audience should focus on the oral presentation or on the slides accompanying it; listeners cannot do both. This affects decisions about what to say in person and what should be written on slides. If the slides are the focal point, the briefer should never read them aloud, but instead supplement them with words that help listeners grasp their messages. The slides themselves should be crisp and clear, not so overloaded with words that their main points are hard to decipher.

The briefer should be prepared for a wide range of audience reactions, from support to hostility, and from enthusiasm to inattention. The length of the briefing should be tailored to the situation and the audience. Cabinet-level briefings normally should take only 10 to 20 minutes. Staff-level briefings should last no more than 40 to 60 minutes. Ample time should be left for questions and dialogue. The briefing should begin by quickly posing its key issues and offering its main judgments. It should then present the material that supports these judgments. It should close with a reminder of the key judgments and a statement on where future analyses should go. Briefings may be glossy and high-tech, but they should never be circus acts designed to hoodwink the audience. The best briefings are straightforward, professional, honest, and candid.

This chapter has provided an introduction to the theory of strategic evaluation, addressing the simple case of designing a policy in order to pursue a single goal. It highlights the importance of good policy analysis and the demanding requirements of carrying it out. Policy analysis cannot be pursued by taking shortcuts. The proper path is that of thoroughness, patience, and persistence. The reward can be a product worth reading and heeding.

Notes

[1] For a historical appraisal of NATO decisionmaking, see Ronald D. Asmus, *Opening NATO's Door: How the Alliance Remade Itself for a New Era* (New York: Columbia University Press, 2002). For examples of the early debate over NATO enlargement, see Ronald D. Asmus, Richard L. Kugler, and F. Stephen Larrabee, "Building a New NATO," *Foreign Affairs* 72, no. 4 (September/October 1993); and Owen Harries, "The Collapse of 'The West,'" *Foreign Affairs* 72, no. 4 (September/October 1993). See also James M. Goldgeier, *Not Whether But When: The U.S. Decision to Enlarge NATO* (Washington, DC: Brookings, 1999) and George W. Grayson, *Strange Bedfellows: NATO Marches East* (Lanham, MD: University Press of America, 1999). For the author's views, see Richard L. Kugler, *Enlarging NATO: The Russia Factor* (Santa Monica, CA: RAND, 1996).

[2] In the wake of terrorist attacks on the United States, a consensus has emerged on the need to reorganize the U.S. Intelligence Community. One step has been to create a new National Intelligence Director who will have increased authority over Intelligence Community budgets and personnel. Notwithstanding the importance of such steps, an equally important challenge is to strengthen the accuracy and insights of intelligence estimates. The terrorist attacks of September 11, 2001, were unforeseen not only because interagency structures did not function properly but also because of a failure of imagination and intellect. See *The 9/11 Commission Report, Final Report of the National Commission on Terrorist Attacks Upon the United States* (New York: W.W. Norton, 2004).

[3] For analysis of defense budget issues, see chapter 16 of this book.

[4] For analysis of critical reasoning as a tool of scientific thought, see Marx W. Wartofsky, *Conceptual Foundations of Scientific Thought: An Introduction to the Philosophy of Science* (London: Macmillan, 1968).

[5] See Irving M. Copi and Carl Cohen, *Introduction to Logic* (Upper Saddle River, NJ: Prentice Hall, 2005). For a useful list of common fallacies of reasoning, see <www.datanation.com/fallacies/index.htm>.

[6] Theories from the fields of political science and international relations can often provide valuable frames of reference for employing the reasoning process in this arena. A core problem is that many such theories are focused on explaining international dynamics in abstract ways, rather than on offering specific policy guidance of the sort needed in strategic evaluations. A good example is the academic debate between idealists and realists, which often is conducted without a specific appraisal of how both theories can be used, and combined, to shape U.S. policy.

Chapter 5
Evaluating Strategies for Multiple Goals

U.S. national security policies abroad are part of U.S. national security strategies—action agendas composed of multiple policies intended to advance several goals at the same time through the vehicle of an individual policy for each goal, with all policies harmonized. Strategy analysis endeavors to design several policies that operate largely in separate domains yet blend in mutually supporting ways under the guidance of an overarching strategic concept.

Strategy analysis is more than normal strategic evaluation on steroids. It is an endeavor unique unto itself. It is more complicated than normal strategic evaluation because it requires the crafting and coordination of not just one but several policies. Beyond this, strategy analysis requires wide-ranging thought not commonly found in less ambitious analyses and frames of reference that are more comprehensive and synthetic. Strategy analysis is often more original and creative than analysis that considers only one policy activity and goal. Strategy analysis normally is not reactive; instead of trying to cope with a situation, it tries to seize the initiative and mold future situations in favorable ways. Analysis of single policies can do this, too, but strategy analysis is steeped in this logic to a greater extent because its thinking is farther-reaching. Strategy analysis is especially demanding of substantive knowledge and analytical talent. Most often, analysis of a single policy takes place within a larger strategic framework that helps set the parameters for its work. The purpose of strategy analysis is to create that larger framework. This is the heart of the difference between the two.[1]

This chapter turns from analysis of policy for a single goal, discussed in chapter 4, to analysis of complex strategies that pursue multiple goals. The chapter first discusses the essential characteristics of strategy—its multiple goals and multiple policies. Three main types of strategy—global, regional, and functional—are defined. The chapter then turns to the specific contributions that can be made by strategic evaluation, and the main challenges to analyzing a complex strategy: evaluating probable benefits and costs, assessing inherent tradeoffs, and predicting the relative likelihood and timetable of success for different options. Ways to portray the results of the analysis are outlined. The chapter ends with a brief illustration of the use of decision trees to portray how strategies may be modified as their programs unfold because such flexibility will increasingly be necessary in the fluid world of the early 21st century.

This chapter argues that in assessing strategies, analysts can use the same procedures identified in chapter 4 for assessing policies (create a conceptual framework, perform the analysis comparatively, and then distribute it through written products and briefing). But in assessing strategies, considerably greater attention must be devoted to how the conceptual framework treats goals and subordinate policies. In policy analysis, only one goal must be defined, and only one policy must be selected among a set of competitors. In strategy analysis, multiple goals must first be defined, weighed in importance to each other, and prioritized. Then, policies must be designed for each goal and harmonized to support each other. The result is a set of alternative candidate strategies, all of which pursue the same goals but with differing emphases, policies, and prospects. All of these strategies must, in turn, be compared in order to determine which strategy is the best choice. Once a set of such strategies is developed, the analysis can then employ the categories of evaluation and analytical techniques of this chapter in order to carry out its business.

Figure 5–1. **Basic Model of a Strategy for Pursuing Multiple Goals**

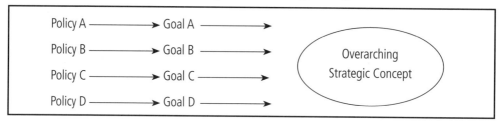

Using a Strategy to Pursue Multiple Goals

The need for a strategy composed of several policies arises when multiple goals are at stake. In theory, a single policy can be shaped to pursue several goals at the same time provided it does an acceptable job of advancing all of these goals. But often this is not the case. Typically a single policy may perform well at achieving one goal, but it might have little positive impact on other important goals in the strategic calculus or even inflict damage upon some of them. Any single policy can pose painful tradeoffs in which some critical goals must be sacrificed in order to attain others. A strategy seeks to surmount this problem of incompatible goals and unwanted negative consequences by designing an individual policy for each goal, then weaving these separate policies together to create an overall strategic construct that best advances all of the goals being sought (see figure 5–1).

An example will help illustrate the point. Suppose the United States is pursuing the goal of enhancing the military capacity of an ally to defend itself against an enemy threat to its borders. The United States could attain this goal by allowing the ally to buy modern American tanks and combat aircraft so as to elevate its military forces to self-sufficiency. But this military assistance program might have downsides; it might overload the ally with expensive defense purchases that its struggling economy cannot afford. It might motivate the enemy to strengthen its military forces, thereby triggering an arms race. It might alarm friendly neighboring countries, causing them to fear that the entire region is becoming unstable. Taken together, these downsides confront the United States with a dilemma: either allow the ally to remain vulnerable to invasion by offering it no military assistance, or provide it assistance at the expense of major damage in other arenas.

These dilemmas can be handled by concocting a multipronged strategy that enables the United States to provide the necessary military assistance, accompanied by parallel policies aimed at shoring up its other goals. In addition to sales of weapons to the ally, the United States might lower trade barriers with it and arrange for it to receive financial assistance from the World Bank and other institutions to help its economy grow even in the face of higher defense spending. The United States might also initiate arms control negotiations with the enemy, thereby opening an avenue to preserve a stable military balance and avoid an arms race. The United States might pursue diplomacy aimed at enhancing regional collective security to reassure other countries that their region is not being destabilized. By forging a strategy of multiple policies, the United States can pursue one goal without unduly damaging other important goals. Performing complex functions of this sort is a primary reason for creating such strategies. The challenge facing analysis is to design strategies that work when conditions are complicated.

The 2003 invasion of Iraq provides a real-life example of the challenges and problems that can arise in designing national security strategies in troubled regions. The main U.S. goal of invading Iraq was to eliminate Saddam Hussein's regime, its menacing regional conduct, and any WMD. But the situation mandated careful attention to other goals as well. Whereas the Gulf War of 1990–1991 had been easier to mount because a broad international consensus favored ejecting Saddam Hussein from Kuwait, the 2003 crisis saw no such consensus in favor of using force to remove him from power. As a result, the United States was compelled to forge a complex strategy aimed at advancing multiple goals.

One goal was to convince the United Nations (UN) Security Council of the need to invade Iraq in the near future. Another goal was to mobilize a large international coalition to support the effort, including Britain and other European allies. A third goal was to elicit acquiescence from France and Germany, which opposed the invasion. A fourth goal was to assure other Arab countries in the Middle East that their own security would not be endangered by a U.S.-led invasion and that their region would be better off without Saddam Hussein. A fifth goal was to avoid hampering the war on terror elsewhere, including in Afghanistan. A sixth goal was to ensure that the invasion did not derail the Israeli-Palestinian peace process. A seventh goal was to ensure that after the invasion had succeeded, the U.S. presence in Iraq would produce a stable, democratic government. An eighth goal was to use the invasion and continued presence to stimulate the advance of democracy across the greater Middle East. A ninth goal was to achieve this complex political-military agenda without diverting U.S. military forces from other global commitments or allowing crises to arise elsewhere, such as on the Korean Peninsula.

Owing to these multiple goals, the United States was active almost everywhere seeking help or trying to persuade doubters while rushing military forces to the Persian Gulf. In the end, it launched a successful invasion with the support of Britain and others, but at the cost of damage to its relations with the UN and Europe. Afterward came a troubled period that suggested that a peaceful, democratic Iraq would be a long time in coming. The rest of the world remained at peace for the time being, but U.S. military forces were bogged down in a lengthy commitment. Historians will be debating the U.S. strategy, its effects, and the forgone alternatives for a long time. It stretched the art of the possible and accepted tradeoffs on behalf of a preemptive war deemed vital by U.S. policymakers. The experience illuminates how difficult the act of crafting and implementing such a complex strategy can be in an unpredictable world of competing crosscurrents and multiple actors with interests of their own.

The Essence of Strategy

The term *strategy* conjures images of a planned, coordinated set of actions aimed at charting a successful course in a demanding situation. A key feature of a strategy is that its multiple actions are not independent of each other, but highly interdependent. None of them stands alone. Each derives part of its rationale from those of the others. Their ultimate success is determined by how they interact to form a sensible game plan. For example, a football coach typically designs an offensive strategy and a defensive strategy for an upcoming game. His design for the former is affected by his design for the latter, and vice versa. If one succeeds, the other is more likely to succeed. If one fails, the other is more likely to fail.

In the national security arena, strategy is commonly associated with military thinking. A military force attempts to formulate a clear, coherent strategy to guide its battlefield operations in war. Early in World War II, for example, the German Wehrmacht pursued a strategy of blitzkrieg to overwhelm Poland and France. During 1944–1945, by contrast, U.S. and Allied soldiers pursued a broad-front strategy as they marched across France to conquer Germany. These two strategies called for military forces to be employed in very different ways.[2]

In contemporary world affairs, U.S. national security strategy is more than solely military. It pursues a broader definition of security than just deterrence and defense. It includes such other instruments as diplomacy, alliance management, trade, and multinational institutions to pursue not just security goals, but also political and economic goals, all of which are combined in order to advance national interests and democratic values. Modern-day strategy analysis can thus be complex.

The relationship between strategy and policy merits further exploration. The definition of strategy employed here says that strategy provides the framework for pursuing policies. This is strategy with a capital *S*. Some observers call this grand strategy, but a better term may be goals-oriented strategy; not all strategies are grand or extensive in their coverage, but they all focus on pursuing multiple goals. Policies themselves can require strategies—that is, schemes to implement them and achieve their subordinate objectives. This is strategy with a small *s*, or operations-oriented strategy, which conveys a sense of tactics and activity. The difference between the two can be illuminated by recalling the U.S. Civil War. From early 1864 onward, President Abraham Lincoln and General Ulysses S. Grant pursued a policy of defeating General Robert E. Lee's Army of Northern Virginia. This policy had an accompanying operational strategy of fighting a series of bloody attrition battles aimed at destroying Lee's forces and seizing the Confederate capital of Richmond. But this policy and strategy were embedded in a larger approach for waging and winning the Civil War as a whole. It called for a coordinated series of offensives not only in Virginia, but also along the Mississippi River, in the Tennessee Valley, in General Sherman's march to the Atlantic, and in the naval blockade of the South. This larger approach amounted to a strategy with a capital *S*: a grand strategy or goals-oriented strategy.[3]

For the United States, developing goals-oriented strategies with a capital *S* is important because of how the international system has changed. During the Cold War, the global structure was so frozen in bipolarity that, over time, U.S. national security strategy became set in concrete. That is no longer the case. Bipolarity has passed into history, and the current international security system lacks such a clear structure. To the extent a structure exists, it resides in a loosely organized democratic community that covers about one-half of the world, with a better-organized inner core of allies at its center. Outside the democratic community, however, the world is largely shapeless and amorphous, unformed by such traditional notions as unipolarity, bipolarity, or multipolarity. Perhaps a structure will eventually emerge, but that time lies in the distant future.

Meanwhile, overall U.S. national security strategy will be a fluid and constantly shifting construct, as will be the component strategies that fall under the rubric of global strategy. Strategy development will mostly take two forms: first, harnessing the resources of the United States and its alliance relationships in order to strengthen the democratic community and to advance common interests and goals in geographic areas outside this community; and second, applying these resources to influence and mold the amorphous, often dangerous world outside the democratic community. Forging new and fluid strategies in these two arenas will be an ongoing challenge for the future that will demand a steady stream of insightful strategic evaluations.

Future strategies will need to be crafted in the context of a globalizing world. Globalization is not a policy or an ideology but rather an empirical trend of profound importance. An accelerating increase of cross-border flows in such areas as trade, finances, investments, technology, biomaterials, technology, communications, information, cultural values, and interpersonal contacts is drawing the far corners of the world closer together. Previously separated regions are coming into closer contact, interdependencies are growing, and the world is becoming a single stage upon which many actors play important roles. Globalization compels the United States to see the world in holistic terms rather than viewing regions separately. It means that the United States needs to design an overall national security strategy plus subordinate strategies. This family of national security strategies will have to be integrated in order to protect U.S. interests and to advance American values and visions abroad.[4]

Different Types of Strategies

A family of U.S. national security strategies will have global, regional, and functional components. Global strategies provide a roadmap for how the United States conducts its national security affairs on a worldwide basis. They provide a framework for regional strategies, which define the goals and policies of the United States in the key regions of the world. Functional strategies provide a sense of how the United States should act in such interdependent, multiregional areas as alliance affairs, arms control, and economic aid. All three types of strategies must be designed to work together if overall U.S. national security strategy is to function effectively. The nature of these types of strategies, and their interrelationships, can be illuminated by discussing them sequentially: global strategies, then regional strategies, and finally, functional strategies.

Global Strategies

A global strategy is more than a collection of regional strategies; it sets worldwide goals as well as priorities for each region.[5] An example is the U.S. national security strategy put forth by the Bush administration in fall 2002. Critics often portrayed the strategy of the preceding administration of William Clinton as anchored in liberal premises and the succeeding Bush administration strategy as resting on conservative premises, but it is fairer to say that both strategies reflected their times, and both can be seen as outgrowths of a process that began in 1990–1991 when the Cold War suddenly came to an end. At that time, U.S. national security strategy had been anchored in time-tested concepts of containment, deterrence, forward defense of allies, and flexible response in the face of crises and wars. Almost overnight, this set of concepts was rendered out of date. A new national security strategy anchored in new concepts was needed, but what it was to be was clouded by great uncertainty about the kind of international security system the post–Cold War era was likely to produce.

The 1989–1993 administration of George H.W. Bush began the process of forging a new post–Cold War global strategy. Although mostly preoccupied with such urgent matters as unifying Germany within NATO and winning the Persian Gulf War against Iraq, the Bush administration devoted considerable effort to thinking about how a new global order anchored in stability and peace could be crafted. Concerned that the collapse of the old bipolar order could result in an unstable multipolar system, it concluded that instead of withdrawing into a new isolationism, the United States should remain actively engaged abroad and use its new status as the world's only superpower for constructive purposes. It also decided that current U.S.-led alliances (such as NATO and bilateral alliances in Asia) should be retained and reformed in order to continue serving as valuable instruments for global security management. It rejected the idea of wholesale military disarmament. Instead, it decided to retain a downsized but still potent U.S. military force configured to carry out a regional defense strategy focused on threats posed by such medium-sized adversaries as Iraq and North Korea.[6]

When the Clinton administration took office in early 1993, it inherited a seemingly peaceful world with a bright future. Accordingly, its initial national security strategy was focused on enlarging the democratic community, establishing a partnership with Russia, and taking advantage of globalization's integrative effects. By the time the Clinton administration began its second term in early 1997, however, international trends were taking a negative course. Savage ethnic fighting in the Balkans, the slowing of democratic reforms in Russia, trouble with China and North Korea, renewed Persian Gulf tensions, and the tendency of globalization to leave many poor countries behind were grounds for worry about the future. In response, the Clinton administration adopted a new, more assertive national security strategy focused on shaping emerging trends, responding to current crises, and preparing for an uncertain future.[7] It also set about to fund larger defense budgets in order to strengthen U.S. military forces and encouraged the NATO allies to do likewise.

The new national security strategy of the George W. Bush administration—written in 2002 after the global war on terrorism had been launched—was even more focused on the dangers ahead. It judged that careful attention would have to be given to the world's turbulent security affairs through such traditional mechanisms as diplomacy and military power. The Bush strategy had several interlocking components, each with a wide set of policies and goals, as well as a worldwide focus that resulted in multiple separate regional strategies. Its first component was an activist security strategy aimed at reassuring allies, maintaining favorable balances of power in key regions, dissuading potential opponents from engaging in destabilizing competitions, deterring and defeating aggression by rogue countries, defeating terrorism, and suppressing threats posed by proliferation of WMD systems. Its second component was geopolitical diplomacy aimed at establishing more constructive relations with such big powers as Russia and China and at defusing such regional hotspots as the Indo-Pakistan rivalry and the Israeli-Palestinian conflict. Its third component was an economic strategy aimed at accelerating global economic growth through expansion of free trade and open markets, as well as greater aid and investments in order to help poor economies grow faster. Its fourth component was an effort to promote the spread of democracy by encouraging social reforms and responsible governance in countries led by undemocratic or authoritarian governments. Its fifth component was a bigger defense budget targeted at transforming U.S. military forces for information-era operations. Whether this global, multifaceted strategy will succeed in its ambitious visions and soaring ideals will depend upon future events. But in sharply changing the earlier U.S. strategy through enhanced activism and sterner security measures abroad, it amounted to an ambitious grand strategy.[8]

This strategy is not the only model that could have been adopted. Few conservatives in the Republican Party endorsed outright isolationism, but some had called for a less assertive strategy aimed mainly at defending traditional vital interests and strategic perimeters, thus limiting the risk of U.S. overextension into peripheral zones. In contrast, some American liberals disagreed with the new strategy's departure from Clinton administration premises and policies toward multilateralism and arms control and about its other manifestations of conservative principles. Europeans and others abroad complained about the strategy's tendencies toward unilateralism, its scuttling of such agreements as the Kyoto Accord, its activist attitude toward rogue countries, and its penchant for military solutions to political problems. These criticisms set the stage for intense debates.

All future administrations will need to craft national security strategies that have a global focus. Doing so will never be easy because it is so intellectually demanding, and it always will be subjected to political scrutiny, debate, and partisan infighting. Strategic evaluation can contribute to this enterprise not only by making the intellectual demands more manageable, but also by providing concrete focus to the accompanying political debates. In this sense, it can help make the pluralist process of democracy more informed and thereby more capable of making sound decisions about very complex matters.

Regional Strategies

A U.S. global strategy must always be accompanied by strategies for handling the various regions around the world, each of which must be treated on its own merits. A good example of a regional strategy is seen in how the U.S. Government handles NATO and Europe. All administrations since World War II have had concerted European strategies, and the Bush administration has been no exception. Its dual pursuit of NATO enlargement and defense reform reflected a focused, ambitious strategy. Under U.S. sponsorship, NATO adopted a new strategic agenda at its Prague Summit in late 2002. The new Prague strategy called for NATO military reform in order to develop a better capacity to project power outside Europe while working closely with U.S. forces. To this end, it called for a new NATO Response Force (NRF), a military command focused on the modernization and incorporation of information technologies for transformation, and alliance-wide pursuit of upgraded military capabilities attuned to the new missions ahead. In order to prevent a rift between NATO and the European Union, the Prague strategy called for pursuit of interoperable military forces and close political consultations between the two bodies. In order to accelerate integration of Eastern Europe into the alliance, it called for prompt admission of seven new members, plus intensified partnership activities with other countries still outside NATO. In order to strengthen relations with Russia, it called for a new NATO-Russia Council to increase collaboration with Moscow in the war on terror and other endeavors. A product of intense analysis and debate throughout the alliance, the Prague strategy was a major departure from the past; it sent NATO on a new trajectory for the early 21st century.

Regional strategies for the greater Middle East, South Asia, and Asia have also been common to all U.S. administrations, as have strategies for Latin America and sub-Saharan Africa. The first three regions will be addressed in subsequent chapters, but a few words here about Latin America and sub-Saharan Africa will help illuminate the kinds of issues that must be addressed by U.S. regional strategies. For many Latin American countries, having cast aside military dictatorships in favor of democracy and participation in global economic markets, the main issues are further democratization, economic progress to close the gap between rich and poor, political stability with effective governance and less corruption, financial stability to control inflation, and control of drug trafficking and local violence. An additional issue is regional economic integration, both within Latin America and with North America. The latter goal is reflected in the Bush administration's proposal to expand the North American Free Trade Agreement (NAFTA) to create a Free Trade Area of the Americas, along with bilateral trade agreements with individual countries.

Sub-Saharan Africa, too, presents specific issues for U.S. strategy. Regional prospects there seem dimmer than those of Latin America, but many of the issues and goals are the same: further democratization, economic progress, political stability, effective governance, and regional economic integration. Sub-Saharan Africa also faces the task of pursuing regional security cooperation to lessen the periodic outbreak of violence in the form of ethnic struggles, revolutions and civil wars, small cross-border wars, and mass murder of civilians. In the years ahead, both regions will merit careful attention in the form of not only scholarly research but also policy and strategy analysis both by the United States and by those shaping policy in the region.

Functional Strategies

In this era of globalization, functional strategies—strategies whose focus is not geographic but rather a particular activity—are also increasingly common and important. Defense planning—preparing military forces to carry out national strategy—is part of the process of developing a functional strategy. Alliance reform, containment and deterrence, arms control, democratization, and economic progress are other Cold War–era functional strategies. Today, functional strategies aim to foster such goals as building partnerships, promoting responsible governance, defusing anti-Western ideologies, dissuading potential adversaries, defeating terrorism, halting WMD proliferation, stopping drug trafficking and organized crime, and reducing greenhouse gas emissions. While these strategies have different focal points, all have multiple subordinate goals and policies that must be coordinated to achieve their purposes. All require in-depth analysis on how to develop and implement them. All must be integrated into an overall U.S. global strategy and into regional strategies that may require different ways of carrying them out in each separate region.

Strategy analysis for determining how the United States is to participate in international and regional bodies that perform functional roles will also be a high priority in future years. Such bodies as the United Nations, the Group of Seven (G–7) major industrialized nations, the World Trade Organization (WTO), and others are becoming more important. The challenge is both to enhance their performance and to ensure that legitimate U.S. interests are respected by them. The same applies to arms control: the Anti-Ballistic Missile (ABM) Treaty was cast aside because its Cold War purposes had been overtaken by events, yet control of nuclear arms and containing WMD proliferation remain vital goals that must be pursued, in some cases through new accords. Climate control is another example of the need for strategy. The United States opposed the Kyoto Accord, arguing that it sacrificed valid U.S. interests on the altar of global agreement. But opposition to the Kyoto Accord does not obviate the need for the United States to have a strategy for control of global warming and to cooperate with other nations and multilateral bodies on behalf of this worthy goal. Yet another example of a functional strategy is the building of post-Westphalian international laws that extend beyond the longstanding but increasingly blurry guidelines for state-to-state relationships established by the Peace of Westphalia in 1648. This is another arena where interstate politics could damage valid U.S. interests but, if handled effectively, could create a broader international consensus on new laws for this era of globalization and complex interactions among nations, multilateral bodies, and nongovernmental actors. For the United States, participating in these arenas requires a carefully honed strategy of the sort that requires serious analysis.

Contributions of Strategic Evaluation

The ways in which national security strategies—global, regional, or functional—are put on paper may suggest they are natural events and exercises in the obvious. Normally, however, they are neither dictated by nature nor created out of thin air, and they are not necessarily obvious. Instead, they often are a product of original thinking, deep concentration, and deliberate choice from among a spectrum of options. They are almost always a product of great labor and intense bureaucratic infighting, in which parts or all of other strategies were considered and rejected. Because such strategies are an expression of a country's moral visions and strategic priorities, they are inherently political constructs. In the United States, responsibility for global strategy lies with the President and the National Security Council (NSC) staff, while defense strategy is mostly shaped by the Department of Defense. Strategies are elaborate edifices forged through a weighing and balancing of multiple approaches, and they necessitate making many judgments about the relationships between ends and means and about how to coordinate their diverse features. Creating them often requires a great deal of analytical support.

Strategy statements are intended to convey strategic messages, both to mobilize the support of Congress and the American people and to inform foreign countries of how the United States will be acting in the coming period. They must have strong rhetorical content, and they must be coherent. Strategic evaluation can help make them so.

A strategy should have an overarching concept, a guiding theme, and policies that fit together. Achieving such coherence can be difficult. Strategy studies usually alter an existing strategy in some major way and convey a sense of change. They often are conducted early in a new Presidential administration, before it has fully developed its strategic thinking. As a result, they plow new ground and seek a new consensus. When time is short, the natural temptation can be not to think deeply, but instead to cobble together a motley collection of imperatives brought in by the new team, the wishes of the career bureaucracy, and a few original ideas advanced by outsiders. During a new strategy's formative stages, strategic evaluation can help by subjecting an emerging consensus to critical scrutiny. A good idea is to compare the new strategy to other alternatives that offer different ways of thinking and acting. By placing the new strategy along a spectrum of options, including polar opposites, analysis can help modify and strengthen it. A strategy that can withstand scrutiny during its creation will have a better chance of finding favor in the outside world and standing the test of time.

Strategic evaluation can also help by ensuring that the new strategy's goals are well chosen and clearly defined, that its policies strongly support these goals and are consistent with each other, that its key strategic judgments are sound, and that its priorities are well placed. When strategies fall apart, it is often due to problems in these areas. A single specious idea or wrong-headed assertion with major implications might be used by opponents and critics to discredit the entire strategy, thus causing support for it to dwindle. Even if public support remains strong, problems in these areas can unhinge the strategy as it is being implemented. For example, some policies might not be granted adequate resources or sound leadership. If their implementation falls short of expectations, this can weaken the effects of policies that do succeed. By probing the strategy's soundness, analysis may be able to expose such problems and resolve them before they become fatal.

The challenge of harmonizing a strategy's multiple policies is particularly important. These policies normally do not operate in their separate domains wholly apart from each other but instead overlap and interact, often to a considerable extent. For example, a policy aimed at stabilizing a region's troubled security affairs may falter unless parallel policies for bringing economic progress and democracy to the region also succeed. Likewise, economic progress and democracy-building may not succeed unless the region's security affairs are stabilized and wars are avoided, perhaps through strong U.S.-backed deterrence regimes. Progress in one policy arena thus can aid progress in the others, and these positive effects can be reciprocal. Conversely, however, policies sometimes can work at cross-purposes or even fall into conflict with one another. For example, a policy aimed at enhancing peace through defense preparedness can hinder economic development if it requires key countries to divert funds from domestic investments in industry and infrastructure to military forces.

Another example of conflict is a regional diplomacy and security policy whose reliance upon support by traditional monarchies or authoritarian governments gives them an excuse not to enhance democracy and economic markets. With policies that naturally support each other, steps may be needed to configure those policies so that such support is maximized and made synergistic. With policies that naturally work against each other, steps may be needed to sand off rough edges or to set priorities so that the most important policies are given emphasis. The key point is that the multiple policy gears of a strategy need to mesh if the strategy is to succeed. Analysis can help design these policies so that they mesh as smoothly as possible.

Strategic evaluation can provide further help by evaluating whether the strategy is merely a rhetorical exercise or is actually a feasible construct with a realistic chance of succeeding. Analysis can help determine whether the necessary support from friends and allies is likely to be forthcoming or could be mobilized through special effort. It can assess whether the strategy is powerful and robust or is vulnerable to an adversary's actions, fate, or bad luck. It can assess whether the strategy has necessary flexibility or is stuck with a rigid agenda that would be hard to alter if conditions changed. It can focus on the relationship between postulated actions and desired consequences, offering judgments on whether the strategy's actions are likely to achieve their purposes, and providing metrics to measure whether progress is being made. It can estimate the budgetary resources that will be needed, whether they will be forthcoming, how they can best be invested, and what the consequences will be if they are inadequate. It can provide a sense of cost-effectiveness, including advice on how money and emphasis can be shifted from one policy to another in order to strengthen the strategy's overall performance. By offering evaluation in all these areas, analysis can provide advice on the strategy's prospects for success and can strengthen the strategy in important ways.

Vigorous implementation is often critical to a strategy's success, yet strategy studies often fall short in this key area, leaving design of implementation to follow-on actions or to chance. Implementing a strategy is harder than implementing a single policy, for the simple reason that a strategy is composed of multiple interacting policies. Each policy component of a complex strategy requires an implementation agenda of its own, and all of these agendas must be blended to yield a coordinated and harmonized execution of the strategy. Strategies typically require attention to timing, pacing, synchronization, and choreography. For example, policy A might have to be successfully launched or even completed before policy B can begin, while the manner in which policy B is carried out might depend upon exactly how policy A has unfolded. Political and economic strategists must, like military strategists, develop a strong sense of the need to master the flow of events. An implementation plan can help resolve the problems that inevitably crop up as the strategy is being carried out. Analysis may contribute to a sensible implementation plan by illuminating crucial details.

Analysis can provide valuable insights into how a new strategy might mandate significant changes in the instruments of U.S. national security policy. For example, it might show that changes must be made in the U.S. overseas military presence or regional reinforcement plans. It might show that reforms are needed in U.S. alliance relationships, including how U.S. and allied military forces work together. It might show that U.S. foreign economic policy needs to place more emphasis on regional bodies, grants rather than loans, lessened trade barriers, new forms of International Monetary Fund (IMF) and World Bank assistance, or expanded investments in foreign countries. It might show that the State Department, the NSC staff, the Intelligence Community, or overseas Embassies need to alter how they coordinate interagency policy implementation. Analysis might be able to show how such changes could make the difference between success and failure for the new strategy.

Challenges Facing Analysis of Strategies

Analysis of a strategy employs the techniques of standard strategic evaluation described in the preceding chapter for analyzing individual policies but is more complicated. The fundamental task is the same: to assess the situation and to compare alternative options on the basis of effectiveness, costs, and other performance-related considerations. Strategy analysis, however, is more challenging because it must design individual policies that make sense and also blend policies together so that they advance multiple goals and thereby advance the common purpose. The need to consider multiple policies and goals greatly increases the intellectual demands.

As laid out in chapter 4 for the process of analyzing policies, the intellectual process of analyzing strategies begins with a conceptual framework that defines the strategic challenges being faced, articulates U.S. interests and goals, and identifies a spectrum of strategy options for pursuing the goals. It then compares these options through a reasoning process that specifies subject areas, employs appropriate analytical procedures, and establishes criteria for evaluation. In some cases, the analytical task will be simplified because strategy options already exist in a well-defined form. Then, the task is merely to evaluate them in mechanical terms. But situations often arise in which strategic problems are so new and unexpected that no existing strategies are appropriate. This task is more creative and demanding: forging entirely new, freshly minted strategies and options that can then be subjected to scrutiny. This task can be performed only through original thinking about the relationships between means and ends and between actions and consequences on a large scale.

Additional factors make the task of strategy analysis more demanding. During most of the Cold War, the intellectual scope of strategy analysis was mostly constrained because the bipolar world was largely unchanging. The United States typically was focused on reacting to individual threats, and it possessed well-articulated strategic theories for judging how to react. Today, by contrast, the entire world is undergoing profound changes at a fast pace, and the United States is not merely reacting to events. Instead, the United States now is often trying to be a leading agent of change and to shape the future. Its agendas are also more comprehensive than during the Cold War: instead of trying to contain individual threats, it is now trying to influence how entire regions or functional areas of activity evolve.

This need for assertive and comprehensive strategies is dictated by the nature of world affairs. Bipolarity has faded into history, and no new international structure has arisen to take its place. Outside the democratic community is a chaotic and heterogeneous international community that lacks structure and order and could produce great turmoil and violence. This chaotic situation is not static; it is changing rapidly in response to globalization and other high-tempo dynamics. These changes are not random. As complexity theorists observe, these changes have emergent properties: left on their own, they may eventually produce new structures. Such new structures may have good features, or they might magnify the turmoil, conflict, and violence of today's world. The daunting task facing the United States is to help direct this fluid environment and to do so without a catalog of existing strategic theories for defining how to act in each case.

For these reasons, strategy analysis today more than ever requires creativity, originality, and conceptual rigor to bring intellectual order to the situations being encountered. Analysis must strive to equip all strategies with coherent, well-constructed concepts and theories that show how multiple policies can be forged to pursue multiple goals in difficult and uncertain settings. This presents three particularly important analytical challenges:

- assessing the tradeoffs that are posed when the goals of competing policies and strategies are incompatible with each other

- measuring the costs and effectiveness of policies and strategies when the activities being pursued are so different that they are not easily compared

- developing the program component of a strategy—its action agenda—in enough detail so that senior officials know what they are approving and are able to enforce its implementation.

Assessing Tradeoffs

The task of strategy analysis is easiest when the multiple goals being considered are compatible and in harmony with each other. The task becomes more difficult when the goals are inconsistent or in conflict with one another. A major purpose of defining a strategy is to reconcile conflicting goals by pursuing a separate policy for each goal. Sometimes, however, an optimal blend of policies can be hard to find; the interdependence of policies may make it difficult to pursue optimal courses of action in each case. That is, policy A might offer high effectiveness for goal A, but its actions may preclude design of a policy B that is comparably effective for goal B. For example, if the United States provides robust military assistance to an ally, this step may confine it to pursuing only limited arms control negotiations with the ally's adversaries, rather than comprehensive negotiations that seem otherwise merited, while ambitious arms control agendas could force the United States to scale back military assistance to its allies.

Such situations can give rise to the need for analysis to address critical strategy dilemmas and difficult tradeoffs. In most cases, senior officials will try to find a balance among competing imperatives rather than sacrificing one goal to another. Determining what constitutes a sensible balance is often subjective. Analysis can help make the task easier by assessing the nature of the tradeoffs at stake. Sacrificing a lot to gain a little is one thing; sacrificing a little to gain a lot is more attractive. Analysis can help distinguish between the two.

An example, represented in table 5–1, helps illuminate how tradeoffs can be addressed. It is a case in which three equal-cost strategies are being considered. Rather than grade

Table 5–1. **Strategy Tradeoffs**

	Performance of Strategies		
Strategy Options	**Goal A**	**Goal B**	**Goal C**
Strategy 1	High	Low	Low
Strategy 2	Low	Low	High
Strategy 3	Medium	Medium	Medium

the policies of each strategy in simplistic terms of success or failure, it employs three possible performance scores: low, medium, and high. Thus, it conveys a better sense of degree for judging the tradeoffs imposed by the three strategies, each of which offers different performance characteristics with respect to its goals. Strategy 1 (composed of three policies for each of its three goals) is assessed as offering high performance for goal A, but low performance for goals B and C. Strategy 2 offers high performance for goal C but low performance for goals A and B. Strategy 3 offers medium performance for all three goals.

Which of these strategies is the best choice? The choice depends partly upon the relative importance attached to the three goals. If all are assigned equal importance and priority, then strategy 3 might be seen as best because its three medium scores, added together, match or exceed the overall performance of the other two strategies, which have two low scores to accompany their single high score. By contrast, strategy 1 could be judged as the winner if goal A is accorded significantly higher importance than the other two goals, and strategy 2 could win if goal C is accorded top priority. The choice also depends partly upon policymakers' attitudes toward risk-taking. If they are risk-averse, they will be more likely to choose strategy 3 because, although it does not perform very well in any one area, it does not perform badly in any area. If they are more risk-tolerant, they may choose strategy 1 or strategy 2 because both offer high performance in one area even though they perform poorly in two areas.

Similarly difficult tradeoffs arise often during strategy studies and policy debates. The task of analysis is to try to illuminate them so that senior decisionmakers understand the choices. If analysis makes imaginative use of the techniques available, it can illuminate these tradeoffs in ways that are genuinely insightful.

An especially valuable technique is that of sensitivity analysis, which shows how sensitive conclusions are to variations in key assumptions. For example, sensitivity analysis can be employed to show how the rankings assigned to strategy options vary as a function of the importance assigned to the multiple goals relative to one another. It can also be used to show how such rankings vary as a function of assumptions about risk-taking.

Typically, a strategy option that is attractive across a wide range of assumptions will be a better choice than an option that makes sense only for a narrow range of assumptions.[9]

Evaluating Costs

Even when the individual policies of a strategy do not create difficult tradeoffs with each other, problems can arise when the thorny matter of costs is addressed. In the example shown in table 5–2, strategy 1 performs better than strategy 2 across the board, and strategy 2 performs better than strategy 3. If the strategies imposed equal costs, the

Table 5–2. **Cost Tradeoffs**

Strategy Options	Costs	Performance of Strategies
Strategy 1	$30 biållion	High for all goals
Strategy 2	$20 billion	Medium for all goals
Strategy 3	$10 billion	Low for all goals

choice would be clear. But in this example, strategy 1 costs more than strategy 2, while strategy 3 is the cheapest.

Which strategy is the best choice ultimately boils down to judgments about performance aspirations, willingness to pay costs, and acceptability of marginal returns. Strategy 1 may be preferred if policymakers insist upon stellar performance irrespective of costs. Strategy 2 may be chosen if they prefer a balance of adequate performance and affordable costs. If they are not hungry for major achievements and want to limit costs, strategy 3 may be deemed best.

The task of analysis is to illuminate the choices and tradeoffs open to senior officials, a task that can be performed by displaying simple measures of aggregate cost and performance, but the task of developing such measures of merit is not to be taken lightly. Calculating budget costs is straightforward, if credible expenditure estimates are available. The main imperative is to ensure that the same cost categories are used to evaluate each strategy (such as acquisition costs plus operations costs for 5 years). Measuring performance, however, is often more difficult. How does an analyst know how likely it is that a policy will succeed to one degree or another? The answer is often not obvious. Many strategy studies have disappointed senior officials because of their failure to address it in explicit and credible ways.

Performance measures are important because the results of most strategies are neither total success nor total failure, but somewhere in between. Predicting relative success or failure becomes crucial to a comparison of competing strategies. Achievement of military and economic goals is often easiest to measure because such indicators as numbers of weapons modernized or growth in gross domestic product can be quantified. Achievement of political goals can be easy when the goal is clear and simple, such as the signing of an alliance security treaty, an economic accord, or an arms control agreement. But it can be far harder when the goal is nebulous, such as achieving a high degree of U.S. diplomatic influence in a foreign capital. In such ambiguous cases, judgments might have to be made about the defining characteristics of success; a well-reasoned judgment will be far more useful than a vague or sloppy one.

Measuring the degree to which a policy will attain a goal can be difficult even when only one policy and one goal are being considered, but it becomes more difficult when strategies composed of multiple goals and multiple policies are under review. Often the goals will be so different that the same measuring sticks cannot be used. For incommensurable goals, different measures of merit must be designed for each goal. For example, military modernization of allied forces must be measured by different metrics than those used for arms control.

To establish comparable standards of measurement, it is useful to create a common scale for gauging all policy-goal relationships. Ranking policies in terms of low, medium, and high performance is one suitable approach. A more sophisticated approach is reflected in figure 5–2, which measures the current state of affairs for each goal as well as the expected outcome after the policy is implemented. The result can be a refined sense of how each policy and strategy is expected to bring about changes for the better.

For strategy 1, policy A is deemed likely to elevate achievement of goal A from a low score now to a medium score in the future. Policy B is deemed likely to elevate goal B from near-zero to a medium score. Policy C is judged likely to elevate goal C from low to high. The performance predictions for strategy 2 differ from strategy 1 for the goals being pursued. By displaying all policy-goal predictions with a similar metric, this chart provides a composite picture of the situation confronting each strategy and its potential ability to succeed. The result is a summary portrayal of how these two strategies and their component policies are likely to work if they are implemented fully. In this case, neither strategy stands out as the clear winner. Both strategies elevate performance for all three goals in comparable ways in terms of overall magnitude. Whereas strategy 1 attains only one high score, strategy 2 attains two high scores, yet it also records one low score, a failing not suffered by strategy 1. Senior officials might select either of these strategies or might instead ask for an appraisal of whether additional resources might produce further improvements. Regardless of the decision, the analysis will have accomplished its purpose by presenting a useful synthesis in clear, easily understood terms.

Developing a Program

The final challenge facing strategy analysis is to develop and assess a program agenda for the strategy options under review. A program is a set of concrete actions taken in order to execute a strategy. It can have military, economic, diplomatic, and political features. It is the main vehicle for determining how the strategy is implemented and whether it succeeds.

Figure 5–2. **Measuring Ability of Strategies to Achieve Goals**

	Degree of Goal Achievement				
	Near-Zero	Low	Medium	High	Near-Perfect
Strategy 1					
Policy A/Goal A		O ⟶ OO			
Policy B/Goal B	O ⟶		OO		
Policy C/Goal C		O ⟶		OO	
Strategy 2					
Policy D/Goal A		O ⟶		OO	
Policy E/Goal B	O ⟶ OO				
Policy F/Goal C		O ⟶		OO	

Key: O is current situation; OO is estimated outcome if policy is pursued.

Developing a program is important for two reasons. Analysts normally can neither gauge budget costs accurately nor predict whether and how a strategy will succeed unless the implementation agendas of its component policies are identified with some precision. During a typical strategy study, programs for each option are sketched in general ways in order to create an aggregate sense of their actions, costs, and impact. Once a single strategy option is selected, intensive analysis then gets under way to define the program in the detail needed for government agencies to implement it.

The program development phase is hugely important, and it requires hard work, time, and a willingness to take pains with details. Preparing a program for a single policy can be difficult enough; developing individual programs for the multiple policies of a comprehensive strategy is even more difficult, let alone developing integrated programs for several entirely different strategies, each of which requires a unique program of its own. Crafting the implementation program can take more time and effort than defining the strategy and analyzing its core features.

Investing time and effort into this grubby stage of the process often pays rich dividends because issues key to the strategy analysis often arise here. This is particularly the case when affordability is a critical concern and cost comparisons play a big role in selection among the options. The success of a strategy may hinge on getting the details of programmatic implementation exactly right. Many brilliantly conceived strategies have flopped because the programs to carry them out were not well designed or properly implemented.

Beyond this, even when a strategy is approved by the President and Cabinet members, it can mutate into a quite different strategy if the concrete acts of implementation take a different course from the one originally decided upon. More than one President has been left wondering how a strategy personally approved by him turned into something very different and disappointingly ineffective once its implementation was placed in the hands of the bureaucracy. Avoiding this dispiriting outcome is a compelling reason for crafting the program in considerable detail at the same time that the strategy is developed.

As many experienced government officials know, the program often is the policy or strategy, which otherwise can be little more than words on paper. The military component of a strategy might include such diverse steps as selling weapons and support systems to an ally, providing training and education to its military personnel, stationing U.S. forces on the ally's soil, enhancing U.S. mobility assets so that reinforcements can be sent in a crisis, and conducting joint training and exercises with U.S. and allied forces. The economic component of a strategy aimed at helping an ally might include grants for purchase of equipment, loans for development of infrastructure, financial guarantees for underwriting investments by private businesses, lowered trade barriers to encourage exports and imports between the United States and the ally, and educational scholarships for students to study in the United States. The political and diplomatic component might include a host of activities, such as signing a formal defense treaty or executive agreement, holding summits between national leaders and regular meetings of foreign and defense ministers, and undertaking efforts to enhance the ally's role in such international institutions as the United Nations, the World Bank, or the IMF.

All of these activities must be articulated, made coherent, and carefully coordinated as they are carried out. The more that is known about them during the stage when the strategy is being developed and evaluated, the better. The challenge facing strategy analysis is to provide this information early enough so that senior officials have it at their disposal when top-level decisions are being made. Success at this endeavor is often the bellwether in determining whether a strategy analysis will succeed in enduring ways or instead passes from memory shortly after it is written.

Portraying Results of Strategies

Although handling details is important, the bottom line in most strategy studies is whether they do a good job of portraying the likely strategic results of the options being examined. Strategies are judged not by how they operate (their means) but by how well they succeed (their ends). Senior officials naturally will want to select the strategy option that promises to perform the best at achieving national goals. Especially when the available options create tough choices and tradeoffs, they turn to strategy analysis for guidance. The task of rendering this guidance is made complicated because it requires a forecast of future events, often amidst considerable uncertainty. Making such a forecast is particularly difficult in a strategy analysis because it must consider multiple policies in pursuit of multiple goals. Yet this responsibility cannot be dodged if the study is to be relevant to high-level decisions.

In making a forecast of strategic results, a good way to begin is by taking stock of the degree to which the multiple goals being pursued by the United States share a common purpose. Typically, a strategy's multiple goals are tied together in order to help support an overall strategic concept; this provides a sense of direction and destination for the effort as a whole. For example, a regional strategy may aim at elevating the peace, stability, and prosperity of that region as a whole; or it may aim at preserving the region's current level of peaceful stability and prosperity, in the face of countervailing pressures in its underlying security affairs and economics; or it may aim at preventing the region from descending into turmoil and chaos as a result of dangerous trends. The strategy might even aim at all three outcomes: adjusting to ongoing trends, preventing decline, and elevating the region insofar as possible (see figure 5–3). Clarifying this strategic concept helps provide a meaningful metric for judging the performance of each strategy option.

Figure 5–3. **Alternative Strategic Concepts**

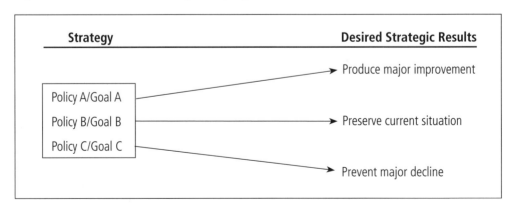

Strategy	Desired Strategic Results
	Produce major improvement
Policy A/Goal A	
Policy B/Goal B	Preserve current situation
Policy C/Goal C	
	Prevent major decline

Such strategic concepts are important because the regional agendas confronting contemporary U.S. national security strategy vary considerably from one another. During much of the 20th century, U.S. strategy for Europe aimed at trying to stabilize a continent that, owing to its turbulent geopolitics, had become a cockpit for global calamity, producing two World Wars and the Cold War. Today, however, Europe is rapidly becoming a model of democratic unity, peace, and progress; this presents the United States with challenges, opportunities, and problems wholly different from those of only a few decades ago. Contemporary Asia has also become more stable, although it is making slower progress than Europe in its politics and security affairs. In marked contrast, the greater Middle East is now highly unstable and is endangered by trends that could make it even more volatile. Strategy analyses for these three regions are thus likely to be guided by quite different strategic concepts that capture the different U.S. aspirations for each region. The same applies to any other type of strategy analysis—being clear about the strategic concept is critical to forming an insightful appraisal of how each strategy option is likely to perform.

Although strategy analyses should always endeavor to use robust methodologies and relevant empirical data, future forecasts inevitably will be anchored in subjective judgments; they cannot rely on mathematical proofs or laboratory experiments. Often a single forecast will not be possible because the outcome will be a variable that is affected by many factors apart from U.S. actions. For example, U.S. strategy might be expected to achieve highly successful results if events go well, but considerably less impressive results if events outside the control of U.S. policy go poorly. When a range of forecasts is appropriate, the analysis can employ a probability distribution to help educate senior officials about the alternative prospects facing them (see figure 5–4).

Portraying a sense of time horizons can also help senior officials gauge the strategy options open to them. Even if a strategy is judged highly likely to perform well, success will rarely come overnight. U.S. strategy in Europe during the Cold War, for example, took 40 years of sustained effort. Strategy options may perform differently as the future unfolds.

Figure 5–4. **Alternative Outcomes: A Probabilistic Forecast**

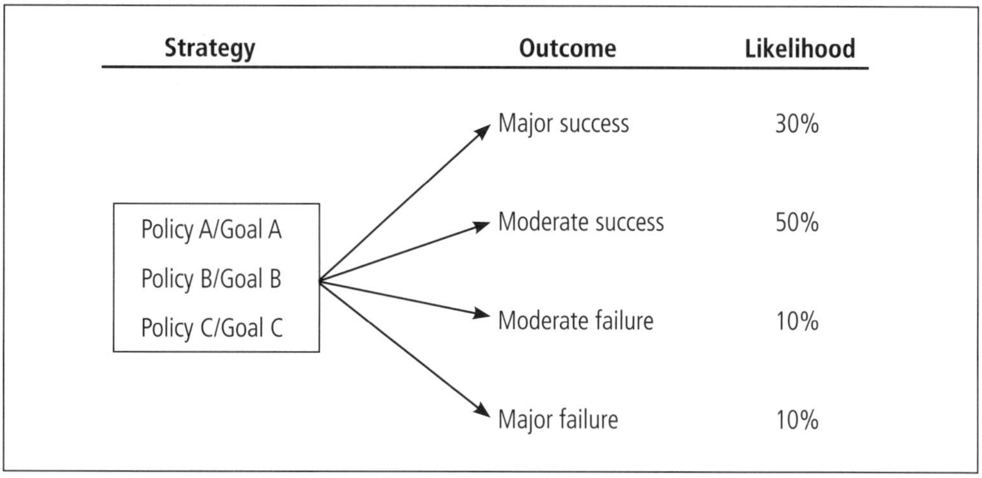

Strategy	Outcome	Likelihood
	Major success	30%
Policy A/Goal A	Moderate success	50%
Policy B/Goal B		
Policy C/Goal C	Moderate failure	10%
	Major failure	10%

Figure 5–5. **Time Horizons for Future Forecasts**

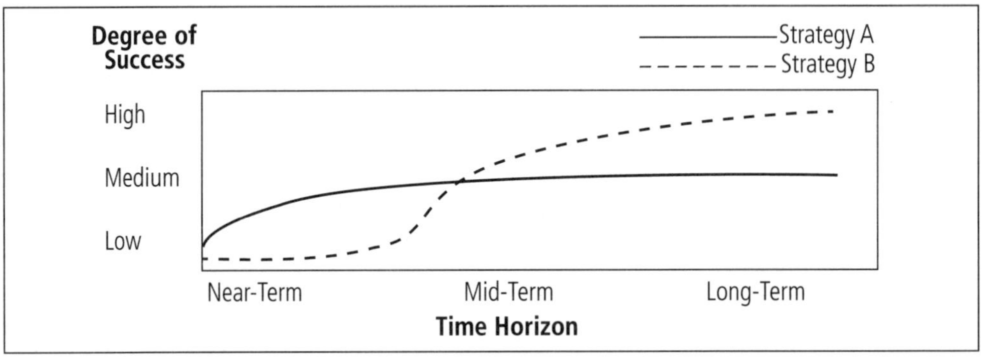

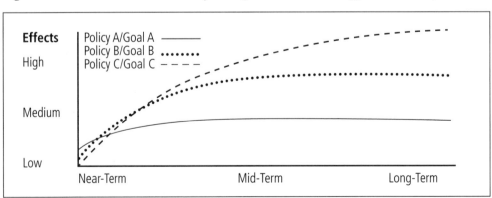

If so, this judgment should be made clear to senior officials. Figure 5–5 displays two equal-cost strategy options with different time horizons. Strategy A delivers moderate success in the near term, but little more beyond. Strategy B produces less success in the near term, but considerably greater success in the long term. The decision depends not only upon the strategic aspirations of senior officials, but upon their time horizons as well. If they need results quickly, they might opt for strategy A. If they can afford to wait longer, they may opt for strategy B because it ultimately delivers more.

Strategy analysis can enhance the sophistication of its forecasts by showing the manner in which the separate policy components of a strategy option contribute to outcomes, both individually and collectively. Figure 5–6 illustrates a strategy that unfolds sequentially in its actions and consequences. Policy A, aimed at goal A, starts having positive effects quite quickly. Then, policy B, aimed at goal B, begins taking hold in the mid-term by building upon the foundation laid by policy A. Finally, policy C, aimed at goal C, gets the job fully accomplished in the long term.

Different strategies and their component policies may perform in radically different ways. The key point is that by making these differences as clear as possible, strategy analysis can help educate policymakers about the options facing them and the strategic results likely to be experienced.

Figure 5–6. **Contributions of Policy Components to Strategy Performance**

Using Decision Trees to Analyze National Security Strategies

The need to blend multiple policies in pursuit of multiple goals has been a continuing feature of U.S. national security strategy for many years, and it promises to remain a demanding consideration far into the future. Quite apart from the intellectual difficulty of forging strategy in a chaotic and nebulous world, an additional factor is likely to make the task of strategy development more complicated in the early 21st century than it was during the Cold War. In today's world there can be no such thing as a perfect strategy— one that does not need improvement—nor a permanent strategy that never needs changing. During the Cold War, strategies were seldom perfect or permanent, but international conditions often permitted them to be better developed, more thoroughly worked out, and longer lasting than today. During the Cold War, the United States could develop an "engineering" approach to strategy: it concentrated on its actions rather than their goals and strategic rationales. This approach has now faded into history. In the early 21st century, developing and implementing strategies is likely instead to be an iterative process of constant reexamination, tinkering, and sometimes wholesale shifting of gears.

Perfect strategies are unlikely now because too many complexities, imponderables, and tradeoffs surround the process of relating means to ends and of assessing how actions beget consequences. As new strategic problems are encountered and entirely new strategies must be crafted, mistakes and misjudgments will be inevitable. Consequently, the United States will often launch a new strategy, take stock of its performance after an initial trial run, and then alter its features in one way or another. Through an iterative process of successive approximations, it will gradually fine-tune the strategy and achieve its goals. Analysis can help contribute to this process of constant adjustment by employing decision trees, a technique often used by operations research, but that can be used, in simplified form, by strategic evaluation. Decision trees portray branches and sequels to show how strategies can be altered over time. (The mathematics of decision trees is discussed in chapter 18.) A node is a point on a decision tree where a preceding line of activity or flow of events reaches a stage at which it can take more than one direction, including new directions. The terms *branches* and *sequels* refer to U.S. military plans in a crisis. A branch is a departure from an existing strategy or plan in a different direction. A sequel means follow-on actions after the initial actions are completed.

In recent years, the U.S. Government has frequently shifted its strategy for virtually all regions in response to changing conditions, not merely pursuing branches and sequels, but casting out entire existing strategies in favor of new and very different strategies. For example, the Clinton administration entered office with a strategy aimed at befriending Russia without altering NATO's role in Europe a great deal. Within 2 years, it had shifted strategy by deciding to work toward enlarging NATO into Eastern Europe while trying to work out an understanding with Russia, which was no longer viewed as a full-scale partner. Something similar occurred in Asia: initially, the Clinton administration criticized China for its failure to democratize, but shortly thereafter, it began seeking to integrate a still-authoritarian China into the Asian economic system. The Bush administration has shown a similar tendency to shift gears. Initially, it expressed its intention to remain aloof from Middle East security affairs. Within 3 years, it began to assert U.S. influence with force into the security affairs, politics, and economics of that troubled region. In Asia, meanwhile, the Bush administration ceased viewing China as an imminent adversary and began trying to collaborate with it to stabilize the dangerous Korean Peninsula. Some criticized both administrations for unclear thinking, but such strategic shifts have become common and doubtless will affect future Presidencies as well.

Frequent shifting of U.S. strategy has become necessary because today's world is experiencing changes that are both fast and systemic. The information age and globalization have accelerated the pace of change far beyond anything experienced during the Cold War. Trends that once took a decade or two to unfold now take only a few years to manifest themselves. Change is affecting not only the superstructure of the global security and economic order, but its underlying foundations as well. What marks today's world is the rapid rate at which it is changing and the uncertainty of its future shape. Some observers expect the world to become increasingly integrated around democratic values, a competitive world economy, and a stable security architecture. Others predict a chaotic, formless world characterized by both integration and fragmentation. Still others predict evolution toward a new multipolar structure, followed by a new bipolarity. The existence of so many different but plausible forecasts drives home the point that the future seems capable of producing remarkable variations that differ radically from today's world.

A rapidly changing world necessitates that, even as the United States frequently adjusts its strategies, it must always think globally because once-separated regions are now drawing closer together into webs of interacting dynamics. Events in one region can greatly affect other regions, and the United States must continually take these interactions into account. Likewise, U.S. strategy must address not only the near-term consequences of its actions, but the long-term consequences as well. The Clinton administration offered the term *shaping* as a main strategic concept for molding the future. The Bush administration did not use this particular term, but its national security strategy made clear its intent to mold the future because preserving the global status quo is not an option. The real issue is how a new and different global system will evolve in the coming years. The central strategic task is one of guiding and controlling global change so that it produces a peaceful world rather than a world of conflict and turmoil.

Strategy analysis can employ the techniques of policy analysis articulated in chapter 4, but it must first create an elaborate conceptual framework of multiple goals and associated policies before these techniques can be employed. Regardless of whether strategies are defined with a capital *S*, or are called grand strategies or goal-oriented strategies, the key point is that they pursue multiple goals with a separate policy for each goal. They must be evaluated in terms of their ability to use multiple policies to achieve these multiple goals. This is the major difference between strategy analysis and policy analysis, which has a narrower focus.

The need to shape the future, rather than be victimized by it, mandates U.S. national security strategies—global, regional, and functional—that take the initiative and that use power on behalf of conscious purpose. These strategies must be more than a collection of platitudes, slogans, and partisan rhetoric; they must provide a compelling analysis of how U.S. interests and goals can best be pursued in response to changing conditions abroad. Even though the United States is a superpower, it does not have resources to squander in poorly conceived pursuits. Efficient use of scarce resources and effectiveness at pursuing multiple goals mandate careful analysis of choices for all types of strategies.

Beyond the need for efficiency and effectiveness, crafting future national security strategies in this era of great complexity and surprising changes will never be easy, and it will always be subjected to political debates and partisan advocacy. The need to craft effective policies while harnessing the productive forces of democratic pluralism is a core reason why strategic evaluation must remain an important tool of statecraft. When performed properly, strategic evaluation can help spell the difference between strategies that are wise and command widespread consensus, and those that fail.

Notes

[1] For technical analysis of how to address multiple goals, see Ralph Keeney and Howard Raiffa, *Decisions with Multiple Objectives: Preferences and Value Tradeoffs* (New York: John Wiley and Sons, 1976).

[2] Whereas the German strategy of 1940 concentrated large forces at the center of its advance in the Ardennes forest, the Allied strategy of 1944 distributed its forces more evenly across a wide front. The Germans aimed to break through British and French defenses in order to carry out envelopment in the rear areas, while the Allies endeavored to advance by applying steady pressure across the German front line. Both strategies worked, but they embodied different approaches to offensive warfare.

[3] See James M. McPherson, *Battle Cry of Freedom: The Civil War Era* (New York: Oxford University Press, 1988).

[4] For portrayals of globalization, see Thomas L. Friedman, *The Lexus and the Olive Tree* (New York: Farrar, Straus, and Giroux, 1999); Daniel Yergin and Joseph Stanislaw, *The Commanding Heights* (New York: Simon and Schuster, 1998); Richard L. Kugler and Ellen L. Frost, *The Global Century: Globalization and National Security* (Washington, DC: National Defense University Press, 2001).

[5] Establishing worldwide goals is an important function of global strategies: an example would be that the United States should prevent a multitheater alliance against it from emerging. Establishing regional priorities is also an important function; an example would be choosing whether more attention should be devoted to the Middle East and less to Europe.

[6] See James Baker, *The Politics of Diplomacy: Revolution, War, and Peace, 1989–1992* (New York: G.P. Putnam and Sons, 1995).

[7] See William J. Clinton, *A National Security Strategy for a Global Age* (Washington, DC: The White House, 2000).

[8] George W. Bush, *The National Security Strategy of the United States* (Washington, DC: The White House, 2002). Also see "U.S. National Security Strategy: A New Era," in *Foreign Policy Agenda: An Electronic Journal of the U.S. Information Agency*, December 2002; Colin L. Powell, "A Strategy of Partnerships," *Foreign Affairs* 83, no. 1 (January/February 2004). For an academic appraisal of U.S. strategy, see Robert J. Art, *A Grand Strategy for America* (Ithaca, NY: Cornell University Press, 2003).

[9] Sensitivity analysis is employed to determine the degree to which main judgments and recommendations are vulnerable to wholesale overthrow by changes in key assumptions and calculations. Assume, for example, that a study's main conclusion stems from the assumption that the value for a key variable is 0.50. Sensitivity analysis would determine whether the conclusion changes if the value rises to 0.75 or declines to 0.25. Sensitivity analysis is a staple of systems analysis and operations research, but it also is employed in strategic evaluation.

Chapter 6
Forging National Security Strategy

Developing an overall national security strategy is the highest order task of strategic evaluation. A national security strategy is focused on the big picture and provides a sense of the whole. Aimed at protecting the homeland and advancing national interests and values abroad while responding to challenges and opportunities, it expresses the visions and aspirations of the United States on a worldwide basis. It strives to ensure that all of the myriad actions taken abroad by the United States serve a common purpose and form a collective enterprise. National security strategies are produced by assessments of not only the global goals being pursued but also the *strategic functions* that the United States must perform worldwide and the multiple *instruments of power* at its disposal. Strategic functions are the activities that the United States carries out abroad in pursuit of its goals and that are intended to influence how the international system evolves. Instruments of power are the resources available for carrying out these functions and their associated activities.

Once a national security strategy is created, it provides the framework for designing a large set of subordinate strategies and policies, each of which must be equipped with its own features. Creating a viable national security strategy requires a careful synthesis of functions and instruments to achieve the many goals being pursued. Performing this synthesis is an ongoing responsibility of strategic evaluation; it repeats itself in different forms from one Presidential administration to the next. Fifty years ago, the U.S. Government was struggling to synthesize its global goals, functions, and instruments. It continues to do so today, and it doubtless will be doing so years from now. Designing national security strategies will continue to be as demanding as it is important, requiring high-level reasoning that is wide-ranging and far-sighted. Creating and evaluating such strategies can be accomplished with the methods of chapters 4 and 5, but the process of conceptualizing, reasoning, and appraising a national security strategy is conducted in broader terms than most other analyses.

Just as chapter 5 argues that strategy analysis is more than normal policy analysis writ large, this chapter contends that analysis of national security strategy is more than normal strategy analysis writ large. Because it necessitates the blending of many ideas and calculations, it requires integrative reasoning of the most demanding sort. It also requires thinking from the top down rather than from the bottom up, for a sound national security strategy cannot be crafted merely by stapling together a set of subordinate strategies in the hope of achieving coherence. Strategic evaluation of national security strategies begins with an understanding of the global situation and the global goals being pursued by the United States. Then, it requires a careful assessment of how these goals can be pursued by performing key functional activities, each of which is carried out by a coordinated set of instruments. Such an assessment can give rise to a spectrum of alternative national security strategies that can then be compared using the evaluative techniques of chapters 4 and 5, with the aim of identifying the best alternative.

Ultimately the act of deciding upon a national security strategy necessitates political judgment on a grand scale. No strategic evaluation can hope to prove, in formal or mathematical terms, that one strategy is better than another. But strategic evaluation can hope to sharpen the generalizations, propositions, and calculations that form alternative strategies. In doing so, strategic evaluation can help ensure that the alternative strategies are all internally coherent—and that the differences among them, including their tradeoffs—are clearly spelled out so informed choices can be made.

Key to forming and evaluating national security strategies is the assessment of how global functional activities and instruments are to work together in order to achieve U.S. goals. Accordingly, this chapter outlines and illustrates analytical methods for assessing the critical relationship between functions, instruments, and goals—in other words, the relationship between means and ends. It begins by briefly discussing this relationship in conceptual terms, focusing on the U.S. role as a global leader, not an empire-builder. Next, it describes the three main strategic functions performed by U.S. national security strategy today. Then, it discusses the three main instruments of power employed by this strategy (see table 6–1). Finally, it shows how strategic evaluation can shape different types of national security strategies for responding to a wide spectrum of global conditions, and how each strategy can be equipped with its own strategic concepts and theories for guiding its functional activities and use of instruments.

A main message of this chapter is that if the United States emerges with a national security strategy composed of coherent strategic theories in each area of major functional activity, it will be in good position to shape subordinate strategies and policies in all areas of endeavor. It also will be in good position to employ its instruments and resources wisely in responding to the world's challenges and opportunities. Designing such a national security strategy at each historical juncture is not easy, but strategic evaluation provides a viable methodology for accomplishing this vital task.

Table 6–1. **How Instruments and Functions Carry Out National Security Strategy**

National Security Goals: Secure and prosperous U.S. homeland, cohesive democratic community, stable global security system, progress toward economic prosperity and freedom

Strategic Functions: Leader of democratic community and alliances, architect of global and regional security affairs, global developer of world economy and poor regions

Policy Instruments: Political diplomacy, military power, economic strength

---

Overview of U.S. Functions and Instruments in Today's World

Strategic evaluation can play an important role in designing overall national security strategy, but only if it is used in properly broad ways. Just as lesser-order policies and strategies must be anchored in a plausible theory of how instruments and functional activities can be employed to bring about favorable consequences resulting in achievement of desired goals, so do national security strategies and the theories underlying them require application of this methodology in more encompassing ways. The process also requires careful attention to contemporary changes in functions and instruments and how they are best brought together.

During the Cold War, the main U.S. strategic function was dealing with the ideological challenge posed by communism in a bipolar world. Today, the United States performs three somewhat more diffuse functions. First, it acts as a leader of the democratic community and its system of alliances. Second, it acts as an architect of global and regional security affairs for the purpose of containing new-era dangers and threats in unstable regions. Third, it acts as global developer, seeking to enlarge the world economy, reduce poverty in poor regions, and promote democratization. Determining how it should perform these three functions is a matter of debate and analysis. The Clinton administration and the Bush administration acted in somewhat different ways; what they shared, and what doubtless will be a bridge to future administrations, is the need to develop a coherent approach to these core functions, which go a long way toward defining the U.S. role in world affairs.

Strategic functions are not performed in the abstract, nor can they be analyzed that way. While the manner in which they are carried out reflects national goals and priorities, it also depends on how the United States assesses the instruments of power at its disposal and the capacity of these instruments to attain its goals. No country can reasonably aspire to goals that lie far beyond its physical capacity. A country whose reach exceeds its grasp—Nazi Germany is an extreme example—typically suffers major failure and can damage its security. Working within their limits, most countries strive to strike a reasonable balance between their ultimate aims and what their resources permit them to achieve. In essence, the wise country views national security strategy as the "art of the possible," as well as the desirable.

Nonetheless, all countries try to gain maximum strategic mileage from the instruments and resources at their disposal. Policies and strategies that make effective use of available instruments will be able to achieve more. This axiom applies to all countries, even the United States: although it is a superpower, its powers are not limitless, and it can afford neither to live beyond its means nor to strive for more than can be accomplished. Thus, it has a major incentive to craft policies and strategies that employ its instruments and resources as effectively as possible because doing so matters greatly in determining how much can be achieved abroad. Its need to employ multiple policy instruments in many different areas of overseas activity compounds the challenges.

The United States employs three main instruments today: political diplomacy, military power, and economic strength. The manner in which they are brought together and applied to carry out the three core strategic functions determines both the nature of U.S. national security strategy and its effectiveness.

A Superpower and Global Leader . . .

A good place to begin a discussion of functions and instruments for national security strategy is by taking stock of the global strategic situation facing the United States today. A commonplace observation is that the end of the Cold War in the early 1990s washed away the Soviet military threat, leaving the United States as the world's sole superpower. The subsequent decade saw the United States reject a return to isolationism. Instead, it chose to continue asserting itself as a leader on the world stage. During this period, its economic and military power grew to the point where the United States had no peers: no other country could match its strength, its global activities, or its worldwide visions.

In some quarters, this development has given rise to the charge that the United States is a new imperial power in quest of a global empire, akin to the historic empires of Rome or Britain.[1] Some observers condemned this alleged development, while others celebrated it. Closer inspection, however, reveals that this portrayal does not square with reality, nor does it accurately frame the policy and strategy issues ahead. The strategic situation facing the United States today demands global activism, but differs radically from the situations that motivated empire-builders of past centuries. The United States is clearly a geopolitical actor that employs its powers in order to attain its strategic purposes in many regions. Equally clearly, it often engages in coercion of its adversaries. But this does not mean that it is an imperial power or that it presides over an empire in traditional terms.

The difference begins with geography. Past empires were anchored in the Eastern Hemisphere, where countries are connected by land, which leaves them vulnerable to direct invasion by each other. Because the United States resides in the Western Hemisphere and is protected by two huge oceans, it does not have to worry about neighboring states invading its borders. Empire-builders of the Eastern Hemisphere were often motivated by a desire to secure strategic zones around their borders in order to keep enemies at bay. A classic example is the Russian Empire, which expanded partly due to defensive motives. By contrast, the United States enjoys friendly relations with its immediate neighbors, Canada and Mexico, both of which have far smaller populations. Moreover, the United States is a strong naval power that easily dominates the maritime sea lines on its coasts. Today the United States does worry about terrorist attacks and bombardment by intercontinental nuclear missiles, but these are different worries than the fear of being conquered and occupied by an invading army. Absence of this fear strips away any motive for the United States to build an empire in order to create a territorial buffer zone around exposed borders.

When the United States was created in the late 1700s, it had a tiny population that sought to insulate itself from the outside world. Its only attempt at imperialism came in the late 1800s, when it occupied the Philippines and some Pacific islands. After World War I, it again withdrew into isolationism, but it soon experienced the disastrous consequences of trying to insulate itself from a world suffering from economic depression and fascism. After World War II, the United States asserted itself on the world stage because it felt endangered by communist expansionism, not because it sought new territories to control. In contrast to past imperial powers, it is one of the most self-sufficient countries on earth. Although its population has grown to nearly 300 million—double its size in World War II—its population density is still less than that of Europe and most other continents. It occupies a continent that is, even now, only partly settled. It invites large-scale immigration of foreigners because so much of its land is still unoccupied. Its main path to growing strength and stature remains that of internal development, not external expansion. It has no need to pursue *lebensraum* overseas for lands on which its people can live. It is also amply endowed with natural resources and thus does not need conquered territory in order to feed its people and fuel its economy. While it must import some resources—for example, half its oil—it has long since learned that these resources can be acquired more cheaply by normal trade and commerce than by conquest.

Beyond this, its population and economy have become so large that the United States no longer worries about being readily overpowered by a coalition of adversaries at places where its vital overseas interests are at stake. A century ago, it is true, the United States worried that Germany might dominate Europe and turn that continent's huge resources against the United States. Today, by contrast, this imbalance of power no longer exists. The U.S. population is nearly three-quarters that of Europe, and its economy matches Europe's in size. Within a few decades, its population will nearly match that of Europe and its economy may be 30 to 50 percent bigger. All other continents, similarly, trail far behind the United States in economic and technological strength. The United States could be menaced by a superpower rival in command of a multiregion alliance, as during the Cold War, but such a global threat no longer exists, nor is one likely to reappear any time soon. Because the United States no longer fears being overpowered by foreign countries or alliances, it has no need to dominate peaceful regions or to keep them weak and divided.

Traditional empires often were designed to impose weakness and dependency on subjugated countries abroad. This is the opposite of what the United States needs and seeks in today's world. For the past 50 years, U.S. strategy has tried to make its allies stronger in economic and military terms, not weaker. The strategic reality is that because the United States has a productive workforce, it can perform effectively in a hotly competitive global economy. It therefore has a compelling reason to see friendly foreign countries become wealthy so that they can import its products and thus stimulate its own economic growth. Beyond this, the United States has an incentive to see its friends and allies become militarily stronger so that they can better defend themselves without major U.S. help. In essence, the United States benefits when overseas regions become peaceful, wealthy, and self-sufficient. This is not the strategic calculus of traditional imperial powers, which sought to suppress and exploit foreign countries, not elevate them.

. . . But Not an Empire-Builder

The idea that the United States presides over an "empire" today is based on a misinterpretation of what the word means. The dictionary defines *empire* as a large territory under the absolute authority and coercive domination of a power that rules according to its own interests and dictates. This definition comes nowhere near to describing U.S. relationships with foreign countries today. The United States has security treaties and alliances with 60 countries inhabited by 1.2 billion people. All of these countries are fully sovereign, not occupied lands or vassals of the United States. They could withdraw from these treaties if they chose to do so. They maintain these treaties because they benefit hugely from their defense ties to the United States: not only greater security but also lower military costs. U.S. interests are served by these alliances, but the interests of those countries are served as well. Indeed, a case can be made that many allies get the better of the bargain by engaging in "free rider" tactics.

All of these U.S.-led alliances, moreover, operate on the basis of democratic decision processes, not American domination. The United States does have substantial influence over countries with which it engages in multilateral planning for combined defense strategy, forces, and operations. But in Europe, Asia, and elsewhere, alliance members have substantial influence of their own and ample latitude to protect their interests. Fifty years of raging debates—in most of which the United States pressed its allies to strengthen their contributions—are ample testimony to the democratic nature of these alliances. The historical record shows that these debates were largely resolved through bargaining, compromise, and consensus-building, not the imposition of U.S. views. Moreover, these debates were usually resolved with a distribution of benefits to all participants, not just the United States.[2]

Sometimes countries do disagree with U.S. actions: the bitter debate over the 2003 invasion of Iraq is an example. Some countries, or factions within them, worry that the United States has acquired too much power and is too free to behave according to its own instincts. But no country, not even France, has proposed to withdraw from its military alliance with the United States. Some foreign governments—adversaries and a few allies—charge that the United States sometimes behaves like a rogue hegemon in world affairs. But such allegations are not the norm. Indeed, many countries spend far more time worrying that the United States will abandon its commitments to them than that it will somehow abuse them or otherwise misbehave on the world scene. The strategic reality is that a security alliance with the United States remains desirable. Countries that already possess such an alliance are reluctant to part with it, while many other countries would welcome the opportunity to enter into such an alliance, as illustrated by Eastern European enthusiasm for NATO enlargement.

The reasons for this pro-alliance stance are obvious: the United States has a good record of respecting the interests of friends and allies and of acting to promote stable regions, global democratization, and a prosperous world economy. Its friends and partners have generally accepted the proposition that when the United States acts in assertive ways that employ military power, it is usually defending not only its own safety and legitimate interests, but also those of close allies that are endangered. For many countries, alliance with the United States brings security in a dangerous world, without a sacrifice of sovereignty, nor the compulsion to pay economic homage to the United States. Although some countries help offset the cost of stationing U.S. forces on their territory, they reap the benefit of lower spending on their own forces, and they remain free to compete with the United States in the world economy. Indeed, America's biggest competitors on world markets—Europe and Japan—are also its strongest military allies. With its allies gaining as much or more than the United States gains, this does not conform to the traditional interpretation of an imperial power or an empire.

Perhaps the United States can be accused of having imperial visions in the sense that it is a vigorous defender of its own democratic values and an active proponent of worldwide democracy. It has shown a willingness to employ military power against countries that try to export antidemocratic ideologies by force. But trying to build and safeguard a global community of democracies is different than trying to establish a hierarchical empire ruled by Washington in the ways that Rome ruled its empire. Democracy implies consent by the governed and equal rights for all nations, large or small. An "empire" of democracies would not be an empire at all, but a community of nations. The difference is vast, and it goes to the heart of contemporary U.S. national security policy and strategy.

Three Strategic Functions

If the term *imperial empire-builder* does not define the U.S. role in world affairs today, what term does capture this role? *Superpower* is commonly used, but it measures only physical strength, not activities or purposes. Perhaps *global leader* is the best term, but it must be accompanied by the purposes on behalf of which leadership is to be exerted. With purposes in mind, the U.S. leadership role can best be characterized by delineating the three key strategic functions that it performs around the world. The first strategic function of the United States is to lead the democratic community and alliance system so as to foster its unity, protect its security, advance its values, and bolster its prosperity. The second U.S. function is to act as a major regulator and architect of global and regional security affairs, to ward off new-era threats, lessen other chaotic dangers, and establish a foundation of peaceful stability in such turbulent places as the Middle East and South Asia. The third U.S. function is to promote steady growth and integration in the world economy, to lessen poverty in poor regions by fostering effective governance and markets, and to encourage the spread of democracy to new countries and regions. These three functions—community builder, security architect, and global developer—may not capture everything that the United States does abroad today, but they do express the strategic essence of the U.S. role in contemporary world affairs.

The United States, of course, is not the only country that performs these functions. What distinguishes it from other countries is sheer scale: the United States is involved almost everywhere to one degree or another. Owing to its security policies, it is especially active in Europe, Asia, and the greater Middle East. Its role in South Asia is growing, as are its activities in Latin America. The same holds true in the former Soviet Union, Central Asia, and the Balkans, regions once regarded as outside the U.S. strategic perimeter. The only big region where the United States does not yet play a major leadership role is sub-Saharan Africa, but even there, it is often active in trying to promote peace and development.

In virtually all of these regions, U.S. activities are growing, not declining. This trend is due partly to expanding U.S. interests in many places. It is also partly due to the dynamics of a globalizing world, whose fast-paced changes and contagious systemic properties are drawing the United States ever outward. It is also partly due to the wishes of many countries that are seeking greater U.S. involvement in their regions in order to aid their own causes. Thus, the United States now finds itself involved in many places where it carries weighty responsibilities and pursues ambitious agendas. It finds itself trying to reassure partners, reform alliances, nurture communities, build new partnerships, create new institutions, dampen security dangers, contain threats, promote economic growth, and encourage democracy in virtually all parts of the world simultaneously. While the United States is not an empire-builder, it is carrying considerable weight.

Why so many burdens for a country whose own vital interests can, arguably, be defined in far more limited terms? The answer does not lie in excessive U.S. imperial appetites that, some charge, rival those of Julius Caesar or Queen Victoria. Instead, the answer lies in the nature of the modern world itself. The United States has come to its current role not eagerly but reluctantly. Most recent Presidents have entered office intending to set limits on American global involvement, only to reverse course because circumstances gave them no alternative. They did so largely because all countries are now irreversibly enmeshed with the outside world. As the world's strongest and most globally entangled country, the United States has little practical choice but to perform these three strategic functions as effectively as it can with the resources at its disposal. This does not mean that the United States must be involved everywhere and carry all of the world's burdens on its shoulders, but it does necessitate a comprehensive national security strategy of global engagement and leadership.

Globalization is making today's world a single big stage on which many actors and activities play influential and interdependent roles in shaping the future. As a result, the three strategic functions of community builder, security architect, and global developer must be performed on a worldwide basis by somebody. If they are not performed, many countries will suffer, not just the United States. Few other countries are willing or able to perform these functions on the scale required. Indeed, even global and regional institutions lack the requisite strength, individually or collectively. To an important degree, the United States has become a global superpower because there is a power vacuum that demands responsible, effective leadership. The United States has frequently been dragged into this role, often unintentionally and against its original preferences. Nevertheless, it finds itself saddled with the responsibility to perform these functions until alternative sources of power and purpose can emerge. This promises to be a time-consuming task that will last decades or longer.

Future U.S. national security strategy will need to take into account how all three functions can interact to help move the world toward peace and prosperity. By acting as a leader of the democratic community and its alliances, the United States not only nurtures common values and bonds, but also helps make global security affairs more peaceful. This is the case because U.S. security guarantees to many countries, especially in Europe and Asia, help protect them, thereby reducing incentives for them to act in self-protecting and power-asserting ways that could trigger multipolar tensions. To an important degree, U.S. security guarantees are the glue that holds the democratic community together, thus enabling it to grow closer in political-economic terms and to contemplate common action outside its borders.

Elsewhere in the world, U.S. strategic functions can help produce peace and prosperity in different yet important ways. U.S. efforts to promote stable security relations with big powers and to help stabilize chaotic regions do more than help reduce the frequency of wars. They also can help establish a foundation of peace that enables democratization and economic growth to take hold. Conversely, progress toward democracy and prosperity can help lessen the propensity to violence and war.

A key point is that these three U.S. strategic functions go hand in hand. Performing all of them is necessary because they interact and reinforce each other in influencing how the world evolves. Performance of them individually and collectively must respond to the temper of the times, with due regard to requirements and feasibility in each case. There is no simple formula for prescribing how these strategic functions should be carried out from one decade to the next. This is why a coherent, constantly evolving U.S. national security strategy, anchored in sound strategic reasoning, will be needed for each distinct period as the future evolves.

For the United States, dealing with today's world is difficult because its goals for all three functions are hard to accomplish. Its democratic alliances continue to defend old Cold War borders that are no longer threatened, and have been slow to reform in order to project power into unstable regions where their contributions are now needed. Creating regional security architectures is difficult partly because of challenges in establishing cooperative relations with China and Russia. But the more serious problem is chaotic turmoil along the southern arc of instability, which gives refuge to today's principal terrorists, tyrants, and proliferators of WMD. Likewise, progress toward economic prosperity and democracy in many underdeveloped regions—along the southern arc and elsewhere—is proving to be slow. Even though allies and other actors have been trying to help the United States, the troubles encountered in today's complex world are taxing its power and leadership capabilities.

The degree to which the United States will continue to be willing and able to perform these three strategic functions is uncertain. What can be said is that, notwithstanding its superpower status, it lacks the physical strength needed to get the job done without considerable exertion. Indeed, the United States seems overloaded in an era in which its responsibilities are growing even as the role of the nation-state is declining. Power, after all, is relative. It is measured not in terms of physical assets, but in terms of the ability to achieve goals at affordable cost. The United States clearly is the world's strongest country in physical assets—it fields the world's best military, and its economy is about 25 percent of the world's total—but its assets are not limitless. They are often stretched thin because the United States is the world's most extended country in diplomatic and strategic terms. It strains to get its global jobs done, and it has little margin of safety for performing inefficiently. This is the core reason why it must make wise and effective use of the instruments of power at its disposal. Compelled to stretch its resources in a globalizing world, it has no choice but to think carefully about how to gain the maximum strategic mileage from them.

Three Instruments

Political diplomacy, military power, and economic strength provide the United States with impressive assets for carrying out its strategic functions around the world. In order to be effective, the strengths and weaknesses of these three instruments must be understood. To maximize their influence and effectiveness, they are best viewed as members of a team, each of which has a specialized role to play in a coherent approach that blends their unique roles. Shedding analytical light on their new-era roles and relationships is a key function of strategic evaluation.

Political Diplomacy

Political diplomacy is a hugely important instrument in U.S. national security strategy on both a daily basis and over the lengthy course of years and decades.[3] The term *political diplomacy*—which includes public and private diplomacy—refers to the use of commitments, negotiations, pressures, and similar tools to influence how foreign countries and international institutions behave in world affairs. The United States publicly engages in political diplomacy when the President and Cabinet members give speeches on U.S. foreign policy. Most of the activity, however, takes place behind the scenes, in private meetings and communications with foreign officials. The goal of political diplomacy is to induce allies and adversaries to pursue courses of action that reflect U.S. interests, values, and visions. The challenge lies in achieving favorable outcomes at a price that the United States can afford to pay. Few achievements are easy, and there is no guarantee of success; the United States must often engage governments with whom it does not have identical interests and goals. Political diplomacy thus involves salesmanship, negotiations, and bargaining.

Complexities of Political Diplomacy. The United States employs political diplomacy in virtually all aspects of its national security activities abroad. In leading its democratic alliances, one of its most important instruments of political diplomacy is that of making security and defense commitments to allies and partners. In exchange for a U.S. commitment to help defend allies if they are attacked, it asks for reciprocal conduct by its allies, such as defense preparations that are adequate to enable them to carry their share of the burdens, or agreement on common strategies for handling security challenges. The normal result is a negotiated bargain of reciprocal commitments that defines how the alliance will operate in peace, crisis, or war. NATO, for example, is anchored in a negotiated bargain, as are U.S.-led alliances in Asia and elsewhere. The ultimate goal of diplomacy aimed at creating such a bargain is to ensure that the interests of both the United States and its alliance partners are elevated in significant and mutually beneficial ways.

On whole, the United States has been remarkably successful at building and maintaining security alliances. The result has been not only protection of allies and vital U.S. interests, but also an important indirect contribution to stable regional security affairs.

Because they enjoy security protection from the United States, many allies are able to defend themselves without building the provocative military forces that might trigger competitive rivalries with their neighbors. That Germany and Japan possess neither nuclear weapons nor offense-postured militaries—a key contributor to regional stability both in Europe and in Asia—owes heavily to their security treaties with the United States. But this important strategic gain is purchased at a political cost: the United States is frequently drawn into complex regional security affairs in ways that require it to back its allies. Wanting to avoid signaling lack of commitment to one ally in ways that might be misinterpreted as weak resolve by others, it sometimes lacks the flexibility needed to make accommodations with adversaries. The task of protecting allies while also negotiating with adversaries often makes the job of political diplomacy doubly difficult.

The United States also engages in political diplomacy when it participates in international institutions. In the security arena, the United States participates in the United Nations, international peacekeeping efforts, various multilateral arms control endeavors such as the Nuclear Non-Proliferation Treaty (NPT) and the accords on chemical and biological weapons, and other multilateral efforts such as environmental protection. In the economic arena, the United States participates in the WTO, the G–7 and G–8 groups of major industrialized nations, the World Bank, the IMF, and regional economic bodies in Latin America and Asia. In all of these institutions, the United States employs its diplomatic instruments to advance its interests, goals, and values. It often finds itself dealing with a host of countries that sometimes share its interests but may frequently oppose them. Because the United States commands both power and respect in many quarters, over the years it has often, but not always, been successful at accomplishing its purposes. Recent problems with the United Nations, the Kyoto Global Warming Accord, and the International Criminal Court are ample testimony to the fact that many countries sometimes oppose the United States and that they are capable of joining forces to frustrate its aims.[4]

U.S. diplomacy is stretched to its limits in dealing with big powers outside the Western alliance system, and especially in grappling with such adversaries as tyrants, rogues, and terrorists. The U.S. diplomatic dialogue with Russia and China is governed by interests that are partly harmonious and partly at odds. This requires persistent efforts by the U.S. Government to dissuade these countries from menacing behavior while encouraging them to cooperate with the United States in areas of common understanding. U.S. diplomacy must engage in a delicate balancing of firmness and accommodation. By contrast, U.S. diplomacy toward such adversaries as Iran and North Korea is guided by unequivocal concepts such as containment and deterrence. A main intent is to use threats of opposition and retaliation to warn such countries not to commit aggression. Even so, the United States also employs negotiations with them aimed at defusing regional tensions and promoting arms control. As a result, its political stance toward adversaries embodies both confrontation and the search for limited accords, in a balance of firmness and accommodation.

Strategic Challenges of Political Diplomacy. While the challenges facing political diplomacy could consume many pages, a few basic points merit mention here. Because the United States is often in a leadership role during situations where great issues are at stake, its political diplomacy is held to a higher standard than that of most other countries. U.S. diplomacy relies partly on the appeal of American values and visions, as well as American economic and military power, which are essential ingredients of its credibility. But U.S. diplomacy also relies heavily upon the wisdom and persuasiveness of the ideas and calculations that underlie it. Diplomacy requires deep thought, not snap judgments based on superficial appraisals. Typically, it will succeed only when it is guided by a clear sense of goals and by a detailed understanding of the actions needed to achieve them. Often, the United States has succeeded because its diplomatic strategy met this demanding standard. On occasion, it failed because its diplomatic strategy fell short of doing so.

Experiences of the past quarter-century illuminate the challenges that confront the United States as it practices political diplomacy on a global scale. When the Reagan administration took power in the early 1980s at the height of the Cold War, it made U.S. national security strategy more assertive, launching a big military buildup and challenging the Soviet Union's quest for superiority in Europe and other key regions. This shift touched off enormous controversies in relations with allies and adversaries. The Reagan administration adhered to its assertive military stance, but it also gradually developed greater diplomatic skill, building consensus among its alliances and pursuing arms control negotiations with the Soviet Union. The eventual result was a great success at winning the Cold War with the Western alliance system still intact and united.

The administration of George H.W. Bush largely focused on consolidating this Cold War victory while laying the foundations for a stable global order in the new era. Its political diplomacy achieved considerable success in forging a multilateral consensus for unifying Germany within NATO, dissolving communist rule in Eastern Europe, and liberating Kuwait from Iraqi occupation. The Clinton administration successfully used political diplomacy to enlarge NATO and unify Europe with Russia's agreement but was not equally successful in the Middle East and Asia. When the administration of George W. Bush took power in 2001, it was confronted with an increasingly dangerous world. It responded by making U.S. strategy more assertive in ways reminiscent of the early Reagan era, while withdrawing from international agreements, such as the ABM Treaty and the Kyoto Accord, that it viewed as not serving legitimate U.S. interests. After the terrorist attacks of September 11, 2001, it launched wars against Afghanistan and then Iraq. The result of this shift in strategy was great international uproar not only from adversaries, but from allies as well. Future results will depend whether U.S. political diplomacy can mobilize widespread consensus around new strategic concepts.

In the years ahead, the best guide to an effective diplomacy will be thorough strategic evaluations that help sort out good strategies from bad. The tasks of diplomacy have become more complex, less clear, and more prone to major changes than during the Cold War. Fresh and discriminating thinking is needed more today than in the past, when diplomacy commonly focused on preserving the status quo rather than on creating entirely new security architectures. In each case today, diplomacy must be anchored in a clear understanding of U.S. goals and priorities and must also have an accurate appraisal of the interests and proclivities of the countries being engaged. The aim of U.S. diplomacy will generally be to persuade a foreign government to act in ways favored by the United States, whether to influence an ally to act in accommodating ways, or to persuade an adversary not to act in threatening ways. In both situations, the United States will aspire to shape the acts and attitudes of a foreign government by employing persuasive arguments as well as carrots and sticks. Doing so requires an accurate appraisal not only of how that government thinks, but also of how U.S. actions will affect its appraisal of the options available to it, and of how it can be motivated to behave in the desired ways.

In addition to understanding the motives of other countries, U.S. diplomacy must also be based upon a sense of how to bargain and negotiate effectively with them. In most diplomatic interactions, a happy outcome reflects some, but not all, of what each side originally wanted, and in most, both sides must make concessions if they are to receive concessions in return. The distribution of benefits will depend not only upon the physical strength and the determination of each participant, but also upon the skillful handling of the bargaining process by both. The more skillfully the United States negotiates, the more often it will come away from the bargaining table with rewards. Knowing when to concede and when to stand firm is key to successful negotiations with adversaries, and often with allies as well.

Such considerations often make the crafting of a sound diplomatic strategy difficult. Especially when the United States is departing from the status quo, the proper diplomatic strategy will not normally be obvious or dictated by the situation. Instead, the United States will need to weigh alternative strategies and select the option that promises to work best in advancing its interests while also being attractive, or at least acceptable, to negotiating partners. A diplomatic strategy must often be composed of multiple features that call for different types of activities on behalf of a common purpose: for example, military measures aimed at deterring adversaries, coupled with offers of arms control negotiations with them. Tradeoffs will often need to be weighed: for example, the act of mobilizing widespread international support for a U.S. initiative might enhance its legitimacy, but it could also reduce U.S. flexibility to act. Conversely, acting alone or with only a few partners may offer considerable flexibility, but at the cost of loss of legitimacy or of additional support when the going gets tough. Thorny issues such as these require careful analysis every time a complex diplomatic strategy is crafted.

In summary, political diplomacy is an indispensable instrument for the United States as it performs its three strategic functions of community builder, security architect, and global developer. Political diplomacy is important for mobilizing widespread support for U.S. policies, for lessening regional frictions while isolating adversaries, and for promoting the goal of democratization and economic development of poor regions. Because the United States plays a leadership role in so many endeavors, the skill and persuasiveness of its diplomacy heavily influence the ability of the international community to join together to address common global problems. The quality of its political diplomacy thus matters greatly in determining whether U.S. interests are advanced and whether progress in international affairs is achieved. The task of strategic evaluation will be to help ensure that this quality remains at a consistently high level.

Military Power

The effectiveness of U.S. political diplomacy is highly dependent upon the strength of U.S. military forces. Military power provides political diplomacy with much of its credibility, is indispensable in coercing enemies, and is also vital in reassuring allies that American commitments can be relied upon. However, military power cannot be applied effectively unless it is guided by wise political diplomacy. This clearly is the case in peacetime, when the principal role of military power is political and diplomatic. But it also holds true in wartime, for wars are fought in order to achieve political and strategic objectives. Political diplomacy and military power thus should not be seen as separate instruments, but rather parts of the same toolkit.[5]

In peacetime, when politics and economics are dominant, military power is not at the leading edge of U.S. global strategy. But even then, it always sits in the background, casting a shadow over U.S. foreign policy. When security issues take precedence, military power moves to the foreground, and it is dominant when crises must be managed and wars must be fought. In peace or wartime, the United States spends far more money on military power than on its other instruments. Taking care to ensure that these funds are spent wisely is vital. Once military forces are fielded, the main challenge is to fit them into the overall fabric of national security strategy, whether in peace, in crisis, or in war. Analyzing how military power can best contribute effectively to this strategy will be one of the ongoing challenges confronting strategic evaluation.

New Strategic Challenges for Military Power. Military power can be a marvelously effective instrument when it is applied wisely, but it could also lead to disaster if it is employed on behalf of poorly conceived strategic principles. Like political diplomacy, it too requires sound thinking, and this must take place before military power is applied, not after military operations have begun. In this arena, acting before thinking is almost always a recipe for disaster. The main intellectual challenge is one of accurately gauging the relationship between military actions and political consequences. What matters is not the amount of military power employed, but rather whether it will achieve the strategic goals for which it is being used.

Decisions on how to build and use military power in peacetime and how to employ forces in combat must be guided by a coherent sense of strategy. This has been true for centuries. Gustavus Adolphus, Charles XII, Peter the Great, Frederick the Great, and Napoleon were all master political-military strategists as well as brilliant battlefield leaders. Strategy ruled the wars of the 20th century, and it will rule the wars of the 21st century, too. As it did throughout the Cold War, it is likely to have a major impact on many political confrontations that do not erupt into war, as well as on the peacetime evolution of the global security architecture. For the United States, like other countries, military power will not stand apart from strategic affairs, functioning as an instrument to be used only as a last resort; it will instead function as a major contributor to how these strategic affairs are conducted.

While its importance is unabated, strategies for how to use military force during the early 21st century seem likely to differ from those of the late 20th century. One reason is that the information era and new technologies are rapidly changing military forces, doctrines, and operations. Globalization and other new-era dynamics are also changing the strategic politics of peacetime confrontations and warfighting operations. During the Cold War, U.S. defense strategy was preoccupied with saving democracy from communism and deterring a mammoth Soviet threat. Today, U.S. defense strategy finds itself coping with a host of smaller adversaries on behalf of values and visions that, while often vital, do not amount to an equivalent ideological call to arms.

The nature of warfare itself is also changing. During the Cold War, U.S. defense strategy was largely planned around waging continental wars at fixed geographic locations where its vital interests and those of adversaries coincided. The United States now finds itself preparing to conduct expeditionary missions for a variety of specific purposes to an ever-shifting array of distant locations and unfamiliar places. Whereas military missions in the past were mostly led by ground forces, today they are often characterized by ground, air, and naval forces working jointly. U.S. adversaries are also showing new ways of fighting in the form of asymmetric strategies aimed at countering the strengths of the U.S. military by seeking out its weaknesses rather than meeting it head-on.

The U.S. military also finds itself waging war much more often. During the span of the Cold War, the United States engaged in shooting wars only twice, in Korea and in Vietnam. It has already fought twice as many wars in just the 12 years from 1991 to 2003. Moreover, the number of peacetime military missions abroad has grown, creating an operations tempo that is taxing the U.S. military and requiring a much greater use of reservists than in the past. A future of frequent and demanding peacetime operations coupled with regular small or medium-sized wars may become the norm, not an aberration.

Today's conflicts—in peacetime and wartime—are proving to be highly political in more complicated ways than in the past. Past wars and peacetime confrontations, of course, often were political in their aims. Indeed, Clausewitz said that war is a continuation of politics by other means, and Bismarck demonstrated it. Yet while politics set the stage for past military conflicts and warfighting strategies, it tended not to intrude deeply onto the battlefield and how operations were carried out. This task was mostly left to generals, unless the politicians were themselves generals. In today's world, by contrast, politics seem to intrude ever deeper into military operations. This certainly was the case in Kosovo and Afghanistan. It also has proven true in Iraq, where politics guided not only the invasion for the purpose of regime change, but also the difficult pursuit of democracy-building in the reconstruction of Iraq afterward.

The growing importance of politics in military operations in a chaotic world means that the United States will need to be skilled at the art of applying military power to political effect. As the Iraq war showed, the United States possesses ample military power to defeat any contemporary enemy on the battlefield. Achieving its political-military goals in peacetime and wartime, however, is a different and more difficult matter that requires expertise in how to employ military force with political and strategic goals uppermost in mind. The United States will also need to take care not to foster the impression, common in some quarters, that it is an overbearing, unilateralist hegemon. This will require diplomatic finesse, respect for international law, and a willingness to work within multilateral coalitions. For these reasons, the art of employing military power in effective and legitimate ways promises to become even more demanding in the future.

Strategic evaluation thus will have a robust role in assessing how to make wise use of military power as an indispensable but volatile instrument of national security policy and strategy. Multiple conflicts of great variety are likely to arise; strategies for handling them will be hotly controversial; choices will seldom be clear-cut. The task facing strategic evaluation will be to make sense of the associated issues and options. It will need to perform this task with approaches that not only are different from the past, but that also change shapes and colors with great frequency. Even Clausewitz and Bismarck would be tested by the coming challenges.

Performing New-Era Strategic Missions. The strategic effectiveness of U.S. military forces will largely depend on their capacity to perform overseas missions in the coming years. Many of the most important missions will arise in peacetime. U.S. forces will be charged with the responsibility of reassuring allies by carrying out security commitments to them, building partnerships with new friends, dampening competitive regional military dynamics, dissuading potential opponents from engaging in destabilizing conduct, and deterring adversaries from committing aggression. While U.S. forces have been performing such missions overseas for years, future missions will need to be performed in different ways. Most will be carried out by U.S. forces that are stationed overseas. The prospect means that the composition of the U.S. overseas presence will need to change as well, a conclusion reflected in the Bush administration's announced plan to alter this presence in future years through a smaller but better distributed posture.

Basic principles of how the U.S. overseas military presence seems likely to change merit brief discussion here (details are addressed in chapter 20). Throughout the 1990s, the United States kept about 100,000 troops in Europe, 100,000 troops in Northeast Asia, and 25,000 troops in Asia. While this posture suited U.S. strategic purposes then, the new strategic environment calls for new design standards. Threats in Europe and Northeast Asia are fading, so fewer forces will be needed there for traditional border defense missions. Smaller and differently structured forces and military bases are likely to be needed for a new purpose: providing regional hubs for projecting power into distant regions that are endangered. U.S. forces in both Europe and Northeast Asia will need to be highly mobile and capable of working closely with friends and allies to encourage them to develop complementary capabilities.

Meanwhile, U.S. force requirements in other regions may rise above their former levels. In the Persian Gulf, much will depend upon how the reconstruction of Iraq unfolds, but the entire region seems likely to remain unstable in ways requiring the presence of U.S. forces for some time. A growing U.S. military presence in Southeast Asia also seems likely, and the war on terror will continue to require a U.S. presence in Afghanistan and elsewhere in South Asia. Growing U.S. military activity in the Balkans and Central Asia seems probable, and missions in Africa may rise in frequency as well. The U.S. presence there may not be large and permanent, but rather small, fluctuating, and marked by austere military installations to which U.S. forces will deploy on a temporary basis. Even so, the prospect of fewer forces stationed at traditional locations, coupled with more forces periodically deploying to new locations, adds up to a major change in the U.S. overseas presence. Crafting sound policies and programs in this arena will be an ongoing challenge for strategic evaluation.

A demanding analytical agenda will also have to address the thorny issues surrounding how U.S. military power can best be employed during crises and wars. Clearly the decision on whether to use force at all must be made on the basis of a strategic evaluation that ascertains the need to do so, the wisdom and propriety of doing so, and the ability to succeed at acceptable cost. However, once a decision to intervene has been made, a similarly thorough strategic evaluation will be needed to determine exactly how to do so. The manner of intervention—including the way in which military force is teamed with political diplomacy—will have a major impact on success or failure. The lack of any universally accepted standard for deciding whether and how to intervene necessitates that each crisis be carefully examined on a case-by-case basis.

Wise strategies are needed all across the spectrum of conflict, from peacekeeping operations to waging major regional wars. The demands posed by the interventions in Bosnia and Kosovo have turned opinion against peacekeeping in some quarters. The continuing need to perform peacekeeping missions seems, however, to be a permanent feature of modern world affairs. Even when allies carry the bulk of the load, some degree of U.S. leadership and participation will often be necessary. In many cases, peacekeeping will not be limited to dampening violence, especially in cases of savage ethnic conflicts that cannot be regulated simply by separating warring factions and drawing demarcation lines. Nation-building may be viewed with skepticism by some, but nonetheless the violence caused by ethnic conflicts and other intrastate rivalries can be dampened in many cases only by building competent governments, capable military forces, effective law enforcement, functioning economies, and delivery of services such as health care, food, electricity, and water. Recent experiences in the Balkans and Afghanistan underscore this, and the postwar presence in Iraq, which has required a major effort at stabilization and reconstruction, reinforces this lesson. U.S. military forces are likely to need improved capabilities and strategies for nation-building as such missions become increasingly necessary.

The war on terrorism is a new kind of war requiring its own approach to employing military power. This long struggle at the far corners of the world has already precipitated invasions of Afghanistan and Iraq and numerous small military actions elsewhere. It has also required multinational coordination of intelligence and law enforcement, as well as other activities. It has mandated vigorous homeland defense measures in the United States, including creation of a new Department of Homeland Security, and close coordination of Federal, state, and local law enforcement agencies. The kinds of operations created by the war on terror are likely to become a permanent feature of the new strategic terrain, requiring new practices in the use of U.S. military power.

Waging major regional wars will also continue to require not only wise choices about whether and when to launch them, but also well-conceived strategies and new military operations for carrying them out. Today, launching such wars typically requires mobilizing a broad multinational coalition of support, both to create political legitimacy and to provide capable allied military forces that can work alongside U.S. forces. Mobilizing multinational support is easiest in response to an act of aggression by a rogue country. However, as the invasion of Iraq shows, it becomes far harder against threats that are imminent or gathering, but where aggression has not yet occurred, and when a U.S.-led military operation takes the form of a preventive or preemptive attack. In such cases, a strategy for preparing the political terrain before the war can be as important as actually fighting the war. The debate over whether to invade Iraq was so contentious partly because, although a consensus had already built in the United States and Britain in favor of regime change in Iraq, no parallel consensus had emerged elsewhere. In contrast, there was little international outcry when, 4 years earlier, the United States led a NATO effort to use military power to eject Serbia from Kosovo, even though public revulsion against Slobodan Milosevic's regime in Serbia was not as great as that against Saddam Hussein's regime in Iraq. The two experiences illustrate the importance of creating new legal and political standards for employing military force against imminent or gathering threats and assuring that these standards are agreed upon on an international basis.

Conducting regional wars also requires an effective strategy. Success is not automatically ensured simply because U.S. and allied forces enjoy a preponderance of military power. Even high-tech U.S. forces can encounter troubles when their battle plans are unwise, when wily enemies can counter them with asymmetric strategies, or when joint operations do not mesh well. A battlefield strategy must not only defeat the enemy militarily, but also achieve U.S. political goals for the war. Harnessing military means to achieve political ends is not easy. Such new U.S. operational concepts as network-centric warfare, rapid decisive operations, and effects-based operations are intended to fracture the cohesion of enemy forces, deny them viable battlefield options, and eliminate their capacity to continue fighting. These concepts are designed to employ U.S. forces jointly in ways that win wars quickly with few U.S. and allied casualties. But they are military standards, not an airtight formula for political success. They must be accompanied by a coherent political strategy. Ensuring that high-tech, high-speed U.S. force operations are brought into harmony with U.S. political goals and diplomatic strategy will continue to be a demanding challenge for the future.

The pursuit of political goals in wartime also requires sound war termination strategies. The ways in which a war terminates often shape the subsequent political and strategic climate. Whereas successful war termination can mean that the fruits of victory last many years, unsuccessful war termination can result in creation of new problems as bad as those eliminated by a victorious war. War termination strategies are typically of three types: restoration of the status quo ante; imposition of a coerced political settlement in which the defeated enemy retains its sovereignty but loses its capacity to commit aggression again; or unconditional surrender accompanied by prolonged occupation of the enemy's territory. The experiences of the past 60 years show examples of all three strategies at work, their attractions, and their liabilities. None stands out as perfect for all circumstances. Strategic evaluation must help identify the strategy that seems best suited for the occasion at hand.

Of these strategies, restoration of the status quo often provides the least satisfactory solution, as when the North Korean regime remained in power after the 1953 armistice. Yet sometimes this is the most that can be achieved. Imposition of a coerced political settlement offers the attraction of attaining core U.S. goals without having to pay the price of total victory and occupation. Yet because it typically results in a bargained settlement with adversaries that are thirsting for revenge, it has potential perils. The Versailles Treaty after World War I, for example, disastrously set the stage for World War II.[6] The Persian Gulf War of 1991 produced a coerced settlement that left Saddam Hussein in power and saw 12 years of trouble followed by a second war against his regime. Unconditional surrender and occupation is the only strategy likely to forestall subsequent trouble from the defeated adversary. The occupations of Germany and Japan after World War II are successful examples of this strategy; both countries emerged as prosperous democracies. The recent cases of Afghanistan and Iraq are examples of the difficulties that can be encountered when occupied countries are not primed for rapid reconstruction. Unfortunately, such cases may be common in the future.

Military power will remain a vital instrument for carrying out U.S. national security strategy. Clearly the United States will need sufficient military power to defeat its adversaries and otherwise attain its strategic goals in world affairs. But military power is not an instrument for all purposes, nor is preeminent military power a guarantee that U.S. goals will be achieved even in situations where it is useful. The United States will need a coherent strategy not only for preparing its military forces, but also for employing them effectively in peace, crisis, and war. Developing such a military strategy, and integrating it into overall national security strategy, will remain one of the principal challenges facing strategic evaluation.

Economic Strength

The idea that the United States uses its economic activity abroad in order to foster its national security strategy is not often thoroughly analyzed by academic textbooks, which typically consider either security affairs or economics, but not both. Yet the strength of its economy plays a major role in enhancing its status as the world's sole superpower. Without an economy totaling about $11 trillion per year, its annual defense budget of over $400 billion would not be possible. Beyond this, the United States promotes a growing world economy not only to bolster its own prosperity, but also to enhance its security by making the rest of the world more stable. Such an economic strategy is not new: during the Cold War, the United States pursued a strategy of helping alliance partners in Europe and Asia become wealthy capitalist democracies so as to strengthen their contribution to the containment of communism. Overall, this strategic effort proved highly successful. It played a large role in making both regions more stable, and ultimately it helped convince the Soviet Union to abandon communist rule.

Today, U.S. national security strategy employs trade, commerce, and market competition to help make its traditional democratic allies wealthier. But an equally important goal has become that of elevating poor countries and regions, in the hope that such progress will make them more peaceful and democratic. To this end, the Bush administration announced in 2002 an increase in annual U.S. foreign aid by 50 percent over the next 3 years and proposed to channel this aid through a new Millennium Challenge Account that would target aid explicitly toward fostering effective governance, markets, and economic growth.[7] It also seeks to reduce global trade barriers in the hope that impoverished regions will benefit from enhanced exports and imports. Its ambition is for the economies of impoverished regions to grow by 10 percent annually in the coming years. Achieving this lofty goal may stretch the art of the possible, but it reflects the current U.S. view that economic instruments, as well as the health of the world economy, are a key part of U.S. national security strategy. The challenge facing strategic evaluation is to integrate U.S.

foreign economic activities into its portrayal of how national security policy and strategy can best be carried out in a globalizing world.

Role of Imports and Exports. The U.S. dollar may play a major role in strengthening the world economy by providing a stable currency for international transactions, but the United States exerts its biggest impact on the world economy through its imports and exports as well as its foreign investments (see table 6–2). Nearly 15 percent of U.S. national income each year is spent on imported products. Nearly 10 percent of annual U.S. earnings comes from the sale of exported products abroad. In addition, bank loans, direct foreign investments, and the activities of multinational corporations add to the total; many experts conclude that about 25 percent of the U.S. economy is tied to the world economy.[8] In recent years, the United States has been importing products and services totaling about $1.2 trillion to $1.5 trillion annually, and exporting about $1 trillion in products and services. The result has been a big trade imbalance that grew from $250 billion in 1998 to roughly $500 billion in 2004; a beneficial effect, however, has been to stimulate global economic growth. U.S. imports play a major role in providing overseas markets to many countries that rely upon exports to propel their economic growth. Of these annual U.S. imports, about $250 billion comes from services, and the remaining $1 to $1.25 trillion comes from merchandise. This merchandise includes industrial supplies and capital goods (about $600 billion), automotive vehicles ($210 billion), consumer goods ($325 billion), plus foods and products.[9]

Table 6–2. **U.S. International Trade in Goods and Services**

	2000	2003
Imports	$1,404 billion	$1,482 billion
Exports	$1,046 billion	$ 993 billion

Source: U.S. Department of Commerce online displays, Washington, DC, 2003.

The bulk of U.S. commercial activity is carried out with wealthy countries abroad. Of the $1.2 trillion of imported merchandise in 2003, about $260 billion came from Europe and $410 billion came from Asia, including Japan, China, and other Asian countries that have been registering fast economic growth in recent years. The United States also imported over $400 billion of merchandise from Western Hemisphere countries. Although Canada is its biggest trading partner in the Western Hemisphere, the United States also imported about $250 billion from Latin America, accounting for about 10 percent of that region's income. U.S. imports from less wealthy regions are far smaller. Even counting oil imports, the United States in 2003 imported only about $55 billion from the Middle East, $37 billion from Africa, and $16 billion from Central Asia, mainly because underdeveloped regions do not produce much of the kind of sophisticated merchandise bought by Americans. An additional reason is that high tariffs and other trade barriers prevent these regions from selling agricultural products to the United States, still less to Europe, whose trade barriers against agricultural products are even higher. Such sales might otherwise help lift them out of poverty.

These data suggest the extent to which U.S. imports help propel the world economy. Also important are U.S. financing, foreign investments, and technological innovation. Today's worldwide economic growth through exports and imports owes much to over five decades of sustained U.S. efforts to reduce trade barriers. U.S. imports of goods and services play a major role in enabling the world economy to grow each year. If, for example, the United States reduced its annual imports to a lower level that matched its exports, the effect would be to drain up to $500 billion from annual economic growth in regions outside the United States. Since these regions today are growing at the combined rate of about $1 trillion each year, this could cut their growth rates in half, from about 3 percent annually to only 1.5 percent. In essence, the world economy would be limited to growing only at about the rate needed to match rising population. Such a draconian cut would remove funds that are badly needed by foreign countries for investments in their economic infrastructure. The negative impact thus would be magnified by an accelerator and multiplier effect. Such a negative impact, of course, is merely hypothetical: U.S. imports and exports are not expected to decline. But this calculus does suggest the important role played by the U.S. economy in elevating the world economy and the prosperity of many regions, contributing to greater stability and peace in global security affairs.

Foreign Economic Aid. In recent years, U.S. foreign aid, as measured by the Organization for Economic Cooperation and Development (OECD), has totaled about $10 billion per year. This aid is intended for humanitarian assistance, economic development, and security assistance. The Millennium Challenge Account proposed by President Bush is intended to add $3 billion to this total by 2005 and $5 billion by 2010. This increase, if fully funded, could diminish (but not end) accusations that the United States commits too small a portion of its wealth to help poor countries around the world. Moreover, the U.S. Government argues that OECD performance measures do not count nearly $13 billion annually of other sorts of U.S. aid that flows to Eastern Europe, the Baltics, and Israel, or that takes such forms as cultural exchanges, support for international organizations, public broadcasting, propagation of democratic values, and funds for the Export-Import Bank, the International Monetary Fund, the Overseas Private Investment Corporation, and foreign military training (a form of assistance although not humanitarian aid). Such aid brings the U.S. total to about $23 billion each year, thus making the U.S. Government the world's biggest donor in absolute totals. Other wealthy countries, such as Japan, Germany, Britain, France, and Italy, each offer from $6 billion to $12 billion in comparable aid. While these figures represent a larger percentage of their gross domestic product (GDP) than the comparable figure for the United States, their higher protectionist trade barriers dampen imports from poor regions.[10]

In addition to official aid, the United States provides the rest of the world with about $34 billion each year in private funds. This includes about $7 billion in donations from private and voluntary organizations, $4 billion from foundations and corporations, $1.3 billion from colleges and universities, and $3.4 billion from religious organizations. The rest—about $18 billion—comes from individual remittances, often in the form of money sent by foreigners working in the United States to their home countries. If such private remittances are counted, total U.S. "assistance"—defined in the broadest terms—comes to about $57 billion each year. This amount totals about 0.5 percent of GDP. Citing the OECD standard that 0.7 percent of GDP is the appropriate level, critics argue for more U.S. aid. However, it can be argued that, because the United States shoulders a disproportionate share of the common defense burden, it should not be asked to keep pace with other wealthy democracies in foreign aid.

The worldwide total of OECD-monitored aid is about $100 billion annually, but these contributions are exceeded by the roughly $200 billion to $300 billion of investment capital that flow to poor regions from banks and lending agencies. Multinational firms add to the total with funds to develop industrial plants and other facilities. Such investments, however, are highly volatile; they rise when the world economy is expanding, but shrink when recessions take hold. Regardless of whether investment assistance is provided by governments or by private institutions, it helps trigger sustained economic growth only when recipient countries can offer effective governance, functioning market economies, and productive workforces. Without these conditions, although foreign aid can help alleviate poverty and improve health conditions, it cannot be expected to make recipient countries wealthy

Foreign Military Assistance. As part of its foreign aid, the United States provides military assistance to friends and allies. Currently, this program totals about $4 billion per year. About $3.8 billion is devoted to foreign military financing (FMF), which provides U.S. guarantees of loans to countries seeking to buy U.S.-made military equipment, such as jet fighters and tanks. In addition, the United States provides about $100 million per year in military grants for military hardware and for education and training of foreign military officers at U.S. military schools. The bulk of this military assistance goes to two countries: in 2003, Israel received about $2.2 billion and Egypt about $1.3 billion. Even so, the United States uses its remaining FMF, International Military Education and Training (IMET), and Military Assistance Program (MAP) funds to pursue military outreach programs to many friendly countries in virtually all regions. A key trend of recent years has been outreach programs to new partners in Eastern Europe and in the Balkans. A military assistance program is also being pursued in the former Soviet Union for training and education and for denuclearization through the Cooperative Threat Reduction effort. Several countries in the Middle East and South Asia benefit from IMET and FMF, as do countries in Latin America, Asia, and Africa. In Latin America, for example, the United States is providing enhanced military aid to Colombia as part of its effort to suppress drug smuggling. Because most of these countries are not wealthy, the assistance they receive from IMET and FMF is quite valuable in giving them access to some types of U.S. equipment and to formal military education for their officer corps.[11]

Supplementing this military aid effort is U.S. Government support for the sale by U.S. weapons manufacturers of advanced military equipment abroad. During the 1990s, the United States sold between $15 billion and $20 billion in weapons abroad each year, or about 45 percent of a global market that stood at $45 billion annually. By 2003, however, global sales had dropped to about $20 billion, for multiple reasons. These included completion of existing procurement programs and a trend toward buying less expensive equipment due to declining defense budgets and slower economic growth worldwide. Although the United States retained its share of the smaller global market, its annual sales had dropped to about $10 billion by 2003. Of this amount, key customers were Saudi Arabia (over $4 billion annually), Taiwan, South Korea, Egypt, Israel, India, and Pakistan. U.S. military sales may rise again as a result of the war on terror and as many countries need to start replacing outdated equipment. In particular, future deployment of the U.S.-made F–22, F–35, and F/A–18 E/F fighter jets should find a big market among wealthy U.S. allies in Europe, Asia, and the Middle East.

U.S. military assistance and sales are criticized in some quarters for contributing to global tensions, but consideration of the full effects should lead to a different conclusion. U.S. military aid packages are closely scrutinized by the State Department and other agencies to ensure that they help meet the legitimate defense needs of recipients and do not pose offensive threats that could trigger regional military competition. Restrictions on sales to South Korea, Taiwan, Pakistan, and India are evidence of U.S. sensitivity on this score. At the same time, provision of defensive equipment to friends and allies can enhance their self-defense capabilities, reduce the risk of aggression against them, and thereby help strengthen regional stability. A good example of success in this area has been U.S. military assistance to South Korea over many years, which has enabled Seoul to build a powerful defense establishment for protecting its exposed borders while not justifying North Korea's fears of an offensive threat against it. U.S. military assistance to Taiwan is another example of a successful, carefully calibrated program for legitimate defensive purposes. An added strategic benefit is that military assistance and weapons sales significantly enhance U.S. influence with the governments of recipient countries and improve the capacity of their military forces to work with U.S. forces in common missions. The reality is that if the United States did not offer such assistance and sales, other countries would claim the market and its associated political influence. Britain and France today sell about $5 billion in weapons abroad each year, Russia and China about $4 billion. All four would be eager to sell greater quantities of weapons. Given the tradeoffs, the U.S. effort may be better than the alternative.

In summary, these economic instruments provide valuable tools for carrying out U.S. national security policy and strategy. Imports and investments abroad have the greatest impact on the world economy, but because they are heavily influenced by market dynamics, the U.S. Government has less control over them than over other economic instruments. They function as strategic tools whose positive effects are slowly manifested by gradual elevation of the prosperity of multiple countries and regions. By contrast, foreign economic aid and security assistance are under U.S. Government control and can be harnessed to support its policies and strategies abroad. Their activities can be directly targeted, and their effects are often quickly visible. The problem is that they are funded at only modest levels, less than one-tenth of what the United States spends on preparing its military forces. Many observers argue that greater amounts could profitably be spent on foreign aid and security assistance. Whether or not bigger budgets will be funded in the future, foreign aid will need to be planned and allocated efficiently in order to achieve maximum effect. Contributing to this enterprise will be an important role for strategic evaluation.

Positive and Negative Use of Economic Instruments

Economic strength is commonly viewed as a positive instrument of U.S. national security strategy; it can help bring enhanced security, democracy, and peace to endangered regions. Yet it also can be used as a negative tool, an instrument for helping deny strength to adversaries. During the Cold War, the United States regularly sought to deny the Soviet Union and its allies access to the world economy and modern technologies to keep them from assembling greater military power. On whole, the effort succeeded, aided by deep flaws in the Soviet Union's system of centralized management that stifled its economic growth. In the current era, negative instruments have mostly taken the form of sanctions aimed at punishing rogue countries in economic terms and at denying them access to WMD technologies. The record on sanctions seems mixed. They did not compel Saddam Hussein's regime to respect UN Security Council resolutions fully; critics charge that their main effect was to punish the Iraqi people, not the regime. In other cases, such as Libya and Serbia, they may have been more successful. Sanctions must be studied on a case-by-case basis.

Another possibility is positive economic inducements; an example is the offer to China of admission to the World Trade Organization and other international economic bodies in exchange for its pursuit of a constructive diplomatic agenda in Asia and elsewhere. The targeted country gains access to the world economy to enhance its economic growth, but it must reciprocate by respecting strategic interests of the United States and its democratic partners. The attraction of this strategy is that it can have powerful effects when the targeted country values its economic growth more than foreign policy adventures. The risk is that the targeted country will behave responsibly during the period in which it is achieving economic progress, but then return to its unfriendly policies with improved military assets. Here too, complicated dynamics, relationships, and tradeoffs must be addressed. Rather than a simple-minded strategic doctrine applied mechanically to all cases, the United States must analyze each situation on the basis of its unique features.

Blending Functions and Instruments in Creation of a National Security Strategy

There can be no question that political diplomacy, military power, and economic strength provide the United States with potent instruments for trying to direct where the world is headed, but they are not powerful enough to guarantee desired outcomes. They are instruments of influence, not of domination. The United States may be a superpower, but it is often underpowered in relation to its extensive global agenda and to the responsibilities it bears in many regions. Because its resources for carrying out its national security policy and strategy are not infinite, it must take care to employ its instruments as effectively as possible.

In order to do so, the United States must combine its instruments so that they work in mutually reinforcing ways. Each operates in only a limited domain. Political diplomacy can aspire to influence interstate politics, but without military strength, it often cannot aspire to mold regional security affairs. Military power can help shape a region's security affairs, but it cannot guide the region's future economic progress and democratization. Economic policies can help elevate a region's prosperity, but they cannot solve its security dilemmas. Together, however, these three instruments can influence the main dynamics that control the future of many regions: diplomacy, security affairs, and economics.

As a practical matter, U.S. national security strategy in virtually every key area of activity employs a combination of these instruments in order to pursue its purposes abroad. This is the case for all three core strategic functions: community-builder, security architect, and global developer. In its efforts to nurture the democratic community, the United States employs military commitments to help make its alliances secure, economic trade to make them more prosperous, and political leadership to reform them in order to pursue new missions. In its efforts to create stable regional security architectures, the United States employs military power to reassure some countries and deter others, economic negotiations to encourage multilateral collaboration, and political diplomacy to defuse conflicts and promote arms control. In its efforts to promote global development, the United States uses military aid to help create foreign militaries capable of self-defense, economic aid to establish market economies, and political diplomacy to encourage adoption of democratic governments.

A significant analytical challenge, therefore, is to design a proper blend of all three instruments that responds to the issues and goals at stake in each functional area. U.S. policymakers face the tasks of committing an appropriate level of resources for each function and instrument and of specifying activities that are likely to achieve the goals being pursued. Policymakers must also ensure that these three instruments are coordinated with one another: policies for employing political diplomacy, military power, and economic strength must operate in parallel and aim at common targets. Achieving such coordination among instruments and activities, although not easy, can greatly enhance the chances of strategic success. Indeed, effective coordination can result in synergy; the combined powers can achieve more than the sum total of their individual powers.

The task of employing multiple instruments on behalf of a common purpose requires a strategic theory in each major area of functional activity. The term *strategic theory* means a set of concepts and postulates that defines the mechanisms by which a coordinated series of activities will achieve the consequences being sought and the goals being pursued. In other words, a strategic theory provides an integrated set of directives that defines how the United States should act functionally as it employs multiple policy instruments across a broad spectrum of interrelated endeavors.

A strategic theory thus is more than a prioritized set of goals. Its hallmark is a cluster of arguments that defines how and why a series of coordinated actions will achieve those goals. It describes a framework of actions and consequences that the U.S. Government can employ to guide its conduct in national security affairs. It can thus be used to develop subordinate strategies and policies aimed at achieving its goals. A classic example of strategic theory is deterrence, which postulates that the United States can hope to prevent an enemy from committing aggression by threatening to inflict unacceptable losses on it in retaliation. Deterrence is just one strategic theory: an effective U.S. national security policy and strategy require multiple strategic theories, coordinated in mutually reinforcing ways, to guide policies, strategies, and resource commitments.

During the Cold War, the United States achieved considerable success at creating such strategic theories. The process of creating them involved prolonged thinking, analyzing, and debate. But eventually the United States crafted strategic theories for defending Europe and NATO, for protecting its allies in Northeast Asia and its interests in the Persian Gulf, and for containing the Soviet Union while pursuing arms control negotiations with it. To a considerable degree, these strategic theories were responsible for the United States winning the Cold War. Without them, the United States would have been adrift, and it might not have won the contest, regardless of the instruments and resources at its disposal.

In the early 21st century, the United States will require equally compelling strategic theories in order to guide its national security activities in all three key functional activities of community-builder, security architect, and global developer. A great deal of intellectual effort has already been devoted to creating such theories. The national security strategies of all three Presidential administrations since 1988 reflect this effort. But considerable additional progress is needed. The United States is still struggling in all three areas. Confronted with a world that is changing rapidly in confusing ways, it is trying to understand the new challenges facing it and to craft enduring strategic theories for handling them that will apply not only to periodic crises but also to the flow of multiple trends over a period of years and decades. Fiery debates are taking place over the strategic basics of how a superpower can best perform its leadership functions in a globalizing world of promise and peril.

Strategic theories for individual functions must be embedded in a U.S. national security strategy that provides a sense of the whole. The central strategic challenge facing the United States in today's world is twofold: to prevent deterioration, chaos, and loss of control; and to propel as many parts of the world as possible toward a future of growing peace, prosperity, and democracy. In order to accomplish this twofold purpose, a truly global U.S. national security strategy will require an integrated approach to all issue areas that responds to the situations at hand, sets realistic goals, and pursues actions likely to achieve these goals in affordable ways. The road ahead cannot be illuminated simply by a strategy of soaring rhetoric that expresses idealistic visions without specifying how real-life problems can be handled in practical ways. Nor can national security strategy focus too narrowly on one functional area at the expense of others, or set goals for all of them that are too modest. U.S. national security strategy will need to be anchored in a composite view that strikes a balance between realism and idealism. It will need to put forth approaches in all issue areas that specify how resources can best be allocated with well-considered priorities. This is a tall order, and a significant challenge for strategic evaluation that is focused on the big picture.

Strategic evaluation should not view a candidate national security strategy in pristine isolation, but instead should examine it in relationship to other alternatives that may be vying for official recognition. A critical issue is not whether a candidate strategy is perfect—no strategy can be perfect—but whether it is a better choice than its competitors in terms of appropriateness, responsiveness, internal balance, performance, and feasibility with the resources at hand. If a candidate strategy has been officially sanctioned but its internal features are not yet fully developed, strategic evaluation can make an important contribution by articulating not only its core strategic concepts and theories, but also the strategies, policies, plans, programs, and budgets that are needed to bring it fully to life. A national security strategy will be fully defined only when these vital internal features are articulated.

Table 6–3 helps provide a spectrum for viewing how alternative national security strategies can be crafted. It displays three different strategic situations that might be encountered in future world affairs. In the middle is the contemporary world, with its current mixture of dangers and opportunities. To the left is a more difficult and dangerous world than now, and to the right is a more peaceful and promising world. The left-hand column displays the three major areas of U.S. national security affairs: community-building, security architect, and global development, followed by illustrative strategic concepts for each case. These concepts can be used to develop associated strategic theories. A composite U.S. national security strategy thus can be assembled from the elements in the column below each global situation. The result is three different illustrative U.S. national security strategies, each of which responds to a different global situation that might be encountered in the coming years. Its concepts are illustrative and do not capture all permutations and combinations, but the table does suggest how current U.S. national security strategy and its alternatives could be appraised. It suggests that an overall strategy should include concepts in each of the functional areas cited here. It further suggests that

Table 6–3. **Composite U.S. National Security Strategies**

Global Security Conditions

	Worse Conditions	**Today's Conditions**	**Better Conditions**
Community-Building and Alliance Relations			
	Border defense and cohesion	Moderate progress toward outward-looking stance	Major progress toward global collective security
Global Security Architecture			
Big-power relations	Contain and deter threats	Build stable relations	Achieve major partnership and integration
Southern arc of instability	Defeat threats	Defeat threats and promote regional stability	Achieve regional peace and security
Global Development			
World economy	Prevent recessions and depressions	Promote moderate sustained growth	Promote fast growth
Poor regions	Contain poverty and preserve democracy	Reduce poverty and promote democracy	Achieve fast growth and democratization
Overall U.S. National Security Strategy	Protect vital interests in a dangerous world	Suppress chaotic dangers and enlarge zones of peace	Build global peace and security

this strategy is likely to change in response to fluctuations in the global environment. Current U.S. strategy is, in fact, essentially as reflected in the central column: one of suppressing chaotic dangers such as terrorism, while steadily enlarging the zones of peace. Its core strategic concepts are to promote alliance reform, to establish stable relations with such big powers as Russia and China, to defeat threats and enhance stability along the southern arc, and to reduce poverty while promoting democracy in poor regions. But this strategy is not necessarily a permanent one.

If the world changes in some major way, U.S. national security strategy will need to change as well. If a more dangerous world evolves, U.S. strategy will need to become more assertive and threat-focused, while reining in its idealistic aspirations. Conversely, if a more peaceful world emerges, U.S. strategy will have the flexibility to enlarge upon its aspirations by pursuing more ambitious goals in all key areas. Regardless of what the future holds, the task of strategic evaluation will be to help create a set of integrated strategic concepts and theories for each of these functional areas. Doing so will enable U.S. policymakers to design appropriate policies and strategies in each case, and to determine the mixture of instruments and resources that should be applied.

The strategy alternatives and associated strategic concepts put forth here help illustrate the need to think about U.S. national security strategy in comprehensive and flexible terms, and to think in terms of options that must be judged in relationship to each other. During the Cold War, the United States needed a global strategy because it faced a global threat. Although it no longer faces a single global threat, it still needs a global strategy because the world is drawing closer together. Diplomacy, military power, and economic policies cannot be viewed separately, nor can regions be viewed as separate and distinct from one another. The functional roles played by the United States can no longer be viewed through different strategic lenses. All of these factors in the modern world must now be seen together in terms of the composite future that they seek to mold. This creates a demanding challenge for strategic evaluation as it carries out its responsibility of contributing to the development of a sensible U.S. national security strategy for today and tomorrow.

Analytical Challenges Facing Strategic Evaluation

Creating U.S. national security strategies will be a continuing challenge in the years ahead, because the world is changing so rapidly that U.S. strategy cannot be fixed in concrete, but must be constantly evolving. Part of the challenge will be to define the achievable goals to be pursued at each juncture, as well as to determine the proper blend of instruments to be employed. An equally important part of the challenge will be determining how U.S. strategic functions are to be carried out on a global scale. The United States will face the continuing task of judging how to perform these functions individually, how to allocate resources among them, and how to integrate them to form a cohesive whole. This does not promise to be easy because these functional activities will not often blend readily together; they must be shaped and molded with coherent concepts in mind. Once alternative national security strategies are defined, they must be compared on the basis of their performance and cost-effectiveness.

Strategic evaluation is an excellent method for performing these analytical tasks. But because it must be up to the challenges that lie ahead, it cannot rely upon the comfortable formulas of the past, not even those of the recent past. Above all, it must be able to think in ways that are rigorous, synthetic, and innovative. As chapters 4 and 5 stressed, strategic evaluation is not a narrowly focused exercise in precise measurements and number-crunching, but a widely focused exercise in conceptualization, reasoning, and judgment. This is doubly the case for designing national security strategies, which is truly an exercise in looking at the heavens through a wide-angle telescope, and then making judgments.

Notes

[1] The "Imperial America" literature includes Dimitri K. Simes, "America's Imperial Dilemma," *Foreign Affairs* 82, no. 6 (November/December 2003); Andrew J. Bacevich, ed., *The Imperial Tense: Prospects and Problems of American Empire* (Chicago: Ivan R. Dee, 2003); Patrick Karl O'Brien and Armand Clesse, *Two Hegemonies: Britain 1846–1914 and the United States 1941–2001* (Aldershot, UK: Ashgate, 2002).

[2] For a classic appraisal of the bargains that underlie alliances, see Robert E. Osgood, *NATO: The Entangling Alliance* (Chicago: University of Chicago Press, 1962).

[3] Political diplomacy is a subset of diplomacy as a whole. It focuses on the high-level interactions of nation-states in the strategic realm. Recent histories of U.S. political diplomacy include James Baker, *The Politics of Diplomacy: Revolution, War, and Peace, 1989–1992* (New York: G.P. Putnam and Sons, 1995); Warren Christopher, *In the Stream of History: Shaping Foreign Policy for a New Era* (Palo Alto, CA: Stanford University Press, 1998); Madeleine Albright, *Madame Secretary* (New York: Miramax Books, 2003).

[4] During 2001, the Bush administration pulled away from the Kyoto Accord on greenhouse gas emissions, charging that it was biased against legitimate U.S. interests. It also drew away from the International Criminal Court, charging that it did not respect the legal rights of U.S. citizens. Both steps triggered protests from circles supporting these accords, which continued to garner widespread support despite U.S. opposition to them.

[5] For an appraisal of the need to integrate political diplomacy, military power, and economic strength into a seamless web for U.S. national security policy, see Stephen J. Flanagan, Ellen L. Frost, and Richard L. Kugler, *Challenges of the Global Century: Report on the Project of Globalization and National Security* (Washington, DC: National Defense University Press, 2001).

[6] See Gregor Dallas, *1918: War and Peace* (Woodstock, NY: The Overlook Press, 2001).

[7] *The National Security Strategy of the United States of America* provides an explanation of the Millennium Challenge Account.

[8] For analysis, see Richard L. Kugler and Ellen L. Frost, *The Global Century: Globalization and National Security* (Washington, DC: National Defense University Press, 2001). For a cogent analysis of how the U.S. and European economies are becoming increasingly bonded, see Daniel S. Hamilton and Joseph P. Quinlan, *Partners in Prosperity: The Changing Geography of the Transatlantic Economy* (Washington, DC: Center for Transatlantic Relations, The Johns Hopkins University, 2004).

[9] Data drawn from U.S. Department of Commerce online displays, Washington, DC, 2003.

[10] See Carol C. Adelman, "The Privatization of Foreign Aid," *Foreign Affairs* 82, no. 6 (November/December 2003); Lael Brainard et al., *The Other War: Global Poverty and the Millennium Challenge Account* (Washington, DC: Center for Global Development/The Brookings Institution, 2003). Department of State, *The Full Measure of Foreign Aid* (Washington, DC: Department of State, 2003), discusses the differing U.S. and OECD criteria for measuring foreign aid.

[11] Department of State, *The Full Measure of Foreign Aid* (Washington, DC: Department of State, 2003).

Chapter 7
Crafting Strategy for Alliance Leadership

The specific contents of future U.S. national security strategies will undoubtedly twist and turn in response to unfolding global events of the early 21st century. As the United States performs the core strategic functions discussed in the previous chapter, however, three basic challenges seem likely to be a continuing preoccupation: managing and reforming alliances; handling the world's principal threats to global stability and peace, in hot spots such as the greater Middle East and elsewhere; and pursuing economic progress and democracy, especially in regions that lack both. The first of these three challenges is addressed in this chapter and the latter two in the chapters that follow. Together, these three chapters provide a framework for understanding key security challenges ahead and for determining how strategic evaluation can contribute to analyzing U.S. policy and strategy for performing its key functions of alliance leader, security architect, and global developer.

Crafting U.S. policies and strategies for leading its worldwide system of alliances is one of the biggest roles played by strategic evaluation methods and, increasingly, one of its biggest challenges. For decades, the United States has relied heavily upon its alliances in Europe and Asia to help pursue an ambitious agenda for managing global security affairs. While this effort has often been highly successful, it has required a great deal of strategic labor to forge common activities that give life to these alliances and enable them to operate collaboratively. The UN debate of early 2003 over whether to invade Iraq, pitting the United States and Britain against long-time allies France and Germany, shows that such collaboration can no longer be taken for granted.

It is no accident that today the United States faces relatively tranquil situations in Europe and Asia but confronts major difficulties in the greater Middle East. A key reason is that while the United States has long benefited from well-established, functioning alliances in Europe and Asia, it has no such alliance in the Middle East, nor does it seem likely to be able to create one any time soon. If the United States were somehow to lose its European and Asian alliances, the likely result would be a major setback not only to its own interests, but also to peace worldwide. Even if these alliances are simply retained in their current configuration, they risk becoming less and less capable of handling the global dangers that have begun to arise outside their borders. The better option lies in trying to reform these alliances to extend their beneficial effects to dangers in distant areas.

Even the best conceived U.S. policies and strategies cannot cure all of the ailments and constraints that bedevil alliances. But they offer the promise of helping tilt the balance from confrontation to cooperation, and of transforming drift and decay into progress and growth. The task of designing such policies and strategies, as well as gauging their prospective performance, remains a critical enterprise for strategic evaluation. Doing so requires that strategic evaluation address alliance management with the problems and prospects of reform in mind.

This chapter begins by appraising the role of strategic evaluation methods in crafting U.S. policies and strategies for managing alliances in the years ahead. It then uses these methods to appraise issues and options facing NATO in Europe and to offer a brief assessment of future directions for U.S.-led alliances in Asia. (Alliance partnerships in the Middle East are addressed in the following chapter.) Along the way, the chapter offers some prescriptions for U.S. actions to bring about necessary changes to its alliances and partnerships in both regions. Regardless of how specific recommendations are appraised on their merits, this chapter illuminates the point that because strong alliances will be needed in the coming era, today's alliances will need to be reformed by invigorating them with innovative ideas that have achievable prospects. The challenge facing strategic evaluation is to contribute to this important agenda.

The Analytical Enterprise

Strategic evaluation of U.S. policy and strategy for alliance leadership employs the methods articulated in chapters 4 and 5. But whereas a normal strategic evaluation will focus mainly on U.S. policy and strategy, strategic evaluation of alliance leadership must also focus on the policies and strategies of alliance partners. The reason is that such an evaluation typically aims to find common ground on which the United States and its allies can agree so they can cooperate. As a result, this form of strategic evaluation can be complex because the goals and preferences of multiple actors, not just the United States, must be taken into account and harmonized.

Strategic evaluation of U.S. policy and strategy for alliance leadership is an exercise in complexity: almost always, multiple goals must be weighed and prioritized, and multiple activities must be coordinated in order to achieve the desired effects. Such an evaluation tends to be undertaken when the alliance is in trouble and new solutions are needed. Typically, these solutions will require new capabilities, which in turn demand political-military reforms such as new doctrines, different decision procedures, revised burdensharing arrangements, or better military forces. The task of strategic evaluation begins by identifying how specific U.S. interests and goals at stake are affected by emerging problems and challenges. When there is a need for responsive action, strategic evaluation then generates a spectrum of policy and strategy options with different types of solutions to address how to achieve the goals being pursued. It evaluates each of these options as to performance, tradeoffs, and controversies, typically by a dual standard—not only whether they will solve the problems at hand, but also whether they can command internal consensus within the alliance.

Finally, strategic evaluation develops plans and programs for implementing the option that seems most attractive or most likely to be chosen. Program details must be evaluated as to costs and effectiveness, while the interests and capacities of multiple alliance members must be balanced as well. The importance of addressing such details cannot be overemphasized. Often debates between the United States and its allies are conducted in terms of competing strategic visions, but when common solutions are pursued, the discussion focuses on details, especially military details, which can have an intricate quality of their own. The most influential strategic evaluations are often those that master such details in ways that illuminate ground for common action. For this reason, this chapter treats not only strategic fundamentals, but also the thorny details of military strategy and forces, which often become the ultimate focal point of alliance decisionmaking.

The U.S. Government is a major consumer of strategic evaluations for alliance management and reform because it has been a leading architect and member of peacetime security alliances since World War II, and it remains so today. The entire saga has been filled with a rich blend of frustrations and rewards, and a continuing need for fresh analyses of issues and options. Nothing in the current global environment suggests anything different for the future. Alliances are not going away—they will remain vital to the success of U.S. national security policy and strategy. But they can operate effectively only if the United States leads them wisely and persuasively, and if other members react constructively. This important reality also seems unlikely to change anytime soon.

Alliance leadership requires coherent, overarching U.S. strategies for both Europe and Asia, coupled with a set of subordinate policies for a multiplicity of accompanying issues. The effect is to create a continuing requirement for strategic evaluations that are both tightly focused and broadly integrative, as chapter 5 suggests. Creating such policies and strategies is complicated because of not only the complexity of the issues but also the bureaucratic battles within the U.S. Government over goals and priorities. Often the biggest battles are fought over the perennial issue of whether to cling to the status quo or to pursue vigorous reforms. Status-quo strategies have the advantage of not rocking the boat or ruffling allied feathers. By contrast, reform strategies offer the promise of making important improvements, but they are difficult to carry out, and they can require considerable effort. Determining how much effort the U.S. Government is willing to expend is part of the calculus, as is a careful assessment of what the political traffic will bear in terms of the willingness of allies to respond to U.S. leadership. When reforms are being pursued, the challenge often is one of judging how much can realistically be accomplished without overloading allies with too many U.S. pressures in ways that backfire by causing a negative reaction.

While status-quo strategies sometimes are adopted, serious consideration of reform strategies is an ever-present imperative. This is especially the case for NATO and Europe. Since the 1970s, most Presidential administrations have basically favored the status quo in Asia but have consistently chosen the path of alliance reform in Europe. A core reason is that Europe and NATO have been buffeted by more strategic changes than have Asia and the U.S. alliances there.[1] In Europe, the Carter administration pursued the Long-Term Defense Plan for NATO; the Reagan administration sought deployment of Pershing II missiles and ground-launched cruise missiles on European soil; the first Bush administration sought to unify Germany within NATO; the Clinton administration sought to enlarge NATO. All eventually got their way, but only after political battles with allies across the spectrum of opinion. The current administration also has pursued a reform agenda in Europe, including further enlargement of NATO and reconfiguring of European military forces for expeditionary missions outside Europe. Future administrations are similarly likely to face challenges of promoting NATO reform. As changes take place in Asian security affairs, the reform imperative may spread there as well. Indeed, changes already are beginning to occur in Asian alliances, and they may accelerate in the years ahead. If so, they will need to be guided wisely.

Crafting effective U.S. policies and strategies for alliance leadership has never been easy, especially when reforms are being sought, and it has become harder in recent years. During the Cold War, collaboration among allies was easier because the Soviet threat menaced all alliance members and could be countered only by intimate cooperation among them. Even so, the United States and its allies often fell into disputes over how to act, and these disputes were resolved only after considerable pulling and hauling on all sides. In today's world, the absence of such a clear threat makes alliance management all the harder, for it requires alliance partners to find common ground in shared goals, interests, and strategic calculations. Such common ground can be found, but it is more elusive.

Alliance management is so hard for the simple reason that multilateral cooperation of the sort mandated by permanent peacetime coalitions does not come naturally. Peacetime alliances exist because they enable their members to advance their own interests as well as common causes. Normally, they are anchored in strategic bargains: reciprocal agreements by which members make commitments to each other and all participants come away judging that they have benefited from the transaction. Such an alliance cannot endure unless each member is rewarded with security and status and is also content to see its partners grow more secure, powerful, and prosperous. Even then, countries may pay a heavy price to belong to an alliance: decreased independence and sovereignty, entangling commitments, acceptance of controversial policies, heightened exposure to risks, and a willingness to share influence over major defense decisions.

Why, then, would a country belong to an alliance in an era that lacks the major external threats of the Cold War? One obvious reason is that new threats are arising, including terrorism, ethnic warfare, rogue country attacks on overseas interests, and WMD proliferation. In addition to helping defend against these threats, alliances bring its members other strategic benefits. By pooling the resources of multiple nations, alliances can lessen the costs that each nation must pay to defend itself and otherwise to pursue its security goals. Equally important, alliances can enable all members to pursue wider strategic horizons and more ambitious goals than if they acted alone. There is safety and effectiveness in numbers: alliances magnify the strategic powers of their members in more ways than one. But these attractive payoffs are realized only if alliance members can reach agreement on how to act together so that their efforts are complementary and mutually reinforcing.

Alliance members cannot always agree on how to act in combination. Sometimes, policy and strategy choices are so obvious that all members reach similar conclusions on their own, but this tends to be the exception. The more typical reality is that at the start of a policy and strategy debate, alliance members may harbor different instincts, predilections, and calculations. They must engage in intense dialogue in order to find common ground. Decisions ultimately reached are often influenced by the give-and-take of alliance politics.

But they can also be influenced by analytical reasoning that illuminates common ground in areas where the participants did not initially know it existed.

Because the United States is the leader of its alliance networks, it is regularly expected to play a constructive role in searching for common agreement on policy and strategy. By virtue of the simple fact that the United States is a superpower and commits major resources to its alliances, it usually has substantial influence over its partners. But it is unlikely to be able to coerce them into acting in ways that go against their interests and instincts. As a result, in seeking to advance its own goals, it must find approaches that advance the goals of alliance partners sufficiently that they will cooperate with the United States. Often the United States will employ negotiations, bargains, and compromises in order to help find common ground. To the extent that it can also marshal arguments, calculations, and data showing how its preferred approaches will benefit its alliance partners, its task of persuasion is made easier.

Creating sound ideas and persuading allies by reasoning with them is where strategic evaluation enters into the picture of U.S. alliance leadership. Strategic evaluation can play an especially weighty role when the United States is putting forth new policy and strategy departures for its allies to consider. For the United States, leading alliances is easiest when they are merely chugging along, satisfied with the status quo. But a different situation arises when the United States wants allies to change course in major ways. Innovative change can permit an alliance to pursue new opportunities or react to new dangers, but it may also require an alliance to embrace fresh visions, to expend additional resources, to accept new commitments, to participate in altered burdensharing arrangements, or to run added risks. Members may want to cling to established practices and may doubt the necessity or desirability of shifting course. In situations such as these, the United States must often rely on persuasive arguments to help carry the day. A key role of strategic evaluation is thus not just to help ensure that the United States adopts sensible policies and strategies, but also to help it mobilize the firm allied support that is needed for powerful common policies to emerge.

Strategic evaluation of alliance policy and strategy thus faces unique demands. In many areas of national security affairs, strategic evaluation is narrowly focused on how the United States can best apply its resources in order to attain its goals at the expense of enemies and adversaries. Strategic evaluation of alliances, by contrast, must address not only how to advance the collective good, but also how to persuade multiple partners that their own good fortune is advanced by the actions favored by the United States. This is no minor feat, and it may require sophisticated analysis. The bigger the alliance, the more sophisticated must be the analysis.

To a degree not widely appreciated, sophisticated strategic evaluation has often played an instrumental role in U.S. alliance leadership. The United States has won many policy and strategy debates not only because it was the biggest country with the most resources, but also because it had developed a reputation for offering sensible ideas backed by sound thinking. In the future, it will need to preserve this reputation even as allies are increasingly inclined to second-guess its thinking and to go slow on reforms. To do so, the United States will need to continue proffering excellent strategic evaluations.

New Strategic Problems and Imperatives

In order to set the stage for using strategic evaluation to discuss reform-oriented policy and strategy options, the new strategic problems and imperatives confronting U.S. goals for its alliances must first be addressed. To those who view U.S. national security affairs in terms of grappling with enemies, the idea that coherent policies and strategies are needed for dealing with close allies may seem foreign. Yet the existence of an elaborate alliance system in many regions that spans the globe did not arise by accident. Rather, it reflects a conscious U.S. design and an immense effort that goes back decades. Well-articulated policies and strategies in this arena have always been in demand and will continue to be so far into the future. Concocting them will require intense analysis; just as successful marriages require hard work, so do alliances and larger communities even if they share common values and visions.

In the years ahead, two goals will dominate U.S. policy and strategy toward its alliances: preserving them so that they can continue to perform traditional missions that are still important, and reforming them so that they can better perform new-era missions, including outside their borders. Determining how the United States should lead its alliances toward these goals requires a clear understanding of the multiple functions that these alliances performed in the past and how their roles are shifting. Alliances exist partly to help advance U.S. interests and goals abroad. In particular, they enable the United States to ensure that vital regions do not fall under the control of powerful enemies who could then harness valuable resources for menacing the United States directly. Even so, the main function of alliances traditionally has not been to protect the United States, but to protect its allies. Alliances have been primarily judged by whether they brought safety and security to exposed, vulnerable members that might otherwise have succumbed to coercion and attack. Thus far, U.S. alliances have mostly passed this test easily, partly because the United States has always made it clear that unflagging defense of its allies is a bedrock principle of its national security strategy. Sometimes the United States is accused of being too militaristic abroad, but close inspection shows that when it rattles sabers and beats war-drums, the purpose is usually not self-aggrandizement, but protection of endangered allies.

By protecting allies through the collaborative mechanisms of deterrence and defense, alliances also perform additional functions. U.S. military protection during the 20th century has enabled such historically controversial allies as Germany and Japan to defend themselves without acquiring nuclear weapons or offensively postured armies and navies. The world today would be considerably less stable if these and other allies had been compelled to fend for themselves. The result would have been a more multipolar world of increased regional tensions, with rivalry between Germany and Russia and between

Japan and China. For obvious reasons, this is a function that is still needed in a world where a slide back into unstable multipolarity remains a worry.

While alliances are military bodies, they also, perhaps ironically, facilitate the pursuit of arms control. This is so partly because they allow members to defend themselves with smaller and less capable forces than otherwise might be needed. The result is lowered force levels, less paranoid worry, and less feverish preparations for distant possibilities. When an alliance has confidence in its military security, moreover, its members are more willing to enter arms control negotiations with adversaries and to sign multilateral accords to limit or outlaw dangerous weapons. To an important degree, today's nuclear arms treaties, the Nuclear Non-Proliferation Treaty, and the conventions banning chemical and biological weapons reflect judgments by many allies that, because the United States provides them extended nuclear deterrence coverage, they do not need to possess such weapons. This, too, will be of continuing value.

The traditional functions of alliances fall under the rubric of border defense, and indeed, the alliances inherited from the Cold War were originally designed to defend the borders of their members against attack. They were not created to project power outside those borders. The core problem today is that, although some alliance borders (such as that of South Korea) still need defending, new-era threats are arising in distant areas. Today, terrorists can strike at victims on the other side of the world. If tyrants were to acquire long-range missiles equipped with nuclear weapons, they would be able to bombard vulnerable countries a continent or more away. Moreover, the United States and its allies have truly vital interests at stake in places far beyond their borders, including access to Persian Gulf oil and protection of valuable economic investments. Equally important, the United States and its allies have reasons to be concerned when distant regions plunge into chaotic turmoil that can produce new threats and violence.

Today's alliances are not configured to deal with these new realities. Their inability to act assertively in distant areas, because common capabilities and willpower are lacking, means that the functions of countering new threats, protecting key interests, and dampening chaotic turmoil are entrusted to the United States and a few like-minded partners such as Great Britain. With nobody to help them, they risk overstretch and a power deficit. The recent record is littered with examples of this dynamic. The United States finds itself trying to suppress multiple threats in distant places such as Afghanistan, where its actions would have been unimaginable in the 1990s. Although the United States has benefited from the help of some allies, the resources most have committed constitute only a small fraction compared to resources they still earmark for defending Cold War borders that are no longer directly threatened by invasion.

This inward focus by many allies on defense of their own territory can result in failure to address challenges outside their territory, challenges that are not only geopolitical but also value-laden. Indeed, some critics charge that it results in a failure to support adequately the cause of promoting democratic values across the globe—a goal endorsed not only by the United States, but by many allied governments as well. Today's alliances do not exist in a strategic or moral vacuum. Their original rationale may have been military self-defense, but more fundamentally, they are an outgrowth of the democratic community of nations and an instrument for serving the community's larger interests and values. Although not all

U.S. allies are democracies, the vast majority of them fall into this category, and the trend in recent years has been toward alliances that are all-democratic or mostly democratic. NATO is willing to admit as new members only countries that have at least promising democratic credentials. Increasingly, the same characterizes U.S.-led alliances in Asia; most members have adopted democracy in recent years. In Latin America, as well, democratic credentials are increasingly demanded as a ticket for admission to cooperative regional endeavors sponsored by the United States. Even in sub-Saharan Africa, the United States has been making clear its preference for dealing with democracies. The exception has been in the Middle East and Persian Gulf; even there, however, U.S. policy now favors the installation of democracy wherever possible.

For the United States, a strategic imperative of the early 21st century is to nurture this democratic community and its alliances for purposes that go beyond self-defense and defeat of threats. A hope is that a strong democratic community can not only ward off external dangers, but also spread its influence and values outward, to enhance peace and prosperity both for its members and for the world at large. Some skeptics doubt the viability of this vision, but there can be no doubt that the Cold War was won because the democratic community held together. The end of the ideological challenge posed by communism was followed by a spread of democracy and free markets to new corners of the world; democracy came to countries throughout Eastern Europe and Latin America, was further consolidated in large parts of Asia, began implanting itself in Russia and nearby Eurasia, and started its initial sprouting in sub-Saharan Africa. By century's turn, about one-half of the world's countries were democracies with free markets, a huge achievement that marked the most fundamental way in which the Cold War was won.[2]

Although some presumed, in the early days after the fall of the Soviet Union, that democracy would soon sweep over the rest of the world, further progress has slowed, and some backsliding has occurred. Democracy's triumph thus is not destined to be speedy, and it may not be inevitable either. Indeed, a momentous ideological struggle pitting democracy against radical Islamic fundamentalism and other neofascist belief systems is under way in places far beyond the democratic community's borders. Winning this battle not only in military terms, but in political and economic terms as well, holds the key to determining whether the 21st century will be an era of peaceful prosperity or instead a descent into dark chaos and turmoil. This will be harder to achieve if today's alliances remain narrowly focused on old-style border defense. Normally, democracy cannot be installed at gunpoint. Military alliances can, however, help propagate democratic values by working with the defense establishments of countries poised on the brink of democratization. More important, they can help lay a foundation of security that permits democracy and markets to take root and grow. But alliances cannot perform these important functions if they remain narrowly focused on defending traditional borders.

At the same time, the existing democratic community and its alliances must also handle the risk that the strong inner core of this community—North America, Europe, and democratic Asia—could be pulled apart by strains arising from within. If not handled wisely, economic competition and internal political rivalries could put the United States at odds with Europe, Japan, or both. Avoiding this outcome must be a high priority, for losing the democratic community's unity and its alliances would be a bad setback in itself and could damage the ability of the democracies to work together in handling the dangers and opportunities posed by events outside their borders. It could also damage their ability to cooperate on lowering trade barriers and pursuing other joint economic endeavors. As a result, their prosperity could be damaged.

For these reasons, keeping the democratic community and its alliances intact is a far better idea than allowing them to fall apart. Whereas America's alliance network in Asia has been functioning mostly free from major controversy in recent years, the same cannot be said for NATO and its underlying U.S.-European collaboration. Skeptics have been predicting that NATO is doomed to collapse because of new conflicts between the U.S. and European strategic agendas. This pessimism is not necessarily an accurate prediction of future transatlantic affairs, but it is credible and worrisome enough to be taken seriously.

The contentiousness of the debate over Iraq is the source of much concern. Taking offense when France, Germany, and some other European countries refused to join it in throwing down the gauntlet to Iraq, the United States questioned their steadfastness and loyalty. In turn, those countries not only challenged U.S. strategy toward Iraq, but also accused it of unilateralism, hegemony, and even unlawful conduct. What resulted was a loud "dialogue of the deaf" against a background of mounting public anger on both sides of the Atlantic. When the history of this debate is written, it is likely to conclude that while both sides put forth valid strategic arguments as well as unfair accusations, neither side showed its customary willingness to engage in dialogue and compromise. In the process, the diplomatic reputations of both sides were damaged, as was NATO's cohesion, far beyond the issues at stake.[3]

If the transatlantic bond fractures, a distant risk is not only that the United States and Europe will no longer cooperate on the world stage but also that they might even become strategic rivals as well. During the debate over Iraq, French President Jacques Chirac gave the impression that he had such a rivalry in mind when he called upon European countries to join with France in an effort to form a global counterweight to U.S. power. This notion offended many Americans, not least because it meant that fewer European allies would be available to help the United States in performing its global security duties. Chirac's suggestion, however, seemed at odds with Europe's own interests, and most European governments quickly distanced themselves from it. Even so, this vision appeals to fashionable anti-American sentiment in some quarters and will remain part of the European dialogue in the years to come.

The debate over Iraq suggests that the difficulties facing NATO can best be explained by addressing events that have been unfolding at two different levels: that of interests, goals, and strategy, and that of underlying political psychology. Both phenomena need addressing because they may be pulling the alliance in opposite directions. Notwithstanding the struggle over Iraq, the United States and Europe still seem to share common interests and goals in today's world. In Europe, they agree on unifying the continent under the flags of both NATO and the EU. Their membership in NATO is held together by a mutually profitable transatlantic bargain of reciprocal political-military commitments that was originally forged in the 1950s and periodically updated as the alliance evolved. As a result, the global dilemmas of the United States are eased by a stable Europe with NATO at the helm of its security affairs, while Europe benefits from the U.S. strategic presence in Europe and its leadership of NATO. While their strategies in the Middle East diverge in some respects, the differences are not so wide that they cannot be harmonized if both sides choose to work together. These considerations thus provide hope for a continued close transatlantic relationship.

The impact of recent trends in transatlantic political psychology, however, is less reassuring. In the 2003 debate, some Europeans accused the United States of adopting an arrogant and patronizing attitude toward Europe. Meanwhile, skeptical Americans accused Chirac and German Chancellor Gerhard Schroeder of strutting their egos on the world stage and pandering to narrow domestic constituencies at the expense of their national interests, not to mention the good of the Western community. Perhaps each side misjudged the motives of the other. Yet the reality is that without thoughtful judgment and conduct on both sides of the Atlantic, the existence of shared interests and goals may not be enough to keep the alliance intact. Clearly, the United States will need to act with care toward Europe and to be cognizant of Europe's changing views, while the Europeans must reciprocate toward the United States. This is the lesson of history: countries have often fallen away from allies as a result of misguided behavior rather than incompatible interests. What must not be lost is the spirit of dialogue, compromise, and accommodation that has successfully guided the alliance through many tough debates of the past.

The reasons why Chirac's vision is unhealthy for Europe deserve mention. To skeptics, the idea that Europe, still struggling to unify itself, can hope to win a global power struggle with the United States seems fanciful, unwise, and unnecessary. Such an agenda could backfire on its European proponents. If they try to organize an anti-American coalition outside Europe, the United States might retaliate by organizing a global coalition against them. In any such contest, the United States would be the likely winner or would at least be able to checkmate Europe's ambitions. The United States has too much power, too many friends, and too many ties to multiple regions for it to be brushed aside even by a newly assertive Europe. In many quarters of the world, memories of Europe's colonial and imperial days weigh more heavily than worries about possible American imperialism. Moreover, most countries would not want Europe to help defend them when instead they could have the same task performed by a more powerful and trustworthy United States with an excellent reputation for delivering on its commitments to allies.

Evidently Chirac understood these realities, for even as he railed against alleged American hegemony in 2003, he also declared that he wanted to keep the transatlantic alliance intact. What he failed to explain was how this goal could be accomplished if Europe were to unite under France's leadership to contest U.S. power worldwide. Apparently his main aspiration was limited to clipping the wings of the United States in order to prevent it from acting assertively counter to Europe's predilections. But since Europe is gunshy about using military and economic power in old-style geopolitical ways, it is unclear how the consequences of a wing-clipped America serve Europe's interests. A weakened United States could be compelled to appease its enemies or at least treat them less firmly, to Europe's detriment. Chirac and his sympathizers offered the proposition that Europe could use its own noncoercive power—diplomacy and economic aid—to compensate for the diminution of coercive U.S. power, including its military strength. But to skeptics, this idea seems anchored in a hope and prayer rather than a sober-minded appraisal of modern security politics; the main effect might not be a more peaceful world, but instead a more violent world that would unleash terrorists and tyrants who want to victimize not only the United States but Europe as well.

Beyond this, Europe could suffer the loss of the sort of U.S. involvement in Europe that has made the continent more unified and prosperous. The United States might react by seeking to divide Europe, pitting countries against each other with the same old-style politics that brought such past grief to the continent. Even absent direct U.S. meddling, the EU might fall apart; in powerful ways not often realized, the U.S. presence helps keep the EU bonded. In particular, it helps ensure that Europe's small powers can join collective institutions without worry that they will be dominated and victimized by their bigger neighbors. Without U.S. involvement, the natural dynamic of Europe could be reversed toward fragmenting re-nationalization and creation of a new, unstable balance of power. Fear of this dynamic is a major reason why so many Europeans wanted the United States to lead NATO 50 years ago. It remains a valid reason for keeping the United States involved in Europe today rather than turning the United States into a rival of Europe. It also is an equally valid reason for keeping NATO alive.

A sensible conclusion of pro-alliance thought is that, instead of clipping the wings of the United States, the Europeans should learn how to fly alongside the United States, and it should make room for them. There are ample incentives for keeping NATO and other alliances intact rather than allowing them to disintegrate into a multipolar world that would break up the democratic community. An entirely different matter, however, is whether these alliances will muster the resolve to reform themselves so that they become better able to deal with new security dangers of the early 21st century. The very need to pursue such reforms is questioned in some quarters. This particularly is the case in European and Asian countries that want to keep their Cold War alliances intact, yet do not want to employ these alliances to embark upon new ventures.

Such views, moreover, are not confined to these countries: even some Americans argue that trying to work with these countries is both impossible and unnecessary.[4] In their eyes, the United States has become such a dominant superpower that it can act unilaterally and no longer needs the help of allies. This assertion, however, disregards the political legitimacy that allies can confer on U.S. actions, much less the raw fact that the demanding U.S. global agenda threatens to exceed America's national security resources. Help from allies is needed to make up the difference between what the United States wants to accomplish abroad and what it can achieve by itself. In today's world, the central issue is whether allies will be ready to help the United States when they are needed. Most often, the United States will need allies not to defend old Cold War borders, but instead to help perform distant missions. Keeping allies willing and able to provide this help is one of the biggest challenges confronting U.S. national security strategy today, for while the United States cannot afford always to act unilaterally, neither can it embrace multilateralism unless the groundwork has been laid.

The democratic alliance system inherited from the Cold War is a magnificent creation, but its traditional border-defense philosophy is no longer aligned with the demands of the new era. These place a high premium on assertive security involvements elsewhere. The alliance system in Europe and Asia has been, on the whole, slow to adopt the necessary reforms in strategic and military terms. As a result, it remains an asset of questionable relevance to the new era. Unless it pursues reforms, its usefulness is destined to decline further, raising doubts about the desirability of keeping it alive and functioning.

For the United States, the task of leading alliances toward reform has always been difficult, and is now more so than ever. One reason is that because the old Soviet threat from the Cold War has vanished, leaving Europe's borders secure, the incentive for transatlantic collaboration now rests in common interests and nebulous distant-area goals rather than grave and proximate threats to survival. Such incentives are not often powerful enough to overcome impediments. Another reason is that large alliances are slow to change simply because they are big and cumbersome. A third reason is that many allies balk at the prospect of distant-area missions and prefer instead to focus on their own regions, entrusting the responsibility for handling distant areas to the United States while remaining aloof from its controversial actions.

Weighing against these constraints are countervailing considerations. Most European countries continue to value NATO and their ties to the United States; they are not blind to new-era dangers, and they are willing to contemplate reforms. Participation in U.S.-led reforms can allow them to strengthen their security, update their militaries, and remain on good terms with the United States. Much depends upon the prevailing political climate within each country. European governments that are typically conservative and centrist are more prone to pursue NATO reforms than are liberal governments or others with strong anti-American constituencies. Defense ministries tend to favor reforms, while foreign ministries are often ambivalent, finance ministries chary, and parliaments divided. As a result, alliance reform—not only in Europe, but elsewhere—while a viable goal, will continue to be a demanding enterprise.

These imperatives suggest that strategic evaluation will need to focus on U.S. policies and strategies for keeping its alliances intact and not allowing them to dissolve or slide into irrelevancy. But this is a minimalist and undemanding agenda. It can be accomplished by designing U.S. policies and strategies that go through the motions of shoring up these alliances while bypassing them when vital security challenges must be met. The more important and demanding agenda is that of taking the assertive, controversial steps needed to reform these alliances in ways that propel them into the 21ˢᵗ century. The ability of strategic evaluation to master this difficult agenda will go a long way toward determining its relevance.

Reforming NATO: Guiding the Troubled U.S. Partnership with Europe

Once strategic problems and imperatives facing an alliance have been analyzed, strategic evaluation moves to the critical task of appraising a spectrum of U.S. policy and strategy options, and then putting forth concrete ideas for plans and programs in order to carry out the best option. Such a procedure makes sense in evaluating U.S. approaches to guiding NATO's future. Although the case for a reform strategy—aimed at creating an improved NATO that can do a better job of projecting military power and strategic involvement to regions outside Europe, including the Middle East—seems apparent when the alliance's troubles and deficiencies are acknowledged, this is not the only strategy that could be adopted by the United States. Two other strategy options are, first, to downgrade the alliance in U.S. national security strategy and reduce its profile in Europe, or second, to maintain the current status quo of NATO as mainly a border-defense alliance devoted to Europe's unification, while working with a small number of European countries willing to help create ad hoc coalitions for operations in distant areas. Although some American critics prefer either downgrading the alliance or clinging to the status quo, both of these strategies suffer from serious liabilities. Whereas the former would unnecessarily sacrifice a still-valuable alliance, the latter would confine U.S. leadership to tinkering at the margins at a time when substantial changes are needed.

Embracing a reform strategy because it is better than the alternatives, however, leaves critical questions unanswered. Exactly how should a reform strategy take shape? What goals should it seek, and what activities should it carry out? Should it be narrowly focused by seeking only a limited set of departures, or should it be broadly focused by seeking a comprehensive set? Should it move slow, fast, or at medium speed? What should be its agenda for the short term, the medium term, and the long term? How can it both strive to meet critical requirements for reform, yet work within the limits of the possible when the politics of allied countries are taken into account? Such questions require answers if coherent reform strategies are to be launched and successfully carried out.

Currently, the U.S. Government is pursuing a middle-ground strategy of reforming NATO. More specifically, it is seeking a moderate yet meaningful set of reforms that are gradually paced, rather than either minor steps or an ambitious cluster that could be impossible to achieve.[5] Some version of this reform strategy seems likely to continue guiding U.S. policy and strategy in the coming years. The task of determining exactly how to pursue this strategy, and how to equip it with concrete ideas that have the potential to succeed, promises to be an ongoing challenge for strategic evaluation and for policymakers alike. The agenda ahead can be illuminated by examining the prospects for meaningful political reform of NATO, and then by addressing three key tasks: enlarging NATO while strengthening its collaboration with the EU, transforming NATO's defenses for new missions, and configuring NATO to become involved in the Middle East.

Prospects for Reforming NATO

The United States will have a major impact, but NATO's evolution will also depend upon how the Europeans react to the challenges at their doorstep. If the United States and the Europeans increasingly quarrel over strategic policies, NATO could lose relevance, slip to the backwaters of contemporary strategic affairs, and even fall apart entirely should transatlantic differences become too big to manage. Even if this deterioration is avoided, NATO might continue only as an alliance that is devoted to consolidating Europe's unification but performs no other serious functions. In such a case, while it would provide the United States with a limited set of potential partners for emerging situations, NATO would not, as an institution, act to deal with security challenges outside Europe. By contrast, the reform alternative calls for NATO to undergo the military and strategic transformation that would allow it to play a vigorous role outside Europe. This could take different shapes, ranging from an alliance that performs peacekeeping and similar duties while the United States and Britain perform the heavy lifting in defense affairs, to an alliance in which the Americans and Europeans share military power-projection responsibilities more equally than now.

Most pro-NATO observers conclude that, while the alliance must remain capable of fielding "cherry-picked" ad hoc coalitions, it should also improve its capacity to act as an institution outside its borders. They also recommend that while role specialization should be pursued in niche areas, the burdens should be shared more equally: virtually all members, not just the United States and Britain, should be capable of fighting wars in distant areas. For the United States, pursuing reforms needed to create these capabilities seems better than clinging to the status quo and risking that NATO's relevance will decline. This may be easier said than done; it will require effective policies and strategies that both the United States and Europe will support.

Fortunately, the United States has considerable influence over its allies in urging them not only to preserve NATO but also to reform it in strategic terms. After all, the United States is protecting not just American interests in distant areas, but common interests as well. A good example is access to Persian Gulf oil, which Europe and Asia need even more than the United States does. The United States also carries out critical security commitments in Europe that hugely benefit allied countries: it provides extended nuclear deterrence coverage over virtually all of Europe, still an important and risky contribution. It provides about 80 percent of NATO's usable military forces for contingencies around Europe's periphery. Kosovo, for example, was liberated because of U.S. military power, not European power. U.S. military contributions to NATO help the Europeans defend themselves at far less expense than would otherwise be the case. The $100 billion to $150 billion that they save annually is roughly equal to the amount that they spend on the EU: in effect, the money they save by participating in NATO allows them to fund the EU without digging deeper into their pocketbooks. For this reason alone, they have an incentive to keep NATO alive because NATO is still the source of valuable U.S. security commitments to Europe.

Beyond this, the U.S. political presence helps encourage European unity because it guarantees the security of East European countries, serves as both a counterweight and a bridge to Russia, and reassures many small European countries that they will not be unfairly dominated by Germany or other big continental powers. Because most allies are reluctant to offend the United States in ways that might risk a lessening of these important contributions, this gives the United States substantial influence over their security policies. As a practical matter, moreover, NATO normally cannot act unless the United States leads assertively; NATO is too big and cumbersome, with too many small members, for decisive action. Consequently, most European countries expect strong leadership from the United States, value it, and often try to heed it.

The United States thus has the influence to persuade the Europeans to act, but because they are sovereign powers, it has neither the authority to compel them nor the leverage to coerce them. When the United States wants NATO to act, it must employ its influence to build a widespread consensus in favor of this step. Doing so in today's era of distant missions has proven difficult, however, because, apart from Britain, many European countries have had different policy predispositions for responding to terrorism, rogue tyrants, and WMD proliferation. Since the terrorist attacks of September 11, 2001, the United States has become more prone to use power assertively against these threats, while many Europeans remain reluctant to do so.

This difference in strategic attitudes has several causes. One reason cited by some observers is that Europe was not victimized by the attacks of September 11, and thus was less galvanized to respond. More fundamentally, Atlantic Community members have drifted apart in their strategic mentalities. Whereas the United States has always been a global power, the Europeans have focused on their own continent since losing their 19th-century empires. Owing to its great wealth, its growing economy, and its rising population of nearly 300 million people, the United States emerged as a confident superpower willing to embrace new global causes and to confront new threats. By contrast, Europe is not growing in population, and the economies of some big countries, such as Germany and France, have been mostly stagnant, growing slowly or not at all for nearly a full decade. The result has been a lack of self-confidence across much of Europe, and some envy of the United States; these attitudes have boded ill for multilateral collaboration.

Equally important, Europeans have been mostly preoccupied with the demanding agenda of unifying their own continent and building the EU by both deepening and enlarging it. This effort has left their leaders with little energy for military missions outside Europe, especially those that might fray their internal consensus. Rather than aspiring to a working partnership between the EU and NATO, some Europeans see the EU as an alternative to U.S. domination in NATO. They fear that remaining active in NATO will slow the EU's quest for unity and global influence. In addition, Gaullist France, as well as Germany to a lesser degree, employs anti-Americanism as a foil for defining European identities and asserting an independent stance around the world.

Even among countries not breathing fervent anti-Americanism or talking of building a global coalition against the United States, some tend either to ignore new threats or to employ a diplomatic strategy of appeasement and reconciliation in order to defuse them. Others are merely inclined to free-ride on U.S. efforts in other regions, entrusting responsibility to it while feeling free to criticize. Such sentiments do not reflect opinion in all or even most of Europe, but they have infected the liberal and conservative ends of the political spectrum in many places, and they have begun to influence foreign policy in several European capitals.

The forecast that NATO is doomed to fall apart may be too gloomy, but whether the alliance can recapture its former vigor, or even remain relevant, is unclear. Reforming NATO will be, at best, difficult. The debate over Iraq resulted in fully three-quarters of NATO's current and prospective members supporting the United States and Great Britain. Opponents—France, Germany, and a few others—claimed to have public opinion on their side, but in terms of governmental stances, they were not nearly in the majority. Even so, the days evidently are gone in which the United States could expect the so-called Quad (Britain, Germany, France, and itself) to serve as a board of directors for pursuing energetic NATO policies. Of this group, only Britain remains closely aligned with the United States. As a result, the United States is likely to turn to Britain and to other countries, perhaps Italy and those of Eastern Europe, to exercise leadership and consensus-building. The United States may be able to mobilize informal, shifting coalitions of support for the security issue of the moment, but whether it will regularly be able to mobilize the entire alliance to act is in question.

This troublesome prospect could change if Europe awakens to the dangers of new threats, or if transatlantic consultations are able to identify more common ground on practical policies. Until then, the United States will need to be effective at devising reform policies and strategies that, in addition to addressing new requirements, are well focused and capable of eliciting support from a critical mass of allies. The future analytical agenda for U.S. policy toward NATO and Europe will be quite different from the past. A new kind of U.S. policy thinking will be needed, and a new type of strategic evaluation will be needed as well. The old arguments for motivating principal allies of the past will need to give way to new arguments to persuade a new cast of characters to follow U.S. leadership. Often, the main targets of persuasion will no longer be Paris and Berlin, but instead capitals to the east and south, including those that are new to NATO.

Enlarging NATO and Collaborating with the EU

Despite the charges of ennui and drift often hurled at NATO, the alliance has, in fact, shown impressive vigor in transforming itself politically in order to perform the still valuable task of helping unify and democratize Europe. The process of NATO enlargement began with adoption of the Partnership for Peace (PFP) program in 1994, and accelerated when three new members—Poland, the Czech Republic, and Hungary—were admitted in 1999. The admission of these countries encouraged efforts by other countries to join. After a stiff 4-year debate, NATO adopted the "big bang" theory of further enlargement at the Prague Summit of 2002 by offering admission to seven new members at once. Led by the United States, NATO agreed to admit four Central European countries and the Baltic states of Lithuania, Latvia, and Estonia, thus marking NATO's entry into the territory of the former Soviet Union.

NATO's enlargement is not yet necessarily complete. Although NATO has fallen out of favor in Paris and some other West European capitals, it remains a popular alliance elsewhere on the continent. Advocates call for admission of such well-established, wealthy countries as Sweden, Austria, Switzerland, and Finland. Several Balkan countries are knocking on the door. Ukraine at times seems to be inching closer to membership. The idea of admitting Russia is also occasionally discussed, even though the prospect of NATO agreeing to defend the eastern and southern borders of Russia seems a stretch of imagination for both. Although the predominant vision is to limit NATO to the European continent, the alliance could expand to 30 members or so in about a decade.[6]

NATO has already grown to a body of 26 members that covers virtually all of Europe. Skeptics worry that such an increase will dilute NATO's capacity to function as a credible military alliance by transforming it into the kind of loose collective security pact that, in the 1930s, meant failure for the League of Nations. Defenders argue that NATO has the capacity to be both large and effective in its traditional terms. The goal of being both large and militarily effective will confront the alliance with continuing policy and strategy challenges in the coming years. In principle, there is no reason why an alliance of 26 members or more cannot operate as effectively as an alliance of 16 to 19 members if the additional members are willing to participate and carry out their commitments. But the sheer mathematics of the situation dictate additional labors aimed at finding common strategic ground and creating usable capabilities.

An equally worrisome challenge facing U.S. policy is that of determining how NATO and the EU are going to collaborate as both seek to unify Europe under their respective flags. Shortly after NATO's 2002 Prague Summit, the EU extended offers of admission to 10 new members, including many of the countries also slated to join NATO. This enlargement has turned the EU into a body of 25 nations that, like NATO, covers virtually all of Europe. Moreover, the EU is not only broadening, but also deepening. Creation of the Euro currency and other steps have already transformed the EU into a full-fledged economic union, complete with common monetary and fiscal policies. Economically, the EU roughly equals the United States, with an annual GDP of $10 trillion. However, the United States has a higher standard of living, as measured in per-capita GDP, and the growth rate in many European economies, including Germany and France, has been lagging behind that of the United States in recent years. Meanwhile, the EU struggles to cast aside barriers to greater competitiveness and stronger internal markets, but it is already a global economic powerhouse.

The next big step for the EU would be political union. Currently, its members are struggling over whether the EU is to be a loose confederation of sovereign countries or instead a truly federal structure similar to that of the United States. The EU has a long record of gradually inching toward greater political unity: its recent efforts to adopt a constitution are a further manifestation of this trend. The EU is also striving for a greater strategic union by trying to create common defense and foreign policies. This step may be the hardest to accomplish because it would require sacrifice of national sovereignties that have until now been jealously guarded. But there is some progress even here, in the creation of EU executive organs for security policy and military forces for some missions.

In recent years, the EU has been striving to create its own military arm in the form of a European Rapid Reaction Force (ERRF) for so-called Petersberg tasks (humanitarian and rescue tasks, peacekeeping, and use of combat forces in crisis management, including peacemaking). The ERRF is to include a ground corps of 60,000 troops plus air and naval units that bring the total to about 100,000. Efforts to create it are being carried out under the mantle of the EU's European Capability Action Plan and Headline Goal for 2010. The ERRF may initially take the form of a smaller force of about 20,000 troops that would be similar in size to NATO's Response Force. It might have a real warfighting capability, and as the larger ERRF emerges over time, it is likely to broaden beyond Petersberg tasks as well. Recently, the EU also reached agreement to create 10 to 15 small battle groups of battalion size (1,500 troops apiece) as light infantry for combat missions in Africa and elsewhere under a UN mandate. These military efforts are all in their early stages, and their progress is uncertain. But eventually the EU is likely to develop military prowess, which will make the need to square the EU's strategic role with that of NATO all the more urgent.

Some Europeans who are cool toward NATO hope that the EU will counterbalance and rival the United States in strategic terms. While this view is not officially embraced by most European governments, the alliance's future will undoubtedly be affected by whether NATO and the EU can cooperate or will instead compete with each other for status and international influence. The most likely result of strategic competition between them may be that neither body emerges triumphant, and the effectiveness of both is diluted. The ingredients of an effective complementary relationship, by contrast, are waiting to be assembled if the United States and Europe take advantage of the opportunity. If Europe is to be fully unified within a functioning transatlantic community of democracies, it will require a firm foundation of security from which closer economic and political union can be pursued. This reality suggests that there should be a division of labor in which NATO functions as Europe's premier military alliance and main provider of security, while the EU is mainly responsible for economic and political unification but has usable military capabilities of its own.

Such a complementary division of labor would not mean that the EU lacks a separate strategic identity; European countries would not lose their sovereign right to pool their forces and use them for their own purposes, although they would also have to meet their obligations to NATO. Because NATO would remain an alliance under U.S. leadership devoted mainly to being prepared for war, there would be some security tasks, such as peacekeeping, for which it is not the best equipped entity. The EU can undertake a valuable strategic role by performing these tasks. Moreover, EU unification can help strengthen European military forces and their contribution to NATO by, for example, creating multinational combat formations, pooling scarce logistics assets, and pursuing common research and development. The main challenge is to ensure that, as the EU becomes stronger in military terms, NATO's defense preparations are not neglected, but instead enhanced, and that NATO remains fully capable of discharging its own responsibilities both inside and outside Europe. Provided this challenge is mastered, a separate EU identity can work not only to NATO's advantage, but to the advantage of the United States as well.

This type of working relationship between NATO and the EU will not just happen by the natural dynamics of the situation. It will have to be created by hard, patient labor on both sides of the Atlantic. Most governments are already aware of this reality. The challenge is one of identifying, adopting, and implementing the necessary policies and strategies. This is the logic of a strategic vision aimed at keeping NATO alive and healthy as Europe unifies.

Ensuring that the EU and NATO work together in the military sphere as the EU acquires its own defense identify will be a high priority goal in the years ahead. Today, EU and NATO defense staffs are engaged in regular consultations about their plans and programs. While such consultations will remain important, they need not define the outer limits of collaboration. In principle, there is no reason why EU military formations cannot be assigned NATO missions even as they remain available for purely EU operations. The Eurocorps, originally created in the mid-1990s to help promote European unity, now functions as a NATO-assigned unit. Likewise, the EU's ERRF and new battle groups could, once fielded, be made available to perform NATO missions. Beyond this, the idea of having the EU join NATO as its 27th member might gain traction in the coming years. While many thorny political obstacles would have to be overcome, EU membership in NATO would lay to rest the view that these two institutions are competing with each other. It would enable EU military forces to benefit from U.S. and NATO guidance on such issues as defense transformation, and it would open the door—in the long term—to NATO eventually becoming an alliance of the United States and the EU if such a vision is favored on both sides of the Atlantic.

While specific policies can help promote a collaborative NATO–EU relationship, the future will be heavily determined by underlying attitudes on both sides of the Atlantic. Some Americans fear the EU, but in the past, such illustrious leaders as Dwight Eisenhower and George Marshall were big proponents of European unification because they saw it as the cure for Europe's fragmentation and weakness. The same stance makes sense today: the EU can be a positive force on the world stage provided it collaborates with the United States and respects NATO's continued importance. The challenge facing Europeans is to ensure that the EU functions in this capacity. If such positive attitudes are adopted on both sides of the Atlantic, they can set the stage for sensible collaborative policies to be adopted.

Transforming NATO's Defenses

Despite its success at pursuing political transformation inside Europe, NATO has made considerably less progress at preparing itself for new defense and security missions outside Europe. While there are encouraging signs of change today, the 1990s were mostly a lost decade in this critical arena. NATO started out well, adopting a new strategic concept at the Rome Summit of 1991 that called for a downsized but reformed military posture that could perform the new missions of the post–Cold War era. At the time, talk of mobile, flexible European forces was in the air. Encouraged by this trend, the United States agreed to keep 150,000 troops in Europe (the target was later reduced to 100,000 troops) that would continue working closely with allied forces. But in the succeeding years, little progress was made. European forces grew smaller, but they did not become appreciably better at performing new missions because of capability shortfalls in power projection, long-distance strike operations, and interoperability with U.S. forces. By way of comparison, where the U.S. military was capable of projecting fully 700,000 well-armed military personnel for global missions, the Europeans were at best capable of projecting only about one-tenth of this amount in comparable time. Even this limited capability, moreover, resided mainly in British and French forces; the other European militaries were not serious participants in the power-projection mission.

The frustrations of the 1990s resulted largely from the political unwillingness of most European countries, apart from Britain, to accept security responsibilities outside their continent. As a result, European military forces failed to develop an improved capacity to project power long distances, leaving them unable to work closely with U.S. forces in performing new missions. By the late 1990s, U.S. military forces began transformation, adopting information age technologies and doctrines. The effect was to raise questions about the physical interoperability of U.S. and European forces (their capacity to operate together regardless of where they were deployed). Some Americans became alarmed that the transatlantic gap in military capabilities would soon grow to the point where U.S. and European forces could not wage war together even if their political leaders ordered them to do so.[7] A deeper fear was that the alliance was headed toward political irrelevancy, if not the graveyard.

This problem had its origins in the late 1970s: the fall of the Shah of Iran exposed the oil-rich Persian Gulf to its own instability and to Soviet pressure. Facing a still-serious Soviet military threat in Central Europe, NATO reached an agreement whereby the United States, already proficient at swift power projection, would defend Western interests in the Gulf. The Europeans, in turn, would take up more responsibility for defending their own borders, and thus compensate for any diversion of U.S. forces to the Gulf. This division of labor made sense at the time, but when the Cold War abruptly ended a decade later, its rationale evaporated. Even after downsizing their Cold War forces, the Europeans still had over 2.4 million troops on active duty—nearly double the U.S. level—plus plenty of modern weapons and sizable combat formations totaling over 50 divisions, 3,000 tactical combat aircraft, and 300 naval warships. Yet the Europeans continued to prepare mainly for fading border-defense missions.

No European states other than Britain and France contributed heavily to the 1991 Gulf War. When the Kosovo War erupted 8 years later, U.S. forces provided over two-thirds of NATO's military power even though the conflict took place on Europe's periphery and within range of European airbases. Several European countries volunteered to help with the war in Afghanistan against the Taliban and al Qaeda terrorists, but the United States turned most offers aside, saying that European forces were not adequately prepared for the task. After the initial fighting proved successful, several European countries deployed forces for peacekeeping, and NATO later became involved, but this important mission did not diminish the reality that when the main battles of the 1990s were being fought, most Europeans militaries remained on the sidelines.

The war in Iraq showed the benefits of working with Europeans and the difficulties as well. In the political debate prior to the 2003 invasion, the United States received support from Britain, Spain, Italy, and others, but faced stiff opposition from Germany and France. During the war, Britain contributed substantial military forces that fought effectively, while other European countries contributed at the margins. Turkey's response, however, was a disappointment; it denied U.S. ground forces the option to invade Iraq from the north. In the early postwar occupation, Britain and Poland made major contributions, as did a number of other countries; again, however, France and Germany stood on the sidelines.

These experiences show that NATO force improvement plans can be designed on paper, but getting them implemented by the Europeans is far harder.[8] Forging a U.S. policy and strategy to surmount this problem requires a balancing of many goals. One goal is to achieve the necessary military reforms and capability enhancements in affordable ways that do not drive European defense budgets through the ceiling. A second goal is satisfying the United States about fair burdensharing while not overloading European governments with more than their constituencies will bear. A third goal is ensuring that the Europeans will be required to commit meaningfully to future crises, yet still have the latitude to refrain from specific operations that their political leaders do not want to join. A fourth goal is to balance authority relationships between the Americans and Europeans in crisis operations so that the former can lead while the latter can wield influence commensurate with their responsibilities.

A fifth goal is to strengthen NATO's force posture in appropriate ways while also allowing room for the EU to develop an independent military capacity. A sixth goal is working out a sensible division of military labors that provides for effective forces, yet yields a satisfactory multinational response to advance the legitimate interests of all participants. A seventh goal is to weave together the often-differing stances of individual European countries. For example, the British have been enthusiastic contributors, but the French have been willing only if their influence in NATO is increased to an extent unpalatable to the United States. The Germans have been cautious, while smaller member-nations have wanted to participate only in ways that do not overtax their small defense budgets. New members, although eager, do not yet have the capabilities to contribute in other than niche roles.

Owing to these multiple goals, some of which pull against each other, U.S. strategy has been faced with the difficult task of developing harmonized policies that promise a powerful military response yet reflect the concerns of the European nations enough to elicit their cooperation. This task is not hopeless, for some European countries are more amenable to defense reforms than others, and even in countries with stingy finance ministries, reform-minded military authorities are often willing to work with the resources available to them. Even so, progress will not be made unless attractive military improvement strategies, plans, and programs are crafted to illuminate the path ahead—a worthy task for strategic evaluation.

Five alternative strategies emerged during the 1990s that still frame the defense and military options today. Each of these options requires multiple policy components attuned to the multiple goals noted above. The first, least ambitious option—"status quo plus"—calls for the Europeans to remain mostly focused on continental defense missions, but for a few willing countries such as Britain to form ad hoc coalitions with the United States that could operate outside NATO's integrated command in handling crises beyond Europe. The second option, a division-of-labor approach, also calls for reliance on these ad hoc coalitions, but seeks greater efforts by European countries to field forces that could perform peacekeeping, occupation, and stabilization duties. Under the third option, European countries would pursue role specialization to a limited degree, but NATO would become better able to perform at least limited expeditionary strike missions. Under this option, several European countries would jointly develop a small strike posture of 20,000 to 60,000 troops that could be used under NATO's integrated command, or as a strong contributor to U.S.-led coalitions. The fourth option is more ambitious. It calls for the Europeans gradually to develop an improved portfolio of military assets in multiple areas for power-projection missions, with a total of about 250,000 troops. The fifth option is the most ambitious: Europeans would broadly match U.S. force contributions to expeditionary missions on Europe's periphery and the Middle East, with 500,000 troops available for ground, naval, and air formations.

Because each of these options has both distinct attractions and distinct liabilities, they pose tradeoffs that mandate careful appraisal: an essential step in any strategic evaluation when several options exist and the winner is not obvious. The "status quo plus" option of ad hoc coalitions accommodates the difficulty of persuading the Europeans to act strongly, but it leaves NATO in a state of declining relevance. The second option tries to take advantage of peacekeeping missions that the Europeans seem willing and able to perform, yet it leaves the United States and Britain with excessive warfighting burdens, and does nothing to upgrade NATO's capacity for such expeditionary strike missions as already have occurred in Afghanistan and Iraq. The ambitious fifth option, with a major European power-projection force, responds to new military requirements and solves the burdensharing issue, but is probably far more ambitious than the European public would countenance.

This leaves the third and fourth options as choices that are politically feasible yet that would significantly move NATO into the expeditionary strike game. Currently, NATO is earnestly pursuing the third option, but elements of the fourth option are under consideration. If this effort succeeds, it will be bucking the tide of recent history. Owing to their ambivalence about defense preparedness and operations beyond their continent, the Europeans did little more than pursue "status quo plus" during the 1990s, despite pleas by the United States and NATO Headquarters for them to do more. When NATO Headquarters first began addressing this issue in the early 1990s, it did so in relatively ambitious terms. It created two headquarters for two combined joint task forces (CJTFs) that could be deployed either inside or outside Europe. It also earmarked a NATO Reaction Force that was led by an Allied Rapid Reaction Corps (ARRC) and could draw from a large pool of 10 ground divisions plus 350 combat aircraft and nearly 100 naval combatants. In addition, it called for other forces to be upgraded in modernization and readiness. However, the CJTFs remained mostly paper creations. While the ARRC was organized with a capacity to command four divisions, half of it was composed of U.S. and British forces, while the other half was populated by other European forces that did not possess the necessary mobility, logistics support, and modern technologies. Other NATO forces made even less progress as European defense budgets declined in real terms. NATO issued fine-sounding communiqués at summit sessions, but it was unable to take the concrete steps needed to enhance its military capacity.

As the 1990s came to an end, the Europeans began showing signs of realizing their need to do more. Frustrated by the political-military problems encountered in the Balkans and determined to enhance its own defense identity, the European Union decided to create its ERRF for Petersberg tasks. Subsequently, the EU and NATO reached a "Berlin Plus" agreement that allows the ERRF to draw upon NATO military assets for agreed-upon operations that NATO declines to undertake. As the EU was thus making strides toward creating the ERRF, NATO proposed a Defense Capability Initiative (DCI), which the Europeans agreed to adopt at the Washington Summit of 1999. Less ambitious than earlier NATO plans, the DCI called for moderate European investments in such high-priority areas as mobility, logistics, information systems, smart munitions, and missile defense. Over the following 3 years, however, the DCI stalled due not only to lack of European enthusiasm, but also to its lack of focus. The DCI had scattered its proposals across the entire European force structure; it did not concentrate on creating the specific forces that would actually be used for crisis response.[9]

The events of September 11, 2001, motivated the Europeans to take another step forward in recognition that the new threats had become unavoidable. They were also alarmed by the fact that the United States chose to fight the counterterrorist war in Afghanistan largely without them, which suggested that Europe and NATO might be left permanently on the sidelines. Their most important action was to support NATO's decision to invoke its Article V collective defense clause, which legally enabled it not only to organize homeland defenses against global terrorism, but also to employ military force outside its border against terrorists and their sponsors. As subsequent events showed, this declaration did not mean that the Europeans were rushing to prepare their forces for new missions, or that NATO had overcome all the barriers to reaching a common political accord for individual crises. Yet NATO's Article V declaration cleared away any lingering doubt that the alliance had a new strategic purpose: projecting power outward in order to defend itself from distant threats.

At the Prague Summit of 2002, NATO acted to remedy the lack of focus of the 1999 Defense Capability Initiative by embracing a bold transformation agenda, partly inspired by the continuing transformation of U.S. military forces. This agenda aimed at overcoming the main limitations that prevented European forces from projecting power outside Europe and operating with U.S. forces there. Alliance-wide endorsement of this agenda was sought by the United States, but critics were surprised by the willingness of many European members of NATO to embrace it. The Prague agenda faded into the background when the debate over Iraq erupted a few weeks later, but the agenda was still being pursued during 2003–2004 under the leadership of a new Supreme Allied Commander Europe, U. S. Marine Corps General James Jones.

The centerpiece of the Prague agenda was a decision to create a new NATO Response Force composed of 3 rotating joint force clusters, each of 21,000 troops. For any 6-month period, one NRF will be on duty, another will be training for future duty, and another will be standing down from previous duty. While on duty, each NRF will have a deployable headquarters, a ground brigade, a fighter wing, a naval strike force, and logistic support assets. The idea behind the NRF was to field a small, mobile, and affordable force, manned mostly by Europeans, that would have a potent capacity for swift power projection, interoperable information networks, lethal strike operations, and expeditionary missions alongside U.S. forces. The NRF was designed to complement the EU's ERRF (performing different missions) and to provide a volunteer posture that European countries could join in a manner that reflected their predilections. It was intended to function not only as a high-readiness NATO strike force, but also as a vanguard for promoting transformation of a large set of European forces as they rotate through NRF duties of 1-year duration. Fielding the NRF was to be a key goal of a new NATO Allied Transformation Command (ATC) and a Prague Capabilities Commitment (PCC) that would replace the DCI. The Prague Summit declaration called for this agenda to be carried out by 2006, leaving NATO better prepared to face the world later in the decade.[10] As of late 2004, progress was encouraging because major parts of the NRF had already been fielded and the ATC had been created, although the PCC was making only slow progress. The NRF is projected to reach full operating capability in 2006.

The NRF will consume only a tiny portion of European forces potentially available to NATO. As table 7–1 shows, European members of NATO today field almost 2.4 million active-duty troops, 63 division-equivalents, 3,400 combat aircraft, and 276 naval combatants. While the forces of longstanding members from northern and southern Europe have declined somewhat in recent years, the forces of new members have made up the difference. Some military experts claim that only the forces from Northern Europe have the weapons and other assets needed for modern combat operations. Even by this standard, however, the Europeans field large forces: 925,000 personnel, 18 division-equivalents, 1,255 combat aircraft, and 150 naval combatants. In addition, Italy's forces (200,000) are fairly modern, and the forces of other countries—from the southern region and Eastern Europe—can perform important missions where they have niche capabilities.

The idea that the Europeans can improve their forces for new missions despite anemic budgets and other limitations is questioned by skeptics. Although these critics have recent history on their side, Europe's defense budgets are bigger than often realized, and force reductions can free funds for investments. Nor is there such a huge gap in new military capabilities that U.S. and European forces cannot be made interoperable. Many European countries are now buying modern command, control, communications, computer, intelligence, reconnaissance, and surveillance (C^4ISR) systems that can be networked with U.S. systems. The weapons and smart munitions of the best European militaries are comparable to those of the United States. Although the Europeans lack adequate mobility forces, long-distance logistic support assets, and specialized assets in such areas as air-to-ground targeting, defense suppression, and all-weather/day-night operations, only limited numbers of these assets are needed to field the small NRF and other forces that might be used for expeditionary missions. Such assets are affordable, while intensified training regimes can close the gap in modern doctrines. The real challenge is to focus these improvements on the forces that will be used for such missions, rather than scattering them across Europe's forces.

Table 7–1. **NATO Forces of European Members**

	Active Manpower	Division Equivalents	Tactical Combat Aircraft	Naval Combatants
Northern Europe	925,000	18	1,255	150
Southern Europe	990,000	31	1,400	110
New Members	450,000	14	745	16
Total	**2,365,000**	**63**	**3,400**	**276**

The logic of its future military requirements suggests that NATO's new defense agenda should not be limited to fielding the NRF. A strong case can be made that NATO should also create a small NATO Special Operations Force (NSOF) of about 1,000 troops from multiple countries that could be used for multiple special operations missions such as gathering intelligence, spotting targets for airstrikes, conducting limited actions against terrorists, and advising foreign militaries. Such an NSOF might be composed of an inner core of 300 troops, plus an outer network of about 700 to 1,000 troops. Multiple European countries including Britain and France already possess elite special operations forces that could contribute to an NSOF.

Likewise, NATO will need to make progress on upgrading its High Readiness Forces (HRF), which will follow the NRF into combat when major combat operations are carried out. Today, European members of NATO field about 12 ground divisions that ostensibly are deployable and could be used for HRF missions, but in reality only 2 or 3 of these divisions are truly deployable, and even these would deploy slowly. NATO needs better capabilities, but as a practical matter, it does not need fully 12 divisions along with commensurate air and naval forces. A ground posture of five or six European divisions (supplemented by one or two U.S. divisions) would meet most future requirements, even for multiple simultaneous contingencies. Because such European combat forces already exist and have adequate stocks of modern weapons, such a posture can be fielded with such affordable, low-cost steps as acquiring modern information networks, sensors, and smart munitions; multinational logistic units for expeditionary missions; and strategic lift assets (airlift and sealift) from the commercial sector.

NATO also should strive to create a Stabilization and Reconstruction Force (SRF) of European units to operate alongside its NRF and HRF. Such units would be configured to deploy after major combat has ended and peace must be established in an occupied country by quelling insurgent opposition, establishing civil order, and restoring such services as electrical power, sewage systems, and health care. Post-invasion Afghanistan and Iraq show the importance of these missions. European countries have ample manpower in such relevant areas as light infantry, military police, civil engineers, health care, and civil administration. The challenge is to organize these assets so that they can be readily available when needed. An organized, on-call European force of about two division-equivalents (35,000 troops) for stabilization and reconstruction (S&R) missions would help meet this requirement. In addition, NATO should organize European assets for performing defense and security sector development (DSSD), both as part of an occupation mission and for peacetime outreach toward new partners in the Middle East seeking help in building modern, democratic militaries.

In summary, the option of creating an NRF gets NATO into the power-projection business, but the expanded option would provide a bigger, better portfolio of assets including NSOF, NRF, HRF, SRF, and DSSD. That may sound daunting, but when details are considered, its total of about 250,000 troops involves only 10 percent of Europe's active military forces, or 16 to 18 percent of its active ground power. This option could be pursued gradually over a period of 5 or 10 years, avoiding the risk of overloading Europe's budgets and willpower. This option is affordable because it mostly requires reorganizing existing forces rather than creating new forces and equipping them with expensive weapons.

Moreover, the Europeans could generate the necessary funds by retiring unneeded border defense forces and applying the savings to investments in power-projection and expeditionary missions. To be sure, these priorities add up to a demanding agenda, but with willpower and commitment, they are feasible.

With these considerations in mind, a new NATO military concept, anchored in a five-tier hierarchy of forces, can be articulated. At the top of this hierarchy would be the NSOF and NRF plus a new U.S. military presence in Europe that provides a parallel capability for prompt, long-distance strike missions (see chapter 20 for analysis of the future U.S. presence in Europe). In the middle would be NATO HRF units: European forces and U.S.-based reinforcements that could supplement the NRF and U.S. quick response forces when major combat operations must be launched. At the bottom would be a NATO stabilization and reconstruction force and defense and security sector development assets, composed of European and U.S. units that could be used for occupation missions as major combat operations are coming to an end. EU forces could be assigned missions in all of these areas. The effect of this new military concept would be to give NATO an integrated capability to perform initial strike missions, followed by major combat operations, followed by stabilization and reconstruction missions, either sequentially or in whatever combination is required by the situation.

Transforming NATO for Middle East Involvement

Even if such an ambitious defense agenda is pursued, it will count for little unless NATO also undergoes a parallel strategic transformation that leaves it better prepared politically to carry out new security missions outside Europe, including in the Middle East. Here, too, practical steps are needed if progress on this goal is to be made. Such a strategic transformation must begin by crafting a shared transatlantic set of attitudes about the application of power and purpose in the Middle East. The United States and Europe do not need to agree on everything in this critical arena, but if they are to work cooperatively, they must agree on basic principles; otherwise, they will continue to be at odds not only when crises erupt, but on a day-to-day basis as well. Progress can be made if NATO writes a new Strategic Concept to replace the outdated version adopted in 1999. While NATO studies and documents can help speed progress, forging a shared set of principles requires continuing dialogue and will not be achieved overnight. But perhaps gains can be made if more Europeans awaken to their own responsibilities and the United States shows a willingness to treat them as equal partners outside Europe.

The United States and Europe will need to reach a better understanding of the menaces posed by such new-era threats as terrorism, rogue tyrants, and WMD proliferation. The damaging debate over Iraq was partly a product of differences in threat perception. In 2003, the United States saw Saddam Hussein's regime as a ringleader of an "axis of evil" anchored in a new-era form of violent, antidemocratic neofascism. By contrast, many Europeans questioned the extent of this threat and whether it was a direct menace to their own continent. Whether the United States was exaggerating the threat or the Europeans were blind to it can be debated, but what is clear is that the wide gap still separating them must be closed.[11]

The shared set of attitudes must include not only common threat perceptions but also a common understanding of the legal standards for using military force and going to war. Many Europeans still cling to the Westphalian principle of 1648 that war is legal only when cross-border aggression has already occurred. By contrast, the United States and Britain have been moving toward a new legal standard under which it is also permissible to topple malignant governments when they have committed genocide against their own people or to launch preemptive wars when it is amply clear, even before external aggression has occurred, that threats are grave, gathering, and imminent. It was this standard, not just WMD proliferation, that the U.S. and British governments used to justify their invasion of Iraq, and against which France and Germany protested.

Unless there is resolution of these two differing interpretations of international law regarding the use of force, they will be the ingredients for further misunderstandings between the United States and Europe. Encouragement comes from two developments. In the Balkans, the Europeans went to war to push Serbian dictator Milosevic out of Kosovo even though his genocide was internal, not cross-border aggression. In the Persian Gulf, the United States and Britain went to war against Iraq after 12 frustrating years of containment that seemed on the brink of failing and after seeking UN approval. Both experiences suggest that the transatlantic gap on standards for using force may not be as wide as it seems. If a common stance can be forged, it is likely to be a sensible blending of approaches that recognizes both the importance of international law and the wisdom of acting to prevent gathering storms from exploding with full fury.

Creating a shared strategic mindset, however, must go beyond defining threats and the standards for waging war against them. In addition, the United States and Europe will need to reach a better agreement on common goals and strategy in the Middle East and elsewhere. The invasion of Iraq signaled that the United States has become willing to use military force to topple tyrants and that it seeks to install democracy in the Middle East. By contrast, while the Europeans favor democracy in principle, they are less willing to confront tyrants and terrorists and are more prone to use traditional diplomacy to pursue their goals. To a degree, the debate between Americans and Europeans is a matter of how to blend coercive instruments with diplomatic persuasion and of how to blend confrontational politics with accommodation. But it also is a product of differences over whether the Atlantic Community should seek to remake Middle Eastern politics in a new mold or instead accept the situation there as it exists, without ideals or illusions. By tradition, Americans tend to be idealists, while Europeans lean toward practical acceptance of presumably immovable realities. Reconciling these two strategic approaches sufficiently to permit common action is critical.

In today's globalizing world, the reality is that the Middle East will not become stable if it remains mired in the status quo. It will need to pursue a future of change anchored in a stable security architecture, steady democratization, and economic progress. On this matter, American visionaries who favor activist Western engagement seem to have logic on their side, although their reach may exceed their grasp. Yet European skeptics are also correct in favoring caution and prudence. Western makeovers of the Middle East have been attempted before: beginning in idealism, they have always deteriorated into some-thing that looked like imperialism to an outraged Islamic fundamentalism. Regardless of the balance to be struck between assertiveness and restraint, there is ample room for blend-ing military power and diplomacy, as well as other instruments, in a common strategy. But this strategy should not deteriorate into an approach in which the United States is the "bad cop" and the Europeans are the "good cop." Such an approach is a recipe for continued trouble in transatlantic relations, as well as strategic failure to attain common goals. The situation calls for a strategy in which the United States and Europe share both coercive and persuasive duties, while sensibly drawing upon their respective strengths.

In order to carry out such a strategy, NATO's strategic transformation will require the alliance to adopt more flexible ways to make decisions regarding when and how to intervene in the Middle East and other regions outside Europe. Currently, the alliance abides by the principle that unanimous decisions must be achieved before it is authorized to act. This principle arguably made sense during the Cold War, when NATO's borders were threatened and any violation of them would have triggered the automatic agree-ment to defend them. But when this principle is applied to gray-area situations outside Europe, it can be a recipe for paralysis. Such situations may easily allow a few countries that do not want to act decisively to use their veto powers to frustrate the wishes of a large majority. Moreover, the unanimity principle delegates too little authority to coun-tries willing to assume responsibility for security missions outside Europe, and it gives too much authority to those countries not accepting comparable responsibility. As a result, those members who bear this responsibility cannot even employ NATO's machinery to plan future crisis operations, much less be confident of carrying the alliance with them when they perceive a need to act.

Thus far, NATO has relied upon such informal practices as the "silence procedure" to prevent paralysis. Under this practice, a member who disagrees with a broad consen-sus refrains from voting, thereby allowing NATO to act without formally approving the step. Another procedure has been to employ the Defense Planning Committee (DPC), instead of the North Atlantic Council (NAC), to make defense decisions. Since France, a member of the NAC, is not a member of the DPC, this procedure allows NATO to act even when the French disagree. Both finessing procedures have their limits. The silence proce-dure works only when dissenters are willing to remain silent. The DPC works only when the sole barrier to action is France, not some other country. With NATO now enlarged to 26 members as it tries to grapple with nebulous security affairs outside its borders, neither procedure is a reliable solution to the problem of future paralysis.

Creation of more flexible NATO decision procedures should be anchored in the principle that mission-performing members need greater authority but that their en-deavors should still be subjected to careful scrutiny by the alliance as a whole. This for-mula means that NATO's basic strategic concepts would still be adopted only through unanimous agreement. But it also means that mission-performing countries should be allowed to use NATO's integrated command to plan future operations at their discretion, subject to approval by NATO's Secretary General. When crises erupt, NATO could then rely upon a model similar to that employed by the UN Security Council, which gives veto power only to permanent members and demands only majority support when the permanent members agree to act. Instead of creating "permanent members," however, NATO could adopt a principle whereby a small group of countries with well-established track records for accepting responsibilities in major mission areas is given special status. In order to launch a crisis response, this "Committee of Contributors" would have to agree unanimously to act: any of them could veto action. But when they agree that NATO should act, only a solid majority of the remaining members of the total membership would be needed to authorize action. NATO would no longer be paralyzed by the unanimity principle. Instead, it would be able to respond to crises when its leaders and most of its members judge that there is a need to act.[12]

Finally, NATO's strategic transformation requires a multilateral agenda of action in the Middle East and elsewhere. Instead of merely providing a reservoir of military power for informal "coalitions of the willing" to operate outside NATO, it needs to be able and willing to project military power in wartime under the NATO flag and with an integrated command. It needs to be ready to participate in long-lasting postwar occupation, stabilization, and reconstruction missions. It needs to be able to provide an ample number of troops to help the United States and Britain so that they are not left alone in the Persian Gulf and elsewhere. It needs to allocate the burdens for new-era missions fairly, while taking advantage of role specialization by which members apply their unique capabilities.

In addition, NATO needs to become more active in the peacetime military affairs of the Middle East. It can do so by employing its PFP program in Eastern Europe as a model for the new Istanbul Cooperation Initiative (ICI) that was adopted at the Istanbul Summit. Such an initiative would not be intended to prepare Middle Eastern countries for admission to NATO, but would endeavor to help their militaries perceive the benefits of democracy, peace, and professional dialogue with NATO members. It would have to be carried out in ways that focus on self-defense and that avoid creating new threats to Israel and other countries. It could begin with a small circle of trustworthy countries and then gradually grow as additional countries express interest and prove their capability. Such a NATO outreach effort has been contemplated before but has never taken hold, due to suspicious skepticism in the Middle East and a lack of passion among key NATO nations. But if the war in Iraq and a renewed Palestinian-Arab peace process were to change attitudes in both quarters, the ICI is an idea worth pursuing.

In June 2004, as NATO's members met at the Istanbul Summit, the prevailing spirit was one of healing the rift over Iraq, welcoming seven new members, and launching NATO upon the path of involvement in the Middle East. The summit adopted parts of the military and reform agenda described in these pages, including the ICI. It is to be hoped that NATO may now pursue its new Istanbul agenda vigorously, rather than letting it languish with new ideas that are adopted but not implemented.

Reforming Alliance Relationships in Asia

Concern for alliance management will not be limited to reform of NATO. Asia must be factored into the equation. Here, too, careful evaluation of strategy options, plans, and programs will be needed as the future unfolds. Unlike Europe, where a large multilateral alliance exists, America's alliance system in Asia is composed of bilateral alliances with a number of countries, each of which is anchored in its own reciprocal strategic bargain in which both participants profit. These Asian alliances have not been hotly debated lately, but as this region evolves, U.S. security alliances there will need to evolve as well. Asia is one of the most dynamic regions on earth, experiencing profound economic and political changes. Authoritarian China is emerging as a regional great power, Japan is beginning to reawaken in strategic terms, and other Asian countries are becoming wealthier while building stable democratic governments. Thus far, however, the U.S. network of bilateral alliances in Asia has not adjusted to these trends, clinging instead to its Cold War structure. The question is whether this alliance system will deteriorate or even shatter or can instead be guided to a new, stable shape that fosters integration, peace, and prosperity.

One risk is that today's Asian security system will give way to an intense bipolar rivalry pitting the United States against China in a struggle for supremacy, with America's allies clinging to its skirts for protection. An equal risk is that Asia will slide into an unstable era of fluid multipolarity in which China, the United States, Japan, the Republic of Korea, and other countries all lack firm security anchors such as a network of interlocking alliances. These countries, left to their own devices, might maneuver against each other and head toward a future of accelerating WMD proliferation and the threat of a deadly WMD-armed confrontation. Far better would be a future in which U.S.-led alliances enable the Asian democratic community to draw closer together and to enlarge in ways that would ultimately result in China's integration. U.S. strategy for alliance leadership in Asia should focus on preventing the disastrous outcomes and fostering the desirable outcome.

Helping guide Asian security affairs toward a favorable outcome is partly the responsibility of the United States as it continues to play the role of superpower leader in this complex region. Taking into account the strategic trends at work in Asia and the inclinations of its allies, the United States has two broad options for alliance management. Either it can cling to the status quo while modifying it only at the margins, or it can try to reform these alliances in order to make them better suited to meeting the challenges ahead. The status quo remains the choice of some observers, but the major changes taking place in Asia coupled with new directions in U.S. defense strategy are elevating the attractiveness of the reform option.

If a reform strategy is chosen, a main strategic task for the United States will be to broaden its existing bilateral alliances in northeast Asia to focus more widely on the Asian–Western Pacific region as a whole. Another task will be to shift, to some degree, from bilateral alliances to multilateral ties across the entire region. In assessing how to approach these tasks, strategic evaluation must deal with the Asian region as a whole, but it also will need to analyze each bilateral relationship on its own, with due regard for U.S. goals and the sensitivities of each country. Alliance reform in Europe may be hard, but alliance reform in Asia will be harder yet. However, the winds of change are slowly gaining force. The challenge is to guide change in sound directions.[13]

The bilateral U.S. security relationship with Japan remains a bedrock of U.S. policy and strategy in Asia and a foundation for the Asian security system as a whole. Maintaining close security ties to Japan will be key to preserving an influential U.S. role in Asia, and ensuring that Japan plays a constructive role in regional affairs will be key to fostering Asian stability. As during the Cold War, the essence of the U.S.-Japanese security relationship is that the United States provides extended nuclear deterrence coverage over Japan plus help in safeguarding conventional defense of its borders. The United States also supports Japan's quest for economic prosperity through vigorous exports and imports. For its part, Japan provides most of the conventional forces for its own self-defense and respects U.S. leadership in Asian security affairs.

Thus far, this relationship has been comfortable for both countries. Japan certainly has benefited because it has been made secure from external threats while also becoming wealthy. The Asian security system has benefited because Japan no longer plays an expansionist role of the sort that led to World War II. With Japan playing a low-profile role and possessing only enough military power to defend its borders, the Asian security system has been freed from one of its major historical sources of tension. Today, most Asian countries are relieved that Japan is no longer a major power-broker. Many Japanese, too, are relieved because this demanding role is being played by the United States in ways that redound to Japan's benefit. Content with the status quo, Japan thus far has shown no signs of the level of discontent with the United States like that now shown by France and Germany.

Yet Japan's security environment is changing. During the Cold War, Japan clung to the United States because it feared a military threat from the Soviet Union. With the Soviet Union gone and Russia possessing far less power in Asia, Japan has become far more secure. Japan, however, confronts two new threats: North Korea's potential acquisition of nuclear-armed missiles and China's emergence as a regional big power could menace Japan's safety as well as its privileged role in Asian security and economic affairs. Japan's natural reaction is to turn to the United States for protection from these new threats. The United States has an incentive to provide this protection in order to ensure that Japan is not pushed into crossing the nuclear threshold or building offensively oriented military forces. Making sure that Japan remains protected will be an ongoing challenge for the United States, not only because it requires the deployment of large U.S. military forces in Northeast Asia, but also because it compels the United States to treat China and North Korea firmly, resulting in perpetual tensions with both. For example, if the United States must deploy regional missile defenses in Asia in order to protect Japan from attack, this could turn up the heat in U.S. relations with both China and North Korea.

Even as the United States continues to protect Japan, it has incentives to find ways for an increasingly powerful Japan to play a constructive role in Asian security affairs. Thus far, Japan has been a security consumer, not a security provider. Yet it has ample military power to become a provider of regional security in partnership with the United States. With a population of 127 million people and an economy of $4 trillion, Japan has a defense budget that, at $43 billion, is significantly larger than that of France or Germany. With 239,000 active troops, it fields about 12 divisions, 280 combat aircraft, and 70 major naval combatants. These forces are armed with modern weapons, but because they are configured for self-defense, they lack the C⁴ISR assets, mobility forces, logistic support, and aircraft carriers that would be necessary to project power far beyond

Japan's borders. Japan could, however, easily afford to acquire such assets: its defense budget is only about 1 percent of its GDP, considerably below the 3.5 percent of GDP spent by the United States. A new role as a security provider thus is potentially within its grasp, should Japan so choose.

Japan already is moving slowly in this direction. The Japanese government is seeking a permanent seat on the UN Security Council, and its Liberal Democratic Party favors altering Japan's pacifist constitution to provide greater flexibility for military operations outside its borders. Its decision in early 2005 to express public concern about a potential Chinese threat to Taiwan marked an important departure in Japan's outward-looking mentality. But this step was a logical extension of other, less noticeable steps taken in preceding years.

In 2003, Japan put its first spy satellite into space and is otherwise strengthening its intelligence agencies. It is also working with the United States to create local missile defenses. Japan agreed to send 600 noncombat troops to Iraq to help participate in reconstruction duties, and it is participating in studies with the United States on ideas for expanding their joint military cooperation to broader missions. Japan's military forces have been extending their military reach in recent years. Its naval forces now operate on a wider maritime perimeter around Japan's borders than a decade ago, and it has accepted the limited role of providing logistic support to U.S. forces in the event of a new Korean war. Japan's navy is building a small helicopter carrier of 13,500 tons that could broaden its capacity to perform maritime missions. Japan has begun providing troops for select peacekeeping operations in Asia, and in future years, it may be cooperating with the United States and other countries in other missions, such as naval patrols to stop piracy and trafficking of WMD materials. While nobody wants Japan to develop major expeditionary combat forces, limited steps in this direction might include, for example, Japan fielding a small strike force similar in size to NATO's 21,000-member NRF.

Two guiding strategic imperatives are at work here. If Japan develops better forces for power-projection missions, they could help lessen the burdens now being shouldered exclusively by the United States. Such Japanese forces could help U.S. forces patrol Asian waters in peacetime and react to crises in wartime. The second imperative is that while such forces must be large enough to be militarily significant, they must be small enough to reassure other Asian countries, including U.S. allies, that Japan is acting constructively, not menacingly. Determining how to strike a sensible balance between these two competing imperatives seems likely to be an issue requiring continuing close attention in the coming years.[14]

The strategic calculus facing the United States in shaping its future alliance ties to South Korea is both similar and different. South Korea remains unquestionably vulnerable to North Korea. Public attention recently has been riveted on North Korea's efforts to acquire nuclear weapons and long-range missiles, but less noticed is that North Korea also poses a major conventional military threat; its big army of 35 divisions, 3,500 tanks, and 10,000 artillery tubes is poised near the demilitarized zone (DMZ), only 25 miles from Seoul.[15]

South Korea is far from defenseless. Its population is double that of North Korea and its economy is 20 times bigger. South Korea's military posture of about 25 well-armed divisions and 538 combat aircraft seems ample to defend its borders across a peninsula that is only 200 kilometers wide and ruggedly mountainous. Yet South Korea still needs U.S. military help in order to deter and defeat aggression. Although U.S. ground forces are being withdrawn from areas near the DMZ, these forces and more could still be needed to provide counterattack options, if necessary. Moreover, in event of a war, sizable U.S. air forces, naval forces, and logistic support forces would also be needed. For these reasons, a continuing U.S. military role in helping defend South Korea will remain a major feature of the U.S.–Republic of Korea (ROK) security relationship for some time.

However, North Korea does not seem capable of continuing to menace South Korea and Northeast Asia forever. Impoverished and saddled with a totalitarian government that cannot create a productive economy, it may eventually collapse of its own weight, and such a collapse has been quietly expected by observers for some time. The strategic task would then shift from defending South Korea to unifying the Korean Peninsula. Thereafter, the U.S.–ROK defense relationship would need to be reconsidered. Critics of this relationship expect that U.S. forces would leave and the U.S.–ROK security treaty be torn up, but a unified Korea would still need U.S. protection against China and other dangers. Moreover, this powerful country could make useful contributions to regional security affairs if some of its forces were reconfigured for power-projection roles and could cooperate with U.S. and Japanese forces in performing such missions. U.S. bilateral defense relationships with Japan and South Korea could then become the basis for a new multilateralism aimed at creating a new and more stable Asian security system.

Along the vast Asian crescent south of Japan and Korea, the United States has four compelling strategic priorities: defending allies with which it has security treaties, maintaining freedom of navigation along the maritime sea lines, protecting Taiwan, and ensuring control of the zone stretching from the Philippines to Singapore. Fulfilling these priorities will remain a demanding task that stretches U.S. military power in Asia to its limits. If Japan and South Korea could be motivated to help the United States perform the necessary missions in military, political, and economic terms, the result would be fewer burdens for the United States, a more stable Asia as China grows in power, and a more secure geopolitical setting.

U.S. bilateral ties with Southeast Asian countries—including the Philippines, Indonesia, Malaysia, Singapore, and Thailand—also merit close watching with a similar calculus in mind. Other than Australia, a close military ally of the United States, these countries have traditionally sought a more distant relationship. U.S. forces withdrew from the Philippines in the early 1990s. In recent years, the United States has been pursuing improved military ties with these countries, all of which field relatively small military forces that are mainly configured for self-defense. Progress, though noteworthy, has been limited and slow. Enhanced bilateral ties in such niche areas as counterterrorism and peacekeeping make sense, but greater progress could be made if these countries can be motivated to cooperate with the United States in forging stronger multilateral ties. By pooling their forces for regional security missions and working with the U.S. military, these countries could take important steps toward making their own region and all of Asia more stable.

Crafting Visionary Strategies That Work

For both Europe and Asia, the alliance reform strategies articulated in this chapter have political and military features that can be pursued in the near term, the medium term, and the long term, at a pace that responds to strategic needs and political circumstances. These strategies could help create new transatlantic and transpacific relationships between the United States and its allies that are anchored in new strategic bargains. During the Cold War, NATO's strategic bargain was one in which the United States and its allies made reciprocal political-military commitments to each other in order to make Europe secure while protecting U.S. interests. The early 21st century could see a new transatlantic bargain in which the United States supports a harmonious relationship between a still-healthy NATO and a stronger EU in Europe, while the Europeans respond by working with the United States to help stabilize the Middle East. A new strategic bargain in Asia could call for the United States to continue defending its traditional allies against new threats, while they work with it to broaden bilateral treaties and create multilateral partnerships to help bring security to all of Asia and other regions as well. If these new relationships and their underlying bargains can be created and are equipped with the necessary political-military capabilities to perform new missions, they will help keep America's alliances with Europe and Asia intact and render them better able to deal with tomorrow's global security challenges.

Regardless of how these particular reform strategies are appraised, a need to reform U.S. security alliances already exists in Europe and is emerging in Asia. Alliance reform makes sense in both regions, not only to strengthen security, but also to employ military integration as a tool to help keep alliances together at a time of foreign policy strains. In order to bring about these achievements, alliance reform strategies will need to be both visionary and practical. They will need to put forth ambitious agendas that fully respond to the new security environment, yet are realistically achievable and work effectively when they are implemented.

The challenge facing strategic evaluation is to contribute to this important analytical enterprise. Good ideas are no guarantee that the future can be successfully navigated, but they will help tilt the odds in that direction. Strategic evaluation has an opportunity to contribute good ideas to the analysis of future U.S. policies and strategies for leading and reforming its alliances in the early 21st century. Indeed, no other analytical methodology can match its strengths in this arena. But to stay relevant, strategic evaluation will need to keep abreast of the issues and options confronting these alliances. Outdated analytical methods such as those that focus, for example, on employing alliances for traditional border-defense missions will need to give way to new methods capable of addressing the thorny issue of reform for the projection of power and purpose outward into unfamiliar and dangerous terrain. Likewise, proposals for military reform of alliances will need to be accompanied by concrete plans and programs that help bring them to life and make them serious candidates for adoption. If strategic evaluation can master such a demanding agenda, it will have served its purposes in this critical arena of thought and action.

Notes

[1] For a history of NATO's early years, see Don Cook, *Forging the Alliance: NATO, 1945–1950* (New York: Arbor House/William Morrow, 1989).

[2] For analysis of the spread of democracy, see Samuel P. Huntington, *The Third Wave: Democratization in the Late Twentieth Century* (Norman, OK: University of Oklahoma Press, 1991).

[3] For an analysis of alliance frictions in the Middle East before the George W. Bush administration, see *Allies Divided: Transatlantic Policies for the Greater Middle East*, ed. Robert D. Blackwill and Michael Stürmer (Cambridge, MA: The MIT Press, 1997). For a political analysis of recent debates, see Strobe Talbott, "From Prague to Budapest," *Foreign Affairs* 81, no. 6 (November/December 2002).

[4] For a skeptical view of the transatlantic relationship, see Robert Kagan, *Of Paradise and Power: America and Europe in the New World Order* (New York: Vintage Books, 2004).

[5] Notwithstanding charges that the Bush administration neglected NATO from 2001 onward, it was a leading architect of further NATO enlargement as well as the defense reforms adopted at the Prague Summit of 2002 and the Istanbul Summit of 2004. Like the Clinton administration, it pursued moderate defense reforms along with enlargement.

[6] See John Gillingham, *European Integration 1952–2002: Superstate or New Market Economy?* (New York: Cambridge University Press, 2003).

[7] See, for example, *Transatlantic Transformations: Equipping NATO for the Twenty-first Century*, ed. Daniel S. Hamilton (Washington, DC: Center for Transatlantic Relations, The Johns Hopkins University, 2004). See also C. Richard Nelson and Jason S. Purcell, *Transforming NATO Forces: European Perspectives* (Washington, DC: The Atlantic Council of the United States, 2003); *Transatlantic Interoperability in Defense Industries: How the U.S. and Europe Could Better Cooperate in Coalition Military Operations*, ed. Jacqueline Grapin (Washington, DC: European Institute, 2002); Ronald D. Asmus, "Rebuilding the Atlantic Alliance," *Foreign Affairs* 82, no. 5 (September/October 2003).

[8] For analysis of NATO's military problems, see David C. Gompert et al., *Mind the Gap: Promoting a Transatlantic Revolution in Military Affairs* (Washington, DC: National Defense University Press, 1999).

[9] See NATO press releases "Washington Summit Communiqué," April 24, 1999; "Defense Capabilities Initiative," April 25, 1999; "The Alliance's Strategic Concept," April 24, 1999.

[10] See NATO press release "Prague Summit Communiqué," November 15, 2002; "President Bush Thanks Germany for Support Against Terror," remarks to Special Session of the German Bundestag, Berlin, May 23, 2002; Hans Binnendijk and Richard L. Kugler, "Transforming European Forces," *Survival* 44, no. 3 (Autumn 2002).

[11] See Hans Binnendijk and Richard L. Kugler, "Dual-Track Transformation for the Atlantic Alliance," *Defense Horizons* 35 (Washington, DC: National Defense University Press, November 2003).

[12] See Leo G. Michel, "NATO Decisionmaking: Au Revoir to the Consensus Rule?" *Strategic Forum* 202 (Washington, DC: National Defense University Press, August 2003).

[13] See Morton Abramowitz and Stephen Bosworth, "Adjusting to the New Asia," *Foreign Affairs* 82, no. 4 (July/August 2003); William T. Tow, *Asian-Pacific Strategic Relations: Seeking Convergent Security* (New York: Cambridge University Press, 2003).

[14] See Eugene A. Matthews, "Japan's New Nationalism," *Foreign Affairs* 82, no. 6 (November/December 2003).

[15] See Jonathan D. Pollack and Young Koo Cha, *A New Alliance for the Next Century: The Future of U.S.–Korean Cooperation* (Santa Monica, CA: RAND, 1995); Michael E. O'Hanlon and Michael Mochizuki, *Crisis on the Korean Peninsula: How to Deal with a Nuclear North Korea* (New York: McGraw-Hill, 2003); Kim Dong Shin, "The ROK–U.S. Alliance: Where Is It Headed?" *Strategic Forum* 197 (Washington, DC: National Defense University Press, April 2003).

Chapter 8
Pursuing Stability in a Dangerous World

In performing its role of global security architect, the United States must grapple with dangers facing the international security system. Crafting U.S. strategy for dealing with these dangers is one of the most important and difficult challenges facing strategic evaluation. Dangers that already exist must be handled wisely because they directly threaten U.S. security interests and those of close allies and could worsen if allowed to fester. Nor can potential dangers of the future be ignored; they could erupt into major problems if they are not handled wisely today. Coping with these dangers, let alone eradicating them, is difficult because their underlying causes are complex and do not lend themselves to easy remedies. Clearly, the United States should take the initiative in its strategies for managing these dangers. But what should these strategies be? The answer is not always clear: all strategies involve a complicated mix of potential solutions, constraints, drawbacks, tradeoffs, and uncertainties. Weighing and balancing these options is a key role for strategic evaluation.

In addressing this subject, this chapter begins by discussing the role played by strategic evaluation in developing U.S. policy and strategy for handling those parts of the world that produce serious dangers. Most of its pages then examine two important policy and strategy issues that arise from today's dangers: how the United States should deal with Russia and China, and how it should deal with dangers arising not only from the greater Middle East, but also along the entire southern arc of instability, which begins in the Balkans, passes through the Middle East, North Africa, and Persian Gulf, and stretches to south-central Asia and the East Asian littoral. Whereas dealing with Russia and China is an exercise in managing big-power relations in order to avert potential dangers, handling the greater Middle East and southern arc of instability is a matter of handling a host of existing dangers, such as terrorism, rogue countries, and WMD proliferation. To the extent that the United States is capable of handling both challenges, it will be better able to create a stable global security system today and tomorrow; to the extent it fails to do so, it will face greater troubles ahead.

Developing and assessing U.S. policy and strategy for each of these challenges requires a particular form of strategic evaluation. Chapter 8 appraises alternative U.S. policies and strategies in both domains, but its purpose is not to put forth a fixed blueprint for how the United States should respond. Instead, it strives to illuminate the issues and options that strategic evaluation must address in analyzing the whys and wherefores of dealing with an endangered world. Its main theme is that options across a wide spectrum should be continuously examined on their merits, for the best choice will depend upon how the situation is perceived, what the United States is trying to achieve, and whether specific courses of action will actually bring about the desired consequences and achievement of goals. A third danger, poverty and the lack of democracy and effective governance in key regions, is addressed in chapter 9, which assesses policy and strategy for the U.S. function of global developer.

Contributions of Strategic Evaluation

Although some observers argue that the United States and the democratic community should try to wall themselves off from the world's turbulent regions, this hope is ill founded and unwise. In the information age of accelerating globalization, such walls no longer exist and cannot be created. Like it or not, the United States and its democratic partners are irretrievably vulnerable to events taking place in distant areas. Their physical safety is at risk, along with their economic prosperity, unity, and democratic values. Moreover, their own interests are moving steadily beyond their borders and the old Cold War strategic perimeters into once-remote areas. The stability of the global security system can be disrupted by events there, and the world economy can be greatly damaged, too. The United States and its allies have no choice but to look outward and act accordingly.

As the world's sole superpower, the United States has a responsibility for trying to create stable security architectures both globally and in key regions. Performing this function is difficult because the world has become a more dangerous place. Only a few years ago, the post–Cold War world seemed relatively safe, but after September 11, 2001, this sense of safety evaporated. Whereas President Clinton had spoken of the opportunities for peace posed by a globalizing world, President Bush pointed to an "axis of evil" that menaces peace and democracy. In response, U.S. policy and strategy for dealing with the modern world's dangers, as well as its opportunities, has become a subject of renewed debate. The intensity of the controversies about the exact nature of the dangers facing the United States and about how best to address them is a clear indication that this important subject is not yet well understood and that deep thinking about it is likely to be needed for many years to come.

While the two issues of big power relations and the southern arc instability do not encompass all of the security dangers facing the United States and its allies, they cover much of the spectrum. If the United States can learn how to handle emerging trends in these two areas, it will go a long way toward taming the world's principal dangers. As recent experience shows, however, the United States is already confronting challenges sufficiently difficult to tax the talents of both Democratic and Republican administrations. Optimists are hopeful about what the United States can accomplish, but pessimists are doubtful, while agnostics do not claim to know what the future holds. Perhaps it is fair to say that as matters now stand, the 21st century appears equally capable of producing sustained peace and prosperity or descending into conflict and violence. If the United States can act wisely and effectively, it may be capable of making the difference. This is a key reason why a sound U.S. national security strategy in this arena is so important today.

The two policy and strategy issues addressed in this chapter differ from each other in their particulars, but what unites them is that both arise amidst uncertainty about their dynamics and trends and about how the United States can best address them. In the past, the United States often confronted great national security challenges, but the causes, effects, and proper strategic responses to these challenges usually seemed clear. During the 20th century, the United States knew how to act in dealing with fascism and communism, once it had concluded that they posed grave threats to the survival of democracy. No such convenient clarity exists in dealing with current issues. Even knowledgeable observers find themselves confused and in disagreement with each other. A main task for strategic evaluation is to bring greater intellectual order to these issues in order to help U.S. policymakers see them not only on their individual merits, but also in terms of how they interact in today's complex, fast-changing world. Grasping their interactions—real and potential—is vital to dealing with them, both individually and collectively.

Strategic evaluation has important contributions to make in this arena. It can contribute by helping improve understanding of how and why developments in these two arenas pose problems, and of where the future may be headed. Equally important, strategic evaluation can help examine the multiple policy and strategy options available to the United States in both areas, and illuminate their pros and cons. Present trends suggest that the United States will seek to improve political relationships with Russia and China while remaining prepared for any downturns, and to increase its involvement with Middle Eastern and other nations along the southern arc of instability so as to promote both stable security affairs and democracy. Strategic evaluation can help provide guidance on how both strategies might best be designed and how their subordinate policies and plans can best be carried out.

Strategic evaluation of these two dangers employs the methods put forth in chapters 4 and 5, in a manner that responds to the issues at hand. Analyzing policy and strategy for big-power relations and the southern arc will differ from analyzing U.S. conduct within its alliances. When the subject is handling alliances, strategic evaluation focuses on the goal of preserving and reforming them through the vehicle of forging consensus among the United States and its allies. By contrast, analyzing U.S. responses to global security dangers often requires assessing how adversaries and potential adversaries can be pressured and coerced.

To say that strategic evaluation in this arena focuses solely on pressure and coercion, however, would be too narrow a formulation. In handling big-power relations, U.S. strategy normally includes not only a measure of coercion, but also the tools of persuasion and bargaining in order to bring about a shared commitment to peaceful outcomes. In dealing with the greater Middle East and southern arc, U.S. strategy partly is focused on suppressing threats, but it also must address how to create stable regional security systems that are making progress toward economic progress and democracy. Thus, U.S. strategy for both big power relations and chaotic regions must be multifaceted: anchored in multiple goals, in diverse policies for achieving them, and in appropriate plans, programs, and budgets. All of this confronts strategic evaluation with a demanding agenda that may get more complex as the future unfolds.

The Basics of Policy and Strategy for a Dangerous World

If the United States fails to grapple successfully with the dangers emerging in the early 21st century, one reason may be that it lacks adequate resolve and resources. But another reason may be that it has failed to muster adequate understanding of the strategic situation facing it. First and foremost, the role of national security policy and strategy is to provide the critical ingredient of clear, purposeful thought so that effective action can follow. Without sound ideas, action is likely to fall short or fail outright, irrespective of how many resources are committed.

In the past, the United States has often proven itself remarkably successful at engineering the rigorous implementation of its national security policies and strategies. Its failures—the Vietnam War is a classic example—arose from a faulty understanding of what it was confronting, what it could hope to achieve, and how it could achieve success. This lack of clear understanding led it to pursue activities that, in retrospect, look painfully flawed. This experience is incentive enough for thinking deeply and clearly—as well as soberly and humbly—about what the United States intends to do in this arena today and tomorrow.

Wise ideas and successful actions must be anchored in an accurate understanding of the fundamentals of strategy for handling the contemporary world's dangers. As earlier chapters explained, national security strategy for these dangers requires an overarching strategic concept and theory, a set of integrated strategies for handling each major danger, a coordinated set of policies for pursuing each strategy component, and a choreographed plan for action that unfolds logically over an extended period of time. Such a strategy should be anchored in the premise that because the globalizing world is changing rapidly, a main task is to guide the process of change rather than attempt to stop it. This strategy also requires a sense of direction and of the goals to be sought—not necessarily a firm plan for ultimate success, but a flexible vision of how today's dangers can be handled, coupled with a plan for encouraging global progress while preventing major deterioration. Such a vision should be idealistic, but it also should be realistic; it should focus on aims that are realistically achievable in order to ensure that priorities are set wisely and scarce resources are allocated properly.

Compared to tranquil times, dangerous times call for a strategy that is more determined and energetic. Dangerous times also demand a strategy that is soundly focused, for there is less room for misjudgment and little margin for error. When dangerous times are also complex times, they require a strategy that is sophisticated and elaborate. Such a strategy must concentrate on the most important dangers, understanding their true nature and the dynamics giving rise to them. Perhaps President Bush was right in fingering terrorists and today's tyrants as ringleaders of an axis of evil because this declaration gave concrete focus to his global strategy. But the risk is that if this formula is interpreted too narrowly, it will mistake symptoms for underlying causes and will circumscribe U.S. activities too tightly or direct them ineffectively. Conversely, if this formula is interpreted too broadly, the United States might try to achieve too many goals at once and thereby lose focus. The same holds true for all intellectual formulas that might be applied to today's world: all are vulnerable to flawed understandings about the world itself and to resultant policy errors.

Does the United States truly understand the underlying dynamics that are driving today's dangers? Undeniably, the United States has more information at its disposal than any other country. But information is not the same as awareness or understanding. The disturbing degree to which the United States has been caught off guard in recent years suggests that its awareness is sometimes less than perfect. On several occasions, the United States has been surprised by the maneuverings of Russia and China. On some occasions, those countries took actions opposed to U.S. interests and policies, and on others, they unexpectedly drew closer to the United States. What holds true for these two big powers applies even more strongly to dealing with the southern arc of instability. The terrorist strikes of September 11, 2001, which emanated from the southern arc, caught the United States by surprise partly because of its own failures of imagination and intellect. Four times during 1990–2003, the United States was compelled to fight regional wars in this zone: in Kuwait, Kosovo, Afghanistan, and Iraq. All four wars caught the United States by surprise: U.S. planners had expected none of them a few years before they occurred. Moreover, the strategic causes of these wars—regional aggression in the Persian Gulf, ethnic conflict in the Balkans, global terrorism launched from Afghanistan, and the perceived need for preemptive intervention against Iraq—were not well understood before they produced military conflict. More fundamentally, the degree to which Islamic fundamentalism has incorporated deep anger at the United States and the democratic world seems to have escaped the attention of most U.S. officials until it became blindingly obvious.

Perhaps being caught by surprise is an unavoidable reality of today's confusing world. But a continued failure to understand the basics of how and why the world is evolving will lead to continued trouble in U.S. national security policy and strategy. Unless the United States understands the basics, it will be unable to take advantage of the opportunities ahead, risking a steep global descent. Unless the United States handles events carefully, the future could bring multiple cascading troubles: deteriorating U.S. relations with Russia, China, or both; mounting strategic chaos along the southern arc of instability that gives rise to new threats; and unrelenting poverty in freedom-starved regions that offer so little hope for progress that they produce massive uprisings. In the eyes of pessimists, the great risk facing world order is that these problems could all metastasize and propel the 21st century into a new Thirty Years' War or worse. Conversely, optimists judge that if these problems can be mastered, or at least kept under control, the 21st century stands a reasonable chance of becoming an extended era of peace as democracy, economic progress, and multilateral community-building fulfill their promise.

U.S. national security strategy needs to address all of these problems in patient and sustained ways with a judicious balance of activities. It cannot afford to focus on one problem to the exclusion of the others, or to become so fixated on today's crises that it loses sight of tomorrow's troubles, which may be different. While winning the war on terror is vital, dispatching today's terrorist cells and rogue dictators will not produce a peaceful world if the southern arc remains a boiling cauldron, the United States falls into rivalry with China, or impoverished regions explode in a frenzy of ethnic violence and failed governance. Nor can the future be made stable simply by establishing friendly relations with Russia, China, and other great powers while hoping for the best elsewhere, if other unstable regions go up in flames.

The United States cannot hope to succeed solely by maintaining cooperative relations with big powers and quelling new threats as they arise on an individual basis. In this era of accelerating globalization, the world's problems are more than purely geopolitical. Friendly relations with big powers can help establish a stable structure for global security affairs, and the act of suppressing threats can remedy the troubles of the moment. But friendly big-power relations merely create a framework structure, not an entire edifice, and quashing threats without draining the swamps where they breed means that new threats will arise to take their place.

For these reasons, U.S. national security strategy must address these problems in their fundamental elements and give due regard to each. The United States does not possess an endless reservoir of resources, so it cannot aspire to perfection in all key areas. But it should aspire to sufficient success so that none of the problems generate the critical mass of fiery energy that would destroy the world around it. Above all, the United States needs to ensure that these problems do not begin to feed off of and magnify each other. The risk is a world in which the United States is squared off against China and Russia while trying to suppress a multiplicity of small and medium-size threats along the southern arc while impoverished Africa and South Asia go up in smoke.

Because such a world is not a mere nightmare but a plausible scenario of catastrophe, it should be taken as a benchmark of a future to be avoided. Preventing such a world, while working hard to build a better future, is a compelling reason for a U.S. national security strategy focused on handling all of these dangers in parallel and mutually reinforcing ways. It also is a reason for the United States to work closely with its democratic allies and partners. Multilateralism is necessary because American unilateralism simply cannot muster the resources, or perhaps the willpower, to handle this demanding, multipronged agenda by itself.

U.S. national security, then, has its work cut out for it in a dangerous, fast-moving world of globalization and change toward an uncertain future of variable outcomes. Strategic evaluation thus also has its work cut out for it because today's endangered world cannot be reduced to the simple formulas and clear-cut prescriptions of the Cold War, nor the illusionary respite of the 1990s. Moreover, strategic evaluation must address the bottom line: performance in achieving goals. While U.S. policies and strategies must pass the test of intellectual coherence, what matters is whether they actually achieve their desired results. Past policies and strategies seemed to make sense on paper, and then failed to achieve their goals; U.S. history in the Middle East is loaded with examples of frustrated aims and policies gone awry. For this reason, strategic evaluation needs to focus intently on the likely relationship between actions and consequences, with due regard to potential consequences that are both intended and unintended. This too makes strategic evaluation a complex exercise in calculations and projections. It is against this background that the balance of this chapter addresses, first, relations with Russia and China, and then troubles in the greater Middle East and southern arc of instability.

Strategy for Managing Relations with Big Powers: Russia and China

Relations with Russia and China have long been a subject of major intellectual skirmishing in the United States. Countless books have been written on this subject, and many have had an impact on U.S. strategic choices.[1] Contemporary relations are changing in response to larger developments in world affairs and are headed in new and unknown directions. Because the relationships are rapidly evolving, a different type of thinking will be required. Analyses via strategic evaluation methods have a golden opportunity in this arena if they can accurately portray the underlying factors at work and help craft sensible strategies for dealing with them.

Dealing with any big power requires a well-reasoned strategy composed of multiple policies that pursue multiple goals in a coordinated fashion, posing the analytical task described in earlier chapters. The task goes beyond handling Russia and China: Europe is steadily becoming a big power in its own right, not just a collection of small and medium-sized countries. Japan is a big power in Asia with global economic reach. India is a new big power with growing influence in South Asia and elsewhere. The United States has not traditionally had a separate big-power strategy for dealing with India, at least not one that was widely heralded and analyzed. But now that India is gaining economic strength and has acquired nuclear weapons, it will need to be addressed in a focused, strategic way. Should the United States attempt to befriend India, which—although relations have been improving lately—has traditionally not been a warm partner of the United States? Should the United States try to contain India? Or should it try to facilitate a role for India in South Asia and elsewhere that satisfies its aspirations for growing status, while contributing to regional and global peace?

The leading big powers, however, remain Russia and China. In the coming years, U.S. relations with these two countries will have a substantial impact on the evolution of the global security system. A key task of strategic evaluation will be to help chart the future course of these relationships. This task promises to be more difficult than in the past because today's relations with Russia and China are more complex and nuanced than during the Cold War's bipolarity, and more prone to shifting changes of fortune.

Major changes have occurred since 1990, many of them for the better. During the Cold War, U.S. relations with the Soviet Union were often marked by intense ideological competition, persistent geopolitical rivalry, and sustained military confrontation. By contrast, today's Russia is trying to become a democracy, and it no longer leads a military alliance against the United States. China still has a communist government, but it is trying to build a market economy at home; it seeks flourishing trade relations with the wealthy capitalist countries; and its diplomacy is no longer animated by extremist ideology or paranoid fears of Western imperialism. Both countries have begun pursuing foreign policies aimed at protecting and advancing traditional national interests. Yet the pursuit of national interests has an assertive logic of its own, and it can be defined in ways that enhance stability, make trouble, or both.

Both Russia and China are big powers with a significant capacity to influence regional and global security affairs. While Russia's power has been declining over the past decade, China's power has been steadily growing; this dual trend has important dynamics and implications because it is altering relationships between them as well as how each sees the outside world. The future conduct of these countries is a question whose answer the United States will aspire to influence for many years to come. If Russia and China work in harmony with the United States and its allies across the board, this will lessen the challenges facing U.S. global strategy and enhance prospects for peace. If they are a mixture of partner and adversary, this will have effects that both ease and sharpen the strategic challenges facing the United States. If they oppose U.S. interests and menace U.S. allies, this will increase U.S. strategic burdens and portend trouble for the future.

U.S. Goals and Strategy Options

The United States approaches Russia and China with multiple goals in mind and with priorities that depend upon what is thought to be both necessary and feasible. Obviously, the bedrock goal is to protect the American homeland from nuclear attack: both Russia and China are nuclear powers with intercontinental missiles. An equally essential goal is to protect close U.S. allies that neighbor these two countries in Europe and Asia. A third goal is to ensure that Russia and China do not join together against the United States and instead have stable relations with each so as to protect and advance other U.S. interests in regional security affairs and economic affairs. How this third goal is defined and pursued depends upon the nature of relationships with them. If Russia or China is acting in ways that menace U.S. interests abroad, then the U.S. goal will be to frustrate those efforts. If they are cooperating with the United States in key places, then the goal will be to reciprocate. If they are trying to gain membership in the responsible community of nations and to join the world economy in ways that respect free trade agreements, the U.S. goal will be to welcome and help them.

Dealing with Russia and China in today's murky world raises crucial issues. Some observers portray the current global structure as unipolar because the United States, as the world's sole superpower, enjoys unusual predominance in resources and leverage. Yet the term superpower breaks down when the particulars are examined. As a practical matter, U.S. power is often stretched thin by global responsibilities, and the United States often finds itself unable to bend and mold events to its liking.

Beyond this, unipolarity, even to the extent it does exist, is a historical anomaly that does not seem destined to last long. The natural inclination is for other big powers, like Russia and China, to try to impose their own imprints on the emerging global order. In this sense, Russia and China are natural "strategic challengers" in today's international system. But what does this mean, and what does it foretell? Some geopolitical theorists argue that Russia or China is destined to be a troublemaking rival of the United States. But perhaps the United States can work with these two countries in ways that shore up prospects for peace and progress. The answer is probably not knowable, for the simple reason that outcomes will be strongly influenced by the actions of each of the main participants as well as by imponderable events. The task facing the United States is to determine and implement the strategies that seem most likely to bring about favorable consequences; then it must hope for the best.

The three U.S. goals and their relative priorities give rise to a wide spectrum of potential U.S. options for dealing with Russia and China. At one end of the spectrum is a strategy of confrontation that would apply when relations are stuck at rock-bottom. At the other end of the spectrum is a strategy of cooperative integration to be followed when relations are warm. In the middle of the spectrum is a strategy, by turns firm and forthcoming, of geopolitical management for when relations run both cold and warm. While a confrontational strategy was applied consistently during the Cold War, today's atmosphere has opened the door to the other two strategies. Most likely no single strategy will be permanently appropriate to both countries. Until conditions become better defined, the United States is likely to need to remain flexible in its choice of these strategies and capable of shifting back and forth among them. This fluid situation, in turn, mandates that analysis be capable of assessing all three strategies and how to pursue them not only for the moment at hand, but with an eye on molding the future as well.

These three strategies come equipped with subordinate concepts, each of which requires a separate policy, all of which must be harmonized together. A strategy of confrontation has four components: containment, deterrence, defense, and limited arms control negotiations aimed at keeping military rivalry in bounds. Its essence is firm political and military pressure designed to keep the targeted country contained, coupled with diplomacy aimed at preventing war and arms races. A strategy of geopolitical management for the gray middle ground embodies such concepts as balance of power, dissuasion, equilibrium, and limited business partnerships of a strategic nature. This strategy strives to warn the targeted country not to transgress, but refrains from threatening it overtly. It protects U.S. and allied interests, but shows respect for the legitimate interests and aspirations of the targeted country. It is willing to enter into limited strategic deals in areas where the United States and the targeted country have common interests and compatible policies. The third strategy, cooperative integration, abandons pressures and warnings in favor of a positive embrace. It aspires to create a warm and regular partnership that applies across many issue areas, and generally welcomes the targeted country's admission into multilateral political and economic bodies and into the democratic community itself.

Since the Cold War's end, the United States has tried to move beyond permanent confrontation with Russia and China to create the best relationships possible, but it has shifted back and forth between geopolitical management and cooperative integration. This has been due to fluctuation not only in U.S. attitudes but also in the behavior of Russia and China. The future will depend heavily upon whether these countries continue to zigzag or whether instead each settles into a single sustained model. An abrupt return to the poisonous animosities of the Cold War seems improbable any time soon. But beyond that, only time will tell. History shows ample cases of big powers that settled their differences and drew close together: Britain, France, and Germany after World War II offer a recent example. History also shows cases of big-power relationships that started out peacefully and then slid into polarized rivalry: the behavior of these same European countries between 1880 and 1914 is a classic example. These two cases suggest that over the long haul, big-power interactions are driven not by atmospherics and aspirations at any single moment in time, but by enduring interests, strategic aspirations, power balances, strategy, and diplomacy. The same likely will hold true for future U.S. relations with both Russia and China.

Trends in Russia and China

Comparing Russia to the Soviet Union in the Cold War, its population today is only two-thirds as large; its economy is only one-half as large, although now rebounding; and its army is only one-fifth as large. This huge loss in physical power at a time when a new government and economy are being built initially left Russia searching for a new strategic identity and foreign policy. Shortly after Russia emerged from the ashes of the Soviet Union in 1991, it pursued a foreign policy of Atlanticism toward the United States and Europe. It proclaimed its ambition to create a democracy with a market economy, to downsize its military, and to pursue diplomacy aimed at partnership and integration with the Western democracies. Then in 1993–1994, Russia's domestic politics began drifting backward toward restored central rule, while its march toward a market economy was stalled by vested interests and an accelerating collapse of its GDP. Its foreign policy began talking tough in terms of pursuing Russia's state interests, its need to restore control over its neighbors on former Soviet soil, its desire to keep an arms-length relationship with the United States and Europe, and its opposition to what it alleged were hegemonic U.S. designs around the world. For the remainder of the 1990s, a period when European diplomacy was marked by struggles over NATO enlargement and the Balkans, Russia under President Boris Yeltsin adhered to this standoffish attitude, although it rejected any return to Cold War or "Cold Peace."[2]

When Vladimir Putin replaced Yeltsin in 2000, Russia's government stabilized into a quasi-democracy and its economy slowly began recovering. With the controversy over NATO enlargement and the Balkans largely settled, Russia's foreign policy again began exploring notions such as expanded strategic partnerships, new nuclear arms control agreements with the United States, and gradual integration into Europe. When the global war on terror erupted in 2001, Russia allowed U.S. military forces to use bases in Central Asia in order to strike the Taliban and al Qaeda in Afghanistan, a step that would have been unimaginable only a few years before. While Russia did not support the U.S. invasion of Iraq in 2003, it did not actively interfere once the invasion was launched. Whether this tone in Russian foreign policy will remain dominant is unpredictable, but many U.S. observers judge that the door remains open to warming relations, provided that Russia can find a legitimate way to satisfy its interests in a world where it has lost much of the power that the Soviet Union had during the Cold War, and provided that the United States reciprocates with appropriate overtures.

Russia's future foreign policy will be influenced by its domestic politics. By late 2004, Russia was a democracy in the sense that its president and parliament were still chosen by popular elections, and the Russian economy was still moving toward market capitalism. Even so, Putin was steadily consolidating the reins of power into his hands by strengthening presidential authority, elevating domestic security agencies, diminishing the autonomy of regional governors, imprisoning capitalist chieftains, and suppressing dissent. The brutal terrorist attack at Beslan in fall 2004 gave him arguments for further power-grabbing in the interest of domestic safety, a justification that seemed to find favor among many Russians. Putin insisted that his internal changes would not alter Russia's stance toward the United States and its allies. This trend toward growing presidential power in Russia could, nonetheless, have an impact on foreign policy, resulting in efforts to draw Belarus and Ukraine back into Russia's orbit, while imposing greater control over the Caucasus and Central Asian countries that once were part of the Soviet Union. Putin's crude attempt in late 2004 to block the election of Viktor Yushchenko to the presidency of Ukraine ultimately failed, but it worried European and American observers.

Short of any reappearance of an imperial ideology, Russia's foreign policy is likely to be guided by a pragmatic, hard-headed sense of national interests. For the immediate future, Russia's main strategic task is unquestionably to shore up its domestic order and internal security while adjusting to the loss of superpower status and empire. The long term, however, seems capable of producing a Russia that either draws closer to the Western democratic community or that, having regained its internal balance and restored some of its lost power, returns to the assertive practices of the tsars. In the interim, its security strategy will not be focused westward on Europe or eastward on China and Asia, but southward. This is the case because Russia today confronts unstable conditions along its southern borders, especially in Chechnya as well as other countries that are heavily Islamic. Russia's southern focus seems to give it common strategic ground with the United States, which now has a comparable focus on the southern arc of instability. These common preoccupations might provide a framework for growing collaboration between the two countries in dealing with terrorism and other matters.

China's strategic intentions have been less clear. Perhaps this has been the case because China is pursuing a complex, uniquely Asian agenda. At home, its government is struggling to preserve authoritarian rule while building a market economy that attracts foreign investors and conducts flourishing trade in the world economy. In its national security strategy, China is trying to advance its interests gradually while determining how it can employ its power to best advantage in the future. China's attitude toward the United States reflects this complex agenda: it seems to want peaceful relations with the United States, joining it in some security endeavors; it participates responsibly in the UN and has gained admission to the WTO and other multilateral economic bodies. China wants to avoid war on the Korean Peninsula, and because it is deeply suspicious of Japan, it does not seek a wholesale U.S. withdrawal from Asia, which could alarm Japan into becoming a nuclear and full-fledged regional power. Yet it continues to want to bring Taiwan into its orbit and otherwise to assert a sizable maritime zone of strategic influence along the length of its Pacific coastline. This ambition translates into a desire, often expressed in the public writings of some strategic thinkers, to weaken the U.S.-led cluster of bilateral alliances in the western Pacific that stretches from Japan to Australia and Thailand.

This adds up to a conscious geopolitical agenda of the sort that Talleyrand or Metternich could understand; however, the big question about China is not its behavior today, but its strategy and actions tomorrow. China's physical power is steadily growing. Already its population numbers over one billion people, making it the world's largest country. China is still poor, with an annual per capita GDP of only about $3,000. For the past decade, however, its annual growth rates have been 10 percent or more. Even if its growth rate slows, China's economy will steadily expand, making its people far better off than they are now. This trend will also enable China to accelerate its effort to transform its huge but obsolescent military into a modern force with the ability to project power beyond its borders.[3]

China is already using its limited funds and technologies to create improved naval, air, and missile forces capable of power projection. This military plan is unlikely to come to fruition until 2010 or later, but when it does peak, it will give China other strategic options than the inward-looking continental mentality that has governed its foreign policy for centuries. Some observers fear that China may then seek to confront the United States and its allies in a showdown over who runs Asian security affairs. To the extent that this fear is valid, the United States may be in a race against time to determine whether China can be integrated into the existing U.S.-led Asian security and economic system before acquiring the ambitions and power to threaten the destruction of that system. If China can be integrated into the existing system, its future evolution can be moderate and gradual. But if China emerges as an imperial power intent on overthrowing the system, a wholesale redesign of U.S. policy, focused on containing China and better protecting U.S. allies in Asia, will be necessary.

Appraising the Strategy Options

Barring descent into confrontation, improbable any time soon, U.S. strategy toward Russia and China is likely to be a shifting blend of geopolitical management and cooperative integration for the foreseeable future. Two key questions are likely to dominate U.S. thinking: To what degree can limited business partnerships on selected issues with Russia be broadened into regular strategic partnerships on many issues, accompanied by that country's admission into the democratic community, and to what degree can a murky geopolitical relationship with China be stabilized so that it does not descend into deep rivalry in the long term, and perhaps can be turned into sustained cooperation? These core issues will have to be readdressed regularly because no single strategic theory is likely to be adequate for dealing with either country on a permanent basis.

Strategic evaluation will need to probe into the reasoning that seems to motivate each country. During the Cold War, the national security policies of both countries often could be explained with relatively straightforward and unchanging propositions. This is no longer the case. Both countries are now being animated by complex, ever-changing calculations that respond to their shifting domestic situations and their fluid external environments. A policy that exists today may be gone tomorrow. The strategic reasoning that underpins a set of policies one year may give way to a different set of judgments and priorities the next year. Rather than rely on traditional theories of what motivates these two countries, the United States will need to employ sensitive antennae capable of discerning how the motives of each are evolving.

The same need for deep-thinking analysis applies to gauging the likely impact of U.S. behavior on both countries. During the Cold War, U.S. analyses of how to deal with the Soviet Union often settled into a polarized debate between two schools. Whereas one school of thought advocated firmness to deter Soviet aggression, the other advocated accommodation to keep the peace. In today's world, neither of these single-minded theories of actions and consequences is likely to apply all or even most of the time.

Events of the past few years suggest that sometimes the reaction of China and Russia to U.S. overtures will be positive and forthcoming. When the United States proposed to scuttle the ABM Treaty inherited from the Cold War in order to pave the way for deployment of a thin missile defense shield, critics expected Russia to provoke a crisis.

Yet Russia accommodated the new U.S. stance and negotiated deeper reductions in offensive missiles. Sometimes, however, the reaction to longstanding U.S. policies will suddenly become negative. This is especially likely with China. For example, China has begun showing more sensitivity on the issue of U.S. collaboration with Taiwan than during the Cold War. Evidently, China judges that its growing power permits it to be more assertive in warning Taiwan of the limits of what China will accept, while Taiwan has become more assertive about declaring its sovereign control over its own affairs. U.S. strategy toward China and Taiwan has not changed a great deal, but the sensitivity surrounding these issues has gone up a notch or two, and the associated strategic calculations have become more complex.

Recent experience shows that in an era of ambiguous geopolitical relationships, when big-power dealings blow hot and cold, the United States may find itself employing firmness in one issue area and accommodation in another at the same time. The art of strategy will require expertise at this finely balanced diplomacy, but the United States, which often has tended to see foreign countries as either friends or foes, rather than a mixture of the two, has not always been good at this. When the United States has attempted such diplomacy, its efforts have often aroused great confusion and controversy abroad, and generated intense debate within its own executive and legislative branches, making it even harder to carry out diplomacy coherently or consistently.

The entire strategy of geopolitical management, especially as it applies to China in Asia, will require serious analysis because such nuances are so foreign to U.S. strategic thought and historical experience. This strategy begins with the premise that the United States must consistently be aware of its need to prevent Russia and China from joining together to oppose it. Since the early 1970s, when President Richard Nixon journeyed to China, the United States has shown skill at prying these two former allies apart and not provoking them to move back together. It will need to continue doing so in the years ahead. Yet the United States will also need to guard against the risk that these two big powers might turn against each other as a result of rivalry over control of their joint border areas, a possibility because of China's growing power and Russia's weakened condition. A U.S. strategy of keeping Russia and China sufficiently apart, but at peace with each other, will require consistent expertise.

A brief look at this strategy's other core components also illustrates the need for serious analysis. The idea of establishing a military balance of power in order to maintain stability has long historical roots that show its necessities and difficulties, but the balancing act may be anything but easy. Whereas too little military power can lead a potential adversary to underestimate U.S. resolve, too much power may unduly alarm it, provoking a destabilizing response.

Beyond this, exactly how is military balance to be measured in the information age? A main goal of power-balancing is to establish a distribution of military forces that discourages such countries as Russia and China from aggressive conduct yet does not menace their own safety. In the past, such balances could be measured simply by comparing the sizes of the armies and navies on both sides. Typically, a potential aggressor had to amass a large numerical superiority over countries that enjoyed the advantage of being on the defense. Thus, a stable balance was mathematically achievable by the defense without unduly menacing the other side. But such simplicity is no longer the case now that there is no main geographical point of confrontation, and now that, when even outnumbered, small high-tech forces can win or inflict great damage from long distances. The key point is not that the term *balance of power* no longer has meaning, as some have suggested, but that it must now be calculated in different and more subtle ways.

A similar judgment applies to the idea of dissuasion. This concept differs from deterrence, by which irreconcilable enemies are contained by formidable military resistance at locations where they might transgress and by threats of heavy retaliation in the event they actually commit aggression. By contrast, the intent of dissuasion is firmly to signal a potential adversary not to behave in ways that could turn it into a real adversary. But exactly how is this delicate act to be accomplished without either suggesting that the United States is weak or making it appear to be a permanent adversary? This question must be answered on a case-by-case basis. If it can be answered, dissuasion is a viable strategic concept in today's world because it operates in that gray area between rivalry and friendship. But it requires careful thought, both to define it for specific situations and to carry it out in the subtle ways required.

The aim of seeking a political equilibrium to help stabilize a geopolitical relationship is fraught with similar challenges. The idea here is that in addition to insisting that U.S. and allied interests be respected, the other country's legitimate interests must be treated with similar respect in return. But defining which interests are legitimate can be difficult, for this is often seen as relative and subjective. A further difficulty is that respecting the targeted country's legitimate interests may necessitate some sacrifice of legitimate interests of the United States or its allies. Indeed, a core challenge for U.S. strategy toward Russia and China is that some attempts to accommodate their wishes may come at the expense of their neighbors, many of whom are U.S. allies. For example, granting China's wish for a zone of security along its coastline could compromise the security of Japan, Taiwan, and a host of other countries friendly to the United States.

The dilemma of balancing the interests of close allies against efforts to accommodate Russia and China has bedeviled U.S. strategy for many decades and is likely to continue to defy easy solution. A core feature of the modern security system, inherited from the Cold War, is that neither Germany nor Japan, the aggressors of World War II, possesses nuclear weapons or offensively postured militaries. Indeed, apart from Britain and France, few Western democracies have military forces capable of projecting sizable power far beyond their borders or conducting nuclear strikes against adversaries. This major contribution to global stability continues to exist only because the United States provides its allies with nuclear deterrence coverage and conventional defense commitments. The U.S. responsibility for the security of the numerous countries to which it has treaty commitments, however, limits its ability to enter agreements with Russia and China that could expose those allies to danger. If a political equilibrium with Russia and China is to be sought, it will have to be the kind of arrangement that leaves close U.S. allies as well protected as before. This requirement lessens the room to accommodate the geopolitical aspirations of those two big powers.

The idea of pursuing limited strategic partnerships with Russia and China also has its rewards and perils. Recent experience with both countries shows that such relationships are possible and useful, even if they do not translate into enduring partnerships across many security issues. But for a limited partnership to work, both sides must profit in strategic terms. Sometimes both sides will automatically profit because U.S. interests will be identical to those of its partner. But in other cases, the United States may face pressures to enter into bargained arrangements and to pay a price, including side payments, in order to secure the cooperation of Russia or China. The price may or may not be worth the gain. For example, in exchange for Russia's help in the war against terrorism, Moscow might seek U.S. acquiescence to its military campaign in Chechnya and to its intrusion elsewhere in the Caucasus. Gaining Russia's diplomatic help in the Middle East could result in pressure to support its political and commercial interests there. At a minimum, such tradeoffs should be scrutinized closely because, in the strategic world, the value of limited partnerships depends on the immediate bottom line, not visions of mergers in the future.

These considerations do not mean that a strategy of geopolitical management is impossible. In gray-area situations where neither full-scale confrontation nor cooperative integration is a viable choice, it may be the only strategy available to the United States. Its concepts provide a rich and mutually reinforcing menu of policies, provided they can be pursued successfully. The key point is that this strategy, like all strategies for dealing with Russia and China, will require intensive analysis of a sort that has not been common.

The future of U.S. relations with Russia and China is uncertain, but with wise handling on all sides, a stable outcome seems within grasp. Much will depend upon how Russia and China evolve internally. Russia may be more likely than China to embrace democracy, but the sharp edges of China's authoritarian order seem likely to soften over time to increase pluralism. Equally important, neither Russia nor China seems likely to embark upon imperial or expansionist policies in the coming years. Russia is likely to focus on consolidating its current position in Eurasia while trying to safeguard its southern regions from radical Islamic fundamentalism. China may gain greater physical power to assert its influence in Asia and the Pacific, but it has always been a continental power, not a maritime power. Provided China keeps to the Asian mainland and the United States remains a maritime power, the two countries are not likely to fall into enduring strategic conflict.

The prospect of improving relations with Russia and China, however, does not mean that these two countries will become regular partners of the United States as it grapples with security challenges along the southern arc and elsewhere. Although partnership may sometimes be possible, at other times Russia and China may oppose U.S. policies, as in Kosovo or Iraq. The challenge will be to contain such localized conflicts rather than allow them to escalate into larger confrontations that undermine the basis of strategic relationships with both countries. The bottom line is that a future of improved geopolitical relationships will require diplomatic finesse by the United States as well as by Russia and China. Strategic evaluation can help equip the United States with the necessary judgment to play its role in the process. In particular, it can help bring clarity to the strategy that the United States is employing in any period of time, reducing the risk that two or more incompatible strategies will be employed at the same time. Likewise, it can help the United States forge coordinated policies for its overarching strategy, and help ensure that the multiple actions taken in several different arenas will achieve their intended consequences. Devising clear strategies and implementing them effectively is the best way for the United States to achieve its strategic goals in handling big-power relations that promise to be murky and fluid for a long time to come.

Strategy for the Greater Middle East and Southern Arc of Instability

In contrast to relations with Russia and China, entirely different issues arise in forging a U.S. strategy for the greater Middle East and the entire southern arc of instability, which includes the Middle East and Persian Gulf, the Balkans, and North Africa, as well as south-central Asia and the East Asian littoral.[4] The very concept of a southern arc of instability did not appear in any official U.S. publication until the DOD *Quadrennial Defense Review Report* of 2001.[5] Much has been written and published about the greater Middle East and other regions on an individual basis, but the idea of analyzing them together is new. Thus, strategic evaluation has an opportunity here to create and integrate original material about a truly critical subject. This will especially be the case in the aftermath of the U.S. invasions of Afghanistan and Iraq, which have altered the strategic terrain along the southern arc, and whose long-range consequences are hard to determine but are likely to include active U.S. involvement for many years.

Dealing with this area will confront the United States with big strategic challenges over the coming years. This vast and heterogeneous zone comprises multiple regions that differ greatly from each other, yet have one feature in common: turbulence in a globalizing era as all of them are becoming more important to world affairs. Twenty years ago, much of this zone was at the backwater of the Cold War: only the Persian Gulf figured importantly in U.S. security strategy. Today, it is the front line of the world's most dangerous security politics.

In this zone, threats of terrorism and WMD proliferation intersect in a setting of great chaos: its fluid, amorphous lack of structure and order. This zone is not unipolar, nor bipolar, nor multipolar, but instead a shapeless mass in motion, headed toward an unclear destination. Apart from U.S. commitments to a few countries, there are no major multinational defense alliances or even loose collective security pacts. In this setting of structural anarchy, virtually every country is on its own, vulnerable to events inside and outside its porous borders. The southern arc is thus a profound security vacuum—a nearly total absence of security—in which military power is ample for major violence, multiple military imbalances may tempt aggressors, and there are many predatory appetites. No other strategic zone in the world has such a complex, risky blend of angry U.S. adversaries, seething ethnic hatreds, radical Islamic fundamentalism, religious quarrels, boiling tensions, exposed allies, vulnerable resources, dangerous security rivalries, intractable ideologies, ineffective governments, tradition-bound societies, booming populations, and weak economies.

The United States mostly kept aloof during the Cold War because, apart from the Persian Gulf, it regarded the southern arc as largely outside its perimeter of vital security interests. But this detached attitude has been washed away by globalization and related dynamics that have elevated the southern arc's role in strategic affairs. The United States has, of course, long been committed to Israel's security, to ensuring Western access to Persian Gulf oil, and to having friendly relations with as many key southern arc countries as possible. But these interests are now supplemented by a larger strategic concern. The military threats emanating from the southern arc—from terrorism to WMD proliferation and cross-border aggression—are increasingly capable of striking not only close allies, but also the U.S. homeland itself. Beyond this, the southern arc is so large and centrally located—it bridges Europe and Asia—that its instability threatens to engulf other regions, to damage both Europe and Asia, and to poison hopes for progress in big power relationships. A turbulent, violent southern arc has the potential to destabilize the entire global security architecture.

The wars in Afghanistan and Iraq demonstrate that the United States can no longer keep aloof from the greater Middle East and southern arc. The role it plays in both countries will significantly shape the future. The United States, having chosen engagement, must now determine how it should stay engaged not only in Afghanistan and Iraq, but in other places as well. Developing a coherent strategy for this entire geostrategic zone is anything but easy: multiple goals must be pursued, effective theories must be forged for how best to advance them, and calculations must be made regarding the resources to be committed. Tradeoffs must be assessed and priorities established. A viable southern arc strategy must be embedded in a larger global strategy aimed at mobilizing the democratic community to help, while managing relations with Russia and China so they are not damaged and, perhaps, even contributing to stability and progress along the southern arc. Strategy formation for the southern arc and its multiple regions will be a challenging long-term intellectual and analytical task.

Dealing with the greater Middle East and the southern arc will become more difficult for two reasons. The first reason is that, owing to radical Islamic fundamentalism and other dynamics, this vast zone is likely to be highly turbulent in the coming years and capable of producing violence directed at the Western democracies. The second reason is that the United States is now involving itself in Middle Eastern and southern arc affairs to a considerably greater degree than was the case during in the 1990s. The decision to launch a preemptive war against Iraq in 2003 suggests that future U.S. military interventions may increase in frequency and, in cases of grave threat, may take place even before adversaries have committed aggression. More fundamentally, the United States has begun trying to alter the basics of politics and economics in the Middle East and elsewhere in the hope of creating stability, peace, and democracy. Exactly how the United States will pursue this quest remains to be seen; it will be a product of the strategic choices the Nation makes in the coming years.[6]

Goals, Dilemmas, and Strategy Options

In the greater Middle East and southern arc, the United States has five dominant goals. The top-priority goal is to defeat global terrorism and its sponsors, to halt the proliferation of WMD into the hands of dangerous rogue states, and to deter other forms of rogue country aggression. The second goal, also a high priority, is to protect close allies such as

Israel and the friendly nations of the Persian Gulf and to ensure unfettered Western access to Gulf oil. A third goal is to preserve and expand the U.S. circle of friends and partners, including such important countries as Turkey, Egypt, and Jordan, and to promote a greater spirit of multilateral collaboration in key regions. A fourth goal is to help defuse local conflicts, such as the Indo-Pakistan rivalry, that threaten to spread outward. A fifth goal is to promote democratization and economic progress in the hope that such changes can contribute to a more stable security climate.

Pursuing each of these goals is a complex enterprise that requires not only considerable energy, but also a coherent sense of policy and strategy in each area. After September 11, 2001, defeating global terrorism emanating from the southern arc became a consuming activity, with military strikes against terrorist strongholds, enhanced homeland defenses, rigorous law enforcement in many places, and diplomatic cooperation among many nations. Slowing WMD proliferation and discouraging aggression by rogue countries has also become a demanding activity, as in Iraq and Iran, requiring a blend of politics, diplomacy, and military force. Enhancing U.S. influence, building partnerships, and expanding multilateral collaboration in a strategic zone that erects barriers to such efforts require delicate diplomacy and patience. Defusing southern arc crises that are deeply embedded in cultural, ethnic, and religious hatreds calls for a prolonged U.S. diplomatic campaign. Encouraging democratization and economic development previously attracted less public attention, yet it too is an important process requiring years of persistence.

For the past decade and more, these five goals have confronted the United States with strategic dilemmas. These goals are incommensurable in the sense that they operate in somewhat different strategic domains: achieving military security, for example, is different from promoting faster economic development and democratization. Moreover, some of these goals are not only incompatible with each other, but also in outright conflict at times. A classic dilemma has been that of protecting Israel while also maintaining friendly relations with other Middle East countries, including conservative Arab sheikdoms in the Persian Gulf. If the United States tilts in one direction, it pays a price in the other. For example, dealing with Iraq during 1991–2003 posed many dilemmas. Following the removal of Saddam Hussein, dealing with the new Iraq may create dilemmas of its own; relations with Iran and Syria also promise to be complicated. Another dilemma has been that of using democratic India's growing power to help stabilize South Asia, while not alienating Pakistan or motivating it or other Islamic governments to lessen their support for the United States in the war against terror. Yet another dilemma has been that a number of the countries whose support for the war on terror is needed are sometimes reluctant participants when it comes to confronting WMD proliferators, or are prone to using their participation in one arena in order to extract U.S. concessions in the other; Syria and Iran are examples. All these dilemmas make it harder for the United States to attain its strategic goals in the Middle East and South Asia.

A further dilemma is presented by efforts to promote democratization in a zone where the United States continues to rely upon traditional and even authoritarian regimes for support of its security policies. Some critics urge the United States to withdraw its support from these governments, but this is no guarantee that they would then be replaced by democratic regimes that would move their countries into the 21st century and also work cooperatively with the United States. If democratization takes a populist course, it runs the risk instead of handing power in key countries to Islamic fundamentalists who would oppose the United States and would stifle further political and economic progress within their borders. Yet if democratization produces responsible governments, it can be key to long-range prospects for peace and prosperity.

Many Islamic societies in the greater Middle East and the southern arc deeply resent being left out of the benefits of globalization's economic progress, yet they have been unwilling or unable to make the social changes needed to become competitive in the world economy.[7] To some of them, Islamic fundamentalism is the answer, even if it is anchored in absolutist values from an earlier century. The problem is that while fundamentalist movements are willing to ride populist support to power, they show a distinct aversion to respecting free expression when it threatens to remove them from office: the behavior of Iran's religious leadership is an example. Many are deeply hostile both to U.S. policies and to U.S. interests and cultural values. Furthermore, fundamentalist Islamic regimes are typically not predisposed to creating the market mechanisms that are needed for economic progress in their countries. The United States thus finds itself with another dilemma: it favors democracy in principle, but when it backs traditional regimes out of necessity, it fears that democracy might bring Islamic fundamentalists to power, thereby dampening hope for liberal social values.

Added to these dilemmas is the complication that the United States lacks a collective security alliance along the southern arc and often has trouble mobilizing consistent help there. Partners tend to join U.S.-led efforts on a selective and ad hoc basis rather than sign on in principle to support a wide range of activities. The United States therefore finds itself having to mobilize and sustain a large number of different coalitions, varying in size and commitment, to support its policies. An additional complication is that the southern arc is beset with major problems that stubbornly resist efforts to solve them. Progress there tends to be glacial and to require considerable patience and persistence. As a result, the five U.S. goals constitute a big agenda that will be hard to pursue successfully along the southern arc.

The requirements and difficulties flowing from these goals provide a conceptual framework for analyzing three illustrative U.S. security strategies for the greater Middle East and southern arc: a key task of strategic evaluation once the situation has been sized up. These strategies span a continuum from less U.S. activism to more. The first option is a strategy limited to defending vital national interests. It calls for supporting the two highest priority goals: suppressing dangerous threats and protecting key allies and Western access to Persian Gulf oil. Because it relegates the other three goals to lower priority, this is a limited option aimed at achieving essential aims while controlling costs and not overextending the United States on behalf of more idealistic visions. The second, more ambitious option is a strategy focused on defending vital interests plus promoting region-wide security and stability. Along with the measures of the first strategy, it includes strong efforts to improve U.S. diplomatic ties in the region, to enhance multinational collaboration, and to defuse local conflicts. The third and most ambitious option is a strategy of protecting interests, promoting security, and accelerating development. In addition to addressing the southern arc's security affairs along the same lines as the other two strategies, it includes the far more idealistic goal of promoting democracy and economic development.

To a degree, these three strategies are simplistic stereotypes. Virtually any U.S. strategy will include elements of all five goals. For example, even a strategy focused mainly on defense of vital interests will include some diplomatic outreach, activities to resolve important local conflicts, and efforts to encourage regional development. The issue here, however, is one of emphasis, ambition, resources, and commitment. These three options differ greatly from each other in this regard. The first option is a minimalist strategy. In aspiring to protect core U.S. and allied interests, it does not aim to cure the southern arc's ills wholly or even partly. The second option has higher aspirations, calls for broader efforts, and will be more costly in time and resources. In addition to protecting U.S. and allied interests, it seeks to enhance U.S. influence in the region, to strengthen the political capacity of the countries of the southern arc to work together to help themselves, and to cool local hotspots. The third option is a maximalist strategy. It is the most costly of the three options, yet has the ambition of healing the southern arc's ills in ways that could greatly lessen or eliminate the dangers the region poses to global security.

In the past, the United States has tended to vacillate between the first and second strategies. But in the aftermath of the Iraq war, its actions in the Middle East suggest increased emphasis on the maximalist third strategy. This was corroborated by President Bush's fall 2003 speech endorsing a "forward strategy of freedom" for the Middle East. His promise was that instead of merely attending to regional security affairs and not challenging the basic political order, the United States would begin promoting democracy across the region. By early 2004, the U.S. Government was speaking in terms of establishing an organization similar to the Organization for Security and Cooperation in Europe (OSCE) and relying on a more outward-looking NATO, as well as other institutions, to encourage freedom, democracy, and multilateral cooperation in the greater Middle East. In his inaugural address of early 2005, President Bush trumpeted the cause of promoting human liberty not only in the Middle East but also globally. Whether such an ambitious strategy of widespread democratization can succeed is debated in some quarters, but to the extent it is seriously pursued, it will challenge strategic evaluation as never before.

While these three strategies differ in their ends and means, they have one feature in common: suppressing the threats posed by terrorism, WMD proliferation, and rogue countries. Achieving this goal is not only critical in itself, but also is essential to pursuing broader goals for regional security and development. Dealing with these threats requires sophisticated strategies that include the application of U.S. military power but mandates other instruments as well, all of which must be blended to provide a coherent approach.

Defeating global terrorism of the sort posed by al Qaeda begins with homeland security, vigorous international law enforcement, and military strikes against terrorist camps. Thus, the United States created a Department of Homeland Security and is strengthening its Intelligence Community, working closely with law enforcement agencies of many countries, and employing its military forces in concert with allies in multiple places. Coping with terrorism also requires using international law enforcement to disrupt organized criminal groups that engage in smuggling illegal arms and narcotics, money laundering, and other offenses. The reason is that organized crime is both a threat in itself and provides terrorist groups access to money for funding their operations. In addition, the wellsprings of terrorism must be dried. This requires pressure on countries that harbor, sponsor, or otherwise support terrorism: the kind of firm pressure that compels them to cease their conduct. Equally important, persistent efforts will continuously be needed to lessen the extent to which terrorism is seen as a legitimate and effective expression of grievances—real or imagined—by Islamic fundamentalists in the Middle East and elsewhere. An across-the-board effort that includes all of these activities will remain necessary for the foreseeable future.

A similar judgment applies to controlling the spread of WMD, especially nuclear weapons. While nuclear proliferation has unfolded more slowly than had been expected some years ago, many observers warn that it is now poised to accelerate, and could result in nuclear weapons falling into the hands of such unpredictable countries as North Korea and Iran and of terrorists. Instruments for preventing nuclear proliferation include the Nuclear Non-Proliferation Treaty and the International Atomic Energy Agency (IAEA), which help enforce inspection regimes, coupled with programs to secure existing weapons inventories in Russia and to interdict the flow of WMD materials to countries seeking them. Treaty enforcement efforts cannot rely solely upon inspections and global policing, but must also include multilateral diplomacy and, when necessary, sanctions against offending parties. In extreme cases, military strikes against nuclear production facilities might be necessary, but only as a last resort when peaceful efforts have failed. More fundamentally, efforts to halt or slow nuclear proliferation must also address larger regional security conditions. Even rogue countries will seek nuclear weapons only when possessing them will strengthen their capacity to pursue their strategic goals, such as intimidation of neighbors or prevention of outside intervention by the United States and its allies. Endangered countries will themselves acquire nuclear weapons only when alternative sources of protection, such as U.S. nuclear deterrence coverage, are lacking. To the extent that U.S.-led management of regional security affairs can lessen these incentives, it will help reduce the likelihood that proliferation of nuclear, chemical, and biological weapons will accelerate in the coming years.

The need for sophisticated, balanced strategies also applies to dealing with rogue countries: those willing to commit aggression, sponsor terrorism, proliferate WMD, or otherwise contribute to violence and instability. The U.S. invasions of Afghanistan and Iraq have removed those two countries from the list, but some remain—Syria, Iran, and North Korea are examples—and others could arise in the future. Past experience shows that a light touch, employing only forthcoming diplomacy and economic incentives, often will not be sufficiently firm to motivate such countries to change their behavior in the ways desired. Yet experience shows that excessively heavy-handed efforts can backfire and make the situation worse. Future strategy therefore will require a combination of firmness and restraint, coupled with artful blending of carrots and sticks. Even when the goal is something short of the removal of outlaw regimes, well-conceived strategies can aspire to contain them, preventing them from causing damage.

Recent experience shows that in extreme cases, military intervention may be the only viable strategy against a rogue country that poses an imminent threat or a grave and gathering threat. Yet logic and experience also show that military intervention for purposes of preemption or prevention should be a last resort that is taken only after major efforts to avoid war are unsuccessful. No simple strategic doctrine can be articulated to govern such interventions, but the criteria of legality, necessity, and likely success are good guideposts.

Whether global terrorism, WMD proliferation, and rogue regimes can be successfully combated in the years ahead remains to be seen, but clearly, suppressing them is vital to pursuing broader strategies of security and progress in the greater Middle East and the southern arc of instability. Equally clearly, however, they are best fought not only by attacking them directly, but also by guiding regional security affairs in directions that remove incentives for them to grow and multiply. This reinforces the need to assess U.S. policy and strategy options with a broad perspective in mind.

Appraising the Strategy Options

What does strategic evaluation have to say about how to appraise the three strategy options for the greater Middle East and the southern arc of instability? Analysis can explore their aims, their theories of performance, their attractions and pitfalls, and their costs and benefits. But analysis alone is unlikely to be able to single out the best choice. None is obviously a winner or loser over the others. All pose tradeoffs that must be weighed and balanced in such key areas as goals, resource commitments, and expected effectiveness. Analysis can, however, discuss the strategic basics in ways that help shed light on the goals and the potential effectiveness of each option. For example, although the huge zone of the greater Middle East and the southern arc has fewer resources than Europe and Northeast Asia, and its complex problems are less responsive to outside intervention, strategic evaluation can point out that the United States is hardly powerless in this zone. It has allies who can be persuaded to help, based on their individual preferences in the various issue areas, such as the need for oil, fear of terrorists and WMD, willingness to use diplomacy or military power, and commitment to political reforms.

A balanced assessment of problems and prospects is key to evaluating all of these strategies fairly and insightfully. Over the past decade, the United States has had to struggle continuously to protect its vital security interests in the greater Middle East and elsewhere along the southern arc; thus far, it has been reasonably successful in this arena. While it has not been able to defuse the Israeli-Palestinian conflict or the Indo-Pakistan rivalry, it has been able to help keep the lid on both, and neither has exploded into full-scale war. The United States has encountered difficulties in promoting multilateral cooperation, but signs of progress have come from cooperation between Israel and Turkey, and in the Persian Gulf, where the Arab sheikdoms have been slowly drawing closer together and the Saddam Hussein regime has been removed from Iraq. The United States has encountered the biggest barriers in promoting democracy and economic progress. Yet although authoritarian regimes and Islamic fundamentalism resist them, the tides of history seemingly favor democracy. In addition, many governments understand that if they are to profit in the world economy, they must modernize their own economies and embrace market capitalism.

With these considerations in mind, skeptics of deep U.S. involvement in the greater Middle East and the southern arc might judge that it requires hard labor with uncertain results. By contrast, proponents might judge that the importance of the effort is worth the costs and that even moderate gains justify the expense. These polar-opposite judgments help provide a frame of reference for evaluating the three strategies in analytical terms. The first strategy—limiting U.S. involvements to defense of vital interests—responds to the skeptics, yet it too requires considerable U.S. effort, including a willingness to combat threats and even to wage war. Thus, this is not a strategy of aloofness and disengagement. Its drawback is that it lacks vision and may turn on an excessively narrow interpretation of long-term U.S. interests. Moreover, it offers no way to address problems when they would be easier and less costly to solve, before they grow to the point of threatening U.S. and allied interests.

Compared to the first strategy, the second strategy of promoting stable security affairs offers added attractions at moderately increased costs, both budgetary and diplomatic. But in seeking to resolve such local disputes as the Israeli-Palestinian rivalry and the Indo-Pakistan feud, it aims to achieve goals that have for years been beyond the reach of U.S. foreign policy and the United Nations. Efforts to enhance multilateral collaboration among countries may make sense on paper but may not be very fruitful because few of these countries trust each other enough to collaborate. The third strategy—security and development—offers the appealing vision of improving basic political and economic conditions in the greater Middle East and the southern arc. But it runs the risk of throwing a great deal of U.S. money and diplomatic effort at troubled conditions that will improve slowly at best, and perhaps too little to make enough difference in the security arena in the near to mid-term.

If cost effectiveness is the standard of evaluation, policymakers who employ systematic analysis might opt for a well-focused version of the second strategy, coupled with aspects of the third strategy where it can be pursued in affordable, effective ways. Much would depend upon expectations of the U.S. capacity to pursue and actually achieve its five key strategic goals. Such an analysis might conclude that, although the United States would be unable to achieve all of its goals any time soon, it could perhaps aspire to keep the lid on this dangerous zone and to achieve significant progress in key areas. If the United States can quell new-era threats, protect allies, and ensure access to Persian Gulf oil, this would be a worthy accomplishment. If it can also move local conflicts toward settlement and enhance multilateralism in ways that support U.S. interests, better yet. It might even make meaningful progress in promoting democracy and economic development. An ambitious strategy thus has potential advantages because it offers higher potential payoffs even if it falls short of its ideal aims. Whether the United States should be willing to pay the added costs and absorb the risks of such a strategy, however, is a decision for policymakers rather than analysts.

Regardless of the strategy chosen, it will be composed of multiple goals supported by multiple policies. The more ambitious the strategy, the larger the number of goals and policies needed, all of which elevate resource requirements. Because most U.S. goals could be pursued in various ways, strategic evaluation can help survey the policy options in each case and contribute to informed decisions about them. Analysis can help ensure that the multiple policies chosen to support the strategy are harmonized and coordinated with each other. For example, if the third strategy is chosen, its defense, diplomatic, and economic components will need to be forged into a coherent whole. Analysis can help achieve this coherence.

Selecting among the policy options for each goal is complicated because of the multiplicity of choices available. As the Iraq case shows, threats posed by WMD-proliferating rogue states can be addressed in different ways: UN-approved arms control regimes, inspections, and sanctions; political pressure by the United States and its allies; stiff economic sanctions; preemptive military strikes; or outright invasion and occupation. Similarly, defusing local conflicts might make use of multiple diplomatic approaches, such as those employed with the Israeli-Palestinian conflict, ranging from step-by-step negotiations to seeking comprehensive settlements. Thus far, none of these efforts have succeeded with the Israeli-Palestinian situation, but earlier efforts to forge Israeli accords with Egypt and Jordan did succeed. Economic development, too, can be pursued in different ways, including financial aid, lowered trade barriers, direct foreign investments, currency support, and educational programs aimed at creating a skilled workforce. The key point is that strategic evaluation can help determine which policy option makes best sense, both in its own right and in the context of the overall strategy. It can also focus attention on the relationship between actions and consequences, to safeguard against unwise choices and identify credible reasons to believe that when strong actions are taken, they will produce the desired results. Such contributions can help increase the odds that future U.S. strategy along the southern arc will be an exercise in success, not frustration.

The Role of Allies and Partners

Perhaps the United States could pursue a strategy that was solely focused on protecting its vital interests by acting unilaterally. But this minimalist strategy seems too narrowly conceived, and the more ambitious strategies certainly cannot be accomplished if the United States acts alone. Major sustained help will be needed, both from European allies and from friendly countries in the Middle East and along the entire southern arc. A core problem is that the United States does not possess a multilateral alliance network or even many bilateral alliances in this vast region. Such bilateral security ties as it has with some countries in the region tend to be limited in scope and size, and focused narrowly on the defense of those countries. They cannot easily be turned into mechanisms for promoting region-wide security or serve as the basis of an enduring multilateral body for pursuing this goal over the long term.

During the 1950s, the United States tried to create such a multilateral alliance in the form of the Central Treaty Organization, which fell apart shortly after it was created, due to growing Arab nationalism, inter-Arab rivalries, and Arab-Israeli conflicts. Creation of a new alliance of this sort may make sense now, perhaps using the coalition of 1991 as a model. But such a creation may not be politically feasible for some time. A similar idea is to create a regional security body similar to Europe's OSCE. But here, too, it may not be realistic to expect much. Until events prove otherwise, a better approach may be for the United States to build upon its existing bilateral ties to create stronger partnerships with broader horizons. It could begin slowly, expanding incrementally over a period of years, ultimately developing into multilateral cooperation encompassing the Middle East, the Persian Gulf, and South Asia.

In the Middle East, the United States already enjoys close relations with Israel and with Turkey, a member of NATO. But the Iraq war of 2003 showed the limits of Turkey's willingness to support controversial assertions of U.S. power in its region even when the purpose was to eliminate a proximate threat. Turkey will remain a valuable partner, but unless its attitude changes, this partnership will have limited scope. The same applies to Israel: although a powerful and trusted friend, it is preoccupied with its own self-defense and currently is prevented by Arab politics from playing a larger or more constructive role in regional security affairs. As for other Arab countries, much will depend upon the Israeli-Palestinian peace process. Provided progress is made toward an enduring peace with a Palestinian state, perhaps U.S. partnerships with Egypt and Jordan can be broadened into instruments for regional security.

In the Persian Gulf, much will depend upon how Iraq evolves. If it emerges as a pro-Western democracy, a close U.S.-Iraqi relationship will be possible, and it could become an anchor for multilateral collaboration in the Gulf. Short of this, the United States will rely on its existing security relationships with Saudi Arabia, Yemen, and other Gulf states. Although Saudi Arabia has begun seeking greater distance from the United States, the other Gulf countries are serving as reliable defense partners, providing the United States with valuable military infrastructure and a launch-pad in the region. Perhaps the Gulf Cooperation Council could become a stronger framework for multilateral collaboration with the United States.[8]

In South Asia, the United States earlier relied upon close ties to Pakistan and "cool but correct" relations with India. Pakistan's drift toward Islamic fundamentalism narrowed cooperation with the United States, but recently its government has restored close ties. India is emerging as a regional powerhouse. Because it remains an adversary of China and no longer can draw upon Russia for meaningful support, it has been moving closer to the United States. As this relationship matures, India can become a more valuable partner. But India is mostly focused on its own South Asian region, which it aspires to dominate. Whether India would be willing to play a constructive, activist role across its region and elsewhere in a manner that supports U.S. goals is less clear, but that is a conceivable outcome if relations with it are carefully nurtured.

Given these complex politics, the prospect of creating a multilateral body along the southern arc that replicates NATO does not look promising any time soon. But now that the United States is asserting itself in the greater Middle East and has removed a nemesis in Saddam Hussein, a new regional security politics can be expected, perhaps with new opportunities. Even if a multilateral body cannot be created, and solid, far-sighted bilateral relationships remain hard to establish, the United States may be successful at expanding upon existing partnerships. It may thus create a pool of friendly cooperators—a "virtual network of allies"—that it can rely on to be flexible, pragmatic, and attuned to U.S. leadership on a shifting array of issues. This could create the necessary climate for bigger steps later and, in combination with help from Europe and NATO, might provide enough multilateral cooperation to help the United States perform its function of security architect.

Crafting Strategies That Work

The United States will continue facing a menu of strategy options for dealing with Russia and China and for grappling with the southern arc of instability. The options chosen may vary over time, but they will be heavily influenced by the strategic situation in both arenas. Regardless of the situation, the strategy will always be dominated by U.S. goals, values, and visions, and by U.S. willingness to commit resources. The ideal outcome is one in which Russia and China are steadily integrated into the Western community and the southern arc steadily moves from instability to peace, prosperity, and democracy. What it will strive to avoid is a disastrous outcome such as confrontation with Russia or China, along with mounting chaos and violence along the southern arc. The likely outcome lies somewhere between these two poles.

The United States can be expected to pursue a dual strategy aimed at improving cooperative relations with Russia and China, while actively involving itself along the southern arc to promote stable security affairs there, as well as economic progress and democratization to the extent possible. Both strategies would demand many years of skillful U.S. performance and attention to the many tasks of implementation. The main challenge will be to assemble packages of policies and associated activities in both arenas that are affordable, feasible, and successful. A key part of this challenge will be to calculate carefully so that U.S. efforts actually trigger the consequences needed to achieve their goals, rather than misfire or backfire. Practitioners of strategic evaluation can play a helpful role not only by applying cost-effectiveness standards, but also by thinking innovatively and clearly, and by keeping an eye out for a cumulative pattern of successes or failures. In order to contribute usefully, however, they will need to produce analyses of a sort not called for in the past. A future of changing intellectual horizons—embodying breadth and depth—lies ahead.

Notes

[1] For an optimistic assessment of the capacity of big powers to achieve stable relations in a multipolar setting, see Charles W. Kegley, Jr., and Gregory Raymond, *A Multipolar Peace? Great-Power Politics in the Twenty-first Century* (New York: St. Martin's Press, 1994). For a pessimistic account, see John J. Mearsheimer, *The Tragedy of Great Power Politics* (New York: W.W. Norton, 2001).

[2] See James M. Goldgeier and Michael McFaul, *Power and Purpose: U.S. Policy Toward Russia After the Cold War* (Washington, DC: Brookings, 2003); Tom Bjorkman, *Russia's Road to Deeper Democracy* (Washington, DC: Brookings, 2003); Daniel Triesman, "Russia Renewed?" *Foreign Affairs* 81, no. 6 (November/December 2002); and Bobo Lo, *Vladimir Putin and the Evolution of Russian Foreign Policy* (London: Oxford University Press, 2003).

[3] See Evan S. Medeiros and Taylor M. Fravel, "China's New Diplomacy," *Foreign Affairs* 82, no. 6 (November/December 2003); David Hale and Lyric Hughes Hale, "China Takes Off," *Foreign Affairs* 82, no. 6 (November/December 2003); and Charles Wolf, Jr., et al., *Fault Lines in China's Economic Terrain* (Santa Monica, CA: RAND, 2003)

[4] Recent analyses of U.S. strategy in the Middle East include Kenneth M. Pollack, "Securing the Gulf," and Joseph S. Nye, "U.S. Power and Strategy After Iraq," *Foreign Affairs* 82, no. 4 (July/August 2003); Michael Scott Duran, "Palestine, Iraq, and American Strategy," *Foreign Affairs* 82, no. 1 (January/February 2003); and William B. Quandt, *Peace Process: American Diplomacy and the Arab-Israeli Conflict Since 1967* (Washington, DC: Brookings, 2000).

[5] See *Report of the Quadrennial Defense Review 2001* (Washington, DC: Department of Defense, 2001).

[6] As of early 2004, the U.S. Government, many European governments, and several international institutions were calling for a coordinated strategy aimed at fostering economic progress, effective governance, and democracy-building across the Middle East. Left unanswered was the issue of how such a strategy should be constructed with the resources available. The idea of such a strategy initially was given mixed reviews by Middle Eastern countries, which often seemed more interested in economic progress than democracy-building. But as of early 2005, this effort seemed to be making headway, with democratic elections in Afghanistan, Iraq, and Palestine, plus promises of elections in Egypt and Saudi Arabia.

[7] For a history of Islamic fundamentalism in the Middle East, see Bernard Lewis, *The Middle East: A Brief History of the Last 2000 Years* (New York: Touchstone, 1995). For a recent appraisal, see Barry Rubin, "The Real Roots of Arab Anti-Americanism," *Foreign Affairs* 81, no. 6 (November/December 2002). For an analysis of cultural conflicts, see Samuel P. Huntington, *The Clash of Civilizations and the Remaking of World Order* (New York: Simon and Schuster, 1996).

[8] For analysis of U.S. strategy in the Persian Gulf, see Richard D. Sokolsky, ed., *The United States and the Persian Gulf: Reshaping Security Strategy for the Post-Containment Era* (Washington, DC: National Defense University Press, 2003).

Chapter 9
Promoting Economic Progress and Democracy

The function performed by the United States of fostering global development attracts less public attention than the other two major functions, reforming alliances (discussed in chapter 7) and orchestrating security affairs (discussed in chapter 8). Behind the scenes, however, the function of global developer increasingly occupies the attention of senior U.S. officials, who are coming to view it as a key component of national security strategy. The reason is simple. Long-range prospects for world peace depend partly upon three interconnected issues: whether the world economy grows steadily, whether underdeveloped countries rise out of poverty, and how widely democracy replaces dictatorships. The United States has a strategic incentive to support favorable trends in all three areas, not only to advance its own prosperity and security interests, but also to help make the world a better and safer place as globalization accelerates. The question is how the United States can best shape its policies and strategies in this complex, difficult arena in order to attain its goals.

Strategic evaluation will be needed far into the future to help produce policies and strategies that are well conceived and likely to be effective. During the early 1990s, a common argument was that sustained global development could be taken for granted because an irresistible tide of market economics and democratic values would make progress inevitable. Events since then have dampened this optimism. Today, the world economy is growing, but many countries are not climbing out of poverty, and democracy is under assault from competing ideologies. These troublesome events do not mean that the quest for steady progress should be abandoned, but progress will be achievable only if governments pursue activist policies that help overcome the barriers ahead. The United States is not the only country facing this challenge, but because it is among the most important countries in the global calculus, its need for sound, effective policies and strategies that play a leadership role is paramount.

This chapter begins by discussing contributions of strategic evaluation in this arena. Then it discusses the world economy and identifies the problems that U.S. leadership must address. Next, it examines the situation of poor countries and identifies the ways in which U.S. policies can have an effect. Finally, it addresses prospects for the spread of democracy. In all three areas, it appraises contemporary trends as well as the strategy options open to the United States. It does not offer a specific blueprint, but instead suggests how strategic evaluation can help illuminate the options ahead to lend coherence to overall U.S. national security policy and strategy.

This chapter's theme is that, while major progress in promoting global development may be hard to achieve in the coming years, wise U.S. policy and strategy choices, in cooperation with other countries, can help pursue this goal. Activist U.S. strategies will be needed in all three areas: promoting a growing world economy, greater prosperity for poor regions, and further democratization. An active policy is required because passivity could result in unfavorable trends across the board and because activism can help foster faster progress. Activist strategies will often need to embrace moderate goals in the near term, rather than aim very high or very low, and should focus on achieving cumulative successes over the long term, rather than a fast-paced, great leap forward in a single period of time. Such strategies will normally need to be flexible, periodically changing their features in response to shifting conditions rather than rigidly relying upon one-dimensional thinking. Appealing visions and internal coherence will be standards for judging old and new strategies, but the fundamental decision criteria will be practical: whether, and to what degree, each strategy will successfully attain its goals during its life span.

In addition to activism, moderate goals, and flexibility, U.S. policymakers will need to think in holistic terms. They should view activities in all three development areas as potentially cross-fertilizing if their effects are designed to be mutually reinforcing. Thinking holistically also requires a concerted effort to focus on the connection between goals for promoting global development and goals for managing global security affairs. In the coming years, developments in each arena likely will have a profound effect on the other. Keeping this relationship in mind, capitalizing on its opportunities, and avoiding its pitfalls will be critical to pursuing simultaneously global development and global peace.

Contributions of Strategic Evaluation

In the past, studies of global economic development and democratization were normally conducted by economists and political scientists who specialized in these particular areas. Scholars of security affairs and geopolitics typically stayed on the sidelines because they saw no major implications for their studies. Governmental policymakers often adopted a similar stance. This intellectual separation no longer applies in the contemporary world because events in these two arenas are now too interactive to be ignored. Indeed, they can greatly affect each other for good or ill. For example, the Middle East is making slow economic progress partly because its security affairs are unstable; economic prospects for many countries there are not bright. As a result, strategic evaluation has become an appropriate method for studying economic development and democratization, and for assessing their consequences for security affairs.

In this arena, strategic evaluation employs the methods that were outlined in chapters 4 and 5. It begins by appraising how international conditions are evolving and how they are affecting U.S. goals and interests. Then, it generates a spectrum of policy and strategy options for pursuing goals. Next, it assesses these options in terms of their capacity to attain these goals. It conducts this assessment in terms of likely consequences, effectiveness, costs, tradeoffs, feasibility, and other considerations. When one or more options stand out as viable candidates for adoption, it develops plans, programs, and budgets in order to illuminate their specific details and implications.

Strategic evaluation must take into account the unique issues that arise in this arena. Analyzing U.S. policy and strategy for global development is different from analyzing how the United States leads alliances and orchestrates security affairs. Because different goals must be pursued and different challenges addressed, a special conceptual framework must be crafted. Yet this conceptual framework cannot stand wholly apart from the frameworks used to address management of alliances and security affairs. The best evaluations of policy and strategy for development are those that can readily be connected to alliances and security affairs so that assessments in all three functional areas can be brought together to create an overall U.S. national security strategy. The key point is that development policies and strategies should be evaluated with their larger strategic implications in mind.

Evaluation of policies and strategies for promoting global development must also be cognizant of limits on the capacity of the United States to influence worldwide trends in the immediate future. When the United States sets out to reform its alliances or to shape regional security affairs, it often can aspire to exert considerable influence and to achieve substantial results fairly quickly, within a few years, if not a few months. In the development arena, by contrast, the United States confronts phenomena that are often more complex and less malleable. Additionally, its own instruments and resources tend to be less potent. As a result, it may be able to aspire only to a limited degree of influence and to success that is achieved only gradually over a period of many years. Its inability to wave a magic wand for instantaneous results, however, does not mean that it is confined to operating at the margins of relevance. The challenge facing it is to employ its resources as effectively as possible in order to achieve tangible progress in any single period, thus setting the stage for additional progress later.

Setting achievable goals and employing resources effectively requires wisdom in choosing U.S. policies and strategies to help manage the world economy, elevate poor countries out of poverty, and promote further democratization. Wisdom, in turn, requires a blending of idealism and realism, the ability to separate truths from myths, the insight to distinguish good theories from bad theories, and a capacity to focus on practical achievements that have cumulative effects. Wisdom also requires thinking flexibly because strategies that work for one period have a way of not working in the next. The task of strategic evaluation is to contribute to this enterprise.

Managing the World Economy

Managing the global economy is an important task in itself, and it also sets the stage for determining how the United States can best promote economic development of poor regions and global democratization. Consequently, strategic evaluation must take into account not only complex economic considerations, but complex political considerations as well. The task is not only to promote a growing world economy in which the United States prospers, but also to use global economic growth as an instrument to help shape a stable security environment in which nations are better able to cooperate peacefully rather than move in the direction of strife and war.

Whereas the Clinton administration was a vocal advocate of helping the world economy to grow, the Bush administration became so engrossed in the war on terror that its stance on the global economy often fell off the front pages of newspapers. Yet the Bush administration, too, has pursued long-range goals and policies similar to those of its predecessor. Aware of globalization's dynamics, both administrations aspired to encourage sustained growth of the world economy. Both expressed hope that global economic growth would not only bring enhanced prosperity to many regions, but also make the world more peaceful, thereby contributing to U.S. national security. Both used free trade, international markets, multilateral bodies, and associated policy tools as instruments to keep the world economy growing while warding off threats of recessions. Future U.S. administrations seem likely to continue such policies, but the details of how the United States should act will continue to be debated and analyzed, giving strategic evaluation a role to play.

The World Economy and Global Security Affairs

An appraisal of U.S. policies for managing the world economy can begin by assessing the strategic relationship between economics and security. For valid reasons, U.S. national security strategy is anchored in the premise that the spread of economic prosperity will help make the world a safer place. While this expectation is true to a point, it should not be carried so far that it oversimplifies complex realities and leads to blindness toward different possibilities. As a general proposition, a growing world economy can help enhance prospects for peace over the long term. But by itself, greater prosperity will not tame today's chaotic security affairs or prevent individual wars from erupting. The fact that the modern world remains violent, even though it is more prosperous than 50 years ago, rebuts the notion that wealth can be relied upon to bring peace. Moreover, today's globalizing world economy is proving to be part of the problem as well as part of the solution because it is leaving behind frustrated losers even as it creates winners. The relationship between the world economy and global security thus should not be presumed to operate on a single track that always promotes peace.

Economic progress does not necessarily bring peace for the simple reason that man does not live by bread alone. Human conflict can take place for many reasons that transcend economics, such as religious values, ethnic identities, border disputes, or political domination. While economic integration may help bring about political integration, it does not always do so. Moreover, integration can bring closeness without unity; indeed, it can help fan disunity, as is shown by ethnic groups that fall into violence when they intermingle. Merely because countries carry out commerce with each other is no guarantee that they will remain at peace, much less form a political community. In 1914, Europe was highly integrated in commercial terms, yet it plunged into World War I. In 1940, Germany and the Soviet Union signed the biggest trade deal in their history, but a few months later, Hitler invaded the Soviet Union.[1]

History shows that economic commerce produces peace when countries take parallel steps to settle their strategic differences and to create shared political values, visions, and institutions. Economic integration thus may be a necessary contributor to political integration and harmony, but it is not a sufficient condition. Much depends upon what happens in the political arena for reasons that often have little to do with economics. The great clashes of the 20th century were driven mainly by political and ideological struggles that swept aside any shared interests in peaceful commerce. Today's quest to expand the global democratic community stems mainly from a commitment to human freedom rather than a sure-fire scheme to become wealthier; similarly, Islamic fundamentalism is deeply opposed to Western cultural values, even though Western economic institutions are often capable of producing great wealth. The future of the world will be determined by how these political agendas are pursued. The world economy will be only one variable in the calculus, and not even the most important one.

Moreover, it should be remembered that even today in the world economy, countries mostly compete with each other rather than cooperate. To be sure, global economic management requires governments to cooperate in establishing common institutions and laws for regulating their interactions, and countries share an interest in cooperating to ensure that the world economy does not plunge into recessions or depressions that damage everybody. Nonetheless, the world economy is ruled by competitive market dynamics and national profit-seeking, not by theories of collective good in which all countries take moral responsibility for each other. The democratic community, including the Atlantic Alliance, is held together by common political and social values, but in the economic arena, its members are competitors to a significant degree. They are interested in their own fortunes first, and in the fortunes of their partners second. The same calculus applies virtually everywhere.

Fortunately, the competitive spirit is moderated by the realization that international economics is not a zero-sum game in which the rich always steal from the poor or where only a few can profit. When some countries become prosperous, they can help poorer countries become wealthier by importing more of the latter's products. Nonetheless, all countries compete with each other for control of market share, and the strongest performers often gain the lion's share of rewards. The countervailing idea that a hotly competitive world economy can bring enhanced prosperity to many nations stems from the theories of David Ricardo and others.[2] Their core argument is that if each country specializes in its areas of comparative advantage, all will be better off by allowing free trade to guide their competitive interactions. In essence, they argue, a rising tide will lift all boats. However, while this theory is true in aggregate terms, it does not mean that all countries will profit equally or that all will become prosperous. To the contrary, those countries with better access to natural resources and more productive workforces will outperform less endowed countries in ways that bring them greater profits.[3] Countries with fewer resources, less productive workforces, and little of value to sell abroad can find their economies stagnant or even shrinking.

The logical implication is that economic competition can give rise to conflict and war as well as peace, especially when competition produces a hierarchy of winners and losers, and when the losers seek to employ military coercion to improve their lot. This was often the case during the past 300 years. This period is littered with examples in Europe and elsewhere of economic nationalism and mercantilism and with wars launched on behalf of imperial economic expansion. For example, World War II in Asia erupted partly because Japan's efforts to establish a sphere of economic control menaced U.S. strategic interests. It is a recent idea that countries should compete peacefully in the global economic marketplace and should refrain from using military power to enforce their claims; this idea is not yet shared by all countries. Saddam Hussein invaded Kuwait in 1990 intending to seize control of its oilfields, and he may not be the last to think in these terms. For example, control over scarce water resources could be a cause of war in several regions.

Other things being equal, however, prosperous economic times enhance prospects for peace because countries have hope for the future and are more willing to collaborate. Conversely, bad global economic conditions can leave countries worried, more willing to use military power to protect their economic interests, and less prone to cooperate. Yet these are general tendencies, not deterministic laws of world politics. The reality is that nations can fall into political conflict for many reasons that transcend economics. Wars can erupt even when economies are growing and becoming more integrated through commerce, as World War I shows. The role of economics in global security affairs thus needs to be kept in perspective, but it is nonetheless an important role.

Interest in global economic cooperation first appeared during the 1930s. The Great Depression was triggered by unstable financial relations when Austria's Kreditanstalt Bank failed, touching off financial collapses elsewhere. The main response by the United States and others was to establish protectionist policies that accelerated the downslide, thereby leading to the Wall Street plunge and the collapse of economies everywhere. In Europe, the resulting poverty and social chaos bred fascism and Nazism. In Asia, Japan succumbed to a nationalist crusade to control markets and resources in China and Southeast Asia. World War II was caused by nationalist aggression and racism, but in important ways, the stage was set by a poorly functioning world economy.

After World War II, the United States had the wisdom to see the close connection between global security affairs and the world economy. Faced with the Soviet military threat, it fashioned a security regime of containment and deterrence in Europe and Northeast Asia, but it also aimed to bond the Western countries in a web of cooperative economic relationships that would avoid the protectionism of the 1930s and promote mutual prosperity. It created the Bretton Woods Accord and the Marshall Plan, supported the European Common Market and the General Agreement on Tariffs and Trade, and fostered the economic recovery of Germany and Japan. After the Korean War, it defended South Korea with U.S. forces, allowing the Republic of Korea to focus on economic development, and it encouraged other allies to develop their economies under the mantle of U.S. military protection, coupled with favorable trade agreements.[4]

This largesse was motivated by more than generosity. The United States correctly judged that its global security agenda could be achieved only if its key allies gained the economic strength necessary not only to defend themselves, but also to create the internal social stability that would allow democracy to take hold. For example, Germany and Japan both became democracies partly because their security was assured and their economies were prosperous. Not coincidentally, increasing the wealth of its allies had a beneficial impact on the U.S. economy by creating partners capable of importing products from the United States. During the Cold War, Ricardo's theory of comparative advantage and mutual profit worked marvelously well for the entire Western alliance in both security and economics.

During the early 1970s, however, the Western community's economic ties seemed to be eroding. The principal reason was that Western Europe and Japan had rebuilt their economies from World War II devastation and were competing with the United States.

The old rules that favored their economic growth while allowing them to draw upon huge quantities of U.S. assistance no longer made sense because they left the United States at a disadvantage. The worst features of this one-sided relationship, however, were ameliorated by policy changes, negotiations, and reciprocal agreements in the late 1970s and 1980s. For example, the United States began floating the dollar in order to achieve better exchange rates for exporting its products. It also pressured the Europeans and Japanese to lower their trade barriers to U.S. products. Partial success in this effort resulted in agreements whereby allies, in addition to accepting variable exchange rates, would help offset the cost of stationing U.S. troops on their soil and would buy American-built weapons.

Creation of the G–7 in the mid-1970s was a major step because it established a forum for coordinating exchange rates, energy policies, and other economic priorities. Progress toward lower trade barriers helped increase world trade. Another influential trend was the resurgence of the U.S. economy in the late 1980s and 1990s. Many observers had been warning that the European and Japanese economies were overtaking the U.S. economy and that this threatened to create rivalries that could shake the foundations of the Western alliance system. But as the U.S. economy gained strength in the 1990s, talk of rivalry with Europe and Japan faded, and U.S. political relations with them settled into a period of comfort in both politics and economics.

When the Cold War ended, it left intact this long-established and still-flourishing Western community of powerful security alliances and close economic relationships. Since then, the United States has been endeavoring to build upon this foundation by enlarging the democratic community, promoting free trade, and drawing more countries and regions into this zone of peace. In the economic realm, it has supported such organizations as the WTO, NAFTA, the Association of Southeast Asian Nations (ASEAN), the Asia-Pacific Economic Cooperation (APEC) forum, the Southern Cone Common Market (MERCOSUR), and such proposals as a Transatlantic Economic Partnership and a Free Trade Association of the Americas (FTAA). It has also been pursuing the Doha Talks (the latest stage in world trade talks) in order to lessen trade barriers and create new agreements not only to promote its own interests but also to expand the web of Western cooperation to other regions. Although recent frustration with the Doha Talks and FTAA progress has led to renewed U.S. interest in bilateral agreements with individual countries, the quest for multilateral agreements will remain important.

Such efforts need to be kept in strategic perspective; multilateral agreements aimed at managing the world economy cannot, by themselves, bring global peace. They cannot win the war on terror, or deter tyrants, or stop WMD proliferation. Indeed, many chaotic regions may require establishment of a foundation of stable security relationships before economic cooperation, free markets, and flourishing trade can take hold. At a minimum, political and economic progress normally must go hand in hand. However, the idea of promoting global economic growth in the hope that it will help tilt the odds in favor of peace—not necessarily everywhere, but in some places—makes sense. In today's world, the challenge facing the United States is to help guide the globalizing world economy toward an era of sustained growth in ways that ease political frictions, not exacerbate them. This goal can be accomplished only by coherent U.S. approaches plus cooperation with other countries; the modern world economy, if left to itself, will not necessarily continue growing in the desired ways.

The World Economy Today

Although the world economy is showing steady growth under the impetus of globalization, it faces two core problems that have strategic implications. First, its continued growth cannot be taken for granted because it remains vulnerable to recessions and contractions that become magnified by globalization. Even during periods of sustained growth, the world economy expands slowly by 3 to 4 percent per year, with wealthy countries growing at 2 to 3 percent annually and poor countries averaging 4 to 5 percent annually. This slow growth rate can bring major improvements over a period of decades, but not instantaneously. Second, the world economy is sharply divided between the rich and the poor. The gap between them is cavernous, raising questions about prospects for global peace. Whether the poor are getting poorer as the rich are getting richer can be debated. But while some poor countries are making fast strides, many are barely staying afloat in today's globalizing economy. To compound the problem, the regions that are the most economically stressed also tend to have highly unstable security affairs. The task of handling these two problems frames the global economic agenda facing the United States.

As table 9–1 shows, today's world economy has an estimated value of $34 billion to $45 billion annually, as measured by the sum of all countries' GDPs. The lower figure uses exchange rates for currencies as the basis for comparison, and the higher figure results if purchasing power parity (PPP) is used. Although both standards are useful, PPP may be a better measure because it gauges the capacity of countries to buy goods and services within their domestic economies. Its effect is to close the gap between poor countries and rich countries a bit.[5]

Table 9–1 illuminates the extent to which the world economy is bifurcated and hierarchical in its distribution of wealth and productivity. The wealthy democracies in North America, Europe, and Asia have only about 24 percent of the world's population, yet they possess about 64 percent of its wealth in PPP and buying power. By contrast, the rest of the world has 76 percent of its population, yet possesses only about 36 percent of the wealth. The result is a major difference in GDP per person (GDP-P). The wealthy democracies have a GDP-P of over $19,000 annually, while in the rest of the world it is only about $3,500 (the average in nonwealthy, nondemocratic regions ranges from $1,200 to $10,000). The gap between the rich and the poor thus is quite large and has increased greatly over the past century or two since the industrial age began. These aggregate statistics conceal important differences among the rich and the poor. Within the wealthy democratic community, the United States and Canada are wealthier, on a per capita basis, than Europe and democratic Asia. Even Europe is no monolith: wealthy countries such as Britain, France, Germany, and other northern European countries have a GDP-P of $22,000 to $35,000 annually (almost as much as the United States and Canada), while the countries of southern and eastern Europe cluster between $10,000 and $20,000. In Asia, Japan and Australia have a GDP-P of $20,000 to $30,000, but South Korea and Taiwan are less wealthy, at only $10,000 to $15,000. The differences among poor regions are even greater. Judged on a global scale, Russia/Eurasia, Latin America, and the greater Middle East are middle class, with a GDP-P of $6,000 to $10,000. By contrast, the regions of nondemocratic Asia, Central/South Asia, and Africa are far behind, with a GDP-P of just $1,000 to $3,000 annually. In these regions, nearly 60 percent of the world's population lives in poverty because they have not yet benefited from the industrial age, much less the information age.

Today's hierarchy is a product of history, not just accelerating globalization. Two centuries ago, nearly all countries and regions were mostly agricultural and were similar to each other in wealth. What caused the change was industrialization, which gradually brought wealth to the Western countries and a few others, but not to the vast majority of the world. Countries profiting were those possessing the natural resources, climate, geographical

Table 9–1. **The World Economy, 2004**

	Population (millions)	Exchange Rate Measure of Gross Domestic Product (GDP) in $trillions	Purchasing Power Parity Measure of GDP in $trillions	GDP per Person
Wealthy Democracies				
North America	317	11.0	11.0	$34,700
Europe	567	9.7	11.6	$17,108
Democratic Asia	604	5.7	6.1	$10,100
Subtotal for wealthy democracies	1,488 (24% of global total)	$26.4 (79% of global total)	$28.7 (64% of global total)	$19,288 (average)
Rest of World				
Russia/Eurasia	221	1.9	2.2	$9,955
Central/South Asia	1,432	0.8	3.4	$2,374
Non-Democratic Asia	1,465	1.3	4.1	$2,800
Greater Middle East	320	0.8	2.3	$7,188
Latin America	522	2.0	3.3	$6,322
Africa	650	0.3	0.8	$1,231
Subtotal for rest of world	4,610 (76% of global total)	$7.1 (21% of global total)	$16.1 (36% of global total)	$3,492 (Average)
Global Totals	**6,098**	**$33.5**	**$44.8**	**$7,347 (global average)**

advantages, stable governments, cohesive societies, and skilled workforces necessary to make the most of industrialization. Gradually, they strengthened their industrial base, societies, and governments to the point of creating economic systems capable of sustaining growth through their internal dynamism. As their wealth grew, they steadily became richer than the rest of the world, still mostly agricultural countries that lacked comparable productivity. By the last half of the 20th century, the consequence was an economic hierarchy, even before globalization appeared on the scene. Today's globalization is modifying this hierarchy, but it did not create it.

In this hierarchical setting, national wealth is determined primarily by how economies perform at home, yet the past two decades have seen international commerce become increasingly important. This trend is likely to intensify in the coming years. The United States is not the only country with 25 percent of its economy devoted to trade and commerce; Western Europe and Japan fall into the same category. Countries in Asia and Latin America are also becoming more internationalist in their outlooks. China's fast growth (about 10 percent annually in recent years) is primarily the result of increases in its exports and foreign investments. This trend, however, is not manifested everywhere. The recent appearance of Western hotels, businesses, and food chains in the big cities of many far corners of the less developed world can convey the impression that local involvement in the world economy is greater than it actually is. Many poor countries still lack products to sell abroad and incentives to attract foreign investments; they stand outside the energetic activity taking place on the global scene and profit little from it.

Table 9–2 helps illustrate the major differences in international activity today by displaying exports as a share of GDP. A key point is that the wealthy democracies conduct about 77 percent of the world's exporting and thus earn most of the profits. The less

Table 9–2. Exports as Share of GDP in Regional Economies, 2004

	Percentage of GDP	Total exports (purchasing power parity) in $billions
Russia/Eurasia	12	$264
Central/South Asia	2	$68
Non-Democratic Asia	9	$380
Greater Middle East	10	$203
Latin America	11	$363
Africa	9	$72
Rest of World (not counting the wealthy democracies) Sub-Total	8	$1,350 23% of total
Wealthy Democracies	17	$4,488 77% of total
Global Average, Total	13	$5,838

developed regions export a far smaller volume, and thus earn smaller portions of their national economies: only about 23 developed regions export a far smaller volume, and smaller portions of percent of world export profits. Africa and Central/South Asia earn particularly small shares of the export market, barely over 1 percent each.

The wealthy democracies are the main beneficiaries of economic globalization for additional reasons. Fully 50 percent of global exports flow back and forth among the wealthy democracies, which provide each other with attractive markets. Another 35 percent flows between the wealthy democracies and underdeveloped regions. In terms of trade with each other, by contrast, the underdeveloped regions account for only 15 percent of the world export market. Beyond this, international economic activity takes many forms other than exports and imports. It also includes multinational corporations, foreign investments, private lending of investment capital, purchases of stocks and bonds, currency speculation, and other activities that may result in trillions of dollars flowing around the world on a daily basis. The vast majority of this activity takes place among the wealthy democracies, bypassing other countries.

These data do not mean that underdeveloped regions are cut out of the world economy altogether. Their participation has grown in recent years and doubtless will continue growing in the future. But they do not reside at the center of the world economy, nor do they benefit fully from the many stimuli of economic globalization. Some countries, such as China and its Asian neighbors, have proven successful at exporting homegrown products while also attracting foreign investments to their soil. Thus far, they have been winners in the globalization sweepstakes. Russia may be springing back to economic life. India and some other countries have succeeded at establishing export industries and services in a few urban areas, but not across their entire economies. However, many other countries, especially in Africa and the Middle East, have not yet been able to generate exports, attract foreign investment, or jump-start their own economies. Thus far, they have been losers in the globalization sweepstakes. Put another way, globalization seems to be passing them by.

Many regions and countries have become aware that command economies and high tariffs lead to slow growth and continued poverty. An international consensus has emerged that market economies, free trade, and vigorous export policies are better for gaining prosperity in the globalizing world economy. The result will likely be a better capacity for the world economy to grow at sustained rates. Even when sustained growth occurs, however, the rate of growth is not nearly fast enough to transform poor countries into rich countries or even middle-class ones overnight. Since 1990, annual growth rates for poor regions have tended to be 3 to 5 percent during non-recession periods. Over a period of 10 years, this sustained rate can increase national wealth by 35 to 60 percent. But if a poor country has a GDP-P of only $3,000 in the first year, it will still be only $4,000 to $5,000 a decade later. Population growth, moreover, may diminish this increase. As a result, it will still be a poor country when judged by the standards of the wealthy democracies, even though its citizens may have a better standard of living than during the previous decade.

Whether today's gap between rich and poor is seen as shrinking depends upon the technical standards of evaluation employed, but clearly it is not going to disappear any time soon. Table 9–3 is an illustrative forecast of where the world economy may be headed in the future if the growth rates of recent years continue to apply.

Table 9–3. **Illustrative Global Economic Forecast (in 2004 Dollars)**

	2004			2014			2024		
	Population	GDP	GDP-P	Population	GDP	GDP-P	Population	GDP	GDP-P
Wealthy Democracies	1.3B	$29T	$22,300	1.4B	$37T	$26,400	1.6B	$47T	$29,375
Rest of World	4.6B	$16T	$3,500	5.3B	$26T	$4,906	6.1B	$38T	$6,229

Presumptions: wealthy democracies will grow by 2.5 percent annually, and other regions will grow by 5 percent; wealthy democracies will experience an annual population growth of 1 percent, and other regions, 1.5 percent.

The table shows that, under certain assumptions, the wealthy democracies will grow wealthier, with a total GDP that grows from $29 trillion in 2004 to $47 trillion two decades later, and annual per capita income that grows from $19,300 to $29,735 (GDP-P).

The less developed regions in the rest of the world will experience a GDP growth that is similar in total amount, rising from $16 trillion in 2004 to $38 trillion in 2024. Although they benefit from annual growth rates of 5 percent, faster than the 2.5 percent rate for the wealthy democracies, the latter benefit from a higher foundation in 2004. As a result, each cluster gains about $20 trillion in GDP by 2024. What is of note, however, is the growth in GDP-P for poor regions, which is forecast to rise from $3,500 in 2004 to only $6,229 in 2024. In other words, even though GDP more than doubles, per capita wealth increases by only 78 percent. The reason is population growth, which reduces the wealth available to each individual. As a result, these poor regions remain relatively poor: the gap in per capita wealth between rich and poor grows by 43 percent between 2004 and 2024, from $16,000 to $23,000. This forecast suggests that even if the poor will be wealthier in absolute terms, they will still be poorer in relative terms.

This illustrative forecast is merely one of many that could suggest different futures, positive or negative. It helps illustrate broad trends in the world economy over a long period of time. While it projects a relatively happy future for the wealthy democracies, it suggests that the signs are less hopeful for the rest of the world. It conceals great variations among regions: China and Russia, for example, and maybe some other countries might gain significantly greater prosperity than average, but the average represents the large majority of countries and regions that are not benefiting from globalization with increased growth rates at or above the 5 percent global average. This forecast suggests that, while these countries and regions may slowly gain, they are not going to be elevated into the ranks of the wealthy and contented any time soon.

The looming issue for national security affairs is what this scenario does to the odds for future global peace. It does not suggest that poor regions are destined to sink into a Malthusian squalor of teeming, hopeless masses. However, it suggests that many will find themselves left behind by a globalizing, high-tech economy that is making the wealthy democracies even richer, but not providing comparable help to them or transforming their lives. This scenario could be a prescription for mounting frustration and anger in many quarters of the underdeveloped world, with considerable resentment of the United States and its allies. Thus, this scenario does not seem likely to produce a future of global peace, and it could produce the opposite. The problem is that globalization produces rising expectations in many regions, which are followed by frustration when these expectations are not met.

Over the course of a decade, a country might experience a 50 percent gain in GDP and even GDP-P, yet still be denied the benefits of modern life and find itself ever further behind the rich countries. This clash between realities and expectations can breed frustration. Tensions can rise even more in countries that grow slowly or not at all. Globalization can also exert pressures on societies to alter their traditional values so as not to lose competitive standing in world markets. As recent experience in the Middle East shows, the resulting stresses can cause antisecular, anti-Western backlashes in traditional countries that do not want to leave the past, yet resent not being wealthy. All of these factors will cause stresses in some underdeveloped regions as globalization accelerates.

As table 9–4 shows, a hypothetical future of sustained growth at 5 percent per year for 20 years would not affect all regions equally. Russia and its Eurasian neighbors would make a meaningful recovery, with a GDP-P of $19,426 by 2024, making the region middle-class. Their economies would probably allow them to pursue meaningful integration with the European Union. Latin America would also make substantial progress, with GDP-P rising to an average of $12,330; development of better manufacturing industries and services might well permit its growing integration with the North American economies.

The Middle East similarly could achieve an average GDP-P of $14,022, but this forecast is misleading because most of the gains would be in oil-rich countries. Others, such as Egypt, might attain an average GDP-P of only $9,500. Nondemocratic Asia's average per capita wealth is projected to be only $5,461, but China's could be higher, at $9,000 or so. The effect could be dangerous: China might still be economically frustrated while

Table 9–4. **Regional Growth Forecasts**

	2004		2014		2024	
	GDP (in trillions)	GDP-P	GDP (in trillions)	GDP-P	GDP (in trillions)	GDP-P
Russia/Eurasia	$2.2	$9,960	$3.6	$13,921	$5.7	$19,426
Central/South Asia	$3.4	$2,374	$5.5	$3,317	$8.8	$4,630
Nondemocratic Asia	$4.1	$2,800	$6.6	$3,913	$10.7	$5,461
Greater Middle East	$2.3	$7,189	$3.8	$10,045	$6.0	$14,022
Latin America	$3.3	$6,322	$5.4	$8,835	$8.6	$12,330
Africa	$0.8	$1,231	$1.3	$1,720	$2.1	$2,401

nonetheless rich enough to acquire greater military power and challenge the economic and political order in Asia. Central and South Asia could be similarly frustrated. India, too, might gain enough economic strength to increase its military power, thus enhancing its status as the dominant power in the region and a strategic challenger on the global stage. The great loser in this forecast is Africa, with an average GDP-P of only $2,401 by 2024. This could set the stage for considerable chaos if underfunded and overburdened governments fail to cope with rising populations, rampant poverty, and local violence.

A rosier future could be achieved if growth rates for these regions could be accelerated from 5 percent annually to 7 to 10 percent (similar to China's growth rate during the 1990s). Although this goal is embraced by the U.S. Government and the United Nations, achieving it will not be easy.[6] Indeed, even 5 percent annual growth rates may prove difficult to sustain because of the world economy's volatility. The Asian "financial flu" of 1997 showed how troubles in one region could have contagious effects worldwide. International financiers began withdrawing their capital when they sensed impending trouble as a result of flawed government policies in Thailand, Indonesia, and other Asian nations. That flight of foreign capital resulted in the collapse of those countries' currencies, stalling economies and raising unemployment. The entire global economy was soon affected and growth rates slowed. Similar jolts, such as Mexico's crises of the 1980s and 1990s and Argentina's crisis of 2002, have had comparable impacts on other regions.

The wealthy economies of the United States, Europe, and Japan are influential drivers of economic growth in poor regions. While the United States showed consistently strong growth through most of the 1990s, Europe and Japan were in the doldrums, growing only slowly. Whether Europe and Japan can shake off impediments to growth, such as excessive government control and lack of reliance on competitive markets, remains to be seen. The U.S. economy, too, is a question mark. While it is projected to continue growing, the recession of 2001–2002 showed that it remains vulnerable to the business cycle as well as to contractions when bubbles burst, as in the information technology sector. Under the Bush administration, the United States reduced taxes and interest rates to attempt to generate the savings and investments that are keys to sustained growth, but the United States seemed to reach the limits of such instruments. A devaluation of the dollar, which was under way by 2003, will stimulate exports, but this step carries risks if, as a result, the dollar is no longer perceived to be a reliable international currency.

A core problem is that the world economy continues relying heavily upon the U.S. economy as its engine of growth. While the United States has played this role through its heavy imports and foreign investments, an unintended byproduct has been a growing U.S. current-account imbalance. Through the vehicle of foreign investments in U.S. stocks and bonds, the United States has been borrowing money abroad in order to finance its imports. As a result, it is no longer a creditor nation but rather a debtor nation. To a degree, these debts are offset by foreign investments and profits earned abroad by U.S. corporations, yet if the current account deficit becomes too large, foreign investors might lose confidence in the dollar and reduce their investments in the U.S. economy. Such a development could damage its capacity to continue powering the world economy.

In order for the world economy to continue growing steadily, it needs other powerful engines. The economies of Europe and Japan figure prominently in this equation, but they will not become economic engines unless they return to sustained growth. Some observers argue that for this to happen, Europe must reduce its welfare programs and deregulate its labor markets, and Japan must strengthen its banks and stimulate growth. Other impediments also threaten continued global economic growth. For example, China and other Asian economies rely upon devaluation of currencies in order to stimulate their exports, but this reduces the capacity of other countries to export their own products to them. Trade barriers, protectionism, and subsidies in China and elsewhere also impede global growth. The Doha Talks were intended to reduce these barriers in order to enhance investments and growth of poor economies, but the collapse of the talks at the 2003 WTO meeting at Cancun, Mexico, suggested that further progress may encounter resistance from both rich countries and poor. In fall 2004, a WTO agreement on reduction of protectionist barriers offered hope of restored momentum, but the ultimate outcome remained unclear.

If the United States, Europe, and Japan were all to plunge into recession at the same time, it could trigger a prolonged global recession that would be hard to shake off even with active governmental policies aimed at stimulating growth. Some analysts fear such a global depression. While a dramatic downturn seems unlikely, periods of recession and slowed growth are real possibilities. If they occur, the result could be a stuttering world economy that grows vigorously for brief periods and then stalls, resulting in an average global economic growth rate of just 3 to 4 percent annually over the coming decades. Poor regions would then achieve growth rates of 5 percent or less, not the 7 to 10 percent growth rates that could mean major progress toward global prosperity.

Implications for U.S. Policy and Strategy

For the United States, shaping policies and strategies that not only serve its economic interests, but also promote global economic growth in ways that enhance prospects for stable security affairs, will be a continuing challenge. Doing so will require the United States to consider a wide range of factors in shaping its responses. Its highest priority will be to ensure its own economic prosperity in an era of growing dependence upon exports, imports, and the world economy. Lessening the trade imbalance by increasing exports is likely to be a key goal of the Bush administration and its successors. Achieving this goal does not promise to be easy because many countries, especially in Asia, continue to rely heavily upon export strategies and resist lowering their protectionist barriers and internal subsidies. Europe, too, clings to protectionist agricultural policies.

Some observers call for the United States to challenge these policies directly and insist on major change. Yet the United States has important dealings with many of these nations in national security affairs, making it reluctant to provoke trade wars or similar economic confrontations. This is clearly the case with Europe and Japan, but it is also true for China. If major progress is not achieved in the Doha Talks, the United States has unilateral instruments at its disposal, including reciprocal trade barriers and further devaluation of the dollar to stimulate exports and impede imports. Such steps, however, run counter to the desire to keep the dollar strong and to seek lowered trade barriers on a worldwide basis.[7]

Ensuring that the global economy continues growing at a solid sustained rate, while avoiding shocks and recessions, will remain another top U.S. priority. Success in this endeavor is important not only to promote greater worldwide prosperity, but also to help reduce geopolitical tensions in many troubled regions, including the greater Middle East and South Asia. Here, too, this agenda will not be easily accomplished, and it will require wise U.S. policy and strategy choices for many years. Effective use of U.S. instruments to help regulate international financial flows, to dampen financial crises before they become global, and to encourage aid and investments in slow-growth regions will be important. In this arena, close cooperation with multilateral partners will be key because the United States cannot guide the world economy by itself.

An important issue will be how the United States makes use of multilateral institutions. Clearly the United States will need to work closely with such global institutions as the WTO, World Bank, and IMF. Many observers expect that considerable progress can also be made through involvement with regional institutions. In Asia, such institutions as ASEAN and APEC provide a vehicle for multilateral collaboration between the United States and its partners. In the Western Hemisphere, NAFTA thus far has been a success. A central issue is whether NAFTA and a Free Trade Association of the Americas can be steadily expanded to integrate a widening set of Latin American economies more closely with North America. New bilateral accords and creation of a Central America Free Trade Association have been pursued to help achieve this goal. Some observers urge creation of a transatlantic free-trade zone. All such regional bodies offer opportunities for progress, yet they also risk dividing the world economy into competing trade blocs that erect barriers to one another. For this reason, a main challenge facing U.S. strategy, as well as that of other countries, will be to balance bilateral agreements and regional endeavors with global initiatives so that the result is an integrated world economy, each of whose separate regions capitalizes upon its own strengths.

Success at selecting a proper institutional mix, of course, will need to be accompanied by parallel success at pulling the global economic levers of influence effectively. This agenda requires expert judgments at determining how to blend many instruments, such as currency exchange rates, interest rates, lending practices, financial flows, and aid policies in order to keep the global economy, as well as its regional economies, operating steadily upward. The technical details are beyond the scope of this chapter, but it suffices here to underscore the importance of ensuring that these decisions add up to a coherent strategy that achieves its goals, rather than misfires or backfires.

From time to time, an existing strategy, anchored in a particular mix of institutional preferences and substantive practices, might need to give way to a new, better strategy that is anchored in a different mix. The key point is that at all future junctures, a clear strategy will be needed. Handling such issues will be both an economic challenge and a political one involving high-level diplomacy. This is a core reason why the United States must view international economic policy in the context of its foreign policy and national security strategy. In today's world, global economics and global security affairs are not separate and distinct. Instead, they are two sides of the same coin; they greatly affect each other, for better or worse. Progress in one area can bring progress in the other, but they can also disrupt one another. For most regions, the challenge is one of simultaneously making progress in both economics and security affairs of a sort that produces parallel, reinforcing effects. The need to integrate economics and security requires continued efforts to promote close interagency coordination within the U.S. Government. It also calls for a new form of strategic evaluation that blends global security and global economics.

In the past, national security experts and global economic experts tended to work in separate domains, each animated by analytical theories and strategic calculations that had little to do with the other. Such thinking may have been appropriate for the 20th century or the industrial age, but it no longer is a viable proposition for the 21st century, the information age, and the era of globalization. These two analytical disciplines need to be brought together, and the sooner the better. The Clinton administration took initial steps to forge a new interagency process that integrated security and economics.[8] The Bush administration took additional steps.[9] Yet success in this arena will require continued effort.

Pursuing Economic Progress for Poor Regions

The United States will continue to be concerned about fostering faster economic growth of poor regions not only because this goal is a moral imperative, but also because it has major implications for security affairs: less poverty can help breed more peace. The issue is not the importance of this goal, but achieving it with the resources at hand. While the economies of many poor countries are growing, their growth rates are slow, perhaps 4 to 5 percent per year, while their populations are rising at 1 to 2 percent per year. China's recent economic growth rate has exceeded this, and the Bush administration has called for a goal of 10 percent annual growth in poor countries, a rate aimed at bringing major progress in a decade, rather than the two to five decades that would be required at current growth rates.[10] The task of pursuing economic development in poor regions is thus one of encouraging and aiding these countries to grow faster by employing the levers of influence that can help attain this goal.

Analysis of strategy options can begin by noting that within the undeveloped world, poverty is relative, as are future expectations. Latin America, the Middle East, Eastern Europe, Russia, or "backward" parts of Asia may seem poor in the eyes of North Americans and Europeans, but judged by global standards they are middle-class. Annual GDP-P averages $6,000 to $10,000, people normally have food and shelter, and many of these regions are making strides toward joining the world economy. Where poverty is truly profound is in sub-Saharan Africa and South Asia, where annual GDP-P is only $1,000 to $3,000. There, such basics as food, shelter, and medical care are often not available. China is an anomaly because its economy is growing much faster than those of most other poor countries. Elsewhere, regional pockets, such as certain commercial zones in India, are adapting to the modern economics of the information age. Most regions, however, lack the indigenous resources, exports, and foreign investments to grow rapidly. Thus far, they have been losers, or at least not winners, in globalization.[11]

As table 9–5 shows, the economies of poor regions differ appreciably from those of other regions. The wealthy countries of North America, Europe, and democratic Asia have small agricultural sectors, moderate industrial sectors, and large service sectors. Middle-class countries tend to be dominated by industry, with moderate agriculture and service sectors. By contrast, poor countries have large agricultural sectors, with less industry and services. A core problem is that their agricultural sectors, for the most part, are not modern: they are neither highly profitable nor fast growing because domestic demand is static and their exports are limited by high protectionist barriers elsewhere. Their industrial sectors tend to be small in scale and do not generate the sophisticated industrial products and other merchandise that sell on the world market. They mostly create the kinds of services that sell in their pre-modern economies, but few that are in high demand in global markets.

Table 9–5. **Composition of Economies**

	Agriculture	Industry	Services	Total
Wealthy Countries	4%	30%	66%	100%
Middle-Class Countries	15%	50%	35%	100%
Poor Countries	40%	25%	35%	100%

Thus, helping these economies adapt so as to grow faster will require modernization of all three sectors to stimulate these countries' domestic economies and generate marketable products for exports. Their agricultural sectors need to be made capable of producing sufficient food for an urbanizing population while being reduced in size so that more workers can turn to industry. Their industries need to be enlarged and modernized, and to be made capable of producing merchandise and other goods for export. Their service industries must be expanded and altered to create information-age products that are in demand on world markets. Because these countries typically lack skilled workforces and their governments lack expert administrative skills, the requirement to enhance all three sectors means that single-dimension strategies focused on one sector will not suffice. Orchestrating phased, balanced growth in all three sectors, however, is a difficult challenge for any development strategy. Achieving three goals at the same time is normally far harder than pursuing only one goal. Doing so can take a considerable period of time even when governments, foreign investors, and internal markets work in harmony. Almost everywhere, governments of poor countries have been trying to master this challenge, but thus far, their efforts have succeeded only partly.

For the United States, pursuing global development requires different approaches to the two parts of the undeveloped world because elevating middle-class countries is inherently easier than rescuing an impoverished bottom-tier economy. Critics often say that the United States should greatly increase the amount of its financial aid to the very poor. In response, the U.S. Government in 2002 decided to increase its loans and grants each year and to seek debt relief for poor countries. But disappointing past experience shows that, apart from the beneficial effects of humanitarian aid in the form of food and medicine, loans and grants often are not used wisely, and they may have little tangible effect on poverty. Moreover, even if the United States, Europe, and Japan quintupled their annual aid, the effect would be to elevate the aggregate wealth of poor countries by only

1 percent. Over the long haul, the real solution is to help middle-class and impoverished countries reshape their economies so that they perform better and grow faster. This is the path that South Korea and Taiwan followed and that China is successfully following now. The thorny issue is determining how this goal can best be achieved and how U.S. strategy could help pursue it.

In deciding upon how to react to the challenge of global poverty, the United States has three broad strategy options. All three options for pursuing economic development of poverty-stricken regions should be appraised on their merits by strategic evaluation. The first option is to treat this endeavor in minimalist terms, confining it to a distinctly secondary status in U.S. national security strategy. The second option is to upgrade this endeavor in moderate ways that are ambitious but affordable and focused on concrete achievements. The third option is to enhance greatly the importance and priority of this goal and fund a major increase in resources for it. During the Cold War, the United States was so preoccupied with other demanding strategic priorities that it mostly pursued the first option. Liberation from Cold War pressures is now enabling it to pay closer attention to this endeavor. Pro-development critics often argue that the third option should be embraced, but practical realities, including limited resources, pose constraints. Current U.S. strategy falls into the category of the second option, even though the Bush administration's declared goal of a 10 percent annual growth rate for poor countries suggests loftier visions.

Lofty visions, however, while desirable, are no guarantee of success. Much depends upon the exact ways in which economic progress for poor countries is fostered. Fortunately, analysis of this task is aided by the existence of numerous economic theories about how to achieve faster growth. The challenge facing strategic evaluation is to sort out these theories, separate the outdated from the forward-looking, and achieve a sensible blend of their recommendations.

Only 25 years ago, a prevalent economic theory held that progress was best pursued through a strategy of command economies and national autarchy. This theory held that a government should run its country's economy and should establish high trade barriers, thereby permitting the domestic economy to grow shielded from outside competition. For example, Latin American governments often adopted this theory, as did governments in sub-Saharan Africa and the Middle East. The Thatcher and Reagan revolutions in Britain and the United States, coupled with Japan's success, gave rise to the opposite theory: that for countries to become wealthy, their governments should divest themselves of public ownership, create internal capitalist markets, and emphasize exports.

This theory, in turn, gave way in the 1990s to the theory of globalization, which held that the impersonal dynamics of a hotly competitive world economy could stimulate supply, demand, competitiveness, and faster growth almost anywhere. Governments, it was thought, could sit back and watch as, by the postulates of David Ricardo and Adam Smith, a rising tide lifted all boats. By the late 1990s, however, globalization was losing its romantic appeal. While it did help accelerate growth, it also sometimes intensified recessions and triggered chain reactions in which economic trouble in one region made big trouble for the entire world economy. Moreover, globalization often seemed to be harming poor countries as much as helping them, because they lacked the money to buy new technologies, the infrastructure to attract foreign investors, and the access to foreign markets to export their agricultural products. Disappointing experience thus showed that, globalization or not, poor countries must have the wherewithal to compete successfully if they are to profit in the world economy.

With globalization's reduced aspirations came new theories of how to use government, markets, and international institutions to enhance competitive performance and ward off the negative effects of globalization. Efforts were undertaken to use the WTO and such regional bodies as NAFTA and ASEAN and to buffer the negative effects of fast capital flows and financial transactions. In addition, under the so-called Washington consensus of the late 1990s, the IMF, World Bank, G–7, and wealthy governments would compel poor countries to undertake reforms, however painful, to lessen their internal barriers to progress; they would be pushed to improve their banking practices, strengthen their legal systems, stabilize their currencies, balance their budgets, and trim social welfare. When this theory of internal reform began faltering and backfiring, contemporary theorizing turned to a new prescription: knock down trade barriers, provide targeted aid to poor countries capable of employing it wisely, switch from loans to grants, improve infrastructure, and strengthen educational systems in order to create more productive workforces.

Economic analysis will doubtless generate more new theories and counter-theories. The art and science of fostering development may very well improve along the way. Strategic evaluation can contribute to this enterprise not only by appraising new economic theories, but also in two other ways. It can ensure that U.S. national security strategy is designed to harmonize its economic policies with its strategic endeavors in the areas of politics, diplomacy, and military affairs. Likewise, it can design ways for the United States and its partners to establish, in key regions, a foundation of stable security affairs so that economic growth can accelerate. The key point is that the challenge of crafting sensible strategies for elevating poor regions out of poverty will be with the United States for a long time to come, and strategic evaluation can help address it in more ways than one.

Strategy for Promoting Democracy Wisely

For the United States, the goal of promoting faster economic growth for poor regions is only one part of a two-part agenda. The other item on the agenda is promoting democratization in regions still ruled by totalitarian ideologies, dictators, monarchs, or traditional authoritarian regimes. Not coincidentally, these regions mostly tend to be poor or at best middle-class in economic terms. A key U.S. hope is that democratization will not only bring human freedom, but will also help create the private property and robust markets that are essential for economic progress. A related hope is that the combination of democratization and economic growth will make regions more peaceful by creating common political values and economic contentment. Democratization is thus seen as both an end in itself and a means to an end.

In his inaugural address of early 2005, President Bush trumpeted the spread of liberty and democracy as a central theme of his second term in office. Critics panned his address as a revolutionary and starry-eyed departure in U.S. foreign policy, but he stood on the shoulders of past Presidents. Before him, President Clinton publicly declared democratic enlargement to be a major goal of his foreign policy. In his stirring 1961 inaugural address, President Kennedy called upon the United States to lead the cause of democracy against communism. In the early 1940s, President Roosevelt led a global war against anti-democratic ideologies of Nazism and fascism. During World War I and afterward, President Wilson called for an idealistic U.S. foreign policy anchored in promotion of democracy and the Four Freedoms. Indeed, the Founding Fathers viewed the Declaration of Independence and the Constitution as models of liberty for the world to follow.

In the modern era, Presidential administrations from Woodrow Wilson onward have promoted democratization, but with varying strategies and expectations. Virtually all of them experienced some measure of success, but also found the going tough and the act of setting priorities anything but easy. Analysis of contemporary strategies is needed not only because pursuing this goal remains a demanding challenge, but also because the United States, in the eyes of critics, seems to have difficulty finding a proper place for democratization in its overall national security strategy. Some critics accuse U.S. foreign policy of being so engrossed in global power politics that it relegates democracy-building to the back seat, preferring to coddle dictators while it allows multinational business corporations to exploit the world's poor. Other critics hurl the opposite charge: that the United States is too prone to try to impose its values, which leads it to interfere too often in the internal politics of nondemocratic countries in ways that have counterproductive consequences.

The polar-opposite nature of these charges suggests that neither of them is fully true, and that U.S. foreign policy is somewhere in between. Striking a balance is not always easy because global trends fluctuate, frequently requiring the United States to alter the specifics of its stance. The job of strategy is, however, to maintain this balance, while the role of strategic evaluation is to help it do so by clarifying U.S. goals, showing how they best can be achieved, and identifying where they are not achievable.

The need for balance arises in democracy-building because this goal is subject both to soaring hopes and to real-world impediments. Not long ago, the collapse of Soviet totalitarianism, along with the spread of democracy in Eastern Europe, Latin America, and parts of Asia and sub-Saharan Africa, created the impression that democracy was destined to sweep over the entire world. Between 1980 and 2000, as table 9–6 shows, the number of fully democratic countries in the world doubled, while the number of nondemocratic governments declined appreciably from 41 percent of the global total to just 26 percent. By 2000, nearly half of all countries were fully democratic, and nearly 75 percent were partly or fully democratic.[12]

Of the 88 fully democratic countries in 2004, 71 of them (80 percent) are located in the Western Hemisphere, Europe, and Asia. By contrast, democracy has not yet expanded significantly into the Middle East and South Asia, where there are only four fully democratic countries. Africa is slightly better on the democratization scale, with nine countries that are counted as fully democratic. In Asia, by contrast, only a few countries are not democratic to one degree or another. However, one of them is China, with a total of about 1.3 billion people; there, a communist government still rules the biggest country on earth. In total, about one-half of the world's people live under democratic rule.

Table 9–6. **Spread of Democratization**
(Number of Countries, Percent of Total Countries in the World)

	1980		1990		2000	
Fully democratic	43	27.7%	61	36.3%	88	46.1%
Partly democratic	48	31%	39	23.2%	53	27.7%
Subtotal	91	58.7%	100	59.5%	141	73.8%
Nondemocratic	64	41.3%	68	40.5%	50	26.2%
Total (number of countries in world)	**155**		**168**		**191**	

This bifurcated pattern raises the issue of whether democracy can be installed everywhere. Doubters often say democracy requires preconditions. Some say that a country must already be industrialized and wealthy; others say that it must already be steeped in Western political and cultural values. The extreme versions of both arguments are wrong. Obviously, an industrial economy is not a precondition. The United States became a democracy in the late 1700s, when it was an agrarian country and industrialization had not yet begun. Germany and Japan became democracies while still struggling to recover from the devastation of World War II. Nor are Western values an absolute precondition: Indonesia and Turkey are the world's two biggest Islamic countries, and they are both democracies. So is India, which is mostly Hindu.

Yet the critics seem partly right. While democratization is not a deterministic process governed by rigid laws, it is affected by such underlying conditions as a country's political culture, its society and values, and its economic system. Favorable conditions, such as a civic culture, a homogenous society, and a market economy with private property, create fertile terrain for democracy to take root. Unfavorable conditions, such as authoritarian ideologies, ethnic hatreds, and hostility to private property, create infertile terrain that reduces the odds for democracy being adopted, much less succeeding. Moreover, a democracy must be able to govern effectively once it is installed. If it fails to provide security or achieve economic progress, it risks being overthrown because it lacks the credibility that begets sustained popular support.

While democracy has made great strides on fertile terrain, progress has begun to slow on infertile terrain, and there has even been backsliding. Latin America, until recently a crown jewel of democratization, has seen a populist regime of questionable democratic allegiance take power in Venezuela, a strong-arm government in Peru, political instability in Argentina, and internal violence coupled with drug trafficking in Colombia. New democratic regimes in parts of sub-Saharan Africa have been surrounded by neighbors afflicted with corrupt governments, military takeovers, and multiple ethnic wars. Democracy has not recently expanded in Asia beyond the cluster of countries now practicing it. In the greater Middle East, the number of democracies is very small, just Israel and Turkey, while Central Asia and the Caucasus are sliding back into authoritarianism, Russia seemingly is becoming a quasi-democracy at best, and China is on the improbable path to having an authoritarian government with a market economy.

The slowdown of democratization is due partly to the resistance of dictators, monarchs, and authoritarian regimes, and partly to the failure of some new democracies to create the economic miracles that were anticipated of them. It is also partly due to underlying cultural and political factors. In Africa, rampant poverty, incompetent governments, and stubborn ethnic frictions make societies too unstable to support the pluralist values of democracy. In the Middle East, fundamentalist Islamic values seemingly bar the way to democracy being widely adopted (Turkey is, so far, the only Middle Eastern country that is both Islamic and democratic). In Iran, the traditional regime of the Shah was overthrown by a populist uprising in the late 1970s, but it was replaced by a theocratic regime that has stifled representative democratic changes that might pave the way to regime change. Elsewhere, monarchies and authoritarian governments in the Middle East cling to power partly with the rationale that the alternative to them is Islamic theocratic regimes similar to that of Iran.

As of early 2005, however, democratic prospects in the greater Middle East seemed to be taking an upswing. Successful democratic elections in Afghanistan, Iraq, and Palestine were important events that sent a powerful signal across the entire region. Afterward, Egypt and Saudi Arabia announced partial steps to allow for elections, and a democratic revolt in Lebanon put pressure on Syria to remove its occupying military forces from that country. Optimists responded to these hopeful trends by proclaiming the dawn of a democratic era in the Middle East, but pessimists did not predict wholesale changes any time soon. Clearly, if democracy is to install itself across the greater Middle East and permanently take root there, it will have to overcome many powerful barriers along the way.

Together, such problems seem to create formidable barriers to democracy in many regions where underlying conditions do not favor its adoption. In Europe and the United States, democracy appeared only after societies had experienced the Renaissance, the Reformation, and the Enlightenment, as well as political and social changes that resulted in the middle classes seizing power at the expense of the aristocracy as well as the lower classes. In addition, realization grew that democracy was needed to safeguard private property and wealth-gathering by individuals, which were key to empowering capitalism. Whether other societies in the contemporary world need to undergo a similar progression can be debated, but one proposition seems valid: the presence or absence of favorable social, political, and economic conditions does have a powerful bearing on whether democracy can take hold.

The recent slowdown, accompanied by some hopeful signs in the Middle East, Ukraine, and elsewhere, has in turn raised questions about how the United States could reignite democratic expansion or at least help to consolidate the gains already made. Should the U.S. strategy toward democratization be passive, relying on U.S. democratic values to set an example, but trusting to historical forces to get the job done? Or should the United States be an activist, encouraging democracy's spread? If an active role is best, should the United States use friendly persuasion to influence countries standing on democracy's doorstep to enter the fold? Should it offer rewards and other positive incentives, or should it instead try to coerce doubters? Should it urge authoritarian governments and monarchies to adopt democracy in a single revolutionary leap, or to advance gradually, one step at a time? Such questions require answers before a wise U.S. strategy can be forged, and strategic evaluation can help answer them.

Three different U.S. approaches for spreading democracy are possible. The first strategy is to promote democracy in minor ways at the outer margins of U.S. national security strategy. The second approach is to promote democracy in moderate ways that have equal status with the other components of U.S. security strategy, and that focus on concrete, step-by-step improvements. The third possibility is to promote democracy in ambitious ways that are a dominant element of security strategy and aspire to sweeping, across-the-board improvements as quickly as possible. Choosing among the three strategies has recently been a bone of contention among the warring groups of skeptics, pragmatists, and visionaries in the U.S. debate. Because no single strategy is automatically superior to the others, all of them merit careful analysis.

In today's global setting, the first strategy, placing minor emphasis on democratization, suffers from three problems. It could be seen as betraying America's own democratic values; it would neglect an enterprise that can contribute to achievement of other national security goals; and it would fail to take advantage of opportunities that may lie ahead, particularly in the greater Middle East. By contrast, the third strategy of a full-court press for democratization suffers from the opposite problems. It could be seen as a form of American cultural imperialism; it might result in Washington paying too little attention to other national security goals; and it might have counterproductive effects in some places if it overplays its hand. This leaves the second strategy of pursuing democracy in moderate, achievable ways. President Bush appeared to have such a strategy in mind when, after his 2005 inaugural address, he indicated that democratization would be one element of U.S. national security strategy, but not the only element, and that it would be pursued responsibly with concrete achievements in mind.

The future may see the United States pursuing a mixed strategy. Such a strategy might be dominated by the second option but include elements of the other two options in regions and circumstances where they apply. Regardless of the mix of options chosen, the strategy must pass the test of coherence and be fleshed out with appropriate activities, plans, and programs. All three instruments of U.S. foreign policy can support this enterprise; diplomacy may be used to good effect, economic aid could also help, and military power might sometimes provide security guarantees that keep new democracies safe from predators. Provided that a U.S. strategy for democratization is backed by appropriate resources, its effectiveness at achieving its goals will matter as much, or more, than its exact blend of idealism and realism.

Forging a coherent strategy requires clearing away the mythology of sweeping claims and exaggerated expectations that has surrounded democracy-building in recent years. Above all, dealing with these expectations requires being clear about what "democracy" means and about the reasons for favoring its adoption. While there are many definitions of democracy, most theorists say it exists when a country provides for popular election of officials and safeguards certain basic human rights for its citizens, such as the rights of life, liberty, and the pursuit of happiness. These, however, are minimal conditions. A more demanding condition is a government that makes public policy decisions through an open process of debate and that produces policies that aim to advance the common good, not just the interests of a few.

Regardless of how it is defined, democracy centers on responsive government and respect for human freedom. While it protects the right to private property, it is not necessarily synonymous with success at creating capitalist markets, or at fostering a wealthy economy. Indeed, some democratic governments have performed poorly in the economic arena. Because of its uneven track record, democracy should not be favored solely because of its alleged ability to perform economic miracles, for it is not always a miracle worker in this arena. Remembering this distinction is key to a wise U.S. strategy because if it views democracy as a political means to an economic end, it will risk being guided by flawed expectations and misplaced priorities.

U.S. strategy also needs to acknowledge that democracy is not synonymous with Madisonian federalism, the form of government enshrined in the U.S. Constitution with its American-style separation of powers. The democracies of Britain, France, and other European countries differ from the U.S. model in their constitutions, structures, and practices. Most have prime ministers who are guided by parliaments, not powerful Presidents who lead strong executive branches and set the agenda for legislation. Most European countries have centralized governments, with fewer powers allocated to regions and provinces than in the United States. Most have multiparty systems, not two-party systems as in the United States and Britain. Aspiring democracies thus have many models to draw upon in seeking to create democratic structures that reflect their own societies, cultures, and values. Regardless of the model, the core goal is both to protect human rights and to foster economic growth, not to achieve the latter at the expense of the former.

Equally important, U.S. strategy should acknowledge that democracy is not necessarily synonymous with peace and progress. Merely because a country engages in popular elections of its leaders does not mean it has become a full-fledged democracy that protects human rights within its borders. An intolerant populist majority can elect demagogic leaders who are then empowered to oppress minorities and who snuff out further elections. For this reason, such a democracy is not necessarily a "liberal democracy" at home. For similar reasons, the sweeping proclamation that democratic countries never go to war with each other nor attack other neighbors carries a reasonable idea a step too far. Liberal values at home may, and often do, translate into liberal values abroad, but a democracy exists mainly to safeguard constitutional rights of citizens within its borders. These internal values do not necessarily mean that the peoples and governments of all countries will always apply the same values and rights to their neighbors, democratic or otherwise. In theory, a country can be liberal at home and illiberal abroad. After all, foreign policy exists to advance national interests, which sometimes can come at the expense of other countries' interests and even their safety.

In fact, when democracy first appeared in Europe during the 19th century, it was often accompanied by a populist culture widely seen as a progenitor of xenophobic nationalism, militarism, imperialism, and war. The European and North American democracies have since tamed themselves of such instincts to a considerable degree, but in other places today, prevailing ethnic hatreds and intolerant religious ideologies create an atmosphere for such malignant behavior regardless of whether a country is a democracy. Indeed, populist impulses can make a new, immature democracy more likely to go to war than a traditional monarchy guided by an instinct for cautious foreign policy.[13]

Nor should democracy be seen as always providing new allies for the United States or fostering flourishing communities of multilateral cooperation. Depending upon their assessment of their interests and priorities, some new democracies may indeed welcome close ties to the United States, but others may aspire to a neutral stance and a distant relationship. Still others may fear the United States, or despise its culture, or resent its alleged hegemony, or simply not agree with its strategic priorities. As for community-building, the transatlantic institutions that unite Europe and North America provide a model for optimism, but this community was a product of unusual circumstances and was achieved only after many years of patient effort. Elsewhere, the impulse to build communities, and the conditions to support them, are not nearly so strong. Some governments may be more jealous of their own sovereignty, an instinct that does not evaporate because democracy has taken root.

The bottom line is that analysis of U.S. strategy should treat democracy-building as a worthy goal but also as an enterprise that requires a well-honed strategy. As a goal it should be fitted wisely to the other components of national security strategy, with a clear sense of strategic priorities and of cause-and-effect relationships. Analysis, experience, and common sense have valuable observations to offer. While fostering democracy in new places can lay the foundation for other good things, such as economic growth, warm relations with the United States, and peaceful communities, they are not guaranteed, and even a happy result often comes later rather than earlier.

Some advocates claim that the United States should encourage the spread of democracy and use the pressures and incentives at its disposal to this end. Some advocates further claim that the United States sometimes should seek the overthrow of fanatical, aggressive dictatorships by military force, and attempt to implant democracy on their soil. While this rationale was part of the U.S. strategy for invading Iraq, its applicability on a consistent basis seems dubious. Democracy is not normally an idea to be advanced at gunpoint; such a practice has a way of alienating the peoples and countries being influenced, causing them to see democracy as an instrument of subjugation, not liberation.

Moreover, sometimes democracy is best advanced with a sense of caution, especially when dealing with countries that are not bent on aggression. U.S. demands for speedy democratization could damage relations with important countries such as China, leading them to crush democratic roots within their borders and to oppose U.S. policies abroad. Friendly traditional or authoritarian regimes should not be shunned because they are not democracies, provided they show proper respect for international law abroad and good governance and expansion of human rights at home. Doing otherwise could damage U.S. strategic interests more than it helps democracy, and it could hinder democratization, too. Yet common sense and experience also suggest that it is important for the United States to promote progress even in once-authoritarian places that do not take naturally to democracy. Such democratization successes as Germany, Japan, Spain, Portugal, Turkey, South Korea, and Taiwan show that the effort can be worthwhile.

Experience and analysis also suggest that the United States should not always demand instant democracy, or even push for it in places where it is remote. As South Korea and Taiwan show, sometimes strongly traditional countries should build democracy one step at a time. Democracy best takes root when the groundwork includes a solid middle class, an integrated society, a civic culture, and a functioning government that can protect the country from external and internal danger, enforce the rule of law, control inflation, and establish sound banking and business practices. When these conditions do not exist, prudence suggests that they should probably be created first, before the adoption of democracy in all its aspects. Otherwise, the consequence can be the discrediting of democracy because of its alleged incompetence at handling problems not of its making, as has happened in Russia and some Latin American countries.[14]

Strategic evaluation can aid U.S. strategy by keeping such observations in mind. Beyond this, it can expose false myths and misleading claims. It can research the likely consequences of competing approaches. It can help the United States weigh and balance alternative options. It can contribute to the design of a well-targeted strategy for democratization. It can show where democracy is a viable near-term proposition, where instead it must be pursued slowly, and where it is unlikely to take root any time soon. It can offer valuable insights on how and where to act, and what to avoid that might backfire or otherwise do more harm than good. Analysis can best support democracy-building by providing a credible, sensible theory of how to achieve success in this important arena.

Crafting Strategies that Work

For the United States, promoting global economic growth, prosperity for poor countries, and democratization makes sense not only as worthy goals in themselves, but also because success could help lessen national security dangers. President Bush was right in his inaugural address of 2005 when he said that American liberties will not be secure until human liberty is better safeguarded around the world. The same judgment applies to the importance of promoting global economic progress, for it will affect not only America's prosperity, but also its safety.

In the era of globalization, the United States faces the challenge of integrating its national security strategies with its global development strategies so that they work together in complementary fashion. As a result, a holistic approach is needed, not only for blending development strategies with security strategies, but also for integrating the three different aspects of development policy so that they work together. Success at promoting a growing global economy can help set the stage for poor countries becoming more prosperous, which can help encourage them to adopt democracy. Likewise, adoption of democracy and market capitalism can help poor countries to become wealthier, which can help empower global economic growth. For such chain reactions to take place, however, they must be encouraged by wise strategies.

Crafting sensible strategies for global development requires a commitment to activism because passivity is a recipe for failure. It also necessitates being idealistic and realistic at the same time. Above all, it requires pragmatism and a focus on the practical consequences of U.S. action. In this arena of complexity, frustration, and slow progress, the United States will require policies that apply resources in ways that attain tangible progress toward the goals being pursued. The challenge facing strategic evaluation is to help ensure not only that U.S. policies and strategies in this arena are equipped with adequate resources, but also that they deliver concrete results.

In the coming years, U.S. strategies in all three areas of development will normally need to embrace moderate goals, rather than aim lower or higher. Moderate strategies do not offer miracles overnight, but they avoid the risk of paralysis, and they can produce cumulative effects that gradually build over time. Reliance upon cumulative effects, in turn, virtually guarantees that in all three areas, no single strategy will apply equally in the near term, the middle term, and the long term. Instead, strategies will need to shift periodically in response to changing conditions. The art of strategy analysis will thus require a capacity to gauge how strategies should unfold over a period of years, changing colors and contours as they evolve.

Irrespective of the various strategies for global development adopted as the future unfolds, strategic evaluation will need to evaluate them continually. Years ago, global development was often viewed as lying outside the boundaries of security affairs. Whether this view made sense then can be debated, but it has passed into history now. In today's world, the trials and tribulations of global development have a major bearing on how the global security system will evolve, for good or ill. This prospect is ample reason for careful strategic evaluation to analyze strategies for global development and democratization, their impacts, and their implications for future security affairs in an era of fast-paced and surprising changes. Although this agenda may be a new one for strategic evaluation, it will be crucial to a hopeful outcome.

Notes

[1] For a history of European political and economic affairs during the early 20th century, see David Thomson, *Europe Since Napoleon* (New York: Alfred A. Knopf, 1962). A detailed economic history is provided by Shepard Bancroft Cole and Charles Woolsey Cole, *The Economic History of Europe* (Boston: Heath, 1947). For analysis of Europe's political and diplomatic collapse before World War I, see Barbara Tuchman, *The Proud Tower* (New York: Bantam Books, 1967).

[2] The trade theories of David Ricardo, a 19th-century economist, can be found in standard textbooks on international economics.

[3] See Paul R. Krugman and Maurice Obstfeld, *International Economics: Theory and Practice*, 4th ed. (Reading, MA: Addison-Wesley, 1997).

[4] See Robert Gilpin, *The Political Economy of International Relations* (Princeton, NJ: Princeton University Press, 1987), and *The Challenge of Global Capitalism: The World Economy in the 21st Century* (Princeton, NJ: Princeton University Press, 2000). For a historical account of global economic policy during the Cold War, see Paul A. Volker and Toyoo Gyothen, *Changing Fortunes: The World's Money and the Threat to American Leadership* (New York: Times Books, 1992).

[5] Global economic forecasts are published by the United Nations, World Bank, and International Monetary Fund. For a convenient display of annual global gross domestic product data, see International Institute of Strategic Studies (IISS), *The Military Balance 2003–2004* (London: IISS, 2003). Economic data in this chapter are drawn from these sources.

[6] The Bush administration's national security strategy of 2001 was most noted for establishing new security principles, but in its sections on global economic leadership, it also endorsed the goal of achieving 10 percent annual growth rates for poor economies. It did not provide a fully articulated strategy, plan, or program for achieving this ambitious goal.

[7] See Jagdish Bhagwati, "Don't Cry for Cancun," *Foreign Affairs* 83, no. 1 (January/February 2004); Jagdish Bhagwati, *In Defense of Globalization* (New York: Oxford University Press, 2004); Susan Esserman and Robert Howse, "The WTO on Trial," *Foreign Affairs* 82, no. 1 (January/February 2003); C. Fred Bergsten, "A Renaissance for U.S. Trade Policy," *Foreign Affairs* 81, no. 6 (November/December 2002); Joseph Quinlan, "The U.S. Trade Deficit: A Dangerous Obsession," *Foreign Affairs* 81, no. 3 (May/June 2002).

[8] See the Clinton administration national security strategies during its tenure, including *A National Security Strategy for a Global Age* (Washington, DC: The White House, 2000).

[9] See the Bush administration's *Economic Report of the President* (Washington, DC: The White House, 2003). See also Steven Radelet, "Bush and Foreign Aid," *Foreign Affairs* 82, no. 5 (September/October 2003); Bernard K. Gordon, "A High-Risk Trade Policy," *Foreign Affairs* 82, no. 4 (July/August 2003).

[10] While the Bush administration's national security strategy endorsed this goal and sought to increase American economic aid to poor countries, it did not aspire to the great increases of aid that would, themselves, bring about 10 percent increases in gross domestic product. The implication was that the bulk of the work would have to be done by other instruments, including multilateral aid, foreign investments, and most importantly, by growth-oriented policies by poor countries.

[11] See International Monetary Fund (IMF), *World Economic Outlook*, October 1999 (Washington, DC: IMF, 2002); The World Bank, *World Development Indicators 2000* (Washington, DC: World Bank, 2000); Nicolas van de Walle, *Economic Globalization and Political Stability in Developing Countries* (New York: Rockefeller Brothers Fund, 1998); World Bank, *World Development Report 2004* (Washington, DC: World Bank, 2004); World Economic Forum, *The Global Competitiveness Report 2002–2003* (London: Oxford University Press, 2003).

[12] See Samuel P. Huntington, *The Third Wave: Democratization in the Late Twentieth Century* (Norman: University of Oklahoma Press, 1991).

[13] See Fareed Zakaria, *The Future of Freedom: Illiberal Democracy at Home and Abroad* (New York: Avon, 2004); Edward D. Mansfield and Jack Snyder, *Electing To Fight: Why Emerging Democracies Go to War* (Cambridge, MA: The MIT Press, 2005); Edward D. Mansfield and Jack Snyder, "Democratization and the Danger of War," *International Security* 20, no. 1 (Summer 1995), 5–38.

[14] For analysis, see Barrington Moore, Jr., *Social Origins of Dictatorship and Democracy: Lord and Peasant in the Making of the Modern World* (Boston: Beacon Press, 1993), plus many other scholarly writings on the sources of democracy.

Part II—Systems Analysis

Chapter 10
Overview

Basic U.S. national security policies and strategies are shaped by policymakers who apply political and strategic analysis. But once such policies and strategies are crafted, the demanding business of carrying them out is often given to managers and economists, who typically must make many difficult decisions regarding how resources are applied in order to pursue the policies and goals that have been endorsed. One of the principal analytical methods that they commonly use is systems analysis, which is a technique for assessing complex plans and programs, and for helping determine how large sums of money—often billions of dollars—can best be spent on them. In the defense arena, systems analysis includes, for example, methods for assessing military balances, requirements, and force posture priorities, using such economic decision models as the curve of diminishing marginal returns and the program optimization model. Systems analysis deals with macro-choices, not micro-details. Its purpose is to help get resource allocation decisions roughly right, while preventing them from being precise but wrong. It can be used to block bad ideas, but it also is often used to help foster good ideas, including innovations whose time has come.

Systems analysis especially is used to help shape defense plans, programs, and budgets, but it also can help analyze other foreign policy and national security efforts that employ significant money and resources. Systems analysis is similar to operations research, which is examined in the final third of this book, in that both are instruments for cost-effectiveness studies, and both are used to help make programs more effective and more efficient. Systems analysis, however, is broader-gauged than operations research. It commonly is employed when the task involves multiple assets and activities and one or more goals. By contrast, operations research is employed for analysis of one or a few assets or activities. In defense policy, for example, systems analysis might be used to determine how to assemble air transports, cargo ships, and prepositioned equipment into an overall strategic mobility program. Operations research might be used to determine how many air transport C–17 aircraft should be bought. Systems analysis thus has a wider focus, and considers more complex issues, than operations research. Typically it is the method of choice when senior U.S. Government officials must make decisions on large, expensive defense plans and programs that involve multiple elements.

Keeping an Eye on Defense Resources: The Stakes are High

While national security policy is a public good, it does not come free of charge; the national security business costs money, and lots of it. The Department of Defense alone spends over $400 billion annually, and the expenses of other agencies, including the State Department, the Intelligence Community, and the Department of Homeland Security, add to the total. This money must be extracted from the Federal treasury and the taxpayer. Money that is allocated to national security cannot be spent on other worthy endeavors, such as roads and schools, or returned to the common citizen in the form of tax cuts that could augment savings and investments. The Federal budget is not a bottomless horn of plenty, nor is the United States is so rich that it can afford to waste money on national security. President John F. Kennedy once said that the United States should find out what military forces are needed and then buy them as inexpensively as possible. His remark remains as true today as it was in 1961, for defense policy and for the entire national security business.

The idea that the United States should economize in this arena does not sit well with those who feel that because national security is so important, it should be given whatever resources are needed to meet requirements and quell threats. While these sentiments are understandable, the fact is that requirements are hard to pinpoint precisely, and national security is impossible to guarantee with certainty. For example, even a fully prepared military force that enjoys a high probability of winning a prospective war will still have some chance of losing if the breaks go wrong. Because dangers and risks will always exist, the task is one of reducing them to acceptable levels and manageable proportions. Although there is a big difference between being well-insured and poorly insured against threats, it is impossible to define a precise level of resources above which success is guaranteed and below which failure is certain. Almost always, it is better to have more resources. The principal issue is the confidence that the United States wants in its national security endeavors, and the levels of expense that it is willing to bear in order to gain this confidence. Like it or not, these are economic judgments made at the margins, where extra capacity to pursue strategic goals must be balanced against the added expense, and where the opportunity to invest in one area must be weighed against the sacrifice of another.

As a practical matter, national security policies are seldom funded to the maximum. As experienced government executives know, even high-priority programs typically receive only about 70–85 percent of the resources that arguably could be spent on them. Their managers are expected to make up the difference by stretching their money as far as possible and get the best performance feasible. The extent to which funds are tight, of course, varies with the times. During the Carter administration and the early years of the Clinton administration, national security spending was kept low and funds were unusually tight. During the Reagan era, spending increased greatly and an expanded agenda became possible. The same has applied to the Bush administration since 2001. But even during periods of fiscal largesse, the Department of Defense and other agencies seldom get all the money they want and arguably could use. There always are compelling incentives to spend money as effectively and efficiently as possible.

Indeed, spending wisely can matter as much, or more, than how much is spent on critical endeavors. Experience shows that a poorly constructed national security program can receive all the money it needs and still fail. The U.S. military in the Vietnam War suffered from lack of vision, not lack of money. The French Army lost to the German Wehrmacht in 1940 not because it lacked weapons, but because it did not have an adequate grasp of how to counter-maneuver against a blitzkrieg attack through the Ardennes forest. It is far from the only army that experienced defeat because it failed to hedge against surprising events by developing adequate agility. The United States today has the biggest defense budget and the best military in the world, but this advantage is no guarantee that it will win future wars if it does not apply its money and forces sensibly. The wise use of resources can, however, matter a great deal in fostering enhanced performance, and can help make up the difference when funds are short. Throughout the Cold War, NATO's military forces never had more than 70 percent of the funds that many argued were needed for defenses in Europe. Yet over the years, NATO developed a reputation for spending its limited funds wisely. It gradually built a stronger military posture to the point where, by the late 1980s, the Warsaw Pact's fabled military superiority was fading. NATO may have lacked adequate money, but it won the Cold War by employing its assets effectively: a lasting monument to sound planning that combined military wisdom and economic common sense.

Although systems analysis largely has acquired a reputation of being a tool for cost-cutting, it can be employed with equal impact to help create greater effectiveness in U.S. military forces and operations. Indeed, systems analysis has made many lasting contributions in this arena. Its positive contributions during the Cold War are too numerous to list, but include path-breaking analyses of nuclear war, the military balances in Europe and Korea, defense of the Persian Gulf, and priorities for building U.S. conventional forces. Since then, systems analysis has helped encourage numerous innovations in U.S. military forces, and is now being used to help guide defense transformation. Regardless of how it is used, it is best seen not as a tool composed of economic curves and mathematical equations that are applied in mechanical ways, but instead as a way of thinking in orderly, systematic terms. Typically, it makes its most valuable contributions when it is employed to bring conceptual order to a new and complicated issue that had theretofore been indecipherable. When it provides such intellectual coherence in ways that help produce better policy decisions, it performs its mission, irrespective of whether the ultimate consequence is less spending, or more spending, or different spending.

Contents of this Section

This section focuses on the role of systems analysis in defense planning and program evaluation. Systems analysis can be applied to many national security endeavors besides defense policy. But because the defense budget is so large, systems analysis typically plays its biggest role in this arena. Defense planning focuses on the relationship between strategy and force posture, while program evaluation helps guide resource allocation in macroscopic ways. Systems analysis is capable of making important contributions to both functions. In doing so, it can help discern the economic problems and challenges facing the U.S. military, and it can help forge sensible solutions to them. It can help ensure that the U.S. force posture is well designed to carry out national defense strategy, and it can help guide the creation of major defense programs so that U.S. military forces become as effective and efficient as possible. It can help spell the difference between a military posture that is only marginally effective in carrying out U.S. defense strategy and one that is highly effective. As such, it is a natural friend of wise political leadership and professional military judgment.

This section has six chapters. Chapter 11 provides a theoretical overview of the key analytical methods typically employed by systems analysis for both defense planning and program evaluation for resource allocation. The other five chapters illuminate how systems analysis can be applied to evaluating contemporary issues and options in defense planning and programming. Chapter 12 examines systems analysis methods for helping shape the overall size and composition of U.S. conventional forces. Chapter 13 examines the role of systems analysis in guiding defense transformation, the process of implementing major changes in forces and major increases in capability as part of a transition from the industrial age to the information age. Chapter 14 shows how systems analysis can help to assess the changing roles of air and ground forces in joint expeditionary warfare, and how to make appropriate changes, especially in ground force structures, to carry out these new roles. Chapter 15 examines the role of systems analysis in charting the modernization of air and naval forces through the procurement of new weapon systems. Chapter 16 surveys the role of systems analysis in helping chart future U.S. defense budgets and their allocation of funds among internal claimants.

Sometimes systems analysis can be used as a stand-alone technique, for instance, when the issue being examined does not require a larger strategic context and when great attention to details is not necessary; an example of this is in chapter 14, which deals with combined air-ground operations. But when both context and details are needed, systems analysis is best used in concert with strategic evaluation and operations research in ways that produce a truly multidisciplinary approach. Chapters 12 and 13 are examples of systems analysis being employed along with strategic evaluation. Chapters 15 and 16 are examples of systems analysis being blended with operations research. Together, the six chapters of this section help illuminate the prospects and limits of systems analysis, both standing alone and working alongside its brethren.

A central theme emerges from this section: although many systems analysis methods will remain relevant, new methods anchored in new concepts and techniques will be needed, because the core issues facing the defense community—issues regarding the interplay between strategic requirements and resource priorities—are mutating rapidly. A new form of defense planning and program evaluation, one significantly different from the approaches of earlier years, is being mandated by major changes taking place in U.S. defense strategy and transformation policies. The challenge facing systems analysis is to preserve useful methods while creating new ones. This is a fitting challenge for an established discipline that already has proven its mettle, yet must demonstrate its innovative vigor for an era that will mandate a robust combination of mature steadiness and youthful energy.

Chapter 11
Methods of Systems Analysis

Systems analysis can be illuminated by first portraying its theoretical components and then examining how it is applied in concrete ways to defense planning and program evaluation. This chapter performs the first of these tasks. It begins by discussing the contributions of systems analysis in the defense arena. Next, it examines the essence of systems analysis: its focus on systems of military assets, activities, and outputs. It then discusses methods of systems analysis that are commonly employed for addressing such crucial defense planning issues as force balances in key theaters. Finally, it discusses economic models of choice, often employed by systems analysis to help guide program evaluation.

Chapter 11 thus portrays theoretical methods in the abstract. It describes how the methods of systems analysis can be employed to help define the problems and challenges facing the U.S. military and to determine how to pursue cost-effective strategic and programmatic solutions. As this chapter shows, systems analysis is composed of a family of methods. They should be employed selectively to respond to the analytical challenges at hand. These methods can help shed light on U.S. military posture, programs, and budgets, subjects that are exceedingly complicated and require great skill to analyze. Defense policy deals with deciding how to employ U.S. forces today and how to build forces for tomorrow. Systems analysis can contribute to immediate questions of force employment, and it is especially useful in addressing questions about the future U.S. military posture, to assure that it will be capable of meeting challenges 5 to 10 years from now and beyond. Making wise decisions in the force development arena is critical to future national security. When used properly, systems analysis can help tilt the odds toward wisdom not only in setting goals, but also in applying money and resources sensibly.

Contributions of Systems Analysis

A brief discussion of how systems analysis contributes to decisionmaking can help set the stage for discussion of this methodology and its various components. Systems analysis was originally created to help the U.S. Government make wise economic choices in using scarce resources. It was first introduced in the Pentagon during the early 1960s by Secretary of Defense Robert McNamara, who used it in vigorous and controversial ways. McNamara created a systems analysis staff in the Office of the Secretary of Defense, and installed a planning, programming, and budgeting system to guide the formation of the DOD budget. From there, systems analysis spread throughout DOD and elsewhere in the national security community. In one way or another, most defense agencies continue to employ this method today to help forge their budgets and programs.[1]

During the McNamara years and afterward, systems analysis made many contributions to U.S. nuclear force planning. Another classic use of systems analysis was in assessing the

NATO/Warsaw Pact conventional military balance in Central Europe during the Cold War. This contribution paved the way to major improvements in NATO defense strategy. The common perception had been that NATO was hopelessly outgunned by a vastly larger Warsaw Pact force of 90 ground divisions and 4,200 combat aircraft. Systems analysis punctured this illusion by pointing out that although NATO's combat forces were numerically smaller than those of the enemy, they had better weapons, readiness, and logistic support, thus appreciably narrowing the difference in overall combat power. All things considered, the forces were closer to balance than superficial comparisons had suggested. This meant that a viable forward defense was feasible if NATO did a better job of organizing its forces and applying its investment resources in highly leveraged ways.

Another case of positive impact was the role of systems analysis in defining how the Persian Gulf could be defended. When this issue first surfaced in the late 1970s and early 1980s, many observers felt that the Gulf was too distant from the United States, and threats too near it, for the U.S. military to be able to perform serious missions. Surface appearances suggested that the Soviet Union and such nearby rogue states as Iraq could seize the Persian Gulf oilfields before the United States could stop them. But once again, misleading surface appearances gave way to a more favorable appraisal when the details were considered. Systems analysis pointed out that potential attackers were constrained by distance, bad terrain, and their own lack of ready forces and logistics support. Systems analysis further showed that if U.S. tactical air forces were sped to the Persian Gulf, and if mobility forces were strengthened enough to be able to move ground forces there in a few weeks, U.S. combat forces could deploy fast enough to get the job done. The historic result was the decision to create the Central Command military posture, which went on to win the 1991 war against Iraq.[2]

Dramatic examples like these are the exception, but systems analysis often plays a quieter role in helping settle bureaucratic wars over budgets and programs. Systems analysis is a common technique for determining what level of resources should be allocated to individual programs to increase them or to scale them down. It also can help strike an optimal balance in allocating resources between two or more competing programs, such as between ground and air forces, an issue that spawns endless debates within the Pentagon. It has similarly been useful in helping resolve bureaucratic disputes and striking programmatic balances in other departments as well.

Systems analysis has a reputation for peering through a fog of confusion and obfuscation to ask the right questions, which is the first step toward getting the right answers. What makes systems analysis especially useful is that it offers an opportunity to see a strategic situation or a U.S. military operation as a whole, rather than only in parts. Its capacity to view matters holistically is important because an analysis that sees only part of the picture risks serious misinterpretation, a fault of many narrowly focused studies. For example, U.S. military operations cannot be properly understood by looking only at ground forces; air forces and naval forces must be considered as well. When systems analyses have succeeded in the past, the reason has often been that they saw the entire picture and thus were able to craft better responses.

A systems analysis can address multiple goals or a single dominant goal. Even in that case, however, multiple sub-objectives must often be assessed according to appropriate standards of evaluation. Regardless of the number of goals and objectives, systems analysis typically focuses on multiple force elements and programmatic activities. This capacity to assess multiple forces and activities that work together toward one or more goals is a hallmark of systems analysis. As a result, systems analysis can be a complex undertaking; it requires a searching appraisal of how diverse activities produce military performance in various forms. Systems analysis requires comprehensive concepts, analytical models that portray input functions and output characteristics, measures of effectiveness and criteria for evaluation, and quantitative data. Systems analysis is not an easy methodology to master, but it can have considerable analytical power.

Essence of Systems Analysis

Systems analysis is, simply stated, the analysis of systems.[3] This definition may sound trite or even tautological, but it reveals the essence of the method, which scrutinizes systems closely in order to determine how they can be made to work better. While there is no standard recipe for using this method—each study must be tailored to its specific purposes—systems analysis normally is carried out through a two-stage process. First, it determines how the subject takes the form of a system. Sometimes systems have distinct and obvious shapes in the real world (for example, a U.S. military organization). Other times, they are more difficult to discern (for example, two military forces fighting each other in new and unanticipated ways). On still other occasions, they are mainly intellectual constructs imposed upon reality to help organize it conceptually (for example, a regional security system or economic system). Systems analysis devotes considerable attention to determining how the system operates and what it produces. Next, systems analysis applies planning methods and economic models of choice in order to determine how the performance of that system can be improved in desired ways. Typically, these economic models take the form of graphical curves or simple arithmetical formulations that portray costs and effectiveness of policy and program options under consideration. The famous

Figure 11–1. **Illustration of a System**

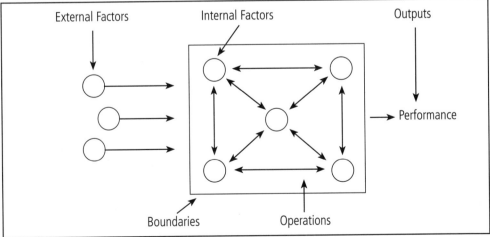

curve of diminishing marginal returns, discussed below, is one example of an economic model of choice.

A system, stated abstractly, is any set of regularly interacting factors and activities that has definable boundaries and that produces measurable outputs (see figure 11–1). For example, the human body is a system; viewing it this way has greatly helped medical science create cures for illnesses. A system can be large or small, and it can be composed of many different features, including variables, constants, structures, functions, and values. Regardless of its size and makeup, a system is a living entity (or at least can be usefully viewed this way) that does something important in ways that affect both itself and the world around it. The key point is that its internal factors are powerfully bonded in ways clearly separating them from the outside world, and it produces results that are important and worth manipulating. While external factors may affect how the system operates, its internal factors have the most influence on outputs and performance.

In the national security arena, a good example of a system is a large military force. It is a concrete organization, it has unique assets, it has a doctrinal ethos, it has regular operating procedures, it performs specific functions, it easily can be distinguished from its surrounding environment, and it produces something tangible: combat power, the capacity to wage war against opposing military establishments. Likewise, two military forces fighting on a battlefield can be conceptualized as a system composed of two organizations interacting in patterned ways. Figure 11–2 illustrates a system of U.S. military forces that face adversary forces. The U.S. posture is composed of multiple components that operate together in battle to produce combat power against the enemy.

Systems such as these have easily recognized physical characteristics. Other systems may be more nebulous but, for the purposes of analysis, they are systems all the same. An example is a regional security system composed of neighboring countries that interact in regular ways that produce war or peace. Another example is the world economic system, which governs the flow of commerce among nations. Yet another example is U.S. foreign aid, a system of activities that provides loans, grants, and other support to needy countries. Regardless of whether they are concrete or abstract, the properties of such systems can be examined in order to help determine how money can be spent to pursue national security policies and goals.

Figure 11–2. **Illustration of a Military System**

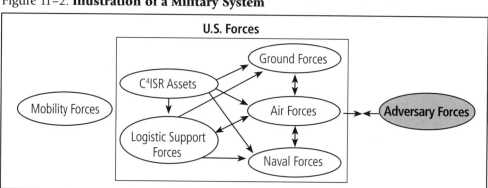

Systems analysis in the defense arena mostly focuses on two issues: the nature of the military environment and the combat situations in which U.S. forces are likely to operate, and steps that can be taken to improve the effectiveness or efficiency of U.S. forces. In addressing both issues, systems analysis often uses models to help guide its inquiries. A model is a set of postulates, data, and inferences that are intended to portray a system, how it operates, and how its products can be improved. For example, the mathematical equation $y = 5ax + by + z$ can be a model if it purports to describe some real-life phenomenon. The same applies to almost any graphical curve. Whether verbal, formal, or mathematical, a model is a miniature representation of a system. It does not attempt to portray all of the manifold features of a complex system, but tries to capture just the core features of the system that must be understood because they play key roles in determining how the system operates and how its outputs can be controlled.

A model normally strives for both parsimony and analytical power so that it is user-friendly but also capable of producing meaningful results. A model can be as simple as an equation or graph, or it can be highly elaborate and complex, such as a dynamic computer simulation with dozens of interactive differential equations. What matters is not the complexity of a model, but its analytical power, relevance, and capacity to generate insights that can be used for decisionmaking. Some of the most successful models have been written on the backs of envelopes, while an elaborate computer model may be too complex for users to understand or prone to colossal error because mistakes in its postulates, equations, or data were impossible to detect.

A systems analysis might use a single model for study, or more than one model, or a large family of models. Typically, a systems analysis will employ one model to portray a military environment in which U.S. forces are operating, and then a second model to help make judgments about resource allocation. For example, a study might employ a model of combat to generate a forecast of how a hypothetical war might unfold. Based on the results, it might then employ an economic decision model to help determine program priorities for strengthening U.S. forces for fighting such a war. Such models sometimes draw upon the techniques of operations research. Although systems analysis has a more macroscopic focus than operations research, they are not mutually exclusive disciplines but can be complementary. Systems analysis often employs the methods of operations research in order to enhance its depth and detail, especially when macro-judgments are dependent upon micro-details as, for example, when decisions about the number of weapons to buy hinges upon the lethality of those weapons in small-unit engagements.

In addition to models, systems analysis also requires measures of effectiveness (MOEs) and criteria of evaluation in order to assess the performance of a force posture or program. For example, one MOE might be the number of enemy targets destroyed per day; another might be the amount of terrain defended or seized per month. MOEs, usually stated in quantitative terms, must be derived from the defense goals being pursued, and they must provide an accurate measure of whether these goals are, in fact, being achieved. By itself, an MOE does not measure whether a force is operating effectively, and therefore MOEs must be accompanied by criteria for judging effectiveness. For example, one criterion might be destroying 80 percent of an enemy's armored force in 2 weeks. Another criterion might be occupying an enemy's country and toppling its government in a month. Like MOEs, criteria of evaluation must stem logically from the defense goals being pursued. A good systems analysis will strive to ensure that its MOEs and criteria of evaluation can be used to gauge the degree to which defense plans and programs are attaining the goals assigned to them.

The analytical models, MOEs, criteria of evaluation, and graphical curves employed by systems analysis to help make decisions about defense planning and program evaluation must be generated through intense analytical work to assemble accurate data on costs and effectiveness. In order to use this data effectively, systems analysis employs a variety of tools, ranging from simple back-of-the-envelope calculations to static models to dynamic computer simulations of the sort used in operations research. In a systems analysis, being technically accurate is important, but before such accuracy can be attained, conceptual power and insight must first be achieved. What matters most in a good systems analysis is the intellectual order that it brings to a problem: its ability to get things approximately right and thereby avoid gross error. Thus, for quantitative data and economic curves to be useful, they must rest upon investigation and appraisal. Systems analysis works best in the hands of people who pay close attention to how systems operate.

Systems Analysis for Defense Planning

Defense planning focuses on the relationship between strategy and force posture. It is meant to ensure that U.S. defense strategy is sound and well focused, and to ascertain what type of U.S. military posture is needed to carry out that strategy. In performing these two tasks, analysts seek to create a framework of coherent defense plans that enables programs to be evaluated. Decisions on how to invest money in order to strengthen military forces cannot be made until the force posture and defense strategy are clarified. Systems analysis can contribute to defense planning in a variety of important ways, each of which requires methods suited to the occasion. Over the years, use of systems analysis for defense planning has resulted in a family of five key methods that have important applications:

- strategy analysis, which compares alternative strategies
- force balance assessment, which compares the size and strength of two opposing forces
- requirements analysis, which assesses how many U.S. and allied forces are needed to attain defense goals
- force posture analysis, which assesses alternative forces structures and mixes
- capability-based analysis, which determines how a flexible and modular force can be built to handle a wide spectrum of demands.

Methods of Strategy Analysis

National security strategy articulates a synthesis of ways to employ the main instruments of power—political diplomacy, military power, and economic strength—to pursue strategic goals in world affairs. Defense strategy is a component of national security strategy. Its purpose is to provide strategic guidance on how military forces can best be built and employed in order to achieve national goals in global security affairs during peace, crisis, and war. Crafting a defense strategy is a complex undertaking. Equally demanding is the task of comparing alternative defense strategies in terms of performance, costs, feasibility, and tradeoffs. The strategic evaluation methods described earlier in this book play a role in this enterprise, but systems analyses are important too. Indeed, defense strategies are best built through a *combination* of strategic evaluation and systems analysis.

Systems analysis can contribute by focusing on the ways in which alternative strategies apply means to achieve ends, and on the mechanisms by which military actions are expected to produce desirable strategic consequences. Systems analysis may often help distinguish faulty logic in some strategies from insightful reasoning in others. During the Cold War, for example, systems analysis played a role in helping resolve the debate between massive retaliation and flexible response. It raised critical questions about the assertion that the threat of massive nuclear retaliation could deter not only nuclear aggression, but conventional aggression as well. Systems analysis helped point out that a nuclear-armed adversary might calculate that it could conduct conventional aggression without fear of a nuclear reprisal because the resulting escalation could destroy the United States and its allies. Accordingly, systems analysis lent credibility to the argument that stronger conventional defenses and a strategy of flexible response were needed in order to achieve across-the-board deterrence. Systems analysis also helped make the case that adequate conventional defenses were affordable in economic terms because Soviet forces were not irretrievably superior to U.S. and allied forces. By showing that conventional defense was an economically viable alternative, as well as a strategic necessity, systems analysis cemented the case for switching U.S. strategy from massive retaliation to flexible response.

In today's world, the goal of conventional defense is taken for granted, but many issues arise regarding the nature of U.S. defense planning on behalf of this goal. For example, a critical issue has been the number of regional wartime contingencies that U.S. forces should be prepared to handle simultaneously. Should U.S. forces be prepared to wage only one regional war at a time, two simultaneous wars, or three or more wars at the same time? The answers to these questions depend partly upon strategic evaluations of adversaries' goals and strategies in contemporary world affairs. But the answers also depend upon U.S. goals, risk-management standards, and economic judgments. Being prepared for multiple wars provides greater capabilities and insurance than being prepared for only one war, but it also is more expensive than a one-war strategy. Systems analysis addresses the questions about force sizing by assessing the exact relationship between strategic goals and economic costs in this arena, by identifying risks and tradeoffs, and by helping determine the point at which adequate security is attained and additional insurance would not be worth the cost. In other words, systems analysis can help provide a sense of the marginal costs and benefits for alternative defense strategies and force postures.

Thus far, U.S. defense strategy for the post–Cold War world has chosen to field enough military forces to wage two concurrent regional wars: not one war, not three wars. This decision partly reflects judgments about the likelihood of multiple wars erupting at the same time, as well as U.S. strategic goals in key regions. But it also reflects an economic judgment that a two-war posture is a cost-effective choice, and that whereas a one-war posture would provide insufficient forces, a three-war posture would be too costly for the insurance it would provide. To an important degree, systems analysis is a source of this economic judgment; it ratifies the argument that while the benefits of a two-war posture are sizable, the marginal benefits of being able to wage an additional war might not be worth the cost of acquiring this capability.

Systems analysis can contribute to the appraisal of defense strategies in both peace and war. Defense strategy is intended to provide a choreographed and coordinated set of military actions that result in the achievement of multiple national goals. Systems analysis can scrutinize strategies to ensure that the prescribed actions make sense and are appropriately combined and coordinated. Over the years, systems analysis has been instrumental in helping determine how military forces could be built and employed to promote such peacetime goals as containment, deterrence, forward defense, flexible response, and alliance reform. Along with operations research, systems analysis has been used to help plan the U.S. overseas military presence, rapid reinforcement programs, security assistance policies, multilateral defense plans, and alliance defense improvement agendas. In all of these complex arenas, development of defense strategy requires the capacity to assess multiple activities and to guide program evaluation. In these arenas, there will doubtless continue to be a need for systems analysis well into the future.

Systems analysis also can contribute to the evaluation of force operations in wartime. Determining exactly how to employ military forces on the battlefield can be a difficult task full of uncertainties and controversies. Systems analysis is not necessarily a good tool for generating battlefield employment options—this is normally the province of professional military judgment—but it can help contribute to the appraisal of these options by assessing their likely effectiveness, costs, and risks. For example, it can help compare the relative merits of a strategy that relies mainly upon air power to a strategy that employs a balance of air and ground forces (an issue that arose in the wars in Kosovo and Iraq). It can be used to compare linear and nonlinear operations, or sequential and simultaneous operations. By illuminating the strong points and drawbacks of each battlefield strategy, systems analysis can help senior political and military officials make judgments about their worth in specific circumstances.

The key point is that while systems analysis is not necessarily a good technique for creating alternative defense strategies in peace and war, it provides useful methods for evaluating them. The choice of strategy is often a close call that involves weighing and balancing complex tradeoffs. Systems analysis offers three important advantages in this arena: the capacity to develop a holistic understanding of the security environment in which defense strategy is operating; the capacity to assess strategy alternatives in terms of their activities and consequences; and the capacity to apply economic reasoning to the choice of strategy to highlight the force needs, resource implications, and budget costs of each option. Sensible use of these tools can help spell the difference between sound choices and mistakes.

In this day and age, high-level DOD studies seldom focus on defense strategies in the abstract, but instead address alternative strategies and force postures. For such a study, the best approach is normally to generate a spectrum of options that present distinct strategic choices in terms of goals, force levels, and spending. Table 11–1 illustrates a spectrum of options that are more ambitious and less ambitious, as well as the current strategy and force posture. Once such a spectrum of options is created, the task of analysis is to compare them in terms of ability to attain national goals, military effectiveness, confidence levels,

Table 11–1. **Alternative Strategies and Force Postures**

	Less Ambitious Defense Strategy	Current Defense Strategy	More Ambitious Defense Strategy
Strategic Concept	Prepare for one regional war plus small contingencies	Prepare for two regional wars	Prepare for two regional wars plus small contingencies
Force Posture	20% smaller than now	Same as now	20% larger than now
Budget	10% smaller than now	Same as now	15% larger than now

tradeoffs, uncertainties, budgetary policies, and other considerations. Doing so can illuminate the key issues and choices for senior officials, helping them make decisions in a balanced manner that takes into account strategic performance and economic constraints.

Methods of Force Balance Assessment

Systems analysis makes one of its most important contributions to defense planning by assessing military force balances in regions of likely wartime contingencies, or where peacetime military competition might influence political-strategic trends. Assessing force balances—the relative strength of adversary forces and U.S./allied forces—is important for obvious reasons. Developing an accurate appraisal of force balances is critical to forging sound strategies, building effective defenses, and pursuing sound programs. An insightful assessment of force balances may spell the difference between U.S. military responses that achieve their goals and those that fall short or are wide of the mark. Accurate assessments can reduce the risk of underestimating dangers, overestimating them, or misconstruing them in ways that result in unwise decisions for forces and programs.

Producing accurate force balance assessments is often anything but easy. Adversary forces are typically structured so differently from U.S. and allied forces that comparisons are not obvious. Prevailing assessments of the balance may be anchored in flawed judgments that resist appraisal because they are deeply and unquestioningly held. Even when minds are open to new insights, force balance assessment can be demanding and time-consuming. It requires attention to many details and a capacity to employ techniques that compare differing military assets in terms of common performance parameters. It requires a thorough knowledge of force characteristics on both sides, along with quantitative data that portray the full range of factors that merit consideration. Because accurate force balance assessments can be invaluable, however, systems analysis has pioneered this endeavor.

A systems analysis of a force balance begins by conducting a thorough appraisal of mobilization and reinforcement rates for both adversary and U.S./allied forces. When a crisis erupts, the forces of both sides may not be arrayed against each other along a border or some other defense line. Instead, many may be a considerable distance away. In order to begin fighting, they must be moved from the rear to forward areas. This can be time-consuming, because military forces are large and cumbersome. A ground force of 10 divisions can field 300,000 troops, 4,000 tanks and infantry fighting vehicles, 2,000 artillery tubes and mortars,

100,000 trucks and small vehicles, and ammunition and other supplies; the total weight is 3 million tons. For an impending war, a critical advantage may accrue to the side that does the best job of transporting its forces swiftly to the battle zone. If the adversary succeeds in deploying its forces faster than U.S. and allied troops, it may gain a decisive temporary advantage even if it lacks a meaningful edge in fully deployed equipment and manpower. If fighting erupts before U.S. and allied forces are fully deployed, the adversary might be able to translate its temporary advantage into victory. Creating an effective military strategy thus begins with ensuring that U.S. and allied forces can deploy to the battle zone fast enough. Deploying rapidly can be a challenge to allied forces stationed miles from the battle zone, and even more so for U.S. forces thousands of miles away in the United States.[4]

Appraising mobilization and reinforcement rates requires consideration of many interacting variables. The readiness of forces on both sides must be analyzed carefully, for this can make a major difference in deployment rates. A military force that is fully trained and equipped may be ready to move within a few days of notice, while a force that lacks adequate training and well-maintained equipment may require weeks or months of preparations before it can move. Another consideration is the amount of equipment: infantry forces can be easier to move than armored forces because they have less heavy equipment to transport, and forces with modest logistic support assets can be easier to move than forces equipped with massive stocks and supplies. Yet another factor is the capability of mobility forces on both sides. If one side possesses an advantage in trucks, railroad cars, air transports, or ships, it will be able to move faster than its opponent. A final consideration is the political capacity of governments to make the decision to order mobilization and reinforcement. If one side can make this decision in just a few days, it will be able to deploy its forces faster than an opponent that requires many days and weeks to decide.

All of these considerations must be taken into account in producing an assessment of how many forces each side can deploy in the space between "M-Day" (mobilization day), "C-Day" (movement day), and "D-Day" (the day on which war begins). Table 11–2 illustrates the results of a typical analysis of mobilization and reinforcement rates in a wartime contingency. It assumes that M-Day and C-Day are the same, and that D-Day could begin at any time between M-Day and M+60. It suggests that if adversary ground forces deploy to the battle zone quickly while U.S. and allied forces deploy slowly, the result will be an adverse military balance in the critical initial 30 days. If the adversary attacks at M+30, when its forces are fully deployed, it might have a serious prospect of winning because insufficient U.S. and allied forces would be available to mount a stalwart defense on D-Day. But if the deployment rates of U.S. or allied forces were accelerated, the result would be a less dangerous situation. Although U.S. and allied forces are still outnumbered in divisions at M+30, the difference shrinks from an adverse ratio of about 3:1 to an improved ratio of 1.67:1. Even though outnumbered by 1.67:1, a force of 15 divisions might be able to mount a stalwart defense if it could protect the terrain assigned to it while generating enough combat power to halt the enemy's advance and to inflict destruction upon it. Achieving faster buildup rates is, therefore, a focus of many mobility programs aimed at fielding more air transports, cargo ships, and prepositioned equipment.[5]

Table 11–2. **Illustrative Buildup Rates for Ground Divisions (in Theater)**

	M-Day	M+15	M+30	M+60
Adversary Forces	5	15	25	25
U.S./Allied Forces: Slow Buildup	2	5	8	15
U.S./Allied Forces: Faster Buildup	4	9	15	20

Presumptions: M-Day (mobilization day) and C-Day (movement day) are the same, and D-Day (battle begins) can occur at any time.

Once mobilization and reinforcement rates have been determined, the next stage of analysis is comparative evaluation of forces and capabilities on both sides. Once again, many variables must be considered because military forces are so diverse and complicated. Surface appearances can be misleading, and things are often not what they seem: one side can appear to have larger forces than the other side when some assets are counted, but smaller forces when all assets are counted. For example, a force with a 2:1 edge in tanks may nonetheless be outgunned by a force that enjoys a 3:1 edge in air forces. The guiding rule of systems analysis is to count all assets on the battlefield, not just some of them.

Owing to its emphasis on comprehensiveness, systems analysis typically employs diverse methods in order to compare forces that might fight each other in combat. Static methods appraise the physical characteristics of forces and weapons. The advantage of static methods is that they are simple and transparent; their disadvantage is that they do not measure actual performance on the battlefield. For that, systems analysis typically will employ dynamic methods, such as computer simulations adapted from operations research. Dynamic methods can provide insights into how forces might fight in battle, but they lack the simplicity and transparency of static methods. Their results can be driven as much by their own mathematical equations as by the strengths and weaknesses of the forces on both sides. Both static and dynamic methods thus have roles to play. Typically, systems analysis will employ both and will search for common ground between them. If a force assessment is anchored in similar results from both methods, it stands a better chance of being correct than if it employs only one method.

When static methods are used, comparative force evaluation typically begins by counting the number of ground divisions, fighter wings, and ships fielded by both sides, but such simple indicators can generate misleading conclusions. As table 11–3 illustrates, this is particularly true when land warfare is being analyzed and comparisons must be made between ground forces. Ground divisions come in differing sizes and shapes. Adversary divisions often have about 12,000 troops, but a U.S. or allied division often fields 16,000 or more troops. Thus, a force of 25 enemy divisions might field 300,000 troops, and a U.S. or allied force of 15 divisions will field 240,000 troops, reducing the numerical disadvantage from 1.67:1 to 1.25:1. Rear-area logistic support assets that are not assigned to divisions must also be considered. If each enemy division has 10,000 troops in logistic support, its

25 divisions will field 250,000 such troops. If each U.S. and allied division draws upon 20,000 logistic troops, its force of 15 divisions will have fully 300,000 troops in logistic support. When troops from divisions and rear-area logistic support are added, each of the two force postures in this example fields about 550,000 personnel, thus producing equality in manpower. Beyond this, the manpower contributions from air forces must also be considered. If the adversary deploys only 10 tactical fighter wings, each with 4,000 aircrew, its air posture will total 40,000 aircrew. If U.S. and allied forces deploy 20 fighter wings of 8,000 aircrew apiece, this will total 160,000 personnel. When ground and air forces are added together, the U.S./allied force no longer faces a numerical disadvantage in this example. Instead, it enjoys a small advantage of 670,000 troops versus 590,000 troops.

Table 11–3. **Illustrative Comparison of Forces: Combat Units and Manpower**

	Adversary Forces	U.S./Allied Forces
Divisions	25	15
Fighter Wings	10	20
Total Manpower	590,000	670,000

A manpower count alone may still give an incomplete picture, however, and therefore the weapons fielded by both sides must also be counted. Here, major differences often arise because ground divisions from different countries are often equipped in different ways. Whereas some divisions may have more tanks and artillery tubes, others may have more infantry troops and antitank weapons. Fighter wings from one country may have more combat aircraft than fighter wings from another country. For example, adversary fighter wings often possess 40–45 aircraft, while a U.S. Air Force wing has 72 aircraft. In table 11–4, the adversary force of 25 divisions has a roughly 1.25:1 advantage over the U.S./allied force in ground weapons (17,300 to 13,725). But the U.S./allied force enjoys a numerical advantage in tactical combat aircraft of 3.2:1 (1,280 to 400). The effect of this airpower advantage is to offset the adversary's lead in ground weapons. The reason is that in situations conducive to use of air forces, two or three U.S. fighter wings can deliver as much ordnance for land warfare as a heavy Army division. In its final category ("Total Weapons"), table 11–4 assumes that 180 combat aircraft (2.5 wings) are roughly equal to 920 ground weapons (one division). As a result, it shows that the overall ratio of weaponry—counting ground and air weapons—is about 1:1, with the U.S./allied force having a slight lead.

A numerical comparison of weapons inventories may be misleading, too, because it says nothing about the quality of the weapons fielded by both sides, or about many other factors such as doctrine and training that affect the capabilities of the two forces. These factors can have an impact on the force balance if they benefit one side more than the other. Typically, U.S. and allied forces will enjoy a qualitative edge—sometimes a major edge—over opponents. The effect can be to give them decisive battlefield superiority even

Table 11–4. **Illustrative Comparison of Forces: Key Weapons**

	Adversary Forces	U.S./Allied Forces
Divisions	25	15
Fighter wings	10	20
Combat aircraft	400	1280
Tanks, infantry fighting vehicles	10,200	6,975
Artillery tubes	3,100	1,750
Antitank weapons	4,000	5,000
Total Ground Weapons	17,300	13,725
Total Weapons	19,344	20,267

in situations where their numbers are not greater than those of the opponent or even fall short. Table 11–5 illustrates how this can be the case. It displays the cumulative effects of six qualitative factors that have an impact on force capability: weapons quality, firepower rates, C⁴ISR, doctrine, training, and sustainment. Assuming that the U.S./allied force enjoys a 1.25:1 advantage over the opponent in each area, thus adding .25 points to the U.S./allied force, the table displays an overall composite capability index.

Assuming the cumulative effects for U.S./allied forces are additive, the table displays a force imbalance of 2.5:1 in favor of U.S./allied forces, even though the numerical ratio is 1:1. The cascading effects of qualitative advantages have been witnessed in such recent wars as *Desert Storm* (1991) and the invasion of Iraq (2003). In both cases, U.S. and allied forces fielded numbers of troops and weapons similar to those of the Iraqi military, yet quickly overpowered it. The opponent was badly outclassed because its military force had far less quality and capability. Whether U.S. and allied forces will enjoy such advantages in future

Table 11–5. **Illustrative Impact of Qualitative Factors on Force Capability**

	Adversary Force	U.S./Allied Force
Size of force	1.00	1.00
Weapons quality	1.00	+.25
Firepower rates	1.00	+.25
C⁴ISR	1.00	+.25
Doctrine	1.00	+.25
Training	1.00	+.25
Sustainment	1.00	+.25
Composite Capability Index	*1.00*	*2.50*

wars is unknown. The key point is that when force balances are being assessed, these factors must be taken into account, and systems analysis provides such methods. These methods are only as reliable as the data, assumptions, and calculations that go into them, but when the inputs are sound, these methods can shed considerable light on a complex, otherwise indecipherable subject.

Methods of Requirements Analysis

A *requirement* is a statement that defines how many U.S. forces and capabilities are needed for a specific purpose, such as to defend against a specific enemy threat or to perform a particular mission. Requirements play an important role in defense planning because they help determine the goals that are to be pursued by U.S. forces and the standards by which U.S. defense preparations are judged. Requirements are partly determined by professional military judgment, but systems analysis often plays an important role as well. Systems analysis can add specificity to judgments that otherwise might be stated abstractly. It can help verify or refute judgments put forth by military professionals. It can help gauge the confidence levels and risks that accompany the process of defining requirements. It also can provide the assistance of economic reasoning to this process. For these reasons, the methods employed by systems analysis will remain important for the appraisal of requirements.

The analysis of requirements does not determine with absolute certitude how many military forces are needed to guarantee success. As a practical matter, dangers and risks will always exist when preparations are being made to fight wars. Even when U.S. forces are so decisively superior that victory is virtually assured, there will be risks: casualties might be high, or wars may be won in troublesome ways that create adverse political conditions afterward. The task of force planning is to reduce risks to acceptable proportions, and to provide desired levels of confidence and insurance. Judgments about force commitments are inevitably influenced by economic considerations: the cost that must be paid in order to be adequately insured. The process of making these judgments has often generated intense political controversy in DOD and the U.S. Government. This certainly has been the case for nuclear forces, but it also holds true for conventional forces. Within DOD, for example, debates often take place between combatant commanders, who want larger forces in order to reduce risks in their domains, and senior Pentagon civilian and military leaders, who must allocate resources and distribute risks among multiple commands.

The analysis of requirements and risks is a technical process that cannot be reduced to simple formulas or algorithms. Each contingency and mission must be examined closely on its own merits in order to discern the relationship between U.S. force commitments and confidence in success. Defense operations take place in a realm of variables, not constants. Requirements for virtually any war can vary considerably as a function of many factors including the goals and strategies of the competing sides, the size and strength of enemy forces, the effectiveness of allies, the nature of weather and terrain, and sheer luck. This means that U.S. force needs can vary widely depending on how these factors are expected to play out on the battlefield. A U.S. military commitment that seems likely to succeed if events go as expected could fail if many things go badly wrong. The only way to avoid vulnerability to a cascade of improbable events is to commit extremely large forces to each war. But the U.S. force posture is not large enough and faces too many competing missions to permit such extreme commitments in each case. The result is that analysis must operate in a world of unknowable events and must deal with probabilities rather than hard estimates of outcomes. The number of U.S. forces committed in each contingency will depend upon technical judgments about these thorny issues. The same applies to the process of determining requirements for the U.S. military posture as a whole, for it too is an exercise in gauging confidence levels, risks, performance, and costs.

A main contribution of systems analysis is to provide technical analysis of how different levels of U.S. force commitments affect the probabilistic distribution of battlefield outcomes. Systems analysis, supported by operations research, has methods that are suited to analyzing requirements in terms of variables, uncertainties, confidence levels, insurance, and economic constraints. Systems analysis can thus help transform intense political infighting over these issues into an exercise in focused inquiry that can make difficult judgments at the margins. For example, it can help determine whether an existing force commitment for a particular contingency has a 50 percent probability of success or instead an 80 percent probability. Likewise, it can help determine whether commitment of 10 percent additional forces can elevate the chances of success from, say, 50 percent to 60 percent, or instead as far as 80 percent. Analytical inputs of this sort can be definitive in helping senior officials make tough decisions about committing military forces in order to reduce risks and elevate confidence.

The static measures and dynamic techniques of systems analysis must be applied on a case-by-case basis. Often the best analytical judgments result when several different methods point to the same conclusion. One of the advances of systems analysis in recent years has been scenario-space analysis. The idea behind this method is to display how warfighting outcomes and U.S. force requirements are sensitive to the interplay of events on the battlefield. Figure 11–3, for example, illustrates how a U.S./allied military force might fare in a war as a function of variations in the effectiveness of enemy forces and in its own operating conditions.[6]

Figure 11–3 suggests that if the enemy fights poorly and a given number of U.S./allied forces benefit from favorable operating conditions, the probability of success will be 80

Figure 11–3. **Scenario-Space Analysis of Battlefield Outcomes**

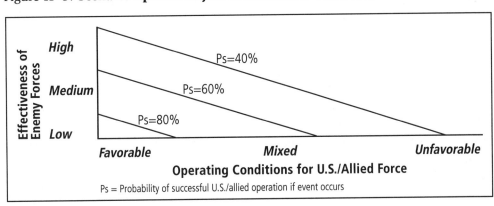

percent. If the enemy fights better and U.S./allied operating conditions are less favorable, the probability of success will fall to 60 percent. If the enemy fights very well and operating conditions are very unfavorable, the probability of success will fall to 40 percent. What this figure suggests is that the U.S./allied posture committed to this war possesses enough assets to succeed if it fights effectively and if it gets enough breaks. The figure also suggests, however, that if events improbably go badly, this force could suffer reversals or even be defeated. The issue of whether additional U.S./allied forces are required depends upon whether policymakers are willing to accept a measure of risk or instead want to be better insured against improbable but costly events.

How alternative force commitments result in differing levels of risk, confidence, and insurance can often be shown by military performance curves. For example, figure 11–4 illustrates a force commitment of a given number (say, four) of divisions (the existing posture) in a particular contingency with a medium probability of success (40 percent) in dangerous situations. Option A offers to elevate the probability of success to about 70 percent by increasing force commitments to, say, seven divisions. Option B offers to increase the probability of success to about 85 percent, through increasing force commitments 250 percent, say to 10 divisions. Three issues arise: Does the existing posture of four divisions provide adequate confidence and insurance? Does option A provide enough extra confidence and insurance to justify the added force commitment? Does option B provide enough more confidence and insurance to justify its added force commitment? Displaying options in these terms of incremental benefits and costs helps show senior officials the choices.

Figure 11–4. **Military Performance Curve Confidence Level as a Function of Force Commitment**

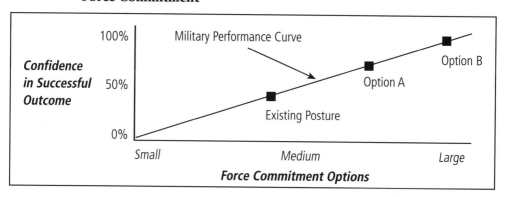

The usefulness of military performance curves to policymakers can often be enhanced by providing a sense of the goals and achievement standards mandated by U.S. defense strategy. For example, figure 11–5 shows a band of strategic goals. At the bottom of this band is a minimum level of achievement: it specifies the lowest level of confidence that national strategy is willing to accept, regardless of the cost, in this particular area of defense planning. At the top of the band is a preferred level, which identifies a performance that, if less than perfect, is desirable if it is affordable. The solid line shows how confidence of success rises as a function of the amount of force committed, ranging from small to large.

Figure 11–5. **Military Performance Curve with Strategic Goals**

The line suggests that a small commitment is insufficient, a medium commitment may be big enough, and a large commitment may be unwise because its extra benefits are not worth the added costs. This appraisal could change if the band of goals and standards were elevated upward. Then a medium posture might be inadequate and a large commitment might be necessary, irrespective of its costs. Bands of this sort should be used regularly because U.S. defense strategy postulates different levels of confidence for different areas of preparedness. For critical areas, high confidence may be essential, while in other areas, medium confidence may be acceptable.

Methods of Force Posture Analysis

Even when agreement is reached on force requirements for a wartime contingency, it does not necessarily specify the exact kinds of forces that should be committed. This is especially true in today's world where ground, air, and naval forces can all be used to wage land warfare, and where choices can be made between long-range and short-range fires. In preparing for each contingency, critical choices must be made that involve difficult tradeoffs and force balancing. Sometimes a single force component will be the best option for performing the mission. Most often, however, the best option will be a mix of ground, naval, and air forces to provide an optimal blend of short-range and long-range fires. Exactly which mix to employ is a complex issue that requires in-depth technical analysis because the answer can vary from contingency to contingency.

Systems analysis, supported by operations research, can contribute to force posture analysis by employing static and dynamic methods. Suitable methods must be chosen on a case-by-case basis. Often, dynamic simulations will be used because combat ebbs and flows in ways that call for different force applications at succeeding stages. For example, the early stages of a war might call for nearly exclusive reliance upon airpower and long-range fires, with little use of ground forces and short-range fires. The middle stages of the war, with meeting engagements between U.S. and adversary forces, may require a balanced combination of the two. When the war reaches its final stages, air forces and long-range fires may be less useful, as ground forces and short-range fires claim center stage. A dynamic of this sort occurred during the 2003 invasion of Iraq, and it may be repeated in future wars. Decisions on the proper force mix can be made only by taking into account all stages of combat. Dynamic analysis can illuminate how the different stages of warfighting pose unique and fluctuating needs for each force component.

What applies to individual contingencies also applies to analyzing the U.S. military posture as a whole. In the past, a common practice was to commit a standard mix of U.S. forces to most wartime contingencies. For example, 5 Army divisions, 1 1/2 Marine divisions and air wings, 10 Air Force fighter wings, and 5 Navy carrier battlegroups (CVBGs) would be committed to each major theater war (MTW). This one-size-fits-all practice has now faded into history. The new reality is that unique force packages must be tailored for each individual contingency. In some cases, the proper force mix will be one-third each ground forces, naval forces, and air forces. The invasion of Iraq roughly fit this pattern. In other cases, a different mix will be needed. The Kosovo war was fought exclusively by air and naval forces; ground forces played virtually no role. Some future wars may be fought with airpower backed on the ground only by target spotters. Other wars may require virtually all ground forces, with air forces and missiles playing little role. Peacekeeping operations are likely to fall into this pattern, as will stabilization and reconstruction operations that occur after combat has ended. For example, the Kosovo war was won from the air, but sizable ground forces had to be deployed afterward to secure the peace.

The need to prepare individual packages for each contingency has major implications for determining how the overall U.S. force posture should be sized and configured. Because the one-size-fits-all model cannot be used for every contingency, it cannot be used to prepare the overall force posture: the force posture cannot be configured simply as a larger version of a standard model for individual contingencies. Instead, the U.S. force posture must now provide a robust, flexible portfolio of modular assets that can be combined and recombined in ways suited to the unique demands of each situation. Moreover, the force posture must contain enough assets for each component to ensure that the demands of all situations can be met. This reinforces the need for a diverse array of assets. It also calls for careful analysis not only to ensure that the overall force posture is adequately large, but also to ensure the adequacy of each of its components.

The implications of this need for flexible forces are illuminated in table 11–6. It displays a spectrum of warfighting scenarios. In the middle of the spectrum is a major theater war that requires a standard mix of one-third each U.S. ground, air, and naval forces. MTW A requires a different mix: more ground forces, accompanied by fewer air and naval forces. MTW B requires yet a different mix: mostly air and naval forces, with fewer ground forces. The table also displays the existing U.S. force posture divided into two standard packages. A key point shown by the table is that if a standard MTW erupts, a standard package can be deployed for it, but if one of the two other MTWs occurs, a different force package would have to be assembled by selectively drawing upon assets from both of the standard packages. Such tailored force packages can be assembled only if the existing military posture is modular in ways that allow it to be combined effectively as needed. Equally important, the force posture must always possess sufficient assets for each component to ensure that the demands of each situation can be met.

Table 11–6. **Illustrative Force Needs for a Spectrum of Major Theater War Conflicts**

	MTW A	Standard MTW	MTW B
Force Needs	9 Divisions 5 Fighter Wings 2 CVBGs	6.5 Divisions 10 Fighter Wings 5 CVBGs	2 Divisions 15 Fighter Wings 8 CVBGs
Existing Force Posture: 50% Allocated to Each Standard Package		*Standard Package 1* 6.5 Divisions 10 Fighter Wings 5 CVBGs *Standard Package 2* 6.5 Divisions 10 Fighter Wings 5 CVBGs	

In the example illustrated in table 11–6, the current U.S. force posture possesses the assets to wage either a standard MTW or MTW A and MTW B, provided the proper repackaging is accomplished. This example, however, is a simplified version of a more complex dynamic: future conflicts may take many different forms than those illuminated here, requiring different force levels and mixes. The challenge facing the United States will be one of continually reviewing, updating, and altering its defense posture so that it possesses a sensible mix of forces that ensures that sufficient assets for each component are always available. The demands of sizing and configuring U.S. forces in order to provide such a portfolio of modular assets are significantly different from the past, when contingencies seldom changed and standard force packages endured for years. Today's defense planning is more complex, and proper analytical methods will be needed in order to perform this new type of defense planning.

Systems analysis can contribute to this enterprise, but many of the methods inherited from the past will not be suitable to the new era. New methods will have to be created that permit analysis of force posture options in terms of portfolios, modularity, and flexible repackaging. Decisions about the size and composition of each force component will need to be informed by a new kind of systems analysis that evaluates force components in terms of a wider spectrum of conflicts and missions. The process of creating new analytical methods for this task has gotten under way in recent years, but additional steps need to be taken, and other new methods must be developed. Systems analysis has long been suited for optimizing the U.S. defense posture in order to serve a narrow range of purposes. It will need to make innovations in its own methods in order to evaluate how the future posture can best be built to serve a wide spectrum of new purposes. Responding to this challenge helps frame the agenda ahead for systems analysis.

Methods of Capabilities-Based Analysis

An important innovation in defense planning of recent years is the shift toward capabilities-based planning (CBP), which can help facilitate the new emphasis on creating a flexible portfolio of modular assets. While this shift sometimes is portrayed as an abandonment of old-style threat-based planning, this portrayal is misleading because CBP is actually focused on determining how to counter future threats. What CBP abandons is the old-style use of a few single-point scenarios and their specific threats as the sole basis for shaping U.S. forces. Recognizing that single-point scenarios can place force planning in a straitjacket and create blindness to other situations that might be encountered, CBP endeavors to prepare U.S. forces to counter a wide spectrum of contingencies, threats, and specific enemy capabilities. It asks: "What types of U.S. military capabilities will be needed to handle this wide spectrum of contingencies and threats?" It seeks to shape future U.S. military forces so that they have the flexibility, adaptability, agility, and versatility to perform in a variety of different ways, with the exact response tailored to each separate occasion.

In order for CBP to be carried out, it will require a new form of systems analysis called capabilities-based analysis (CBA), a major challenge. Analytical work on CBA has only begun in recent years, and much ground remains to be covered, but the outlines of this new methodology are discernible in the work of Paul K. Davis at RAND.

Davis' recent landmark book, *Analytical Architecture for Capabilities-Based Planning, Mission-System Analysis, and Transformation*, uses the technique of analyzing U.S. forces in terms of their capability to carry out certain key missions and operations that regularly arise in modern-era warfare.[7] Davis reasons that if U.S. forces have the requisite capabilities to perform these missions and operations in generic ways, they should possess the necessary portfolio of assets that can be tailored to the unique demands of each contingency. If transformation is focused on the design of new-era capabilities for these missions and operations, the resulting force posture will be able to cope with the wide spectrum of challenges ahead.

Acknowledging that capabilities-based planning must be conducted in terms of a system of capabilities, Davis makes use of an innovative conceptual tool called a spider chart. Figure 11–6 is a simplified version of Davis's chart. It posits 10 generic mission-performance capabilities needed by U.S. forces. For each type of capability, an axis radiates outward from the center—zero capability—to a high point of 10 units of capability. Based on a postulated desired level of performance in each area, a line connects each level, forming a completed perimeter around an aggregate space or zone of capabilities needed for each era. In figure 11–6, a dashed line shows the new era; a solid line shows the predominant emphasis of the Cold War. The spider chart thus displays visually the need for a dramatic shift of emphasis. Cold War planning emphasized a particular space of capabilities. By contrast, new-era defense planning should emphasize a different combination of capabilities that are attuned to the threats and operations ahead. A main implication is that new-era CBP should focus not only on different missions and operations than during the Cold War, but also on different forces and programs.

Davis's CBA methodology employs scenario-space charts (as in figure 11–3) to illuminate likely outcomes of combat as a function of enemy capabilities and the extent of U.S. force deployment before combat begins. For each generic contingency, across a wide spectrum, Davis employs dynamic force assessment techniques to gauge how current U.S. forces would be likely to perform. His scenario-space charts indicate a zone of favorable situations in which U.S. forces are likely to perform well and a zone of unfavorable

Figure 11–6. **Spider Chart of Future Capabilities**

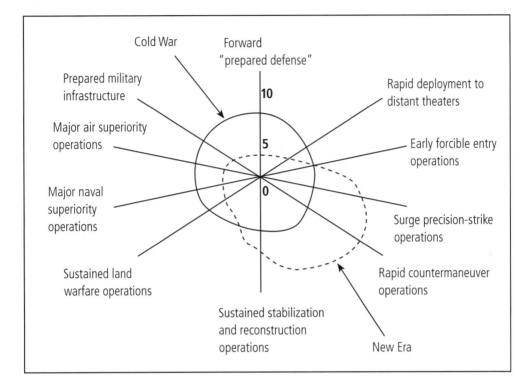

situations in which they would be likely to perform less well or even fail entirely. Using the same tools, Davis then shows how alternative force improvement packages could enhance the performance of U.S. forces to increase the zone of success and diminish the zone of failure. Finally, Davis combines the results of each contingency to show whether each force improvement package could produce positive results across the board, and how they stack up in comparison to each other in terms of overall cost-effectiveness.

Davis's CBA methodology is a major step in the right direction, but CBA is not yet a fully mature methodology. The great promise of CBA is that it can improve judgments about how aggregate U.S. military capabilities can be shaped for flexibility, adaptability, and modularity. The challenge is to develop this methodology so that it takes its place as a major tool of systems analysis for the new era.

Systems Analysis for Program Evaluation and Resource Allocation: Economic Models of Choice

Whereas defense planning using the methods described above determines the force posture needed to carry out national strategy, the tools of program evaluation help determine how funds and other resources should be allocated in order to provide the requisite capabilities in such areas as readiness, modernization, and sustainment. Systems analysis provides a set of methods that can be used to help perform program evaluation for resource allocation to illuminate the cost-effectiveness of alternative options. As such, it provides a bridge between the force posture and the defense budget.[8]

A *defense* program can be defined as a set of weapons systems and associated assets and activities that interact to perform military operations to achieve specified goals. Table 11–7, for example, displays an illustrative program for a tactical air force. As it suggests, air operations require not only fighters and bombers, but also other assets such as support aircraft, pilots and crews that are trained properly, service support assets to keep aircraft flying, airbases capable of functioning in combat situations, and ample stocks of munitions and fuels. Unless all of these assets are present in adequate numbers and quality, the air operation will perform ineffectively or even shut down.

Table 11–7. **Tactical Air Program**

Combat Aircraft
- Fighters
- Bombers

Support Aircraft
- Command and control aircraft
- Refueling tankers
- Reconnaissance aircraft
- Defense suppression aircraft
- Search and rescue aircraft

Adequate numbers of pilots and aircrews

Training for pilots and aircrews

Service support: maintenance, intelligence, planning

Airbase operations

Munitions and fuels

Other supplies

The DOD budget is officially divided into 11 major programs: strategic forces; general purpose forces; C[4]I and space; mobility forces; guard and reserve forces; special operations forces; research and development; central supply and maintenance; training, medical, and other activities; administration; and support of other nations. Each of these categories, in turn, has multiple constituent programs. For example, general purpose forces include active-duty ground, naval, and air forces, and each of these has many programs of its own. A program can be large or small, ranging in costs from a few billion dollars to $100 billion annually or more. A program could be a procurement effort that buys several tactical fighters, or one that buys just a single aircraft along with its support assets. What matters is that a program, regardless of its size, has multiple parts—program elements—all of which must operate together.

The task of program evaluation is to allocate budgets and other resources in balanced ways to ensure that all of these program elements are properly prepared. Although program evaluation often focuses on the internal composition of individual programs, it also engages in the business of assessing how resources can be allocated among multiple programs that may be competing for funds and assets. For example, it might assess how resources can best be allocated among air, land, and naval programs. Regardless of the scope, the purpose of program evaluation is to allocate resources as efficiently and effectively as possible. In order to aid program evaluation, systems analysis measures costs and effectiveness of program elements and entire programs. It then employs economic models of choice in order to shed light on how resources can best be allocated at the margins. Five models of economic choice, each with its associated analytical methods, play important roles in program evaluation:[9]

- the model of diminishing marginal returns
- the comparative performance model
- the tradeoff model
- the program optimization model
- the time-phased investment model.

Model of Diminishing Marginal Returns

The model of diminishing marginal returns is widely used in evaluating how much of a single program or program element should be bought. For example, it can be used to help judge whether 300, 600, or 900 new aircraft of a particular type should be acquired. Its premise is that while initial investments may produce major increases in performance and benefits, at some juncture the rate of return begins to diminish. Figure 11–7 displays a typical curve of diminishing marginal returns. It shows that through the medium zone of acquisition, effectiveness and benefits rise rapidly: the upward slope of the curve is steep. As a result, each additional increment of resources for the program yields substantial increases in effectiveness and benefits. But as the program becomes large, the slope declines and the "knee of the curve" is reached. This is the point where each additional increment of resources provides smaller and smaller returns. Above that, the curve flattens and barely rises, reflecting the fact that each additional increment provides only a minor gain in benefits.

Figure 11–7. **Diminishing Marginal Returns Model**

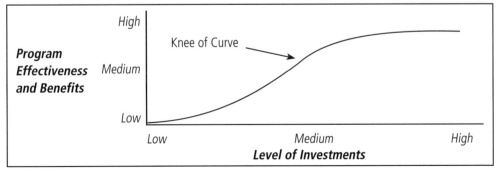

Policymakers often employ this model to determine when investments in a program should be halted. Typically, the knee of the curve is the chosen point, because up to this point, investments produce major benefits, but after it is reached, further investments will not produce enough additional gain to justify the added expense. This presumes that national defense strategy is served by the level of effectiveness that falls at the knee of the curve. If national strategy mandates a higher performance level, however, then additional investments may be mandated even if the costs are high and marginal returns are low. But in cases where the knee of the curve offers a cost-effective investment strategy and an identifiable point for terminating investments, the analysis of diminishing marginal returns provides an excellent tool for program management. It is often used as a tool for comparing investment strategies of competing programs. The guiding premise is that if all programs are funded to the knee of the curve—not lower or higher—then DOD'S money is likely to be well spent. The curve of diminishing marginal returns is relatively simple to create, transparent in its criterion of evaluation, easily understood by policymakers, and highly illuminating. For this reason, it is regularly used for program evaluation.

However, not all defense programs produce this exact curve. In its standard form, the curve begins with a flat slope, then transitions to a quickly rising slope, then returns to a flat slope at high levels of investment. Other curves are possible: curves of linear returns, or increasing returns, or slower-rising returns, or curves that produce plateaus. In each case, analysis should conduct a careful appraisal of how program effectiveness changes as a function of investment costs. Sometimes the standard model might apply, but sometimes not. Every study should aim to create technically accurate curves that reflect reality, regardless of whether they reflect the standard model.

Comparative Performance Model

The comparative performance model is used to show how two different programs compare in terms of cost-effectiveness (where the curve of diminishing marginal returns would be used to evaluate single programs). This model can be used in a variety of ways. For example, it can be used to compare programs on a variable cost–variable effectiveness basis. In this case, the model portrays programs in terms of rising costs and effectiveness, as shown in figure 11–8. It allows the reader to judge whether the benefits of each option are justified by the costs.

Figure 11–8. **Variable Cost–Variable Effectiveness Model**

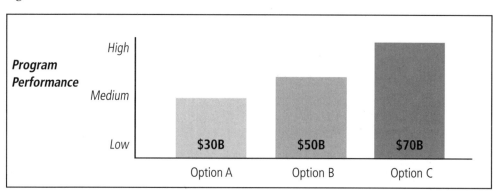

The program performance model might compare programs on the basis of variable effectiveness and equal costs, or equal effectiveness and variable costs. In the first case, as shown in figure 11–9, option A is more cost-effective than option B because it performs better and costs the same. In the second case, option A is better because it performs equally but costs less. This model is most useful when a distinct "either-or" choice must be made between competing programs. The comparative investment model provides a clear-cut criterion, is transparent, and provides analyses that are easy to understand. For these reasons, it too is a favorite of systems analysts.

Care must be taken in applying cost-effectiveness data for this model because sometimes programs differ from each other in how their costs accrue and how they perform. A critical task, for example, is ensuring that costs are measured accurately and compared fairly. A typical program incurs several different kinds of costs: research and development, procurement, and annual operating costs once it is fielded. Normally, the best cost figure is that of life-cycle costs, which measures costs for the entire duration of the program's life. Regardless of the cost metric chosen, it must be applied to all competing programs. For example, if analysis measures life-cycle costs for option A and only procurement costs for option B, option B will appear to cost less than option A even though their life-cycle costs might be identical.

Similarly, care must be taken in employing MOEs to gauge the effectiveness of competing options. If a single MOE is employed, it should measure the key performance characteristic of the weapons systems and forces being considered. Often, multiple MOEs should be used when performance in more than one domain is important. For example, a weapons system might look highly attractive when only its capacity to destroy enemy targets is measured, but less attractive when its ability to survive in the face of intense enemy fire is considered. Regardless of the MOEs used, they must be applied equally to all program options to order to ensure a fair comparison. If weapon A is highly lethal in combat and weapon B is highly survivable, they should be compared in terms of both metrics. The importance of using a family of metrics can be illustrated by recalling the case of tank modernization in the late 1970s. At the time, the Army was considering not only its own M–1 Abrams, but also the German Leopard and the British Challenger. Compared to the M–1,

Figure 11–9. **Comparative Performance Model: Two Versions**

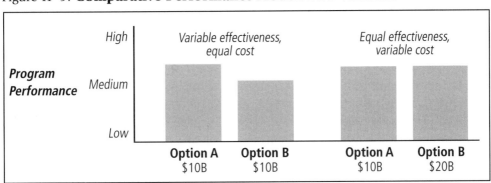

the Leopard had better tactical mobility and the Challenger had better survivability. The M–1, however, was judged the best choice because it did a better job of combining fire-power, mobility, and survivability. All three metrics had to be considered in order to reach this conclusion.

The need to analyze cost-effectiveness carefully can be illustrated by a case in which DOD is preparing to spend $50 billion to modernize its tactical air forces, and it has a procurement choice between two different fighters. Fighter A is equipped with medium-level technology and has a life-cycle cost (including both acquisition and operations) of $125 million per aircraft. Fighter B is configured with more sophisticated technology and has a higher cost of $220 million per aircraft. Thus, $50 billion will buy either 400 models of fighter A or 227 models of fighter B. Moreover, fighter A has a slightly higher daily sortie rate of 1.2; fighter B's rate is 1.0. If numbers of aircraft and total daily sortie rates are the MOE (as shown in table 11–8), fighter A is clearly the better choice by a ratio of 2:1 or more.

Table 11–8. **Comparison of Options Based on Numbers of Aircraft and Sorties**

	Fighter A	Fighter B
Total cost	$50 billion	$50 billion
Unit cost	$125 million	$220 million
Number of aircraft	400	227
Sorties/day per aircraft capability	1.2	1.0
Total daily sorties	480	227

The drawback of this kind of comparison is that it considers only numbers of aircraft and sorties, not the qualitative performance of the two weapons. When qualitative performance is considered, the two fighters in our example differ in ways that reflect their relative costs and differing technological components. Judged on an individual basis, fighter B is the better aircraft for three reasons: better radar and air-to-air missiles make it superior to fighter A in dogfights; it carries twice as many smart bombs to drop on ground targets; and it has stealth features, which make it less vulnerable to enemy air defenses. Such considerations must be taken into account in a dynamic assessment that includes the full range of factors that influence air operations and performance over the entire length of a war. Such an analysis, for example, might show that over the course of a one-month war, fighter B, owing to its superior performance characteristics, could destroy more enemy air and ground targets than each fighter A, and will have less chance of being shot down. When MOEs of enemy targets killed and U.S. aircraft lost are used, the force of 227 fighter Bs emerges as more cost-effective than the force of 400 fighter As, as shown in table 11–9.

Whether the best choice is fighter A or fighter B depends upon the MOEs used, and these, in turn, depend upon the missions, purposes, and goals that are guiding the program evaluation process. If the main goal is to deploy a large number of fighters in order to perform multiple missions in different locations, fighter A might be the best choice. But if

Table 11–9. **Comparison of Options Based on Performance Characteristics for One-Month War**

	Fighter A	Fighter B
Total cost	$50 billion	$50 billion
Number of aircraft	400	227
Sorties per day	480	227
Enemy targets destroyed in 30-day war*	3,135	3,411
U.S. aircraft lost in 30-day war	60	15

*Illustrative estimates of enemy targets destroyed are based on a dynamic calculus that takes into account available sorties for ground attack missions, the ability to detect targets, the accuracy and lethality of munitions, and other factors.

the goal is to maximize combat power in a single war, fighter B could be the best choice. The key point is that when the comparative investment model is used, a detailed examination of multiple performance characteristics and MOEs might yield insights that, while counterintuitive, lead to better decisions.

Indeed, careful analysis might yield the conclusion that the best choice is not one option or the other, but instead a combination of the two. In this case, for example, a mixture of fighter A (268 aircraft) and fighter B (75 aircraft) may be a more cost-effective option than investing all $50 billion in one aircraft or the other, as shown in table 11–10.

If so, this would be nothing unusual. Systems analysis often concludes that when two competing programs are performing similar missions, a mixture of them is wiser than an "either-or" approach. This can be the case, for example, when two weapons have different performance characteristics that allow one weapon to perform well in one situation, and the other weapon to perform well in a different situation. Acquiring two types of weapons can provide excellent capabilities for both situations.

The Tradeoff Model

Systems analysis employs the tradeoff model to help balance resource distribution among the multiple elements of a single program. On a bigger scale, it can be used to judge how resources can best be shifted at the margin between two existing programs, both of which would continue being funded at significant levels. This model aspires to measure

Table 11–10. **Comparison of Three Options (Assuming 30-Day War)**

	Only Fighter A	Only Fighter B	Mix of 268 Fighter A and 75 Fighter B
Cost	$50 billion	$50 billion	$50 billion
Number of Aircraft	400	227	343
Enemy Targets Destroyed	3,135	3,411	3,573
U.S. Aircraft Lost	60	15	45

tradeoffs in terms of marginal returns and opportunity costs. That is, it seeks to determine whether the marginal benefits of investing additional resources in option A exceed the lost opportunity of not investing additional resources in option B, or of transferring resources away from that option. The purposes of the tradeoff model are to provide a tool for challenging how resources are traditionally allocated among competing categories and to help ensure that when shifts are made in resource allocation, the benefits truly exceed the costs.

Tradeoff analysis is not a favorite within governmental departments that value continuity in the distribution of money and resources. But it is a valuable method for aiding reformers who want to challenge the status quo. It can become particularly important when new threats, new missions, or new technologies create reasons for shifting resources from one program to another. An example occurred early in the George W. Bush administration, when senior political leaders decided to channel a larger portion of DOD's growing military budget into space systems, C⁴ISR, and missile defenses rather than distribute the money among the military services as had traditionally been done. The effect was to accelerate transformation in these areas, albeit at the expense of slower progress in other areas such as modernization of ground, air, and, naval forces.

The idea of judging marginal returns against opportunity costs is unquestionably an important economic concept for defense analysis and management. It rises to the fore especially when programs are in direct competition with each other over budget shares, and when the choice is not one of canceling one program in favor of another, but instead of shifting resources at the margin between them. An example was DOD's decision in 2001–2002 to shift procurement funds away from ground weapons and to devote them instead to accelerating modernization of tactical air forces. Figure 11–10 illustrates the tradeoff model. It suggests that the marginal returns of investing in option A exceed the opportunity costs of not investing in option B by a wide margin of 2:1. Often, however, the advantage gained by shifting resources from one program to another will be less distinct. In such a case, systems analysis must devote detailed attention to measuring and comparing marginal gains and opportunity costs. Sometimes the marginal gains are not greater than the opportunity costs, but less, and damage would be done by shifting resources. The core purpose of the tradeoff model is to provide analysis that helps illuminate these choices as accurately as possible.

Figure 11–10. **Tradeoff Model**

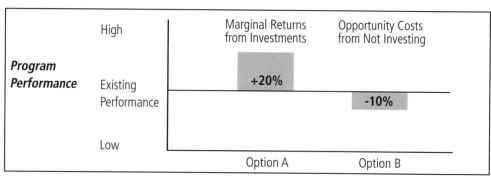

The tradeoff model is easiest to use when the programs being examined are commensurate with each other: when they operate in similar domains and can be compared using the same MOEs and criteria of evaluation. For example, tanks, artillery tubes, and cruise missiles can be readily compared when all three weapons have the same mission of destroying enemy ground targets. The tradeoff model becomes harder to use when the programs operate in such different domains that they cannot readily be compared. For example, aircraft carriers are hard to compare to heavy air transports such as C–17s. Whereas the former provide maritime supremacy, the latter deliver equipment and supplies to distant locations. Despite their different purposes, they might have to be compared when there is insufficient money to fund both of them and a choice between them must be made. Imaginative use of systems analysis techniques can sometimes create a common measure for comparison, but when this is not possible, tradeoff analysis can boil down to comparing how two different programs stack up in relation to their curves of diminishing marginal returns. When one program is already being funded well beyond the knee of its curve, and funding for another program is short of its knee, a case may exist for shifting funds from the former to the latter.

Program Optimization Model

The program optimization model is employed when the task at hand is to blend two or more elements, such as weapons systems, to form a composite program, rather than choose one over the other. Examples would be procurement of a combination of two different tactical fighters rather than one fighter, or buying a combination of naval cruisers and destroyers rather than one or the other. This model is employed in cases where a robust mixture of complementary elements makes sense. A mixture of investments is appropriate when some of everything is needed, and when a combination of measures will produce better performance than investing solely in a single weapon. For example, a naval force of 50 cruisers and 50 destroyers may perform better than an equal-cost force of 75 cruisers, or of 150 destroyers. The task of the program optimization model is to determine the optimum combination: the number of assets from each element that should be acquired in order to maximize performance.

This model is important for systems analysis because, in the real world, program evaluation often requires blending two or more measures rather than investing in only one. The Air Force, for example, traditionally flies two or more types of fighter aircraft, not just one. The Navy deploys a combination of cruisers, destroyers, and frigates. The Army fields tanks, infantry fighting vehicles, and attack helicopters, not just one type of weapon for armored warfare. For all three services, the task of planning their future modernization strategies requires deciding upon the proper combination of new weapons to be purchased in each category: should the Air Force, for example, purchase 600 F–22s and 2,200 F–35s, or instead 300 F–22s and 2,800 F–35s? The program optimization model can help illuminate the cost-effectiveness of alternative combinations.

This model is easiest to employ when only two weapons or other program elements are competing with each other for a fixed amount of money. It starts from the premise that both weapons are subject to the curve of diminishing marginal returns. It therefore postulates that buying a balanced combination of both weapons is likely to be more

Figure 11–11. **Comparison of Investment Strategies**

Effectiveness Index

Combination of
A and B

All A or All B

100

50   100

0

Cost $B

	Comparative Cost-Effectiveness		
	All A	All B	Equal mix A and B
Index score	70	70	100
Cost	$100B	$100B	$100B

cost-effective than investing solely in one weapon. Figure 11–11 illustrates this calculus. It shows that whereas an equal combination of weapons A and B will produce a score of 70, a program composed of all A or all B scores only 40 points. The reason for this difference is that both A and B are subject to diminishing marginal returns. The combination program invests in both A and B at the steep part of the curve. Because it is not at the point of diminishing marginal returns, it yields higher overall effectiveness. In the example shown in figure 11–11, a 50–50 mixture of A and B may be an optimal strategy. But this equal distribution may not always be the right one: the proper distribution is a variable that must be treated on a case-by-case basis. The proper mix might be 75 percent of one weapon and 25

Figure 11–12. **Optimal Investment Strategy**

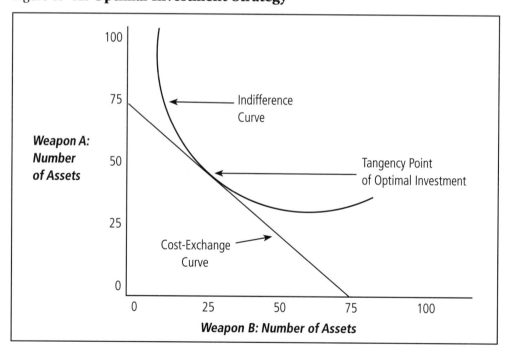

percent of another. The program optimization model provides a general approach for determining the optimal mix in each case. It does so by employing a graph with two curves, and by seeking the intersection of them. As shown in figure 11–12, the first curve is a cost-exchange curve. It measures the manner in which investments in weapon A can be exchanged at equal cost for investments in weapon B. It thus shows the various combinations of A and B that can be procured for a fixed cost: for example, 75 of A, or 75 of B, or 37 of each for a fixed cost of $50 billion (here A and B are presumed to have equal unit costs). The indifference curve is a line on which any combination of A and B will produce the same overall effectiveness, for example, an index score of 100. The implication is that a decisionmaker should be indifferent to any force mix along this line because, cost aside, all mixes will perform equally well. On this graph, the optimal mix of weapons is the tangency point at which these two curves intersect. This point is optimal because no other mixture of programs will provide higher performance at equal cost or equal performance at lower cost.

The tangency point is the point at which the marginal rate of transformation (MRT) equals the marginal rate of substitution (MRS). This formula means that the rate at which A can be transformed into B along the cost-exchange curve (MRT) is equal to the rate at which A can be substituted for B along the indifference curve (MRS). At this point, the slope of the two curves is equal. The reason why this tangency point is the optimal investment strategy can be demonstrated by examining figure 11–13. It portrays a situation in which $50 billion is available for investment. Options for spending this amount are displayed along the cost-exchange curve (here, a straight, solid line). In order to show how this model is employed to make decisions, the chart displays two indifference curves: indifference curve 1 (solid line) provides higher effectiveness than curve 2 (dotted line). Because the goal is to maximize effectiveness, the optimal mix is the point on the cost-exchange curve that touches the highest possible indifference curve (indifference curve 1). Any other point on the curve would intersect with a lower indifference curve (here, curve 2),

Figure 11–13. **Cost-Exchange Curve in Search of Highest Indifference Curve**

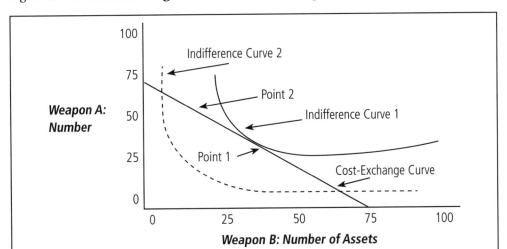

thus producing less effectiveness. Point 1, the tangency point with indifference curve 1, is that point. By contrast, point 2 intersects with indifference curve 2, which provides less effectiveness.

The same conclusion is reached if the issue is examined from the reverse angle. Figure 11–14 examines a situation in which the goal is to achieve an effectiveness score of 100 at the lowest possible cost. It shows an indifference curve that provides this score. It also shows that this indifference curve intersects with cost-exchange curve 1 (a solid line) at point 1. This is the optimal investment strategy, because if any other point along the in-difference curve is chosen, it will fall on a higher cost-exchange curve: for example, point 2 on cost-exchange curve 2 (dotted line). Thus, the cost of achieving a score of 100 will rise if an investment strategy different from that falling at point 1 is chosen.

Such graphs can be used to shape program investment strategies in which only two weapons are being compared, but a more complex calculus must take place when multiple weapons or other program elements are being examined. The process is illustrated by considering an example in which $30 billion is available for investment in a defense pro-gram. Five different weapons are under consideration, each costing the same amount per unit but with differing operating characteristics and capabilities. Figure 11–15 provides a matrix for showing how they perform. The top of the chart lists the five weapons systems, A through E. Each cell of the matrix represents an incremental investment of $2 billion, and each cell provides a score in utility points showing the output performance of the relevant weapons system (derived, for example, from a computer simulation). The columns show how performance for each weapon changes as a function of the increment being purchased. The chart shows that for the first $2 billion spent on weapon A, the performance will be worth 10 points. Reading downward, for the next $2 billion, the performance will be worth 7 points, and so forth. If $16 billion is spent on weapon A, the total performance (33 points) can be gauged by adding the scores for its 8 cells. A key point is that weapon A

Figure 11–14. **Indifference Curve in Search of Lowest Cost-Exchange Curve**

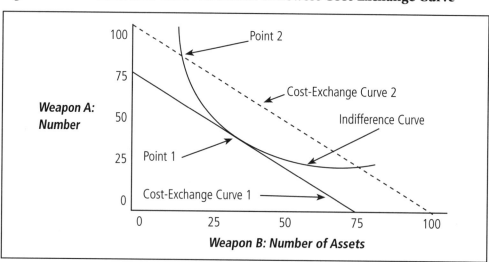

Figure 11–15. **Performance of Weapons as Function of Investment Effort (Utility Points)**

		Weapons Systems					
		A	*B*	*C*	*D*	*E*	*Total*
Investment Increments of $2 billion	*1)*	10	8	6	4	**3**	31
	2)	7	6	5	**3**	2	23
	3)	5	5	**3**	2	2	17
	4)	4	**3**	2	2	2	13
	5)	**3**	2	1	1	1	8
	6)	2	1	1	1	1	6
	7)	1	1	1	1	1	5
	8)	1	1	1	1	1	5
	Total	*33*	*27*	*20*	*15*	*13*	*n.a.*

NOTE: Investing $30 billion in weapons A and B only nets 59 utility points. Investing $30 billion in first 3 increments of all 5 weapons nets 71 utility points. Investing $30 billion according to Optimal Strategy nets 75 utility points.

is affected by diminishing marginal returns: for each additional increment of investment, marginal performance declines. The same applies to all five weapons.

As figure 11–15 shows, weapon A clearly is better and more cost-effective than the other four weapons. Weapon B comes in second place, weapon C in third place, and so forth. Yet the chart also shows that because weapons A and B are particularly affected by diminishing marginal returns, an investment strategy of buying only A and B would be sub-optimal. A budget of $30 billion would permit 15 cells of weapons A and B to be bought (for example, 8 cells of weapon A and 7 cells of weapon B). Their total utility score would be 59 points. This score, however, would be less than provided by a strategy that buys the first three increments and cells from all five weapon systems. In this event, the total utility score would be 71 points. Yet, the figure shows that this strategy would be sub-optimal because it buys cells of weapons C, D, and E, whose scores are lower than competing cells of weapons A and B. For example, cell number 4 for weapon A has a score of 4, which is higher than all three top cells for weapon E.

These considerations suggest that a complex investment strategy of acquiring different numbers of all five weapon systems would be optimal. But how can an optimal investment strategy be determined? This is shown by the diagonal line. It is drawn on the chart below the score of 3 for each of the 5 weapons to indicate that all 15 cells above the line should be bought, and no cells below the line should be bought. If this investment strategy is followed, the total score will be 75 points, or better than the other two strategies that provide 59 and 71 points. This strategy is optimal, and the line is placed where it is, because the total score cannot possibly be improved through re-allocating resources by exchanging a purchased cell for an unpurchased cell. For example, if cell number 5 of weapon A were exchanged for cell number 3 of weapon D, three utility points would be lost and only two points gained. The total score would fall from 75 points to

74 points, a net loss. The same prospect of net loss applies to all other possible trades—the loss would exceed the gain.

A key feature of this optimal investment strategy is that in the final cell purchased for each weapon, the utility score is the same: 3 in each case. This similarity is no accident. Rather, it reveals a standard rule-of-thumb for determining an optimal investment strategy: generally, it is reached when the ratio of marginal productivity (*MP*) to marginal costs (*MC*) is the same for the last item (*n*th item) in all categories of investments. In this case, the ratio of marginal productivity to marginal costs is 3:2 (3 utility points and $2 billion) for each of the five weapons. When a strategy is anchored in this standard, it is an optimal strategy because any other strategy would result in the marginal gain being less than the opportunity cost, and thus, a lower total score. This standard, which derives mathematically from the formula *MRT* = *MRS* for two-variable problems, can be expressed in the following general terms:[10]

> An optimal strategy is when *MP/MC* is identical for the *n*th investment item in all categories, or: $MP_a/MC_a = MP_b/MC_b = MP_c/MC_c = ... MP_n/MC_n$

Table 11–11. Composition of Optimal Investment Strategy

	Weapons Systems (presumed $100 million each unit)					
	A	B	C	D	E	Total
Increments and cells purchased	5	4	3	2	1	15
Total funds invested	$10 billion	$8 billion	$6 billion	$4 billion	$2 billion	$30 billion
Total weapons bought	100	80	60	40	20	300
Total utility points	29	22	14	7	3	75

This standard does not imply that total investments in each category will be equal. Indeed, they normally will not be, when the candidate weapons systems have differing performance characteristics and differing curves of diminishing marginal returns. In the example discussed here, table 11–11 displays the amount of money invested in each weapon, the number of weapons acquired assuming each weapon costs $100 million, and associated utility points for each weapon. The result is a program costing $30 billion that procures 300 total weapons, with each of the 5 weapons bought in some numbers, but in differing numbers. Here, the program includes 100 models of weapon A, 80 of weapon B, 60 of weapon C, 40 of weapon D, and 20 of weapon E. This composite program may be complicated, but it is optimal, because no other composite program could generate a performance score this high.

This example is typical of many defense programs. Most are composed of multiple different weapons and associated assets. In many cases, some numbers of all weapons and assets must be acquired for the program to operate effectively: for example, multiple support assets are required for a new weapons system to perform effectively. But the number of weapons and assets in each category is a variable, not a constant. The task of program evaluation is to forge an overall investment strategy that allocates available funds so as to produce the most effective program possible. Normally, such a program will involve different levels of funds, and procurements in all categories. The mathematical rule shown here—MP/MC for all nth items—is a conceptual tool. It requires good data for costs, effectiveness, and marginal performance curves. Used in proper ways, aided by sound professional judgment, it provides a reliable economic model of choice for determining how to assemble efficient and effective defense programs.

Time-Phased Investment Model

A complete program evaluation often requires an investment strategy for determining how programs can best be pursued over a lengthy period of time. Typically, a large defense program takes many years to field. For example, a program to procure 1,500 tactical fighters or 5,000 tanks might take 10 to 15 years. Because performance in the interim years matters in the defense calculus, carrying out the program in an efficient and effective manner during this prolonged period can be quite important. The time-phased investment model provides an analytical tool for thinking in these terms. Figure 11–16 shows how this model is intended to work by displaying two different programs that achieve the same effectiveness after 10 years but produce markedly different results along the way. Because the balanced program produces greater effectiveness during most of the implementation process, it performs better than the unbalanced program.

Figure 11–16. **Effects of Alternative Time-Phased Investment Strategies**

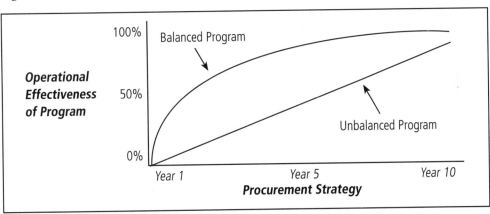

The model begins with the premise that much depends upon the availability of funds. A 10-year program will not usually receive 10 percent of its funds each year. Instead, it may receive a smaller portion of funds in the initial years and a larger portion in later years, because defense budgets often increase over a period of years. Regardless of how funds become available, this model seeks to invest them so that program performance is maximized during each year of the cycle. For example, if a program includes tactical fighters, smart munitions, and logistic support assets, this model will seek to acquire a mix of all three assets in each year so that a small but effective posture is fielded within the first 2 or 3 years. This model would seek to avert an unbalanced strategy that would acquire all of the program's fighters first, then its smart munitions, and only later its logistic support assets. Such a strategy would mean that the program would achieve operational effectiveness only in its final years. A balanced strategy might initially acquire one-third of the assets in all three categories to permit one-third of the posture to begin operating within 3 or 4 years. Afterward, balanced packages could be bought at regular intervals.

Figure 11–17. **Time-Phased Procurement of Two Weapons**

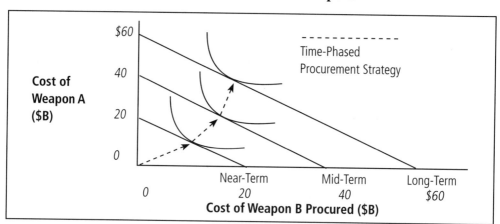

Within the framework of a balanced procurement strategy, the time-phased investment model seeks to allocate funds at each stage to achieve maximum marginal returns. That is, it seeks an optimal investment strategy for each phase of the procurement process. This can be illustrated by a program composed of two different weapon systems. The time-phased investment model employs indifference curves, cost-exchange curves, and tangency points in order to determine an optimal strategy. It applies these tools across a period of time; the results may suggest different investment strategies at different stages of the program. In figure 11–17, for example, the optimal mix in the near term occurs with most funds spent on weapon B. In the mid-term, an equal mix of spending on each weapon is optimal. In the long term, the optimal mix would result in funding tilted toward weapon A. The program thus starts with mostly weapon B being procured, but then shifts gears, ending with weapon A being mostly bought.

Table 11–12. **Utility Points for Time-Phased Procurement of Multiple Weapons**

| | Weapons Systems | | | | | | |
	A	B	C	D	E	Total utility points	Cost
Near-term package	17	14	6			37	$10 billion
Mid-term package	9	5	5	4		23	$10 billion
Long-term package	3	3	3	3	3	15	$10 billion
Total	29	22	14	7	3	75	**$30 billion**

The model would apply the same logic of time-phased optimality to programs involving multiple components. Table 11–12 displays the case of five weapons discussed earlier. This time, it employs optimality standards to divide the composite program into three successive stages. At each stage, it displays an optimal package costing $10 billion. The implication is that if the entire program is acquired in this way over a period of years, the result will be optimal performance along the way, not just at the conclusion.

Use of the time-phased investment model can result in a typical portrayal of how funds are spent among five weapons, as shown in figure 11–18. In this example, spending in the initial years focuses mostly on weapons A and B, then shifts to weapons C and D, and finally culminates in an emphasis on weapon E. Over the full period, similar amounts are spent on all five weapons, but in differently phased ways in order to achieve an optimal investment strategy that maximizes productivity along the way.

Figure 11–18. **Time-Phased Program Flows**

Note: Spending over 10 years for each of the 5 weapons programs totals $100 billion.

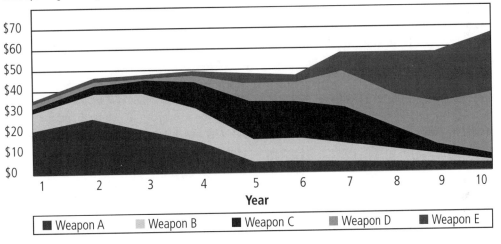

Applying Systems Analysis

Systems analysis offers a set of potent methods that can be used for force planning and program evaluation, as well as for other public policy issues in the defense sector and elsewhere. It has an unmatched ability to probe deeply into force operations while keeping the big picture in view, and its economic models of choice are capable of clarifying the options and tradeoffs of many complex programmatic issues that are crucial when large sums of money are at stake. Analysts need to remember, however, that more is involved than selecting one or more of these methods from the shelf and then using them like a cook uses a recipe to prepare a meal. Systems analysis requires that analysts possess a solid understanding of the subject area as well as the issues and options at stake. In many studies, moreover, the methods of systems analysis must be configured specifically for the study being conducted. In this era of fast-paced changes in world politics and military affairs, analysts must be prepared to think, analyze, and write in new ways.

Systems analysis has a long track record of impressive accomplishments, but it cannot continue contributing unless its users embrace changes in its methods, practices, and perspectives. Provided it evolves in appropriate ways, it is a methodology for the future.

Systems analysis faces its biggest agenda of change in methods that are employed to assist defense planning. Its methods for strategy analysis, force balance assessment, requirements analysis, and force posture analysis are mainly inherited from the Cold War. While some are still relevant, others need conceptual retooling. Although new methods have been evolving in recent years, additional progress is needed before they can lay claim to the same relevance and insight as the methods that they are replacing. As for economic models of choice, they are agnostic about the times and circumstances. As technical constructs, they can be used as well today as they were used decades ago. But they need to be configured with data and assumptions that reflect modern-day issues before they can be used to produce reliable results.

The need for change and reform in systems analysis should not obscure a deeper truth. Systems analysis is not merely valuable to defense planning, but essential. The defense budget and force structure are too complex to be managed without it. No amount of human knowledge and experience can substitute for its presence when it is functioning properly. This is the reason why it was adopted in the first place, and why it exerted such major influence in past years. The solution to the problems facing systems analysis is to solve them, not to banish the method in the hope that something else can take its place.

The following five chapters on applied methods suggest ways in which systems analysis can be updated to address the challenges of defense planning and program evaluation in the coming years. Together, they call for a new type of systems analysis that can address flexible forces, military transformation, expeditionary warfare through joint operations, and growing investment spending in a setting of stretched budgets.

Notes

[1] Classic books in this field include Charles J. Hitch and Roland N. McKean, *The Economics of Defense in the Nuclear Age* (Cambridge, MA: Harvard University Press, 1963); Alain C. Enthoven and K. Wayne Smith, *How Much Is Enough: Shaping the Defense Program, 1961–1969* (New York: Harper and Row, 1969); E.S. Quade, ed., *Analysis for Military Decisions* (Chicago: Rand McNally, 1964); E.S. Quade and W.L. Boucher, eds., *Systems Analysis and Policy Planning: Applications in Defense* (Chicago: American Elsevier Publishing Co., 1968).

[2] Systems analysis was required to play a critical role in defining Persian Gulf defense plans because, prior to the late 1970s, the United States had no organized military forces and command structures for operating there. Steps to rectify this deficiency were initiated when Secretary of Defense Harold Brown launched a landmark study, using systems analysis, on creating capabilities for limited contingencies there. Initially, the 1979 study focused on an Iraqi invasion of Kuwait, then addressed a Soviet invasion of Iran, and ultimately considered a spectrum of contingencies. The initial decision was to create a Rapid Deployment Joint Task Force but it was superseded by the creation of Central Command during the early 1980s. Equally important, the 1979 study and its successors resulted in allocation of a sizable force of divisions, fighter wings, and carrier battlegroups to Persian Gulf scenarios. As DOD funded programs for mobility and other assets, this force structure came to life with real capability for Gulf operations. It was this force structure, reinforced by additional units, that rushed to the Gulf in 1990 to carry out *Desert Shield* and *Desert Storm*.

[3] The term *systems analysis* has been defined in various ways by observers over the years. Gene H. Fischer defined it as inquiry that systematically examines relevant objectives and alternative policies or strategies for achieving

them, and compares quantitatively the economic costs, effectiveness, and risks of the alternatives. While the various definitions differ in their particulars, all focus on the use of systematic investigation of complex issues for the purpose of helping make economic decisions on major programmatic issues. Such definitions are broadly consistent with the definition used here. In the past, systems analysis and operations research have sometimes been portrayed as being the same or, if distinctions are made, systems analysis has typically been defined as dealing with a wider set of goals and activities, and operations research as dealing with a narrower set. Although efforts to draw clear distinctions are helpful, the reality is that there is no sharp demarcation line between systems analysis and the other two methods, strategic evaluation and operations research. Rather, systems analysis overlaps with both. In its core essence, nonetheless, it is separate and distinct, a reality that becomes apparent when these three methods are actually put into practice. See Gene H. Fischer, *Cost Considerations in Systems Analysis* (Santa Monica, CA: RAND, 1971).

[4] During the 1970s, analysis of mobilization and reinforcement rates had an especially powerful impact on U.S. defense planning for defense of Central Europe. The result was a landmark series of studies illuminating the many complexities that affect the rate at which military forces can mobilize and deploy to a crisis zone at a long distance. Results of these studies are presented in Secretary of Defense Annual Reports to Congress during the 1970s and 1980s.

[5] The issue of a proper force ratio for forward defense was a matter of continuing debate and analysis during the Cold War, when focus was mainly directed at NATO's Central Region. While few argued that NATO had to match the Warsaw Pact in numbers of divisions in order to produce a 1:1 force ratio, many initial studies were conservative, calling for a 1.25:1 ratio (Warsaw Pact: NATO), which would require 72 NATO divisions. Later analysis reduced this estimate to ratios that ranged from 1.40:1 to 1.67:1. As NATO's modernization got under way and other programmatic improvements were made, confidence grew in NATO's ability to mount an initial forward defense with 50 or 60 divisions, a force ratio of 1.80–1.50:1 (Warsaw Pact: NATO). Despite this trend toward less demanding force ratios, at no time was the belief widely shared that a 2:1 ratio (just 45 NATO divisions) would be adequate. The more basic insight stemming from this debate was that the desired force ratio is a variable, not a constant. In the view of most analysts and using most quantitative techniques, much depends upon such factors as the terrain, the defense concept, the interaction of attacker and defender strategies, the impact of air power, and the qualitative performance characteristics of forces on both sides. Thus, the ratio that applied to Central Europe during the Cold War might not apply to other theaters and periods of history. Each situation must be considered on a case-by-case basis with due regard for its unique features.

[6] For an insightful analysis of scenario-space analysis, exploratory analysis, and related techniques, see Paul K. Davis, "Uncertainty-Sensitive Planning," in Stuart E. Johnson et al., *New Challenges and New Tools for Defense Decisionmaking* (Santa Monica, CA: RAND, 2003), chapter 5.

[7] See Paul K. Davis, *Analytical Architecture for Capabilities-Based Planning, Mission-System Analysis, and Transformation* (Santa Monica, CA: RAND, 2002).

[8] Although public attention is often focused on defense policy and budgets, programming is typically the activity that captures greatest attention within the Department of Defense. The programming guidance issued by the Secretary of Defense spans the gap between abstract policies and budgetary details, determining how defense funds are allocated on behalf of national goals. In response to this guidance, the Services write program objective memoranda (POMs) that spell out how their funds are to be spent each year. Issue papers written by the Office of the Secretary of Defense staff to challenge aspects of the POMs are often exercises in systems analysis.

[9] Standard microeconomic textbooks that address welfare economics and political economy provide supporting analysis for these and other models. See, for example, Edwin Mansfield, *Microeconomics: Theory and Applications*, 5th ed. (New York: W.W. Norton, 1985). See also textbooks on public policy and management science, such as James L. Riggs, *Economic Decision Models for Engineers and Managers* (New York: McGraw-Hill, 1968).

[10] The mathematical progression is shown in appendix A to this chapter.

Appendix A: Mathematical Progression

The mathematical progression from $MRT = MRS$ to $MP_a/MC_a = MP_b/MC_b$ can best be illuminated by using a concrete example to create a general formula.

The concrete example involves two weapons systems: B on the x axis and A on the y axis. At the point of tangency between the cost-exchange curve and the indifference curve, the slopes of the two curves are identical. This is the same as saying that $MRT = MRS$. Assuming this:

- if spending on weapon B is reduced by $2 billion, the result will be a loss of 10 units of effectiveness from weapon B.

- in exchange, spending on weapon A will increase by $2 billion, and because of the identical slopes, the result will be a gain of 10 units of effectiveness from weapon A. If this is the case, then:

MRT = +$2 billion (weapon A)/-$2 billion (weapon B) = -1 (the slope)

MRS = +10 units (weapon A)/-10 units (weapon B) = -1 (the slope)

In the MRT equation, MRT = marginal cost of weapon A/-marginal cost of weapon B, or $MRT = MC_a/-MC_b$ = +$2 billion/-$2 billion.

In the MRS equation, MRS = marginal productivity of weapon A/-marginal productivity of weapon B, or $MRS = MP_a/-MP_b$ = +$10 billion/-$10 billion.

If $MRT = MRS$, then: $MC_a/-\dot{M}C_b = MP_a/-MP_b$

These two equations can be transposed to: $(MC_a)(-MP_b) = (MP_a)(-MC_b)$

Further transposition yields the final equation: $MP_a/MC_a = -MP_b/-MC_b$ which yields $MP_a/MC_a = MP_b/MC_b$

This equation holds true for two weapons. It can be generalized to include any number of weapons in the following way: $MP_a/MC_a = MP_b/MC_b = MP_n/MC_n$.

Chapter 12
Sizing Conventional Forces

Contributing to high-level decisions on the size and composition of U.S. conventional forces has long been one of the main roles of systems analysis. In this arena, critical issues arise about the interplay of strategy and resources, many of which are amenable to treatment by systems analysis. For example: how big should the U.S. conventional military posture be? How many principal combat formations, such as divisions, fighter wings, and carrier battlegroups, should the United States field in order to meet national security needs? More fundamentally, how much is enough? How can the United States know when its forces are too big, or too small, or about the right size? What intellectual standards should it employ to make these judgments? What are the criteria by which it should gauge military adequacy, today and tomorrow?

These important issues have been hardy perennials of the U.S. defense debate for many years, and decisions on these issues will continue to play a big role in shaping the size of the defense budget and the effectiveness of U.S. national security policy. These decisions also will help shape the future global security system in peacetime, and they will determine whether the United States wins its future wars. A posture of too few forces would create dangers, but having too many forces would waste money, diverting funds away from readiness and modernization. Making sound decisions on such issues is thus vital not only for the security of the country, but also for the health of U.S. military as a whole.

Systems analysis cannot prescribe the size and composition of the force posture in a mathematical sense, for these decisions depend heavily on political and strategic judgments. Systems analysis can, however, help bring analytical discipline to the process by which these decisions are made. It can illustrate the strategic consequences of alternative force levels by showing how different options offer different levels of confidence and insurance, and at what costs and risks. It can show how the flexibility of the U.S. military might be enhanced by equipping the force posture with a diverse portfolio of assets rather than designing it to serve a single purpose. It can also show how different approaches to striking a balance between quantity and quality will perform, thereby providing options for employing the resources that will be available. These are worthy contributions to an area of defense planning that requires clear thinking in a political and bureaucratic setting where such thinking can be at a premium.

This chapter begins by discussing the agenda of change facing systems analysis as threat-based planning gives way to a focus on flexible capabilities for multiple missions. Then it discusses the historical evolution of force sizing constraints from the Cold War through today, including the focus on two regional wars in the 1990s. Finally, it discusses the challenges facing systems analysis as it confronts new-era issues in force sizing and defense planning.

An Agenda of Change in Systems Analysis

A method traditionally employed by systems analysis has been first to identify enemy threats arising in specific wartime contingencies, and then to use quantitative techniques to determine the number of U.S. forces required to defeat these threats. Although this method worked well in past years, in the future it must be supplemented by new analytical approaches. A key reason is that the intellectual standards employed by the U.S. Government to shape its force posture are changing. Traditional standards have already been relegated to the dustbin by big changes in the Department of Defense and U.S. national security strategy. Previously the force was sized on the basis of threat-based planning anchored in a few specific and long-identified contingencies, but today it is being sized on the basis of capabilities-based planning oriented toward multiple crises and many types of operations. The issue is no longer how the force posture can be optimized to perform a few dominating missions against certain large threats, but instead, how it can be made flexible enough to perform diverse operations and a wide spectrum of missions, often against small to medium threats.

Determining how best to achieve this flexibility is easier said than done, especially when large forces of high quality must be maintained with constrained resources. Because size and quality can both be expensive, they often compete with each other at budget time. A larger military posture will normally provide greater flexibility than a smaller posture, because it provides more room for a diverse portfolio of assets. Maintaining large forces, however, can drain funds away from investing in the new weapons and training that permit the development of new doctrines. Conversely, enhancing the quality of one set of forces can be so expensive that insufficient funds remain to keep another type of force in the military posture at all. The consequence can be a well-equipped but relatively small force that lacks necessary size, diversity, and flexibility.

The tension between size and quality creates an incentive to strike a sensible balance between the two. But exactly how is this balance to be achieved? The idea of reducing the size of the force to free funds for greater investments and more training appeals to some. Yet the modern era demands a sizable military posture of ground, naval, and air forces that can carry out a high operational tempo even in peacetime and remains ready to perform multiple simultaneous missions in wartime. If the defense budget does not grow, tough tradeoffs may arise because of the difficulty in preserving an adequate quantity of diverse forces while steadily improving their quality with new and expensive equipment. Systems analysis will be called upon to help create a sound theory of force size and force mix, and to help illuminate the tradeoffs between quantity and quality.

The emerging situation dictates that new methods for applying systems analysis to sizing and designing forces must be created. In addition to the switch from threat-based planning to capabilities-based planning, other changes are at work. The days are gone when the force posture could be sized by creating some simple theory of aggregate requirements, such as being prepared for two regional wars, and imposing it from the top down. Future sizing decisions will have to be made partly from the bottom up. That is, key strategic decisions about overall force levels will need to be based on carefully considered and well-supported judgments about the internal composition of the conventional defense posture: whether it provides a sufficiently robust, modular portfolio of different types of forces that can be combined and recombined for use in constantly shifting ways for performing major combat operations (MCOs) and a large number of other missions. The adequacy of the force posture as a whole can no longer be gauged independently of knowing whether its constituent parts make sense. Indeed, possessing the right constituent parts and organizing them effectively may be at least as important as the total size of the force posture.

Thus, U.S. defense planning faces a threefold challenge in this arena: continuing to refine new force sizing standards so that the focus is on future strategic purposes, not those of the past; maintaining a force posture that is not only adequately large in aggregate, but also has the internal diversity and flexibility to perform an ever-shifting array of missions across a wide spectrum; and doing so affordably so that sufficient funds are available for spending on qualitative improvements. Even with a growing defense budget, meeting this challenge will confront senior defense officials with thorny dilemmas in the coming years. The dilemmas will become more difficult if, as is possible, future defense budgets quit growing, thereby leveling off in ways that confront DOD with tough choices about priorities.

The traditional economic models of choice employed by systems analysis—models that gauge tradeoffs by weighing marginal returns against opportunity costs—can still be used to help meet this challenge. But such models can be useful to evaluate force options only if the underlying issues are conceptualized properly, relevant systems are analyzed insightfully, and competing priorities are appraised wisely. The task facing systems analysis is to provide new analytical methods and new knowledge for helping grapple with complex options and tradeoffs that go to the heart of modern-era defense planning. In this important arena, an agenda of analytical innovation lies ahead.

Force Sizing in the Cold War: Focus on European and Global Wars

The best way to illuminate the agenda ahead is to look at the legacy of the past. Many of today's analytical methods for force sizing were created during the Cold War and then modified for the early post–Cold War period. The core force sizing method of threat-based planning, applied to a few specific contingencies, had four components. First, analysts would identify a limited set of plausible and demanding contingencies in which U.S. forces might be called upon to wage war. Second, they would form an intelligence estimate of the threat: the forces, capabilities, and battle plans that the enemy would bring to each contingency. Third, they would ascertain the number of U.S. and allied forces that would be needed in order to defend against these threats. Fourth, they would use the results to shape the size of the overall U.S. force posture and its internal composition as well. The expectation was that if the resulting posture was capable of performing its missions in these canonical contingencies, it could handle most other crises and wars, which were treated as "lesser included cases."[1]

Threat-based planning of this sort, critics alleged, risked becoming overly preoccupied with a narrow set of contingencies at the expense of neglecting other, different events that might erupt. But because it was well suited to systems analysis, it permitted penetrating inquiry into the full set of considerations that determine defense preparedness. It allowed force planners to make quantitative calculations about the numbers of divisions, fighter wings, and carrier battlegroups needed for defense against an attacking enemy force of a given size and capability. It allowed them to make similarly precise calculations about such important matters as mobility forces, logistic support assets, and war reserve stockpiles. It thus served as a convenient mechanism for determining full-fledged defense programs and their budgets. It also permitted cost-effectiveness comparisons of alternative weapons and programs by judging them on the basis of their ultimate rationale: their capability to perform missions in actual combat. As a result, threat-based planning helped bring a badly needed degree of intellectual rigor to defense planning.

During the Cold War, the most influential contingency was a Soviet/Warsaw Pact invasion of Central Europe, which became known as the "NATO contingency." This contingency rose to prominence in the mid-1970s, during the period after the Vietnam War when DOD was searching for a new, enduring rationale to guide strategic planning in response to the growing military competitiveness of the Cold War. The contingency postulated a Warsaw Pact invasion of Central Europe and the flanks after only a short period of mobilization and warning. The presumed goal of the Soviet Union was to overrun Western Europe quickly before the democracies could mobilize their superior industrial strength for a prolonged conflict. The nearby presence of large enemy forces in Eastern Europe and the western Soviet Union seemed to provide the wherewithal for a Soviet invasion.

Concern about such an invasion had been present in Western defense circles in the 1950s and 1960s, but worry grew when the Soviets began mounting a major modernization effort aimed at giving their forces the mechanized weaponry and offensive doctrine that would be needed for a conventional war. A principal concern was that the Soviet military might mimic the German Wehrmacht strategy of blitzkrieg in World War II by concentrating against NATO's exposed linear defense, punching through at vulnerable points, and then exploiting the rear areas to defeat NATO's forces in detail. During the later stages of World War II, the Soviet military had shown skill at turning the tables on the Germans, becoming adept at maneuver war themselves. When evidence became available that the Soviet military was returning to a strategy of breakthrough and maneuver for use against NATO and configuring its forces accordingly, concern mounted in Western circles.[2]

Never before had a hypothetical contingency been subjected to so much analysis of not only its broad parameters, but also its myriad details. The size and timing of the enemy threat was studied in great depth, along with the characteristics of allied forces, in an effort to establish a framework for determining U.S. force requirements for the forward defense of West Germany's borders. Once this framework was established, DOD analysts carefully examined a range of U.S. military options in order to identify the most effective responses that would make the best use of the funds available. Over the course of several years, a rich analytical paradigm was built that made a lasting contribution to refining U.S. defense planning. By the late 1970s, this paradigm helped channel the Carter administration's limited defense funds. Under the Reagan administration, the paradigm was employed to guide growing defense budgets. This paradigm had its drawbacks and critics, but seen in the light of history, it was instrumental in helping U.S. military forces recover from the Vietnam War, regain their strategic vision, and begin the long, successful march to their supremacy today.

The paradigm began springing to life when analysts determined that the realities of the Central Region military balance were not what they had been presumed to be. Surface appearances suggested that the Warsaw Pact, with its 90 heavily armed combat divisions, had an imposing advantage over NATO of 2.4:1 in ground forces. As of the late 1960s, NATO's deployed posture of about 37 divisions did not appear to be big enough to mount a strong defense of West Germany's lengthy, curving border of 750 kilometers. The presumption had been, therefore, that Soviet and Warsaw Pact forces could easily penetrate NATO's defenses and quickly conquer all of Western Europe. But as the 1970s unfolded, closer inspection by systems analysts suggested a more nuanced appraisal. Analysts and senior military officers concluded that NATO did not, in fact, have to match the enemy in total numbers of divisions, tanks, and artillery pieces. Owing to its qualitative advantages in airpower, readiness, logistics, favorable terrain, and defensive positions, NATO could aspire to a successful forward defense if it could reduce the force ratio disparity from 2.4:1 to 1.5:1 or so. In other words, NATO would stand a good chance of stalemating an enemy attack by 90 divisions if it could assemble the equivalent of 60 divisions.[3]

Systems analysis showed that the United States and NATO had viable options for pursuing this goal by taking advantage of defense resources that already existed but were not being used optimally. The most important consideration was that, although the United States permanently stationed only 5 2/3 Army divisions in Central Europe, it possessed over 30 active and reserve divisions based in the continental United States. Many of these formations were officially committed to NATO in a war, but they deployed too slowly to be available against a short-warning enemy attack that might be launched with 2 to 4 weeks of mobilization. Systems analysts proposed speeding their reinforcement rate by prepositioning the equipment for six armored divisions in Europe, thus allowing their personnel to fly there quickly in a crisis. Analysts also sought to strengthen U.S. airlift and sealift in order to permit other Army units to deploy faster as well. The goal, ultimately embraced by DOD, was to be able to deploy 10 Army divisions in 10 days and several more divisions within 30 days. Once these programs were implemented, the result promised to be a tangible improvement in the force balance, although it was still not enough to remedy the gap between capabilities and requirements.

Supported by DOD senior civilians and military officers, systems analysts crafted other innovative programs aimed at making further improvements. One of these programs sought to enhance the contribution of U.S. air forces to the land battle. Most U.S. and allied air forces stationed in Europe would be needed to win the air battle, but the United States had an additional 10 wings of fighter aircraft based in the United States that were candidates for rapid reinforcement and ground attack missions. DOD facilitated this effort by allocating funds to deploy munitions, build aircraft shelters, and preposition other assets at allied air bases that were big enough to absorb U.S.

aircraft that would deploy there in a crisis. These aircraft, many of them tank-busting A–10s, were equipped with the avionics and weapons needed to destroy enemy armored formations, thus providing the equivalent of ground units.

Another program equipped U.S. Army units with new armored vehicles, artillery that could fire large amounts of lethal munitions, and a new mobile defense doctrine. Enhanced quality in these areas provided the equivalent of more quantity. Under another program, NATO asked the European allies not only to modernize with new weapons, but also to supply more of their reserve formations with better equipment, including tanks and artillery pieces, to make them viable participants in NATO's defense strategy. The Germans and several other countries responded by fielding several additional combat brigades, further enhancing NATO's defense prospects.[4]

As table 12–1 shows, this four-pronged improvement effort enabled NATO to make major progress as the Cold War entered its final years. By the late 1980s, NATO could strengthen its ground posture from a force of 37 divisions to the equivalent of 55 divisions within a month of mobilization. Moreover, its once-brittle linear defense had given way to a more robust posture that combined a strong frontal wall with mobile reserves that could help contain enemy breakthrough attacks. The Warsaw Pact's decreasing ability to win by a speedy war of maneuver meant that a conflict could deteriorate into a grinding attrition contest in which NATO would benefit from its stronger logistic support assets, an area in which the enemy did not excel.

Table 12–1. **Status of NATO's Defenses in Central Europe, Late 1980s**

Existing NATO Posture	37
U.S. Army Reinforcement Program	5
U.S. Air Force Reinforcement Program	5
NATO Ground Modernization: U.S. and European	4
European Mobilization of Reserve Forces	4
Division-Equivalents Available by M+15/30 or D-Day	55
Division-Equivalents Needed for Successful Defense	60

During the period that these remedial programs were initially under way, NATO's posture was not fully assured. But although NATO still faced risks, the Warsaw Pact now faced looming risks of its own, coupled with the prospect that a conventional war would be costly and dangerous. With NATO gaining more modern weapons and smart munitions, the Warsaw Pact was being outpaced in the arms competition. It faced the prospect that, sooner or later, NATO would be capable of defeating it on the battlefield. This achievement was not accomplished overnight. It took at least 15 years of patient effort and considerable expense. In retrospect, however, it was a stellar achievement that owed a great deal to planning on the basis of threats and contingencies, and to the contributions of systems analysis.

During the early 1980s, the NATO contingency grew into a global contingency as U.S. defense strategy focused on the prospect of a worldwide war with the Soviet Union and its allies. While war in Europe remained the centerpiece of this global plan, potential conflicts in the Persian Gulf, Northeast Asia, and at sea were also assessed. This global contingency reflected the premise that if the Soviet Union provoked war with the United States, it might attack in more regions than just Central Europe. An accompanying thrust against the Persian Gulf oilfields was deemed plausible, as was Soviet military action against Japan and a North Korean invasion of South Korea. Serious fighting over control of the seas, including U.S. maritime lines of communication to Europe and Northeast Asia, was deemed likely. Planning even postulated that the U.S. Navy might take the fight to the Soviet Navy by going on the offensive and engaging in horizontal escalation in order to sweep the seas clean of Soviet forces.[5]

A main effect of this global contingency was to add the Persian Gulf to the two theaters—Europe and Northeast Asia—that would have to be defended concurrently with big U.S. forces. Simultaneity was nothing new to U.S. defense strategy. During the 1960s, DOD had pursued a "two-and-a-half-war" strategy that was animated mainly by potential wars with the Soviet Union in Europe and with China in Asia. During withdrawal from Vietnam in the early 1970s, the Nixon administration endorsed a "one-and-a-half-war" strategy, planning for a major war in Europe along with a smaller conflict elsewhere, such as the Korean Peninsula. Later in the 1970s, as the NATO contingency grew to prominence, staying prepared for another conflict elsewhere, such as Korea, remained a goal of defense planning. A core reason was reluctance to become so narrowly focused on Europe that the U.S. military would not have the forces and flexibility needed to handle even one other crisis.

The Reagan defense strategy, nonetheless, was a big departure from the prevailing norm. It elevated the number of major theaters to be defended from two to three, and called for concurrent defense of all three theaters against large, short-warning enemy attacks. The strategic effect was to elevate U.S. force requirements and the budgets needed to meet these requirements. While critics complained that the threat was being inflated, this global contingency provided a strategy anchor for the big defense budget increases sought by the Reagan administration. It also provided a basis for rebutting claims that the Reagan administration was so focused on achieving nuclear supremacy that it was neglecting conventional defenses or commitments to allies that were directly threatened by the Soviet Union. Beyond this, the contingency helped DOD chart a balanced modernization of its military posture that, instead of creating added strength for its own sake, sought tangible strategic payoffs in overseas geographical locations where U.S. power directly confronted Soviet power.

Illustrative U.S. force allocations for a global conflict during this period are displayed in table 12–2. In addition to the global strategy that this planning framework helped foster, it also provided an analytical rationale for the Reagan administration's decision to enlarge the conventional force posture. Its defense program added 2 Army divisions, 4 fighter wings, and 2 CVBGs while also endeavoring to build a 600-ship navy. The role of systems analysis in this calculus was to help ascertain force needs in each of the three theaters. Broadly speaking, systems analysis supported the notion that if the strategic goal was a global defense posture, then this force expansion made sense, as did an al-location of sizable forces to each of the theaters. Indeed, careful appraisal of the relevant force balances justified the judgment that although U.S. and allied forces were adequate or nearly so in each case, nowhere would they possess a solid margin of safety until the Reagan administration's modernization program was completed. The larger question was whether the Soviet Union, having started a big war in Central Europe, would see advantages in escalating it into a global conflagration. Debate on this issue swirled during the mid to late 1980s without reaching a firm conclusion one way or the other. The debate ended only when the Cold War drew to a close.

Table 12–2. **Illustrative U.S. Force Allocations for Global War, 1980s**

	Active Divisions	Fighter Wings	Carrier Battlegroups
Europe	12	20	5
Persian Gulf	7	11	4
Northeast Asia	2	3	3
Total	21	34	12

Sixteen Army Reserve Component divisions, most of which were either committed to Europe as later-arriving reinforcements or with-held as strategic reserves, are not shown. Also not displayed are a Marine Reserve Component division and two to three Navy carriers that would have been unavailable for early wartime duties because they were in shipyards being repaired or overhauled.

Force Sizing in the 1990s: Focus on Concurrent Regional Wars

The end of the Cold War brought a huge upheaval to U.S. standards for force siz-ing. The collapse of the Soviet threat meant that significant reductions could be made in U.S. nuclear forces, conventional forces, and combat units deployed in Europe. But although Europe was becoming secure, other regions remained turbulent where lo-cal rogue powers posed threats to U.S. interests and allies. As of 1990, the two princi-pal rogue states were Iraq and North Korea. Both were heavily armed countries led by governments with a record of menacing conduct. As a result, the United States could not afford to disarm in some wholesale way. This situation gave rise to a new issue: how much military power and capability should the United States still possess in the post–Cold War world? Answering this question became the focal point of analysis and debate aimed at creating new force sizing standards.

The task of creating new standards was initially taken up by the George H. W. Bush administration, then carried to completion by the Clinton administration. After mak-ing clear that Russia and China were not regarded as enemies, the Bush administration fastened on regional wars against medium-sized enemies as the basis for its defense planning. Its regional defense strategy singled out the Persian Gulf and Northeast Asia as likely sites for regional wars. But it also decided to leave 150,000 troops in Europe (down from the Cold War level of 330,000) as a hedge against potential instabilities there. The core goal of the Bush administration was to craft a strategy and force posture that could meet the requirements of the new era with a smaller defense budget than during the Cold War, while ensuring that the United States remained a global power by having the capacity to operate in multiple theaters.[6]

The climactic events of 1990–1992 added further definition to this regional strategy. The dissolution of the Soviet Union and its subsequent disarmament ended any serious threat to Europe by a reconstituted Russian military. However, the unraveling of Yugoslavia resulted in the eruption of savage ethnic fighting in the Balkans, raising the prospect that U.S. and NATO forces might be needed there. In the Persian Gulf, the *Desert Storm* campaign ejected Iraq from Kuwait, but Saddam Hussein remained in power in Baghdad, potentially capable of using his battered but still large army to invade Kuwait again if the United States turned its attention elsewhere. In Northeast Asia, although Japan was no longer menaced as during the Cold War, the Korean DMZ remained tense. Indeed, the totalitarian North Korean regime seemed to slip further into hostile paranoia, and remained capable of employing its big army to invade South Korea at the drop of a hat.

The effect was to solidify support for the Bush administration's decision to retain a Base Force capable of meeting the requirements of this regional strategy. The Base Force was about 75 percent the size of the Cold War posture: surprisingly big in the eyes of critics but, in the view of the Bush administration, well attuned to the new era. The active Army was downsized from 18 to 12 divisions, while the Marine Corps retained its 3 active divisions. The Air Force was reduced from 34 active and reserve fighter wings to 26 wings, plus about 100 strategic bombers newly configured for conventional war. The Navy was reduced from 15 aircraft carriers and 530 major ships to 12 carriers and 435 ships. The overall effect was to reduce U.S. active-duty military manpower from a peak of 2.1 million in the late 1980s to 1.6 million by 1994. The DOD budget was projected to decline to about \$270 billion by 1993, considerably below its Cold War peak of about \$350 billion (fiscal year 1993 dollars). The new downsized defense posture was intended to provide sufficient forces to wage regional wars in the Persian Gulf and Korea, and also provide a margin of insurance for small events elsewhere, such as strife in the Balkans or the U.S. invasion of Panama in 1989.

When the Clinton administration took power in early 1993, it launched a Bottom-Up Review (BUR) by DOD that preserved the essence of this regional defense strategy but modified its features in the direction of lower force requirements. The BUR embraced the goal of being prepared for two concurrent regional wars (referred to as major regional conflicts [MRCs]) in the Persian Gulf and Korea. Compared to the Bush administration, it saw less need to preserve an extra margin of insurance with forces beyond those needed for the now-canonized two MRCs. Accordingly, it further reduced the Army to 10 active divisions, the Air Force to 20 fighter wings, and the Navy to 11 or 12 aircraft carriers, with the total inventory projected to shrink to about 350 ships. DOD manpower levels were scheduled to decline to about 1.4 million by the end of the 1990s. The Clinton administration planned to keep the DOD budget at a level of about \$250 billion annually, allowing inflation gradually to reduce the total in real terms as the 1990s progressed.[7]

The Clinton team proposed that the two-MRC strategy would meet its military requirements by allocating virtually all active-duty forces to the concurrent contingencies of regional wars in the Persian Gulf and Korea. It set the goal of being able to deploy about one-half of the total force posture to each theater swiftly and simultaneously to meet short-warning attacks in both places. It therefore authorized programs to keep active forces at high readiness and to enhance DOD's strategic mobility assets by acquiring more prepositioned stocks, sealift, and airlift. Critics complained that the BUR force posture was too small to provide any flexibility for other crises. Rejecting this criticism, the Clinton team pointed out that it would continue deploying 100,000 troops in Europe and that small forces could be used to handle other contingencies so long as either the Persian Gulf or the Korean Peninsula was calm. Compared to the Bush strategy, the BUR strategy thus accepted an additional margin of risk, a tradeoff that systems analyses at that time pointed out: the BUR posture would be prepared either for two concurrent regional wars, or for one regional war plus smaller conflicts elsewhere, but it could not handle both two regional wars and smaller conflicts at the same time.[8]

During its second term, the Clinton administration undertook a Quadrennial Defense Review (QDR) in early 1997. The *QDR Report* put forth a new defense strategy of "shaping, responding, and preparing." A main effect was to broaden DOD's focus beyond being primed to "respond" to regional wars, in order to address how U.S. military power could be used to help "shape" peacetime engagement with new friends and to begin "preparing" for future transformation. The original BUR formula of being prepared for two regional wars (now called major theater wars [MTWs]) was nonetheless retained. The force posture remained constant, apart from measures to elevate the readiness of 15 Army reserve component brigades. The defense budget was to be kept mostly flat at about $250 billion annually, providing no additional funds for procurement to modernize an aging force, by living off the Reagan legacy of modern weapons.

The Clinton administration's decision to continue relying upon the two-MTW standard for force sizing was a target of mounting criticism from several quarters. Some critics felt that DOD was overinsuring against a highly improbable event because two regional wars were unlikely to erupt at once. Other critics felt that the standard so locked the entire force posture into its two hypothetical wars that not enough forces were free for handling the host of smaller but demanding conflicts and missions beginning to sprout up with growing frequency. Still other critics charged that the two-MTW standard would keep the military services from transforming their forces for the information age.[9]

Despite these criticisms, the two-MTW standard maintained its grip on DOD's force planning process for a number of reasons. First, while it created a ceiling above the force posture to bar expansion, it also created a floor that prevented major reductions. Second, it provided a convenient framework for the services, the regional commands, civilian programmers, and analytical staffs to pursue their various aims at budget time. Third, it provided a familiar and usable frame of reference for making judgments about priorities and for promoting integrated joint defense planning. A fourth reason was that it provided ample leeway for making arguments in favor of buying new weapons, strengthening readiness, and otherwise improving the force posture, so it could be used to support calls for new programs and bigger defense budgets. A fifth reason was a widespread belief that if the force posture could meet the demanding standard of being prepared for two regional wars at the same time, it would probably be capable of meeting almost any other type of challenge. A sixth reason was that mobilizing an internal DOD consensus behind a different approach was difficult. While few people liked the two-MTW standard, few strongly opposed it, and virtually nobody agreed on what should replace it. The final and most important reason was that DOD strategists were genuinely worried about Iraq and North Korea: while aware that other crises might erupt, their dominant goal was to send a powerful deterrent signal to those two adversaries, and to be fully prepared if they committed aggression. The two-MTW standard served this purpose admirably.

As the Clinton administration's tenure drew to a close, this strategy was fraying at the edges because so many new missions were arising. Peacekeeping missions in Bosnia, counterterrorist strikes in the greater Middle East, the increase of peacetime engagement missions in multiple theaters, and the demands of remaining ready for two regional wars contributed to a significant upsurge in the operational tempo of U.S. forces, leaving some active and reserve units drained of energy. Then came the Kosovo War of 1999. The United States deployed no ground forces to the conflict, but it did commit sizable air and naval forces that nominally were earmarked for the two canonical regional wars. Use of these forces in Kosovo was possible because both the Persian Gulf and Korea were stable at the time. Even so, for a brief period some Pentagon officials are said to have resisted the idea of intervening forcefully in Kosovo because this step might weaken deterrence in those other two theaters. The experience highlighted the shortcomings of locking the entire force posture so rigidly into two hypothetical, improbable wars that insufficient forces were available for real-life emergencies elsewhere. It also fueled critics' charges that the force posture was too small or was improperly organized to handle the growing strategic demands of the new era.

The Clinton administration resisted pressures to alter the defense strategy or the force posture, but late in its tenure, it did begin elevating the defense budget with real spending increases and inflation offsets. In particular, it significantly enlarged DOD's O&M budget to provide added funds for training, exercises, and crisis deployments. It also raised pay for military personnel. It began adding more funds for procurement in order to start buying the new-generation weapons systems that were emerging from the research and development process to replace old weapons inherited from the Reagan years that were beginning to wear out. By the time the Clinton era ended, the defense budget had risen to $300 billion, but even so, critics were calling for additional increases of $50 to $100 billion annually. Equally important, calls were being made to alter the regional defense strategy and the force posture in order to make them more relevant to changes in the world. In early 2001, the task of determining how to configure a new strategy, force posture, and defense budget faced the incoming George W. Bush administration.

Toward a New Defense Strategy and Force Sizing Standard

Shortly after arriving at the Pentagon, Secretary of Defense Donald Rumsfeld and his civilian team launched a full-scale review of the U.S. defense strategy, force posture, and budget. The results became available when the *QDR Report* of 2001 was released shortly before the terrorist attacks of September 11. The report charted a path to a major increase in the defense budget, which was to rise to $400 billion by 2005, with additional increases envisioned afterward. Initial funds were slated for spending on increased military pay and training to increase readiness quickly, and for investments in missile defense, homeland security, and counterterrorism. Long-term spending on research, development, and procurement was slated to rise significantly as well, in order to promote modernization and eventual transformation of U.S. forces for the information age.[10]

Accompanying this budget increase was a new defense strategy that replaced the two-MTW standard with a fresh approach to force sizing. Compared to the Clinton strategy, the new Bush strategy de-emphasized peacetime engagement, but otherwise pursued similar strategic goals abroad: assurance of allies, dissuasion of destabilizing military competition, deterrence of aggression, and defeat of enemies in war. The new strategy, however, announced that reliance upon threat-based planning would be replaced by an emphasis on capabilities-based planning. In essence, this meant that U.S. forces would no longer be tailored to deal with threats arising in specific contingencies. Instead, they would be sized and designed to counter generic enemy capabilities that could be faced in a wide set of circumstances, many of them impossible to forecast in advance.[11]

In addition, the new strategy announced a marked shift in the geographic focus of U.S. defense planning. Whereas the Clinton strategy had focused on Europe, Northeast Asia, and the Persian Gulf, the new strategy concentrated heavily on the huge southern arc of instability stretching from the Middle East to the East Asian littoral. The strategy identified the dangerous southern arc as an area not merely of hypothetical concern, but also as a growing locus of U.S. defense planning in peace, crisis, and war. It noted that the United States currently had few military assets there and that permanent stationing of big forces in peacetime was not politically feasible because few allies would be willing to host them. Accordingly, it announced that the U.S. overseas military presence would be reoriented to facilitate operations along the southern arc by developing bases, reception facilities, and infrastructure for temporary deployments there. It said that large forces and bases would be retained in Europe and Northeast Asia, but these assets would be re-oriented from performing stationary defense of old Cold War borders to providing hubs for projecting power outward to distant areas along the southern arc. It called for the repositioning of some naval forces and equipment stocks from Europe to Southwest Asia and the Pacific region.

The new strategy also called for improvements in the capacity of forces stationed in the United States to deploy swiftly to distant places along the southern arc that lack a well-developed military infrastructure. It called upon the regional military commands to develop plans and programs to facilitate this reorientation. In essence, the strategic vision thus articulated was one of expeditionary warfare. Instead of planning to position U.S. forces permanently at fixed overseas locations for decades, the new strategy instructed the military to prepare itself for temporary power-projection missions to an ever-shifting array of new geographic locations. This capacity for expeditionary warfare was to be provided by a combination of a new overseas presence and a better capacity to move highly mobile forces swiftly from the United States to places where they would join overseas-stationed forces to perform a broad spectrum of missions.

The new strategy dictated that U.S. forces should be configured to achieve forcible entry against enemy threats despite access-denial tactics and asymmetric operations. After gaining access, U.S. forces should be prepared not only to defend allied borders, but also to undertake offensive operations aimed at defeating the enemy, denying it sanctuary and, if necessary, occupying its territory. Such operations were to be carried out jointly, with all service components working closely together. But whereas the earlier emphasis on continental operations had largely been led by ground forces supported by air and naval forces, the new strategy postulated that some joint operations along littorals might be led by air and naval forces, with ground forces relegated to a supporting role. Indeed, the strategy articulated a vision of long-range strikes from the air and sea using smart munitions and cruise missiles to soften up the enemy before ground and air forces would deliver the coup de grace in close combat.

To help guide this switch to new-era defense concepts, the new strategy replaced the old two-MTW standard for force sizing with a new model that came to be called a "1-4-2-1" standard. This new standard said that U.S. forces no longer would be sized and designed exclusively for the two canonical regional wars of the 1990s. Instead, U.S. forces should be sized for four interacting purposes. First, they should be capable of performing homeland security and defense missions. Second, they should be large enough to carry out normal peacetime and crisis response missions, short of major regional wars, by the overseas combatant commands in such geographic areas as Europe, the Middle East/Persian Gulf, South Asia/Southeast Asia, and Northeast Asia. Third, they should retain the capacity to conduct strong, fully effective defense operations in two concurrent regional wars that might occur in the Persian Gulf and Korea as well as elsewhere. Fourth, U.S. forces, while defending in one regional war, should have the capacity to undertake a counteroffensive in the other regional war that could decisively defeat the enemy and occupy its territory.

This new standard meant that U.S. forces for overseas operations should be sized to provide three clusters of capabilities. The new standard implied that the military posture should be large enough to provide sufficient forces to wage offensive warfare in one theater and defensive warfare in a second theater, with sufficient additional forces to carry out normal peacetime operations elsewhere. For example, the posture should be large enough to pursue a counterattack in the Persian Gulf, to mount a strong defense in Korea, and at the same time to carry out a significant agenda of peacekeeping and daily alliance management in Europe. Compared to the old two-MTW standard, the new standard thus sought greater flexibility from the existing posture by making a significant number of forces available for other missions even as two regional wars were being deterred or fought. The precise allocation of forces was not made public and, in any event, would depend upon the circumstances of the moment. But hypothetically, simple arithmetic suggested that as many as one-fourth of existing forces could be withheld from commitments to regional wars and used for other purposes.[12]

In itself, the new force sizing standard did not point the way to either force increases or contractions. It implied that much would depend upon how the detailed requirements in each area were interpreted. If anything, it seemed to create a rationale for keeping forces at roughly current levels because while it provided room to alter commitments for major regional wars, it elevated commitments for other purposes. What the new standard focused on was the need to distribute forces among multiple missions so that all of the missions could be performed in adequate strength. It implied, therefore, that the force posture should be both adequately large and diverse, with a balanced array of assets, to meet the complex demands of the early 21st century.

A core purpose of the new strategy and force sizing standard was to make U.S. defense plans more flexible so that, in addition to deterring big regional wars, forces could be used for the full set of important but often less demanding global missions that arise so frequently. For example, U.S. forces could now be used to intervene in such places as the Balkans without undercutting plans for defense of the Persian Gulf and Korea. This new approach was put into effect 3 months after QDR 2001 was adopted, when U.S. forces were dispatched to Afghanistan in order to overthrow the Taliban and hunt down al Qaeda after the terrorist attacks of September 11. The new standard initially passed this test with flying colors: success was achieved in Afghanistan, and neither the Persian Gulf nor Korea erupted into war. When the Iraq war was fought a year later, U.S. forces continued to perform peacekeeping in the Balkans and Afghanistan, and while political tensions on the Korean Peninsula heated up, war did not break out there. This experience suggested that the new force sizing standard, with its new distribution scheme, could work effectively.

In important ways, this new force sizing standard was merely the tip of the iceberg with major implications for how the entire force posture was to be designed. The old strategy dictated that U.S. forces should be optimized for fighting two regional wars in specified contingencies. To the extent that flexibility was achieved, it would come as a byproduct of preparing for these two wars. The old strategy pursued optimization for a few missions, at the potential expense of flexibility for other missions. It did not discount specific contingencies entirely, but they played a lesser role in the planning process.

By contrast, the new defense strategy sought to liberate force planning from this straitjacket. Instead of being primed for only a select class of big wars, it declared, U.S. forces should be prepared to conduct operations across the entire spectrum of military conflict: from peacetime alliance management and peacekeeping operations at one end, to medium-sized conflicts in the middle, including strikes against terrorists and WMD, to regional wars or even bigger conflicts at the other end, and including postwar stabilization and occupation duties. Above all, the new strategy's leitmotif of joint expeditionary operations for full-spectrum dominance placed a premium on flexibility, agility, versatility, and adaptability. Each of these terms had its own meaning, but together they suggested something profoundly important: in the future, the U.S. military should be designed not just to perform one or two missions exceptionally well, but also to be able to perform a much larger set of diverse missions with effective skill. Moreover, the U.S. military should become capable of shifting gears and performing swift U-turns by quickly switching from mission to mission.

The new strategy emphasized modularity as a key goal of force planning. A military force possesses modularity when its constituent elements are self-contained, can perform their operations without outside help, and can be substituted for each other without degrading the performance of associated units. An Army division, for example, has high modularity when two of its three infantry brigades can be detached and their places taken by an armored brigade and an air assault brigade, thus creating a composite division of multiple different brigades. The same applies to air and naval forces: modularity allows them to incorporate different types of units and capabilities in response to shifting missions. The main purpose of modularity is to permit the flexible design of a wide range of tailored force packages, thus enhancing flexibility and adaptability.

The new strategy and force sizing standard thus marched boldly into a new era of force planning and programming. It meant that U.S. forces must have the capacity to be continuously packaged and repackaged for ever-shifting purposes; they must be capable of being combined, torn apart, and then swiftly recombined for missions that might change yearly or even monthly. This fresh guidance implied that what mattered was not merely the overall size of U.S. forces, but their internal composition as well. In essence, the new strategy called for a broad portfolio of differing capabilities that could provide considerable diversity and flexibility.

The immediate consequences for the size of the force posture became evident when the *QDR Report* was released. During DOD's internal debates, consideration evidently was given both to enlarging the posture in order to enhance its assets and to contracting it by 20 percent or so in order to save money for investments in modernization and transformation. But the rising defense budget lessened the need to set painful priorities in this area. In the end, a decision was made to retain the existing posture in its overall size, but to seek ways to reorganize it for added flexibility and capability. Apart from a few minor additions and subtractions, the military services thus came away from the strategy debate with the same forces as before. A core reason was that the existing posture, while far from perfect, was shown to have a fair degree of flexibility because it already possessed a diverse portfolio of assets, the fruit of having multiple services each pursuing its own designs. But notwithstanding this bow to continuity, the new strategy and force sizing standard opened the door to potentially big changes in the future as transformation unfolds.

The future will determine how force sizing standards will unfold, but frequent change is likely. The 1-4-2-1 standard already seems to have been partially overtaken by events. The first two numbers (1 and 4) seemingly will still apply because the United States will need to continue defending its homeland while employing four combatant commands to carry out its normal overseas operations. As for the standard of being capable of waging two concurrent regional wars, the overthrow of Saddam Hussein's regime means that one traditional likely adversary—Iraq—has been eliminated. But North Korea remains a potential wartime adversary, and other adversaries can be imagined. For this reason, U.S. defense strategy likely will continue embracing a two-war standard. Major change, however, seemingly lies ahead for the final number: being prepared for only one postwar occupation. As of late 2004, the United States remained in both Iraq and Afghanistan while still performing peacekeeping duties in the Balkans. Additional duties of this sort seemingly lie ahead. For this reason, U.S. defense strategy may need to possess the capacity to occupy two Iraq-sized countries at the same time. This would suggest that a 1-4-2-2 standard may be appropriate. Perhaps some different formula can be found, but the larger truth may be that no simple arithmetical formula can capture the full complexity of force sizing in the coming years.

Regardless of the force sizing standard employed, the emerging strategic environment seemingly dictates a need for a future force posture that is as large, or even larger, than now. If more forces are needed, a main reason will be that U.S. ground forces need enlarging in order to provide more assets for multiplying expeditionary missions, including the occupation duties of stabilization and reconstruction (S&R). In theory, this need for additional ground manpower could be met by reducing the size of the Air Force and Navy. While some steps of this sort might be pursued (for example, some Air Force reductions as new aircraft enter the inventory), there are constraints on any wholesale reliance on this practice. The primary reason is that current levels of Air Force and Navy active manpower are needed to field the combat formations of both services. Because sizable air and naval forces will be required for a host of purposes (including future wars that may place a premium on their assets), DOD is unlikely to look with favor on major cutbacks to either service. As a consequence, enlargement of the Army and Marine Corps combat forces will likely need to come from reorganizing the current assets of both services or from enlarging DOD's overall manpower, rather than reducing the Air Force and Navy in major ways. The need for continuing strength from all force components helps frame the debate on the future size and composition of the U.S. military as well as its need for high quality.

The Future Role of Systems Analysis

Although future administrations will doubtless modify the Bush strategy and force sizing standard, the emphasis on adequate size and flexibility seems here to stay because it is the only way to keep the U.S. military attuned to the requirements of a fast-changing world. Even so, debates about the U.S. conventional posture are likely to rage for many years. Systems analysis can contribute to the studies and debates that lie ahead, helping to insure that U.S. forces have the necessary size, composition, and flexibility. Systems analysis has the potential to contribute a great deal, because the decisions ahead are best approached by viewing the force posture as a whole, not as a collection of separate parts. The force posture is a system that must be tailored to provide the size, diversity, and other characteristics needed. Only by viewing the force posture as a system of interdependent parts will it be possible to design individual components that will add up to an integrated whole.

However, for systems analysis to make a sustained contribution, it must put into practice new analytical methods. Systems analysis can employ traditional models of economic choice, but it must first illuminate crucial systems, performance metrics, options, and tradeoffs. Three types of systems analysis, with associated methods, are likely to be needed in order to:

- help identify force requirements for a wide spectrum of contingencies, not just regional wars, and evaluate alternative force levels in terms of their capacity to perform under a variety of circumstances

- apply portfolio concepts to the design of future forces so that they possess a diverse set of assets to provide substantial flexibility and adaptability

- evaluate how U.S. military forces can best be improved through qualitative enhancements such as introduction of new technologies and weapons systems, and examine the tradeoffs between force quantity and quality.

Analyzing Aggregate Force Requirements

Although there is no clear demarcation line between adequacy and inadequacy, the size of the force posture matters in determining the degree to which military requirements can be met. A main task facing systems analysis will be gauging how much confidence and insurance in the face of an uncertain future are offered by the existing military posture and by potential alternatives. Given the emerging new U.S. defense strategy, systems analysis will have to examine force needs for waging major regional wars and for carrying out missions across the entire spectrum of operations.

In the coming years, systems analysis is likely to show that the peacetime mission of alliance management will continue to demand significant force levels. Although future U.S. deployments in Europe and Asia are uncertain, most likely 50,000–70,000 military personnel will remain in Europe and about 100,000 will remain in Asia, with an additional 20,000 or more in the Persian Gulf, in order to lead alliances and otherwise pursue peacetime political-military goals. Significant peacekeeping operations are also likely to arise frequently, and experience in the Balkans shows that such an operation typically requires the commitment of 10,000–30,000 personnel. Medium-sized crisis operations and wars will impose distinct requirements that vary in size: although limited airstrikes against terrorist camps and facilities may require only a few tactical aircraft and a few ships carrying cruise missiles, bigger operations against an adversary's WMD assets could require larger forces, perhaps two or three fighter wings, one or two CVBGs, and special operations forces. The invasion of Afghanistan was a medium-sized operation, but it required several fighter wings and carrier battlegroups, plus eventual commitment of ground troops capable of operating in brigade strength. The Kosovo war, another medium-sized event, required even larger air and naval forces, although ground combat forces were not committed until after the conflict had been won and peacekeeping became necessary.

Notwithstanding the growing importance of such missions, preparation to wage major regional wars and similar major combat operations is likely to remain a factor in the force sizing calculus. Throughout the 1990s, systems analysis supported the prevailing judgment that a large force of 6 to 7 divisions, 10 fighter wings, and 4 or 5 CVBGs could be needed to wage war in either the Persian Gulf or Korea. However, the victory over Iraq in early 2003 was won with joint forces only about two-thirds this size. In this conflict, U.S. forces were able to bring their technological prowess fully to bear, and Iraqi forces did not fight well. While future opponents may put up stiffer resistance, Operation *Iraqi Freedom* suggests that U.S. defense strategy may no longer need to plan to commit fully one-half of its military posture to fight a single regional war. Yet the operation also shows that postwar occupation duties can impose larger requirements than originally anticipated. Months after Saddam Hussein had been toppled, 130,000 U.S. forces remained in Iraq trying to stabilize the countryside and help build a democratic government.[13] Future contingencies will vary, but systems analysis is likely to find that future regional wars can be fought with forces that are no larger, and perhaps somewhat smaller, than the forces planned during the past decade.

Although analysis of specific requirements for missions all along the spectrum will matter in the force sizing calculus, strategy judgments about aggregate force needs will depend greatly on assumptions about the number of peacetime and wartime missions that U.S. forces must be able to perform concurrently. For as long as the United States remains a global power with involvement in multiple theaters, the need for simultaneous operations will remain. The calculation of force needs for such operations will always be a variable, not a constant, varying with changes in the total number of operations that U.S. strategy aspires to be capable of mounting at once. While the 1-4-2-1 concept may be altered, U.S. force requirements are likely to remain similar to the current posture or even larger. However, the current posture is not set in concrete: the options of deploying larger or smaller forces will remain viable choices that are likely to be debated intently in the coming years.

Table 12–3 helps illustrate the alternatives available to the United States by displaying three different force postures. Option A is the current force posture. Option B displays a posture that is about 20 percent smaller. Option C displays a posture that is about 20 percent larger. These three options offer different levels of capability for carrying out simultaneous operations in the current strategy. Compared to option A, the status quo, option B pares away capabilities, resulting in reduced confidence but, say its proponents, not fundamentally undermining the strategy. Option C provides added capabilities, but not enough to elevate U.S. military capability for a vastly more ambitious strategy. These three options have different costs attached: option A is funded by existing budgets, while option B would generate annual savings of about $40 billion, and option C would elevate expenses by about $40 billion annually.

Table 12–3. **Alternative U.S. Conventional Defense Postures**

	Option A Current Posture	Option B 20% Smaller Posture	Posture C 20% Bigger Posture
Active Divisions (includes Active Army and Marine divisions)	13	10.4	15.6
Fighter Wings	20	16	24
Carrier Battlegroups	12	9.6	14.4

Choosing among these options involves making judgments about relative strategic performance and cost-effectiveness. Systems analysis can help by providing insights about the marginal costs and benefits for each option. More fundamentally, it can counter the temptation to compare options in terms of a single fixed theory of requirements. Instead, its analyses can compare the options in terms of confidence levels, margins of insurance, risks, and tradeoffs. An example of such an analysis is illustrated in figure 12–1, which displays a strategic space of requirements rather than a pinpoint estimate. It shows how requirements for U.S. forces and their capabilities can vary as a function of the strategic conditions being encountered. It gives a bird's-eye view of how different force levels stack up against threats, requirements, and uncertainties that might be faced.

On the Y axis, the chart displays strategic conditions facing U.S. forces ranging from favorable—perhaps a single contingency in which the enemy force fights poorly—to

Figure 12–1. **Confidence Levels Provided by Alternative U.S. Force Postures**

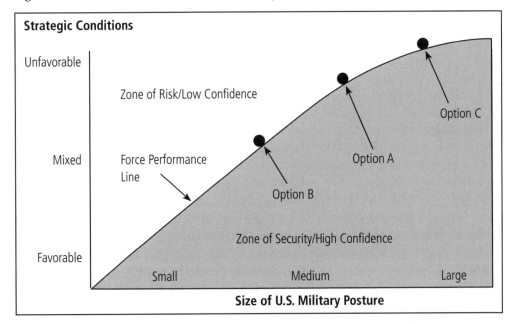

unfavorable, perhaps three simultaneous contingencies against three formidable enemies. On the X axis, the chart shows alternative force sizes ranging from small to large, including options A, B, and C as shown in table 12–3. Whereas a favorable situation might require only a small U.S. force to handle it, an unfavorable situation would require a much larger force.

Using data from both axes, the chart shows two strategic zones divided by a force performance line. Below the line is a zone of security, within which U.S. forces are big enough to operate with high confidence of success. Above the line is a zone of risk, within which U.S. forces are vulnerable to failure because they lack adequate size and capability. The line itself presents a statement of U.S. force capabilities. That is, each point along the line reflects the maximum capacity of the associated military posture to defend successfully, given various strategic conditions. The figure shows that as U.S. forces grow larger, the degree of confidence in the security they can provide increases because they can perform their missions successfully in less and less favorable situations. For example, a small force posture can perform successfully only in favorable conditions, a medium-sized posture can handle mixed conditions, and a large posture can handle unfavorable conditions as well.

Likewise, each point along the line also implies a unique theory of force requirements, because it defines the size of the force needed to provide that particular level of performance. The figure shows that U.S. force requirements are a variable: they depend not only upon the strategic conditions being faced but also upon the confidence levels sought, and risks accepted, by U.S. strategy. Thus, only a small U.S. force is required if the goal is merely to provide confident defense in favorable situations; a medium-sized force is required if the goal is to handle mixed conditions; and a large force is required if the goal is high confidence in unfavorable situations.

The figure suggests that none of the three options being considered here provides perfect security. Each provides a particular level of capability and reflects a particular theory of requirements, confidence levels, and risks. Illustratively, the current posture—option A—provides confident defense in about 75 percent of the situations that might be encountered, that is, up to conditions falling between mixed and unfavorable. Option A does not provide high confidence if conditions are worse than the point on the Y axis where the zone of security transitions into the zone of risk. Option B, with its smaller force, costs less but provides less capability and confidence than option A. Option C, by contrast, provides higher capability and confidence than option A. Shown together in the figure, they provide a sense of tradeoffs: greater security in exchange for higher costs, or lower costs in exchange for less security.

In itself, figure 12–1 does not endorse any of the three options; rather, it permits a comparison of their cost-effectiveness. It shows the conditions under which each might be judged as a viable choice or as an option to be rejected. The chart shows that option A makes the best sense if policymakers are satisfied with its 75 percent level of performance, do not want to spend the additional funds for a larger, better-performing posture, and are willing to accept the associated risks. The chart also shows that option B makes sense if policymakers aspire to reduce budget expenses and are willing to accept a lower-performing posture with its greater risks, and that option C makes sense if they want enhanced security and fewer risks at a higher price.

This type of figure is useful because it helps bring conceptual order and clarity to a complex setting that might otherwise overwhelm policymakers with more considerations than they can easily absorb. Charts of this sort typically present economic performance curves so that the assets and capabilities of alternative options can be measured against goals and requirements. Such charts help show senior officials how force requirements vary depending on the strategic goals that they set, and how the choices facing them have alternative consequences. Such charts will be valid only if the analyses that form their key judgments are accurate. The role of systems analysis is to provide the in-depth analysis that makes such charts as accurate as possible.

Analyzing Force Composition

The internal composition of the force posture can be at least as important as its aggregate size. In order to perform multiple and frequently changing missions, the U.S. military needs a portfolio of different assets that can be quickly combined and recombined to generate force packages tailored to the demands of the situation. This need for a robust portfolio helps reinforce the rationale for a relatively large force, around the same size as today's, but it is no guarantee that even with an adequately large posture, all of the specialized capabilities will be fielded in the right amounts. Creating a properly diverse and balanced posture is an ongoing challenge facing defense planning.

Systems analysis can contribute to designing the internal composition of U.S. forces by employing the method of portfolio analysis, which employs techniques similar to those used to create a balanced array of investments—property, liquid cash, stocks, bonds—that respond to needs for both regular income and long-term security. In the defense arena, portfolio analysis aspires to create a wisely balanced array of complementary military assets. It aims to ensure that the entire posture is sufficiently large to provide enough assets in each individual area of force operations, and that such assets are, in fact, available. When new types of specialized assets are needed but the overall posture cannot be enlarged, the job of systems analysis is to help determine how the posture can be contracted in some areas to make room, often a difficult and controversial task.[14]

Suppose, for example, that a contingency arises requiring the deployment of a sizable U.S. military force with considerable combat power. On the surface, the situation might seem to call for commitment of many combat units. But if sending numerous divisions and air wings means that adequate logistic support assets cannot be deployed, the force might lack the wherewithal to fight effectively. Conversely, deploying large logistic support assets might be counterproductive if insufficient combat units are sent. Portfolio analysis is the process of determining how to assemble the proper combination of combat and support assets so that the performance of U.S. forces is maximized.

What applies to force packaging for individual contingencies holds true for shaping the internal composition of the U.S. military posture as a whole. The first issue that arises is the distribution of assets among the four services. Table 12–4 shows the current distribution of combat formations and active military manpower. Portfolio analysis would ask whether each service has enough assets to carry out its missions. It also would ask whether the distribution of assets among the services reflects a sensible balance, or whether some other force mix might make better sense. While the answers to these questions are debatable, today's force mix undeniably reflects a longstanding practice of favoring continuity at the expense of innovation: in essence, the same force mix has been fielded since the mid-1970s, regardless of whether the overall posture is expanding, contracting, or remaining stable. When U.S. forces were enlarged during the Cold War, all services benefited to similar degrees. When forces were reduced afterward, all services contracted by similar margins. Whether such linear practices will make sense in the future seems uncertain: new strategic conditions and defense transformation may create reasons for a new force mix with a different combination of service assets. If so, systems analysis using portfolio techniques can help chart the course ahead.

Any quest for a sound, future-oriented force mix must begin by recognizing that none of the services is automatically entitled to a specific share of defense manpower and

Table 12–4. **Composition of U.S. Military Forces, 2004**

Service	Main Combat Formations	Active Manpower
Army	10 Active Divisions	486,000
Air Force	20 Fighter Wings	354,000
Navy	12 Carrier Battlegroups 12 Amphibious Ready Groups 310 Authorized "Battle Force Ships" (295 actually deployed)	371,000
Marine Corps	3 Active Marine Expeditionary Forces	172,000

resources. Decisions should depend upon strategic needs, which can change from time to time. It is also true, however, that while the current mix reflects the legacy of past priorities, it is a product of strategic judgments that thus far have withstood the test of time because they consistently emphasized flexibility and diversity. Theories about different mixes have often arisen, and normally proved ephemeral, fading when their attractions dimmed or new conditions arose. In 2000, for example, many critics argued in favor of more air and naval forces and fewer ground forces. Today, many such critics are arguing the opposite: more ground forces at the expense of fewer air and naval forces. Only time will tell whether this argument has more staying power than its predecessors.

The argument against major change stems from the valid premise that the current posture has more attractive features than its critics generally acknowledge. In particular, the current force posture already provides considerable diversity for the simple reason that all four services field substantial forces. Owing to its powerful naval forces, the U.S. military is capable of dominating the seas and winning any naval engagement imaginable. Its strong air forces can dominate the skies and contribute importantly to ground battles. Likewise, its ground forces are capable of generating substantial combat power for any land battle. These separate components, moreover, can be blended for joint operations: naval forces can contribute to land warfare, and air forces can contribute to both naval warfare and land warfare. Few other countries have such a diverse, balanced force posture, which is a key reason why the U.S. military is the world's strongest and most flexible fighting force.

Because of these characteristics, the current posture does not seem vulnerable to the charge that it is badly out of balance. Whether it is optimally balanced for the challenges ahead is unclear. Yet a major reallocation of assets from one service to another would not necessarily produce a better mix. Because a tradeoff would have been made (for example, more ground forces for fewer air forces), the U.S. military would be enhanced in one way but degraded in another. If a bad trade is made, the U.S. military's overall flexibility and responsiveness might decline, not increase. All potential tradeoffs thus must be examined on their individual merits. If options can be found to further strengthen the posture's flexibility by altering how resources are distributed among the four services, they should be pursued. A challenge for systems analysis will be to help identify and evaluate such options, with their full implications in mind.

The same need to analyze the current force distribution and options for change also applies to the internal composition of each service, all of which are products of past strategic choices and are not set in concrete. Indeed, there may be greater opportunities for altering force mixes within each service than for altering the balance among the services. All four services are currently undergoing debates about their future structures. The challenge is to conduct these debates wisely so that sound decisions emerge regarding not only how each service is structured in future years, but also how their future structures blend so that their capacity for joint operations is maximized.

Table 12–5 shows how the Army is currently structured in terms of main combat formations and distribution of active manpower. In the recent past, DOD has judged that the Army needs an active force of 34 brigades and regiments to meet requirements for adequate strength, and to ensure that each type of combat formation is maintained in sufficient numbers. For example, the current posture provides three air assault brigades and

Table 12–5. **U.S. Army Active Force Structure, 2004**

Active Brigades/Regiments		Active Manpower Distribution	
Armored	6	Combat Forces	150,000
Mechanized	12	Deployable Support Units	150,000
Air Assault	3	Non-Deployable Support Units	186,000
Armored Cavalry	3	**Total**	**486,000**
Medium Stryker	2	Reserve Component Forces	
Light Infantry	4	Manpower	550,000
Airborne	4	Divisions/Separate Brigades	8/15
Total	**34**		

four airborne brigades. But is this particular force mix suited to strategic requirements ahead, or would a different mixture of brigades perform better? Would more heavy (armored and mechanized) brigades and fewer light and medium brigades make better sense, or the reverse? The Army sparked controversy in 2002 by proposing a long-term plan to transform its entire posture to a single model of medium-weight brigades with light armored vehicles. Critics charged that, without heavy armored forces and light infantry, the Army would be unable to perform its full spectrum of operations. More recently, the Army has begun pursuing the idea of fielding a larger number of smaller brigades (43–48 such brigades); this, too, sparked controversy and a need for continuing analysis.[15]

Similar questions are often raised about how Army military manpower is allocated. Some critics complain that the Army has insufficient "teeth" (combat forces) because its "tail" (deployable support units) is too large and redundant. Other critics note that logistic support units are manned at only 50–65 percent of regular strength and charge that this creates undue reliance upon Reserve Component manpower to make up the difference. Still other critics complain that because the Army allocates 180,000 soldiers to nondeployable support units, such as headquarters and training facilities, too few soldiers are available for overseas deployments in combat formations or support units. It has been argued that the Army's large reserve component posture—550,000 soldiers, 8 divisions, and 15 separate brigades—should be reduced to free more funds for active forces. While these criticisms are debatable, two key points stand out: first, the Army's need for a diverse array of internal assets plays an important role in its need for as many as 43–48 new-style brigades and 480,000 active troops, and second, how these brigades and manpower levels are allocated determines how the Army functions and what types of combat power it is capable of generating. Portfolio analysis can contribute to evaluation of how the Army's force composition should take shape by illuminating requirements and priorities in each functional area.

The Air Force has a combat force of about 200 strategic bombers and the equivalent of about 20 fighter wings (which are now organized into 10 aerospace expeditionary forces).

Table 12–6. **U.S. Air Force Aircraft, 2004**

Bombers	208
Tactical Combat Aircraft (assigned to combat units)	1,450
Reconnaissance and Electronic Warfare	337
Refueling Aircraft	536
Transport Aircraft	722
Total	**3,253**

It also flies a large number of additional aircraft that provide various types of support to air, ground, and naval forces. Table 12–6 displays the distribution of these assets.[16]

The Air Force has been deploying 20 fighter wings not only to generate aggregate air power, but also to fly a mixture of sorties: air superiority, multimission, and ground attack. Thus, 4 wings are equipped with F–15s for air superiority, 13 wings are designed for multirole missions with F–16s, and 3 wings are configured, mostly with A–10s, for ground attack. The need to preserve this varied portfolio plays a role in the Air Force's modernization plan to buy the new F–22 Stealth fighter, the F–35 Joint Strike Fighter, and the F–45 unmanned combat aerial vehicle (UCAV). Likewise, the Air Force total of about 3,250 aircraft comprises not only the 20 fighter wings, but also about 1,600 aircraft needed to support these fighter wings, including reconnaissance, electronic warfare, refueling, and transport aircraft. The Air Force's inventory of 208 bombers provides aircraft for nuclear and conventional roles.

The manner in which functional requirements for air operations are allocated plays a major role in determining the shape of the Air Force and the types of aircraft that it will buy. For the same amount of money, the Air Force could have different distributions of aircraft: perhaps more standoff bombers and fewer tactical fighters, or the reverse. Debates about the Air Force's internal composition are best resolved through the kind of careful analysis of the options and tradeoffs that systems analysis can contribute.

Similar considerations apply to shaping the internal composition of the Navy and Marine Corps. A main feature of U.S. maritime strategy is to keep continuously afloat a force of three CVBGs and three amphibious ready groups (ARGs, composed of amphibious ships with Marine ground troops and strike aircraft). Owing to rotational dynamics and overhaul requirements, a force of three to four carriers is needed to keep a single carrier afloat at all times. ARG requirements are similar. Thus, the Navy posture comprises 12 CVBGs and 12 ARGs. Each CVBG and ARG requires a mixture of submarines, cruisers, and destroyers to act as escorts, plus logistic support ships. The Navy's authorized posture of 2004 is 310 ships: 12 carriers, 55 attack submarines, 14 ballistic missile submarines, 116 surface combatants, 36 amphibious ships, and 77 other support ships of various types. These numbers are not sacrosanct: debates are continuously under way about all of them, and Navy force levels and overseas deployment patterns have been slipping downward in recent years. The future Navy will be determined largely by the types of ships bought, including the numbers of carriers and amphibious ships as well as the mix of traditional combatants and new littoral ships. A key issue is whether the Navy will continue to be animated by traditional sea dominance missions, littoral missions, or a combination of both.

Meanwhile, the Marine Corps is moving away from its traditional emphasis on amphibious warfare to create flexible expeditionary forces capable of joint operations across a wide spectrum of contingencies. Future Marine expeditionary forces may have different combat structures, weapons, and support assets than current forces. In particular, the Marine Corps' longstanding emphasis on amphibious assault missions seems likely to give way to a growing emphasis on capabilities for a wide spectrum of land operations. No matter what lies ahead for the Navy and Marine Corps, naval planning factors and force composition policies will have to be subjected to scrutiny, verification, and modification using systems analysis.

Debates over the internal composition of all four services have been a continuing feature for many years, and are likely to continue far into the future. Controversy and uncertainty will inevitably give rise to a continuing stream of studies aimed at weighing the issues and options. A complaint of recent years has been the lack of low density/high demand (LD/HD) forces in the inventory of all services. These are forces that are few in number but must be used frequently: for example, units for peacekeeping operations, defense suppression and electronic warfare aircraft, command and control aircraft, search and rescue aircraft, and Navy special forces. Identifying requirements for these assets has been easy, but it has been far harder to make room for them by reducing assets in other areas. Similar dilemmas will arise in other areas as the new defense strategy and transformation unfold; an example is the impending acquisition of UCAVs, which could replace some fighter aircraft. Thus, the need for some types of old-era forces may decline as the need for new-era forces grows. Managing this transition promises to be challenging.

The experience of occupying Iraq after the invasion of early 2003 has given rise to another type of new-era requirement: forces capable of performing S&R missions. These missions include bringing security and stability to chaotic areas where enemies may still operate; restoring power, electricity, and water; reestablishing basic governmental administration and social services; and getting the domestic economy running again. These missions require special types of U.S. military assets such as civil administrators, construction engineers, military police, special operations forces, and light infantry, which might not normally be available in adequate numbers when major combat operations are launched. In the coming years, an important issue will be how the U.S. military, especially the Army, reconfigures itself to provide necessary capabilities in these areas without unduly reducing combat forces for wartime missions.

Studies of cross-service tradeoffs and alternative approaches to the internal composition of individual services require use of sophisticated analytical methods. In particular, performance metrics from different functional areas must be weighed in terms of comparable yardsticks. For example, armored divisions and fighter wings have different functions in war, yet when both are employed to destroy enemy ground forces, they can be compared in terms of their impact in this area. While the technical features of performing tradeoff analyses are beyond the scope of this chapter, systems analysis can often generate illuminating results when it uses the concept of marginal return versus opportunity cost to analyze options and compare them. The term *marginal return* refers to the gain that is achieved by transferring existing resources from one activity to another, or from investing new resources in one area rather than another. *Opportunity cost* refers to the loss that accompanies this transfer; for example, transferring resources might result in a gain to capability A but a loss to capability B. When force structure tradeoffs are being pursued, the marginal gain should match or exceed the opportunity cost; otherwise, the change makes no sense and could be counterproductive. Systems analysis is a useful methodology for studies of such tradeoffs because it is well suited to identifying and measuring prospects for enhancing marginal returns and lessening opportunity costs across a broad array of options.

Assessing the Quantity-Quality Tradeoff

Despite totaling nearly 1.4 million active troops, the U.S. military is not amply large when judged in relation to its global requirements; if anything, it is stretched thin. As a result, U.S. defense strategy will continue relying upon both adequate quantity and high quality to perform future missions. In the years ahead, the challenge will be to provide both quantity and quality at the same time with the budgets that will be available. As a result, decisions about the size of U.S. conventional forces will need to be made in the context of judging how best to improve their quality through modernization and transformation. Both types of judgments will have to be made together because future defense budgets may not be large enough to deploy all of the forces that might be needed, while also improving them at the rate that might be desirable. To the extent such constraints exist, the tradeoff between quantity and quality will need to be appraised carefully, with a view toward striking a sensible balance of both. Systems analysis will need to be capable of shedding insights on this tradeoff, with its complexities in mind.

In contrast to the Reagan era, the military buildup being pursued by the Bush administration thus far has not sought to enlarge the conventional force posture appreciably. While it is funding an increase of 30,000 Army troops in order to handle the spike in demand caused by the ongoing presence in Iraq, this increase may be temporary or permanent. For the long haul, the Bush administration currently intends to keep the posture at roughly current levels and to employ growing defense budgets to fund modernization and transformation to enhance U.S. military power through qualitative improvements. For example, acquisition of modern C⁴ISR systems and information networks, new weapons, and smart munitions is intended to strengthen the capability of each division, fighter wing, and carrier battlegroup. In the future, therefore, U.S. forces may be no larger than they are now, but they are intended to be better able to perform their missions.

While the exact degree to which U.S. conventional forces will improve is to be seen, the process will be gradual and cumulative over a period of years. For example, by 2010 or so, a qualitatively stronger U.S. military posture would be able to cover a larger space of requirements: today's zone of risk would contract, and the zone of security would expand. Risks will remain, however, because of remaining constraints on U.S. combat power and because adversaries will be strengthening their own forces.

Although a plan to keep the current military posture constant in size while improving it qualitatively has merit, pressures for force contraction and force expansion are both likely to be part of the political debate for years to come. Such pressures could intensify if the growth of the defense budget slows and DOD must therefore set priorities more stringently, or if international conditions worsen, elevating U.S. force requirements. Tough decisions would then have to be made.

Irrespective of the size of the defense budget, both force expansion and force contraction would affect the amount of money available for modernization to enhance force quality. This tradeoff between quantity and quality must be handled carefully at all times. Both contraction and expansion have vocal proponents in the political process. During the 2001 debate as the QDR Report was being written, some observers argued in favor of reducing the active-duty force by about 20 percent in order to make more funds available for investments in modernization and transformation. They worried that procurement budgets in coming years would not be big enough to fund proposed purchases of tactical aircraft, missile defenses, space systems, and other new weapons. They asserted that a somewhat smaller force would still be large enough to perform key missions, and that U.S. defense strategy would gain from the exchange because the remaining forces would be even stronger in qualitative terms.

By 2004, the school in favor of force expansion had arrived on the scene with equally vocal arguments. Most favored expansion of the Army, some by as much as two divisions, or a 20 percent enlargement of combat forces and up to 100,000 additional troops. Meanwhile, senior Navy officers began quietly lobbying for a long-term expansion to as many as 375 ships, or 20 percent larger than the authorized level of 310 ships. While different types of force expansion may be considered in the coming years, the idea of a 20 percent overall expansion of all services provides a benchmark for considering the strategic tradeoffs involved regardless of the size and scope of expansion. The principal argument for expansion by 20 percent is that more forces are needed to perform a widening spectrum of missions in an increasingly dangerous world. Proponents of this idea argue that DOD can afford to trim its investment plans in order to field more combat formations, because current U.S. forces are already qualitatively superior to enemies and will remain so even with smaller acquisition budgets.

The policy preferences of these two schools of thought may be incompatible, but they both challenge DOD's existing plan for future force levels and modernization budgets. Systems analysis has an important role to play by helping impose analytical discipline upon the resulting debate. Each school of thought tends to dismiss as insignificant the negative consequences of its recommendations, but both approaches would, in fact, impose significant tradeoffs that would have to be weighed in the decision process. Force contraction might free additional funds for procurement, but it would also result in smaller forces and less capacity to perform simultaneous missions. Expansion would provide more forces for more missions, but unless defense budgets grow proportionately, it would also result in slower modernization and fewer qualitative improvements in the coming years. For both courses of action, the issue is whether the gains exceed the losses and result in a net benefit for U.S. defense preparedness. Systems analysis is well suited to helping make this judgment.

A careful analysis is needed because the issue at stake is not the tradeoff between quantity and quality in the abstract, but at the margins in the context of specific circumstances. Experience shows that sometimes, but only sometimes, trading less quantity for more quality is a good idea: the exact details of the exchange matter. The realities of the exchange, moreover, may be different from what is suggested by surface appearances or asserted by advocates. Systems analysis can contribute to the debate by comparing options in terms of a common metric: the capacity to defeat enemies in wartime situations. By applying cost-effectiveness analysis, it can help illuminate whether the marginal gains for each option exceed the opportunity cost, the best criterion for judging whether a net gain, or a net loss, will take place.

The need for careful, discriminating analysis especially applies to the idea of reducing forces in order to fund faster modernization on the premise that a net strategic benefit will result. As figure 12–2 illustrates, if forces were reduced in size by 20 percent in exchange for a gain in quality of only 10 percent, this would be an unwise tradeoff. A sensible tradeoff would be one where the percentage gain in quality matched or exceeded the reduction in quantity. In some cases, for example, a 10 percent force reduction might produce a quality gain of greater than 20 percent if the result were procurement of high-performance weapons and other capabilities that could open the door to new operational concepts.

Even reducing U.S. forces by 20 percent would not, however, liberate $80 billion for modernization (20 percent of a $400 billion budget). The reason is that the cost of several expensive defense programs remains largely unchanged even if active-duty forces are contracted. Examples include programs for C⁴ISR, missile defense, administration, health care for retirees, reserve forces, and research, development, testing, and engineering. A good rule of thumb is that a 20 percent reduction of active forces produces only a 10 percent budget savings, or about $40 billion annually.

Savings of this magnitude would, of course, make more funds available for investment and modernization, but again, the details matter. Today, DOD spends about $140 billion annually on research, development, and procurement. This amount is expected to grow to $170 billion in a few years. A $40 billion increase in funds would elevate this annual investment spending by about 25 percent, a sizable increase that would permit speedier development of new technologies and faster procurement of new weapons systems. But hope that the combat power of U.S. forces would grow by 25 percent seems unlikely to be fulfilled (although much depends upon the new systems acquired). Advanced weapons

Figure 12–2. **Fewer Forces in Exchange for Higher Quality?**

An Unwise Trade		A Sensible Trade	
			+ 20 percent
	+ 10 percent		
- 20 percent		- 10 percent	
Quantity	**Quality**	**Quantity**	**Quality**
20% Fewer Forces and 10% Additional Quality		10% Fewer Forces and 20% Additional Quality	

systems probably account for only about one-third of the strength of U.S. forces. The rest of the strength comes from personnel, training, and doctrine. Thus, a 25 percent improvement in the quality of weapons systems might result in an increase of 10 percent or less in overall U.S. combat power. Even if the increase were more than 10 percent, modernization takes effect only over a period of several years, not instantly. A normal, vigorous modernization effort, as now under way, will increase the overall quality of U.S. weapons by about 3 percent annually. A faster modernization brought about by a 25 percent increase in procurement budgets might increase this to 5 percent annually. Within a decade, overall weapons quality would thus improve by 50 percent rather than 30 percent. But in the near term (3–5 years), the increase would be less impressive because modernization unfolds slowly.

Is a steady increase in quality of this magnitude worth losing 20 percent of force size? Perhaps this would be the case in the long term, but the near term could be a different matter, if smaller forces could not perform as many missions and would face greater danger abroad. Concern about losing valuable forces does not, however, rule out the idea of some contractions in order to accelerate modernization or otherwise improve quality. The point is that this tradeoff imposes opportunity costs that would have to be justified by compelling marginal returns. Perhaps the benefits of some force contractions would exceed their cost, and perhaps not: systems analysis is a tool to enforce disciplined examination of the tradeoffs, and thereby encourage good decisions while resisting bad decisions that might be based on impulse or hazy reasoning.

The same need for careful analysis applies to proposals for enlarging the force posture by 20 percent. This step would undeniably make more forces available for more missions with beneficial strategic consequences. Doubtless virtually all U.S. military commanders would welcome the prospect of having more forces and greater flexibility at their disposal. But would the gain be worth the cost of a slower modernization effort? Such a force expansion would cost about $40 billion annually. The effect could be to reduce future research, development, and procurement budgets by one-third, from $170 billion annually to $130 billion, keeping them at roughly today's levels.

The impact on the buying power of the future procurement budget, now slated to reach $110 billion in a few years, could be even more deleterious. The reason is that about $45 billion of this amount must be spent on such common items as trucks, war reserve ammunition, and replacement items. This steady-state expenditure leaves only $65 billion for major new weapons, equipment, and hardware. It is these discretionary funds that suffer the most when procurement budgets are cut. A reduction of $25 billion to $40 billion owing to force expansion could cut this critical feature of procurement by 50 percent or more, dramatically impeding modernization. With fewer aircraft, ships, and other weapons arriving in the inventory, the qualitative improvement of U.S. forces could slow dramatically. Would a bigger but less superior U.S. military truly do a good job of protecting U.S. strategic interests several years from now?

These cautions do not rule out the ideas of contraction and expansion in the coming years. Indeed, limited steps in either or both directions might make sense. For example, some less-important forces might be retired in order to fund high-priority modernization programs. Indeed, the Air Force is retiring some aging fighters and the Navy is retiring some ships even before obsolescence in order to liberate more funds for investment. Likewise, it might make sense to scale back low-performing modernization programs in order to add some additional forces in critical areas, such as LD/HD and S&R units. Pursuing such limited tradeoffs is part of healthy defense planning. But the pursuit of major tradeoffs—either by large cuts in forces in order to speed modernization or by gutting modernization to order to increase forces—should be subjected to a careful systems analysis of how the benefits and losses stack up. In this critical and contentious arena, long experience shows that careful analysis is the best guide to wise policy.

Future Perspectives

Analytical efforts to determine the proper size of future U.S. forces will need to account for two strategic trends. The first trend is that, owing to their growing quality, fewer U.S. military forces may be needed than before to wage most wars. The second, countervailing trend is that simultaneous contingencies are becoming more frequent in today's chaotic world. As of late 2004, for example, the U.S. military found itself carrying out a major combat and postwar operation in Iraq, while also girding for trouble on the Korean Peninsula, pursuing stability missions in Afghanistan and the Balkans, carrying out counterterrorist operations in many places, performing counterdrug missions in Colombia, and engaging in normal training with allies in Europe and Asia.

If this trend toward multiple missions continues, it clearly will reinforce the need for sizable forces regardless of whether a new standard replaces the 1-4-2-1 standard. The idea that U.S. forces can be reduced appreciably, prevalent as recently as early 2001, has faded. The main issue now is whether the force posture should be enlarged. Budgetary constraints mean that a force enlargement would have to come at the expense of procurement and modernization. Even if the judgment is neither to contract nor to enlarge the posture significantly, this does not mean that the current posture is set in concrete. Within the framework of current manpower and resources, there will be ample room to alter the internal composition of U.S. forces—both within the services and among them—in order to field innovative structures and new force mixes. Determining how to do so will be one of the main challenges facing transformation, the subject of the next chapter.

Notes

[1] The methodology of using scenarios for threat-based planning during the Cold War is discussed in Annual Reports to Congress issued by Secretaries of Defense Robert McNamara, James Schlesinger, Harold Brown, and Caspar Weinberger between the mid-1960s and the late 1980s.

[2] Relevant discussions of maneuver warfare include Major General F.W. von Mellenthin, *Panzer Battles* (London: Futura Publications, 1979); Richard Simpkin, *Race to the Swift: Thoughts on Twenty-first Century Warfare* (London: Brassey's, 1985); and John Erickson et al., *Soviet Ground Forces: An Operational Assessment* (Boulder, CO: Westview Press, 1986). For a discussion of surprise attack in Central Europe, see Richard K. Betts, *Surprise Attack* (Washington, DC: Brookings, 1982). For a discussion of Soviet military strategy, see Thomas W. Wolfe, *Soviet Power and Europe, 1945–1970* (Baltimore: Johns Hopkins University Press, 1970).

[3] See Department of Defense, *NATO-Warsaw Pact Military Balance Study, 1978–1984* (Washington, DC: Department of Defense, 1979, declassified 1985).

[4] For more detail, see Richard L. Kugler, *Commitment to Purpose: How Alliance Partnership Won the Cold War* (Santa Monica, CA: RAND, 1993); Richard D. Lawrence and Jeffrey Record, *U.S. Force Structure in NATO: An Alternative*

(Washington, DC: Brookings, 1974); and William P. Mako, *U.S. Ground Forces and the Defense of Central Europe* (Washington, DC: Brookings, 1983). See also a series of articles published as "Policy Focus: The European Conventional Balance," *International Security* 12, no. 4 (Spring 1988): Joshua M. Epstein, "Dynamic Analysis and the Conventional Balance in Europe," 154–165; Kim R. Holmes, "Measuring the Conventional Balance in Europe," 166–173; John J. Mearsheimer, "Numbers, Strategy, and the European Balance," 174–185; and Barry R. Posen, "Is NATO Decisively Outnumbered?" 186–202. Also see General Accounting Office, *NATO-Warsaw Pact: U.S. and Soviet Perspectives of the Conventional Force Balance*, GAO/NSIAD-89-23A (Washington, DC: U.S. GAO, 1988); Jeffrey Simon, *NATO-Warsaw Pact Force Mobilization* (Washington, DC: National Defense University Press, 1988); Stephen Biddle, "The European Conventional Balance: A Reinterpretation," Survival (March-April 1988); Anthony H. Cordesman, *NATO's Central Region Forces: Capabilities, Challenges, Concepts* (London: Royal United Services Institute, 1988).

[5] For assessment of U.S. defense planning during the Reagan years, see William W. Kaufmann, *Defense in the 1980s* (Washington, DC: Brookings, 1981); William W. Kaufmann, *A Reasonable Defense* (Washington, DC: Brookings, 1986); and Franklin C. Spinney, *Defense Facts of Life: The Plans/Reality Mismatch* (Boulder, CO: Westview Press, 1985). For an assessment of Persian Gulf defense planning during the 1980s, see Joshua M. Epstein, *Strategy and Force Planning: The Case of the Persian Gulf* (Washington, DC: Brookings, 1987).

[6] For more detail, see Richard L. Kugler, *U.S. Military Strategy and Force Posture for the 21st Century: Capabilities and Requirements* (Santa Monica, CA: RAND, 1994).

[7] See Les Aspin, *Report of the Bottom Up Review* (Washington, DC: Department of Defense, 1993).

[8] See William Cohen, *Report of the Quadrennial Defense Review* (Washington, DC: Department of Defense, 1997). For accompanying analysis, see Zalmay Khalilzad and David Ochmanek, eds., *Strategic Appraisal 1997: Strategy and Defense Planning for the Twenty-first Century* (Santa Monica, CA: RAND, 1997).

[9] See Steven Metz, ed., *Revising the Two MTW Force Shaping Paradigm* (Carlisle, PA: Strategic Studies Institute/U.S. Army War College, 2001), for a wide range of criticisms of the two-MTW standard.

[10] See Donald Rumsfeld, *The Quadrennial Defense Review Report 2001* (Washington, DC: Department of Defense, 2001). For a critique, see Hans Binnendijk and Richard Kugler, "Sound Vision, Unfinished Business: The Quadrennial Defense Review Report 2001," *The Fletcher Forum of World Affairs* (Winter/Spring 2002).

[11] As DOD documents made clear, capabilities-based planning involves a switch away from planning on the basis of a few canonical contingencies and threats flowing from them. Yet DOD documents also declare that it is planning on the basis of countering enemy capabilities. Hence, threatening contingencies do not disappear from the equation, but instead a wide variety of them are to be used as one input in force planning. A key feature of capabilities-based planning is that it focuses on shaping the size and nature of U.S. forces in response to their own operational requirements, rather than designing them to counter specific threats in some mechanical way. Its main goal is to foster U.S. forces and capabilities that are highly flexible and adaptable, rather than imprisoned by their design standards to produce only a limited range of operational responses.

[12] See Hans Binnendijk and Richard Kugler, "Revising the Two MTW Standard," *Strategic Forum* 179 (Washington, DC: National Defense University Press, 2001).

[13] As of late 2004, the number was being increased to 150,000 troops. See Eric Schmitt and Thom Shanker, "U.S. to Increase Its Force in Iraq by Nearly 12,000," *The New York Times*, December 2, 2004. This article said: "The American military presence in Iraq will grow by nearly 12,000 troops by next month, to 150,000, the highest level since the invasion last year, to provide security for the Iraqi elections in January and to quell insurgent attacks around the country, the Pentagon announced Wednesday."

[14] Paul K. Davis, David Gompert, and Richard Kugler, *Adaptiveness in National Defense: The Basis of a New Framework*, IP-155 (Santa Monica, CA: RAND, 1996).

[15] See chapter 14 for analysis of Army force structure issues.

[16] For further details, see Donald Rumsfeld, Annual Report to Congress, 2002, and other DOD documents.

Chapter 13
Pursuing Defense Transformation

Contributing insightful analyses to help guide defense transformation in the information age is one of the biggest challenges facing systems analysis and related methods today. While some critics have claimed transformation is just an illusion, within the Department of Defense it is recognized as a serious effort to chart the future of the U.S. military. Transformation is a powerful dynamic that cannot be allowed to unfold willy-nilly; it must be guided by a sound strategy and wise choices about force development even if the outcome is hard to foresee. By exploring the issues and options surrounding transformation, systems analysis can help illuminate the path ahead, but it cannot rely solely on methods and practices of the past. Instead, it must create new methods and practices to help the U.S. military pursue innovation both vigorously and sensibly. To be relevant in this critical arena, systems analysis must embrace changes that parallel the changes now beginning to sweep over military affairs.

This chapter proposes a new systems analysis focused on bringing conceptual order to transformation strategy as a whole. While opposing bad ideas will be important at times, developing and promoting good ideas for pursuing transformation will be essential. Systems analysis should focus not only on acquisition of new technologies and weapons, but also on changes to force structures, operational doctrines, and other key facets of preparedness, all of which will have a big impact on determining whether transformation fulfills its promise of producing new military forces that have technical prowess and perform well in carrying out future U.S. defense strategy. In addition, systems analysis should focus on how to pursue transformation in affordable and achievable ways, rather than allow it to become a hollow exercise in wishful thinking. Similar to all past efforts to improve U.S. military forces, today's transformation will have to live within the boundaries of budgetary feasibility, invest its resources wisely, set priorities, and accept tradeoffs. Systems analysis can help it do so by bringing holistic thinking and economic reasoning to the enterprise.

Accordingly, this chapter begins by explaining the need for a sound transformation strategy and how new types of systems analysis can help create such a strategy. The chapter then surveys several key challenges to be addressed by systems analysis as DOD's transformation strategy matures. The chapter closes by discussing how systems analysis can help policymakers craft a comprehensive transformation strategy that blends improvements in the near term, mid-term, and long term so that their effects accumulate. Provided that systems analysis innovates in its practices, it can help address these issues, challenge the status quo, argue against unwise departures, and promote constructive changes.

Essence of Transformation

The word *transformation* is used regularly in today's defense debate, but often without a real understanding of its meaning. Transformation is meant to prepare U.S. forces for the information age, which will be very different from the industrial age. It embraces bright new ideas, but it is not meant to be a political code by which pet theories can be imposed on defense planning without thorough analysis and debate. Transformation is neither a revolution for its own sake, nor a misleading sound bite to camouflage adherence to the status quo under the pretense of meaningful change. Transformation does not carry with it a predetermined programmatic agenda. It is not, as some observers claim, the wholesale replacement of legacy weapons with exotic new platforms, such as replacing all manned fighter planes with robot-piloted aircraft, or aircraft carriers with missile-firing submarines. Nor is transformation solely the fielding of computers, information grids, global telecommunications, sensors, smart munitions, and space systems. It is not a wholesale shift to air-delivered firepower while the battlefield is emptied of ground forces. Transformation may include some such steps, but its essence is broader and more fundamental.

The Department of Defense describes transformation as "a process that shapes the changing nature of military competition and cooperation through new combinations of concepts, capabilities, people, and organizations that exploit our nation's advantages and protect against our asymmetric vulnerabilities to sustain our strategic position, which helps underpin peace and stability in the world." Using this description, this chapter puts forth the following definition, which helps set the stage for analysis: Transformation is a process of pursuing major changes to U.S. military forces in order to greatly elevate their future combat capabilities for information-age operations. The key terms of this definition—*process, change,* and *capability*—are the principal determinants of transformation's essence. Transformation aims for major changes and improvements, not just minor ones. Transformation is a dynamic and ongoing process, not a static condition with a fixed end. While it is animated by the transition from the industrial age to the information age, it is an emergent process of creative exploration and experimentation whose destination will be determined only as it unfolds over a period of years. It thus provides a visionary guide toward a future of enhanced and relevant capabilities, but it does not yet detail exactly where military forces will be 10 or 20 years from now.[1]

Transformation focuses especially on the employment of modern information networks and the knowledge they carry in order to achieve joint integration of force operations from all components: ground, naval, and air forces. Transformation will not unfold at breakneck speed, for the practical reason that a large and diverse military posture of 1.4 million troops and thousands of weapons systems cannot be reconfigured overnight. Moreover, good ideas take time to sort out, test, and mature before they are ready to be put into widespread practice. Yet if transformation is carried out properly, changes will occur during the foreseeable future. Meaningful changes are already under way and should be apparent by 2010 or sooner; substantial changes will occur by 2015–2020. Eventually the entire defense posture will be transformed to some degree. Regardless of its exact pace, therefore, transformation is not a passing fad. It is destined to be a major occupation of defense planning for many years, and its importance is likely to grow.

Critics debate whether transformation's impact will be revolutionary or evolutionary, but there is no doubt that it seeks to foster truly big shifts in military forces, while striking a sensible balance between continuity and change. As such, transformation encompasses more than the gradual process of recapitalization and modernization that is always taking place, and more than the introduction of new technologies and information systems. It also involves major changes to how U.S. forces are structured, organized, and operated. It focuses on creating new doctrines and operational concepts for employing U.S. forces on the modern battlefield, and on fostering new cultural mindsets in U.S. military personnel. Its ambition is to blend major changes in all of these important areas so that military forces in the information age not only are structured and equipped differently from those of today, but also operate differently, think differently, and fight differently.[2]

In pursuing big changes of this sort, transformation aspires to elevate U.S. forces to a significantly higher level of capability and performance. But transformation does not seek this enhanced capability just for its own sake; as interpreted by DOD, it has clear strategic purposes. One purpose is to ensure that U.S. military forces do not become outmoded because they are clinging to the past, but instead keep pace with a world of technological change around them. A second purpose is to ensure that U.S. forces retain their current margin of dominance and superiority over future opponents, which will be updating their own military forces as they acquire information-era assets. A third purpose is to help U.S. forces be able to perform the full range of their future strategic missions, including missions that may differ markedly from those of today in a world that is globalizing rapidly and contains many new-era dangers.[3]

Transformation thus is driven by both supply-side and demand-side dynamics. That is, it endeavors to take full advantage of the new information networks, technologies, organizations, and doctrines that are bubbling upward from the military services and industrial communities in which they are created. But it also seeks to harness these innovations to produce the new types of forces that can best serve U.S. national security policy and defense strategy in the coming era. The complex challenge of matching new opportunities from the supply side to new imperatives from the demand side will define the multi-year agenda ahead.

This agenda not only makes transformation a difficult enterprise, but also creates a looming risk that it might not succeed. If transformation is not carried out vigorously, it might produce forces that lack the proper technological sophistication and doctrinal prowess. If transformation is pursued vigorously but not sensibly, it might produce forces that, although technologically sophisticated, are the wrong forces for the purposes and missions ahead. In the future, the United States will need not only strong forces, but also the right forces, with the inherent flexibility to adapt successfully to a fast-changing world. Transformation is capable of producing such forces, but such an outcome is not guaranteed.

Making sure that transformation succeeds is a main DOD responsibility. Transformation cannot be left to its own devices. It must be guided by a sound strategy and channeled in sensible directions. The strategic choices made by DOD will determine not only how funds are spent on transformation, but also how future programs and forces take shape under transformation's mantle. If DOD is to succeed, it will need a sensible transformation strategy, equipped with a good set of concepts and ideas, to help guide a large, far-flung bureaucracy of established practices and varying instincts to chart a future of major change, and to master it as well.

Contributions of Systems Analysis

Systems analysis can help transformation succeed by contributing to the task of developing sound strategy, concepts, and ideas. It can still fruitfully employ its classical emphasis on analyzing systems and employing economic models of choice. Likewise, systems analysis can be helpful by playing its time-honored role of debunking unwise ideas and puncturing the inflated and self-serving claims of advocates whose intellectual reach exceeds their grasp, or whose political or military agendas lead them astray. Systems analysis can also continue playing its traditional role of helping bring fiscal discipline and a sense of cost-effectiveness to an enterprise that will need ample doses of both. But if systems analysis does little more than apply the brakes to bad ideas and excess spending, it will not fulfill its demanding responsibilities in the transformation arena. Systems analysis should contribute by helping identify initiatives that make sense, articulating their rationales, mobilizing support for them, and helping determine how they can best be implemented. In essence, systems analysis will need to make clear not only what should be opposed, but what should be favored as well.

In order to perform this role, systems analysis will need to develop new practices and habits of identifying and fostering sensible innovations. In the past, systems analysis has often been used as an opponent of innovation. For example, some civilian overseers employed systems analysis to help block ideas favored by the military services by pointing out their excess costs or questionable effectiveness. While the practice of critically scrutinizing controversial ideas will remain necessary, systems analysis must encourage the military services to pursue innovations that they otherwise might shun. In order to do so, systems analysis will need new methods that illuminate the changes that should be pursued even if they are controversial.

Systems analysis will also need to surmount the understandable tendency to focus solely on new technologies and weapons systems, often seen as the glamour children of transformation. To be sure, new technologies and weapons are important, but they are far from the only variables in the transformation equation. Changes to force structure, organization, and doctrine, wisely blending the old and new, will have a major bearing on whether transformation succeeds. If the U.S. military merely grafts new technologies and weapons onto existing structures, it will not achieve the maximum potential gains in capability. Determining how best to carry out force structure reforms is anything but easy, especially in a political climate where bad ideas compete for attention with good ideas, and where bureaucratic dynamics favor slow, incremental changes. Systems analysis needs to develop and apply new methods to help investigate how new weapons and force structure innovations can combine to propel transformation along the road to success.

Provided it is equipped with such methods and that it focuses on new-era issues, systems analysis is well suited to analyzing transformation strategy and programs. Because of its capacity to think big, it has the ability to see both the supply side and the demand side. But in analyzing transformation in these terms, systems analysis will no longer be able to rely upon its standard practice of first defining a desired end-state, and then identifying a cost-effective program for reaching that end-state. The reason is that transformation is not about end-states, but about guiding innovative changes toward ultimate outcomes that may be inherently unknowable. In dealing with murky futures and undefined end-states, systems analysis will need to be adept at assessing how innovative changes can best be pursued in the near term, the mid-term, and the long term. Moreover, it will need to help determine how transformation policies for each of these three periods can be brought into harmony to support each other, so that options for the future are broadened rather than foreclosed. Determining how to build a new-era military posture gradually but steadily and without a strategic outline of the ultimate product is akin to trying to build a new style of house without a carpenter's blueprint. Doing so will require a new and different kind of thinking from systems analysts, for systems analysis has been a discipline that valued blueprints.

When transformation first appeared on the scene, the public debate was polarized between those who focused on the near term while favoring only gradual change and those who focused only on the long term and wanted to get there by big leaps ahead. Since then, this polarized debate has abated somewhat, but elements of it still linger. The dual risk of these extremes is that either the distant future will be neglected or that security in the near term will be mortgaged on behalf of dim futurist concepts that might not pan out. Often missing in this debate is a measured and purposeful focus on the mid-term—5 to 12 years—during which significant changes will be necessary and possible, with implications that can be analyzed in concrete terms. Systems analysis can contribute to the transformation dialogue by focusing on the mid-term, for (as many senior DOD officials know) that is where the main impact of transformation will be and where a bridge connects the near term and long term.

In addition, systems analysis will need to help craft a transformation strategy that is composed of an integrated family of ideas, rather than anchored in a single idea or concept. While focusing on a single dominant idea would ease the managerial agenda, such an approach would put transformation into a confining straitjacket that would almost inevitably leave the U.S. military well suited for just one strategic purpose, but ill suited for the multiple other purposes required. A transformation effort guided by multiple ideas is the best way to produce the kind of flexible force posture that will be needed. Systems analysis will also need to think in terms of integrating multiple programs and activities, rather than examining them solely on their individual merits. Because transformation will eventually reshape the entire U.S. military posture, it must be guided by a sense of the whole rather than by a set of fragmented or disassociated enterprises that do not add up to a coherent strategy or structure. Above all, transformation must be joint: it must seek to combine the military services so that they can operate as a single team. Systematic, integrated thinking aimed at managing comprehensive change does not come easily to DOD or to systems analysis.

The task of helping craft a transformation effort that is guided by a clear sense of strategy, yet is anchored in a large family of complementary ideas, is one of the most important items on the transformation agenda. Systems analysis can help by asking the right questions and by providing insights on the effectiveness of alternative courses of action. Above all, systems analysis can help focus on how best to push transformation in sound strategic directions. Change is a means to an end, not an end in itself. If transformation is to succeed, it must be pursued energetically, and it must have real meaning, not be encased in a fog of hyped claims and exaggerated expectations. But energy alone will not be enough. A main challenge facing systems analysis is to help ensure that transformation is equipped with a sound strategy and core concepts to produce an integrated family of good ideas, visions, and departures.

Systems analysis can help enable the defense community to keep a close eye on the relationship between inputs and outputs. What matters is not the number of changes imposed by transformation, but the degree to which these changes elevate the combat capabilities of U.S. military forces. Sometimes this important consideration is lost if the bureaucratic process focuses on actions rather than consequences. A normal modernization might be expected to increase U.S. military capabilities by up to 30 percent or so; in contrast, transformation, which includes modernization plus a host of other changes, offers the promise of far greater increase, by perhaps 50 percent or more. Whether to-day's transformation will succeed to such an extent is to be seen, but DOD must have a clear understanding of what the endeavor is yielding in terms of returns. Systems analysis can contribute by developing performance metrics of inputs and outputs, and by using these metrics along with associated data to provide analysis showing how transformation is producing gains in capabilities over the short term, the medium term, and the long term. A management information system of this sort can provide invaluable help to senior officials who want to know what their policies are achieving. Systems analysis is particularly well equipped to provide the performance metrics and data needed to bring such a management information system to life.

Systems analysis can help keep transformation focused on the task of fielding future forces that are well aligned with the requirements of U.S. defense strategy and national security policy. While elevating the combat capabilities of U.S. forces is important, equally important is ensuring that future U.S. forces have the flexibility and adaptability to perform the wide spectrum of missions that lie ahead. As figure 13–1 suggests, transformation can help broaden the capacity of U.S. forces to perform simultaneous missions under increasingly challenging conditions. It can do so by reducing force requirements for individual missions, which frees forces for other missions. It can also enable individual units to operate in more diverse ways, further enhancing force flexibility. Finally, it can ensure that joint forces can carry out many different types of operations, rather than be limited to a narrow script. The combined effect can be to permit the United States to get greater strategic mileage out of its force posture and to stretch its military resources to maximum operational effect.

Figure 13–1. **Transformation's Impact on Capacity of U.S. Forces to Perform Multiple, Demanding Missions**

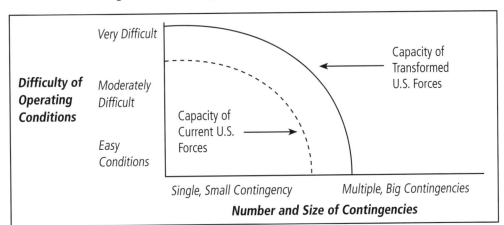

In order for such strategic gains to be realized, transformation needs to be well planned, with careful attention to the types of forces being fielded. Clearly, it should endeavor to strengthen the capacity of U.S. forces to wage futuristic high-tech operations and thereby preserve strategic domination over peer rivals such as China in the long term. But it should also address how to apply transformation to forces and capabilities for performing expeditionary operations in the Middle East and similar regions in the near to mid-term. Such expeditionary operations will include not only major combat, but also peacetime overseas presence, peacekeeping, limited crisis interventions, and postwar stability and reconstruction missions. Determining how to field both future high-tech strike forces and forces designed for more immediate expeditionary operations promises to be challenging. The future U.S. military posture should not reflect one single design standard for high-tech warfare, but instead will need to provide a portfolio of diverse assets for multiple purposes covering a wide spectrum of missions. Systems analysis can help contribute to transformation by addressing how to balance requirements in these important areas.

Remembering History's Lessons

One of the ways that systems analysis and related methods can contribute to transformation is by recalling both the positive and negative lessons of history. Transforming a military force to prepare for the future has been tried many times before; sometimes it succeeded, and sometimes it failed. Remembering the reasons for the different fates is important to guiding U.S. military transformation today.

The classic case of successful transformation was that of the German Wehrmacht before World War II. Rejecting World War I's legacy of static trench warfare, the German military employed a bold blitzkrieg strategy to overpower the ill-prepared French and British armies quickly in the spring of 1940. While the German victory was a testimony to transformation, the full reasons behind its success need to be remembered. Some observers credit the victory to Germany's decision to field tanks and to concentrate them in only about 15 percent of its divisions, which spearheaded the attack. Closer inspection, however, reveals that a bigger transformation had swept over Germany's entire military. The Germans also fielded a large air force configured to provide offensive strikes in support of ground maneuvers. While Germany's few armored divisions had ample tanks, they also were equipped with mobile artillery and motorized infantry that allowed them to speed across the battlefield with all of their weapons at hand. Nor were Germany's infantry divisions neglected: they received modern artillery, antitank weapons, and trucks to carry their troops into battle. Improvements to railroads, bases, and infrastructure allowed the Germans to move large forces across big territories faster than the French and British could respond.[4]

The key point is that the Germans viewed transformation in holistic terms aimed at integrating new weapons and technologies with reformed force structures. They created the operational doctrine of combined arms warfare as the best way to make effective use of their new weapons and structures. By contrast, the British and French were defeated not because they were hopelessly outgunned—their divisions, aircraft, and tanks were similar in numbers and quality to those of the Germans—but because they did not concentrate their tanks, make effective use of their aircraft, or motorize their infantry and artillery. Unable to wage combined arms operations or maneuver warfare, they compounded their vulnerability by creating a linear forward defense that was vulnerable in the Ardennes and that lacked the mobile reserves to contain breakthroughs. As a result, they suffered a calamitous defeat even though they possessed the forces, weapons, and firepower to perform much better. The lesson of 1940 is that transformation is best pursued, and wars are best won, not by acquiring a few new weapons, but by blending new weapons with new force structures and doctrines that together elevate combat capabilities. The more fundamental lesson is that insightful thinking, coupled with a willingness to embrace sensible innovative ideas, is the key to building a transformed military.

The U.S. military had to learn transformation and new-era operations on the fly during World War II. It ultimately won that war, but its many of its successes were due more to its imposing industrial resources than to operational skill on the battlefield. Its air and naval forces were superior to those of opponents, but its ground forces had trouble defeating the German army. Often they had to rely upon artillery firepower and logistic sustainment rather than expertise at infantry, armor, and tactical operations to gain victory in Europe. Whereas the German military used artillery barrages to set the stage for armor and infantry, the U.S. Army often used armor and infantry to set the stage for artillery barrages, and then relied upon replacement troops and weapons to replenish when high casualties were taken. In doing so, it was able to wear the German military down through sustained pressure rather than tactical superiority on the battlefield. As the European campaign drew to a close, American performance in close battles improved, a product of growing experience by units that had been formed only recently. Even so, the experience left critics worried about future wars against tough opponents.

Afterward, as the Cold War gained momentum in the 1950s, the U.S. military set out to pursue transformation in sweeping, holistic terms. Rejecting the conventional combat of World War II, it decided to pursue deterrence and defense on the cheap by embracing nuclear weapons throughout its force. Within a few years, it had nuclearized not only its strategic forces for long-range bombardment, but also its ground, naval, and air forces for tactical combat and theater operations. By the late 1950s, this ambitious and visionary effort had produced a wholly revolutionized force structure armed with new weapons capable of delivering immense nuclear firepower.

The problem was that the perceived usefulness of nuclear options suddenly ceased at the precise moment when this new force posture came to fruition, because the Soviet Union succeeded at deploying a credible nuclear deterrent of its own. The U.S. military was left scrambling to rebuild its conventional forces, and it fought the Vietnam War with forces that were not as well prepared for that conflict as they could have been. The enduring lesson of the 1950s and 1960s is that, while transformation can be pursued expeditiously under the mantle of a single clear idea, that idea must be compelling and possess staying power. Otherwise, the transformed military might be incapable of fighting the wars of the future if they take an unexpected course.

During the late 1970s and 1980s, the U.S. military set about to recover from the Vietnam debacle by rebuilding its forces for the growing Cold War competition with the Soviet Union and its allies. By all measures, this effort was a great success. Whether it was transformational or not, this effort undeniably involved a lengthy process of making major changes to U.S. forces that greatly elevated their combat capabilities to the point where they emerged as the world's strongest military. This effort involved both the acquisition of new weapons and the pursuit of reformed force structures. It was not, however, driven by a single dominant idea or design standard. While it was animated by a clear strategy of becoming prepared to project military power swiftly to zones of confrontation with the enemy, the all-important details of this effort were shaped by a large family of ideas. Indeed, the process was often cacophonous and hurly-burly, with each military service pursuing its own agenda, and with factions within each service competing for resources.

Although this tumultuous process reflected the realities of democratic politics, it seemed to violate the norms of carefully controlled, top-down planning. Yet it succeeded, although historians will debate the reasons why. Some will say that the Reagan administration threw enough money at the problem to overcome all the barriers. But this is not a fully convincing explanation, because even those large sums could have been spent poorly. The more credible explanation is that this process was energized by the presence of many good ideas, enough to provide a sensible focus to the entire Department of Defense and to each military service. An enduring lesson here is that democratic politics is not an enemy of transformation, but if this process is to succeed, it must be driven by sound ideas, often several of them.

The Building Blocks of Transformation Strategy

According to the logic of systems analysis, a coherent strategy anchored in a family of sound ideas is necessary for four compelling reasons. The first reason is that transformation is a hugely complex process. It involves literally hundreds of important changes in multiple areas, all of which must be coordinated. Such coordination cannot be achieved in the absence of a guiding strategy for force development. The second reason is that transformation must strike a sensible balance between continuity and change. A coherent strategy is needed to determine the mix of existing assets that should be retained, obsolete assets that should be discarded, and new assets that should be acquired. The third reason is that transformation can be pursued in many different ways. When the various alternatives are carefully considered, some may make little sense, others may seem sound but not compelling, and perhaps a few may offer the full promise of major gains in capability and flexibility. A strategy is needed to ensure that the best course is selected, because it will not be adopted automatically. The fourth reason is that transformation must be both desirable and feasible. While it must focus on attractive goals, it must also put forth an agenda that realistically can be achieved given the technological, political, bureaucratic, and fiscal constraints along the way. A coherent strategy is needed to maximize gains.

Crafting a coherent strategy must begin by understanding transformation's rationale and imperatives. At its foundation, transformation is built on the premise that the acquisition of modern information systems and networks offers major advantages by greatly enhancing the knowledge and awareness available to military forces. Throughout history, knowledge, or its absence, has been hugely important in determining the outcome of battles and wars. Many commanders have won big battles not because their weapons and troops were inherently better than the opposition, but because they had superior situational awareness. An effort to provide future U.S. forces with large amounts of relevant, applicable knowledge therefore makes great sense. A main characteristic of 21st-century wars is that they will be heavily knowledge-based. The quality of weapons and troops will still matter greatly, but expert knowledge about how to use them will matter more than ever before. If future U.S. forces possess knowledge superiority, their ability to win battles and wars will be greatly strengthened.[5]

Enhanced space systems play an especially important role in transformation strategies for information networking and sharing of knowledge. Improved communications satellites can provide wide bandwidth to link national command authorities with field commanders and their troops, allowing for a voluminous two-way flow of radio traffic, video conferences, and data transmissions. Improved weather satellites will provide a global capacity to monitor weather trends, while better navigation satellites will improve upon today's global positioning system (GPS) technology, which already allows for pin-point identification of ground locations from space. Better intelligence satellites will provide improved photography and communications intelligence. In the future, transformation may yield a space-based radar system that allows for real-time tracking of moving targets almost anywhere in the world. The cost-effectiveness of such systems is a matter for debate, but the technology is already under development.

Information networking is taking place not only in space, but in the atmosphere and on the ground as well. Growing numbers of unmanned aerial vehicles (UAVs) such as Global Hawk, Predator, and Hunter will provide ground, naval, and air commanders with enhanced intelligence about enemy dispositions and U.S. force movements. Better multifrequency wide-bandwidth radios will facilitate effective communications between commanders and field forces, and among the various components, so that air and ground forces can work more closely in real time. Better data displays will provide large volumes of critical information to headquarters staffs and to individual tanks, fighter aircraft, and ships. The growing capacity to transmit such data will permit all combat forces and logistic support units to remain in continuous contact throughout engagements, allowing them to attack enemy forces with greater effectiveness while reducing their own vulnerability and losses to friendly fires.

Information networking strives to create a "system of systems." That is, it seeks to equip U.S. forces with high-powered computers, sensors, communications systems, bandwidth, and data-processing technologies that create several interlocking types of information networks, providing real-time information about enemy forces, terrain and weather, the disposition of U.S. combat forces, and the status of U.S. logistic support and mobility efforts. Such integrated networks offer the promise of enhancing U.S. force capabilities in multiple ways, facilitating, for example, integrated joint operations by multiple force components that previously operated in separate domains, and coordinated, simultaneous operations by highly dispersed forces, even those deployed far from the battlefield, to enhance military teamwork in warfighting.

Another potential contribution is to make U.S. force operations more effective by enhancing their lethality, maneuverability, speed, operational tempo, and survivability. Integrated networks should also make U.S. force operations more efficient. In past wars, battlefield campaigns have often been hampered because forces were used in the wrong places for the wrong purposes. Modern information networks offer the promise of helping ensure that U.S. forces will be allocated at the right time and the right place. Yet another contribution is to provide U.S. forces with enhanced leverage over their opponents, reducing the need to bludgeon the enemy through crude attrition dynamics, and instead enabling U.S. forces to fracture the cohesion of enemy forces by attacking their weak points, reducing the enemy's ability to fight effectively and making it more vulnerable to quick defeat.

While transformation begins with information networking, it does not end there. Acquiring a new generation of ultra-smart munitions and missiles is another important feature. Such existing smart munitions as joint direct-attack munitions, joint standoff weapons, joint air-to-surface standoff missiles, and sensor-fused munitions reflect decisions of a decade ago to seek ways to enhance the lethality of U.S. fires. For over 20 years, U.S. forces have been able to generate large volumes of fires: one of today's Army divisions, for example, can fire 1,000 tons of artillery ammunition per day, and one of today's fighter planes can carry as much ordnance as a B–17 bomber of World War II. The usefulness of these increases was limited, however, by a lack of accuracy, even against targets that could be visually spotted by ground troops and aircraft pilots. Two decades ago, for example, a fighter aircraft stood only a 10 percent chance of actually hitting a target being bombed. This constraint, however, began to fade when new avionics and smart munitions appeared on the scene. Today, a fighter plane has up to an 80 percent chance of hitting a ground target with a smart bomb guided by laser or GPS; an M–1 tank has a similar chance of hitting a moving target. Future generations of smart munitions will elevate single-shot kill probabilities to near their mathematical limit of 100 percent. More important, future munitions will permit accurate fires in day or night and in all weather conditions, and provide high lethality with small explosives and the capacity to penetrate deep bunkers and to destroy other specialized targets. Eventually, transformation is likely to produce usable directed-energy systems (such as high-energy lasers and electromagnetic rail guns), liquid propellants, and other exotic forms of firepower that will further enhance the lethality of U.S. forces.

For all the importance of information networks and ultra-smart munitions, DOD's plan to equip future U.S. military forces with a new suite of weapons systems is the most expensive part of transformation. During 2000–2001, some transformation enthusiasts called for DOD to "skip a generation" by rejecting these new weapons, then well along in the lengthy research and development pipeline, in order to concentrate resources on an entirely new generation of futuristic, exotic weapons that would not be available for 15 to 20 years. This idea was largely rejected by DOD not only because such futuristic weapons were only vaguely conceived, but also because the emerging generation of new weapons promised to contribute importantly to transformation's goals during their life spans. The dual purpose of DOD's modernization plan is to replace aging, obsolescent models and to provide useful capabilities for new-era operations. A dominating feature of this modernization effort is the plan to acquire about 4,000 new fighter aircraft for the Air Force, Navy, and Marines: the F–22 stealth fighter, F–35 Joint Strike Fighter, the F–18A E/F fighter, the F–45 UCAV, and the V–22 Osprey tilt-rotor helicopter. In addition, the Navy intends to increase shipbuilding with a new generation of powerful combatants, and the Army is buying new armored vehicles. The bill will be high, perhaps over $1 trillion over a multi-year period. This modernization effort has begun only recently, but it promises to accelerate by the end of this decade and afterward, bringing a bow wave of growing transformation expenses.

Some critics complain that this modernization effort is not truly transformational because many new weapons systems physically resemble models of the past. Their underlying argument is that real transformation requires new platforms that are radically different from old models: for example, new tanks that weigh only 20 tons rather than 70, new aircraft carriers of 60,000 tons instead of 100,000, or new fighter aircraft piloted by robots, not humans. While valid arguments exist about the design standards of future weapons, this generic criticism misses the point: what matters is not whether new weapons are built differently from old weapons, but whether they deliver the new capabilities and operational concepts needed for information-age warfare. Many of the new weapons systems meet this standard even though they are similar to legacy designs. The same reasoning applies to the criticism that smart munitions render new weapons unnecessary, because existing weapons can use these munitions. However, before smart munitions can be fired against targets, they must be maneuvered into proper position by weapons platforms capable of surviving enemy fires. To use the coming generation of ultra-smart munitions requires enhanced maneuverability and survivability, which are provided by many of the new weapons systems.

New military structures and doctrines will be needed to make effective use of these acquisitions. Transformation would be incomplete if it merely sought to graft modern information networks, new weapons systems, and ultra-smart munitions onto existing military structures and operational doctrines. Transformational reform of structures and doctrines thus is vitally important for all military services. In the future, the main building blocks of military operations may no longer be divisions, fighter wings, and carriers; they may replaced by different formations. However, great care must be taken in pursuing such reforms. A cautionary tale comes from the private sector. Some years ago, many business corporations became so enamored of the information age that they decided to overturn their existing organizations in favor of new structures based on information networks and architectures. While some corporations achieved major gains in productivity, others lost sight of the fact that the purpose of a business is to make saleable products, not to process information. They disrupted their line organizations in ways that resulted in reduced performance, fewer saleable products, and loss of competitive stature in the marketplace; some went bankrupt as a result. In order to avoid a similar fate, defense transformation needs to focus on creating new military structures and doctrines, not on the basis of whether they can operate new information networks and weapons, but on the basis of whether they provide enhanced performance on the battlefield, the ultimate "marketplace" of intense competition. Information networks should be designed to empower old and new structures, not the other way around.

DOD's Evolving Transformation Strategy

Defense transformation strategy needs to reflect all of these imperatives in ways that enhance the warfighting capabilities and flexibility of future U.S. forces. But what is the best strategy for achieving this goal? When transformation first got under way during the Clinton administration, this question was hard to answer because an official strategy had not yet been devised. One of the major contributions of the Bush administration was to craft an initial transformation strategy. In some quarters, this strategy is controversial because it allegedly attempts too much, or too little, or not enough of the right things. This strategy will doubtless mutate as it matures, but at a minimum, it provides at least a worthy model for gauging today's situation as well as the strategy challenges that remain to be addressed.

The 2001 *Quadrennial Defense Review Report* set the stage by endorsing a deliberate, well-planned transformation as a main goal of defense planning. The report made clear that transformation should be pursued vigorously, although the entire force posture would not be uprooted overnight: the official position was that only about 15 percent of the posture would be transformed in the next few years. To guide the process, the *QDR Report* and DOD's subsequent Transformation Planning Guidance endorsed six goals:[6]

- protecting the U.S. homeland and critical bases of operations
- projecting and sustaining U.S. forces in distant theaters against access-denial threats
- denying enemies sanctuary by means of precision strikes
- assuring the integrity of information systems and operations in the face of enemy attacks
- ensuring the capability and survivability of space systems
- leveraging information technology to develop a joint C⁴ISR architecture.

These goals called attention to missile defenses, space systems, information networks, and long-range strike assets in the transformation equation. In order to strengthen
its commitment to pursuing these goals, Secretary Rumsfeld created an Office of Force
Transformation to advise him on DOD's progress and assigned the Joint Forces Command an important role in orchestrating the effort to promote joint operations. Rumsfeld's defense budget for fiscal year 2005 set aside $24.3 billion for transformation and
a 5-year expenditure of $239 billion to fund key transformation initiatives in these ar-
eas. What these six goals lacked, however, was clear guidance on how transformed U.S.
forces would operate on the modern battlefield. Apart from endorsement of precision strike, they said little about how ground, air, and naval forces should be blended
under the transformation mantle.

Joint Vision 2020, published by the Chairman of the Joint Chiefs of Staff, provided
better guidance in this critical area. Under the rubric of "Joint Expeditionary Warfare
for Full-Spectrum Dominance," it identified five key military concepts for joint forces:
joint C⁴ISR, dominant maneuver, precision engagement, full-dimensional protection,
and focused logistics. The services articulated follow-up concepts: effects-based operations, sponsored by the Air Force; rapid decisive operations, sponsored by the Army;
and network centric warfare, sponsored by the Navy. Related joint operations concepts
and joint operating concepts emerged from the Joint Staff, including decision superiority, battlespace awareness, continuous pressure, networked and decentralized operations,
disruption of the enemy through lethal and nonlethal means, and force operations that
are simultaneous, dispersed, and parallel. Together, these concepts expressed common
themes. U.S. forces are to be capable of conducting not only major combat operations,
but also stability operations, homeland security, and strategic deterrence, all in an interagency and multilateral context. Future U.S. warfighting operations are to be conducted
jointly by high-tech forces that employ information dominance, lethal strikes, fast maneuvers, and a high tempo of coordinated actions in order to fracture enemy forces, erode
their will to resist, and destroy them with smart munitions. These concepts said little
about the precise mix of forces to be employed in intense combat, but they suggested
that ground, air, and naval forces would be working closely together as equal partners,
rather than with one component dominating the others.[7]

Along with *Joint Vision 2020* and its accompanying joint documents came service roadmaps that indicated how each of the services planned to pursue transformation within
its ranks. The Air Force roadmap reflected confidence in the growing role of air power
in power projection and expeditionary operations. With a sizable $293 billion invest-
ment budget during 2005–2009, the Air Force roadmap highlighted space activities, information systems, smart munitions, and an ambitious fighter modernization program
as key contributions to transformation. The Navy and Marine roadmap carried forward
an established vision of configuring themselves to project power ashore from the littorals, along with still dominating the seas, as their role in joint operations. The Navy roadmap put forth three new military concepts called Sea Shield, Sea Basing, and Sea Strike
aimed, respectively, at protecting naval forces from new threats, enhancing their ability
to sustain operations from sea platforms, and increasing their ability to carry out strike
operations. Benefiting from a $265 billion investment budget during 2005–2009, the

Navy roadmap also outlined a plan to create new carrier strike groups and amphibious strike groups, to buy more ships with new technologies, and to modernize its air forces with new fighter planes and smart munitions. The Army's roadmap appeared to reflect less certainty and confidence about its transformation future. Hampered by a smaller investment budget, only $120 billion during 2005–2009, the Army initially put forth a plan to limit investments in current legacy forces, to create six Stryker brigades of medium weight, and to devote attention to long-term development of lightweight Future Combat Systems (FCS). When this plan was criticized, the Army modified it by putting forth a plan to reorganize its existing combat forces, creating larger numbers of smaller combat brigades, and to spend additional funds on upgrading them with improved equipment.[8]

All three roadmaps proposed acquisition of new platforms, but in varying ways. The Air Force and Navy roadmaps showed confidence in their ability to make major platform improvements in the near and mid-term. This was mainly because new weapons are ready to emerge in the next few years from their existing, well-funded modernization programs. Even so, both roadmaps encountered criticism. The Air Force was accused of putting forth an overly ambitious modernization plan requiring expensive new aircraft that could strain DOD procurement budgets. The Navy was accused of wanting to construct costly new ships based on old designs. The Marine Corps found its troubled Osprey tilt-rotor helicopter still struggling to prove its safety. Critics derided both the Air Force and Navy for modernizing mostly with legacy platforms. But the Air Force then announced plans to acquire the F–45 UCAV fighter, and the Navy took steps to build small littoral ships and to outfit future carriers with ultra-modern electronics and power systems. The effect was to help undercut the criticisms, but not to silence them.

The biggest proposed change in platforms came from the Army roadmap, whose future vision of 20-ton tanks, infantry fighting vehicles, and artillery tubes suited the advocates of a lighter, more mobile Army. The problem was that because these new weapons are still just ideas on drawing boards, the ability of the research and development community to produce them any time soon seems uncertain. In the meantime, the Army's new Stryker vehicle for armored operations was being criticized for lacking enough firepower and survivability to compete on the modern battlefield. Critics levied the same charge at FCS vehicles, which were designed to fit aboard C–130 transports and might lack the armor or firepower needed to carry out offensive operations against well-armed enemies. The Army responded that these vehicles would be embedded in a system of modern information networks and overhead fires that would enable them to survive and function effectively. But critics doubted the validity of this claim, labeling it as a distant, ephemeral hope rather than a credible analysis of battlefield priorities. Few critics questioned the idea of equipping the Army with some light vehicles, but the idea of outfitting the entire Army with them was widely criticized.

Likewise, the three service roadmaps pursued structural changes in varying ways. The Air Force's proposed changes were the least ambitious, because it viewed its recently created Aerospace Expeditionary Force formations as suitable for the future. The Navy announced structural changes in the form of adding more cruise missiles and other weaponry to its carrier strike groups and amphibious strike groups to make them more versatile. The Army outlined the most far-reaching force structure changes, aimed at not only fielding Stryker brigades, but also increasing the number of its existing brigades by making each of them smaller while equipped with a larger suite of combined-arms weapons. Even so, Army procurement programs did not fare well: the Crusader artillery tube and the Comanche attack helicopter were cancelled on cost-effectiveness grounds. The Army was, as a result, left facing a difficult dilemma: it was without enough money to pursue robust investments, faulted for not pursuing more initiatives, and criticized for the initiatives that it was pursuing.

The Army's troubles aside, however, the three roadmaps suggested that the military services intended to take transformation seriously, and were trying to respond to the guidance of the Secretary of Defense and the Chairman of the Joint Chiefs of Staff. While the roadmaps were criticized as being insufficiently "joint," all services had clearly gotten the message about the importance of acquiring information networks and smart munitions. The Air Force, Navy, and Marines seemed ready to use transformation to field the kind of combat forces called for by *Joint Vision*'s operational concepts. By contrast, the Army seemed to be lagging. Critics accused the Army of being unwilling to make its existing forces more mobile and deployable, and of betting too heavily on the distant FCS program. In the Army's view, however, any lagging was due to lack of adequate funding rather than its own lack of interest or hostility to innovation.

Strategy Challenges Facing Transformation

Viewed through the lens of systems analysis, defense transformation seems to be off to a credible start, with both a strategy and a program to give it life in measured, purposeful ways. Yet DOD's transformation strategy will require further development before it will be fully mature. In addition to the issues already discussed, transformation strategy must master essential challenges in several areas. Providing solutions to these challenges will require insightful systems analysis.

One of the biggest challenges will be determining how to afford transformation and to invest its resources wisely. If transformation is to rise above wishful thinking and hollow promises, it must focus on goals achievable not only in their technical plausibility but also in their budgetary feasibility. During 2001–2005, DOD was heavily focused on developing ideas for transformation, and was not yet fully funding it. As a consequence, transformation expenses in 2005 totaled only about 6 percent of the defense budget. This situation will be changing in future years. By 2009, transformation is projected to consume about 10 percent of the budget, a big sum. Afterward, its expenses will mount as a big procurement effort gets under way, buying new weapons for all the services. A looming worry is that DOD will have trouble funding all of these programs because, owing to competing domestic priorities, its budgets may not be awarded with sustained real growth in 2010 and afterward. To the extent this is the case, DOD will need to find savings elsewhere in its budget that can be devoted to investment, and it may need to set painful priorities in pursuing procurement and transformation. Systems analysis is well suited to addressing issues of affordability and budgetary priorities, which are examined in chapters 15 and 16.

Quite apart from the problem of affordability, transformation is faced with other important issues of a strategic and programmatic nature that have important implications for how the future U.S. military posture is to take shape:

- planning to field forces that can perform both expeditionary missions in the near term and high-tech strike operations in the long term

- ensuring that transformation fosters joint forces and operations

- developing joint training and exercises that advance transformation

- developing improved networks for battlefield operations

- guiding choices between legacy weapons and leap-ahead technology

- developing better mobility programs and overseas infrastructure

- designing spearhead forces for access into hostile hot spots

- encouraging force structure innovations

- strengthening the Army's transformation

- invigorating the research and development process

- strengthening missile defenses and homeland security

- improving capabilities for counterterrorist operations

- transforming the Reserve Component forces

- extending transformation to allies to order to enable multilateral operations with U.S. forces.

Expeditionary Forces and High-Tech Strike Forces

The new U.S. defense strategy and DOD's transformation plan may, to some degree, be at odds regarding the kinds of forces to be fielded in the future. Whereas the former calls for flexible and adaptable forces that can operate in multiple ways and perform diverse missions, the latter thus far has heavily emphasized high-tech strike forces for combat operations involving precise lethal targeting. The problem is that the latter, if pursued too exclusively, may not yield the former. Prior to September 11, 2001, this problem was more theoretical than real. In the years since then, however, the problem has started to become real in ways demanding careful attention to how future forces are built, with two important goals in mind.

Strengthening U.S. forces for waging expeditionary warfare in the Middle East and elsewhere along the southern arc of instability in the near term, while also transforming for strategic domination against opponents in the distant future, will be main endeavors of transformation with different implications for defense priorities. These two goals are strategic partners, not mutually exclusive, but pursuing both of them at the same time may be difficult because of budgetary constraints. In some respects, the capabilities and investments needed for near-term expeditionary operations are different from those needed for long-term transformation. DOD will need to strike a sensible balance among these goals when budget constraints do not permit both to be fully funded at the same time.

As conceived before September 11, 2001, the main purpose of transformation was to prepare U.S. military forces to enhance their strategic dominance over potential adversaries in the long term. Threats were considered to be medium-sized rogue powers and large near-peer rivals, such as China. While generic in principle, one of the key agendas was to create high-tech standoff strike forces aided by information networks, sensors, and smart munitions that can play lead roles in combat. This approach to transformation relies heavily upon air power, naval forces, and related joint assets to win wars. It de-emphasizes the traditional roles of massed ground forces, calling instead for dispersed ground forces to perform land missions. This approach also calls for ground forces that rely on indirect, standoff fires from attack helicopters, missiles and rockets, or other artillery rather than close combat units of tanks and infantry fighting vehicles.

By contrast to such long-term visions, expeditionary wars of the near term will continue requiring different types of transformed joint forces. Such wars will necessitate boots-on-the-ground assets for many missions that require large ground forces for close-in fighting and for performance of S&R missions. Such missions often do not place predominant emphasis on airstrikes across the entire spectrum of operations. As the wars in Afghanistan and Iraq show, this type of war requires more than merely dislocating and defeating enemy units on the battlefield: U.S. forces must also suppress enemy forces that, after losing on the battlefield, retreat into cities, mountains, and forests to conduct guerrilla warfare. S&R missions further require establishing new governments to rule countries occupied by U.S. forces. Ultimately, the military is being tasked not only to win the war, but also to help win the peace locally. These missions are carried out by ground forces operating in complex situations quite different from those envisioned in standoff-strike theory.

Preparing for such joint expeditionary wars is not solely the province of ground forces. It also requires reconfiguring of air and naval assets so that joint operations are possible. Both the Navy and Air Force have been taking steps to meet these new requirements for expeditionary warfare. Yet additional changes may be necessary as new priorities emerge for operations, information networks, forces, weapons, munitions, and support assets.

The key point is that future expeditionary missions will continue to demand unique joint operations, force capabilities, and operational doctrine. Moreover, the force posture best suited to expeditionary operations in the near to mid-term may be different from the posture needed to deal with China or a similar adversary in the long term. A challenge facing transformation will be to field forces that can perform expeditionary missions while providing the adaptability to shift to new threats and different missions over the horizon. While some joint forces and information systems can operate effectively in domains of both expeditionary warfare and future high-tech warfare, this is not true across the entire posture because not all forces are fully adaptable. The solution is not to pursue either expeditionary missions or futurist transformation at the expense of the other, but instead to strike a sensible and evolving balance between them. Doing so will require careful analyses of how to allocate future budgets and how to pursue new technologies and force structures. Basically, transformation must pursue two strategic designs that have different time horizons, not merely one design with only the distant future at stake. (The budgetary implications are discussed later, in chapters that deal with procurement and defense budgeting.)

Fostering Jointness

A major premise of contemporary U.S. defense strategy is that force operations must truly be joint in order to maximize the capabilities of all components. On the modern battlefield, ground forces rely upon contributions from air and naval forces in order to perform their missions. The converse is also true: all components depend upon each other. Beyond this, joint operations offer the promise of synergy by making the whole greater than the sum of its parts and the opportunity to reduce redundancy in many areas. Joint thinking, however, is new to the military services and does not come naturally to them. To a degree, they continue to view each other as rivals at budget time, and as distant partners with separate responsibilities on the battlefield. While transformation is intended to foster joint thinking, the initial roadmaps were service-centered, while DOD's plan was criticized as excessively vague and general.

The accelerating introduction of information networks facilitates joint operations by enabling commanders to blend the operations of multiple components in their battle plans, but there are other and more fundamental issues to be addressed. Among them, joint operations require doctrines and programs that blend precision air fires with fast ground maneuvers in mutually supporting ways. Modern air campaigns, for example, require coordinated operations by units from the Air Force, Navy, and Marines, plus integration with attack helicopters and multiple launch rocket system fires from the Army. Modern ground campaigns require contributions by Army, Marine, and Special Operations Forces (SOF) units. Joint air-ground campaigns necessitate the sophisticated blending of combat and logistics forces from all of these components, which interact far more closely on the modern battlefield than during earlier eras. As the next chapter explains, making full use of airpower's growing capability, while preserving adequate ground strength and creating new ground structures, constitutes an especially important challenge facing joint operations and transformation.

Creating jointness is partly the province of military commanders and their staffs during the preparatory stages of campaign planning, before battles actually begin. But such joint operations cannot be launched unless the forces already possess the necessary physical assets, training, and doctrine. Systems analysis has a role to play in helping ensure that the necessary assets are programmed and budgeted. For example, the presence of interoperable radios can be crucial to helping the Army and Air Force work together in tactical battles. Systems analysis unquestionably favors joint operations because of the obvious gains to defense preparedness and cost-effective use of resources. Systems analysis is well suited to finding low-cost, high-leverage ways to enhance joint force collaboration, such as interoperable C⁴ISR systems, common logistics, and complementary weapons and munitions.

Using Joint Training and Exercises to Foster Transformation

Training and exercises play a crucial role in determining the fighting quality of military forces. U.S. forces are the world's best, not only because of their advanced weapons, but also because they devote considerable money, time, and attention to realistic battle-field training. Although the military services have long trained extensively within their own realms, the coming agenda calls for them to devote substantial effort to joint training and exercises. Jointness in this arena, although not new, will increasingly be required, because modern warfare is fought jointly, modern doctrines and operational concepts are all joint, and the gears of joint operations must mesh. Ground and air forces cannot fight tactical battles of maneuver and fire together unless they train and exercise together.

Using joint training and exercises will be an important part of transformation. One reason is that, whereas transformational programs to field new weapons and technologies can take years to mature, joint training and exercises can produce results quickly, helping transformation produce big payoffs in the near term. Another reason is that operational doctrines are a key part of transformation, and they can be learned and adopted only through extensive training and exercises that reach all parts of the U.S. force. An equally important reason is that new operational concepts and doctrines are often created, tested, and matured during field training and exercises.

Joint training and exercises are excellent vehicles to experiment with new force structures and practices. The characteristics and capabilities of new weapons systems and information networks are often not fully knowable until they have been used extensively in training and exercises. While joint training and exercising is an activity, it also is a program that must be adequately funded, wisely targeted, and carefully planned so that it achieves its goals. Systems analysis commonly has not devoted a great deal of attention to joint training and exercises, but it is so important to operational readiness and transformation that a new kind of systems analysis focused on it makes sense.

Better Networks for Battlefield Operations

While much already has been accomplished, the agenda of continuing to strengthen the U.S. military's information networks for battlefield operations will remain critical for transformation in the years ahead. Two goals merit mentioning: creating better tactical intelligence, and improving logistic support of front-line forces. Determining how to pursue both goals is a matter for professional military judgment, but systems analysis can contribute by virtue of its capacity for thinking in terms of systems that are empowered by information networks.

Today, the U.S. military benefits from far better tactical intelligence on the battlefield than was the case even a decade ago. Equally true, however, the demand for highly accurate, promptly available intelligence is growing at a rapid rate. One reason is that U.S. combat forces operate more rapidly than in the past and need pinpoint data for precise targeting, often in a hurry. Another reason is that adversaries are learning to disperse their forces rather than mass them, thereby making them harder to locate and strike. Force operations in Iraq have seen both of these modern-day phenomena. During the major combat phase, U.S. forces operated rapidly, thereby compelling intelligence assets to work hard to provide data on enemy forces in a timely manner. During the subsequent stabilization and reconstruction phase, enemy insurgent forces dispersed in cities, operated in small groups, and often struck by surprise, thereby testing the capacity of U.S. intelligence to find them. Future contingencies are likely to see more of the same. The solution is partly one of developing better intelligence collection capabilities, but it also is one of developing better networks so that the various types of intelligence—for example, human and sensor-derived—can be integrated and analyzed effectively. Systems analysis has the capacity to contribute by viewing intelligence assets and information networks as a system of interdependent parts in need of further effectiveness.

The same judgment applies to providing timely logistic support to engaged U.S. forces on the battlefield. In the past, logistic supplies could move forward from rear area depots to front-line troops in a predictable steady manner in response to combat operations that often unfolded at a moderate pace. No more. In the invasion of Iraq, U.S. ground forces advanced toward Baghdad at a rapid rate, thereby extending their supply lines beyond previous experience. Their demands for logistic support were erratic and unpredictable, sometimes requiring large amounts of fuel, but other times requiring big infusions of ammunition. Meanwhile, long U.S. supply lines during and after the major combat phase resulted in truck convoys becoming exposed to enemy attacks even though they were transiting rear areas.

Such experiences, which may be repeated in the future, have changed the traditional calculus of logistics. In addition to needing rear-area security, U.S. force operations will also require well-developed information networks that can quickly identify shifting demands by front-line troops and then identify how to meet these demands by drawing upon stocks in multiple locations, not just distant supply dumps. Such new concepts as "sense and respond logistics" (whereby logistics units anticipate front-line needs even before they arise) offer promise of improvements. Systems analysis can contribute by viewing logistic support as a complex system empowered by information networks that need to match modern-era supply to demand.

Overall, information networking will succeed only if several different types of networks can be integrated. Intelligence networks provide information about enemy forces. Communications networks allow U.S. forces to share knowledge among all echelons and components. Operational networks provide data on the status and locations of U.S. forces. Logistic networks provide data on the flow of supplies to combat forces. These networks must be integrated not only to provide proper information flows so that force employment decisions can be made, but also to do so rapidly enough to meet modern-day needs. A current standard of timeliness is near-real-time: close to the time that a force operation takes place. A future standard will be real-time: at the very moment an operation is occurring. Information flows of this speed will be needed because the pace and complexity of force operations is steadily accelerating. Although significant progress has been made, future improvements are needed. The challenge for systems analysis will be to help make them.

Legacy Weapons versus Leap-Ahead Technology

Although DOD's modernization plan is mostly dominated by procurement of so-called legacy weapons, stiff debates arose in the Pentagon over whether some of these programs should be cancelled or pared back in favor of investing in leap-ahead systems involving futuristic platforms and exotic technologies. Some choices resulting from these debates are still questioned. The Army's Crusader artillery tube, for example, was cancelled because of its allegedly old-era qualities, but it might have been, in fact, transformational, because it brought major improvements to long-range artillery fires. Similar debates probably lie ahead as the Air Force and Navy modernization programs swing into high gear.

The principal argument in favor of legacy systems is that they offer major capability gains in the near and mid-term, while leap-ahead systems may take a decade or more to field, but may offer greater payoffs in 15–20 years or more. Leap-ahead advocates are likely to call for the Air Force to purchase fewer F–22 and F–35 aircraft, and more F–45 UCAVs and long-range bombers armed with cruise missiles. In the naval arena, leap-ahead advocates will be promoting a slowdown in construction of current-model carriers, submarines, and surface combatants in favor of investment in improved vessels, power plants, and weaponry for the long term. Their ideal involves ultra-modern and modular ships with far smaller crews than now, plus the deployment of larger numbers of smaller vessels in order to reduce vulnerability to enemy missile fires. For ground forces, the leap-ahead school will favor less spending on upgrades for current tanks and infantry fighting vehicles, but more on developing lightweight FCS vehicles. In general, systems analysis is agnostic in this arena, preferring to anchor choices in technical cost-effectiveness rather than doctrinaire formulas. The reality is that legacy weapons are likely to dominate the force posture for many years, while leap-ahead systems will play niche roles and will grow in numbers. Determining the exact mix of the two will be subject to continuing debate and analysis in the coming years. Systems analysis should participate in this process with the aim of helping field a sensible mix.

Transforming U.S. Mobility and Overseas Infrastructure

For the past two decades, the goal of creating better strategic mobility has been a big concern in DOD, and large sums of money have been spent on this endeavor. However, it has not, thus far, been a major preoccupation of transformation strategy. A contributing reason has been consensus that U.S. mobility forces are now basically adequate to the task and that further big improvements are not needed. Yet when U.S. forces were deployed to the Persian Gulf before Operation *Iraqi Freedom*, they did not seem to move any faster than during *Desert Storm* in 1990. While Iraq was being invaded in March 2003, some U.S. ground units were still offloading at Persian Gulf ports; the equipment for an entire Army division was on ships in the Suez Canal; and some Army units were still in the United States waiting for transport. A significant portion of U.S. ground forces arrived in the theater only after the major fighting had ended. While unusual constraints deriving from political and diplomatic dynamics partly accounted for this situation, it suggests that U.S. mobility capabilities may still not be adequate for new-era requirements.

Part of the solution may lie in acquiring more wide-bodied transport planes. Cargo transports far larger than the C–17 and C–5 (each of which can carry up to 100 tons) are on the drawing boards. Likewise, procurement of more big cargo ships of the large, medium-speed, roll-on/roll-off class could help, as could prepositioning of more equipment in key areas and increased use of afloat stationing for equipment and offshore logistic support. An equally important imperative is to improve the organizational process for deploying to give it better flexibility and adaptability for responding to fast-breaking situations. Prior to Operation *Iraqi Freedom*, DOD had developed a well-oiled plan for deploying large forces to a major Persian Gulf contingency. But the diplomatic and military maneuverings specific to that crisis resulted in this plan being altered in favor of a different deployment with fewer forces, in less time, and to different locations. It placed more emphasis on airlift and allowed less time to mobilize sealift. Perhaps because DOD had trouble shifting gears quickly, the deployment effort unfolded raggedly in places.

This experience highlights the need for a better mobility system anchored in flexible deployment plans so it can be adjusted quickly and efficiently to meet the requirements of the moment. Fortunately, the Persian Gulf deployment of 2003 benefited from an existing infrastructure of bases and facilities. The invasion of Afghanistan, however, was an entirely different matter: bases and facilities had to be created on the fly, even while combat operations were in progress. The Afghanistan experience illuminates the importance of creating more bases and facilities in distant areas where U.S. forces may be deploying in the coming years. Systems analysis provides methods that are well suited to examining mobility requirements and program priorities in these areas.

Designing Spearhead Forces for Access and Limited Strikes

A few years ago, a prevailing worry was that future opponents might develop entry-denial capabilities that could prevent U.S. forces from gaining early access into crisis hot spots. An example might be enemy missiles capable of sinking U.S. ships and bombarding U.S. airbases. Concern about such a threat led some observers to urge that U.S. defense strategy should switch away from forward defense operations to standoff bombardment, such as using bombers to fire long-range missiles from outside the range of enemy defenses. Closer inspection showed this fear to be exaggerated. U.S. forces have been successfully combating access-denial threats for decades, and future enemies do not seem likely to develop the sophisticated weapons systems needed to suppress deploying U.S. forces significantly. For example, U.S. carriers are quite hard to target and destroy from significant distances, while airbases are hard to shut down if they are hardened, and ports are hard to close if they are well developed and properly defended. Moreover, there are likely to be local allied forces present for most contingencies, especially if U.S. forces are helping defend their territory, and these forces can help keep the gate open to U.S. deployments.

Even though the access-denial threat is not a reason for a major change in U.S. military strategy, it is a prospect to be addressed by transformation because it could hinder U.S. force deployments in some cases. As many strategists have recommended, a sensible response is creation of small spearhead forces: U.S. combat units designed to be the spearhead for early entry into crisis hot spots. The deployment of spearhead forces can be assisted by preparatory long-range, standoff bombardment to help suppress enemy defenses. But the spearhead forces must themselves be highly mobile and survivable, while also possessing the combat power to perform their early-entry missions. Navy littoral forces as well as long-range strike assets are well suited for this purpose, provided they can survive enemy missile fires. Amphibious Marine Corps units also are appropriate. Light Army units could play this role, but a better choice might be creation of medium-weight brigades armed with some armor and light logistic support. Air Force units that can deploy with lean logistic support to bare-bones bases are another candidate. All of these forces must be combined to form joint packages tailored to the demands of the situation. Creation of spearhead forces was an early focus of transformation strategy, but seems to have faded in intensity; the idea deserves to be resurrected, and systems analysis can play a role.

A focus on spearhead forces should not be confined to gaining access to crisis zones in order to pave the way for bigger forces. Spearhead forces can also be employed, on their own, for specialized, limited strike operations. A potential example is strike operations against WMD sites on the soil of adversary nations. Such strikes likely would be carried out mainly with air and naval assets, coupled with Special Operations Forces. Advanced capabilities would be required in such areas as real-time intelligence and C^{4}ISR systems, specialized smart munitions including deep-penetrating munitions, and specialized air support for ingress and egress. Acquiring such capabilities seems likely to be a focus of defense planning and programming in future years.

Encouraging Force Structure Innovations

Transformation is already witnessing important force structure innovations. The Air Force has become skilled at packaging tactical fighters, bombers, command and control aircraft, tankers, and support aircraft for such tasks as intelligence, suppression of enemy air defenses, and search and rescue into single organizations for expeditionary operations. With additional assets to enhance capability and flexibility, the Navy is reorganizing its CVBGs into carrier strike groups and its ARGs into expeditionary strike groups. The Marines are configuring divisions and regiments for expeditionary warfare, while acquiring systems aimed at providing a capacity to conduct amphibious assaults from ships to deep inland. The Army is creating medium-weight Stryker brigades as a supplement to its current posture of light infantry units and heavy armored units, while also seeking to deploy smaller, more numerous combat brigades capable of independent action. SOF units are acquiring assets needed to play more important roles in major battlefield operations.

As transformation accelerates and new technologies arrive, opportunities for further innovations are likely to arise. The challenge will be to recognize these opportunities and act upon them, while turning aside ideas with only superficial appeal. Bombers are likely to play roles of growing importance in Air Force expeditionary force structures because they can carry large numbers of smart munitions; the same applies to inexpensive UCAVs because of their capacity to operate in dangerous areas without risking loss of pilots. The Navy likes the idea of gaining greater strategic mileage from carriers and amphibious assault ships. Operating within carrier strike groups, supported by increased numbers of ships and submarines armed with cruise missiles, carriers can be used for multiple purposes other than launching attack aircraft. They can, for example, carry Special Operations Forces and Marines. Amphibious assault ships are, in size, junior aircraft carriers: equipped with ramped flight decks, they could be used to launch F–18 aircraft. The Marine Corps has a growing incentive to emphasize all-purpose brigades, rather than divisions and regiments, as its major military formation. The Army faces major challenges and stressful internal debates in deciding how to transition away from big divisions and corps to reliance on agile brigades and smaller corps-like structures as its principal formations. Because many ideas compete for attention in this arena, the challenge is to sort out the good from the bad in the spirit of innovation. Systems analysis can aid this process by illuminating the effectiveness, costs, and tradeoffs of each idea.

Strengthening the Army's Transformation

Of all the services, the Army's prospects in transformation are least clear. Part of the problem is uncertainty about the role of ground power in a new U.S. defense strategy that intends to extract maximum strategic mileage from air power and naval power. Another problem is that, whereas the Air Force and Navy are both benefiting from new weapons emerging from the RDT&E cycle, the Army has few new weapons ready for procurement in the near term: its loss of the Crusader and Comanche leaves it with only the new Stryker vehicles for modernizing its inventory. A third problem is that the Army's proposed innovations—interim Stryker brigades, smaller combat brigades, and long-term FCS program—have attracted criticism from some quarters. A fourth problem is that the Army's ultimate plan to create a future force anchored entirely in FCS-armed medium-weight brigades seems at odds with the need for flexible, diverse forces. A fifth problem is that the Army's investment budget is comparatively small because so many funds are consumed by manpower, operations, and maintenance for its large force of active and reserve formations. The result is a slow pace of improvement for the Army's current forces, which will be its mainstay for many years. These impediments add up to a troubled Army role in transformation and dissatisfaction from outside critics.

Operation *Iraqi Freedom* showed that strong Army forces will still be needed to fight the major wars of the future. The initial combat phase of that war could not have been won had the Army not been present in sizable strength and capable of powerful offensive operations. How the Army's role in transformation can be strengthened is one of the key challenges facing DOD and the Army. Some critics think that part of the answer lies in scuttling the Stryker brigades and the FCS effort, but this step would deprive the Army of main transformation programs and would terminate initiatives that have merit. To other critics, the answer is increased funding for Army investment in modernization, but this step would require painful belt-tightening in other areas, such as, perhaps, cutbacks in manpower and formations. Still other critics reject the Army's plan for smaller brigades, but call for other approaches to reorganizing the Army's current forces, especially heavy armored and mechanized formations and large logistic support apparatus, to make them lighter, more mobile, and more agile. Because the solution cannot wait years for new weapons and technologies, the Army faces tough tradeoffs and difficult decisions, for which systems analysis can help provide the insightful evaluations of innovative alternatives needed.

Invigorating Research and Development

Although procurement will help empower transformation in the mid-term, R&D is a main engine for pursuing transformation in the long term. Accordingly, DOD's

RDT&E budget has been increased from $48 billion annually to $69 billion in 2005. Increased resources will help, but even so, the RDT&E process is besieged by complaints that it has become old, stodgy, sclerotic, and too expensive. One accusation is that the RDT&E process lacks a guiding strategic concept, leaving it to pursue a wide range of new technologies without a clear purpose in mind. Another accusation is that it takes far too long to produce new weapons. During the 1990s, a typical acquisition program took 11 years to reach initial operational capability, a big increase from the 7-year cycle of the 1960s. DOD is now trying to reduce the average time to 8 years, and over the long haul, to 5 1/2 years, but success is not assured. A third accusation is that the RDT&E process considers too narrow a range of new systems, prematurely closing the door to experimental ideas that merit serious investigation. A fourth accusation is that the RDT&E process produces new weapons that, while lavishly endowed with impressive capabilities, are too expensive to be procured in adequate numbers. Perhaps some criticisms are misplaced: DOD's RDT&E process is the most productive in the world by far, and it has equipped U.S. forces with superior weapons and technologies. Even so, a ponderous, rigid, gold-plated RDT&E process does not square with the vision of transformation being innovative, speedy, and affordable.

How can these problems be solved? Critics advance multiple potential solutions, some of which are now being pursued by DOD. In addition to speeding RDT&E, one idea is to increase funding for the basic scientific research—the first stage of RDT&E—that is responsible for originating innovative ideas for new technologies yet receives only a tiny fraction of the budget. A second idea is to furnish DOD's laboratories with better scientists and more money. A third idea is to focus on simpler designs for new weapons, resisting the temptation to tack on time-consuming additional capabilities as they evolve toward production. The effect presumably would be to speed the fielding of cheaper weapons. Another idea is to pursue spiral development by fielding new technologies as soon as they arrive and steadily improving them afterward, rather than waiting for them to reach full maturity before putting them into the field. Another is to spend more on experimental projects, and to add options to initiate new projects that offer promise, and to halt failed ideas to weapons systems as they move through RDT&E, enhancing the capacity to pursue flexible designs. Still another idea is for DOD to do better at working with the commercial information technology industry, and at organizing multi-company consortia to build new systems at lower cost when new weapons enter production. Such reforms must be forged together to create an overall system of improvements to RDT&E. Systems analysis traditionally has not focused much on the RDT&E process, but it could well do so productively.[9]

Improving Missile Defenses and Homeland Security

When the Bush administration took power in early 2001, it arrived with a determination to speed the deployment of missile defenses to guard the U.S. homeland against nuclear attack and to protect U.S. forces overseas. Accordingly, it increased spending on missile defense programs with a view to fielding them in the near future. It also proceeded to renegotiate the ABM Treaty with Russia in order to allow for limited missile defenses against attacks by rogue nations. Designing and deploying an effective, affordable missile defense system will be a continuing challenge for transformation. As chapter

19 discusses, a limited defense composed of mid-course and boost-phase interceptors appears to be the most cost-effective choice, provided that the technical and engineering problems can be solved.

The terrorist attacks of September 11, 2001, show that the threat goes beyond nuclear-tipped missiles. It also includes traditional forms of terrorism, plus use of nuclear, chemical, and biological weapons that could be delivered by many means besides intercontinental ballistic missiles. The U.S. homeland and U.S. forces stationed overseas are similarly exposed. Addressing this broader terrorist threat, while also deploying limited missile defenses at home and abroad, has become a critical item on the agenda of U.S. defense strategy and transformation. A major homeland defense and security program has been launched amidst worries that the United States is ill prepared and vulnerable. DOD has created the U.S. Northern Command to coordinate defense preparations and to work with other governmental agencies. A new Department of Homeland Security coordinates efforts that previously were distributed among various agencies of the Federal government, the states, and local communities. Consequence-management programs have been launched to deal with terrorist attacks and to increase the stocks of medicines and vaccines for biological and chemical attacks. Although domestic agencies will handle many of the tasks, U.S. military forces must be prepared for important roles. U.S. Reserve forces, for example, will have roles to play in disaster relief and other missions. While that agenda is beyond the scope of this book, it suffices to note here that homeland security is not only a policy goal, but also a program of multiple activities that must be carefully coordinated. Its effectiveness will hinge on whether this program is adequately funded and properly focused, balanced, and integrated. New forms of systems analysis have a vital role to play, not only for defense transformation, but for the entire homeland security effort as well.[10]

Strengthening Assets for Counterterrorism

The war on terrorism that erupted after September 11, 2001, was a "come-as-you-are" conflict. Lacking advance warning, the United States launched a global campaign against terrorists with the assets then available. The need to take immediate action allowed no government agency the time to survey the situation and build new or different assets. Fortunately, DOD was able to draw upon its special forces, which had been strengthened over the past decade for missions that included counterterrorism. SOF troops rose to the occasion and performed superbly in combat missions against the Taliban and al Qaeda in Afghanistan, and in conducting counterterrorism training in the Philippines and other allied countries. The U.S. Government was also able to draw upon the Central Intelligence Agency and other U.S. intelligence agencies, the Federal Bureau of Investigation and other law enforcement agencies, and intelligence agencies of other governments in its rapidly expanding global campaign. At home, the U.S. Government launched a crash effort to mobilize Federal, state, and local law enforcement agencies and to orient them to counterterrorism. Critics initially expressed worry that domestic law enforcement was lagging, but within a few months, major innovations were made and performance improved.[11]

For the most part, this global and domestic effort seems to have worked well: al Qaeda and other terrorist organizations have been set back on their heels, with many of their cells dispersed and leaders arrested. Yet the war on terrorism will be a long conflict, and terrorist groups like al Qaeda have shown signs of recovering from their setbacks and learning new ways to circumvent U.S. suppression efforts. An enduring and deadly competition seems to lie ahead. As its dynamic unfolds, the United States will need to learn how to better organize its counterterrorist assets and efforts and to achieve better performance by its multiple instruments. Because an effective counterterrorism effort will be a continuing imperative, it will require an organized system of activities and a coherent program to carry them out. This is natural turf for systems analysis, although studies employing its methods have been slow to emerge, at least in the public literature.

Transforming the Reserve Component Forces

While the U.S. military's Reserve Component forces are not commonly thought to be a focal point of defense transformation, they merit attention. Numbering 865,000 paid Reservists, they provide nearly 40 percent of DOD's military personnel and cost about $30 billion annually, or 8 percent of DOD's budget. While they may be a bargain at this price, the money spent on them is not available for other worthy programs. With the dramatic increase in DOD's operating tempo in recent years, Reserve Component units and personnel have increasingly been called upon to perform overseas and in missions that earlier were the province of active forces. In key ways, their contributions have been major, yet there are also numerous criticisms about deficiencies and about whether they are worth the money spent on them. Nobody proposes wholly dismantling the Reserves, but senior officials have expressed a desire to get greater effectiveness and efficiency from them, and to search for ways to create a better active-reserve mix.

The Air Force's Reserve Components are valuable because they fly many tactical fighters, tankers, and strategic lift aircraft. The Navy's Reserve component is too small—only about 90,000 personnel—for changes to make much difference. The Marine Corps' Reserve division and air wing seem permanent features of the terrain, and make a useful contribution to defense preparedness. By contrast, the large component of 550,000 National Guard and Army Reserve personnel is a regular target of criticism. The Army Guard and Reserve have many specialized support personnel that have performed invaluable services in key overseas locations. The bulk of Army Reservists, however, are assigned to 8 National Guard divisions, 15 independent brigades, and low-readiness logistic support units that cannot promptly be activated for breaking emergencies. This situation contrasts with the Cold War, when many Reserve brigades and divisions were closely affiliated with active units in order to augment them and maintain satisfactory readiness for key contingencies. After the Cold War, however, this practice fell into disuse, and a "readiness divide" opened between the active and reserve Army. A few years ago, DOD launched a program to enhance the readiness of the 15 independent brigades, but progress has not seemed impressive.

This situation cries out for transformational thinking, provided the complex politics of Reserve affairs can be mastered. Numerous ideas abound for getting greater strategic mileage out of the Army Guard and Reserve. One idea is to elevate the readiness of key combat support and combat service support assets that are needed by the active forces for warfighting emergencies. Some observers favor placing more of these assets in the active force while moving some combat forces to the Reserve structure. A second idea is to recreate the Cold War practice of affiliation and augmentation with active forces in order to enhance the readiness of Guard and Reserve combat forces. A third idea is to assign key homeland security missions to the Guard and Reserve, a practice that already is under way. A fourth idea is to impose major reductions on Guard and Reserve forces, trimming away unready units and freeing the money for investment elsewhere. These and other ideas need to be scrutinized for their costs and effectiveness, and combined to form an integrated program. This area is natural turf for systems analysis methods focused on both enhancing performance and economizing.

Making Transformation Multilateral

Transformation should not be a unilateral endeavor, but must instead be multilateral: the military forces of key allies must be helped to transform in their own ways. One reason is to reduce global apprehension that building ultra-modern forces is part of an American neo-imperial agenda aimed at coercing other countries. A second reason is to help ensure that allied forces can operate with U.S. forces on the modern battlefield. The United States is currently pursuing a multilateral transformation agenda with its European allies and NATO: the new NATO Response Force is an example. A major challenge is to broaden this agenda to key allies in Asia and other regions.

Most allies will not be able to pursue network-centric warfare to the extent the U.S. military can. But many will be able to achieve the lesser, but important, standard of network-enabled warfare: while networks may not determine force operations, they do enhance them. If allied networks can connect with and work with U.S. networks, then allied forces should be able to operate with U.S. forces in complementary fashion. Systems analysis has a long record of contributing to alliance defense reform; many allied militaries have been willing to listen to well-reasoned U.S. advice, and have become skilled at using analytical methods in their force planning. This arena provides systems analysis an opportunity to continue making worthwhile contributions.

Planning the Scope and Pace of Transformation: A Systems Analysis Perspective

Provided these and related challenges are addressed properly, transformation has an opportunity to pay handsome strategic dividends. But for transformation to succeed, it must be carried out effectively. It must be gradual, because transformation concepts are still in the process of evolving and require time and experimentation to mature, nor can the entire U.S. force posture be put through rapid upheaval without unduly damaging readiness. But transformation must also be steady and purposeful to provide a continuing flow of payoffs over the years ahead. It is not a process that can be judged solely by its results 20 years from now. What also matters is whether transformation provides information-age forces and enhanced capabilities in the critical intervening years. Systems analysis has a responsibility to help chart the course of transformation along the dimension of time, because this goes to the heart of transformation's success.

Pursuing a mid-term strategy for transformation is critical because a strategy focused solely on the near term or the long term would suffer from critical shortcomings.

A near-term strategy could produce modest improvements in a few years, but its limited gains could not accelerate afterward. A long-term strategy of leap-ahead measures might produce major gains in 20 years or so, but many of these improvements would come too late to deal with strategic affairs a decade from now. Moreover, even a combination of a near-term strategy and a long-term strategy could leave the country dangerously exposed during the critical mid-term.

As figure 13–2 shows, the promise of a mid-term strategy is that it can produce major benefits for this critical time period that would be neglected by a near-term or long-term strategy. A mid-term strategy can also serve as a bridge between initiatives for the near term and long term. It can help ensure that near-term initiatives will serve the forces that will be operating a decade from now, not just the forces of today. The result can be an integrated transformation strategy with near-term, mid-term, and long-term components that work together in cumulative, mutually reinforcing ways.

Figure 13–2. **Promise of Integrated Strategy for Transformation**

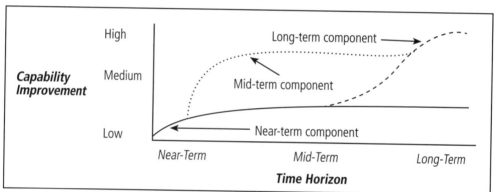

Likewise, a mid-term strategy can help give long-term initiatives greater specificity and relevance. As a practical matter, long-term technologies and systems are hard to design in the absence of experience with the new weapons and doctrines of the mid-term. Can the Air Force reliably design leap-ahead combat aircraft for the long term without first experiencing how best to use the F–22 and F–35? Can the Navy design ships for the third and fourth decades of this century without using ships from the second decade to learn about their assets and limitations? Can the Army design an effective 20-ton tank without first learning how to develop and use a 40- or 50-ton tank? Long-term success in any of these areas is questionable without first mastering the mid-term.

In the final analysis, transformation requires an integrated strategy that addresses all three time periods in ways that produce improvements with cumulative effects. What matters most about transformation is not whether it elevates capabilities for any single point in time, but whether it provides a growing stream of improvements that create enhanced security over a period of many years. As a mathematician might say, it is the total area under the performance curve that counts, not any single point along the curve (see figure 13–3). An integrated strategy should produce near-term gains that provide a foundation for building mid-term gains. These mid-term gains should, in turn, provide a foundation for long-term gains. For example, readiness improvements, new operational doctrines, and information networks in the near term can set the stage for new force structures and modernized weapons platforms in the mid-term. These mid-term innovations can then set the stage for introducing leap-ahead technologies as they become available in the long term. The result can be a cumulative process of transformational improvements that elevate U.S. force capabilities over a sustained period of years. When the results are measured in terms of greater capability and enhanced security, as figure 13–3 suggests, the whole can exceed the sum of its parts.

While such a favorable outcome for transformation is desirable, it is not inevitable. Transformation is a process that could succeed, but it could easily fail or fall flat in a number of different ways, all of which are real dangers. A sound transformation strategy backed by a family of good ideas is needed. Equally necessary is a sound transformation program composed of an integrated set of concrete measures to propel transformation forward. The task of blending changes in training and readiness, operational concepts and doctrines, information networks, force structure innovations, new weapons systems, and leap-ahead technologies will be difficult.

Figure 13–3. **Performance of Effective versus Ineffective Transformation**

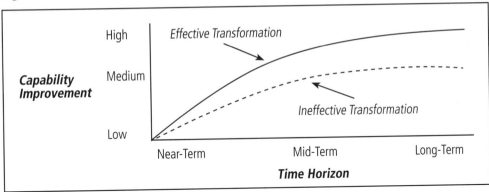

If systems analysis can help craft such a program, it will have made a worthy contribution to the transformation game. But in order to make this contribution, a new type of systems analysis will be needed, one that scrutinizes transformation closely but with a positive agenda in mind, that focuses intently on the emerging issues of the future and that brings insightful methods to bear. Mastering this agenda should be a compelling goal for a new-era systems analysis pointed toward the future.

Notes

[1] Arthur K. Cebrowski, *Military Transformation: A Strategic Approach* (Washington, DC: Department of Defense, Fall 2003). See also Donald Rumsfeld, "Transforming the Military," *Foreign Affairs* 81, no. 3 (May/June 2002). For an

overview of transformation, see Hans Binnendijk, ed., *Transforming America's Military* (Washington, DC: National Defense University Press/Center for Technology and National Security Policy, 2002).

[2] For a critique of transformation and the revolution in military affairs, see Michael O'Hanlon, *Technological Change and the Future of Warfare* (Washington, DC: Brookings, 2000).

[3] Because transformation is being pursued through a combination of changes, its impact on elevating the capabilities of U.S. forces can be understood only by taking into account their interplay, whose effects often will be synergistic and multiplicative. These combined effects must also be taken into account in gauging the capacity of a transformed military to fulfill it strategic purposes, which are both political and military.

[4] For a German perspective on pre-World War II transformation, see Erich von Manstein, *Lost Victories* (Novato, CA: Presidio Press, 1984). Von Manstein, who designed the Ardennes offensive of 1940, argues that the entire German military underwent transformation, not just parts of it.

[5] For analysis, see David S. Alberts et al., *Network Centric Warfare: Developing and Leveraging Information Superiority* (Washington, DC: Command and Control Research Project, 2000).

[6] See Donald Rumsfeld, *Report of the Quadrennial Defense Review 2001*. See also James McCarthy, *Transformation Study Report, Executive Summary: Transforming Military Operational Capabilities* (Washington, DC: Department of Defense, 2001).

[7] See Joint Staff, *Joint Vision 2020* (Washington, DC.: Department of Defense, 2003). See also Joint Staff, *Joint Operations Concepts* (Washington, DC: Department of Defense, 2003).

[8] Office of Force Transformation, *Military Transformation: A Strategic Approach*; Department of the Army, *2004 Army Force Transformation*; Department of the Navy, *Naval Transformation Roadmap 2003*; Department of the Air Force, *Air Force Transformation Flight Plan 2003* (Washington, DC: Department of Defense, 2003–2004).

[9] See Don J. DeYoung, "The Silence of the Labs," *Defense Horizons* 21 (Washington, DC: Center for Technology and National Security Policy/National Defense University, 2003).

[10] For an academic appraisal shortly after September 11, 2001, see Michèle A. Flournoy, "Strengthening Homeland Security," in Binnendijk, ed., *Transforming America's Military*.

[11] See *The 9/11 Commission Report, Final Report of the National Commission on Terrorist Attacks Upon the United States* (New York: W.W. Norton, 2004).

Chapter 14
Mastering Joint Force Operations

The arrival of the information age presents the U.S. military with the demanding challenge of determining how best to blend airpower and ground power for joint expeditionary warfare. Mastering the air-ground interaction is key not only to winning today's wars, but to carrying out transformation for future wars as well. Ever since World War II, the U.S. military has emphasized a robust mixture of air and ground operations in order to win land wars; it employs a larger proportion of air forces for this purpose than any other military in the world. This practice has played a key role in winning past wars and in making today's U.S. military superior to all opponents. It has shaped the balance of air and ground forces that the U.S. military fields today, as well as the forces fielded individually by the Army, Air Force, Navy, and Marines. Preserving and enhancing a powerful capability for joint air-ground operations is an imperative for U.S. defense strategy and transformation. Determining how best to do so is both important and controversial.

Controversy is arising because new technologies and doctrines make the proper path for future transformation uncertain. Air forces—flown not only by the Air Force but by the Navy and Marines and even the Army—are now fulfilling their longstanding promise of being able to destroy enemy ground forces swiftly and effectively. Key issues arise about what this trend means for U.S. ground forces. Should they be relegated to a lesser role because air forces can now perform many of their traditional functions? Or should they continue to play a critical role, work as equals with air forces, and innovate to strengthen their capacity to perform new-era missions? If the latter, how can such changes best be carried out? Is the Army on the right track with its plan to alter how its forces are structured, equipped, and operated? Or does some different approach to Army reorganization and transformation make better sense?

These issues are sufficiently important to merit a careful examination of where transformation seems to be taking the U.S. military. Transformation will result in air forces that are similar in composition to current forces, but even more powerful and better able to contribute to land warfare. Meanwhile, transformation seems pointed toward a future Army that will be significantly different. Today, the Army's heavy forces (armored and mechanized units) deploy slowly by sea, but once they arrive at a distant location, they field large, well-armed brigades that can engage in close combat and carry out major offensives. In the future, the Army's plan calls for a larger number of smaller combat brigades, each of which will be equipped with new lightweight weapons that may be less capable of face-to-face combat with a well-armed enemy. Owing to their advanced information networks and other technologies, future Army forces will be better able to destroy enemy forces from long distances through standoff targeting and air-delivered firepower, but they may be less able to perform close combat missions and offensive campaigns. Because this Army plan is based on new concepts that are fresh and untested, it must be studied carefully before a verdict can be rendered on its soundness. During 2001–2005, the Army made impressive strides toward refining its initial transformation plan, and it doubtless will make further progress in the years ahead. It will need analytical advice, including from systems analysis. Critical questions arise: Does it make sense for the U.S. military to field a joint force that relies mainly on air forces plus ground forces that can fight proficiently at long ranges, but lack a strong capacity for defeating the enemy in close combat? Does an alternative joint posture, equipped with ground forces that still can perform traditional missions, make better sense? The answers to these questions merit serious appraisal of the sort that systems analysis can deliver.

This chapter begins by assessing how systems analysis will need to create and apply new methods of inquiry in order to address these and related questions. Then, it employs systems analysis to examine the future roles of air forces and ground forces in joint expeditionary warfare. Next, it applies systems analysis to examine several critical issues affecting the Army's transformation: its ability to deploy forces swiftly, its plan to create a larger number of smaller brigades, its effort to develop new lightweight weapons, and its capacity to carry out stabilization and reconstruction missions. Next, it briefly discusses issues facing the Marine Corps and Navy as they endeavor to strengthen their contributions to joint expeditionary warfare. It concludes with remarks on future directions for the U.S. military, and for systems analysis, in the arena of air-ground operations.

Along the way, this chapter illuminates the importance of retaining a robust mix of air and ground forces, including well-armed ground forces for close combat, in order to provide the flexibility for a wide spectrum of expeditionary operations. It puts forth some ideas on how to improve transformation of ground forces, but more important, it also offers a basic message. Careful thinking will be needed in order to chart the future wisely. Proposals for change should be examined thoroughly with their full consequences and tradeoffs in mind, not accepted merely because they promise to overthrow the status quo, or offer glamorous new technologies, or satisfy one aim at the expense of others. The goal should be to foster changes that truly make sense and that genuinely will enhance the U.S. military's capacity to wage all forms of joint expeditionary warfare, not just a limited number of them. Because mastering the air-ground interaction is a complex subject, it demands the best that systems analysis has to offer, as well as mature judgment and wise decisionmaking.

New Directions for Systems Analysis

Systems analysis is not needed to tell U.S. military officers how to wage tactical battles and theater campaigns; their professional skills are ample for this task. But systems analysis is able to perform a crucial function. Being prepared for future expeditionary wars requires a program for enhancing the prowess of all services and blending their individual contributions together. This requires a large set of diverse joint assets that will give U.S. forces the new-era capabilities needed. Such a program is likely to include not only new hardware and information networks, but also innovative changes to service force structures.

The program must pursue sound goals with sensible actions, and it must make use of its resources as effectively as possible. Systems analysis can help construct this program.

If systems analysis is to be relevant in this arena, it must anchor itself in the study of expeditionary warfare in today's world. This is a significantly different type of warfare than the U.S. military has been accustomed to preparing for in the past; studying it requires new frames of reference. An expeditionary operation can be defined as a temporary military journey to a distant place for a specific strategic purpose. Expeditionary wars are typically not fought at places where the U.S. military enjoys the advantage of having had years to prepare for positional warfare, as in Central Europe. Such places as Afghanistan and Iraq are wholly new terrain, being encountered for the first time. Often the U.S. military will not have had an opportunity to study such places in great detail, much less prepare the elaborate infrastructure that facilitates positional warfare.

Expeditionary wars, moreover, are typically littoral operations, not continental operations. That is, they are launched from the sea and nearby shore areas, although they may strike hundreds of miles inland, as in Afghanistan and Iraq. Expeditionary wars are often fought against opponents who have serious ground forces but little strength in the air and at sea. Expeditionary wars are not always purely defensive campaigns aimed at rebuffing an enemy cross-border invasion and restoring the status quo ante; while they might begin with a defensive phase, they may transition quickly into offensive campaigns. Their war-termination campaigns can include toppling enemy governments and occupying territory. Their underlying purpose may thus be not merely to protect the borders of allies, but to reshape the geopolitics of countries and sometimes entire regions. Although the warfighting phase of an expeditionary campaign may be brief, the experiences of Kosovo, Afghanistan, and Iraq show that the phase of stabilization and reconstruction can be longer than originally anticipated, with demanding requirements of its own for forces and operations.

Expeditionary wars are power-projection operations in a new sense. They can require that U.S. forces deploy overseas quite swiftly and then strike lethally to bring quick and decisive victory, with few casualties to U.S. and allied forces. The premium placed on both deploying swiftly and striking lethally imposes highly demanding requirements on U.S. forces. In the past, ground forces capable of deploying swiftly typically have been light and not heavily armed; they have lacked the firepower for combat against well-armed opponents. Ground forces with significant firepower are usually big, ponderous, and slow-moving, and take months to deploy overseas to distant locations that lack a prepared infrastructure. Today's expeditionary forces must somehow manage a combination of speedy deployments with enough strength to get the job done: they must be quick, effective, and not prohibitively costly.

Air and naval forces are clearly well suited for such operations. Tactical air forces can deploy overseas quite rapidly, not only because their aircraft can fly to distant spots at high speed, but also because their logistic support requirements are relatively modest. Naval forces can also provide high-leverage performance: carriers, amphibious groups, and other strike formations are constantly deployed around the world, and their seaborne mobility means that they can often converge on littoral areas within a few days. Marine forces are also well suited for expeditionary warfare because of their orientation toward conducting air-ground operations on littorals. The fly in the ointment is Army forces. When they are needed for expeditionary warfare—as is often the case—it is their formidable firepower that is required, and their capacity to seize and hold large tracts of enemy terrain. Light infantry forces can deploy quickly, but they lack the heavy weapons for intense combat. Armored and mechanized forces possess such weapons, but they are hard to deploy swiftly and usually require cargo ships. The process of deploying them has sometimes taken months; the Persian Gulf War of 1991, for example, required 7 months of sea deployments before enough heavy ground forces were finally in place.

Fortunately, most expeditionary wars will not need as many as the nine divisions sent to *Desert Storm*. Even so, Operation *Iraqi Freedom* required deployment of five Army and Marine divisions, amidst complaints that even larger forces were needed. Deploying even one Army corps of three heavy divisions can require the time-consuming movement of one million tons of equipment and stocks. Perhaps if it is successful at fielding lighter weapons, the Army could deploy faster, but the gain is likely to be less significant than proponents hope. Prepositioning of more Army weapons and equipment at locations abroad can help, as can buying more transport aircraft. The biggest gains could be made, however, if the Army can trim away some of its large logistic support assets. Although they were needed to provide sustainment in past conflicts, they may no longer be required in the short, intense expeditionary wars of the future. Whether such steps will be taken depends upon the Army's success at reorganizing and creating new structures for expeditionary war.

For all of these reasons, waging expeditionary wars will often require different joint force packages than have been assembled in the past. This will also mandate that the overall conventional force posture be planned, programmed, and equipped differently than it was for the positional, continental warfare of earlier decades. Above all, the expeditionary, littoral wars of the future will require a joint force posture: sizable forces from all components that can be blended to wage truly joint campaigns in which ground, air, and naval forces are fully networked to carry out integrated, fast-moving, hard-hitting campaigns. Operation *Iraqi Freedom* was such a campaign, and it is not likely to be the last. Because new types of joint forces will be required, a new and responsive type of systems analysis will be needed: a systems analysis of joint expeditionary warfare.

Mastering the air-ground interaction will be critical to deploying swiftly and striking lethally. If systems analysis is to contribute to the study of this imperative, it will need, above all, to think jointly. The act of thinking jointly includes a sharp-eyed focus on the air-ground interaction to ensure that air and ground forces mesh to create leverage and synergy, rather than produce fault lines and seams that expose dangerous vulnerabilities in tough battles. This implies a demanding agenda: in the past, systems analysis has tended to view the services as separate components and to study their individual operations in considerable detail without concern for how they combine to form a warfighting whole. To a degree, this stovepipe mentality reflected the defense community's general satisfaction with how the military services were structured in relationship to one another. It also reflected the fact that the services themselves were mostly preoccupied with their own missions on the battlefield and did not pay a great deal of attention to how they could best work together.

This traditional focus is, however, now changing as joint thinking gradually gains momentum. If systems analysis is to preserve its relevance, it needs to be at the cutting edge of this trend. It is not there yet; most systems analysts are air analysts or ground analysts or naval analysts. Many are aware of the growing importance of joint operations as a paradigm for defense planning, but few yet truly think, analyze, and calculate in joint terms. Becoming an expert on all force components and how they interact is not easy. However, if military officers are expected to master this new art, systems analysts can do the same. Modern-era defense planning needs a cadre of well-trained joint systems analysts capable of shedding insights on expeditionary warfare.

Systems analysts must think about the fundamentals of how air forces and ground forces work together on the modern battlefield. This too implies an agenda of change in how systems analysis is practiced. Systems analysts have often allowed computer models of combat simulations to perform analyses for them. Such models are convenient tools because they can quickly provide a great deal of quantitative data and at least the appearance of meaningful insights. They can, for example, generate data showing how modern tactical aircraft and smart munitions perform in attacking ground targets, and how airstrikes compete with ground forces in destroying enemy formations. But these models can conceal as much as they reveal, and they can give rise to erroneous conclusions if they are not anchored in a sophisticated understanding of how modern tactical battles are actually fought.

Unlike computer models, modern battles are not a shooting gallery in which air forces and ground forces blaze away at enemy targets. Rather, they involve the blending of fires and maneuvers in complex, fast-moving, and sophisticated ways. Joint operations are often aimed at fracturing the enemy's cohesion and limiting its battlefield options in order to make it vulnerable to attrition. To win such battles, air forces, ground forces, and joint operations must mesh together smoothly. Ground forces must compel the enemy to concentrate its forces in open areas where they can be struck from the air. Air forces must help ground forces by disrupting the ability of enemy forces to fire and maneuver, leaving them vulnerable to U.S. ground strikes.

Air-ground coordination must be especially tight when close air support (CAS) strikes are conducted in large numbers. Whereas interdiction strikes hit targets in the enemy's rear areas, CAS strikes hit targets in proximity to U.S. ground forces. Many such CAS strikes are determined by forward air controllers assigned to U.S. Army units at the forward edge of the battle. Other CAS strikes are conducted within a few miles to the enemy's rear of the front line and must be integrated with the fires of Army artillery tubes and attack helicopters. CAS strikes and Army long-range forces thus must be closely coordinated and planned jointly so that their resources are used efficiently and the full set of enemy targets is struck effectively while avoiding friendly fire on nearby U.S. forces. This coordination, moreover, often must be accomplished in constantly changing ways during the heat of battle, rather than choreographed days in advance. Coordination becomes more complicated when CAS strikes are being flown not just by the Air Force but by the Navy and Marines as well, and when ground operations are being carried out by both the Army and the Marines. All of the air and ground components must understand how to carry out CAS, and they must be able to work together.

Complex interactions like these normally are not embedded in computer models. Their existence and their implications can be understood only by human analysts. For example, computer models may not be able to account for the importance of giving forward air controllers adequate GPS devices and multifrequency radios. When this is the case, such factors need to be included in an analysis, not left out because computers cannot portray them. Because of their failure to grasp complex interactions, moreover, computer models sometimes are erected on concepts and equations that are flawed or misleading. A computer model may favor one course for defense planning, and sound human reasoning a different course that may be better. Systems analysts need to be able to understand what their computers are telling them, and to view the results with a sense of battlefield realities in mind. This can be achieved only by thinking first, and then using computers to help calculate, rather than by calculating instead of thinking.

A new type of systems analysis for joint expeditionary warfare will also need to devote considerable attention to ascertaining how to deploy sizable joint forces quickly to distant locations. The timelines for expeditionary deployments may be measured in days and weeks, not months, and such deployments will be to regions that lack reception ports and airbases. Carrying out such operations will necessitate a new approach to force deployments that are not only swift and large, but also flexible and adaptable. Systems analysis will need to address the equally demanding task of determining how U.S. military forces can be prepared for occupation duties of stabilization and reconstruction. Forces employed for this important mission will need to be equipped and trained differently from combat forces. Exactly how they should be structured and outfitted is a question that requires accurate answers from systems analysis.

This new analytical agenda means that systems analysts will need to become expert at examining U.S. ground forces, especially the Army, in fresh terms. Analyzing air and naval forces is easier than analyzing ground forces because the operations, structures, and weapons of the former are comparatively easy to bring into tight conceptual focus. Army forces are hard to analyze because their structures are complex and also in flux, headed toward an unclear destination. Reorganizing Army forces for expeditionary warfare is a difficult and complicated undertaking that involves the blending of new structures with new weapons systems. But building an effective Army for the future—one that can deploy swiftly, fight lethally alongside air forces, and occupy successfully afterward—is an undeniable imperative for U.S. defense strategy in the information age.

Systems analysis can contribute to this analytical agenda by viewing expeditionary forces and operations as a system, and by employing economic reasoning to identify cost-effective programs. Its main business, however, is not likely to be one of identifying programs as "excess" because they are too expensive or inefficient, but rather helping maintain balanced joint force preparedness, and identifying innovative ways to maximize output and performance. This emphasis on enhancing performance is important because expeditionary warfare promises to remain a unique and demanding enterprise full of new challenges and surprising variations. Systems analysis will need to examine the premises of transformation in light of battles that are expected, but it also will need to perform sensitivity analysis of how U.S. forces will fare if future battles unfold in unexpected ways that test the capabilities of each component. In this context, it must help determine how requirements for ground forces are affected in situations when their own weapons for air delivery of firepower and standoff targeting cannot perform with full effectiveness.

Finally, systems analysis can help perform the vital task of comparing current transformation plans for future forces and weapons with alternative proposals that offer different attributes and capabilities. Force plans cannot properly be analyzed in pristine isolation because none of them are perfect; they almost always contain a mix of attractive features and questionable actions. What matters is whether they make sensible tradeoffs and set wise priorities. They are best judged on the basis of whether they are better, or worse, than competing ideas. While systems analysis cannot be the sole approach to evaluating force structures in comparative terms, it can participate helpfully in this agenda, but only if it is successful at applying its methods to the issues and options at stake.

Promises and Limits of Air Power

Systems analysis of joint expeditionary warfare can best begin by scrutinizing the role that can be played by airpower from all the services. The idea of using airpower to wage expeditionary wars has gained prominence because of recent changes in the strategic landscape. During the Cold War, the Air Force and Navy were too preoccupied by serious threats in their own domains, air and sea, to contribute fully to land warfare, which would be carried out largely by the Army and Marine Corps. In the post–Cold War era, severe enemy air and sea threats have mostly faded from the scene. The Air Force and Navy thus have been liberated to focus their air forces, smart munitions, and cruise missiles on contributing to land warfare. This development has allowed the U.S. military to pursue joint operations for land warfare in more diverse ways than before. Prior to the invasion of Iraq, it also gave rise in some quarters to the belief that air forces can substitute for ground forces or even replace them. The presumption is that airpower is cheap and effective, with fewer of the messy complications that accompany use of ground forces. Indeed, some advocates claimed that air forces could win wars virtually by themselves, with ground forces playing at best a minor supporting role. In the aftermath of the war in Iraq, sorting out the truth in these claims is important to defense planning and a key priority for systems analysis. Ongoing improvements to air forces mean that they may be able to win some wars by themselves, but winning demanding wars against well-armed enemies in unfavorable conditions is another matter.

Contemporary U.S. defense strategy already reflects a major increase in reliance upon airpower for land warfare. During the Cold War, the U.S. military's capability for land warfare was provided mainly by the Army's 16 active divisions and the 3 Marine Corps divisions. Since then, the Army has been reduced to 10 divisions, but this loss in firepower has been partly offset by greater contributions from the other services as more of their forces have become available for land warfare missions. Table 14–1 shows how the services now combine to provide an impressive capacity for land warfare. It estimates the amount of ordnance that can be delivered daily against enemy land forces by each service component. While this metric is crude—it says nothing about lethality and other performance characteristics, or about logistic support constraints—it does reveal generally how much each component contributes to aggregate combat power. Whereas during the Cold War, Army and Marine land forces provided nearly 80 percent of the capacity for ordnance delivery, today they provide just 57 percent of the total. The contribution from air forces—Air Force, Navy, and Marine aircraft—has grown from only 23 percent during the Cold War to fully 43 percent today, or about equal to what the Army delivers.[1]

Table 14–1. **U.S. Military Forces and Firepower for Land Warfare**

Component	Ordnance that can be Delivered against Enemy Targets Per Day (in tons)	Percentage of Total
Land forces		57
Army (10 divisions)	12,000	44
Marine Corps (3 divisions)	3,500	13
Air forces		43
Air Force (20 fighter wings and 100 bombers)	7,500	28
Navy (11 CVBGs and combatants armed with cruise missiles)	3,000	11
Marine Corps (3 air wings)	1,000	4
Total	27,000	—

Note: Calculations are based on standard DOD estimates for munitions expended in combat.

In recent years, however, the tonnage of ordnance delivered by air forces has not continued to grow appreciably, nor does it promise to increase as transformation unfolds. The major change is that, owing to information systems and smart munitions, this ordnance can now be delivered with vastly greater accuracy than before, and thus has far greater lethality. Twenty years ago, an Air Force fighter squadron would have been able to destroy only 5–10 ground targets per day. Today, it can destroy 25 targets or more when conditions are favorable. Some years from now, it might be able to destroy 50 targets or more. Moreover, it will continue to strengthen its already impressive capability to attack targets by day or night, to destroy armored formations on the battlefield, to operate in all weather conditions, and to strike within only a few minutes after mobile targets are acquired. Formerly air forces were mostly used to strike stationary targets in rear areas, but with the help of the Joint Surveillance Target Attack and Radar System (JSTARS), an aircraft with moving target indicator radar capable of tracking moving targets on the ground, and sensor-fused munitions, they can now destroy mobile enemy armored formations.[2]

This major increase in lethality has greatly enhanced the contribution of air forces to the land battle. An example will help illustrate the point. A modern enemy with an army of 20 divisions and a supporting infrastructure might offer 40,000 targets. One-half of these targets might be tanks and other armored vehicles that move continuously on the battlefield; the other targets are airfields, radars and air defense systems, supply dumps, headquarters, bridges, and industrial plants that are mostly stationary. Two decades ago, a U.S. air posture of 10 wings could destroy only about 150–250 of these targets per day. Thus, they would have taken 4 to 9 months of continuous bombardment to destroy the entire target system. Today's air posture might be able to destroy the target set far faster, perhaps within 2 to 3 months. When transformation is complete, it might be able to destroy the target system within a month or two. To be sure, these calculations are theoretical and do not reflect the many constraints that can impede airpower and degrade its effectiveness. But they suggest where things are headed. Because most enemies lack a sophisticated air defense system for fending off U.S. air attacks, they are highly vulnerable to this type of intense, accurate air bombardment.

Mathematical calculations such as these lie at the heart of the belief in some quarters that airpower can now win wars mostly on its own, with little help from ground forces. But as experienced systems analysts know, theoretical calculations are not necessarily the same as real-life experience. The defense literature of the past 20 years and more is littered with predictions of high lethality for modern weapons that were not borne out in the face of the impediments and constraints of the battlefield. Actual battlefield experience tends to be a better guide to gauging future performance than mathematical models and field tests. The experience of recent expeditionary wars suggests a mixed record about the performance of airpower. It validates the idea of airpower's growing potency, but it also suggests that airpower is not yet a wonder-weapon for winning all wars quickly and decisively.

Airpower did not win the first Persian Gulf war on its own. While it contributed importantly through a 6-week air bombardment campaign at the start of that conflict, many enemy forces were destroyed in the 100-hour ground campaign that liberated Kuwait in the last few days of the war. The Kosovo war of 1999 was won entirely through airpower's precise targeting with no U.S. or allied casualties, but in ways that gave rise to lingering controversies. Following an intense air bombardment lasting over 2 months, Serbian President Slobodan Milosevic finally withdrew his forces from Kosovo, thereby allowing Albanian refugees to return home and NATO ground forces to occupy Kosovo. Even so, some critics claimed that NATO "won ugly." They questioned whether Milosevic withdrew because of airstrikes, or rather because he felt Russian political support slipping and feared a NATO ground invasion. In any event, the prolonged air campaign gave Serbian troops ample time to abuse the Kosovars brutally, while it apparently did not destroy large amounts of Serbian military equipment in Kosovo. The main destruction was inflicted on Serbia's homeland; damage to industry, roads, telecommunications, and rivers slowed its economic and political recovery even after Milosevic was finally overthrown.[3]

Airpower was also instrumental in winning the war in Afghanistan. Aided by Special Forces that identified targets, U.S. air forces waged a 4-month campaign to pummel enemy Taliban and al Qaeda forces into submission. Friendly Afghan ground forces were also crucial in compelling enemy troops to concentrate where they were vulnerable to airstrikes. Near the end, U.S. Army forces began conducting maneuvers against remaining enemy strongholds. One reason was that airstrikes had not resulted in capture of Osama bin Laden and key Taliban leaders. Another reason was that surviving enemy troops were not giving up but were instead dispersing to mountains and caves where they could not easily be destroyed by airstrikes. In March 2002, Operation *Anaconda* against enemy forces in the Shahikot Valley employed a U.S. Army brigade plus Special Operations Forces and friendly Afghan troops. After an initial ground attack faltered, this 2-week battle was eventually won because air forces flew hundreds of sorties against a dug-in enemy. But this air operation was not marked by the quick, lethal efficiency of earlier air bombardments. Indeed, some U.S. Army officers complained that the air forces did not show high proficiency at CAS strikes. Air officers disputed this claim, but afterward steps were taken to improve air-ground coordination in such battles.[4]

Although the wars in Kosovo and Afghanistan were won principally by airpower, both conflicts were followed by lengthy occupations aimed at securing the countryside, installing democratic governments, and rebuilding the destroyed economies. In contrast to its prevailing roles in the wars, air forces played only secondary roles in these occupations. The heavy lifting was done by ground forces. Sizable U.S. and allied ground forces were committed: 20,000–30,000 troops in each country. Even so, both operations encountered difficulty. The effect was to show that while big ground forces might not be needed to win some wars, they often are needed to win the peace afterward, and that their success is often not easily achieved.

Operation *Iraqi Freedom* was a different test of airpower's emerging role in fighting expeditionary wars. Before the war, press reports suggested that senior Pentagon officials turned aside the idea of committing a very large ground force to carry out the invasion of Iraq. Apparently, their argument was that effective use of airpower could offset the need for a traditionally sized ground force. Even so, the invading ground force of U.S. and British forces was composed of nearly six divisions counting independent brigades. In Operation *Iraqi Freedom*, the air and ground campaigns were conducted simultaneously, not sequentially as in *Desert Storm*, where a long air bombardment preceded ground attacks. The initial air concept of "shock and awe" did not fulfill hopes that the Iraqi government and military would unravel in a few days. But during the 1-month war that followed, air forces flew over 20,000 combat sorties, most of which delivered smart munitions. They destroyed many targets and helped soften up the Iraqi army, much of which deserted rather than face American weapons. Yet it was ground forces that accomplished the lightning drive to Baghdad and ultimately occupied that city and other urban areas.[5]

Afterward, there was little public data showing the roles played by air forces and ground forces, respectively, in destroying multiple Iraqi divisions, Republican Guard units, and irregular forces. U.S. military participants credited both air and ground components with playing big roles. While air forces inflicted considerable destruction through rear-area strikes during the march to Baghdad, ground forces tore apart numerous enemy formations that temporarily barred their path. The bottom line is that Operation *Iraqi Freedom* succeeded because it was a truly joint operation in which air and ground forces played equal roles as indispensable teammates. Equivalent success would not have been achieved if air forces had fought the war mostly alone, or if ground forces had not benefited from major air support. After the war, the experience of Kosovo and Afghanistan repeated itself on a bigger scale. About 150,000 U.S., British, and other allied ground troops remained in Iraq in order to perform occupation, stabilization, and reconstruction missions. Air forces played a reduced role in this phase, even though low-intensity combat was still taking place. This war-termination phase encountered tough sledding, leaving some critics complaining that U.S. forces, despite their large size, were not large enough and were deployed too thinly. The effect was to illuminate the point that when wars are fought, sizable ground forces can be needed for more reasons than one.

This record of four expeditionary wars helps illustrate not only airpower's promise, but its limitations as well. Clearly, air forces are not suitable instruments for many postwar missions of occupation, stabilization, and reconstruction. But recent experience and careful analysis suggest that even during warfighting, air forces can be impeded by numerous real-life constraints. Conditions can sometimes create a big difference between what air forces can achieve in theory and what they can provide in actual practice. The difference between the two is a major reason why the idea of airpower regularly winning wars on its own carries a partly valid insight a few steps too far.

Serious systems analysis of airpower begins by recognizing that it is not unlimited. Only a certain number of bombers, fighter wings, and support aircraft can be committed to individual contingencies. Much depends upon the performance that they can deliver, which depends in part upon the types of aircraft available. For example, F–15 and F–16 fighters can accurately deliver smart munitions from high altitudes, and the A–10 is designed for CAS missions conducted at low altitude. All three types of aircraft, along with AC–130 gunships, may be needed for full-spectrum air operations. Even when a proper mix of aircraft is available, the performance of air forces is also affected by the strategy chosen for employing them. Air strategy involves choosing how to allocate sorties among multiple different missions over a period of time. Typically, allocations change on a daily and weekly basis. Much depends upon whether these allocations are attuned to the war's dynamics. A sound strategy can greatly enhance the performance of airpower; a poor strategy can weaken it. Effective planning can help ensure that sound air strategies are produced, but such strategies do not happen automatically.

Current air strategy is anchored in the premise that U.S. air forces will enjoy total control of the skies that permits them to conduct untrammeled strikes against enemy ground targets. While such air supremacy was the case in all four expeditionary wars, it is a recent development. During the Cold War, the Soviet Union possessed a formidable air defense system of fighters and surface-to-air missiles (SAMs) that threatened to disrupt U.S. air operations and inflict sizable attrition on them. In the Vietnam War, North Vietnam was able to use its thick air defenses to shoot down hundreds of U.S. aircraft. A worrisome possibility is that enemy air defenses might again be effective in the future, making U.S. air operations costlier and less effective. An effective air defense system could inflict attrition on U.S. air forces and compel them to divert aircraft to sweeping the skies clear of enemy fighters, bombing air bases, and destroying SAM sites. The more aircraft devoted to defense suppression, the fewer would be available for striking ground targets, especially early in a war, when critical battles are being fought.

U.S. air forces might also be constrained by organizational impediments. Awareness of these constraints has been a refrain of systems analysis in past years and merits continued attention. While U.S. aircraft are theoretically capable of flying two to three sorties per day, practical constraints limit the actual number to about one sortie per day. Limiting factors include pilot fatigue, maintenance and repair, re-arming and refueling, the availability of adequate stocks of smart munitions, and airbase operating tempo. Shortages of tankers can limit the number of combat aircraft that can be refueled while airborne, and lack of airborne warning and control systems (AWACS) and JSTARS aircraft can limit the number of targets that can be struck per day. The normal result is a metered air operation in which the total number of sorties flown and targets struck is spread evenly over the entire length of the campaign. The effects of such an air campaign build cumulatively rather than instantaneously: airstrikes can inflict great damage over a period of weeks and months, but less in just a few days. Moreover, sorties in the early stages of an air campaign are typically distributed among a number of different missions, such as patrolling the skies and striking industrial targets as well as hitting ground forces on the battlefield. The number of enemy ground combat forces that can be destroyed quickly might thus be limited simply because fewer sorties are allocated to this mission. When critical ground battles must be fought in the early days, sometimes air forces may not be able to make major contributions to them.[6]

The effectiveness of smart munitions may also have limits. Smart munitions have been highly effective in Afghanistan and Iraq, because these wars were mostly fought on the kind of flat desert terrain that makes target identification from the air or ground easy. But identifying targets can be far harder in rugged mountainous terrain, jungles, forests, or urban areas, especially when the weather is bad and pilots cannot see targets on the ground. Unlike radars, lasers cannot guide bombs through rain clouds, and even the GPS requires knowledge of the precise location of targets. When targets cannot be identified, they cannot be struck. Even when they can be seen, prompt bomb damage assessment, to determine whether a target has actually been destroyed, can be difficult. As a result, aircraft may be sent back unnecessarily to restrike targets, lessening the number of sorties available for striking fresh targets.

A more fundamental consideration is political and strategic. Often, air bombardment campaigns are not intended to win through attrition and obliteration, but by the destruction of the enemy's will by convincing it that further resistance is futile. Sometimes, however, enemies can be grimly determined to continue fighting even in the face of relentless air bombardment. The Vietnam War was such an experience; the North Vietnamese continued fighting to victory even after their bomb-cratered landscape came to resemble the moon. Some future enemies might buckle quickly, but others might employ asymmetric tactics to degrade U.S. airstrikes, perhaps by dispersing their forces and hiding them in places where they cannot be easily targeted. Their main hope might be to gain a political victory before U.S. forces are able to destroy them. In some cases, such a strategy might be a viable hope even when the skies are filled with American warplanes.

Beyond this, overall U.S. strategy can dilute the feasibility of relying solely upon airpower. An air campaign makes sense as a sole endeavor only when it promises to achieve the political-military goals being sought by the U.S. Government. But sometimes an air campaign may take too long to succeed or provoke international anger because the enemy's homeland is destroyed while its government and military forces escape largely unscathed. Sometimes U.S. strategy may require the taking and holding of large tracts of terrain rather than the destruction of enemy forces. While air forces are good at destroying targets, they are not good at holding roads, bridges, hills, cities, and supply lines. Nor can they solve the problem of U.S. military police being killed by insurgents and suicide bombers in cities, or small convoys being ambushed while traveling through forests. For such low-intensity battles, U.S. ground forces must bring their weapons with them, not look to the skies for safety.

The key point is not that victory through airpower is an illusion, but that airpower is a variable, not a constant. Its effectiveness depends upon the conditions prevailing for each war. When the conditions are right, airpower sometimes can win wars largely on its own. But when conditions are otherwise, it cannot triumph alone. In these cases, success requires ground forces, sometimes in large numbers and with a powerful capacity for close combat. Clearly, the growing potency of air forces justifies efforts to transform them with new information systems, combat aircraft, and munitions. Nonetheless, the continuing importance of ground forces is a compelling reason for retaining an Army that is an equal partner in the joint force, not a secondary player on the modern battlefield. It also is a compelling reason for ensuring that future Army forces have the capacity to perform the full spectrum of missions ahead, not just some of the missions.

Transforming the Army: Achieving Faster Deployment Rates

When airpower alone is not adequate for winning expeditionary wars, systems analysis suggests that ground forces bring important capabilities that can often be instrumental to joint operations. In contrast to air forces, they can seize and hold terrain features as an invasion is in progress. They can move across land quickly. In Operation *Iraqi Freedom*, for example, the Army's 3ᵈ Mechanized Division raced an astonishing 200 kilometers in only 7 days; it occupied Baghdad, 450 kilometers from Iraq's border with Kuwait, after just 3 weeks. Ground forces can generate a high volume of accurate and lethal firepower. For example, an Army heavy division in intense combat will typically deliver two to three times more ordnance than a fighter wing. Ground forces can also surge their expenditure of firepower; they can deliver it quickly rather than doling it out as air forces normally do. They can maneuver with devastating effect; for example, swift-moving "hammer and anvil" attacks can tear apart a large enemy ground formation in just days or hours. Moreover, ground force operations are not as costly as they used to be: in both *Desert Storm* and the major combat phase of Operation *Iraqi Freedom*, Army and Marine casualties were remarkably low despite the efforts of a large and well-armed enemy. Finally, ground forces are the only component in the U.S. military that can perform major occupation duties, including stabilization and reconstruction.

To capitalize upon their strengths, U.S. ground forces cannot stand still, but instead must undergo transformation of their organizational structures and weapons to work effectively with air and naval forces in joint operations. The challenge is to ensure that Army transformation unfolds in sound ways that remedy current deficiencies while not producing new drawbacks. Systems analysis needs to examine the Army's transformation plan and its alternatives with this criterion in mind.

A principal limitation of ground forces is that they are slow to deploy to distant locations. This especially is the case for heavy forces, which provide the best assets for wars requiring substantial fire and maneuver. An Army infantry division weighs 20,000–40,000 tons, but a heavy armored or mechanized division weighs nearly 120,000 tons. Changes are planned in the size and number of brigades, but today's Active Army of 10 divisions is composed of 33 brigades and regiments, of which 16 are armored or mechanized. Of the remainder, the 101st Air Assault Division has so many helicopters that it weighs nearly as much as a mechanized division. The Army has three light divisions: the 82d Airborne Division, the 10th Mountain Division, and the 25th Light Infantry Division. These light divisions are well suited for jungles, forests, or mountains, but not for desert warfare or other open terrain, and they lack the weapons and firepower to fight intense battles against enemies with armor.

Light infantry can deploy aboard air transports, but armored and mechanized units are so weighty that they must travel mostly by sea. This will remain true even if U.S. air transport capabilities and prepositioned equipment stocks improve in the coming years. The process of loading heavy forces aboard ships, transporting them across thousands of miles of ocean, offloading them, and moving them to forward areas can take weeks or months. During Operation *Iraqi Freedom*, DOD encountered trouble in moving a moderate number of heavy divisions fast enough to meet the timelines for invading Iraq. Systems analysis would suggest that reducing this problem by speeding the deployment of heavy ground forces is a key priority. This solution makes greater strategic sense than factoring ground forces out of the warfighting equation by placing excessive reliance upon airpower. Indeed, airpower normally works best only when ground forces are present in adequate strength. Even granting many of the arguments of airpower advocates, this is added reason for strengthening the role of ground forces in expeditionary warfare, not diminishing it.

Understanding the reasons why Army forces weigh so much is important to crafting solutions for speeding their deployment rates. That an Army heavy division weighs 120,000 tons is not because of the weight of its principal weapons. Its tanks, infantry fighting vehicles, and artillery tubes account for only about 20 percent of a heavy division's weight, while providing over one-half of its combat power and virtually all of its offensive punch. The other 80 percent of the total comes from its other 10,000 items of equipment, including trucks, tactical vehicles, and other assets. The Army also deploys additional logistic support assets to accompany its divisions. Normally assigned to corps headquarters or higher echelons, these assets include support formations with many troops and equipment items, and large stocks of war reserves, such as ammunition, fuels, and other supplies and materials. These assets are certainly important: they include air defense units, corps artillery, military police, ammunition depots, and trucks for transporting supplies to the forward areas. But as table 14–2 shows, they take the weight of a heavy corps from 360,000 tons for its 3 divisions up to 1,000,000 tons or more.[7]

These realities are a principal reason why fielding lightweight vehicles, such as Stryker and FCS vehicles, as replacements for today's heavier Abrams tanks and Bradley infantry fighting vehicles (IFVs) is not itself a solution to the Army's weight problem. Such vehicles, by themselves, would reduce the weight of a heavy corps by only 5 percent or so. Their advantage is that they can be airlifted by C–130 transports, but the Air Force does not fly nearly enough C–130s to lift an entire division of well-armed units, much less a full corps. Heavy divisions and corps would still have to deploy by sealift, and virtually the same number of cargo ships—100 to 150 or more—would be required to transport them. A corps armed with light weapons would not arrive at a distant location much sooner than today's heavy corps, and it would possess far less combat power. An Army corps equipped with Stryker vehicles could probably not have made the dash to Baghdad during Operation *Iraqi Freedom* because it would have lacked offensive punch and the capacity to survive enemy fires. The same constraint applies to proposed FCS vehicles. If the only change is introduction of these vehicles, Army formations would still weigh nearly as much as today but would have less of the offensive firepower and survivability crucial to offensive strikes.[8]

Table 14–2. **Estimated Size and Weight of an Army Heavy Corps**

Units	Personnel	Short Tons
Divisions and Combat Brigades	53,000	380,000
Corps Combat Support/ Combat Service Support	50,000	250,000
Ammunition and War Reserves (War Reserve Munitions and War Reserve Stocks)	——	370,000
Total	103,000*	1,000,000

* An additional 23,000 troops assigned to higher echelons elevate the total corps "slice" to 126,000 troops.

Systems analysis suggests that a better solution to the Army's weight problem is not to strip away tanks and other weapons that would still be needed on the modern battlefield. Instead, the solution lies in determining what parts of the Army's large support assets—over 60 percent of the weight for a corps of three divisions—are needed for expeditionary wars, and whether some of them can be reduced to lighten the corps. These support assets are of two types: combat support and combat service support. Combat support includes such assets as artillery and air defense that provide firepower; combat service support assets mainly are composed of various types of logistic supply units. For both categories, today's support assets still reflect Cold War concepts and are anchored in the assumption that each Army division must be able to wage intense combat against a big, well-armed enemy and must possess almost indefinite staying power for long wars. This assumption called for extensive support assets in such areas as artillery support, maintenance, engineers, medical aid, air defense, cargo trucks, and supply depots. It also produced requirements for extensive artillery stocks and other ammunition, fuels, spare parts, building materials, and replacement weapons. To be sure, the Army will still need assets in these areas for future expeditionary wars, but it will not be fighting the Soviet army or waging intense combat for months on end. The prospect of fighting lesser wars against lesser enemies translates into a need for fewer support assets.

An example will help illustrate how Army support requirements are sensitive to assumptions about threats, the intensity of combat, and its duration. During the Cold War, the Army heavy corps was given enough logistic support to destroy a Soviet tank army of five divisions and to fight a second tank army to a standstill. This design standard led to a requirement that the Army corps be capable of generating about 3,500 tons of artillery fires per day for 30 to 45 days. This high volume, in turn, produced a need for large ammunition stocks, plus multiple truck transport units and depots in order to keep this ammunition flowing to the front lines. The need for quick repair of anticipated damage to many vehicles led to a need for multiple maintenance units, large stocks of repair parts, and extra weapons for replacing those beyond repair. The need for a large air defense brigade reflected fear of attack by sizable enemy air and missile forces. A similar calculus applied to many other areas of logistic support.

Perhaps those assumptions were appropriate to the Cold War, but they seem less appropriate for expeditionary wars, where lesser threats, lower combat intensity, and shorter wars are likely. If future wars are less intense and fought against enemies that are not armed with modern weapons, the Army corps may not need to expend 3,500 tons of artillery ammunition per day. Perhaps 2,500 tons might suffice. This change would reduce the needs for ammunition stocks, truck transport units, and supply depots. The same calculus might hold true for other areas, such as air defense, maintenance, combat engineers, and medical support. A portion of today's logistic support and stockpiles may be redundant, or at least no longer a high priority. For example, huge stocks were deployed for *Desert Storm* in 1991, but many went unused and were shipped back to the United States afterward. During Operation *Iraqi Freedom*, large stocks remained in rear depots because the major combat phase was quicker and easier than originally anticipated. Can the Army drop some of its logistic support in the interest of achieving faster mobility? Can it deploy a trimmed logistic support structure and still be able to win expeditionary wars because it will still field the full panoply of tanks and other potent weapons for short, intense wars? These questions merit close scrutiny of the sort that systems analysis can provide.

Hope for leaner support assets comes not only from changes in modern warfare, but also from the impact of modern information networks. Such networks can greatly enhance the Army's ability to track the ebb and flow of demands from front-line units and to channel the flow of supplies to them from the rear. Before the invasion of Iraq, the Army was using information networks to pursue the concept of "just-in-time" logistic support in order to tailor the process by which supplies were shipped from the United States to overseas locations. As a result of the experience in Iraq, the Army is now using networks to develop the concept of "sense and respond" logistics, which is intended to tailor the flow of supplies from overseas depots to front-line units. Both concepts were originally intended to help ensure that logistic support adequately meets wartime requirements, but perhaps with the help of systems analysis, they can also help economize on logistic support, thereby reducing the extent to which the Army's logistics tail slows down its deployment rates.

The idea of examining the Army's "tooth-to-tail" ratio is nothing new. Thirty years ago, systems analysts began scrutinizing the Army to determine whether the logistics tail could be trimmed in the hope of generating more "tooth," that is, more combat forces. The Army examined its assumptions for support requirements with a similar goal in mind. While some progress was made, it was not comprehensive: Army support requirements and assets are still sizable. Today's challenge is not only to trim redundant logistic support in the hope of fielding more combat forces, but also to help speed the deployment of combat forces that already exist. Meeting this challenge is a key priority for systems analysis because it could help solve the Army's weight problem and thus ensure its continued usefulness in expeditionary wars. Any trimming of Army logistic support must be pursued carefully. During the invasion of Iraq, ammunition requirements were not large, but extended supply lines stretched the capacity of truck transports and maintenance units. This does not mean, however, that major redundancy everywhere is the solution. Instead, the solution is careful analysis that tailors logistic support to the mission at hand by ensuring that requirements are met and excess is avoided.[9]

What sort of standard for size and weight should guide Army deployment plans? In the past, the Army has thought primarily in terms of deploying traditional heavy corps for major combat operations. The traditional corps comprised 3 divisions and 10 brigades, totaled about 103,000 troops, and weighed about 1 million tons. For a major expeditionary war such as *Desert Storm*, deployment of two or three corps was a common practice. If Operation *Iraqi Freedom* is a valid indicator, future major combat operations may be less demanding of forces and support structure. Perhaps the Army can devise a new corps-like structure of five or six traditional brigades (or a larger number of the smaller brigades now being designed). Such a force would be composed of about 50,000–60,000 troops, and together with leaner logistic support, would weigh about 500,000 tons or less. Even armed with tanks and other heavy weapons, it could be sped to overseas locations far faster than a traditional corps of 1 million tons. A single corps-like force of this size likely would be sufficient for most modern-era combat operations if it is equipped with a proper mix of modern information systems, armor/mechanized units, and long-range indirect fire assets. If more combat units and support assets are needed, more could be sent either to enlarge this corps-like structure or to add more corps.

A chief advantage of this corps-like structure is that it would help make Army forces smaller and more modular, allowing them to be deployed in separate packages, rather than as a big mass that must fully arrive before commencing combat operations. The Army, moreover, would be able to maintain several such structures, thereby providing a capacity to respond to multiple contingencies. Currently, the Army has four corps headquarters: XVIII, III, V, and II Corps. If these four corps are retained in the Army's new command structure (discussed below), all of them could be configured for expeditionary missions, with about 50,000 troops apiece along with a modular capacity to expand or contract and to package different combinations of combat and support units.

This idea should be considered, along with others, on its merits. The key point is that the current slow deployment rate of Army forces is a problem that demands a solution, and the solution is not to strip away the weapons that give Army forces their fighting power. Future Army forces will need to be rapidly deployable, but they must also still possess the tanks and other weapons that allow them to engage in close combat and to carry out offensive maneuvers without relying unduly upon airpower. The challenge facing systems analysis and other methods is to find a proper solution, which likely lies in studying how Army forces are organized and supported, not how they are equipped with heavy weapons.

Reorganizing the Army's Combat Formations

While speeding deployment rates will strengthen the Army's role in joint expeditionary operations, efforts to reorganize its main tactical combat formations—brigades and divisions—will also be important. Systems analysis has the potential to contribute here too: not by creating new ideas, but by evaluating these ideas according to their potential effectiveness, downsides, and tradeoffs. In this arena, the winds of change are in the air because the Army is launching an effort to alter how its combat brigades and divisions are organized, and how they operate in a joint setting. Making sure that these changes are carried out sensibly is a challenge facing the Army, and systems analysis too.

In 2001–2002, the Army put forth an initial transformation plan that said little about reorganizing its brigades and divisions. This plan divided Army Active forces into three categories: Legacy Force, Interim Force, and Objective Force. The plan's main focus was on the latter two categories: the Interim Force was to be composed of six Stryker brigades (four Active and two Reserve Component), and the Objective Force was a distant vision of how the Army would take shape when its new FCS vehicles are fully fielded. The Legacy Force, which included the vast majority of the Army's existing combat formations, was largely left untouched with neither new weapons systems nor new organizational structures to improve capabilities for expeditionary warfare. Critics besieged the Army with complaints not only about the Stryker brigades and the FCS systems, but also because the Legacy Forces were left mired in the status quo until sometime in the future when the FCS might be fielded.

Reacting to these criticisms, the Army modified its transformation plan in 2003–2004. The revised plan abandoned the earlier framework of Legacy, Interim, and Objective Forces, instead creating two categories: Current Force and Future Force. It retained the Stryker brigades and seemingly placed less emphasis on any near-term rush to field FCS systems. Its most important change, however, was an ambitious plan to reorganize how the brigades and divisions of the Current Force are to be structured.

One of the Army's goals was to respond to charges that its deployed forces for wartime operations are saddled with too many layers of command echelons. The traditional structure—in which brigades were commanded by divisions, divisions were commanded by corps, and corps were commanded by a field army—made sense in previous conflicts from World War II onward. But it also was a cumbersome structure that, in the Army's view, could be trimmed, flattened, and reorganized now that modern information systems were being deployed. The new Army transformation plan put forth two types of units: Units of Action (UA) and Units of Employment (UE). The main UA is to be a new brigade combat team that will be endowed with a wider spectrum of assets than traditional brigades. The exact nature of the UE formations was defined less clearly, but the Army's plan stated that the division will remain as a principal UE, called UE(x). The plan further said that higher-echelon headquarters would also be created, called UE(y), but it did not specify whether the corps and field army would still exist, or instead would be consolidated into a single headquarters for theater-wide operations. This decision was left to further iterations of the Army transformation plan.

The most prominent, well-defined feature of the Army's plan is its scheme to restructure how combat brigades are organized and operated. A key feature of the Army's plan is to expand the existing active force of 33 old-style brigades to 43–48 new-style brigades, called brigade combat teams. This step is to be accomplished mainly by reducing the size of existing brigades from about 5,000 troops to roughly 3,700 troops, thereby liberating troops for more brigades. A main purpose of this force expansion is to provide a larger number of brigades for carrying out the Army's proliferating missions in expeditionary operations, including the need to rotate brigades regularly when missions continue over a prolonged period. The new brigades are to be highly modular and organized into three types for the immediate future: Heavy (armored and mechanized), Infantry, and Stryker brigades. The Army plan stated that these brigades will be maintained in a tiered readiness structure, with one-third in high-readiness status for deployment, one-third conducting training and exercises, and one-third recuperating from earlier high-readiness status.

Surface appearances suggested that the Army is trading less quality for more quantity by creating more brigades, each of which will be less powerful than traditional brigades. The Army, however, put forth a new design aimed at enhancing the combat power of each new brigade in order to help compensate for its smaller size. In essence, this design aspires to transform each brigade into a true combined-arms formation by transferring to it several assets that previously have been assigned to divisions, such as artillery tubes and reconnaissance assets.

The Army plan specifies that most new brigades will be equipped with two maneuver battalions of four companies apiece, rather than the three battalions of traditional brigades. Each brigade, however, will gain strength by virtue of being equipped with a reconnaissance, surveillance, and target-acquisition squadron, a fire battalion of two artillery batteries, a support battalion of logistic assets, and a brigade troop battalion that will provide command posts, intelligence, and signals units. The implication is that each new brigade will be able to operate as an independent, self-contained unit on the battlefield, without turning to the division for many kinds of support.

The Army's plan is based on the premises that future expeditionary operations should be centered on brigades and that a battlefield force of fully-equipped brigades capable of independent maneuvers will be more effective than a force of multiple, partly equipped brigades tethered to divisions for critical support. In a sense, this design takes the Army back to the regimental combat teams of armored divisions in World War II, which had a similar capacity to operate independently because they possessed both combat battalions and a full set of organic support assets. A key difference is that, in contrast to the past, the new brigade combat teams will possess modern information networks, digitization, and other assets that enable them to coordinate the operations of multiple force elements.

The Army is now implementing this plan to create a larger number of smaller, more powerful brigades, with completion expected in a few years. Systems analysis suggests that this plan offers important advantages, both because the new brigades will be better able to operate independently on the battlefield, and the Army will have more brigades available, including for occupation missions in which regular rotations must take place. Doubtless the new brigades will perform effectively in many combat situations, but whether they will perform effectively in all situations, including highly demanding combat, must be demonstrated through serious analysis, not taken for granted.

The Army's plan for new brigades has been criticized because of downsides and tradeoffs that, it is claimed, may outweigh the gains. One criticism is that this plan strips too many assets away from the division. In the traditional organization, the availability of many combined-arms assets (such as artillery, attack helicopters, and maintenance) allowed the division commander to distribute support among all three brigades in a flexible manner that responded to the shifting tactical situation at hand. The new brigade-centered structure, critics allege, leaves the division underpowered, compromising flexibility on the battlefield because higher-echelon commanders have a reduced capacity to concentrate resources in some areas while lessening them in others.

Another criticism is that the Army's plan overloads the brigade commander and his staff with too many responsibilities. Under the traditional structure, the division commander made many important decisions about how to commit resources and how to conduct complex battle operations. The effect was to free brigade commanders—Army colonels with relatively small command staffs—to focus on the tactical situation at hand. In the new structure, the brigade commander and brigade staff will now have to make many additional decisions about, for example, performing reconnaissance, using artillery and attack helicopters, and carrying out maintenance and resupply. Critics allege that future brigade commanders will be hard-pressed to make such decisions wisely on the fast-paced battlefield of the future.

A third criticism is that the new Army brigades will be too small to fight effectively in intense combat of a sustained nature. Notwithstanding the acquisition of new combined-arms assets, most of the new brigades will have only two maneuver battalions rather than three. The effect will be to reduce by about one-third the number of tanks, infantry fighting vehicles, mortars, machine guns, and rifles at their disposal. This downsizing is coming at a time when the Army is trying to disperse forces across the battlefield, to have brigades maneuver separately from each other, and to require each brigade to cover a larger amount of territory than before. Critics fear that the new brigade combat teams will lack a sufficient quantity of assets, especially in sustained fighting that produces high casualties, thus reducing the tanks and troops at the brigade commander's disposal. Because traditional brigades had more maneuver units, they were able to absorb significant casualties while continuing to fight effectively. Critics worry that the new, smaller brigades will lack this staying power.

A noteworthy alternative to the Army's plan for smaller brigades comes from Colonel Douglas Macgregor, USA (Ret.). In his recent book, Macgregor calls for the Army to anchor its battlefield operations on brigades, and endorses the transfer of combined-arms assets from the division to a new brigade-like structure, which he labels "combat maneuver groups."[10] But Macgregor does not have smaller brigades in mind. Instead, his combat maneuver groups would be larger than traditional brigades, with more manpower and other weapons, including tanks. Macgregor therefore recommends reducing the number of Army maneuver units from 33 traditional brigades to about 25 new combat maneuver groups, plus several reconnaissance strike groups and air assault groups. He also calls for creation of several aviation combat groups composed of attack helicopters and UCAVs (see table 14–3).

Table 14–3. **Proposed Expeditionary Strike Army**

Units	Number of Groups
Heavy Combat Groups	13
Light Reconnaissance Strike Groups	3
Airborne/Air Assault Groups	9
Aviation Combat Groups	7–14
Total	**32–39**

Source: Douglas A. Macgregor, *Transformation Under Fire: Revolutionizing How America Fights* (Westport, CT: Praeger, 2003).

Macgregor's goal is to create combat maneuver groups that can function as "junior divisions" in joint operations. He proposes that these combat maneuver groups should be commanded by a brigadier general with a sizable headquarters staff, and that the Army should disestablish the division as a command echelon. In his design, the new theater command structure would be joint, and it would command these combat maneuver units directly, rather than employing a division headquarters as an intermediary. Macgregor's design is considerably different from the Army plan: because the Army's brigades would be smaller than they are now, they could not operate as junior divisions. Instead, they continue to report to a division headquarters, which would command between three and six of the new brigades.

The Army is now implementing its plan for new-style brigades, but criticisms of this plan mean that it is likely to engender controversy in the coming years. Continuing analysis will be needed, including field tests of the new brigade. If better ideas surface, the Army may decide to alter this plan in various ways as more information becomes available, and as its own views evolve. Clearly, the Army needs a sufficient number of combat brigades to perform its many missions, but just as clearly, each brigade must be properly sized and armed. The subject of how to organize future Army combat brigades and other units is likely to be studied for years to come. Systems analysis has an appropriate role to play in this enterprise by focusing on how alternative formations will actually perform on the battlefield, which is the bottom line in judging their merits

Equipping the Army with New Weapons and Capabilities

The Army's decision to field between 43 and 48 new-style brigades establishes a structural framework for the future, but it leaves critical questions unanswered. How should these brigades be equipped with weapons and other assets? What capabilities should the Army possess in order to carry out joint expeditionary operations? How can the Army best be prepared so that it has a sufficiently wide spectrum of assets to provide proper agility, flexibility, and adaptability? Systems analysis can help address these questions by scrutinizing the Army's plan with an eye on its viability and capacity to meet the requirements of U.S. defense strategy.

The Army's long-range effort for shaping its capabilities is mainly concentrated in its RDT&E effort to create Future Combat Systems. Its FCS plan is shaped by a key premise: the need to field future forces that are networked and rapidly deployable, can enter combat zones from multiple points, and can conduct dispersed simultaneous operations on noncontiguous battlefields. The FCS plan strives to take full advantage of standoff weapons and air-delivered firepower (for example, attack helicopters, UCAVs, long-range artillery, rockets, missiles, and smart munitions), thereby reducing today's reliance upon direct fires and close combat carried out by armor and infantry. The FCS plan relies heavily upon networked architectures, sensors, and unmanned reconnaissance and surveillance systems to provide highly accurate information about the dispositions of friendly and enemy forces, thereby achieving high effectiveness in standoff-strike operations. Its goal is to use these assets to destroy enemy forces before they can come into close contact with U.S. Army forces, thereby avoiding the need for pitched battles at short ranges, where traditional direct firepower still dominates.

The FCS plan is composed of fully 18 new weapons vehicles. They include a tank, an infantry carrier, an artillery tube, a mortar, a command and control vehicle, a reconnaissance and surveillance vehicle, and various vehicles for logistic support operations. This plan also includes a family of robotic vehicles, some armed and some for logistic support. While these 18 vehicles vary in form and function, they share one thing in common: all are intended to be light in weight. For example, the new tanks, infantry fighting vehicles, and artillery tubes are being designed to weigh less than 20 tons apiece, light enough to be lifted by a C–130 transport plane. This goal stands in contrast to current weapons: today's M–1 tank weighs 70 tons, and the Bradley IFV weighs about 35 tons.

Accompanying this emphasis on lightweight vehicles are other important features. Some of these vehicles are to be mounted on wheels, not treads. This will enable them to move at high speed on roads, but it could inhibit their ability to operate on open terrain where a light footprint is important: tracked vehicles create less overpressure than wheeled vehicles. Most of these new vehicles will not provide the thick protective armor of current tanks and IFVs, a sacrifice made necessary by their low weight. They are also likely to be armed with smaller guns than current weapons: the M–1 tank's 120-millimeter gun, for example, will give way to a smaller gun on the new lightweight tank. While much will depend upon how ongoing RDT&E programs evolve, these new vehicles will be lighter and easier to move to distant locations, but they will have less firepower, survivability, and cross-country mobility than their current counterparts. In the FCS plan, this reduction in traditional combat power is to be compensated by information networks and standoff targeting assets that destroy the enemy at long distance rather than by close-in fighting.

The FCS plan, including its information networks and new vehicles, is currently advancing through the early stages of RDT&E. The exact capabilities of the new combat vehicles will become known only when they emerge as testable prototypes in a few years. The Army's transformation plan calls for the initial vehicles to be deployable by

2008, and all 18 vehicles to be available by 2014. Equipping the Army with these new vehicles presumably will take place during 2010–2020 and beyond. In the interim, the Army will continue using its existing weapons, but as the next decade unfolds, they will be steadily retired, ultimately giving way to an Army that is fully armed with FCS weapons.

The Army's FCS plan is visionary by promising to create a future Army that is equipped differently than today and operates differently as well. This plan, however, is being subjected to four major criticisms regarding its implications for the Army's future warfighting prowess. Together, these criticisms suggest that while the Army's FCS plan has attractive features, it may suffer from tunnel vision by being too preoccupied with light-weight weapons and big technological leaps, at the cost of paying too little attention to other important considerations.

The first criticism is that the Army is investing too many of its scarce investment dollars in the FCS plan, thereby resulting in insufficient funds being spent on upgrading current weapons that will remain in the inventory for many years. For example, worthy upgrades to M–1 tanks, Bradley IFVs, Apache attack helicopters, and Paladin artillery tubes have, it is charged, been sacrificed in the interest of funding the FCS plan. This criticism was especially vocal in 2001–2002. Since then, the Army has shifted gears somewhat by channeling more investment funds into upgrading of existing weapons, but even so, critics still complain that the Army is betting too much on the distant future at the expense of the present.

A second criticism is that the FCS is too ambitious in its aims to create new technologies that may stretch the art of the possible beyond what the research and development community can produce any time soon. The networking component of the FCS plan alone is highly ambitious, necessitating extensive bandwidth and other advanced features that have not been contemplated before, much less achieved. The same holds true for many of the new FCS vehicles, which must create and blend several new types of components, such as information systems, armor plating, guns and missiles, engines, transmissions, and stabilization systems, all of which must successfully work together. Critics worry that the entire effort might go bust because it fails to achieve enough technological breakthroughs. They argue that the Army would be better advised to aim for less lofty technologies that offer greater promise of being available when the time comes to deploy them.

The third criticism is that the FCS plan places too much stock in air-delivered fires and long-range targeting, neglecting close-combat capabilities that will still be needed in the future. Critics of this persuasion doubt the feasibility of fielding an Army whose networks, sensors, and standoff targeting assets are so good that close combat will never be necessary. They argue that although standoff targeting can work when the enemy is attacking U.S. positions, it may be considerably less effective when U.S. forces are on the attack and must drive enemy troops from prepared positions. In such situations, critics assert, U.S. Army forces must be capable of delivering shock action and engaging in other features of close combat. Lightweight and vulnerable FCS vehicles, say critics, will leave the Army able to defend, but unable to take the offensive as in *Desert Storm* and Operation *Iraqi Freedom*. These critics are also worried that the combination of smaller brigades and FCS lightweight weapons will make the loss of traditional combat power far greater than it appears to be at first glance. These critics would pursue a revised FCS plan that, while developing lightweight weapons for some Army forces, would also aim at creating heavier, tracked, offense-capable weapons, such as a tank of 35–50 tons rather than 20 tons, so that the majority of forces could remain capable of close battles.

The fourth criticism is that the FCS plan will eventually result in an Army Future Force that is mostly homogenous, at the cost of proper diversity. Although the Army plan says that the Future Force will have a mix of light, medium, and heavy units, critics worry that the design standard of optimizing for standoff targeting and non-contact operations will result in units that cluster around a similar FCS model, resulting in a scarcity of infantry, armor, or other units that are optimized for close contact. These critics value the Army's current diversity: its 33 brigades include 16 armored/mechanized brigades, 3 air assault brigades, 4 airborne brigades, 8 infantry brigades, and 2 armored cavalry regiments. This diverse portfolio, critics argue, provides the Army with considerable flexibility and adaptability. The critics worry that although a mostly one-dimensional FCS force would be able to perform some missions, it would lack the versatility to perform others, especially close contact. They argue in favor of an FCS plan that preserves a diverse mix of formations similar to now, with some light-medium brigades, multiple heavy brigades, and several specialized brigades, with robust capabilities for close contact.

These four criticisms may offer important insights, but much depends upon how the FCS effort ultimately unfolds. Strategic logic suggests that the Army should devote a sufficient portion of its investment budget to upgrading current weapons, that it should pursue achievable technologies, that it should create a future Army that can attack as well as defend, and that it should field a diverse portfolio of brigades rather than a single type. To the extent these criticisms are valid, they argue for shifts in the Army's FCS plan as it evolves. The larger truth is that the FCS plan is still in its early conceptual phases, and it is an evolving creation. It likely will be altered several times as it unfolds. The challenge for the Army will be to make the necessary alterations at the proper time. The challenge for systems analysis will be to provide the insights needed for the Army to react wisely.

New Forces for Stabilization and Reconstruction Missions

Recent experiences in the Balkans, Afghanistan, and Iraq show that in addition to transforming its forces for future combat missions, the Army also needs to upgrade its assets for performing S&R missions. The forces that perform these important postwar missions include formations such as military police, construction engineers, and civil administrators. Such assets normally are in short supply when a combat force deploys for major warfighting, and must be deployed from the United States as wars are drawing to a close. This effort, however, is difficult when sizable S&R forces are required, because the Active Army has a shortage of such assets and has not organized them for S&R missions. When they must be mobilized from Reserve Component formations, this necessitates the callup of thousands of reservists who may lack the necessary equipment, training, and readiness. Rectifying this shortfall will be necessary in order to be properly prepared for future expeditionary wars in which the U.S. goal is not only to defeat enemy forces and overthrow rogue leaders, but also to install democratic governments and market economies afterward.

The goal of better S&R assets can be pursued in different ways. A minimal approach would be to strengthen planning for S&R missions, assign these missions as added duties to existing active combat support/combat service support forces, and upgrade the readiness of selective reserve formations. A moderate approach would, in addition, also add some more S&R assets to the Active Army and Reserve Components: perhaps a few additional battalions of construction engineers, military police, and civil administrators. An ambitious approach would be to expand the Active Army to 11 or 12 divisions with the creation of 1 or 2 new "S&R divisions" or the equivalent of 2 division-sized formations. Perhaps the Army's 7th and 24th Divisions, which have active headquarters in command of Reserve Component brigades, could be used to establish S&R divisions. Populated by a mixture of Active units and high-readiness Reserve Component units from the Army and Marine Corps, these divisions would be capable of standard S&R missions: creating local security, establishing police and law enforcement forces, repairing damage to cities and infrastructure, restoring electricity, water, and sewage, and creating new governmental and economic institutions. The Army would need additional funds and manpower to pursue this approach. The composition of an illustrative S&R division with about 15,000 troops is shown in table 14–4.[11]

Systems analysis can help assess how alternative S&R programs compare in terms of their ability to perform their important strategic missions. Future S&R requirements will depend upon the number of S&R contingencies that might occur at any single time, and

Table 14–4. Composition of Notional Army Stabilization and Reconstruction Division

Units	Personnel
Headquarters (division and brigades)	750
Stryker Battalions with Artillery Company (2)	1,550
Combat Aviation Battalion (1)	650
Aviation Battalion for Logistic Support (1)	650
Military Police Battalions (2)	1,300
Special Forces Battalions (2)	1,300
Construction Engineer Battalions (2)	1,300
Medical Battalion (1)	650
Transportation Battalions (2)	1,300
Civil Affairs/Adjutant General Battalions (2)	1,300
Maintenance Battalion (1)	650
Quartermaster Battalion (1)	650
Ordnance Battalion (1)	650
Training and Security Assistance Battalion (1)	650
Administration, Signals, Air Defense, Psychological Operations and Other Units	1,750
Total	**15,100**

the degree of difficulty encountered in each case. In early 2004, for example, the U.S. military found itself occupying Iraq even while it was carrying out small-scale S&R missions in Afghanistan and the Balkans. Thus, the issue is one of determining how much S&R capability, confidence, and insurance is wanted in a "strategic space" of potential requirements that, depending upon changing circumstances, could range from small to quite large.

Figure 14–1. **Illustrative Performance Capabilities of Alternative Stabilization and Reconstruction Options**

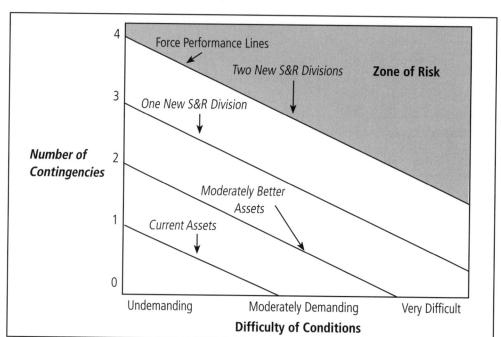

As figure 14–1 shows, the existing capability can handle only undemanding events. A minimalist or moderate effort would create better capabilities for handling more stressful situations, but could still fall short of preparing the U.S. military for multiple contingencies or highly difficult interventions. A program to create an S&R division would significantly elevate U.S. capabilities for such contingencies and interventions (in situations similar to Iraq), but it might still leave a wide gap between assets and requirements if events mandated bigger operations such as, for example, occupying countries considerably larger than Iraq. Figure 14–1 suggests that fielding two S&R divisions might be the best solution, but if budgetary and manpower constraints will permit only one division, this would clearly be better than marginal improvements to the status quo.

Transformation of the Marine Corps and the Navy

Although public attention is focused on the Army, the Marine Corps is also important to future land warfare and joint operations. With three active-duty divisions, the

Marines provide nearly one-fourth of active U.S. ground forces. The Marine Corps was a target for criticism during the 1970s, but it has not provoked much public controversy in recent years, mainly because it has acquired a good reputation for innovating and responding to shifts in U.S. defense strategy. Recently it has been switching from its earlier focus on over-the-beach amphibious assault to a broader spectrum of littoral operations. In Operation *Iraqi Freedom*, Marine forces were able to drive deep into enemy territory as fast as the Army and helped to occupy Baghdad. Like the other services, however, the Marine Corps will need further transformation. Success at this endeavor will require not only careful planning but also adequate funds.

The Marines have shown skill at joint operations. Marine ground forces even bring their own air forces with them: each division has a Marine air wing attached to it, thus creating a Marine Expeditionary Force. Close cooperation of these air and ground forces provides the Marines with substantially greater firepower than is suggested by the inventories of ground weapons, which include artillery plus one or two tank battalions per division. In addition, the Marines are integrated into Navy operations to blend carrier strike assets and cruise missiles with Marine ground and air forces. The Marine Corps and the Navy have a reputation for cooperating more closely than do the Army and Air Force, which have sometimes been at loggerheads in the past.

The agenda ahead for the Marine Corps is not one of wholesale restructuring, but instead continuing to improve upon a transformation process already under way. Ideas for restructuring include proposals to base plans for future operations on independent brigades rather than divisions, and to enhance the flexibility of amphibious strike groups by equipping them with more cruise missiles and other strike assets. At the center of Marine modernization, however, are its programs to acquire the V–22 Osprey (a tilt-rotor assault aircraft) and the F–35 Joint Strike Fighter. A key point is that the Marine Corps will need adequate funds in order to carry out its transformation plans; a natural tendency can be to neglect the Marine Corps at budget time when other programs are beckoning.

The Navy's success at undergoing transformation will also affect future U.S. capabilities for joint expeditionary warfare. Today's Navy was originally created to perform traditional sea-domination missions, but in recent years it has contributed importantly to the U.S. expeditionary operations in Kosovo, Afghanistan, and Iraq. In particular, its capacity to generate firepower with its carrier-launched aircraft and cruise missiles has aided not only the Marines, but the Army and Air Force as well. Under its transformation plan, it will be acquiring new combat aircraft, carriers, amphibious ships, surface combatants, and submarines, most of which will bring enhanced capabilities for expeditionary operations as well as sea domination. A few years ago, the Navy was criticized for not buying ships capable of littoral operations, but its current plan to acquire 56 littoral combat ships will help stifle this complaint. The problem facing the Navy is not the worthiness of its new weapons, but its ability to afford them, a problem faced by the Air Force as well.

Preparing U.S. Forces for Joint Expeditionary Warfare

Joint expeditionary operations seem destined to remain a focal point of the U.S. military for years to come. Transformation should aim to create the types of forces that are best able to perform these operations, and to provide the necessary flexibility and adaptability. Systems analysis should strive to generate the force evaluations needed in order to guide this effort along sensible paths.

Mastering the air-ground interaction in expeditionary wars will be critical to making wise choices. Continuing to improve the combat power of air forces is key, but this cannot be the only item on the agenda. Fielding strong ground forces will also be important because, in many conflicts, their roles will be as vital as those played by air forces. These roles may require close combat and powerful offensives that cannot be accomplished by Army forces that rely mostly on standoff targeting, and thereby lack such traditional weapons as heavy tanks with thick armor and big guns. Because charting the future of the U.S. Army is anything but easy, it merits careful attention by systems analysis and other methods.

Channeling the Army's transformation in sound directions will be important for more reasons than one. If the future Army emerges with forces and weapons that are not well suited to the expeditionary missions ahead, pressure will be placed on the Air Force and Navy to help compensate for the deficiency in capabilities for major combat operations. As a consequence, Air Force and Navy combat aircraft may be diverted from their normal missions in order to provide greater than normal help to the Army, at a potential cost to a flexible air strategy in joint operations. Beyond this, a flawed transformation by the Army could create pressures for the Air Force and Navy to pursue their own transformations in different ways than now being contemplated, perhaps by devoting more attention to close air support of ground forces. The problem is that by the time this is known, both services may be too far along in their transformation plans to shift gears by acquiring different aircraft, munitions, and information systems. In this event, the U.S. military might get the worst of both worlds: a flawed Army plus an Air Force and Navy that cannot make up the difference.

As of this writing, a firm verdict cannot be rendered on the Army's transformation plan. It contains so many fresh concepts and departures that in-depth analysis of it will be needed, along with field experiments that test the new brigades with their new weapons. In the interim, a fair-minded conclusion is while that the Army's plan endeavors to optimize future forces for one dominant style of operations, its lack of emphasis on preserving traditional capabilities for close combat may unduly sacrifice flexibility and adaptability, both of which will be needed in the coming years. An Army that can carry out diverse operations, including in surprising and unfavorable conditions, is far more likely to serve U.S. national security strategy well than an Army that offers only a limited script.

The Army clearly needs to develop the capacity to deploy combat forces faster. Efforts to trim the size of the Army's large support structure seem to make more sense than trying to reduce the weight of its major weapons, which are only a small part of the deployment calculus. Criticisms of the Army's plan to deploy larger numbers of smaller brigades and to field FCS vehicles seem to justify continued scrutiny of these efforts. Perhaps future events will show that the Army is on the right track, but if better ideas can be created in the coming years, they should be adopted and acted upon. Bigger brigades and heavier new weapons may be the solution, but if the Army continues seeking air-delivered fires as a main source of combat power, perhaps it should possess its own air forces for close air support. For example, a successor to the Air Force's A–10 might be given to the Army, making it similar to the Marine Corps, which operates both ground and air units. Regardless of how its future combat forces are structured, the Army needs better capabilities for stabilization and reconstruction missions of the sort that have been required in Iraq and Afghanistan. Remedying the current deficiency in S&R assets seems likely to be important for some time to come.

Together, these issues create fertile ground for systems analysis if it can rise to the occasion by comparing alternative options for force structures and new weapons on the basis of their performance. A main challenge facing systems analysis will be to shed insight on how the air-ground interaction can best unfold in expeditionary wars as the U.S. military continues to transform itself. A related challenge will be to appraise how the future Army can best take shape in the presence of airpower that, while offering growing potency, is not a sole-source solution to all future wars. If systems analysis meets both challenges, it will have proven its mettle in this complex and controversial arena.

Notes

[1] The reason why air forces today provide a greater percentage of deliverable ordnance for land warfare than in the past is not any change in the proportional size of air and ground forces. Instead, the reason is a new force allocation. In the past, many Air Force sorties were consumed in air defense and air superiority missions; Navy carrier-based aircraft were largely allocated to maritime defense missions. Today, both missions consume far fewer air forces, so more aircraft can be allocated to ground attack missions and land warfare.

[2] See David A. Deptula, "Effects-Based Operations: Change in the Nature of Warfare," *Defense and Airpower Series* (Arlington, VA: Aerospace Education Foundation, 2001). For analysis of methodology, see Christopher Bowie et al., *The New Calculus: Analyzing Airpower's Changing Role in Joint Theater Campaigns* (Santa Monica, CA: RAND, 1993).

[3] As Serbian forces withdrew, NATO ground forces entered Kosovo to restore order and prevent further ethnic violence. From that point forward, NATO ground forces, not U.S. forces, carried the main load of peacekeeping there, as in Bosnia. For analysis of the Kosovo air operation, see Benjamin S. Lambeth, *NATO's Air War for Kosovo* (Santa Monica, CA: RAND, 2001).

[4] For analysis of the Afghanistan war, see Norman Friedman, *Terrorism, Afghanistan, and America's New Way of Life* (Annapolis, MD: United States Naval Institute, 2003); Michael E. O'Hanlon, "A Flawed Masterpiece," *Foreign Affairs* 81, no. 3 (May/June 2002).

[5] Williamson Murray and Robert H. Scales, *The Iraq War: A Military History* (Cambridge, MA: Harvard University Press, 2003); Anthony H. Cordesman, *The Iraq War: Strategy, Tactics, and Military Lessons* (Washington, DC: Center for Strategic and International Studies, 2003).

[6] The number of air sorties per day depends heavily upon the duration of average sorties. If an aircraft must fly 2 hours to reach the battlefield, then spend 2 hours patrolling over the battlefield, and then fly another 2 hours to home base, total sortie duration will be 6 hours, and only about 1 sortie per day will be possible. But if the time for each component of the mission is only 30 minutes, total duration will be only 90 minutes, and 2 to 3 sorties per day will be possible. Even when two or three sorties are possible, however, this normally applies only to the initial days of combat. Afterward, sortie rates will decline to about one per day as steady-state operations take hold.

[7] For data, see MTMCTEA Pamphlet 700-5, "Deployment Planning Guide: Transportation Assets Required for Deployment, (Newport News, VA: Military Traffic Management Command, 2001).

[8] The impact of Stryker vehicles and FCS vehicles on unit weight will depend upon the type of units that receive them. Light infantry brigades receiving them will find their unit weight increasing by about 20 percent. Armored or mechanized brigades receiving them will experience a weight reduction of about 10–15 percent. An entire heavy corps would lose only about 5 percent of its weight, because the corps's total weight includes not only combat formations but also support assets, ammunition, and other war reserves. Indeed, the weight of a corps could increase if the loss in armored firepower were compensated by adding artillery firepower. These estimates assume no other changes in force composition.

[9] During the 1960s, the U.S. Army's large logistic support structure was seen as helping offset the Warsaw Pact's edge in combat forces in Central Europe. During the 1970s and 1980s, however, growing questions were being raised about whether too many soldiers were being allocated to logistic support, depriving the U.S. Army and European forces of adequate combat formations for the short, intense war expected to be fought in Central Europe. The core issue was the tradeoff between logistic support and combat forces, or "tail" and "tooth": whereas tail provided sustainment assets for a long war, tooth provided immediately available assets for firepower and maneuver in a short war. During the 1990s, U.S. Army logistic support assets were trimmed, but not much.

[10] Douglas A. Macgregor, *Transformation Under Fire: Revolutionizing How America Fights* (Westport, CT: Praeger, 2003).

[11] See Hans Binnendijk and Stuart Johnson, *Transforming for Stabilization and Reconstruction Operations* (Washington, DC: Center for Technology and National Security Policy, National Defense University, 2003).

Chapter 15
Modernizing Affordably

During the middle and late 1990s, DOD's pursuit of transformation was constrained by low procurement budgets that averaged only $45 billion annually, well below the $71 billion average of the early 1990s. Although the Department of Defense was able to start funding such inexpensive improvements as new information networks and smart munitions, it was unable to begin buying new weapons in large numbers. This constraint has been partly overcome by major increases in procurement spending, initially by the Clinton administration and later by the Bush administration. Procurement budgets today stand at about $75 billion, and they are projected to rise to $100 billion–$120 billion per year late in the decade and beyond. The effect has been to permit the services to begin pursuing a vigorous modernization, not only to replace aging weapons but also to support transformation with new and more capable weapons.

The projected rise in procurement spending, however, does not mean that the modernization problem has been completely solved. Future events will show whether bigger procurement budgets are actually funded, or instead fall victim to fiscal constraints and other priorities. Budgetary adequacy, moreover, is a question of not only available funds but also the number and cost of new weapons being bought. A few years from now, the services intend to be buying new weapons in such numbers that a bow wave of rising expenses may match or exceed the procurement budgets available. This bow wave will peak between 2008 and 2015 and will still be a factor through 2022. Careful planning will be needed to guide modernization so that procurement budgets are not overloaded and critical military requirements are met.

A sign of impending trouble came in January 2005, when DOD began unveiling its plans for the 2006 budget and the 2006–2011 program. DOD spokesmen announced that owing to fiscal constraints and other priorities, including the need for enhanced Army readiness, $30 billion had to be trimmed from procurement budgets over the coming 6 years. The amount was only about 6 percent of total procurement spending for this period, but the cuts were heavily taken from several big-ticket items, including the F–22 fighter, national missile defense, and naval warships. The Pentagon still had the option of restoring the cutbacks by spreading out these programs over a longer number of years than originally planned, but even so, the experience sent a wave of worry through the services because it suggested that further funding troubles might lie ahead.

Air and naval forces have attracted less public controversy than ground forces in recent years, but charting their future is important to the success of affordable modernization and transformation. A key reason is that DOD is investing significantly more money on modernizing the Air Force and Navy—about $559 billion for both—than on the Army (just $120 billion) during the next 5 years for procurement and RDT&E. Increases in the combat power of U.S. military forces thus will depend heavily on the acquisition of new combat aircraft and naval combatants. This acquisition effort, which could cost about $600 billion through 2022, will not happen automatically. Achieving maximum feasible success requires that these large sums must be spent wisely, with cost-effectiveness, balanced priorities, and affordability in mind. Good plans and careful handling of DOD's procurement programs for air and naval forces, as well as ground forces, will be needed for at least the next two decades.[1]

The Procurement Agenda Ahead

Unlike the Army, the Air Force and Navy do not face fundamental questions about how their forces are organized for joint expeditionary warfare, nor do they face accusations that they are not thinking innovatively or that they are pursuing unachievable technologies. Both the Air Force and Navy have robust modernization plans for the mid-term that are anchored in new weapons systems now emerging from the RDT&E cycle. Over the next 10 to 15 years, planned procurement of new aircraft and ships will not only recapitalize a major portion of their aging inventories, but also enhance their combat capabilities and performance of new-era operations. This sweeping mid-term modernization is intended to set the stage for gradual transition to the entirely new systems and technologies expected to emerge from the RDT&E process over the long term.

Appearances might suggest that all is well for both the Air Force and Navy, as they ride the crest of modernization and transformation with well-considered plans for force operations and weapons systems. Beneath the surface, however, budgetary realities make things more complex: both services may be unable to afford the expensive procurement programs needed to bring their future visions to life. The cost of their procurement plans may stretch their investment budgets to the limit or even beyond. If so, both services will need to set priorities in deciding upon the kinds, numbers, and mixes of weapons to buy, and the schedules for buying them over a period of many years.

Handling this challenge will require insightful analyses and wise planning. Systems analysis, supported by operations research, can contribute by applying economic models of choice to program evaluation. In particular, it can employ the curve of diminishing marginal returns, the program optimization model, and the time-phased investment model to good effect. Making a substantial contribution will, however, require that systems analysis be configured to address the complex issues at hand, particularly those connected with acquiring families of new weapons systems that work together to create a high-performance force posture.

This chapter deals with the emerging analytical agenda in this area. It begins by discussing the role of systems analysis in evaluating procurement strategies. Next, it addresses how such strategic considerations as future access-denial threats and U.S. investment priorities provide a framework for assessing procurement proposals. Then, it provides an overall portrayal of DOD procurement budgets and plans. The procurement agenda, affordability constraints, and cost-management options facing U.S. air forces are assessed, and then those affecting procurement of naval ships. These assessments illustrate how systems analysis can employ a step-by-step process to appraise complex procurement issues when multiple weapons systems must be forged into a coherent, affordable package.

Role of Systems Analysis

At first glance, systems analysis would appear to have little role to play in weapons acquisition and procurement. Performance requirements are set by professional military judgment; design features of new weapons are determined by engineers and the defense industry; and the pace of procurement is shaped by available budgets. Within this framework, however, systems analysis can apply economic reasoning and discipline. New weapons are developed, deployed, and improved upon over a long period that can last decades. Ten years or more may be required for the RDT&E process to develop and test a new weapons system. Procurement of a weapon to be bought in large quantities can take an additional decade or longer, because only limited numbers can be purchased each year. Then, once a weapons system is fielded, it may remain in service 20 years or longer, during which it might be upgraded several times with improved components. Systems analysis can influence decisions, by shaping the economic calculus, at all three stages of the cycle: RDT&E, procurement, and mid-life upgrades.

Systems analysis can influence the RDT&E process by examining the theory of requirements that is used to design each new weapon. It can help determine whether this theory is responsive to emerging strategic conditions, and whether it will produce a weapons system that is not only effective but also affordable. In the past, weapons that emerged as too costly could have benefited from scrutiny by systems analysis in this area. Systems analysis can also help compare two or more candidates that are competing, as in the competition between Lockheed Martin and Boeing over the Joint Strike Fighter (JSF) contract. Systems analysis can exert its greatest influence when the time to begin procurement arrives and economic decisions must be made about how many of a particular weapon are to be produced, and at what rate they are to be acquired.

Systems analysis typically plays its biggest role when two or more different weapons systems are being procured and must compete for scarce funds. This requires the preparation of an integrated procurement program that phases the introduction of multiple weapons in balanced, prioritized ways that respond to strategic needs and budget realities. As these weapons pass through their life cycles, systems analysis can help evaluate alternative options for upgrading them with new subcomponents. During roughly two decades of service thus far, for example, the Air Force's F–15 and F–16 fighters have undergone many product improvements in such areas as avionics, engines, aerodynamic features, and munitions, as have the Navy's F–14 and F–18 fighters. The same pattern is likely to unfold for such new fighters as the F–22, F–35, and F/A–18 E/F, and for new ships as well. Carrying out these future upgrades will be key to ensuring that these new aircraft and ships continue performing effectively, to prolong their life spans and defer the need to develop an entirely new generation of weapons.

Systems analysis can contribute because the weapons acquisition process—development, procurement, and upgrading—is strongly influenced by defense economics. Strategic requirements do create the demand for new weapons systems, and technological imperatives determine the supply, but it is budgets and affordability considerations that determine what weapons are bought, the pace at which they are acquired, and the manner in which they are improved during their life spans. Thus, systems analysis has ample opportunities to contribute helpfully, but only if it produces evaluations that are attuned to both the performance characteristics of new weapons and their costs.

Force Operations in an Access-Denial Environment

The first question that systems analysis should ask of new weapons systems is whether they respond to the strategic challenges likely to be encountered during their life cycles. Can they meet future military requirements for performance characteristics, and will they be able to defeat enemy threats directed against them? Critics levy two main accusations at the air and naval weapons now being procured: that they cannot survive in the face of future access-denial threats, and that they are legacy platforms rather than leap-ahead systems. Close inspection shows that both accusations are wide of the mark, although both do raise legitimate issues. The reasons were mentioned in chapter 13; here the explanation is spelled out.[2]

In today's setting, the ability to perform missions during expeditionary warfare is essential for new weapons systems and the forces that employ them. Air and naval forces, with their modern weapons, are attractive for expeditionary warfare partly because of their capacity to deliver lethal fires against enemy targets without risk of major casualties to U.S. personnel. In contrast to ground forces, they also can deploy overseas swiftly and can converge on crisis zones within days, not weeks, and they do not require large bases or facilities on the soil of allies and other countries. Whereas an Army division and its support assets require 30,000–45,000 troops and multiple bases, an Air Force fighter wing can be deployed with 10,000 or fewer airmen, and requires only 1 or 2 airbases. Because a Navy CVBG can operate from the sea, it does not require any land bases apart from distant storage depots and repair docks. Air and naval forces thus are natural candidates for expeditionary operations along the southern arc of instability, where the United States has few allies and, apart from the Persian Gulf, little assured access to bases and facilities. In the distant future, they might also be needed to support U.S. security guarantees to Asian allies in the face of a growing military challenge by China.

Air and naval forces must, however, be able to overcome enemy efforts to deny access to the zones in which they are to operate. Whether they will be able to do so is now disputed in some quarters. When the Bush administration took power in early 2001, some observers predicted that access-denial threats would become formidable in future years: enemy forces could, they said, use missiles and other weapons to sink U.S. carriers and destroy U.S. Air Force bases, making intervention operations impossible. In addition, they feared that an opponent with modern air defenses could prevent operations by non-stealth aircraft over enemy territory because vulnerable aircraft would be shot down. These observers called for a bold change to defend against this new threat.[3] They wanted the Navy to shift from carriers and their fighters to long-range cruise missiles, and the Air Force to shift from fighter aircraft to bombers carrying cruise missiles. Standoff operations and long-distance bombardment, they argued, would allow U.S. forces to operate safely outside the envelope of enemy access-denial threats. In their view, a future U.S.

military posture anchored in standoff bombardment—rather than shorter-range fires of tactical air and naval forces—would provide an effective way to foil a growing threat.

The vision of transformation thus articulated was revolutionary: in addition to arguing for a shift from ground forces to air and naval forces, it argued for air and naval forces that would operate from long distances rather than close to the battlefield. This would require a major change not only in how U.S. forces operate, but also in the force posture itself. For the Air Force, tactical fighter wings would give way to considerably greater numbers of strategic bombers such as the B–2 stealth bomber, as well as transport aircraft for carrying cruise missiles. The Navy's carriers would decline in number, replaced by submarines, surface combatants, arsenal ships, amphibious assault ships, and other vessels that would rely upon long-range cruise missiles, not short-range tactical fighters. This shift, in turn, would mean less reliance upon forward forces, bases, and installations in overseas regions. In the future, according to this vision, U.S. forces would defend allies and other vital interests from far off, not with a forward defense.

This provocative strategic concept is anchored in fear of lethal enemy capabilities for access denial in the years ahead. Closer inspection using systems analysis and related techniques, however, shows that the extreme version of this thesis is overdrawn. It does call attention to the threat of asymmetric strategies that could menace U.S. force operations to some degree. The proper solution, however, is not to abandon an otherwise sound strategy and force posture in favor of a radical new approach that might be unnecessary and has serious drawbacks of its own. Instead, existing forces should be strengthened to counteract the threat. After all, the U.S. military has been in the business of counteracting threats for years without sacrificing its main strengths or its strategy.

A sense of history helps provide perspective on this issue. Throughout the Cold War, the U.S. Navy faced, and surmounted, a major access-denial threat posed by the Soviet Union. The Soviets built a huge naval force of long-range bombers, air-to-ground missiles, nuclear warheads, and attack submarines aimed not only at denying the U.S. Navy access to northern Atlantic waters but also at interdicting NATO reinforcing convoys sailing to Europe. In order to suppress these threats, the Navy greatly increased its defensive capabilities with such systems as F–14 fighters with Phoenix missiles, Aegis cruisers with air defense missiles covering a wide area, and point-defense missiles. The Navy also built P–3 submarine-hunting aircraft, lethal attack submarines, and modern destroyers and frigates. By the end of the Cold War, the Navy had become relatively immune to these threats, to the point of judging that it had the ability to sail close to northern Soviet ports and strike them without risking major losses in return.

On the European continent, too, the Soviet Union assembled a huge force of several hundred bombers, 4,000 tactical combat aircraft, and hundreds of nuclear-tipped ballistic missiles for suppressing NATO airbases, ports, supply dumps, and road and rail networks, all aimed at preventing NATO from mounting a forward defense of West Germany's borders. The United States and NATO countered by erecting a formidable defense screen of AWACS aircraft, modern fighters, the Patriot air defense system, point defenses, and hardened facilities. U.S. and allied aircraft developed the capacity to suppress enemy air defenses by bombing airbases, attacking SAM sites, and shooting down interceptors. By the end of the Cold War, the Soviet air threat was fading, and no one doubted the NATO capacity to reinforce and mount a formidable forward defense. The central lesson is that, on land, at sea, and in the air, the U.S. military chose to confront a serious access-denial threat rather than retreat from forward defense, and it decisively countered a rival with big military forces and modern technology.[4]

If U.S. military forces could thwart such a formidable access-denial threat in the past, the logic of systems analysis leads to the conclusion that it should be able to do so again. Provided that success at this enterprise is possible, the strategic drawbacks of replacing forward intervention with long-range bombardment are obvious. U.S. national defense strategy has always relied on the ability to deploy large American military forces directly onto the soil of allies and friends in order help protect their borders from attack. A deterioration to long-range, standoff bombardment would inevitably lessen the credibility of this commitment by suggesting that the U.S. military might have lost the will and the capability to confront new threats posed by second-tier powers directly. The result could be a loss of U.S. political influence in key regions, thereby encouraging the aggressive instincts of rogue powers, and motivating allies and friends to draw away from the United States.

A good illustration of the possible deleterious consequences is in Asia. Throughout the Cold War, Asian allies valued the protection of the United States against the Soviet threat and other grave dangers. Now that a new era has created different, but mostly lesser, threats, their typical reaction is not to be cowed by such threats, but instead to reaffirm their security ties to the United States. Thus, Asian allies are not giving any impetus to a shift toward a standoff bombardment strategy by U.S. forces. Any such shift would be, instead, driven by a U.S. fear that China will develop formidable access-denial capabilities. While China does not now pose such a threat, and its military currently is struggling just to modernize, advocates of standoff bombardment worry that China could eventually prevent U.S. forces from operating safely around Taiwan, 100 miles from China's shore.

Even if China eventually succeeds in this endeavor to some degree, what would be the political consequences if U.S. forces no longer directly protected longstanding allies, but instead relied on a distant bombardment strategy from Guam, Iwo Jima, and nearby waters? How would Taiwan, South Korea, or Japan respond? They might conclude that the fundamental U.S. security guarantee to them was no longer reliable, and take steps to shore up their own defenses, possibly deploying nuclear weapons. What would happen to the Asian security system if they react in these ways? How would prospects for stable relations with China be affected? The obvious answer is that Asia would become multipolar and less stable, because U.S. bilateral security alliances would have been damaged, and the U.S. capacity to deter and dissuade potential opponents would have been weakened.

Quite apart from these political consequences, in purely military terms the capacity of standoff fires to compensate for the removal of forward-committed forces is questionable. In today's posture, strategic bombers, cruise missiles, and other standoff strike assets provide only about 25 percent of the U.S. military's capacity for air-delivered firepower. The other 75 percent is provided by tactical fighters and attack helicopters, many of which presumably would be retired if the U.S. military were to make a significant shift to long-distance bombardment. Even if long-range strike assets were upgraded significantly, they would probably not possess the firepower, maneuverability, or agility needed to win future wars on their own. Most conflicts would still need a hefty infusion of shorter-range airpower and ground maneuver forces. U.S. conduct of the wars in Kosovo, Afghanistan, and Iraq benefited from standoff bombardment, but forward-committed ground, air, and naval forces were essential for the combat phase and for occupation duties afterward. This is a practical reason for not relying too much on standoff assets: they will not usually be enough to get the job done alone. A posture composed largely of standoff assets would be optimized for one kind of response, but it would lack the flexibility and modularity for a wide spectrum of operations.

Determining how best to respond to future access-denial threats depends upon a technical appraisal of these threats and the ability of U.S. technology to counteract them. The notion that future enemies are busily assembling formidable access-denial threats seems exaggerated. In theory, an enemy could employ a combination of sophisticated radars, cruise missiles, ballistic missiles, diesel submarines, and mines to menace approaching U.S. naval forces. Likewise, a future enemy could theoretically employ missiles, aircraft, and bombs to pulverize U.S. airbases, ports, and facilities. Such an enemy might use modern SAMs in integrated air defenses capable of downing non-stealth aircraft. But creating such threats is easier said than done: it requires advanced C^{4}ISR systems, access to sophisticated technologies, modern missiles and warheads, skilled personnel, sizable forces for these missions, and lots of money to acquire the necessary assets. Such resources are beyond the reach of today's enemies. In the years ahead, access-denial threats may appear, but in most places they are likely to be only modest. This is the case in Asia, and it also holds true in the Persian Gulf and the Middle East.

U.S. military forces will have the wherewithal to counter such threats if they take appropriate measures. In this arena, the best defense may often be a good offense: U.S. strikes against an enemy's forces could help suppress its ability to mount access-denial operations. As for defensive measures, U.S. carriers and amphibious assault ships are already difficult to locate on the high seas, much less target, strike, and destroy. They can be made even more survivable by improvements to their C^{4}ISR systems, air defense missiles, and defensive protection against submarines and mines. Likewise, U.S. airbases can be hardened with such easily afforded steps as air defense missiles, aircraft shelters, runway repair kits, extra runways, redundant communications, hardened maintenance sheds, and units to clear away chemical and biological contaminants. Such practices were followed by the Air Force during the Cold War, and they can be resurrected at a relatively modest cost. Measures of this sort cannot provide a perfect defense, but they can help ensure that U.S. naval and air forces would not suffer prohibitive losses if they were compelled to operate within the shadow of future access-denial threats. The same applies to U.S. ground forces, whose survivability could be enhanced by upgrading rear-area defenses, hardening ports and supply depots, and dispersing ground forces to reduce their vulnerability to WMD strikes.

These considerations do not mean that all efforts to enhance U.S. capabilities for standoff bombardment are unwise. Cost-effective improvements would be eminently sensible. Situations may arise in which U.S. access to forward bases and facilities is denied for political reasons, and standoff bombardment might be the only viable strategy. Standoff bombardment can suppress enemy defenses from far off, paving the way for intervention forces to deploy into forward areas. A balanced mix of standoff bombardment and forward operations makes sense. Standoff bombardment may thus acquire enhanced importance in U.S. defense strategy, but this does not imply that forward-operating forces should be greatly reduced in size and importance. Improvement programs will need to focus on measures to enhance standoff bombardment capabilities, but the capabilities of forces that deploy forward and mount strike operations from nearby or medium distances must also be strengthened. This imperative sets the stage for determining how tactical air and naval forces should be recapitalized, modernized, and transformed in an era when the necessary improvements will not be cheap.

Legacy Platforms versus Leap-Ahead Systems

Determining how to manage the coming procurement effort requires resolution of the debate over legacy platforms versus leap-ahead systems. A legacy weapon is a new platform that carries forward most of the structural features of the weapon being replaced. A leap-ahead platform is one that introduces major new features by embracing several innovative technologies, creating a big difference between old and new platforms in performance as well as appearance. For example, the F–22 is said to be a legacy platform because its features are similar to those of the F–15 it replaces, while the F–45 unmanned UCAV, which will be piloted by robotics, is seen as a leap-ahead system. Controversy arises because many of the new weapons now in the final stages of RDT&E are portrayed by critics as legacy platforms while transformation calls up visions of major changes in weapons, operations, and structures. At issue is whether these so-called legacy platforms should be procured in large numbers, or instead bypassed in favor of leap-ahead platforms that might make possible entirely new types of military operations.

This debate is in serious need of contributions from systems analysis; far from developing a critical appraisal of the alternatives and their cost-effectiveness, the debate has shown signs of deteriorating into a dysfunctional exercise in sound bites and simplistic labels. A good example is the recent debate over the Army's Crusader artillery system, which was cancelled even though the Army viewed it as a major contributor to improved operations. At a cost of about $10 billion—small compared to the F–22 and the F–35 Joint Strike Fighter—the Crusader was intended to provide major improvements over the existing 155-millimeter self-propelled howitzer, the Paladin. In particular, it offered a 50 percent increase in range, an area in which the Paladin does not excel. It also offered greater accuracy and lethality, plus reduced logistic support and faster tactical mobility, allowing it to keep pace with fast-moving maneuvers by the Abrams tank and Bradley IFV. On the surface, the Crusader appeared to be a cost-effective choice, but it was cancelled by civilian DOD officials because of its heavy weight (70 tons) and because it did not seem to fit well into the Army's FCS vision of lighter forces reliant on information networks and air-delivered fires rather than traditional ground-delivered fires.[5]

The decision in 2002 to cancel the Crusader was praised by some observers and criticized by others, and the issue can be argued from either side. The disturbing feature of the debate was that many of the arguments on each side seemed simplistic and misleading. The case for the Crusader boiled down to the proposition that it truly would offer major performance advantages over the Paladin that would justify the spending of scarce Army procurement funds; whether this case was persuasively made can be debated. Likewise, the case against the Crusader at times seemed lacking in substance. For example, it was criticized for being too heavy, yet it was no heavier than the Abrams tank, and given its reduced logistic support needs, it would have decreased the overall weight of heavy Army forces.

As for the argument that the Crusader did not mesh with the FCS plan, the counterargument was made that the FCS is a distant vision of exploratory departures that might succeed or fail, and would in any case produce new systems different from those now being contemplated. The ultimate result might not be an Army of lightweight vehicles, but instead one still partly reliant upon heavy weapons and traditional firepower for its combat capability. If so, the Crusader could have had a functional role to play in the future Army. In the interim, a long period of as much as two decades, it could have significantly upgraded the battlefield capabilities of Army forces, especially by making them more capable of fast-moving offensive operations of the sort often necessary for expeditionary warfare. Had systems analysis played a larger role, it could probably have provided a better appraisal of the issues and options, and it might have led to a different decision.

The need for systematic analysis will apply in even stronger terms as debates mount over the new tactical fighters and naval combatants now poised for procurement. Virtually all of these weapons are legacy platforms in the sense that they perpetuate structural features inherited from the past, such as fixed-wing fighters. Although all of them will be expensive, they offer significant improvements in technology and in performance, even against new-era threats. Yet all of them face competition from leap-ahead systems that may be forthcoming in the future. Critics claim, for example, that traditional fighters and big naval combatants may be obsolescent 20 or 30 years from now, a period in which the weapons now being procured will still be operating. Some of the arguments seem, however, to disregard the extended mid-term of demanding military operations. When the distant future arrives, it may produce a need for new weapons that are different from the leap-ahead systems now being contemplated by advocates.

To what degree should these expensive legacy platforms be procured, or instead be set aside in favor of leap-ahead systems? What balance should be struck between legacy platforms and leap-ahead systems? Most fundamentally, how should scarce investment funds be distributed among RDT&E and procurement? The basic dilemma is that the U.S. military is suffering from a prolonged hiatus in procurement that left it with aging weapons that must be replaced soon. Yet the future offers hazy promises of new technologies and weapons that could be much better than those now ready for procurement. Resolving this dilemma between a bird in the hand and two in the bush will not be easy; the best choices are not obvious. The associated debates cannot, however, be resolved through sound bites, bumper stickers, or generic solutions that ignore the need to make a series of sensible judgments on a case-by-case basis.

A new weapons system should not be procured just because it has been under development for a decade. Yet when such a weapon is eagerly sought by its sponsoring service, it should not be junked merely because the term *legacy platform* is applied to it. The real issue is whether it offers major gains in capabilities for new-era operations in ways that justify its costs, and that make it a better choice than its contemporary competitors. Likewise, leap-ahead systems should not be chosen over legacy platforms just because they have futuristic labels. A leap-ahead system might be a good idea, or it might be anchored in flimsy visions or exploratory technologies that will not pan out. The strategic reality is that while the U.S. military will need new legacy weapons that can meet operational requirements for the coming 10 to 20 years, it also will need leap-ahead systems for the more distant future. Striking a sensible balance between these two imperatives is an important challenge for defense planning; systems analysis must illuminate the tradeoffs.

As a practical matter, most of the new weapons systems now poised to emerge from the RDT&E process are going to be procured, and in significant quantities. The idea of forsaking this generation of modernization in order to leap ahead into a distant, long-term future of entirely new weapons originated when a stable world was expected for the coming 10 or 15 years. The war on terrorism, the invasion of Iraq, and other contemporary dangers overturned this premise and created a need for high-performance U.S. military forces during the near term and the mid-term. The military services will have to modernize with so-called legacy platforms just to replace obsolescent weapons and to acquire new capabilities. Moreover, they will need to gain experience with such new weapons as the F–22 in order to judge how requirements for the next generation should be defined. Otherwise, a leap-ahead strategy could be a leap into the dark.

As experience is gained with these new weapons and product improvements, the military will be in a better position to determine how best to take advantage of new technologies, such as directed energy weapons, that will be maturing in the coming years. When these new technologies and weapons mature, they can be procured gradually and introduced into the force posture, rather than rushed prematurely to compensate for a lost generation of modernization. Weapons such as the F–45 UCAV, the Navy's new littoral combat ship (LCS), space-based lasers, and other hardware can supplement existing weapons, rather than replacing them immediately.

The reality of an accelerating procurement effort, however, means that existing plans are not set in concrete. Much will depend upon the level of procurement funds available, but regardless of the amount, the challenge of reconciling requirements and programs with budgets will be significant. What mix of F–22s, F–35s, F/A–18 E/Fs, Ospreys, and Army attack helicopters should be procured, and on what schedule? What mix of new naval combatants should be bought, and on what schedule? How can room be made for new types of weapons such as the F–45 UCAV and the LCS? The answers will be key to defense plans in the coming years. The opportunity for systems analysis is to employ its ability to assess complex programs and to apply models of economic choice to help guide these decisions.

Recapitalizing and Modernizing an Aging Force Posture

The goal of DOD's procurement campaign is modernization and transformation, but the stage is set by the need to recapitalize in order to replace aging weapons systems. If weapons systems remain in service too long, they can become obsolescent either because their performance characteristics are no longer adequate or because, owing to sheer fatigue and deterioration, they cannot be operated any longer. Intensified maintenance can extend the life spans of aging weapons, but eventually those costs can match or exceed the cost of replacement weapons. The calculus is similar to that of owning a private automobile. As it ages, eventually its maintenance costs will become greater than the expense of buying a new car. At that point, if not before, it should be replaced. This is especially the case if it presents the risk of frequent breakdowns, exposing the driver to difficulty and danger. Within the U.S. military, some fabled weapons systems, such as B–52 bombers and KC–135 tankers, have remained in service for 40 or 50 years or more, but these are exceptions to the rule. Most weapons in frequent use have shorter life spans.

The cost of recapitalizing the U.S. military is high not only because many individual weapons are expensive, but also because the military possesses a large number of them. A crude estimate of the cost of replacing all of today's major weapons systems with similar technology and platforms could be between $1.5 trillion and $2 trillion. This is only the cost of major systems such as fighter aircraft, tanks, and surface combatants. It does not include the significant added expense of buying such secondary items as trucks, jeeps, communications gear, construction materials, and spare parts. Fortunately, major weapons systems are well built and regularly repaired, so they typically remain in active service 25 to 35 years. Even so, the average annual cost of replacing 3 to 4 percent of them each year with equivalent weapons would be about $45 billion–$60 billion, and buying better weapons would add to the cost. Add to this the normal procurement costs of secondary systems and other materials, totaling $40 billion or more annually. Thus DOD seeks an annual procurement budget of $114 billion by 2010, and more later.[6]

Table 15–1. **Major Weapons Systems in Current Inventory**

Army (Includes ground weapons for Marines)		Navy,* Marines**		Air Force	
Tanks	8,023	Aircraft Carriers	12	Bombers	208
Infantry Fighting Vehicles	6,710	Amphibious Assault Ships	36	Fighter Aircraft	2,928
Armored Personnel Carriers	17,630	Cruisers	27	Command, Control, Communications, and Intelligence Aircraft	63
Artillery Tubes	6,900	Destroyers and Frigates	69	Reconnaissance Aircraft	74
Anti-tank Vehicles	2,350	Attack Submarines	55	Major Transports	329
Patriot Launchers	493	Other Ships ***	96	Other Transports	787
Fixed-Wing Aircraft	282	Fighter Aircraft	1,700	Tankers	600
Helicopters	5,200	Other Aircraft	1,300	Trainers	1,640

* The Navy is authorized 310 battle force ships, but its actual inventory is 295 ships.
**Includes air weapons for Marines.
*** Includes ballistic missile submarines, combat logistic ships, and command and supply ships.
SOURCE: Multiple sources, including DOD documents.

Table 15–1 illustrates most of the major weapons systems in the current inventory that the services must replace as they age. Today, ground weapons typically cost from $1 million to $6 million apiece. The total cost for an entire program is high because of the large number that must be procured. Naval ships are quite expensive: submarines and surface combatants, for example, cost between $1 billion and $2 billion each. Owing to their sophisticated technology, the cost of combat aircraft has risen in the past two decades: a modern fighter can cost $40 million to $100 million or more, and such support aircraft as cargo planes, AWACS, and JSTARS can cost $200 million each or more. In addition to buying these aircraft fresh from the production line, the military must also add new components during their life spans in order to enhance their quality. The cost to replace these weapons as they age can often be reduced by extending their normal life spans through service life extension programs (SLEPs), which may add 5 to 10 years of life at about 20 percent of the cost of buying a new replacement. Even with DOD's regular use of SLEP practices, however, recapitalizing each of the services is expensive.[7]

If DOD could acquire new weapons at a replacement rate of 3–4 percent per year, the effect would be to spread procurement costs evenly over 25 to 35 years. Unfortunately, history has conspired to prevent this practice. After World War II, postwar disarmament and low military budgets prevented the military from buying new weapons in adequate quantities. When the Cold War intensified in the early 1950s, all three services set out to replenish their inventories quickly with new weapons. The effort succeeded, but the result was a block obsolescence problem later on, when most weapons bought during that short span had to be replaced at about the same time. After a period of slowed modernization in the late 1950s, the pace picked up in the early 1960s as defense budgets again were elevated. But the Vietnam War intruded: its high costs resulted in major delays in recapitalization and modernization. After the Vietnam War ended, defense spending plummeted downward, further delaying procurement and leaving a rapidly aging inventory. By the late 1970s, the services were poised to begin buying new generations of weapons. The floodgates opened with the Reagan defense buildup of the 1980s. But once again, rapid buying over a brief period set the stage for another block obsolescence problem later. The effect was compounded during the 1990s, when DOD took advantage

Table 15–2. **Age Profiles for Military Aircraft**

Categories	Weapons Systems	Service	Average Age in 2007
Maritime Patrol	P–3C	Navy	31
Bombers	B–52, B–1, B–2	Air Force	30
Tankers	KC–135, KC–10	Air Force	47
Multirole Fighters	F–14, F–18, AV8–B	Navy	16
	F–16, A–10	Air Force	19
Air Superiority Fighters	F–15	Air Force	23
Light Attack Helicopters	OH–58, Kiowa	Army	28

Source: Congressional Budget Office estimates.

of its still-young inventory to take a lengthy procurement holiday, and procurement budgets declined to about $45 billion annually. Most funds were devoted to normal steady-state procurement of secondary items and component upgrades, while procurement of major new weapons slowed to a crawl.

The problem of an aging inventory was already becoming noticeable in the late 1990s, but real concern is focused on 2005–2015 and later, when aging will bring many weapons closer to the end of their natural lives and result in rising maintenance costs. By 2007, most Army weapons will be about 20 years old. Fortunately, the life spans of such ground weapons as tanks, IFVs, and artillery tubes can be extended many years by SLEPs, which the Army is funding. Many Navy ships can and are being extended in the same way. In addition, the Navy's inventory of combatants is still relatively young: by 2007, its destroyers and cruisers will average 15 years of service. The aging of the air inventory is more worrisome because the useful lives of many aircraft, especially tactical fighters, cannot be as easily extended by inexpensive SLEP plans. Table 15–2 shows age projections for Air Force and Navy aircraft. It is important to remember that these are average ages; thus, about one-third of the weapons in each category are 5 to 10 years older, and thus will need replacement sooner.[8]

The military services approach the task of buying new weapons from the perspective of needing to allocate their scarce procurement funds among multiple claimants. Although DOD allocated $74.9 billion of its total budget of $402.6 billion in 2005 to procurement, only about $36.5 billion, or a bit less than half, was available for major weapons systems. The remainder was consumed by many other items that, while important, did not address the problem of an aging inventory of major weapons. In 2005, the procurement budget was distributed among the services as shown in table 15–3. It displays the relatively small share received by the Army, compared to the larger shares awarded to the Navy and Air Force. This distribution pattern reflects the fact that the Navy and Air Force have greater needs for procurement funds because, at this stage, their modernization cycles require them to buy more hardware than the Army. But this pattern also reflects a DOD-wide preference for investing in air and naval forces rather than ground forces because they are expected to make a greater contribution to transformation. If this pattern is carried out over a 6-year period with growing defense budgets, the Army will receive about $70 billion for procurement, while the Navy and Air Force will receive about $180 billion apiece, a big difference.[9]

Table 15–3. Distribution of DOD Procurement Funds, 2005 (Budget Authority)

Army	$10.4 billion
Navy	$27.7 billion
Air Force	$32.6 billion
DOD-wide	$4.2 billion
Total	**$74.9 billion**

Table 15–4 shows how the services allocated these procurement funds among the several categories within their accounts. Only $1.6 billion was spent for Army combat vehicles, but $10 billion was spent for Navy shipbuilding and conversion, and about $24 billion on aircraft for all three services, with the lion's share going to the Air Force and Navy. Notwithstanding this money for new weapons, fully one-half of the DOD procurement budget—$38.4 billion—was spent on missiles and related weapons, ammunition, electronics and communication; secondary equipment such as trucks; and on miscellaneous items. As a result, the rate at which recapitalization can occur is slow for the Army, and for the Navy and Air Force as well.

Table 15–4. Distribution of Service Procurement Funds Among Different Accounts, 2005 (Budget Authority, in $Billions)

Army		Navy		Air Force	
Aircraft	$1.8	Aircraft	$8.8	Aircraft	$13.2
Missiles and Weapons	$1.3	Missiles and Weapons	$2.1	Missiles and Weapons	$4.7
Combat Vehicles	$1.6	Shipbuilding and Conversion	$10.0	Ammunition	$1.4
Ammunition	$1.4	Marine Corps	$1.1	Other	$13.3
Other	$4.3	Ammunition/Other	$5.7		
Total	**$10.4**	**Total**	**$27.7**	**Total**	**$32.6**

An additional constraint is that not all of the procurement funds allocated for major weapons are actually spent on buying new models. In the Army, for example, $1.6 billion of the allocation of $1.8 billion for aircraft went to modifying existing hardware. Of the Army's $1.6 billion for wheeled and tracked vehicles, about $900 million was spent on new Stryker vehicles, but the remainder was spent on modifying existing tanks, IFVs, and other weapons. Within the Navy, the $8.8 billion allocated to new aircraft was divided among new combat aircraft ($5.2 billion) and modifications, spares, and trainers ($3.6 billion). Of the Navy's $10 billion for ship construction, $8.9 billion was spent on new carriers, submarines, surface combatants, and amphibious ships; the remaining $1.1 billion was spent on conversions, overhauls, and auxiliaries. Within the Air Force, only $4.2 billion of its $13.2 billion for aircraft was spent on buying new fighters (24 F–22s at $151 million apiece). The remaining $9 billion was spent on airlift aircraft such as C–17s, C–130s, and other models, plus trainers, modifications, spares, repairs, support equipment, and miscellaneous activities.

The details thus show that, of the $36.5 billion allocated to major weapons systems, only $19.2 billion was spent to buy new weapons. The remaining $17.3 billion, or nearly half, went for modifying and upgrading existing weapons. Of DOD's $74.9 billion budget for procurement, therefore, only 26 percent was allocated to new weapons.

The remaining 74 percent was spent on existing weapons or on procuring the myriad of additional items needed to keep U.S. military forces properly equipped and operating. Of this $19.2 billion, DOD's decision to limit Army investments allowed it to give priority to spending on new tactical aircraft and combat ships ($15.8 billion). This, however, does not go that far, given the costs of new weapons. As a result, DOD's effort to launch a major new wave of modernization for air and naval forces proceeded at a snail's pace: only 74 new fighters and 8 new ships were budgeted in 2005 (the shipbuilding program was subsequently cut to only 5). This is less than the rate needed to sustain normal recapitalization, much less to replace aging weapons rapidly in a posture facing a block-obsolescence problem.

In the coming years, DOD will face growing procurement requirements arising from several areas:

- modernizing the air forces by acquiring large numbers of new fighters, plus expensive support aircraft such as cargo transports and tankers

- building new naval combatants at a faster rate than in recent years

- achieving a faster Army modernization by upgrades of existing weapons, while also buying the Stryker combat vehicles and a replacement for the Comanche helicopter

- fielding national missile defenses at a cost of $8 billion–$10 billion per year, while strengthening space-based systems

- buying enough smart munitions to maintain adequate inventory plus spares and repair parts for all major weapons.

This situation underscores the need for annual DOD procurement budgets to rise to $100 billion and beyond in the coming years. It also sets the stage for analyzing how the challenge of buying new combat aircraft and ships can be met, for budgets may not provide enough funds for all the new weapons that are sought, or that will, in any case, require carefully phased acquisition efforts over many years.

Affording Air Modernization

Counting funds spent on RDT&E and procurement, DOD's current aircraft modernization program of about $25 billion annually includes fully 21 different types of airplanes. Some of these funds are spent on modifications and upgrades of existing weapons: in 2005, for example, $402 million was spent on the F–16 and $317 million on the F–15, both of which have been in the inventory for years. Nonetheless, the heart and soul of DOD's future air modernization effort, and the reason for its rising costs, lies with the six tactical aircraft programs shown in table 15–5. Total RDT&E costs for these programs are likely to be $70 billion to $80 billion, with the F–22 program costing about $25 billion and the F–35, about $30 billion or more. Total procurement costs will be driven by the high cost of each aircraft and the total number of aircraft purchased: an estimate would be $225 billion–$318 billion for 3,588 to 3,762 fighters plus projected acquisition of the V–22 Osprey, helicopters, and UAVs and armed UCAVs. For each aircraft, table 15–5 shows program costs in 2005, total numbers of aircraft likely to be bought for the entire program, estimated cost of individual aircraft, and total procurement costs for the entire posture. In addition to these tactical aircraft, DOD also will need to acquire more C–17 and C–130J transports, replacements for its aging KC–135 tanker fleet, and new C⁴ISR aircraft. This expense could elevate procurement spending on aircraft by an additional $60 billion–$100 billion.

Table 15–5. **Major Aircraft Modernization Programs (Budget Authority)**

Type of Aircraft	Program Costs in 2005 (in $billions)	Number Planned to be Bought	Estimated Unit Cost (in $millions)	Total Procurement Costs (Illustrative— in $billions)
F–22	$4.7	276–450	$115–125	$32–56
F–35 JSF	$4.6	2,852	$45–55	$122–157
F/A–18 E/F	$3.1	460	$58–62	$27–29
V–22 Osprey	$1.8	458	$40–45	$18–20
Army Helicopter	$1.1	650–1,213	$25–30	$16–36
Unmanned Aerial Vehicle, Unmanned Combat Aerial Vehicle	$1.9	?	?	$10–20
Total				**$225–318**

In the public arena, attention has focused mostly on individual aircraft and their costs, with such questions as how many F–22s can be bought at a total program cost of $43 billion. But for all of its importance, the F–22 accounts for only 14 to 18 percent of total aircraft procurement costs in the coming years. The more important issue is the size and expense of the total program for all six aircraft. In the estimate used here and shown in table 15–5, the total cost eventually could be $225 billion–$318 billion, with an additional $10 billion–$20 billion for further RDT&E after procurement begins. The cost could be lower if fewer aircraft are bought or if costs for individual aircraft turn out to be lower because of economies of scale. The cost could be higher if more aircraft are bought or if product improvements result in higher unit costs. If the total expense is within the range displayed here, these 6 aircraft will consume a large portion of DOD's procurement budgets over the next 10 to 15 years and beyond. The expense does not seem formidable when compared to total procurement budgets, which are likely to average about $100 billion per year (in constant 2005 dollars). But a different picture emerges when stock is taken of the lesser amount out of that budget that will actually be available for procuring major new weapons systems: about $20 billion–$40 billion annually. Of this amount, $10 billion–$20 billion will need to be set aside for buying other new weapons such as ships and ground combat vehicles. Thus, about $10 billion–$20 billion might be available for buying new aircraft each year.

The implication is that aircraft procurement will need to be spread out over a period of years and pursued gradually within the limits of the funds available each year. If $10 billion is available each year, the entire air procurement effort could take 23 to 31 years. If $20 billion is available each year, the entire effort could take 12 to 16 years. Current projections suggest that about $15 billion–$20 billion will be available each year, and that a sustained effort lasting 20 years or more will be needed. Regardless of the exact figures, DOD is going to be in the aircraft procurement business for a long time. The challenge will be one of fitting the total procurement effort to the total budgets available over this entire span of time. It will also be one of balancing the acquisition of six different aircraft each year, so that the procurement effort unfolds rationally, and U.S. combat capabilities are elevated as much as possible each year. All six of these aircraft are needed because each of them performs a separate, important military function. Some of each of them will need to be purchased in most years, when they are ready for procurement. Achieving a balanced and integrated procurement effort will be a strategic challenge on a grand scale not only for the services, but for systems analysis as well.

Toward a New "High-Low Mix" of Fighters

The origins of today's controversy over tactical fighter procurement began in the mid-1970s, when the Air Force was selecting its fighter inventory for the future. At the time, the Air Force wanted to buy the high-tech F–15 as its premier fighter, but the high cost of the aircraft ($40 million–$50 million apiece) meant that it could not buy enough to outfit the entire posture. The Air Force therefore chose to pursue a "high-low" mix composed of a limited number of F–15s, a large number of F–16s, and a limited number of A–10s. Procurement of these three aircraft was largely carried out in the 1980s when growing acquisition budgets permitted large-scale buys.

The F–16 was a less impressive aircraft than the F–15. It was limited to firing infrared air-to-air missiles at short range rather than radar-directed missiles at longer range, and it carried a smaller bomb load than the attack-version F–15E. But it was an adequately effective multimission aircraft whose lower cost ($20 million–$30 million) allowed the Air Force to purchase it in ample numbers. The low-cost, slower-moving A–10 was designed to be a highly survivable aircraft configured for ground attack missions, especially tank-busting with its GAU–8 gun. When the F–117 Stealth became available, the Air Force also purchased a limited number of these expensive fighters.

The Navy pursued a similar high-low mix philosophy by buying some expensive F–14s for air defense, a large number of less expensive F–18s for multimission roles, and the least expensive AV–8 Harrier for the Marine Corps. Purchase of the F–15 began in the mid-1970s, followed by the other fighters as they emerged from the RDT&E process. During the Reagan era, the Air Force, Navy, and Marine Corps used their growing procurement budgets to acquire all six aircraft. As of 2004, the Air Force and Navy/Marine inventories included the mix of fighter aircraft shown in table 15–6.

Today, the services are planning to acquire another high-low mix in order to meet their future inventory goals affordably. The Air Force intends to buy a limited number of the F–22 Raptor as its high-tech fighter for sophisticated air defense and ground attack missions, and a larger number of the F–35 Joint Strike Fighter as its lower-tech, more affordable fighter. The Navy intends to buy a limited number of F/A–18 E/Fs as its high-tech fighter, and a larger number of lower-tech F–35 JSFs to meet Navy and Marine Corps needs. As a result, the current DOD program calls for procurement of 740 to 840 high-tech fighters (F–22s and F/A–18 E/Fs) and 2,852 lower-tech fighters (F–35 JSFs). Meanwhile, the Marines are planning to acquire 458 V–22 Osprey tilt-rotor helicopters for assault missions, while the Army may seek to acquire several hundred new attack helicopters in place of the cancelled Comanche. The specific contributions of each aircraft in the context of this overall plan are described next.

Table 15–6. **Air Force/Navy Fighter Inventory, 2004**

Air Force		Navy, Marine Corps	
F–15	736	F–14	142
F–16	1,430	F/A–18	1,032
A–10	220	F/A–18 E/F	88
F–117	51	AV–8	275
F–22	22		
Total	**2,459**	**Total**	**1,537**

Note: Includes aircraft assigned to fighter squadrons plus trainers and spares.

F–22 Raptor

The source of the F–22 Raptor was the Air Force's need for a high-tech fighter to replace the aging F–15, with improved performance characteristics. RDT&E work on the F–22 began in the mid-1980s and accelerated in the 1990s after Lockheed Martin was awarded the contract. A main goal was to produce a new fighter that could dominate air battles by defeating next-generation enemy fighters in air-to-air duels. In addition, the F–22 was designed to be stealthy and to have a supersonic cruise capability without using afterburners. Later in the development cycle, an F/A–22 was designed to carry a large suite of precision munitions for bombardment and ground attack roles, including stealthy attacks against sophisticated air defense systems. When the F–22 finally was produced after a prolonged RDT&E process and various technical problems, it met these design standards, promising to be the best fighter in the world. But it is expensive: the RDT&E effort for the F–22 evidently will total about $25 billion, and initial F–22s are costing about $150 million apiece. By taking advantage of economies of scale and improved assembly techniques, full-scale production offers to reduce unit costs to $120 million apiece (in 2005 dollars) or even less. Some estimates show that if 750 aircraft are produced, unit costs could drop to $75 million–$80 million. Procurement of 339 aircraft is estimated to total about $35 billion–$40 billion.[10]

The high estimated costs prompted a debate within DOD and in the Congress about whether the F–22 is affordable and how many should be bought. Calls to cancel the F–22 were rejected, but the number to be procured was pushed steadily downward. The Air Force initially wanted to buy about 750 aircraft, and then reduced the number to 648. Subsequent fiscal pressures resulted in a further reduction to 438 aircraft, then 380, and then 339: enough to provide one F–22 squadron for each of 10 AEF formations. When Congress imposed a $43 billion limit on total program cost, DOD announced that roughly 280 could be afforded. The number ultimately bought will depend upon costs, but requirements will also enter the picture. The Air Force would prefer to deploy 1 or 2 F–22 squadrons per AEF, which would require between 375 and 750 aircraft. In addition, the Air Force is also considering an F/B–22 that would be able to deliver a larger ordnance load than the F/A–22, plus an EA–22 for electronic warfare missions. If funds are available, procurement of 450 aircraft is plausible. The F–22 was originally slated for procurement at a rate of 24 aircraft per year, but budget constraints are reducing the rate. DOD decisions for the 2006 budget could result in the F–22 program being stopped well short of 280 aircraft. Provided the F–22 survives calls from critics to cancel it entirely, it may continue being bought for several years, when a decision on whether to keep the production line open will have to be made. For as long as the production line remains open, the number of F–22s to be procured may vary from year to year.

F/A–18 E/F Super Hornet

The least controversial of the new tactical fighters, the F/A–18 E/F Super Hornet is a twin-engine, multimission fighter. It is an upgraded version of the F/A–18 C/D, which has been in the Navy and Marine Corps inventory for years. It is replacing the F–14 air interceptor and will be used by the Navy in ground attack roles as a replacement for aging F–18 C and D models. Compared to the latter, the E and F models have many improved performance characteristics, including better avionics, more weapons stations, longer range, and improved maneuverability. For the Navy, the F/A–18 E/F will be the high end of its new high-low mix. It will help provide a high-performance framework within which the less-expensive F–35 Joint Strike Fighter can operate.[11]

Development began in the early 1990s when Congress approved a $4.9 billion engineering and manufacturing development contract awarded to Boeing. Initial flight testing began in the mid-1990s, and proved successful despite some problems. The Navy's original plan was to purchase about 1,000 aircraft, but cost constraints pushed the number down to somewhere between 548 and 785 in the late 1990s. In 2002, DOD again reduced the number to the currently planned 460. Development costs were about $6 billion. The F/A–18 E/F is currently being procured at the rate of 42 aircraft per year, with costs of about $72 million per aircraft. Once the full program is complete, costs are likely to fall to $58 million–$62 million apiece.

F–35 Joint Strike Fighter

The F–35 Joint Strike Fighter is the low end of today's high-low mix, and it will be produced in large numbers. It will replace the Air Force's F–16 and A–10, and also the Navy's F/A–18 C and the Marine Corps' AV–8B. Thus, three different models of the F–35 will be produced: the F–35A for the Air Force, the F–35B with carrier takeoff and landing (COTL) capability for the Navy, and the F–35C with short takeoff and vertical landing (STOVL) capability for the Marine Corps. After a lengthy competition with Boeing,

Lockheed Martin was awarded the F–35 contract in 2001. RDT&E costs, initially estimated at about $25 billion, have risen to over $30 billion. Inaugural flights for all three versions are planned for 2006. Initial operational capability for the Air Force and Marine Corps versions will occur in 2010 and for the Navy version in 2012. All three versions will continue being procured throughout 2010–2020 and beyond.[12]

The Air Force intends to use the F–35, like the F–16, principally as a ground-attack aircraft that also can win aerial dogfights with future enemy aircraft. It thus will complement the F–22. Although similar to the F–16 in size, the F–35 will have many improved performance characteristics, including stealth, agility, better avionics, advanced software, a greater combat radius (690 miles), a better power plant, and a larger capacity to store munitions internally. The Air Force intends to procure 1,763 of the aircraft; the Navy, 480 COTL aircraft; and the Marine Corps, 609 STOVL models. These service plans result in an overall DOD plan to procure about 2,852 aircraft. A few years ago, costs for each aircraft were predicted to be $60 million–$70 million, but costs are now expected to be as low as $45 million–$55 million owing to economies of scale and efficient production techniques. Even so, total procurement costs for the F–35 will be $128 billion–$157 billion, plus $5 billion–$10 billion for further RDT&E.

In addition to the aircraft being produced for DOD, another 150 aircraft will be produced for Britain. Sales to other countries could total fully 3,000 F–35s over the coming decades. If so, this would make the F–35 JSF the biggest, most expensive fighter aircraft program in history. The challenge for DOD will be to generate enough funds to buy the F–35 at the high annual rates needed to replace aging F–16s and other aircraft. Otherwise, DOD may need to devote added funds to extend the service lives of these aircraft until enough F–35s are produced. For the Air Force, budget constraints may necessitate completion of F–22 deployment before the F–35 can be procured in large quantities. For all three services, the F–35 JSF thus is intended to provide a low-cost aircraft that can help solve the affordability problem while also meeting new-era performance requirements. However, it complicates the affordability problem because of the large numbers that must be bought: the F–35 accounts for about 50 percent of DOD's expected expense for tactical air modernization during the coming years.

F–45 Unmanned Combat Aerial Vehicles

Unmanned aerial vehicles have grown from a small DOD program only a few years ago to claim about $2 billion in today's budgets, with larger spending likely in the future. Today, roughly two-thirds of the funds are being spent on RDT&E; only about $620 million is being spent on procurement of 34 UAV aircraft annually. But if a decision is made to acquire more UAVs in order to meet mounting demands, procurement costs will rise. The main purpose of UAVs is to provide tactical reconnaissance. Equipped with cameras, radars, and other sensors, UAVs are capable of long loiter time over battlefields and distant targets, providing commanders with valuable real-time information of a sort not previously available. Three UAVs are now being procured: a tactical UAV (Shadow), a medium-altitude endurance UAV (Predator), and a high-altitude UAV

(Global Hawk). In addition, the Navy is buying a small number of new underwater unmanned vehicles while also developing a broad area maritime UAV.[13]

Apart from attaching Hellfire missiles to some Predators, UAVs today are not being used systematically to attack targets on the ground. This pattern promises to change, however, as RDT&E efforts begin to field UCAVs. The Air Force, the Navy, and DOD agencies are currently spending nearly $700 million annually on UCAVs that can carry suites of smart munitions and can be used as major contributors to ground attack missions. UCAVs will cost less than modern fighters and do not expose pilots to enemy fire, but because they are robot-piloted, they lack the flexibility and responsiveness of manned aircraft. The future of UCAVs will be heavily determined by the extent to which sophisticated computer systems can take the place of pilots, allowing these aircraft to be directed by personnel in distant command posts. The future also will be determined by costs for UCAVs, which promise to rise as their technology improves and as they are provided with additional capabilities for delivering smart munitions.

Some visionaries portray a future in which UCAVs will totally replace manned combat aircraft, but any such development is many years off. In the interim, the military services plan to continue relying principally upon manned fighters and to use UCAVs selectively as they mature and prove their cost-effectiveness. One model envisions a flight of six manned fighters accompanied by one or two UCAV fighters. This could significantly increase the number of smart munitions that could be delivered in a single mission. The Navy and Marine Corps are planning to buy enough F/A–18 E/Fs and F–35s to maintain their current inventories as old aircraft retire. They may well view UCAVs as an option to increase their overall numbers of aircraft. The Air Force, however, is planning to buy just over 2,000 F–22s and F–35s (between 2,043 and 2,143), not enough to replace the 2,459 fighters in its current inventory on a one-for-one basis. Thus, the Air Force may come to view UCAVs as a way to preserve its current overall number of aircraft. Much, however, will depend upon the future technical prowess of UCAVs. In the long term, a UAV/UCAV procurement effort that totals $10 billion–$20 billion is an illustrative estimate.

V–22 Osprey and Army Helicopters

The V–22 Osprey is a tilt-rotor aircraft designed to provide the benefits of both a helicopter and a fixed-wing aircraft. When operating as a helicopter, it can take off vertically, hover, and fly forward at a speed of 100–150 miles per hour. When operating as a turboprop, it can fly at a speed of about 300 miles per hour, with a range of about 500 miles. These features make it ideal for amphibious assault missions that move long distances inland. Because the Osprey can carry 24 combat troops or about 20,000 pounds of cargo, it can be used for both infantry assault and logistic supply. The Osprey has been under development for two decades; its progress has been delayed by technical problems. Safety concerns led test flights to be halted and the aircraft grounded during 2000–2002. Provided the Osprey meets technical and safety requirements, the Marine Corps plans to buy 360 aircraft to replace its CH–46 and CH–53 helicopters, with full-rate production starting in 2006–2007. About 100 additional Ospreys will be bought by the Air Force, the Navy, and the Army for SOF and other missions. The Osprey is expected to cost about $40 million–$45 million per aircraft, a unit cost similar to the F–35 Joint Strike Fighter. Procuring a force of 458 Ospreys thus will cost about $18 billion–$20 billion.[14]

Until the RAH–66 Comanche was cancelled in early 2004, the Army expected to use it as a light helicopter for reconnaissance and anti-armor attack missions. The Comanche had been under development since the 1980s, and the first prototype appeared in 1995. Engineering and manufacturing development began in 2000 and was expected to take 6 years. The Comanche was to have stealth features and advanced avionics and to carry multiple Hellfire or Stinger missiles plus cannons. The Army expected to buy 3,000–5,000 Comanches to replace the UH–1, AH–1, OH–58, and OH–6 helicopters. By 2000, however, the program had been reduced to 1,213 helicopters. Due to subsequent affordability constraints, the program was reduced to 650–850 Comanches through the mid-term, with initial production to begin in 2007. By early 2004, however, the prolonged delays, high costs, and questionable merits of the Comanche led to its cancellation. The Army announced that it would be replaced by purchase of more AH–64 Apache helicopters, which already are being flown in large numbers, while RDT&E would develop a number of new attack helicopter options.

Affordability Options

These six aircraft modernization programs promise to elevate U.S. combat capabilities in important ways and to contribute to transformation. The question is not whether a legitimate requirement exists for them—it does—but whether they can be afforded. Evidence of the affordability problem is seen in the stream of decisions in recent years to scale back the number of new aircraft to be acquired. Whether the current plan can be afforded in its entirety will depend upon several factors. One factor will be the schedule for procuring these aircraft. At the moment, only the F/A–18 E/F and F–22 are being procured in significant numbers; their programs will be completed in a few years. Later in this decade, the V–22 Osprey and additional Army helicopters will enter production, followed shortly thereafter by the F–35 JSF, which will be bought in large numbers, as well as by F–45 UCAVs. Assuming that procurement of these 6 aircraft is spread over 20 years, DOD will need to buy, each year, an average of about 185 tactical fighters and 105 Osprey or Army helicopters. These acquisitions will not, however, be distributed evenly over this period. Owing to the interaction of the six schedules, a bow wave of rising costs will strain DOD's procurement budgets during 2008–2015.

Much will depend upon whether DOD's annual procurement budgets grow as now projected to $100 billion–$120 billion for that period. Even if this budget increase is fully funded, other procurement programs are also likely to be accelerating then and competing for funds. For example, costs for space systems, national missile defense, ship building, and new Army weapons could be rising significantly. The affordability of the air modernization effort thus cannot be taken for granted. To some degree, DOD and the military services may need to consider options for scaling back procurement costs during this bow wave. For example, a reduction in annual air procurement budgets of 10 percent or more may be necessary. Great care must be taken in evaluating these options, for while none are painless, some are less damaging than others. Systems analysis can play a helpful role by appraising the tradeoffs and implications of these options.

The option that offers superficial merits is that of canceling one or more big-ticket items. The program most often fingered for elimination is the F–22 because of its high costs and the relatively few aircraft to be procured. The V–22 Osprey is also cited by critics. However, other considerations argue in favor of keeping these programs alive. First, new programs are normally best cancelled early in their life spans, not after expensive RDT&E programs. If the F–22 were cancelled, a RDT&E program of about $25 billion would go down the drain without providing a major contribution to U.S. combat capabilities. Similarly, the V–22 Osprey has already consumed large R&D sums while producing prototypes with attractive capabilities.

Second, if F–22 procurement were cancelled, this would save $32 billion–$56 billion, but it would deny the Air Force its premier interceptor and ground attack aircraft, compelling it to rely solely upon a less capable aircraft, the F–35 JSF. Moreover, savings from F–22 cancellation would trim procurement budgets mainly during 2005–2010, the period before the bow wave takes effect. The reality is that because the F–22 will mostly be procured earlier, it is not a main cause of the bow wave, and canceling it would not greatly reduce the bow wave. Cancellation of the V–22 Osprey and a Comanche replacement would generate similar savings, but these savings mostly would take place during the bow wave. However, this would deprive the Marine Corps and the Army of new aircraft that are critical to their new operational concepts and transformational goals. The bottom line is that operational requirements create powerful reasons for deploying all three aircraft at least in enough numbers to meet minimum needs.

A second cost-savings option is that of reducing the size of U.S. combat forces, scaling back the need for new aircraft. A reduction of the force posture by 10–20 percent could result in a similar reduction of aircraft procurement needs, from about 3,600 tactical fighters and 1,900 Osprey/Army helicopters to 2,900–3,200 fighters and 1,500–1,700 helicopters. This step would result in total procurement savings of $28 billion–$56 billion over 20 to 25 years, for an average saving of $1.2 billion–$2.4 billion per year. Savings during the bow wave could be higher if procurement schedules were adjusted to focus on this period. The drawback of this option, however, is obvious: it would reduce total U.S. forces and combat capabilities. A few years ago, some observers judged that force cuts would be safe because the world was sufficiently peaceful, but since then, world affairs have become more dangerous, and the frequent call is for larger combat forces, not smaller. The idea of sizable force reductions in order to scale back procurement expenses flies in the face of this requirement, but the high effectiveness of air operations in recent wars may lessen the need for large forces, thus making some reductions possible.

A third cost-savings option is that of stretching out today's procurement plans. For example, this plan might call for average production of new fighters to be reduced from 180 fighters per year to 140 fighters. If applied across the board, this step could result in a reduction of annual procurement budgets for new aircraft from $12 billion–$16 billion to $9 billion–$12 billion. Focus on the bow wave period could result in greater savings then. The drawback of this approach, however, is that it brings its own costs. If fewer new aircraft are procured each year, steps must be taken to extend the life spans of existing aircraft. SLEPs to rehabilitate aging aircraft are not cheap. A SLEP for the F–16, for example, is estimated to cost $5 million per aircraft, and the rehabilitated aircraft gains only 5 or 6 years of life. SLEPs kick the can down the road: a few years later, new aircraft must still be bought. While SLEPs can reduce near-term costs, they do not necessarily reduce long-terms costs, and in the interim, combat capabilities grow at a slower place than is desirable.

A fourth cost-savings option is that of shifting the high-low mix downward. In this option, expensive aircraft would be replaced by less-expensive models, reducing total procurement costs. For example, the F–22 and F/A–18 E/F programs could be replaced by a larger program of F–35 JSF aircraft. In the extreme case, cancellation of 280 F–22s and 460 F/A–18 E/Fs would save about $60 billion. They would be replaced by an equal number of 740 F–35 Joint Strike Fighters at a cost of about $40 billion, producing net savings of $20 billion. Alternatively, the F–35 JSF program for the Air Force might be cancelled in favor of buying a modernized version of the F–16, which might cost $35 million rather than $45 million to $55 million for the JSF. Costs for the entire Air Force program of 1,763 fighters would then be reduced from about $90 billion to $60 billion, for a net savings of $30 billion. The problem with both options is that, while they reduce annual procurement costs, they make the force less capable. If the Air Force and Navy were denied new high-end fighters, they would need to rely solely on the less-capable F–35 JSF. If the Air Force received the F–22, it would still have to rely upon a modernized version of the F–16 that lacks the stealth features and other performance characteristics of the F–35 JSF. Procurement budgets would be lower, but the combat capabilities of the military would be diminished.

When all four options are scrutinized closely, none of them comes across as a satisfactory single solution to the affordability problem. All of them offer to reduce annual procurement budgets, but all impose painful sacrifices to U.S. combat capabilities, either by reducing the size of U.S. forces or by reducing their ability to field new high-performance weapons. As a result, although they might be cost-efficient in budgetary terms, they are not necessarily cost-effective in strategic terms. This conclusion does not mean that the affordability problem is unsolvable. The logic of systems analysis suggests that if savings are needed, a cost-effective approach might be found by blending all four options in ways that draw partially upon each of them.

For example, the size of U.S. air forces might be trimmed 5–10 percent by reducing the number of combat aircraft assigned to the Air Force, Navy, and Marine wings, and by integrating Air Force/Marine Reserve wings with Active wings. The same approach could be applied to Marine and Army units that fly the V–22 Osprey and Apache. A modest stretch-out of the F–35 JSF program and SLEP for some aging aircraft might make sense even if a full-scale SLEP is not a good idea. For all six aircraft types, only about two-thirds of the new aircraft would be assigned to combat units. The rest would be used for spares, attrition fillers, trainers, and maintenance floats. If usage in these areas can be trimmed, smaller procurement programs need not result in main combat forces being denied modern weapons.

These ideas are suggestive. All of them need to be evaluated closely on their merits. The key point is that when difficult affordability problems are not amenable to a single solution, sometimes they can be solved by complex solutions anchored in discriminating program management. Programs combining several partial cost-reduction measures could produce sensible results by working together in ways that achieve the overall goal while not relying too heavily on any single measure, so as not to incur more damage from its drawbacks than necessary. This is the practice that DOD has often pursued successfully in the past. Whether this practice will work again with air modernization is to be seen. But systems analysis suggests that this approach is worth considering as DOD enters a new cycle of expensive air modernization.

Affording Naval Modernization

DOD's rising procurement budgets are a major help to the Navy because they allow it to pursue two goals at the same time: modernization of the existing ship inventory and expansion of the force from the 310 ships that are now authorized to 375 ships. This force expansion has not yet been approved by DOD, but it remains a key Navy goal even though doubts exist about its affordability. Fiscal constraints may prevent growth of the fleet to 375 ships by 2022, but even if substantial shortfalls must be accepted, the Navy is likely to seek some increase in its force posture, perhaps to 325–350 ships. While the Navy's current ships do not face immediate aging problems, they will eventually need to be replaced as they reach the end of their average 35-year life spans. The Navy plans to replace them with a new set of combatants that provide major new capabilities and respond to the transformation imperative. In addition, the Navy plans to halt the steady decline of its ship inventory by buying small littoral combat ships that will help enlarge its posture while also providing an enhanced capability to operate in offshore waters. The effect of this modernization program will be to better enable the Navy to pursue its new operational concepts of Sea Strike, Sea Shield, and Sea Basing, while creating new formations such as carrier strike groups, amphibious strike groups, and surface action groups.

Only a few years ago, it was common to predict that fiscal constraints would result in a smaller Navy of 250 ships or less. The recent rise in procurement spending for shipbuilding offers to reverse this trend, allowing the Navy to stay at its current size or even grow by 15–20 percent. If this buildup is fully funded, the Navy's shipbuilding program will accelerate from the 4 to 5 new ships per year in the recent past, to 8 to 10 ships through 2009, to 13 to 15 ships during 2010–2022. If the Navy is both to replace retiring ships and enlarge its fleet to 375 ships, it will need to buy 207 new ships through 2022 at a cost of about $275 billion. The planned acquisition rate will result in the Navy growing slowly: it will reach 325 ships by 2015 and 375 ships by 2022. During 2022–2033, the Navy will need to buy an additional 87 ships in order to keep its fleet at roughly 375 ships.

The Navy wants a future fleet of 375 battle force ships for the operational goal of deploying 12 carrier strike groups, 12 expeditionary strike groups, 9 surface strike groups, 4 nuclear-powered guided missile submarine (SSGN)/SOF strike units, plus appropriate maritime prepositioning groups and logistic support ships. In the Navy's view, these various formations will be needed to carry out its demanding missions in future U.S. defense strategy. In order to deploy these formations, the Navy's plan to buy 207 new ships through 2022 is composed of a mix of vessels: 4 carriers, 39 attack submarines, 87

Table 15–7. **Navy Force Levels and Construction Plans**

	Deployed Ships, 2005	Construction Plans, 2006–2022	Deployed Ships, 2022
Carriers	12	4	12
Amphibious Assault Ships	36	14	37
Cruisers, Destroyers, Frigates	96	59	104
Littoral Combat Ships	0	56	56
Attack Submarines	55	39	59*
Other Ships	96	35	107
Total	295	207	375

* For 2022, 55 SSNs and 4 SSGNs are deployed.

surface combatants, 14 amphibious ships, and 63 support ships of various types. If the Navy succeeds in its goal to deploy 375 ships by 2022, this enlarged fleet will include 12 carriers, 37 amphibious assault ships, 104 surface combatants, 59 attack submarines (nuclear attack submarines [SSNs] and SSGNs), 56 LCS ships, and 107 support ships. As table 15–7 shows, the force mix thus will be similar to today's posture; the only major change is addition of the 56 LCS ships. Thanks to construction of better ships, as well as the LCS acquisition, however, the future Navy will be more capable than the current Navy.

Achieving this ambitious modernization agenda, however, should not be taken for granted because it could stretch the Navy's procurement budgets to the limit or beyond during the bow wave period and afterward. The Navy may need to consider procurement alternatives, including smaller numbers of new ships and different ships than are now on the drawing board. For example, the Navy will need to recalibrate its plans if it can buy only 155 to 185 new ships instead of 207 by 2022. In this event, it will need to decide whether its future, smaller fleet should be a linear downsized version of its model for 375 ships, or instead should reflect a different mix of ships by preserving some capabilities while sacrificing others. Here again, a sense of management and economizing will be needed, giving systems analysis a role to play.

Current and Future Shipbuilding Program

The Navy's current procurement program of $10 billion annually is divided into $8.62 billion for construction of new ships and $1.4 billion for conversions, overhauls, and auxiliaries. Table 15–8 shows how most of these funds are allocated among the various categories, resulting in eight new ships initially being planned for 2005. The number was subsequently reduced to five ships owing to problems with the Office of Management and Budget and Congress over funding plans. In addition, a Trident fleet ballistic missile submarine (SSBN) is undergoing conversion to conventional roles as an SSGN. In current plans, funds for shipbuilding are projected to rise to about $15 billion in 2008, and to average $15 billion–$18 billion per year through 2020. If these bigger budgets are funded, the effect will be to enable the Navy to pursue its plans to acquire new carriers, amphibious ships, surface combatants, submarines, and other ships.[15] But if they are not fully funded, cutbacks will be necessary.

Table 15–8. **Navy Shipbuilding Program, 2005**

Type of Ship	Number of Ships	Procurement Funds (in 2005 $billions)
Carrier Replacement Program	1	$0.98
DDG–51 Aegis Destroyer	3	$3.45
LPD–17 Amphibious Ship	1	$0.97
Virginia Class Submarine	1	$2.45
Auxiliary Cargo Ships	2	$0.77
Total	**8**	**$8.62**

New Carriers and Amphibious Assault Ships

Public attention to shipbuilding typically focuses on the Navy's biggest, most visible ships: its carriers and amphibious assault ships. Although an aging carrier is being retired early in order to reduce operating costs, the Navy plans to buy its replacement on schedule, and to retain its current force of 11 to 12 carriers and 36 amphibious ships. Whether the early retirement of one carrier will yield a long-term reduction in the carrier force is to be seen. Retention of the current fleet would allow the Navy to deploy about three CVBGs and three ARGs continuously for peacetime overseas presence abroad, because it provides a sufficient rotational base of ships including those recovering from past deployments or preparing for future deployments. In addition, this number of carriers and amphibious ships should be able to fulfill naval requirements for warfighting missions. For example, with a force of 12 carriers, 8 to 10 carriers can deploy overseas in an emergency, providing the capacity to support 2 major combat operations.

Periodically, the Navy is criticized for building carriers that are too large at 90,000 to 100,000 tons. The recommendation advanced by critics is that the Navy should produce smaller carriers of 50,000–60,000 tons that would, it is argued, be cheaper to buy and operate. The Navy's response has been that carriers of this size are needed to be able to carry a full fighter wing: about 54 fighters plus other aircraft for C⁴ISR, refueling, and antisubmarine warfare. In addition, the Navy argues that the carrier itself is only part of the total cost of a CVBG, which includes not only the air wing, but also escorts and logistic supply ships. A smaller carrier would reduce life-cycle costs for the CVBG by only 5–10 percent, the Navy says, yet would reduce capability by 33 percent or more, and thus would not be cost-effective. In response to arguments that big carriers are vulnerable to enemy attack, the Navy argues that modern air defenses protect carriers with high confidence, and that when the details of battle are considered, a larger force of smaller carriers would not have greater survivability than the current force.

For these reasons, the sizes of Navy carriers and of amphibious assault ships seem likely to stay at or near current levels for the future. The Navy plans to buy new carriers and assault ships at a steady rate that allows for replacement of aging vessels reaching retirement age. Even so, debates are likely to continue about the exact composition and costs of new ships in this category. In 2002–2003, senior DOD officials mandated a significant change in construction plans, proposing to build a new carrier, designated

CVN–21, with major upgrades of new transformation technologies. Currently, 7 of the Navy's 12 carriers are *Nimitz* class. The eighth and final *Nimitz* class carrier, CVN–77, is scheduled to be delivered in early 2008. It will serve as a bridge platform for new technologies that are to be incorporated into next-generation carriers. The new CVN–21 will have an integrated topside island with a new multifunction radar, new propulsion plant monitoring improvements, a smaller crew, flight deck enhancements for greater sortie-generation rates, and advanced arresting gear. Construction of CVN–21 is to begin in 2007, and is likely to be complete by 2012–2014. One new carrier should be commissioned every 3–4 years on average to replace retiring carriers as they age.

Construction of new amphibious ships is likely to be affected by similar considerations. Currently, the Navy's fleet of amphibious ships includes 7 LHD *Wasp* class amphibious assault ships, 5 LHA *Tarawa* amphibious assault ships, 11LPD *Austin* class amphibious transport dock ships, and 13 LSD dock landing ships.[16] These ships, though similar in appearance to aircraft carriers, are considerably smaller, at 40,000–55,000 tons apiece. Their mission is to carry Marine ground and air forces for amphibious assault and power-projection missions. For example, each *Tarawa* can carry about 1,900 troops, 100 tanks, 6 AV–8B fighters, 21 helicopters, and 4 landing craft. Other models carry a force mix of similar size in varying combinations. The Navy has enough amphibious ships to keep three ARGs continuously afloat, each with a battalion of troops plus aircraft. If the entire amphibious fleet were mobilized, it could carry about 36,000 soldiers, 65 to 70 combat aircraft, and several hundred helicopters, or more than a full Marine division with support assets and a Marine air wing. Procurement of new amphibious ships has slowed in recent years, but simple mathematics suggests that, on average, one new ship should be procured each year in order to replace aging ships as they retire. For this reason, construction of amphibious ships will be an important feature of Navy shipbuilding.

New Surface Combatants and Submarines

Traditionally, the main role of surface combatants—cruisers, destroyers, and frigates—has been to protect carriers, but in recent years, they have been acquiring major land attack roles as well, with cruise missiles playing a key role. Reacting to rising procurement budgets, the Navy has an ambitious plan to buy new surface combatants in order to modernize and enlarge the current force. Today the Navy has 96 surface combatants; its goal is to enlarge to 104 ships by 2022. Current Navy force levels are shown in table 15–9. Produced during the Cold War, all of these ships are heavily armed with modern weapons. For example, the CG–47 *Ticonderoga* class cruisers carry the Aegis missile defense system, 2 helicopters, 2 5-inch guns, and 122 vertical launch system (VLS) cells for cruise missiles. The DDG–51 *Arleigh Burke* class destroyer typically carries Aegis, 8 Harpoon missiles, 2 helicopters, 1 5-inch gun, and 90–96 VLS cells. The DD–963 *Spruance* class destroyer and *Oliver Hazard Perry* class FFG–7 frigate are configured with strong open-ocean antisubmarine warfare assets, plus other weapons for convoy escort or land attack.[17]

The DD–963s and older FFG–7s and CG–47s are slated for retirement during this decade as they approach the end of their normal life spans. In order to modernize its fleet, the Navy plans to upgrade remaining CG–47s and FFG–7s, and to acquire 10 new DDG–51s,

Table 15–9. **Composition of Surface Combatant Force, 2005**

Ship Class	Number	Type	Tons	Crew Size	Main Missions
DD–963	17	Destroyer	9,300	375	Antisubmarine warfare, land attack
FFG–7	33	Frigate	4,100	221	Escort, antisubmarine warfare
CG–47	27	Cruiser	9,500	410	Air defense, land attack
DDG–51	38	Destroyer	8,400	340	Air defense, land attack

which currently are being produced at a rate of 2 or 3 per year. Its main focus, however, is to buy three entirely new types of ship in the coming years: the DD(X), the CG(X), and the LCS. The DD(X) and CG(X) will both be considerably bigger than the destroyers and cruisers they will replace. The LCS will be a small, speedy vessel of only 3,000 tons; it is a major departure for the Navy, harking back to its World War II-era use of PT boats. Table 15–10 displays these ships and an estimate of procurement costs for each of them.

Whether these new ships are truly transformational platforms is questioned by some critics, but they will be equipped with advanced networks, sensors, munitions, and other new-era technologies. A replacement for the cancelled DD–21, the DD(X) destroyer will be a stealthy, multimission ship configured for land attack. In addition to modern information networks, it will carry 1 or 2 155-millimeter guns that can fire at long ranges, plus up to 128 VLS cells for launching Tomahawk cruise missiles. Configured with such advanced features as an inward-sloping tumblehome hull and a graphite composite superstructure, this electric-powered, highly automated ship will carry a crew of only 150 sailors, far fewer than the 350 aboard current destroyers. Procurement will begin in a few years, and up to 16 DD(X) vessels will be acquired. The CG(X) will be a multimission cruiser focused on air and ballistic missile defense. The Navy is likely to procure between 24 and 32 of these vessels beginning in 2014. The LCS will be a small, "focused-mission" ship with a modular design so that combat systems can be altered for one of three missions: mine countermeasures, antiship operations, or littoral antisubmarine warfare. The idea is to provide a large number of small ships for operations close to enemy shorelines and other

Table 15–10. **Proposed New Surface Combatants**

Ship Class	Number	Type	Unit Cost (in $billions)	Tons	Main Missions
DD(X)	16	Destroyer	$1.3–1.9	16,000	Land attack, antisubmarine warfare
CG(X)	24–32	Cruiser	$2.2	16,000+	Air and missile defense, land attack
LCS	56	Small Combatant	$0.350	3,000	Multiple littoral missions

littorals. The Navy's plans are not finalized, but about 56 LCS ships are likely to be acquired, beginning in about 2010. Total cost for all three ships in the numbers now planned is likely to be between $94 billion and $120 billion.

The interaction of retirements and delivery of new ships will shape the Navy's future force. Through 2010, the surface combatant force will number about 120 ships. New DDG–51s will replace retiring DD–963s and FFG–7s (although some of the latter will remain in the inventory until 2015). Beginning in 2010 or so, DD(X) and LCS ships will begin entering the inventory, followed later by the CG(X). As a result, the surface combatant force will gradually grow in size, ultimately reaching 160 ships or more by 2020. By then, the force will be composed of about 55 DDG–51s, 10 to 15 aging CG–47s, 15 to 20 DD(X)s, 10 to 15 CG(X)s, and 50 to 60 LCSs. The element that enlarges the force thus is the LCS; otherwise, the surface combatant force would stay at around the current level.

The current SSN submarine construction program is focused on acquisition of new *Virginia* class vessels, portrayed as the next generation of attack submarines for maintaining undersea supremacy well into the 21st century. Their missions include surveillance, strike warfare, mine countermeasures, and antisubmarine warfare. These submarines will carry Tomahawk cruise missiles and will be able to conduct long-term surveillance of land areas, littoral waters, and sea-based forces. They are currently being funded at a rate of one per year. The time needed to build the vessel is normally 6 years from authorization to actual deployment. Thus far, seven vessels have been contracted through 2008. Behind the scenes, debates and studies are taking place over the long-term size and configuration of the SSN submarine force. The current force includes 18 SSBN strategic submarines (*Ohio* class with Trident intercontinental ballistic missiles); 4 of these are being converted to conventional (non-nuclear) missions with Tomahawk cruise missiles. The SSN force includes 54 SSGN nuclear-powered guided missile submarines of varying types, including 51 *Los Angeles*-type vessels, two SS–21 Seawolfs, and one submarine for special operations and intelligence missions. The Seawolfs carry up to 45 Tomahawks apiece; the *Los Angeles* vessels carry just 4 to 12.

Because older *Los Angeles* submarines will reach the end of their life spans over the next decade, keeping the force at 55 submarines will require a significant shipbuilding program. Through 2025, roughly 35 new submarines—*Virginia* class or its successor—will need to be funded at an expense of about $75 billion. This is in addition to the seven *Virginia* submarines and one Seawolf already funded. In order to meet this schedule, submarine construction rates will need to increase from one vessel per year to two.

Moreover, some senior Navy officials have argued that 55 conventional submarines are not enough for future missions and have called for additional construction in order to reach a level of about 68 SSNs by 2015 and 76 by 2025. This increase presumably would elevate the Navy's posture from 375 ships to about 395 by 2022. Annual submarine construction rates would thus need to increase to 3–4 per year, and the total expense would rise from $75 billion to $121 billion. Through 2025, submarine construction budgets would need to average about $6 billion per year; they are about $2 billion per year now. Conversely, some analysts say that a smaller submarine force of only 37 vessels would be adequate. This decrease presumably would trim the Navy's force from 375 ships to 357, and it would result in significantly smaller budgets for submarine purchases and slower annual production rates. As of this writing, the model of 55 submarines seems likely to survive both challenges, but much will depend upon operational requirements and available budgets.

The combination of modernizing and enlarging both the surface combatant force and the attack submarine force promises to elevate the Navy's funding requirements for shipbuilding significantly in the coming years. Total expenses for both components could be $165 billion–$241 billion, plus an additional $80 billion–$100 billion for acquiring new carriers and amphibious ships. Funding this naval construction program at $245 billion–$341 billion would require an average of $12 billion–$17 billion per year for the coming two decades, much more than Navy spending on comparable vessels today (about $6.4 billion). Perhaps rising DOD procurement budgets will permit such an increase. If not, ways will need to be found to scale back construction goals and rates in order to match the budgets available.

Systems analysis can help evaluate the options, tradeoffs, and priorities. Perhaps the Navy's force goals can be reduced. The current Navy has an authorized force of 310 ships and a deployed force of 295 ships that seemingly has been carrying out U.S. defense strategy effectively. So one question is whether the future Navy really requires an increase to a force of 375 ships. Is a 20 percent expansion in the size of the Navy truly needed by U.S. defense strategy, or can the Navy safely be asked to operate with a posture the same size as today, or just 10 percent larger? The Navy's plan to grow to 375 ships is anchored in the premise of expanding the number of current models from 295 ships to 319 ships while also adding 56 LCSs for littoral missions. To what degree are diminishing marginal returns at work when the strategic benefits of enlarging the Navy by this amount are analyzed? These questions seem likely to be debated in the years ahead, and systems analysis can help.

Other options to reduce costs may also be examined. One obvious option is to fund SLEPs for existing vessels, to allow the Navy to slow the rate at which new vessels must be constructed. Another option would be to seek a less expensive mix of new surface combatants and submarines. For example, cheaper ships perhaps can be bought by relying upon modular designs and by scaling back on the practice of configuring surface combatants with multiple capabilities, such as counterair, countership, and countersubmarine systems. Still other options are to station more naval vessels overseas or to create multiple crews for each vessel, thus increasing their usage. These approaches have drawbacks, but they could allow the Navy to get more use out of current ships while reducing the number of new ships that must be bought, their individual costs, or both. Here, too, systems analysis has a potential contribution to make, especially if multiple cost-cutting strategies must be used, rather than a single strategy.

Analyses of the future Navy's force size and mix need to be embedded in a larger appraisal of strategic concepts for maritime power in the information age. Currently, the Navy is designed mainly for traditional sea domination. This mission plays a major role in determining the Navy's requirements for carriers, surface combatants, and attack submarines. If this mission continues to animate force planning, the future Navy inevitably will be similar to the current Navy, with the exact number of ships being determined by budgetary realities rather than any change in strategic concepts. But sea domination is not the only plausible concept. For example, the future Navy might instead be shaped mainly to carry out expeditionary strike missions and littoral operations. In this event, its mix of ships might need to change, with more LCSs and fewer carriers and subma- rines. Alternatives such as this, along with the current strategic concept, should be considered by systems analysis in order to help shed light on how to approach the future.

Future Procurement in Strategic and Budgetary Perspective

Judged in strategic terms, the vision of fielding an entirely new generation of fight- ers and warships by about 2020 has considerable appeal. It would allow transformation to couple its new information systems, structures, and doctrines to new weapons with significantly better performance characteristics. It would enable U.S. military forces to re- main the world's strongest by a wide margin. The problem is that this vision might not be fully affordable. If significant budgetary shortfalls arise, DOD is not likely to resolve them by fielding strong air forces at the expense of weak naval forces, or vice versa. Instead, it will aim for the strongest possible capability from both components, as well as from ground forces. The need to strike a sensible balance among these constituencies will man- date the need for a well-focused procurement strategy that pursues important goals but also accepts sacrifices and tradeoffs.

In addressing such procurement issues, the logic of systems analysis says that atten- tion should focus not on individual weapons, but on the large family of new weapons as a whole. It should focus not only on their effectiveness but also on their aggregate costs, and how those costs are distributed each year over a period of many years. One challenge is to pace the annual acquisition of these new weapons so that they fit into available procurement budgets rather than crowding each other out. Another challenge is to make sure that each new weapon is developed and produced within reasonable cost estimates, avoiding cost inflation due to inefficient manufacturing techniques or the ad- dition of expensive new components. If major cost inflation occurs across the board, or if future procurement budgets experience wholesale cuts, the idea of a comprehensive and affordable procurement effort could go up in smoke.

If there are funding shortfalls, there will be a premium on cost-saving strategies. The idea of canceling one or more big-ticket items will have superficial appeal, but because expensive weapons normally must be replaced by an equal number of less-expensive weapons, typically such actions result in smaller net savings, while such cancellations can deprive the military of sophisticated weapons that may truly be needed at least in some numbers. For these reasons, cost-saving strategies should take account of the multiweapon procurement effort as a whole and employ a combination of measures that trim costs in several areas at the margins to yield sufficient cumulative savings. Such strategies, although complicated, may often be the most cost-effective choice. Moreover, they can also focus attention on the $35 billion–$40 billion or more that will be spent each year on such mundane activities as secondary items and spare parts. Here too, care must be taken: a common cost-saving strategy has often been to reduce spending on ammunition stocks in order to free money for new weapons, but as a result, some stocks of smart munitions, for example, have been too low to meet projected wartime requirements. Cost-saving strategies must be optimally designed to allocate pain and risk in balanced, prioritized ways.

Procurement of large numbers of new fighter aircraft and ships clearly promises to accelerate transformation and enhance the combat capabilities of U.S. military forces, but this modernization will be costly, at about $500 billion–$600 billion or more through 2022 and beyond. Whether DOD's rising procurement budgets will be able to afford average annual expenses of $23 billion–$33 billion for these two efforts, while also modernizing the Army, attending to other new strategic priorities, and meeting normal procurement expenses is not clear. Much will depend upon the size of future DOD budgets, as well as their internal priorities, but a prolonged agenda of management, economizing, and careful scheduling of acquisitions will be needed. Along the way, some painful decisions may have to be made in the form of stretch-outs, scale-backs, high-low mixes, and inventory reductions. If so, the challenge will be to pursue these economizing measures without compromising U.S. military preparedness.

This important arena of defense planning and transformation will require serious, systematic thought about how to achieve maximum effectiveness at affordable expense. The task facing systems analysis and other tools is to contribute to the enterprise in helpful ways. Systems analysis can contribute by applying economic models of choice to individual weapons. But its more important contribution lies in providing a tool for seeing the defense procurement agenda as a whole.

Notes

[1] For analysis of the defense acquisition process, see J. Ronald Fox, *The Defense Management Challenge: Weapons Acquisition* (Cambridge, MA: Harvard Business School Press, 1988). See also Jacques S. Gansler, *Affording Defense* (Cambridge, MA: The MIT Press, 1989).

[2] For alternative perspectives, see Clark A. Murdoch, "The Navy in an Antiaccess World," in Sam J. Tangredi, ed., *Globalization and Maritime Power* (Washington, DC: National Defense University Press, 2002), chapter 25; and Norman Friedman, "Globalization of Antiaccess Strategies," ibid., chapter 26. For analysis of methodology, see Paul Davis et al., *Measuring Interdiction Capabilities in the Presence of Anti-Access Strategies* (Santa Monica, CA: RAND, 2002).

[3] Debate over access-denial issues particularly flared during 2001, when the Pentagon's Quadrennial Defense Review was being written, and has remained alive since then.

[4] For more detail on how these air and naval threats were countered, see Richard L. Kugler, *Commitment to Purpose: How Alliance Partnership Won the Cold War* (Santa Monica, CA: RAND, 1993).

[5] For more detail on this debate, see Hans Binnendijk, ed., *Transforming America's Military* (Washington, DC: National Defense University Press, 2002).

[6] A procurement budget of $114 billion would need to grow by about 2.5 percent annually in subsequent years in order to offset inflation. Additional annual increases would be needed to provide for real growth.

[7] For ground and air forces, total inventories significantly exceed the number of weapons assigned to combat units. For example, the Army needs tanks not only for combat divisions, but also for training, maintenance floats, war reserves, and prepositioned stocks. For good detail on U.S. inventories as well as those of other countries, see International Institute for Strategic Studies (IISS), *The Military Balance: 2003–2004* (London: IISS, 2003), a valuable document that is updated annually.

[8] See Congressional Budget Office, *The Effects of Aging on the Costs of Operating and Maintaining Military Equipment* (Washington, DC: Congressional Budget Office, 2001).

[9] See Office of the Under Secretary of Defense (Comptroller), *Department of Defense Budget for Fiscal Year 2005: Procurement Programs* (Washington, DC: Department of Defense, February 2005).

[10] See Michael D. Williams, *Acquisition for the 21st Century: The F–22 Development Program* (Washington, DC: National Defense University Press, 1999). See also Paul Jackson, ed., *Jane's All the World's Aircraft 2003–2004* (Surrey, UK: Sentinel House/Jane's Information Group, 2003).

[11] See *Jane's All The World's Aircraft, 2003–2004*. See also Roman Schweizer, "Big Bucks for the Best There Is: U.S. Sees Brew of Three Aircraft Owning Future Skies," *Armed Forces Journal*, June 2003; John Tirpak, "The F/A–22 Gets Back on Track," *Air Force Magazine*, March 2003.

[12] See *Jane's All the World's Aircraft 2003–2004*; and John Tirpak, "The F–35 Steps Out," *Air Force Magazine*, April 2003.

[13] See *Jane's All the World's Aircraft 2003–2004*.

[14] Ibid.

[15] See Congressional Budget Office, Testimony to Senate Armed Services Committee, Modernizing Tactical Aircraft (Washington, DC: Congressional Budget Office, 1999).

[16] The LHD *Wasp* class is the largest amphibious ship in the world, an improved follow-on to the LHA, a general-purpose amphibious assault ship. The LPD is an amphibious transport dock ship; the LSD is a dock landing ship. See <www.globalsecurity.org/military/systems/ship/>.

[17] See Congressional Budget Office, *Transforming the Navy's Surface Combatant Force* (Washington, DC: Congressional Budget Office, 2003), and *Increasing the Mission Capability of the Attack Submarine Force* (Washington, DC: Congressional Budget Office, 2002).

Chapter 16
Forging Defense Budgets

Analyzing defense budgets is hard work because it requires paying attention not only to broad goals and large programs, but also to the fine details of how money is spent on them. Hard work is especially needed when defense budgets are not large enough to fund all goals and programs, priorities must be set, and the best choices are anything but obvious. This has often been the case in the past, and it promises to hold true in the future. DOD will need to strike a balance between two key transformation goals—being prepared for expeditionary warfare and strategic dominance missions—while finding savings elsewhere in its budget to fund them properly. Because this agenda will not be easy or free of controversy, it will require a boatload of analyses focused on the issues at hand.

This chapter deals with the challenge of shaping future defense budgets and the role of systems analysis in handling it. After first discussing the potential contributions of systems analysis, it views today's DOD budget in strategic perspective, that is, in relation to defense budgets of other countries and to its impact on the U.S. Federal budget and national economy. Next, it examines future DOD budgetary toplines, the total amount of funds that are available to DOD, and the rationale for determining how large the defense budget should be and how fast it should grow. Then, it discusses why the need to pursue the two major goals—preparedness for expeditionary warfare in the near to mid-term and high-tech strategic dominance in the long term—frames the main budgetary challenge ahead. Then, it examines future spending patterns for distributing funds among the services and among competing macroprograms. Next, it analyzes the defense budget from a functional viewpoint, exploring new allocations of funds among such important categories as military personnel, operations and maintenance, construction, RDT&E, and procurement. Finally, it discusses analytical strategies for guiding defense budgets in the future. Along the way, it offers a snapshot of today's defense budgets, where they are headed, and how systems analysts can help assess the options and tradeoffs for new spending priorities.

The Role of Systems Analysis

An assessment of the role of systems analysis can best begin by discussing the contemporary budget scene. During the mid-1990s, annual defense budgets that had shrunk as far as $255 billion presented DOD with many dilemmas in allocating its limited funds among competing priorities. The result was a decision to maintain the existing force posture at high readiness while paring back such investment accounts as RDT&E, procurement, and construction. The situation began to ease during the later years of the Clinton administration, when defense spending was raised to $290 billion per year.

Within 3 years after the Bush administration came into office, it had raised defense spending to about $400 billion. This amount was for the basic defense budget that funds normal peacetime preparedness. Additional costs for the wars in Iraq and Afghanistan were funded through Congressional supplemental spending bills that elevated the total budget to about $440 billion in 2003 and 2004.

For the basic budget—the focus of this chapter—the administration announced plans for a further increase to nearly $500 billion by the end of the decade. About a third of the $100 billion increase through 2005 was needed to offset annual inflation, but the remaining two-thirds represented real growth. A somewhat different pattern of real growth and inflation offsets will apply in the future if Congress agrees to continue elevating the defense budget at the rate now planned by the Bush administration. Of the $100 billion increase needed to approach the proposed level of $500 billion by 2010, about $50 billion will be required to offset inflation, while the remaining $50 billion will provide more real growth of about 2 percent per year.[1]

The public perception that DOD's coffers are being filled to overflowing, however, conceals a more complicated reality of continuing stresses on defense decisionmaking. DOD is receiving more funds, but it also is facing growing demands on those funds. One reason is the need to perform additional missions as part of the war on terrorism in a dangerous and rapidly changing world. Another reason is that a very large and long-postponed backlog of spending on procurement must now be paid off, and this will be expensive. A third reason is that the cost of funding defense is steadily rising. DOD must maintain a skilled workforce of military and civilian personnel, and because this workforce is entirely voluntary, DOD must pay competitive salaries. The steady growth of the U.S. economy in wealth and productivity means that ever-larger salaries must be paid to dissuade good people from seeking higher-paying jobs elsewhere. Likewise, the cost of new weapons is rising, both because of expensive technologies and also because of rising labor costs. For these reasons, the defense budget will need to continue growing not only to offset inflation, but also to provide sustained real growth in at least moderate amounts. Critics who are looking for easy ways to cut future defense budgets are not likely to find many.

However, while DOD has a legitimate need for these bigger budgets and further real growth, the political reality is that the defense budget will not continue skyrocketing. Federal deficits and rising costs for domestic programs make this course implausible. The height of the defense budget's future peak is uncertain, but a leveling off is coming and DOD will not be able to spend its way out of fiscal dilemmas. Even if DOD receives all the money now planned, it will still need to set priorities and make hard decisions on how best to economize in spending discretionary resources. Its efforts to set priorities will be complicated by the fact that the familiar, well-oiled bureaucratic spending patterns of the past will no longer suffice as guidelines for the future. In the past, DOD has been able to allocate a fixed percentage of the budget to longstanding recipients, such as 25 percent to the Army, and 14 percent to command, control, and communications and space assets. Instead, it will need to shift resources among multiple recipients and strike new balances among them. New spending priorities will be needed; a business-as-usual approach will no longer be possible.

Clear thinking will be required so that the United States receives maximum strategic mileage from its defense budgets.

Systems analysis has the potential to make major contributions to decisions on future defense spending, particularly on the task of sizing and allocating future budgets, which will vary, not remain constant. Its economic models of choice provide useful tools for analyzing how best to distribute sums among competing priorities and multiple claimants. Instead of focusing solely on the internal composition of individual programs, systems analysis will need to assess how multiple programs and activities are combined to form the overall defense budget. Macro-budget analysis will be called for on a grand scale, as old spending patterns are replaced by new priorities that have not yet been determined and will shift as the future unfolds.

Making tradeoffs by transferring resource shares from some activities to others requires careful evaluation of marginal gains and opportunity costs. This will necessitate careful thought, analysis, and planning of the sort that systems analysis can help provide. In particular, systems analysis will be called upon to help assess how to make tradeoffs among programs that are not easily compared. An example of what may lie ahead came in fall 2004, when DOD announced its intention to pursue new priorities during 2006–2011. In order to create $30 billion for additional investments in Army readiness and space programs, the Pentagon said that it would remove this amount of money from key procurement programs: the F–22 fighter, new naval destroyers and submarines, the Osprey tilt-rotor helicopter, and national missile defense. Whether the Pentagon made a sound exchange was debated by critics who alleged that similar, less-damaging reductions could have been taken elsewhere. The need to make similarly difficult tradeoffs may arise with growing frequency in the future, and systems analysis will need to help assess them.

Seeing the Defense Budget in Strategic Perspective

Keeping the defense budget in strategic perspective is the first step toward assessing where it should be headed in future years. Is the United States spending too much on defense preparedness, too little, or about the right amount? Although different parts of the political spectrum give different answers, critics of current policies often buttress their arguments in favor of smaller budgets by pointing out the extent to which the United States outspends other countries. A favorite statistic is that the United States today accounts for fully 48 percent of global defense spending: $400 billion of the global total of $835 billion worldwide in 2004. However, this ignores another and equally telling statistic: the U.S. military accounts for only about 7 percent of global active-duty military manpower—1.4 million of the 20.4 million troops worldwide.

One reason for the disparity in spending is that the global figure of $835 billion is based on currency exchange rates. Although the U.S. dollar has been depreciating lately, it remains strong compared to many other currencies. This has the effect of elevating the apparent level of U.S. spending and decreasing that of other countries, especially those countries whose currencies on global markets are weak. For such countries, a better measure is purchasing power parity (PPP), which measures the capacity of currencies to buy goods and services on domestic markets. If PPP is used, total global defense spending would rise to $1,050 billion or so, while the U.S. share would shrink from 48 percent to 38 percent. Equally important are manpower costs: DOD must spend an average of $65,000–$70,000 on each member of the active forces and each civilian employee. Many countries can hire people at one-third of this rate or less. Some use conscription to populate their militaries with soldiers who are paid much less than market rates in their own economies. This allows such countries to field large forces with small manpower budgets. If the United States could buy competent personnel at a similar rate, its defense spending would fall to about $280 billion annually, or 30 percent of the global total at PPP. Currency exchange rates and manpower expenses thus go a long way toward explaining the difference between U.S. defense budgets and those of many countries.[2]

A fairer standard of evaluation might be to compare U.S. defense spending with that of wealthy European, Asian, and Persian Gulf allies, yet even here, appearances are misleading. Today, European members of NATO spend about $160 billion annually on national defense, while fielding 2.4 million troops. In Asia, three countries with close U.S. defense ties—Japan, South Korea, and Australia—together spend about $65 billion and field 977,000 troops. In the Persian Gulf, five close partners of the United States together spend $28 billion and field 205,000 troops. Together, these U.S. allies thus field about 3.6 million troops at an expense of $253 billion annually. Although they maintain larger force structures than the U.S. military by relying heavily upon conscription, their defense spending is fully two-thirds that of the United States: less, but not vastly less.

Even so, critics often point out that whereas these countries typically spend only about 2 percent of their GDP on defense, the United States spends over 3 percent, suggesting that this amount is too large. Yet rather than asking why U.S. spending is so high, one may ask why their spending is so low. The fact is that they can protect their security by spending 2 percent or less of GDP on defense precisely because they are allies of the United States: all of them benefit hugely from U.S. military commitments to their security, which allows them to pocket big savings in their defense budgets. The United States provides extended nuclear deterrence coverage and conventional force commitments to help defend their borders and interests. If these countries lacked the U.S. commitments, they might need to double their defense spending to achieve comparable security. Instead, the United States is obligated to maintain a high level of defense spending in order to help protect them. The difference in defense spending within the Western alliance system reflects not profligacy in U.S. military budgets, but rather the major savings that participation brings to allies. This is one reason why these countries value their alliance ties with the United States, even though U.S. strategy sometimes raises controversies in their domestic politics.

Because the United States has global defense commitments to many allies, it must possess a strong, well-prepared military, which costs a lot to maintain. Judged in relation to these global commitments, the U.S. military is relatively small and is spread thin: critics say that it fields a two-war posture for a three-theater strategy. The U.S. military must, therefore, rely upon high quality to offset its lack of quantity. It must purchase and maintain expensive modern information systems, weapons systems, smart munitions, and other assets. Beyond this, the U.S. strategic situation demands a multifaceted defense posture, which is also expensive. Because the United States is a Western hemisphere country, it requires a large navy, costing about $115 billion annually, in order to control sealanes so it can swiftly project air and ground forces abroad. The United States also needs strategic mobility assets costing about $15 billion annually in order to move its air and ground forces. It must maintain a robust network of information systems, including satellites, to communicate with its overseas forces and provide them critical data, at a cost of fully $55 billion per year. Expenses for these unique strategic requirements add up to nearly one-half of today's defense budget. The United States could have a smaller defense budget if it pared away such assets, but the cost would be a less effective defense strategy and a more unstable world.

The United States needs a larger defense budget than other countries for legitimate strategic reasons. Comparisons with foreign allies thus are misleading. None of them play global roles comparable to that of the United States. The looming need is, if anything, for them to increase their defense spending, not for the United States to slash its own. A better metric for judging the U.S. defense budget is to assess its impact on the Federal budget and the domestic U.S. economy. Critics often argue that the growing defense budget is consuming too much money that otherwise would be available for domestic uses such as lower taxes or discretionary programs. When seen in historical terms, however, the image of an exploding defense budget smothering domestic endeavors does not withstand close scrutiny. During the late 1970s and 1980s, as table 16–1 shows, the defense budget consumed 22.5 to 39.4 percent of the Federal budget and 4.9–7.6 percent of GDP. Today, the defense budget consumes only 17.9 percent of the Federal budget and 3.6 percent of GDP. While this is slightly up from the late 1990s, it is well below that of the Cold War, when heavier defense burdens were carried even as the U.S. economy continued to grow. The same applies to manpower levels: in 1980, DOD employed 2.8 percent of the national workforce, but today it employs only 1.4 percent.

Despite periodic shifts at the margins, the past decades have seen a steady decline in the impact of the defense budget on the national economy. The U.S. economy and population have shown major increases during this period, making the defense effort steadily

Table 16–1. **DOD Impact on the Domestic Economy**

	DOD Share of Federal Budget (percent)	DOD as Share of Gross Domestic Product (percent)	DOD Manpower as Share of Public-Sector Employment (percent)	DOD Manpower as Share of Total Labor Force (percent)
1950	27.4	4.3	28.8	3.4
1960	45	8	31.8	4.9
1970	39.4	7.6	26.5	5
1980	22.5	4.9	16.1	2.8
1990	23.1	5.1	15	2.5
2000	15.7	3	9.6	1.5
2005	17.9	3.6	9	1.4

smaller by proportion. In 1970, the U.S. GDP was $5.2 trillion (in 2005 dollars), the population was about 210 million, and the Federal budget was $1 trillion (in 2005 dollars). In 2005, when the U.S. GDP was about $11 trillion and the population nearly 300 million, the Federal budget was about $2.5 trillion. In other words, the United States is better able to afford a defense budget of $400 billion today than it was 30 years ago, when real defense spending was similar, in constant dollars, to that of today. In the coming years, the Federal budget, GDP, and national workforce are likely to continue to grow, which would provide room for some additional defense spending. None of these trend lines imply that the defense budget is "entitled" to some fixed share of the national economy, but they do mean that when the growing defense budget is seen in perspective, it does not seem destined to smother either the Federal budget or the national economy.

Even so, DOD will not receive whatever budgets it wants. The past years have seen a major rise in entitlements and other domestic spending programs: domestic social and economic spending now totals $1.6 trillion per year. Interest on the public debt totals $176 billion and is rising. These and other programs, together with defense, result in an annual Federal budget of $2.5 trillion, which is expected to climb to $2.9 trillion by 2009. The recent Bush administration tax cuts, coupled with uneven economic growth, have conspired to shrink annual Federal revenues below expenditures, resulting in a budget deficit of over $400 billion in 2005. Provided the economy returns to sustained growth, these deficits could shrink and move the budget from red ink to black ink. Clouding hope for balanced budgets, however, is the prospect that as the baby-boomer generation reaches retirement age, expenses for Social Security and health care will rise steadily, perhaps doubling by 2020. For these reasons, the Federal budget will not generate a surplus for painless additional defense spending. For the coming decade and beyond, the defense budget will need to be anchored in the kind of logic and analysis that persuades a scrutinizing Congress and public of its necessity.

Analyzing the Defense Topline

The defense topline is the total amount of funds that are available to DOD. Decisions about the topline are made not only for 1 year, but for several years—usually 5 to 6 years in firm terms, but with an eye on 8 to 10 years or longer. The United States does not want to waste money by spending too much on defense, but neither should it spend too little, because this could leave U.S. military forces too weak to perform their missions. How much is enough, if the United States wants to be well insured while recognizing that not all risks can be eliminated? Decisions on the topline are made by a two-part calculus: from the top down and from the bottom up. A tentative judgment is made about the aggregate level of funds that are likely to be needed each year for the coming period of 5 to 6 years. This funding profile is then evaluated in light of requirements emerging from the various components of the defense budget. A judgment is rendered that reconciles the two calculations, by adding or subtracting funds here and there. Systems analysis has the potential to contribute to both calculations and also to how they are reconciled, by applying economic models of choice.

Performing the top-down calculus seems straightforward, but the details are not simple in a time of strategic change. When threats and requirements are growing, a funding level that was adequate last year may not be adequate this year, and may be grossly inadequate 5 or 10 years from now, so budgets must increase. When threats and requirements are diminishing, defense spending can be reduced by some amount. But by how much in each case? There are no simple mathematical algorithms for determining adequate budgets. For example, some observers recommend that a fixed percentage of GDP be allocated to defense each year, perhaps 3.6 percent. This approach could provide a sizable budget for the coming year while allowing for slow, steady growth in future years as the national economy expands. This approach also could end the perennial debate over guns versus butter. The problem, however, is that this approach is not responsive to strategic requirements, which are a variable, not a constant.

Over the past 30 years, defense spending has fluctuated between 2.9 percent and 6 percent of GDP. Today's consensus calls for 3.6 percent of GDP to be spent on defense, but this judgment is affected by changing strategic conditions. The same applies to the idea of pegging future defense budgets to rates of growth in the national economy. If GDP were to grow by 3 percent each year in real terms, such an approach would enable the defense budget to grow at a similar rate, but over the course of years, a 3 percent rate might be too much or too little. Moreover, what would happen if the economy were to plunge into recession or to grow at a faster rate? The defense budget could be on a roller-coaster ride driven by the vagaries of national economics, not by strategic requirements. For these reasons, the idea of pegging the defense budget to GDP is only a good place to begin analyzing the topline, not a conclusion.

The Historical Legacy

Perspective on the topline can be gained by examining the historical record. As table 16–2 shows, "current dollars," which include inflation, are misleading. This indicator would suggest that over the past 30 years, the defense budget has spiraled upward from $74 billion in 1970 to $402.6 billion for 2005 (excluding war supplements). A better indicator is that of "constant dollars," which strips away inflation, allowing earlier budgets to be measured using the value of today's dollar as a baseline. This indicator shows more continuity than one might expect: DOD budgets have consistently remained between about $300 billion and about $470 billion since 1960 (measured in constant 2005 dollars). Yet this indicator also shows important variations. Defense budgets have moved upward and downward in response to changing world affairs, DOD's internal needs, and U.S. domestic politics. The budget for each year must be judged in relation to the conditions then prevailing. The key issue is whether each year's budget adequately protected the United States while allowing its military forces to modernize at a satisfactory rate.

Seen through the lens of constant dollars, a defense budget of only $314.8 billion in 1960 was possible because U.S. defense strategy was then anchored mainly in nuclear weapons and the threat of massive retaliation. During 1960–1965, the defense budget moved upward to $340 billion because a buildup of conventional forces was under way. During 1965–1970, a further increase was needed for the Vietnam War. During 1970–1975, withdrawal from Vietnam and force reductions permitted the budget to drop to $306 billion.

Table 16–2. **Trends in Defense Budgets (Budget Authority)** *

	Current dollars in billions	Constant 2005 dollars, in billions
1960	$40.9	$314.8
1965	$49.1	$340
1970	$74.1	$394.2
1975	$85.7	$305.7
1980	$142.6	$330.7
1985	$286.8	$480.7
1990	$293	$423.3
1995	$255.7	$326.5
2000	$290.5	$328.8
2001	$309.9	$340.9
**2002	$345.6	$369.9
**2003	$437.8	$456.8
**2004	$441.7	$450
*** 2005	$402.6	$402.6

* Budget authority (BA) represents the funds that DOD is authorized to allocate each year. A similar term is total obligation authority (TOA), which differs from BA in minor details. BA and TOA are not the same as outlays, which reflect the funds that are actually spent in any given year. Because BA and TOA funds that are allocated in one year may be spent over a number of years, their totals normally differ somewhat from outlays, which can represent several years of BA/TOA funding. This chapter mainly uses BA figures.
** Includes war supplements for 2002–2004.
*** War supplements for 2005 were not available as of this writing.

Rising Cold War tensions resulted in budget growth to $331 billion by 1980. During the 1980s, the Cold War and modernization produced the Reagan buildup, during which the defense budget grew to $481 billion in 1985. The end of the Cold War resulted in the budget declining to $423 billion by 1990 and to $327 billion by 1995. After 1995, the budget again began moving upward, and after 2001, its growth rate accelerated, reaching $402.6 billion in 2005. According to official projections, the defense budget will grow to $488.9 billion by 2009 in current dollars, which includes a projected annual inflation rate of about 2.5 percent during 2005–2009. But in constant 2005 dollars, the 2009 budget will be $443 billion. Of the $87 billion increase in current dollars between 2005 and 2009, $46 billion is thus due to inflation, and $40 billion to real increases. Whereas today's defense budget is similar to that of the Vietnam War, by 2009 the budget will be similar to budgets of the Reagan era.

Over the past 45 years, the historical record shows that at no time was the United States defeated in a war or compelled to withdraw from important security commitments because its military forces were too weak. All of these budgets were approved by

the executive branch, and all passed close Congressional scrutiny. Critics, nonetheless, offer differing appraisals of the details during each period. For example, some judge that
U.S. defense spending was dangerously low in the middle to late 1970s during the Ford
and Carter administrations. The Reagan buildup was intended to correct this problem,
but some charge that it was too profligate and that adequate military preparedness could
have been bought for significantly less. During the early to middle 1990s, the declining
defense budgets of the Clinton administration prompted critics to charge that military
preparedness was being neglected. While the Bush administration argues that its bigger
budgets are necessary, some charge that they are too big and wasteful, while others claim
they are still too small. Similar uncertainties will undoubtedly surround future budgets.[3]

Looking back over the past 45 years, a fair conclusion is that the executive branch
and Congress have always tried to do their best, and that some critics are never satisfied, yet cannot agree amongst themselves on whether individual budgets have been
too big or too small. A core reason is that there is no objective formula for judging budgets or for gauging how much confidence is needed and how many risks should be accepted. Among critics who have taken a serious look at defense planning, however, one
judgment is widely held: wide fluctuations in spending (upward or downward) can
create damage by causing turbulence within DOD. This is the case because a considerable portion of DOD's funds—today, about $250 billion each year—go toward carry-
ing out normal business by paying for people, operations, and maintenance. Because
investment funds must come from the balance, they are highly affected by fluctuations.

When budgets fall to the point where total spending just meets steady-state needs,
investment funds become scarce, forcing DOD to make painful decisions to stretch out
RDT&E and procurement. When budgets rise well above this point, investment budgets
soar, and DOD is able to open the floodgates of procurement. The problem is that, in
its rush to buy new weapons before the gates close again, it may buy them in inefficient
ways that elevate costs or create a block-obsolescence problem of the sort that exists today. It is widely agreed that defense preparedness would be better served by stable, predictable budgets and continuity over the years, rather than cycles of peaks and valleys, which
cause multiple problems.

Rising Costs of Defense

The logic of systems analysis can glean additional insights from historical data by
comparing DOD budgets and military manpower levels. Table 16–3 shows budgets and
manpower for key years since 1960, plus funds spent annually per active-duty soldier. During the 1960s, costs per soldier were stable, but the table shows a steady rise since 1970,
when the average soldier cost $128,571 per year. By 1980, the cost had risen by 25 per-
cent, to $160,300, and during the 1980s, the cost rose by another 23 percent. The pace of
increase was similar during the 1990s, at 15 percent for the decade. The rate of increase has
since accelerated, with costs per soldier rising by nearly 22 percent during 2000–2005. Current projections suggest that by 2009, the increase for the entire decade may be 34 percent.

Table 16–3. **Trends in DOD Budget and Manpower**

	Budget (in constant 2005 $billions)	Active Military Manpower (in millions)	Budget per Soldier
1960	$314.8	2,476	$127,140
1965	$340	2,656	$128,012
1970	$394.2	3,066	$128,571
1975	$305.7	2,129	$143,589
1980	$330.7	2,063	$160,300
1985	$480.7	2,207	$217,800
1990	$423.3	2,144	$197,435
1995	$326.5	1,583	$206,254
2000	$328.8	1,449	$226,915
2005	$402.6	1,458	$276,132
2009 (projected)	$443	1,458	$303,841

Even if the actual increase turns out to be only 20–25 percent, this will be similar to the experience of steadily rising costs for the previous three decades.

Many reasons account for this steady upward trend in costs manifested throughout three decades of changing conditions. Three seem primary. First, the cost of new weapons and hardware has risen as new and better technologies have appeared. Second, the cost of military and civilian salaries has risen in reflection of a more prosperous national economy. Third, the cost of military operations has also risen, due to the expense of modern fuels, building materials, spare parts, and supplies. In itself, this rise in costs does not mean that waste has occurred. On the contrary, the rise is a predictable product of contemporary economic conditions. Indeed, it may be healthy if it is accompanied by a rise in productivity. Economists often calculate the extent to which the U.S. economy experiences productivity growth each year. A 2 to 3 percent annual productivity growth is considered a solid gain. Such gains are normally accompanied by rising prices, for the simple reason that better goods and services tend to cost more to produce than their predecessors. By most measures, the productivity of the U.S. military—its combat power—has risen by an annual rate of 2–3 percent or more. A commensurate rise in costs is thus to be expected. It is not a sign of waste, but the price of remaining the world's strongest military power.

This steady pattern of rising costs suggests how defense budgets should be sized in the future: assuming force levels remain constant, the defense topline should be elevated by about 2 percent per year in real terms in order to pay for naturally rising costs. Such a strategy would not guarantee that defense budgets will be adequately large in any given year, but it does mean that over the course of one or two decades, DOD is likely to receive the resources needed to continue operating and improving at a rate that reflects historical norms. Additionally, the pattern of rising costs suggests that if the defense budget is not increased by 2 percent or so per year, DOD will have to make cutbacks, whether in forces, manpower, operating costs, acquisition, or somewhere else. The only way for DOD to avoid such cutbacks in fiscally stringent times is to cast off less-valued assets and marginally performing programs that it can do without. The reality is that, for most periods, a combination of real budget increases and belt-tightening will be needed, because neither by itself will get the job done.

Future DOD Topline

Table 16–4 shows official estimates of where the defense topline may be headed in the future. In order to offset annual inflation of about 2.5 percent and provide real growth of about 2.6 percent annually, the DOD budget is projected to grow to $488.9 billion by 2009 in current dollars. Toplines for subsequent years will depend upon similar determinations regarding inflation offsets and real growth. If the goal is merely to offset inflation, the topline is likely to grow to $544 billion by 2015 and to $600 billion by 2020 in current dollars. If the goal is to provide real increases of 1–2 percent per year in addition, defense budgets will need to grow higher, perhaps to $600 billion by 2015 and $650 billion by 2020 in current dollars. Much will depend upon the level of DOD's need for funds to pay for personnel, operations, and future procurement, and much also will depend upon the wishes of the President and the Congress.

Table 16–4. **Future Defense Top-Lines (Budget Authority)**

	Current dollars (in $billions)	Constant 2005 dollars (in $billions)
2005	$402.6	$402.6
2006	$423.7	$413.8
2007	$444.9	$424.1
2008	$466.7	$433.8
2009	$488.9	$443

Decisions about the defense topline will remain a political judgment, because there is no objective formula or algorithm for determining future budget levels. Rules of thumb for offsetting inflation and providing real growth can help provide crude estimates, but detailed appraisals of how each DOD budget is constructed will also be necessary. Thus, top-down calculations must be accompanied by bottom-up calculations based on such critical factors as service shares, program funding, and how funds are distributed among such functional activities as personnel, operations, and procurement.

Although public attention is presently focused on defense budgets for 2005–2009, similar stresses and controversies may arise during the period of 2010 to 2020. Many observers expect that the current budgetary growth will level off by 2010 and afterward will be limited to inflation offsets with little real growth. If so, this leveling off will occur at the same time that a procurement bow wave is starting to peak, resulting in a clash between available resources and spending imperatives. The mood among defense planners would change from today's celebration of bigger budgets to concern over how to stretch available funds as far as possible. The need to examine new spending priorities, which is already manifest, could then rise to the forefront of defense management issues.

The Challenge of Pursuing Two Goals with Limited Budgets

Transforming U.S. forces for waging expeditionary warfare along the southern arc of instability in the near to mid-term, while also transforming to ensure strategic dominance of potential rivals in the long term, will be a main challenge facing future defense budgets. Although these two goals are strategic partners, they require different capabilities and investment priorities in some respects. Pursuing both at the same time will be challenging because future defense budgets likely will not contain enough investment funds for all of their endeavors. If so, DOD will need to strike a sensible balance between them by setting priorities and accepting tradeoffs. DOD also will need to search elsewhere in the defense budget in order to find savings that can be spent on these two goals. As a result, the act of handling this challenge will play a major role in determining how budgetary allocation issues and alternatives are appraised in the years ahead.

When the Bush administration decided in 2001 to enlarge the defense budget, its primary transformation goal was to prepare U.S. forces for maintaining long-term strategic dominance over potential peer or near-peer rivals such as China. The events of September 11, 2001, introduced the second goal into this strategic calculus: winning the global war on terrorism (GWOT) by carrying out expeditionary operations in Afghanistan, Iraq, and elsewhere during the near to mid-term. The forces and capabilities required by these goals are similar in some respects, but differ in others. Strategic dominance requires investments in high-tech standoff strike forces that are equipped with modern information networks, sensors, and smart munitions. Because it relies heavily upon air power, naval power, and other joint assets, it de-emphasizes the traditional roles played by massed ground forces. By contrast, the expeditionary wars being waged as part of the GWOT require joint operations by air and naval forces, but they also necessitate substantial boots-on-the-ground assets, including large ground forces for close-in fighting and for S&R missions.

The investments needed to enhance the preparedness of U.S. forces for these two goals are sizable and they differ appreciably from each other. Expeditionary warfare requires investments in such areas as additional ground forces, new Army formations and equipment, new overseas bases and facilities, Special Operations Forces, S&R assets, low density/high demand assets, prepositioned equipment, strategic lift, increased training with new partners, and regular use of Reservists. By contrast, strategic dominance requires investments in missile defenses, space systems, new fighter aircraft and support aircraft, and new naval combatants, including aircraft carriers and amphibious assault ships, cruisers and destroyers, and attack submarines.

A reasonable estimate is that during 2005–2020, preparedness measures for expeditionary warfare will cost $200 billion–$275 billion in constant 2005 dollars. Meanwhile, preparedness measures for strategic dominance (discussed below) will cost another $700 billion–$975 billion. Together, they total $900 billion–$1,250 billion. The problem is that when long-range budget forecasts were originally prepared, they were mostly focused on the second goal, strategic dominance, and did not anticipate such big expenses for expeditionary warfare. Because expeditionary warfare measures must now also be funded, the effect is to enlarge spending requirements to the point where they could significantly exceed the funds available in future procurement budgets.

Unless investment budgets are increased proportionately, a sizable potential shortfall of funds could emerge, and it cannot be handled by minor tinkering. This is why DOD is likely to face tough choices about how to strike a sensible balance among these investment programs, how to set priorities and make tradeoffs, and how to find savings elsewhere. The need to make these choices provides a frame of reference for examining how the defense budget is allocated today, and how it might be reallocated tomorrow.

Analyzing Service Shares and Defense Programs

Determining how defense spending can best be allocated or reallocated is a complicated enterprise that would test any manager or analyst. It requires that senior officials take stock of three broad, overlapping categories of spending: among the service departments, among multiple defense programs, and among line item functional activities. These three categories and their subcomponents give the defense budget the form of a three-dimensional matrix with about 300 cells, each of which must be given appropriate funds every year. A simplified version of the matrix is shown in figure 16–1; it has 220 cells reflecting 11 programs and 5 functional categories in each, for each of the 3 services plus DOD-wide. Given this complexity, the natural tendency of any bureaucracy may be to ease the challenge by establishing fixed distribution rules to allocate funds each year and over several years. Critics accuse DOD of being so mired in this practice that its budgetary distribution patterns seldom change regardless of strategic conditions: each recipient, it is charged, gets the same budget share regardless of circumstances. While this criticism is overly broad, there is no question that many defense budgeters value continuity over change. It makes the task of distributing funds among multiple recipients easier, and it has the added advantage of reducing disruptive political debates over the budget. Senior officials who follow such practices hope that if every constituency gets a predictable piece of the action each year, DOD will benefit from less angry competition and more cooperation.

A large measure of continuity was possible during the Cold War and for the decade afterward, but strategic conditions are now changing rapidly, necessitating new distribution rules and new patterns to allocate funds wisely among the various recipients. New strategic conditions are resulting from changes in world affairs, U.S. national security strategy, and military commitments and missions, as well as transformation priorities, emerging weapons and technologies, and DOD's internal management practices. In today's world, there is no overarching strategic theory for determining the details of how defense budgets should be allocated in response to these changes, nor is it likely that a fixed theory of distribution can be created any time soon. As a result, DOD may face a future of continuous major adjustments to its spending patterns, not merely marginal ones.

Figure 16–1. **The Defense Budget Matrix**

Functions _ _Programs	Military Personnel	O&M	RDT&E & Procurement	Construction and Housing	Other
Strategic forces					
General purpose forces					
Intellligence and communications					
Mobility					
Guard and Reserve					
R&D					
Central supply and maintenance					
Training, medical, and other					
Administration					
Support of other nations					
Special operations forces					

(Cube dimension labels: Army, Navy, Air Force, DOD-wide)

The task of determining how to adopt new spending patterns eases when the defense budget is rising and allows many recipients to be given ample funds. Few recipients complain when their coffers are brimming. But the task becomes far harder when requirements are rising faster than the budget, major shortfalls emerge, painful priorities must be set, and multiple recipients must be frustrated. Today's defense budget is somewhere between largesse and scarcity. Although future budgets will be larger than now, spending requirements are rising as a result of growing costs in such areas as intelligence and communications, operations and maintenance, and procurement. Regardless of whether tomorrow's budgets reasonably match requirements or fall short, budget allocation will be stressful. Resource shortfalls may emerge to one degree or another, and new spending patterns will have to be continuously created and recreated in ways that perpetually upset the budgetary balance.

Service Shares

At first glance, trends in service shares do not seem to reflect changes in spending patterns to the degree being experienced in the other two categories, defense programs and functional activities (see table 16–5). Closer inspection, however, shows important changes at the margins. A shift of only 1 percent in budget share equates today to fully $4 billion per year. When funds are shifted from one service to another, they often come from acquisition accounts, because spending on manpower and operations is far harder to change.

Table 16–5. **Distribution of Service Shares of Total DOD Budget (Budget Authority)**

	Past budget shares (percent)			2005		2009	
	1980	1990	2000	$ billions	Percent of Budget	$ billions (in current $)	Percent of Budget
Army	24.3	26.8	24.8	$97	24.1	$116.4	23.8
Navy	33.1	34.1	31.2	$119.2	29.6	$148	30.3
Air Force	29.3	31.7	29	$120.4	29.9	$142.6	29.2
DOD-wide	13.3	7.4	15	$66	16.4	$81.9	16.7

A $4 billion shift could increase the Army's procurement account by 25 percent and decrease the Air Force's account by 10 percent. Over 5 years, a 1 percent shift means $20 billion: enough to buy 200 new fighters, or 10 new surface combatants, or 3,000 new tanks. For this reason, even shifts as small as 1 percent are taken seriously by defense officials; they indicate significant strategic changes. Table 16–5 shows the distribution of budget shares among the services for 2005–2009, along with a snapshot of past trends.

As the table shows, DOD-wide departments and agencies have doubled their share of the defense budget since 1990. This trend reflects the growing emphasis on joint operations as well as DOD control of expensive joint investment activities in intelligence and space, and in such shared research and development (R&D) and procurement programs as the JSF and Osprey. The budget shares of all three service departments have declined as a consequence: each has about 2–3 percent less than its 1990 share of the budget. The table does not suggest any future wholesale shift, as some have alleged, away from the Army in favor of the Air Force and Navy. The Army will continue to receive about 25 percent of the DOD budget throughout 2004–2009. From 2006 onward, this share might grow somewhat as a result of funding increases being made by DOD. Yet the fact remains that the Army will continue to receive about 4–5 percent less of the budget than the Navy or the Air Force, or up to $20 billion–$30 billion less than either each year. This difference may seem odd, since the Army has about the same number of personnel as the Navy, and 40 percent more than the Air Force. But it is largely explained by two factors: the Navy and Air Force possess more expensive weapons than the Army, and they also perform national missions not performed by the Army, including nuclear defense and strategic mobility. These create a genuine need for bigger budgets.

These differences in total funds are accompanied by similar patterns in the funds available to the three service departments for acquisition, including RDT&E and procurement. As table 16–6 shows, the Navy and Air Force not only possess larger budgets, but also are able to channel larger portions of their budgets into acquisition: 36–44 percent, compared to just 21 percent for the Army, which bears weighty expenses for personnel and operations. This is a big difference in acquisition funds. This pattern has been the case for decades, and it will remain true in the future even if, as now being contemplated,

Army budgets are enlarged about $5 billion per year at the expense of the Air Force and Navy. The Army will have $20 billion–$25 billion for acquisition each year from 2005 to 2009, while the Navy and Air Force each will have more than double that amount. The Army procurement effort in 2005 ($10.4 billion) is slowed not only by a lack of investment funds, but also by the Army's decision to spend heavily on RDT&E for the Future Combat System. By 2009, Army procurement is projected to rise to $16.2 billion, but this will still only be about half what the Navy or Air Force spends ($39.5 billion and $38.5 billion, respectively). Even if the Army receives somewhat more funds than this projection, it will modernize less rapidly than the other two services.

Table 16–6. **Service Acquisition Funds (Budget Authority)**

	Total Acquisition (current $billions) and Percent of Service Budget				RDT&E (current $billions)		Procurement (current $billions)	
	2005		2009		2005	2009	2005	2009
Army	$19.9	21	$24.6	21	$10.4	$8.7	$10.4	$16.2
Navy	$43	36	$56.8	38	$16.4	$13.1	$27.7	$39.5
Air Force	$52.8	44	$57.9	41	$21.2	$22.8	$32.6	$38.5
DOD-wide	$22.1	33	$26.8	33	$21	$25.8	$4.2	$4.4

By 2010 or thereafter, if the FCS program produces on schedule, new combat vehicles will be candidates for Army procurement. The Army will then have to seek additional procurement funds to acquire these new weapons in large quantities. It may be able to find some in its own budget by shifting money from RDT&E or other accounts to procurement. Some funds may come from growing DOD procurement budgets, which are projected to rise to $110 billion or more by then. If the Army finds itself short of procurement funds, its supporters may lobby for additional funds to be transferred from the Navy and Air Force. Regardless of the source, the Army will need more funds for procurement—not as much as the Navy or the Air Force, but enough to meet its needs. An additional $5 billion for procurement and other investments each year, as now being contemplated, would significantly enhance the Army's modernization.

Defense Programs

Spending patterns for the 11 defense programs, each of which involves a cluster of specific activities and purposes, are displayed in table 16–7. The table shows the extent to which defense preparedness is a multifaceted business in which new spending patterns are emerging. In order for the defense budget to be properly balanced, all 11 programs must be funded at adequate levels. The question of how to measure adequacy for each program can be answered by first assessing requirements and cost-effectiveness for each program. Then all 11 programs must be evaluated in relation to each other to determine a sensible overall distribution of funds. DOD has been analyzing these programs, individually and collectively, for the past four decades, so a large record of information, data, and analytical standards allows defense managers to scrutinize each program's internal contents. Even so, comparing them to each other—called cross-program evaluation—is a continuing challenge that does not promise to get easier in an era when underlying strategic premises are changing and new spending patterns are needed. The dilemma is that if one or more programs are to receive additional funds, those funds must be denied to other programs. Tradeoff analysis thus becomes necessary, but it is difficult because programs differ from each other in ways that make tradeoffs hard to measure.

Table 16–7. **Distribution of Program Spending (TOA)**

	2005		2009		Past Allocation (percent)		
	Amount (in current $billions)	Percent of Budget	Amount (in current $billions)	Percent of Budget	1980	1990	2000
Strategic Forces	$8.8	2.2	$9.2	1.9	7.3	6.2	2.5
General Purpose Forces	$144	35.8	$190	38.9	36.8	38.6	36.8
Intelligence and Communications	$55.5	13.8	$64.9	13.3	6.1	9.9	11.1
Mobility	$14.5	3.6	$20.8	4.3	1.6	2.1	4
Guard and Reserve	$31.7	7.9	$39.4	8.1	6.3	6.4	8.5
Research and Development	$45.6	11.3	$48.5	9.9	7.4	8.7	9.2
Central Supply and Maintenance	$23.5	5.8	$25.8	5.3	9.9	9.6	6.5
Training, Medical, and Other	$60.1	14.9	$67.2	13.8	22.4	14.8	16.7
Administration	$10.4	2.6	$14.7	3	1.8	2.3	3
Support of Other Nations	$1.4	0.03	$1.5	0.03	0.04	0.03	0.03
Special Operations Forces	$7.1	1.8	$6.9	1.4	—	1	1.4
Total	$402.6	100	$488.9	100	100	100	100

The historical data show that none of these programs has been awarded an unchanging share of the defense budget consistently over the past 30 years. Virtually all of them have floated upward or downward as DOD has struggled to get maximum strategic mileage from its budgets. The program budget for 2005 is a product of this past experience as well as an appraisal of current priorities. During 2005–2009, significant changes will take place in several programs. For example, the general purpose forces (GPF) program will acquire in 2009 a share that is $13.3 billion greater than its 2005 share. This increase owes mostly to funding of new procurement programs for these forces. Offsetting reductions will be made in six other programs, each of which will see its budget share go down by one-half to one full percentage point. To be sure, most of these programs will receive more funds in absolute terms because the total DOD budget will be growing, but some of this increase will be eroded by inflation. The key point is that marginal benefits from an enhanced GPF program are being purchased at an opportunity cost to the other programs.

As table 16–7 shows, funding for strategic nuclear forces, which consumed over 7 percent of the defense budget during the Cold War, has gone steadily downward in the years since. With the $8.8 billion allocated to this program in 2005, DOD retains a reduced offensive force of ICBMs, SSBN, and SLBM submarines, and bombers that will be able to deploy 2,000–2,500 warheads once downsizing is complete in a few years. Although a budget of $9.2 billion is planned for 2009, this may not be enough for the deployment of national missile defenses now under way. If additional funds are needed, they might be transferred from the R&D program for missile defense, which may be tapering off then. In the distant future, today's missiles and bombers will need modernization and replacement as they age. Thus funding for this program may need to increase, but a return to Cold War levels is not in the cards.

General purpose forces constitute the biggest program. At $144 billion and 35.8 percent of the DOD budget in 2005, it is nearly two and a half times as big as the next largest program (training, medical, and other [TM&O]) at $60.1 billion. This buys the 13 Army and Marine divisions, 10 Air Force air expeditionary forces, 12 carriers and other naval combatants, and other assets that constitute today's active-duty conventional combat forces. The GPF program does not include all U.S. combat forces; it excludes the Guard and Reserve forces and Special Operations Forces, among others. The Guard and Reserve program, funded in 2005 at about $31.7 billion and about 8 percent of the budget, generates 865,000 trained Reservists from all services. Thousands of these Reservists have recently been serving full-time in such distant places as Iraq, Afghanistan, and the Balkans. Critics often portray parts of this program as a questionable investment, arguing that some Army National Guard divisions and brigades are not sufficiently ready to play a meaningful role in U.S. defense strategy and war plans. Whether this area experiences funding increases, or decreases, or internal reallocations is to be seen. The much-praised SOF program has grown since its inception in 1987, but it appears that it will level off at about 1.4 percent of the budget. Even persistent critics of DOD acknowledge the valuable capabilities provided by the SOF program for the war on terrorism and other new-era missions.

The program for intelligence and communications largely escapes public notice, but since 1980 it has grown in size and importance. In 2005, its spending totaled $55.5 billion and was 13.8 percent of the defense budget. Funding for 2009 is $64.9 billion, at a slightly reduced budget share of 13.3 percent. The steady rise in this program reflects the growing role of information networks in U.S. force operations and transformation strategy. Parts of this program are classified, but open-source DOD documents show a vigorous set of acquisition measures. For example, space programs, mostly funded by the Air Force, consume $3.3 billion per year for such measures as new satellites for communications, navigation, and early warning, as well as new launchers for putting them into orbit. In order to improve tactical force operations, the Army is funding nearly 100 measures for new communications and electronic equipment, at a cost of $2.3 billion per year. The Navy and Air Force are spending similar amounts for the same purpose. The promise of this expensive program is that its information technologies and systems can greatly strengthen U.S. military capabilities in the coming years. The drawback is that this program has become expensive. From 2000 to 2005, spending for it rose from $32 billion to $55.5 billion. This major shift of funds may well have been justified, but it undeniably came at an opportunity cost, as those funds were not available for other programs.

The strategic mobility program, small 30 years ago, has grown in funding and importance. The reason has been a concerted DOD effort to speed the wartime deployment of U.S. forces overseas through increased prepositioning, air transports, and cargo ships. In 2005, the mobility program hovered at about 4 percent of the defense budget; the exact amount varies as a function of procurement each year. The R&D program, which funds creation of new technologies and weapons, has likewise claimed a growing share of the defense budget over the past 25 years. Today, it stands at $45.6 billion and claims 11.3 percent of the DOD budget. In future years, its funding is projected to grow modestly, but its share of the overall DOD budget will go down to 9.9 percent. The three programs of central supply and maintenance (CS&M), TM&O, and administration basically define the U.S. military infrastructure in the continental United States. In 1980, these three programs together consumed fully 34 percent of the defense budget, but in 2005, their share had dropped to 23.3 percent. This reflects a persistent effort to trim domestic infrastructure in order to devote more resources to deployable forces and other high-payoff programs. Even so, today these three programs remain large: $94 billion for 2005 and $107.7 billion for 2009. Support of other nations accounts for only a tiny portion of the program budget, but plays an important role in U.S. overseas military activities.

What are the strategic implications of today's spending patterns for these 11 programs? Conceptual order can be brought to this issue by grouping the 11 programs into 2 broad categories: combat programs and support programs. The combat category includes the four programs that directly field combat forces: strategic forces, GPF, Guard and Reserve forces, and SOF. The support category includes the other seven programs that provide various forms of support to the combat forces. While this categorization may oversimplify a complex reality, it helps shed light on the perennial issue of the tooth-to-tail ratio in the U.S. defense budget.

As table 16–8 shows, the defense spending split between combat and support programs has hovered at about 50–50 for the past 25 years. A reduction by 3 percentage points for combat forces during 1990–2000 seems likely to be reversed by 2009, restoring the 50–50 balance. This share of funding for combat programs has been necessary, because the forces require adequate personnel, operating revenues, and modernization, and it has been possible, because DOD has succeeded in keeping support costs under control. While costs for intelligence and communication have risen, DOD has managed to control expenses for administration, CS&M, and TM&O, trimming budget shares for each of these programs.

Table 16–8. **Allocation of Funds Between Combat and Support Programs**

	Combat Programs (in $billions)	**Support Programs (in $billions)**
2005	$191.6	$211.0
2009	$245.5	$244.4
Percent of DOD Budget		
1980	50.4	49.6
1990	52.2	47.8
2000	49.2	50.8
2005	47.6	52.4
2009	50.2	49.8

	Percent of DOD Budget					**Budget (in $billions)**	
	1980	**1990**	**2000**	**2005**	**2009**	**2005**	**2009**
Combat Programs	50.4	52.2	49.2	47.6	50.2	$191.6	$245.5
Support Programs	49.6	47.8	50.8	52.4	49.8	$211.0	$244.4

The data show that DOD has succeeded in preventing a growing infrastructure tail from starving its combat teeth. Even so, DOD continues to spend 50 percent of its budget—over $200 billion per year—on support activities. This is a great deal of money, and some critics say it is too much. Moreover, about one-half of DOD's active military manpower and most of its civilian workforce are employed in these programs, leaving only about one-half of active servicemembers available to deploy overseas in a war: 750,000 of the total 1.458 million in 2005. Many of these support activities are vital to the effectiveness of combat forces, which could not operate without satellites, information grids, cargo transports, well-maintained weapons, and healthy, educated soldiers. However, the money spent on these activities comes at the expense of buying the combat forces bet-ter equipment, training, and stocks. Whether a proper balance is being struck between combat forces and support programs in today's world is unclear, but the question is likely to be asked over and over for many years. If there are shortages in funding for combat forces and their investment priorities, the support programs will be natural candidates for trimming. If they are trimmed, the challenge will be to do so in a sensible manner.

In this era of information warfare, the idea of trimming expenditures on intelli-gence and communications will come across as heresy to advocates of this program. Indeed, its size seems to be growing, not shrinking: in January 2005, DOD decided to add about $1 billion per year to fund sophisticated communications satellites and space-based radars. But to outside critics, an annual budget of about $65 billion per year in 2009 seems quite big: indeed, it will be DOD's second-largest program. At a minimum, its myriad elements deserve close scrutiny, not automatic acceptance simply because they fall into a program of strategic importance for transformation.

A similar judgment can be made about TM&O. On the surface, nobody should question the importance of training U.S. servicemembers and providing them health care. Yet, this program is about the same size as intelligence and communications, and it is full of elements that merit scrutiny to ensure that its funds are necessary and well-spent. Moreover, preventing this program from growing above current projections may be a problem. Today, health care costs about $25 billion: $17 billion for operations and maintenance, the rest for personnel and investment. But with costs for national health care soaring and the ranks of DOD retirees swelling, many observers judge that this expense could double in the coming decade or so. While adequate health care for the U.S. military must remain a top priority, economic reasoning will also be necessary.

Can CS&M be trimmed? It already has been shrunk in past years by belt-tight-ening activities, but at $23.5 billion in 2005, it still remains large as well as complex, a labyrinth that defies ready understanding. Perhaps DOD's ongoing efforts to foster a revolution in business practices can reduce this budget through outsourcing, private contracting, and similar measures. In summary, a fair judgment for all of these sup-port programs is that they provide important services to national defense and de-serve adequate funding. But they also come at an opportunity cost because they draw money away from investment accounts, which need to grow in coming years. To the extent they can be trimmed at the margins, perhaps by $5 billion–$10 billion per year, they would provide valuable savings that could be translated into procurement and other investments, thereby reducing the need for painful sacrifices there.

Functional Activities

Shifting patterns in defense spending are noteworthy in the category of line item functional activities. Over the past 15 years, a main trend has been the rise in spending on peacetime operations and maintenance (O&M), which has grown from 30 percent of the defense budget in 1990 to 35 percent in 2005 even though force posture and manpower have shrunk by about one-third. In the future, a key DOD aim is to elevate procurement spending from $75 billion in 2005 to $114 billion in current dollars by

2009. Whether this aim can be accomplished will depend heavily on whether O&M spending can be kept under control and perhaps even trimmed. The interaction between O&M and procurement will be a key issue for systems analysis for years to come, but the other functional activities will need close scrutiny as well, both to ensure that critical requirements are met and to prevent unnecessary spending.

Table 16–9 shows current and future distributions among the various components, and a snapshot of past trends. Back in the 1980s, spending on military personnel, O&M, and procurement was about equal. In 1989, for example, expenditures for them were as follows: $78 billion for military personnel, $86 billion for O&M, and $80 billion for procurement. Indeed, throughout much of the 1980s, procurement spending exceeded O&M spending. Today, a definite hierarchy exists, and O&M is at the top. It exceeds military personnel by $35 billion, and it is nearly double procurement spending. By 2009, the difference between O&M and procurement is projected to narrow somewhat because of the fast rise in procurement spending, but even so, O&M spending will still be $40 billion higher, at $164.6 billion.

Table 16–9. **Spending Patterns for Functional Activities (Budget Authority)**

	Expenditures (in current $billions)		Trends in shares (percent of defense budget)				
	2005	**2009**	**1980**	**1990**	**2000**	**2005**	**2009**
Military Personnel	$106.3	$122.1	30	27	28	26	25
Operations and Maintenance	$141.2	$164.6	32	30	39	35	34
Procurement	$74.9	$114.0	25	28	20	19	23
RDT&E	$68.9	$70.6	10	12	13	17	14
Construction and Housing	$9.4	$13.7	3	3	2	2	3
Other	$1.9	$3.9	—	—	—	1	1
Total	$402.6	$488.9	100	100	100	100	100

Although the procurement budget is slated to rise to $114 billion in current dollars by 2009, it will still consume only 23 percent of the defense budget, which is lower than the 25–28 percent level of the modernization effort of the 1980s. After 2009, additional increases in procurement may be needed in order to fund the bow wave of weapons buying that will take hold then. Because spending on the other functional activities must increase in order to offset inflation, and to provide real growth in some cases, the implication is that DOD will be struggling to strike a balance among all six areas through 2020 and beyond.

Military Personnel Account, Construction and Housing Account

The military personnel account includes pay for Active troops and reservists, plus about $13 billion for retired pay. As table 16–9 shows, spending on military personnel consumes a smaller share of the defense budget today than it did 20 or 30 years ago. This is mainly because active-duty troop levels have dropped from 2.06 million in 1980 to 1.46 million today. A similar trend has taken place in the DOD civilian workforce, which is funded in the O&M budget: it has declined from about 1 million in 1980 to 673,000 today. The budget share allocated to military personnel is projected to fall from 26 percent in 2005 to 25 percent by 2009, but even so, total spending in this account is projected to rise from $106.3 billion to $122.1 billion by 2009. The increase is needed to fund the annual pay raises necessary to attract qualified people into military service. During the 1990s, military pay rose at an average rate of 3.2 percent per year in current dollars. During 2000–2004, it rose at an average annual rate of 4.8 percent. During 2005–2009, it is expected to rise at 3.4 percent annually, and the same rate will apply to DOD's civilian workforce, which today costs about $50 billion.

During 2004–2009, construction and housing will benefit from a shift of funds totaling 1 percent of the defense budget. The effect will be to restore the shares that these activities had from 1980 to 2000. Today, spending on construction and family housing is $9.4 billion, and it is slated to rise to $13.7 billion by 2009 in current dollars, about a 35 percent increase in real spending. This increase is needed largely because in past years, DOD has fallen behind in updating its buildings, plants, and facilities. Many are aging, so higher O&M spending is needed to keep them usable. Increased spending will allow DOD to accelerate its rate of closing old bases, repairing old plants, and building new plants and family housing, thus lowering O&M spending over the long term.

Efforts to control spending for both military personnel and construction and housing will be challenging. With the war against terrorism and difficult overseas assignments for many servicemembers, a natural tendency will be to elevate military pay above the annual 3.4 percent increases now planned. Such increases doubtless will be merited and perhaps essential, yet they would have a major cumulative impact on the budget. For example, an additional 1 percent increase in a single year would elevate military pay by about $1 billion today. If 1 percent increases were funded each year for 5 years, the effect will be to elevate this account by $6 billion in 2009. Unless the topline is increased similarly, this could drain equal funds away from procurement. A similar calculus applies to construction and housing; if increases in these accounts go beyond those now planned, they, too, could drain funds from procurement. In retrospect, it is unfortunate that DOD was unable to allocate more funds to construction and housing in the 1990s, thereby avoiding the backlog now. A lesson is that it is better to fund increases to this account during a procurement holiday than when procurement, too, is on the rise.

The O&M Quandary

The fact that O&M spending has risen steeply becomes obvious when O&M budgets for the past 30 years are measured in comparable terms. In constant 2005 dollars, DOD was spending $59,700 on O&M per Active servicemember in 1990, a year when military readiness was judged to be high. That figure for 2005 is $97,040. Table 16–10 shows how

this upward trend unfolded. O&M budgets rose from $88 billion in 1990 to $141 billion in 2005 (current dollars), but when measured in constant 2005 dollars, they actually fell between 1990 and 2000, rising again between 2000 and 2005 by $18 billion.
The slight decline in real O&M spending during the 1990s, however, is misleading, because military manpower levels were dropping by one-third then. The noteworthy trend
is the rise in per-capita O&M spending by 62 percent between 1990 and 2005. The rise in
per-capita spending on O&M is not due to the wars in Afghanistan and Iraq, which are
funded by separate Congressional supplemental appropriations. Nor is the main reason
the upsurge in other international activities, such as peacekeeping and engagement with
new countries (for example, training and exercises with partners), that are funded within
the normal budget: in recent years, these activities have cost only about $3 billion–$4
billion per year. One reason is that, in many areas, U.S. military forces are operating at
a higher tempo today than in the past. Part of this increase is due to new missions, but
it is also due to long-established practices that have not been modified to free resources
for new activities. For example, the practice of rotating servicemen to new assignments
every 1 or 2 years, rather than keeping them in parent units for 3 to 5 years, contributes
to high tempo. This upsurge has not, however, produced a major increase in readiness
indicators for combat forces, such as aircrew training hours, ship deployment dates, or
usage rates for ground weapons: most of these indicators have stayed constant or slipped
somewhat downward in recent years. This raises questions about whether the rise in O&M
spending is producing a commensurate increase in U.S. combat power and preparedness,
or instead reflects higher tempo without major benefits in performance and output.

Table 16–10. **Trends in O&M Budgets (Including Health Care)**

O&M Budgets	1975	1980	1990	2000	2005
Current $billions	$26.3	$46.4	$88.3	$108.8	$141.2
Constant 2005 $billions	$93.9	$107.6	$128	$122.9	$141.2
Military Manpower $thousands	2,129	2,063	2,144	1,449	1,455
Per Capita O&M (Constant 2004 $)	$44,100	$52,160	$59,700	$84,820	$97,040

The rise in O&M spending is due to the interaction of multiple factors, no single
one of which dominates. The cost of the civilian workforce, which consumes about $50
billion of the O&M budget per year, is not one of the reasons. Since 1980, this cost (in
constant 2005 dollars) has shrunk from $60 billion to its current level because the civil-
ian workforce has declined from 991,000 to 688,000. Some increase in per-capita O&M
spending was inevitable as force downsizing occurred in the 1990s; some activities such as
military schools and bases could not be trimmed in direct proportion to declining manpower levels. Soaring healthcare costs, which reflect trends in national healthcare owing
to new technologies and higher standards of care, have been a key component of the increase, accounting for $17 billion in 2005 and $22.5 billion in 2009. Other factors have

included rising costs for maintenance of sophisticated new weapons, increased need for repair of aging weapons, and increased costs for military fuels, spare parts, facility upgrades, computerization, education and training, and hiring of contractors. Beyond this, O&M funds are popular within the military services because they are flexible and produce results quickly. When tight lids are not placed on this account, the natural tendency is for O&M spending to rise at whatever rate the traffic will bear. The sheer multiplicity of causes makes O&M spending hard to control; DOD cannot just turn one or two faucets and hope to reduce the flow by much.

The steady rise in per-capita O&M spending has affected all of the services. Table 16–11 shows how the O&M budget was distributed among the services during 2005. It suggests that the O&M budget is not synonymous with the readiness of active combat forces: the account for these forces totals only $59.9 billion, most of which is devoted to force readiness. Even here, moreover, roughly $15 billion is spent on such non-readiness activities as facility maintenance and restoration. Administration and service-wide activities cost $31.5 billion in 2005. Within the services, this account includes about 20 different measures, such as base operations, facilities, manpower, management, commissaries, and the like. Across DOD, this account includes the Office of the Secretary of Defense and the Joint Staff, seven agencies such as Defense Contract Management, dependent education, Special Operations Forces O&M, and $7 billion of classified programs.

A key issue is the future of O&M spending. Current plans envision the O&M budget rising from $141.2 billion in 2005 to $164.6 billion in 2009: a 17 percent increase in current dollars, and a 6 percent increase in constant dollars. O&M's budget share is projected to drop slightly, from 35 percent today to 34 percent in 2009, but O&M will continue to claim a larger share of the defense budget than it did during 1980–2000. The difference between 34 percent (in 2009) and 30 percent (in 1990) is significant: about $16 billion annually in 2009. If these funds could instead be spent on acquisition, for example, they could elevate procurement spending in 2009 from $114 billion to $130 billion, a 14 percent increase that could speed buying of new aircraft, ships, and ground weapons. Doubtless many of the past and future increases in O&M spending were desirable or necessary due to conditions. Whether all of these increases are required is a matter of some debate.

One senior Pentagon official was reported by a newspaper to have complained that "DOD is being eaten alive by O&M costs." If so, he was not alone in his concerns. The Navy is trying to reduce its O&M spending in order to liberate more funds for procurement.[4] Thus far, DOD's main effort to reduce O&M expenses has focused on Base Realignment and Closure (BRAC). The BRAC effort has partly succeeded, but its progress has been slow because of the political controversies associated with base closings and consolidation. BRAC, moreover, is only a partial solution to the O&M quandary. The need to control O&M spending is understood across much of DOD's senior leadership, but any attempt to pursue a DOD-wide effort is constrained by bureaucratic and analytical impediments. Unlike procurement and RDT&E, O&M budgets are not centrally managed, and their myriad expenses are determined at lower levels of the bureaucracy. DOD does not possess an overarching concept, a management information system, an integrated set of performance measures, or data-equipped economic models of choice for O&M. As a result, O&M

Table 16–11. **O&M Budget for Fiscal Year 2005 (Budget Authority, Current $Billions)**

	Army	Navy	Air Force	DOD-wide	Total
Active Operating Forces	16.4	25.4	15.9	2.2	59.9
Mobility	0.5	0.8	3.3	0.1	4.7
Training and Recruiting	3.3	2.6	3.0	0.4	9.3
Administration, service-wide	5.8	4.7	6.2	14.8	31.5
Guard/Reserve	6.5	1.4	6.3	—	14.2
Other *	—	—	—	21.6	21.6
Total	32.5	34.9	34.7	39.1	141.2

* Includes $17 billion for the Defense Health Program plus funds for counterdrug activities, inspector general, and other activities.

spending is hard to evaluate and control. Becoming better at both evaluation and control is imperative if DOD is to prevent the O&M budget from growing further in ways that could eat into its plans for accelerated procurement.

Research, Development, Testing, and Engineering

Surface appearances suggest a picture of health for the RDT&E budget.[5] In 2005, RDT&E had a budget of $68.9 billion, or 17 percent of the entire defense budget. Although the RDT&E budget is expected to be at $70.6 billion in 2009, its budget share will drop to 14 percent; however, this is still well above the 10–12 percent share of the 1980s and 1990s. The RDT&E process is often criticized for being stodgy and slow and for producing "gold-plated" weapons, but its past successes are a main reason why current U.S. military forces are the best equipped in the world. The main purpose of RDT&E today is to develop new weapons and technologies for procurement and transformation in the coming years. The RDT&E budget is divided into service shares and seven functional categories, as shown in table 16–12.

While service shares are important, the functional categories reveal more about how the RDT&E budget is distributed. The first three functional categories—basic research, applied research, and advanced technology development—include activities during the early stages of RDT&E, when research on new technologies and weapons is getting under way. The other four categories—advanced component development and prototypes, system development and demonstration, RDT&E management support, and operational systems development—provide funds for the stages of the RDT&E process when new ideas have taken shape, prototypes are emerging, and the new weapons and technologies are subjected to full-scale testing to determine whether they are ready for procurement. The difference in spending between these two different clusters is substantial. The first three categories receive $10.5 billion, the other four receive $58.4 billion, or 85 percent of the RDT&E budget. Programs now in the latter four categories include such major new

Table 16–12. **Distribution of RDT&E Budget, 2005**

Service Shares		Functional Categories	
		Basic Research	$1.3 billion
		Applied Research	$3.9 billion
Army	$10.4 billion	Advanced Technology Development	$5.3 billion
Navy	$16.4 billion	Advanced Component Development and Prototypes	$15.3 billion
Air Force	$21.1 billion	System Development & Demonstration	$19.3 billion
DOD-Wide	$21.0 billion	RDT&E Management Support	$3.3 billion
		Operational Systems Development	$20.5 billion
Total	**$68.9 billion**	**Total**	**$68.9 billion**

weapons as the F–22, F–35 Joint Strike Fighter, and new ship designs. The reason for spending so much on these later stages is that a great deal of testing, evaluation, and further development must take place after new weapons start to take physical shape, and even after they already are deployed. The drawing-board phase, although critical to success, is less costly because it largely involves ideas, studies, and initial demonstrations, not full-blown development and testing.

Even so, critics question whether enough funds are being allocated to the first three stages of RDT&E. This especially is the case for basic research. A DOD goal has been to set aside 3 percent of the RDT&E budget for basic research, but only about 1.9 percent was allocated in the 2005 budget (Congress subsequently elevated the amount). Whether even 3 percent is enough is itself an issue. Basic research may not have critical results for 5 or 10 years, but it has a major bearing on future technology, weapons, and systems in 10 or 20 years and beyond. Most major breakthroughs, such as stealth technology, come from basic research as well as applied research, not testing of already assembled hardware. From today's small budget for basic research, less than $100 million is spent on in-house research by DOD's laboratories. The rest is contracted to outside sources, mainly universities. An emphasis on outside research is deemed necessary because most ideas for new technologies, especially information systems and networks, are now developed there. Nonetheless, critics wonder whether DOD's laboratories, which once were an engine of innovation in military technology, are being unwisely neglected. Shifting an additional $1 billion to basic research, including more funds to DOD labs, might make sense, and would not appreciably damage other programs.

The RDT&E process is driven by developments on both the supply side and the demand side. That is, it responds to ideas for new technologies and weapons systems that bubble upward from ongoing research, but it also responds to the demands of DOD's civilian leaders and the military services. The result is a diverse mixture of measures. Major items of today's RDT&E effort are displayed in table 16–13, which illuminates the importance attached to intelligence, communications, and space as well as to national missile defense, which together account for nearly one-third of the RDT&E budget. The rest of the list shows spending for major conventional weapons systems. The table accounts for nearly one-half of the total RDT&E budget. The remaining funds are distributed in smaller parcels of various sizes among hundreds of items of various shapes and purposes. In past years, the RDT&E process focused mainly on weapons platforms, but focus has now shifted to information networks, sensors, missiles, and munitions. Individually, items in these categories do not consume much, but collectively, they are a large expense, and will significantly determine the future combat capabilities of U.S. forces.

Table 16–13. **Sampling of Major Items in RDT&E Effort**

	Spending Levels (2005 budget)
Intelligence, Communications, and Space	$13.8 billion
National Missile Defense	$9.1 billion
F–35 Joint Strike Fighter	$4.6 billion
Army Armored Combat Vehicles	$2.7 billion
Navy Ship Design	$1.4 billion
Unmanned Aerial Vehicles	$0.6 billion
V–22 Osprey	$0.4 billion
AWACS	$0.3 billion
Total (47.8 percent of RDT&E total of $68.9 billion)	$32.9 billion

Critics' main question about the RDT&E process is not whether it is capable of eventually producing new weapons and technologies, but whether it can do so quickly enough to meet today's needs. Past years have shown a growing tendency toward ever longer RDT&E efforts before a new weapon finally gets fielded: often 10 years or more to complete all stages of RDT&E. The ultimate result has been impressive new weapons, but during the interim, the U.S. military has had to continue using old and even obsolete weapons. A lengthy, inward-looking RDT&E process also runs the risk, some charge, of producing expensive weapons that may not meet the new requirements that have emerged in the years since the original ideas for them were created.

In order to help correct these problems, DOD is now beginning to pursue a new RDT&E practice called *spiral development*. The idea is to field new systems quickly, even though they may not yet possess the sophistication that would come from a prolonged development cycle. The hope is that by fielding interim new systems swiftly, the military can benefit from them, experiment with them, and provide guidance on how they can be further improved as they continue through the RDT&E process. This way, good systems can be separated from bad systems in the early stages, and the RDT&E community can get mid-course corrections to guide its ongoing efforts. The future of spiral development and associated concepts is to be seen. What seems clear is that today's fast-paced changes in technology and world affairs will no longer permit RDT&E cycles of 10 years or more. Ultimately, DOD aspires to reduce the average cycle to 5 years, but this is a vision, not yet a concrete achievement.

Regardless of whether new practices are adopted, the RDT&E budget will remain one of the most dynamic areas of the defense budget. Although public attention is focused on a few big-ticket items, hundreds of smaller items are continuously transiting through the various stages of RDT&E. Many are destined for procurement, but some do not pan out or are shoved aside by competitors. As a result, the internal components of the RDT&E budget are constantly changing even though overall funding levels and broad distribution patterns may not shift dramatically. In recent years, the RDT&E process has been mainly focused on producing the upcoming new generation of weapons and munitions as well as new information technologies. As this goal is achieved in the next few years, the challenge facing RDT&E will be to shift focus to the next generation of weapons, which is likely to be considerably different from the generation now lined up for procurement. RDT&E will also need to address other new technologies, such as nanotechnology and the biomaterials revolution.

These efforts will ensure that RDT&E remains a major part of the defense budget for the distant future; even so, money spent on RDT&E is not available for other worthy defense programs, including procurement. During the 1980s, the procurement budget was over twice the size of the RDT&E budget, but today the two budgets are close to the same size. By 2009, procurement is slated to be about 60 percent larger than RDT&E, but even so, a robust RDT&E budget will come at the expense of less money for procurement. For this reason, cost-effectiveness standards should be applied not only to the overall size of the RDT&E budget, but to its internal components as well. Like other areas of defense spending, RDT&E needs economic reasoning in addition to scientific vision and engineering prowess. Economic reasoning must include a clear sense of internal program priorities because, even though large, the RDT&E budget is not large enough to fund all measures that arguably could be funded. The RDT&E process must be driven not only by promising future technologies but also by future U.S. military requirements and sensible priorities. Strategic guidance on future requirements is especially important because they shape the products that ultimately emerge. Responding to joint requirements as well as those being developed by the services promises to be one of the biggest challenges on the RDT&E agenda.

Procurement

The main weapons systems of the coming procurement effort were described in chapter 15 and are not repeated here. Rather, this discussion places the growing procurement budget in the larger context of the entire defense budget, its new spending patterns, and its future priorities, to illuminate the challenges facing future procurement. In the mid-1990s, the procurement budget had shrunk to a low of $45 billion per year, but since then, it has grown to about $75 billion for 2005. Under current plans, it will continue rising in the coming years, reaching $114 billion by 2009, and perhaps $120 billion–$125 billion by 2012. After that, procurement budgets may grow slowly in current dollars, but in constant dollars they are likely to stay relatively flat if the overall DOD budget does not receive steady real increases. Even so, procurement is the fastest rising part of the defense budget today. As it grows, its internal spending patterns will change. Today, only about 25 percent of the procurement budget is devoted to new major weapons; the rest is spent on secondary items, steady-state replenishment, and upgrades to existing weapons. By 2012 and beyond, about 55–60 percent of the procurement budget may be available for spending on major new weapons. DOD's aim will be to use these funds for a major modernization of U.S. combat forces during the coming decade and beyond.

Table 16–14. **Alternative Distributions of 2009 Defense Budget (Current $Billions)**

	Reagan-Era Model	DOD Projection	Difference
Military Personnel	$122.2	$122.1	—
O&M	$136.9	$164.6	+ $27.7
Procurement	$156.4	$114.0	- $42.4
RDT&E	$53.8	$70.6	+ $16.8
Construction and Housing	$14.7	$13.7	- $1.0
Other	$4.9	$3.9	+ $1.0
Total	$488.9	$488.9	

The projected rise in procurement budgets should be judged in perspective, because it is not as big as it seems. Although the procurement budget of 2009 will be 23 percent of the defense budget, this is well below the levels of past procurement cycles. An interesting comparison can be made between the projected DOD budget for 2009 and a hypothetical budget whose funds are distributed according to the model of the Reagan era. As table 16–14 shows, the procurement budget for 2009 would be fully $42.4 billion higher if the Reagan-era model still prevailed. The table shows the extent to which lower procurement funds are due to high levels of spending on O&M and RDT&E.

Because today's force posture is smaller than the Reagan era, arguably a procurement budget of only $114 billion for 2009 could provide proportional spending. But this calculus ignores the higher costs of today's weapons, which elevate the spending requirement upward by $20 billion–$30 billion or more. As a result, the projected procurement budgets of future years are not lavish or even well-endowed. If anything, they are small when judged in relation to the need to fund a big bow wave of procurement programs in multiple categories affecting all services. Moreover, it should be remembered that each year, at least $45 billion–$50 billion will need to be spent on secondary items and related assets. This means that in 2009 and beyond, at most $65 billion–$70 billion, not $114 billion, will be available for major new weapons.

A risk is that the projected rise in procurement spending could be crowded out by unplanned increases in such other areas as military personnel, operations and maintenance, or construction. Because those activities will still consume over 60 percent of the defense budget by 2012, an unanticipated 5 percent rise in their expenses could cause nearly a 15 percent drop in procurement spending, which would have serious consequences because it could cut spending on new weapons by 30 percent per year. Conversely, if spending on those other activities were pared by 5 percent, procurement spending or other programs could be increased by significant amounts, and spending on major weapons could rise by 30 percent.

DOD's ability to extract maximum strategic mileage from its future procurement budgets will be greatly influenced by the individual costs of new weapons systems such as the F–35 JSF. To the extent these costs are kept under control, more weapons can be bought in each procurement budget. If their costs grow, fewer weapons will be purchasable. Current cost estimates are based on such factors as expenses for labor, parts, and assembly as well as anticipated economies of scale as industries gain experience and efficiencies are attained. Experience shows that efficient production techniques can lessen expenses. Equally true, however, past experience has shown escalating costs brought about by decisions to add new technologies and capabilities as an entire weapons system marches through production over a period of years.

The interaction between available procurement budgets and spending requirements is illustrated in table 16–15. The table shows that during 2005–2020, $950 billion (in constant 2005 dollars) could be available for buying new major weapons, assuming that procurement budgets do not grow appreciably after 2010 in real terms. Although total procurement spending will approach $1,600 billion, because of other requirements, spending on major new weapons will be limited to the lower amount. Expenses for acquiring new weapons in six categories mean that spending requirements in this period could range from $900 billion to $1,250 billion, depending upon the size of each program and its per-unit costs. As a result, future procurement budgets could be large enough to meet expenses if costs for these six weapons programs fall at the low end of the range. But if costs rise to the high end, a budgetary shortfall of as much as $300 billion could emerge. In this event, DOD might have only 70 percent of the funds that are needed, and thus will be compelled to acquire weapons at a significantly slower rate than now planned. A funding shortfall of fully 30 percent may be unlikely, but even a quite plausible shortfall of 15–20 percent could compel a major adjustment to DOD's plans for modernization.[6]

Significant budget shortfalls would not necessarily force DOD to abandon its planned procurement campaign altogether, or even leave any single measure grossly under-funded. But shortfalls could compel DOD to engage in belt-tightening and stretching-out of its programs, thus delaying the pace of modernization and limiting its scope. While such prioritizing might not fatally undermine U.S. defense strategy or produce deficient forces, it could be painful within DOD and the services, necessitating adoption of management strategies such as SLEP measures for aging systems and high-low mixes for new systems. The problem could be worse if procurement budgets fail to grow to the levels now planned; it could ease either if DOD succeeds in extracting savings from elsewhere in the budget, or if the President and Congress can be persuaded to fund bigger budgets.

Table 16–15. **Future Procurement Budgets for New Weapons versus Requirements for 2005–2020 (Current $Billions)***

Measures	Cost**
Expeditionary Warfare Measures	$85–115
National Missile Defense	$80–150
Army Modernization and FCS	$110–160
Combat Aircraft Modernization	$275–350
Support Aircraft	$75–100
Shipbuilding	$275–375
Total predicted spending requirements	**$900–1,250**
Predicted procurement budgets	$950
Potential shortfall	$0–300

* Author's estimates based on multiple sources.
**Cost estimates reflect alternative assumptions about unit costs and production programs in each category. For modernization programs, cost estimates include costs for buying major new weapons and for upgrading of existing major weapons.

Regardless of future budgets, the tempo of procurement will be accelerating at a rate that will confront DOD with challenges as it spends funds in the six areas of endeavor shown in table 16–15. DOD will need to engage in a careful balancing act to ensure that procurement activities in each area, and the distribution among them, make sense each year. The distribution pattern shown in table 16–15 is merely illustrative: a different pattern of distributing funds among these six areas might make better sense, or the distribution pattern among them could change from one year to the next in response to changing priorities. For all of these reasons, procurement management will have to respond to dynamic changes in priorities, to fluctuating budget levels, and to shifting spending patterns. Because this effort must be carried out within a larger defense budget that is also in flux, it will be all the more demanding. A major task will be to create an optimal investment strategy to help guide procurement.

Analysis of New Spending Priorities

DOD's need to pursue the twin goals of being prepared for both expeditionary warfare and strategic dominance means that its future budgets will be stretched to their limits. This especially will be the case if these budgets do not benefit from real growth to their toplines; this concern applies not only today, but throughout the decade of 2010–2020 and beyond. The likelihood of tight fiscal constraints means that persistent efforts to allocate funds wisely will be needed during a period in which new spending priorities must be shaped. All of this adds up to a demanding analytical agenda ahead.

In retrospect, perhaps DOD pursued high-tech transformation and standoff strike capabilities too zealously during 2001–2004, to the neglect of the Army and other boots-on-the-ground assets for expeditionary warfare. But now that the pendulum is beginning to swing in the other direction, there may be a risk that it will swing too far by cutting too heavily into procurement of new air and naval weapons for long-term strategic dominance missions. This risk could grow if, simultaneously, spending on such other accounts as military personnel, intelligence and communications, health care, RDT&E, operations and maintenance, and construction edges upward, with cumulative effects that compel cutbacks to procurement budgets for all services. To avoid such risks and their damaging impacts, careful scrutiny of the entire defense budget is necessary, with economic reasoning and stiff priorities in mind.

Because DOD is aware of its need to shape new priorities wisely, it acted in early 2003 to reform its long-established Planning, Programming, and Budgetary System (PPBS) for managing the budget. Originally a product of the industrial age and the Cold War, the old PPBS process required that DOD prepare such time-consuming documents as annual Defense Planning Guidance, Service Program Objective Memoranda (POMs), Issue Papers, Budget Submissions, and Five-year Defense Plans. While this PPBS process was extensive, it left limited time for reflective thinking.

The new process is called the Planning, Programming, Budgetary, and Execution System. It establishes a 2-year cycle in which a fully elaborated review is performed in the first, even-numbered year, succeeded by a less-elaborate framework for the second, odd-numbered year of each cycle. This step is intended to liberate more time for in-depth analysis and planning during the second year. Secretary of Defense Donald Rumsfeld further strengthened this streamlined process, announcing two new forms of secretarial guidance to be issued early in the planning cycle. In the new approach, "Strategic Planning Guidance" is to be issued in late fall of even-numbered years to provide clear guidance on overarching strategic and budgetary themes. The following spring, a second document called "Joint Programming Guidance" is to provide detailed directives on spending patterns. DOD announced that the intent of these two documents is to focus greater attention on big strategic issues early in the cycle, and to defer decisions on budgetary details until after strategic matters are first resolved.[7]

Even if this new 2-year planning cycle with its two new forms of secretarial guidance proves successful, further steps could be taken to intensify the focus on transformation. The activities currently sorted into 11 defense programs could be recategorized to provide a better focus on new defense priorities. Table 16–16 proposes a set of new candidates. Of particular note are its categories for joint expeditionary programs, major theater war forces, forward presence and international activities, C4ISR forces, and medical programs; these are all areas of vital concern that justify focused attention. In addition, the old practice of Service POMs could be replaced by writing Joint POMs that integrate separate service activities under a single umbrella in key issue-areas. An example might be a Joint POM written by the Joint Staff on C4ISR programs and information networks, which are key to transformation. Joint POMs could also be written on mobility forces, overseas presence forces, and other areas where joint planning and programming is vital.

A case can also be made for reforming the defense budget's functional categories. Table 16–17 displays a proposed new scheme. It combines pay for military personnel and civilian personnel into a single category. It replaces the O&M budget with a new Operations

Table 16–16. **Toward a Proposed New Set of Defense Programs**

Existing Defense Programs	Proposed Defense Programs
Strategic forces	Program 1: Joint Expeditionary Programs
General purpose forces	Program 2: Major Theater War Forces
Intel and communications	Program 3: Special Operations Forces
Mobility	Program 4: Mobility Forces
Guard and Reserve	Program 5: Forward Presence and International Activities
R&D	Program 6: Strategic Forces and Missile Defense
Central supply and maintenance	Program 7: C^{4}ISR Forces
Training, medical, and other	Program 8: Research and Development
Administration	Program 9: Medical Programs
Support of other nations	Program 10: Central Supply and Maintenance
Special operations forces	Program 11: Personnel, Training, and Development

Budget that no longer contains civilian pay and is divided into two categories: active force operations and other operations. It divides the procurement budget into two categories: major weapons systems and secondary items. It divides the RDT&E budget into two categories: initial and later RDT&E. The overall effect is to better illustrate how the defense budget is spent and how its various categories perform functions and produce outputs.

For all their importance, such reforms to bureaucratic procedures and documents will accomplish little unless they are accompanied by an analytical effort that focuses on issues where strategic policy and spending priorities intersect. In future years, DOD is not likely to be able to spend its way out of fiscal dilemmas, nor can it avoid the need to set priorities and make tradeoffs. As matters now stand, DOD may have trouble funding sufficient investments for both expeditionary warfare and strategic dominance unless savings can be found elsewhere in the budget. DOD will need to ascertain how savings can be created, and how they can best be invested in high-leverage areas of force enhancements, modernization, and transformation for both goals. All programs and functional activities should be examined for savings, including such support programs as intelligence and communications. The account needing the most scrutiny is O&M, not only to extract potential savings, but also to prevent this account from continuing to grow so much that it crowds out procurement and other important investments.

Only careful analysis can answer the question of whether savings can be found within the O&M budget. One conclusion, however, already seems clear. A careful appraisal could lead to a stronger DOD capacity to manage, guide, and control this expensive, far-flung activity, which has often defied efforts to impose management controls and tight fiscal

Table 16–17. **Toward New Functional Categories for the Defense Budget**

Military and Civilian Personnel
Military Pay
Civilian Pay
Operations Budget
Active Force Operations
Other Operations
Procurement
Major Weapon Systems
Secondary Items
RDT&E
Initial RDT&E
Later RDT&E
Construction and Housing
Construction
Housing
Other

discipline. Today, there are few true experts on the entire O&M budget, no strategic theory of O&M, no economic models for appraising its performance, and no textbooks on how to manage it. This absence of analytical frameworks stands in marked contrast to many other areas of defense planning, which are replete with methods and metrics. A core problem in many O&M accounts is that there are no theories of requirements to help set spending ceilings, nor are there curves of diminishing marginal returns to help identify where additional spending would be undesirable. As better analytical tools are built, the O&M process should be configured with an eye to prudent requirements, economic constraints, cost-effectiveness, and tradeoffs. More fundamentally, the O&M process needs coherent strategic concepts with specific goals and priorities, firm fiscal guidance, a management information system that serves senior officials, and strong top-down guidance. Creating such a high-level management structure is what a concerted DOD internal review can hope to accomplish. If the result is savings, so much the better.

If, through savings or further budgetary growth, additional investment funds become available, care must be taken to spend them effectively in order to gain the maximum mileage from them. A top priority will be to apply these savings to procurement to fund modernization of all six major areas (expeditionary warfare measures, national missile defense, army modernization and FCS, combat aircraft modernization, support aircraft, and shipbuilding). To the extent budget shortfalls still exist, the manner in which funds are distributed among these six areas will need to be analyzed carefully. Top priority will clearly need to be given to programs for expeditionary warfare, including the Army and other boots-on-the-ground assets, but the Air Force, Navy, national missile defense, and other important requirements cannot be neglected. A sensible, evolving balance between expeditionary warfare and strategic dominance will need to be struck, perhaps with attention shifting from the former to the latter as the future unfolds.

The task of setting aside old priorities for new priorities, and then making sound decisions about how to allocate scarce funds among these new priorities, is a job for political and military expertise, but it also is a job for systems analysis and related techniques. In theory, a perfect budget is attained when no further internal changes in the distribution of funds would produce a better product: the marginal benefits of adding funds to one account would be matched or exceeded by the opportunity costs of taking those funds away from another account. While such a perfect outcome may be impossible, no serious observer would question the proposition that continuing efforts are always needed to wring better performance from the defense budget. New spending priorities are a principal tool for elevating the effectiveness of the budget in response to changing conditions, and will remain an important feature of the defense dialogue for the future.

If systems analysis can help develop new spending patterns, it will play an important role in the coming era of defense programming and budgeting. The unique strength of systems analysis is that it can draw connecting links from the big strategic picture to defense programs and their budget details. Its economic models of choice provide tools for making judgments about cost-effectiveness and tradeoffs when options for new spending patterns are considered. Fortunately, systems analysis does not need new tools in order to perform this task; the old tools still work well. But these tools need to be configured with the proper concepts and data to address the issues of today and tomorrow. They must be employed by analysts who are attuned to new issues and who have a taste for diving into budget details with innovative spending patterns in mind. This is the challenge facing systems analysis and its practitioners in this important arena, where strategic policy meets the hard reality of determining how money should be spent.

Notes

[1] Official budgetary data for this chapter come from DOD publications. See Office of the Undersecretary of Defense (Comptroller), *National Defense Budget Estimates for FY2005*, and accompanying documents (Washington, DC: Department of Defense, 2004). For a long-term appraisal of DOD budgets, see Congressional Budget Office, *The Long-Term Implications of Current Defense Plans: Summary Update for Fiscal Year 2005* (Washington, DC: Congressional Budget Office, 2004). Budgetary estimates for 2006 and following years will alter these projections somewhat, but the basic issues will remain alive.

[2] For Purchasing Power Parity estimates of international defense budgets, see International Institute for Strategic Studies (IISS), *The Military Balance, 2003–2004* (London: IISS, 2003).

[3] For a critique of the Reagan defense budgets, see William W. Kaufmann, *The 1986 Defense Budget* (Washington, DC: Brookings, 1985). For a critique of U.S. defense spending in the George H.W. Bush era, see William W. Kaufmann, *Glasnost, Perestroika, and U.S. Defense Spending* (Washington, DC: Brookings, 1990).

[4] During 2005–2009, the Navy is trying is trim its O&M spending by about $2.5 billion per year, a 4.3 percent

reduction. Because 75 percent of its O&M budget is spend on active operating forces, the Navy is focusing on early retirement of some ships to create these savings.

[5] DOD's RDT&E budget includes not only research and development, but also the critical steps of testing and evaluation that precede actual procurement and deployment.

[6] See Congressional Budget Office, Testimony to Committee on the Budget, U.S. House of Representatives, Testimony on the Long-Term Implications of Current Defense Plans (Washington, DC: Congressional Budget Office, 2003).

[7] Stuart E. Johnson, "A New PPBS Process to Advance Transformation," *Defense Horizons* 32 (Washington, DC: Center for Technology and National Security Policy, National Defense University, September 2003).

Part III—Operations Research

Chapter 17

Overview

This final section of the book addresses how the methods of operations research (OR) can be applied to defense resource allocation. Rather than provide a definitive account of all these methods and their mathematical models, it introduces several of them to help readers understand how they can be used in policy analysis. The term *operations research* often sends shivers down the spines of the uninitiated: it conjures up images of occult mathematics that are beyond the grasp of anybody not possessing a PhD in the subject. Yet although the mathematical techniques of operations research may be sophisticated, most are not impenetrable. With some effort, anybody with a grasp of simple algebra can understand and use many of them. Learning how to apply these techniques is important because they can help analyze many national security issues, including crucial questions involving the application of money and resources to the achievement of national goals.

While this section focuses on the allocation of defense resources, operations research methods can be applied to a wide range of national security policy issues, including foreign policy issues in which military forces play only a minor role, such as foreign economic aid. They also can be used to examine domestic policies and programs, such as investments in transportation infrastructure and electrical power grids, and they are often used by business corporations in the private sector to help shape capital expenditures and production schedules. Their diversity and flexibility make them valuable tools for all facets of policy analysis where a detailed focus on costs and performance is needed.

Microscopes for Analyzing Operations

Just as *systems analysis* can be defined as the analysis of systems, *operations research* can be defined as research on operations. These definitions may sound redundant, but they capture the essence of both methods. Where systems analysis usually takes a wide focus on large-scale systems, operations research typically focuses more narrowly and in greater depth on individual operations—organized activities—within such systems. For example, systems analysis might assess the entire military force posture in a single theater. By contrast, operations research analysis might assess some aspect of the posture, such as airstrikes or artillery fires. An operations research analysis can study more than one operation at a time, but when it covers multiple operations, it starts being systems analysis. The dividing line between operations research and systems analysis thus is blurred, because these two methodologies can overlap in their focus and techniques. People who practice operations research often employ systems analysis when a broader perspective is needed.

Operations researchers thus can also be systems analysts, and vice versa. In their essence, nonetheless, these are two different methods that are used for different purposes.

Regardless of whether its focus is wide or narrow, operations research provides microscopes for a fine-grained view of how organizations and institutions carry out their tasks and missions. Typically, it seeks to break complex operations into component parts, and then studies how these parts work individually and collectively. When it examines a particular operation that unfolds in sequential stages (for example, a military force performing a specific mission), it identifies each stage, examines how it is carried out, and assesses the factors that determine its success or failure. Then it examines how these stages interact to produce a final result, which is measured in terms of whether the mission's goal is achieved. It strives to produce conclusions and recommendations with considerable precision, and it often attaches specific numbers to its performance estimates, such as "100 missiles have a 75 percent probability of destroying 45 to 50 targets."

For example, in analyzing how U.S. air forces would perform in a particular strike mission, operations research might focus on a number of key factors, such as:

- airbase survivability, including shelters, runways, and storage sheds
- aircraft sortie rates as a function of maintenance levels, munitions stocks, and aircrew availability
- weapons loads of aircraft
- C^4ISR systems and the intelligence provided by them
- the ability of the aircraft to penetrate air defense systems
- target acquisition capabilities, weapons accuracy, weapons lethality, and target vulnerability
- weather and terrain.

Typically, an operations researcher would develop a mathematical equation for portraying each of these factors. He or she would then bring these equations together to form an overall mathematical model for the operation. Next, the analyst would gather quantitative data to determine values for key variables, constants, exponents, and coefficients in each equation. Then, the model and data would be employed to generate predictions of how the air operation would unfold under varying conditions and circumstances. Having produced a basic estimate of the operation, the analyst would then seek to determine how overall performance could be enhanced by improvements in one or more of the contributing areas: how, for example, the number of enemy targets destroyed might be increased by elevating sortie rates, adding more smart munitions, or both. Such an analysis can, when complete, provide a detailed portrayal of what makes an air operation succeed or fail, and how its success could be enhanced through cost-effective improvements in various areas.

Another example illustrates how operations research can shed quantitative light on analytical problems. Suppose the task is to compare how two fighter aircraft will perform in the role of bombing targets on the ground. At first glance, the task is hard because the two aircraft have different performance features: aircraft A has better features in some areas, and aircraft B better features in others. Operations research can bring conceptual order to this problem by identifying the relevant features as variables and by using a simple mathematical model that shows how these variables combine to produce a single output: the probability of one sortie by a single aircraft destroying a single target on the ground.[1] Assuming the factors are independent of each other, the proper technique is to determine overall probability of success (OPS) for each aircraft by multiplying the probabilities of success (PS) for each variable. Analysis employing this technique might show that aircraft A is the better performer by a margin of 0.40 to 0.24, the OPS for each aircraft. Aircraft A performs better because, even though it is less likely to reach its target than aircraft B, its superior ability to find and strike the target more than compensates for that shortcoming. Cases like this are standard subjects for operations research.

Operations research is well suited to studies that are concerned about details and need precise results. This does not mean that operations research is a tool for trivial pursuits: major strategic issues often turn upon seemingly minor details. This can be especially true for military operations, where a 10 percent difference in survivability or lethality can have major implications for the number of weapons systems that should be bought and the amount of money that must be spent on them. In the defense arena, moreover, strategic evaluations and systems analyses must often employ operations research methods in order to provide the performance and cost data needed to evaluate policy options. In such cases, operations research, with its microscopic focus, can be essential in aiding policy analyses that have a broad focus.

Operations research is often seen as synonymous with reams of quantitative data and elaborate mathematical models, but this is not always true. Sometimes just a few numbers and a simple mathematical model may suffice. Operations research is pragmatic and ecumenical in its selection of data and models. What matters is whether the data and models are able to get the job done. While operations research may be characterized by its numbers and formulas, its more important characteristic is its details. It is an excellent tool for probing into the depths of complex operations that would otherwise defy clear understanding. Details often matter not only for small issues, but for big issues as well; when details matter and precise answers are needed, operations research can be a valuable tool.

Operations research frequently requires input data on key performance variables, such as the probability that a missile will destroy a target, or the operational availability of a fighter wing whose aircraft have periodic maintenance requirements. Such input data come from more detailed forms of analysis, such as engineering analysis or field testing. Newcomers are often surprised to find how much there is of such quantitative information in the defense field. Acquiring data is normally not the problem; the main challenge is interpreting it, which is the province of operations research.

Critics sometimes allege that operations research produces false precision—that its pinpoint answers are often not justified because too many uncertainties surround its data and calculations. While this criticism correctly notes that there is a difference between precision and accuracy, it misses an equally valid point: operations research may not always be able to get answers exactly right, but it is a good tool for getting them as accurate as possible, and it is better at this task than any other method. Moreover, policy analyses may not require exact certainty; often, a range of estimated performance parameters may suffice. For example, if the decision is whether to buy 100 or 150 aircraft, an operations research analysis that points to a range of 140 to 160 aircraft may be adequate. A similar response can be made to the parallel criticism that operations research sometimes draws its data from subjective judgments rather than from laboratory experiments or other carefully controlled measurements. While human judgment is not perfect, it is almost always better than nothing, and sensitivity analysis can be employed to show how results vary in response to different judgments. The solution to uncertainty is not to close up shop and remain ignorant, but instead to do the best possible job of creating useful knowledge with the information and techniques that are available. Operations research reflects this practical ethic.

A key strength of operations research is that it can be used in less than ideal conditions to help make better informed policy decisions. Another strength is that it can produce concrete answers to many questions. It is largely responsible for the many volumes of quantitative planning factors that Pentagon officials employ in the force planning and budgeting process. Virtually all major DOD organizations have operations research staffs, some of them large. There are many private consulting firms that perform operations research, operate computer models, and maintain databases for DOD. More money is spent on operations research than on strategic evaluation and systems analysis: it is a big business within the defense community.

Because operations research is not carried out in a laboratory, its practices are always vulnerable to second-guessing, and its conclusions are not necessarily the literal truth. Like any other method, it must be used with intelligence and prudence, and with due regard for its shortcomings and potential abuses. Virtually all operations research methods are suitable for some types of issues but not others. They must be selected in each case with regard for their appropriateness. The methods are only as good as the ideas, concepts, equations, and data that bring them to life; how they are selected, shaped, and applied requires careful thought. Moreover, operations research should not be seen as a methodology for every issue. In national security affairs, it is typically best employed in combination with strategic evaluation and systems analysis, not as a stand-alone technique. But when it is used properly, it definitely is a methodology worth knowing and employing.

Contents of this Section

This section begins with chapter 18, a theoretical chapter that surveys standard operations research methods such as statistical models, probability models, force exchange models, multi-attribute utility functions, decision analysis, game theory, and linear programming. Then, in the first of five applied chapters, chapter 19 examines OR methods for nuclear force planning, especially the mathematics of national missile defense. Chapter 20 shows how multi-attribute utility analysis can be used to study the future U.S. overseas military presence. Chapter 21 discusses how combat models and dynamic computer simulations can be employed to help guide programs to improve conventional military forces. Chapter 22 examines how mobility models, dynamic simulations, and decision analysis can help force planning for crisis interventions and wartime battle campaigns. Chapter 23 shows how a set of methods—cost analysis, linear programming, and decision analysis—can help guide investment decisions for research and development and for weapons procurement.

Sometimes operations research can be used as a stand-alone technique, but usually where a broader context is required, operations research is best embedded in strategic evaluation and systems analysis. Chapter 20, in particular, shows the importance of multidisciplinary approaches in such cases, while chapters 19 and 22 also draw upon multiple types of analysis. Together, the six chapters of this section show the need for new types of thinking and analysis to address the defense resource allocation issues of the future. They also spotlight the most important roles of operations research in analyzing national security policies and defense priorities.

Note

[1] Postulate that four variables are involved that reflect sequential stages of the operation: launching the aircraft, penetrating enemy air defenses, locating the target, and striking it accurately with lethal munitions. For aircraft A, its probabilities for each variable are multiplied in sequential order to determine the overall result: perhaps, 0.7 * 0.8 * 0.9 * 0.8 = 0.40. For aircraft B, its overall result is determined by the same mathematical process, using its probabilities in each case; here, perhaps 0.9 * 0.9 * 0.6 * 0.5 = 0.24.

Chapter 18
Methods of Operations Research

Operations research provides a large family of methods that can be used to analyze national security policy issues when a focus on details is necessary. A quick scan of a typical operations research journal will reveal that its articles often focus on the application of exotic techniques to highly specific and detailed issues, such as management of inventory stocks or scheduling of maintenance procedures.[1] To be sure, such fine-grained studies can be important. This chapter, however, has a different purpose. It strives to show how to use some simple and relatively easy operations research methods to help study big issues at the national level that require policy judgments about costs and effectiveness. In the process, it helps illuminate how operations research can aid systems analyses and strategic evaluations that have a wide focus yet need to zoom in on details to do their jobs well.

A Conceptual Focus

This chapter has a theoretical focus that sets the stage for the five applied chapters that follow. It emphasizes methods that are used for defense planning and resource allocation, which is a major consumer of operations research. These methods can be applied to many other aspects of national security policy as well. This chapter aims to identify the main features of relevant methods, but does not cover all their variations. These methods have analytical power largely because of the way that they bring coherent intellectual order to their subjects, not because of their capacity to crunch numbers. A user who grasps the conceptual foundations and promise of each method will be positioned to choose among them for the study at hand, with confidence that any number-crunching will have meaning.

Once a method is chosen and data have been gathered, appropriate computational techniques must be employed. These techniques are typically graphical, algebraic, or both. An example is linear programming, whose problems can often be solved either by two-dimensional graphics (x-y graphs) or by Simplex, an algebraic procedure for solving multiple simultaneous inequalities. Graphical and algebraic procedures generally yield the same conclusions, but graphics have an advantage: their pictures may be worth thousands of words. Algebraic procedures are more versatile and produce results that are more exact. Both have their uses, and they can reinforce each other.

This chapter identifies several computational techniques, but it does not provide detailed instructions on how to employ them. Such guidance can be derived from standard textbooks. Computer programs or trained technicians who can perform the necessary calculations may be available to the analyst. This chapter provides an introductory overview of operations research methods, not a procedural cookbook for how to employ them for specific studies. The following five chapters provide additional guidance on computations, but they too are mainly conceptual, not exercises in number crunching.

A Spectrum of Seven Methods

This chapter does not pretend to cover the entire field of operations research, which is vast.[2] It surveys seven categories of methods that are regularly employed to assist defense planning and studies of other national security issues:

- statistical techniques

- probability-based models of operations

- force exchange models, including dynamic computer simulations

- multi-attribute utility analysis

- decision analysis

- game theory

- linear programming.

These methods can be used individually or in combination with each other. Often they will be most useful when two or more methods provide different angles of vision yet yield similar results. All of them are anchored in a few conceptual principles and computational procedures that can be readily understood by newcomers. The first three methods—statistical techniques, probability-based models, and force exchange models— are most commonly employed by defense planners in search of basic insights about the performance of weapons systems and military forces. The other four methods are used less often in high-level studies, and they can be somewhat harder to understand at first glance. But with a little effort, they can be grasped in enough depth to know how and when to apply them. Even in cases where they are deemed too exotic to present to senior officials, they can provide analysts with valuable background information in support of results that may be presented to decisionmakers in simpler, more easily grasped terms.

Statistical techniques are used when data on a large number of variables must be gathered and analyzed. Probability-based models of operations are used when performance of weapons or other instruments is strongly affected by chance variations in a few key variables. In the defense arena, these models typically are used for analysis of the performance of U.S. weapons and programs without accounting for the interactive effects of opposition posed by enemy forces. Force exchange models, such as nuclear and conventional combat models, are used when the impact of enemy opposition over the course of a war or battle must be considered. These models come in many varieties, and range from simple to complex. Multi-attribute utility analysis is useful when complex programs must be evaluated in terms of their capacity to achieve multiple goals with different priorities or levels of importance. Decision analysis can be used when policies and programs over a period of time must be assessed, and the twists and turns of chance events as well as subsequent implementation decisions may have a large effect on the outcome. Game theory is often used to analyze how opponents can choose from an array of strategies when they are trying to outfox each other, and can also be used to evaluate such cooperative situations as arms control negotiations. Linear programming uses a set of equations to optimize multifaceted programs when several constraints must be satisfied or several goals must be achieved.

These seven methods share three things in common. Each provides powerful conceptual tools for bringing intellectual order to complex situations; each comes equipped with relatively straightforward mathematical techniques for making calculations about costs and effectiveness; and each generates quantitative results that can either be used by themselves or be fed into studies of broader scope that also employ systems analysis or strategic evaluation. In the national security community, the common practice has been for analysts to specialize in just one of these methods. However, as national security issues become more complex and multifaceted, analysts should aim to possess the multi-disciplinary awareness to use more than one of these methods, and preferably all seven of them. Equally important, analysts should know how to alter and reconfigure these methods as needed to deal with the ever-changing policy challenges ahead. These methods should not be seen as static creations. To be relevant, they need to mutate and grow. A future of change lies ahead for them, as well as for the analysts who use them.

Statistical Techniques: Describing and Explaining Defense Realities

Statistical techniques are of two sorts: descriptive techniques that help portray complex phenomena, and inferential techniques that search for explanations by investigating cause-effect relationships. Descriptive techniques can best be introduced by noting that they are favored not only by physical scientists, but also by social scientists who are trying to discover how large populations are thinking and acting on various issues. Political scientists, for example, may use polling and bell-curve analysis to help make accurate assessments of voter preferences. The dilemma facing pollsters is that populations are often far too large for the opinions of everybody to be sought. Statistical techniques enable pollsters to sample a small part of the population and analyze it to yield information on the entire population. The result can be highly accurate descriptions of how opinions are distributed across the entire population at any moment. A brief discussion of how these techniques are applied to polling will help illuminate their relevance to defense analysis.[3]

The statistical technique of polling mandates random sampling and provides guidance on how large a sample must be taken. A random but representative sample of 500 to 1,000 people may be needed. Such a sample does not allow pollsters to describe public opinion with pinpoint accuracy or air-tight certainty, but by employing simple mathematical calculations to analyze the data drawn from such a sample, pollsters can confidently claim that public opinion lies within a relatively narrow range. For example, they might state with 85 percent confidence that 50 percent of the population favors candidate A and 50 percent favors candidate B, with a margin of error of plus or minus 5 percent in either direction.

The mathematical foundations of this technique are easy to describe. Suppose that in reality, a voting population is equally divided in its opinions on candidates A and B. If a single random sample of 200 people is taken, the result may show a 60–40 split, which is an erroneous portrayal. If multiple samples are drawn, however, the laws of chance dictate that the results of these samples will cluster around the true answer (a 50–50 split), with a few falling various distances away from this mark. As figure 18–1 shows, the result will be a bell-shaped curve (curve 1) whose mean (average result of samples) is close to the 50–50 mark.

Figure 18–1. **Results of Public Opinion Polling Data**

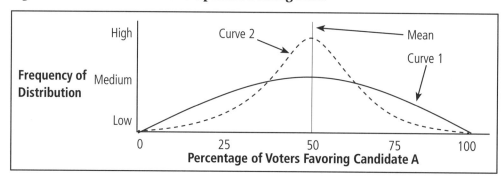

The shape of curve 1 is rather flat, which suggests a greater likelihood of error in a single sample, because the size of each sample is only 200. But if the size of each sample is increased to 500 or 1,000 voters, the results will cluster closer around the true mark and curve 2 will be steeper. It is steeper because, owing to the laws of chance, the larger size of each sample dictates that fewer samples will produce results that diverge sharply from the true mark. The practice of expressing curve 2's results in terms of a confidence level of 85 percent and margins of error of 5 percent plus or minus is a way of saying that if multiple samples were taken, the results in 85 percent of the cases would fall in the range of 45–55 percent for candidate A or candidate B, and that the overall mean for these samples would be 50 percent for each. Of course, there is a theoretical possibility that if only a single sample is drawn and it shows a distribution in this range, it could be erroneously reflecting a different reality (perhaps a 65–35 split). But statistical laws dictate that the odds of such a large error are quite small, less than 10 percent. Thus, pollsters are on solid ground in their confidence that when their sample is large enough, their judgments are statistically sound and accurate with only a small margin of error.

Bell-shaped curves take the shape of a normal distribution curve whose form is dictated by the central limit theorem. This theorem specifies that in binomial situations of chance (such as a flipped coin, which can land just one of two ways, heads or tails), multiple large samples will produce results whose mean clusters around the true odds. The product is a statistical technique that allows analysts to use random samples to generate accurate descriptions in many other domains, not just voting behavior. Defense analysts often use random sampling and bell curves in order to take snapshots in areas such as the time between failures for aircraft engines or the time needed to repair tanks on a battlefield. In these arenas, the universes are large enough to necessitate samples and bell curves as descriptors of reality.

Sometimes, defense analysts are not interested merely in describing situations, but want to explain situations by gauging how causal relationships work. For example, they might want to assess how the amount of repair work devoted to tanks before combat affects their capacity to operate for long hours on the battlefield without breaking down. In order to develop such cause-and-effect assessments, they commonly turn to an inferential technique called *regression analysis*, which provides statistical methods for exploring the relationship between independent and dependent variables.

Regression analysis begins by using data derived from actual experience to generate a graph that broadly displays the relationship between an independent variable x and a dependent variable y. In the example used here (see figure 18–2), the x variable is the amount of repair work devoted to tanks prior to combat, and the y variable is fighting time of these tanks in combat before breaking down. Suppose that a sufficiently large sample from actual combat experience produces the data distribution that is displayed in figure 18–2. Visual observation suggests that a causal relationship exists: y rises as x increases. The relationship appears to be linear in the sense that at each stage of the progression, y increases by about one-half of the amount that x increases. Seeing this relationship, the analyst might accurately judge that the relationship can be expressed by a simple equation: $y = 1/2\ x + c$. Of course, not all relationships will be linear. For example, the equation $y = x^2 + c$ would be curvilinear because the value of y increases as a function of the square of x, thereby creating a line whose slope increases as x increases.

Figure 18–2. **Illustrative Relationship Between Prior Repairs and Tank Endurance in Combat**

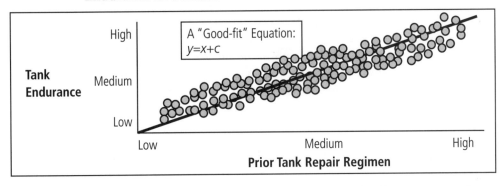

In cases of complex data patterns, choosing an equation that best expresses the relationship between x and y is anything but easy. Regression analysis provides a method for choosing an equation that is better than any other potential equation.[4] To do this, it employs a computational technique called *least squares*, which seeks to draw an equation line that minimizes the amount by which data points deviate from it. It does so by determining the deviation in each case, squaring it, and summing the results to get a total deviation. Least squares endorses this equation line as the best expression of the x-y relationship, because its total deviation is smaller than any other possible line. Figure 18–3 illustrates how least squares works. There, the least squares equation clearly provides a better description of the x-y relationship than does the alternative equation. This is the case not only because it looks like a better fit, but also because in numerical terms, its total deviation is less than that of the alternative equation. Indeed, its deviation will be less than any other alternative equation that might be drawn.

Is a least squares equation proof that the posited causal relationship between the two variables actually exists? The answer is no, because the relationship might be merely correlative, not causal. Some variable other than x might be causing the changes to y, and x might just be along for the ride. Even if a causal relationship exists, the least squares equation might not be the best interpreter of it. Simply because it provides a tighter fit than any

Figure 18–3. **Least Squares Equation**

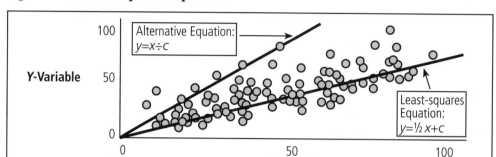

other known equation does not mean that it necessarily must be correct. Least squares equations and related tools of regression analysis are exercises in logical inference, not deduction, and they are subject to the same drawbacks as other inferential techniques. But when they are used competently, they can help improve the storehouse of knowledge in the search for causal relationships.

Regression analysis also provides an elaborate set of theories and techniques for analyzing cause-effect relationships in sophisticated terms. Entire textbooks are written on regression analysis. One technique is analysis of variance, which helps test how other variables may affect the *x-y* interaction for situations of widespread data patterns on the vertical axis (that is, where a wide range of *y* variables exists for each value of the *x* variable). By using mathematical techniques that strip away the impact of other variables, analysis of variance helps focus on the relationship between *x* and *y*. Another technique is multiple regression analysis, which analyzes relationships when multiple causal variables are at work and develops equations for each of them. Systems of many regression equations can be combined to form computer models for analyzing highly complex phenomena, such as national economies. Economists label their version of regression *analysis econometrics*, but the mathematical techniques are the same.

Regression analysis has a role to play in any defense study that investigates the mathematical details of causal and correlative relationships in military affairs. For example, it can help ascertain how such variables as pay, training, family health care, or career-advancement opportunities may affect recruitment and retention of military personnel. It thus permits analysis of how policy changes in each of these areas could improve recruitment and retention. The result might be an entire program of changes to produce improvements beyond what might have been achieved if sophisticated inferential statistical techniques were not employed. The same applies to such other areas as logistical support, maintenance, and professional military education. While DOD is a long-time practitioner of regression analysis, many defense studies could be improved if greater use were made of it.

Probability-Based Models of Operations: Analyzing the Odds

Although descriptive and inferential statistics are helpful to policy analysis, most defense planners make greater use of probability-based models of operations in their labors. These models make use of a type of mathematics called *Bayesian analysis*, which deals with stochastic, or random-chance, events.[5] These models are employed when, as often is the case, the issue in question is a function of probabilities, not certitudes, such as war. For example, they can be used when combat between U.S. and enemy forces is being examined, and events could take several different forms. They are especially helpful when the focus is on how various types of U.S. weapons and forces are likely to perform as they carry out their operations.

A simple example illustrates how these models can be used to help guide analysis of force operations in tactical battles. Suppose that a tactical situation arises in which an enemy tank must be destroyed, and the only way to destroy it is to employ U.S. tanks to shoot at it. How many U.S. tanks are necessary to accomplish the job? If a single U.S. tank has only a 60 percent probability of destroying the enemy tank, more than one U.S. tank must be used, but how many more? This question can be answered by using a simple model derived from the mathematics of probabilities:

$OPk = 1 - Ps^n$

Where:

OPk (overall probability of kill) is the combined probability that multiple U.S. tanks will destroy the enemy tank; and

Ps is the probability that the enemy tank will survive U.S. fires.

Ps is equal to $1 - SSPk$. $SSPk$ (single shot probability of kill) is the probability that a single U.S. tank will destroy the enemy tank (here, presumed to be 60 percent). Thus, $Ps = 1 - SSPk = 1.0 - 0.60 = 0.40$;

n is equal to the number of U.S. tanks firing on the enemy tank.

Thus, for example, if two U.S. tanks fire, $OPk = 1 - 0.40^2 = 1 - 0.16 = 0.84$.

Use of this equation generates table 18–1, which shows that whereas a single U.S. tank will have only a 60 percent chance of destroying the enemy tank, two U.S. tanks will have a better chance (OPk) of 84 percent. If three U.S. tanks are used, OPk rises to 94 percent. If four tanks are used, OPk rises to 97 percent; if five, to 99 percent. The table shows that for each additional U.S. tank added, there are diminishing marginal returns. The table also suggests that regardless of how many U.S. tanks are used, OPk will never reach 100 percent, because there will always be a small chance that all will fail. So how many U.S. tanks should be used? There is no simple answer to this question. It depends upon the goal sought by the U.S. commander and the willingness to commit resources. Two or three tanks might well be used, on the premise that a confidence level of 84 to 94 percent is enough and that more tanks would be a waste of resources. Regardless of the decision, the key point is that this probability calculus has helped illuminate the options available.

Probability models can also analyze tactical battles when multiple U.S. weapons are used to attack multiple enemy targets. Suppose that 10 U.S. fighters are sent to bomb 10 enemy SAM sites. Suppose that each fighter has a 60 percent chance of destroying one site, and that the goal is to destroy six or more sites. Assuming one aircraft is allocated to one SAM site, a simple probability model suggests that six sites will be destroyed: 10 (OPk) = 10 (.60) = 6. But this estimate is an expected value calculus: it assumes that each aircraft

Table 18–1. **Illustrative Kill Probability as Function of U.S. Tanks Used**

Number of Tanks Used	Probability of Kill (percent)
1	60
2	84
3	94
4	97
5	*Total = 99*

will perform as advertised. There is a chance that more than four aircraft could fail. Indeed, there is a small chance—less than 1 percent—that all 10 aircraft could fail. In order to deal with this uncertainty, a more sophisticated probability model can illuminate all of the potential outcomes:

$$Po = \frac{N!}{S!F!} \ (Ps^n)(Pf^n)$$

Where:
Po is the probability of the event occurring (e.g., that all 6 targets are destroyed);
N! (*N* factorial) is the number of targets struck, multiplied in succession (10 * 9 * 8 …1);
S! (S factorial) is the number of successes multiplied in succession;
F! (F factorial) is the number of failures multiplied in succession;
Ps is the probability of success raised to the appropriate n^{th} power (which is determined by the number of successes in each case);
Pf is the probability of failure raised to the appropriate n^{th} power.

Use of this equation generates a binomial distribution of likely outcomes, shown in table 18–2: there is a 47 percent chance that either 6 or 7 targets will be destroyed (the likelihood of destroying exactly 6 is 25 percent). There is a 17 percent chance that 8, 9, or 10 targets will be destroyed. But there is a worrisome 36 percent chance that the mission will take out only half its targets or less, and a 5 percent chance of virtually complete failure, with just 3 or fewer targets, perhaps none, being destroyed. What is the solution to this problem of possible failure? If this risk of failure is deemed unacceptable, the fighters can be sent back to conduct a second bombing of the SAM sites that remain, or if time does not permit a second strike, the number of fighters committed to the first strike could be increased from 10 to 20.

Use of the binomial distribution to call attention to extreme outcomes becomes less important when large target systems are being struck by large numbers of weapons. Because the Central Limit Theorem is operating, the bell-shaped curve becomes steep, and the result will converge on the expected value. In other words, 10 strikes against 10 targets may produce a 15 percent likelihood of destroying only 0–4 targets, but 1,000 strikes against 1,000 targets will reduce this likelihood to 5 percent or less. The binomial

Table 18–2. **Binomial Distribution of Successes**

Number of SAM Sites Destroyed	Probability of Occurrence (percent)
0–3	5
4–5	31
6–7	47
8–10	17
	Total =100

distribution can be essential, however, when a small number of strikes is being conducted and very high levels of destruction are essential. The main effect is normally to elevate force requirements for the mission. The core reason is the need to hedge against low-probability events that, while unlikely, cannot be neglected. In this example, destruction of six or more SAM sites might be deemed essential to pave the way for subsequent airstrikes against other targets. If this is the case, commitment of more strikes makes sense even if expected value calculations suggest that the goal might be accomplished with only 10 aircraft.

In addition to contributing to analysis of tactical battles, probability-based models can offer valuable insights on the selection of theater-wide strategies and associated campaign plans. Suppose that a potential strategy requires execution of five sequential maneuvers, each of which must succeed if the follow-on maneuver is to succeed. If the likelihood of each of them succeeding is 85 percent, this does not mean that the overall likelihood of the entire strategy succeeding is 85 percent. The overall likelihood is, in fact, only 44 percent, because values for all of the events must be multiplied in order to determine the expected value for the entire strategy. Sharp drop-offs of this sort are a reason for being skeptical about complex, demanding strategies even if each component seems quite feasible. Somewhere during the campaign, a negative event is likely to happen, and it could unravel the entire strategy unless remedial steps can quickly be taken. Conversely, expected value calculations can sometimes give good reasons for not being overly worried about an enemy's complex strategy aimed at unraveling U.S. defenses. Even if the enemy has a 70 percent chance of successfully mounting each of 5 phases of an attack, it might have only a 17 percent chance of executing all 5 of them.

Probability-based models can also be used to help gauge force requirements for theater-wide strategies. Such models can provide the quantitative data that allows systems analysts to generate curves of diminishing marginal returns and other economic models of choice to help shape theater defense plans on a grand scale. A main strength of these models is that they offer measures of effectiveness that are focused on outputs. They facilitate a focused appraisal of how the likelihood of success or failure varies if different force levels are committed. They also call attention to a core consideration in force sizing, that not all commitments of equal forces have equal value.

The example shown in table 18–3 illustrates this point with respect to sizing ground forces for a theater-wide land war. It shows a situation in which committing one division will not greatly elevate defense prospects, because the gap between capabilities and requirements remains large: the probability of success rises from 0 to only 10 percent. Committing 3 divisions has high leverage, raising the probability of success to 60 percent. Committing a fourth division has a smaller marginal impact than the second and third divisions, but does elevate the probability of success to 75 percent. Marginal gains coming from a fifth, sixth, and seventh divisions are progressively smaller, even though together they increase the probability of success to 93 percent. Which of these force levels should be chosen? The choice turns on the force goals, confidence levels, and risk-management standards of policymakers. The contribution of probability-based models is not to make their choices for them, but to attach numbers to the tradeoffs facing them.

Probability-based models can also offer insights on how priorities should be attached to programs for acquiring new weapons. They can be used to analyze programs for all three force components: air, ground, and naval forces. In analyzing air forces, they are especially useful in assessing how improvements in such areas as sortie rates, information networking, defense suppression, target acquisition, and smart munitions can elevate the performance of fighter wings. In analyzing ground forces, they can help illustrate how improvements to fire rates and target acquisition can enhance the battlefield performance of artillery, tanks, and attack helicopters. In analyzing naval forces, they can help illustrate how a networked system of defenses, such as sensors, fighter interceptors, Aegis missiles, antisubmarine aircraft and combatants, and passive defenses can protect carrier strike forces against access-denial threats.

Table 18–3. **Illustrative Impact of Force Levels on Battlefield Prospects**

Number of Divisions Committed	Overall Probability of Success (percent)	Marginal Contribution of Last Division Added (percent)
0	0	0
1	10	10
2	35	25
3	60	25
4	75	15
5	85	10
6	90	5
7	93	3

These models can also be used to help analyze cross-component investment strategies for theater warfare. Table 18–4 shows how data from such a model could be used to compare the degree to which 3 different programs of equal cost—500 new tanks, or 100 new attack helicopters, or 50 new fighter aircraft—could enhance prospects for success in 3 different contingencies. New tanks make the greatest contribution in contingency A, while new helicopters contribute the most in contingency B, and new aircraft contribute the most in contingency C. A fourth equal-cost program of investments in C⁴ISR systems performs as well or better than all three other options for all three contingencies. A fifth equal-cost program that combines balanced investments in tanks, helicopters, fighters, and C⁴ISR performs best across the board. Although obvious choices such as this case seldom occur in reality, it is still a useful reminder that mixed programs often perform better than single-focus programs, because their constituent elements are less vulnerable to diminishing marginal returns. A more fundamental point is that probability-based models can help provide the output measures needed to assess such programmatic tradeoffs.

Probability models require precise mathematical statements of expected performance: for example, that weapon A has a 0.60 chance of killing a target, not 0.50 or 0.70. Where do these precise figures come from? When individual weapons and munitions are being examined, the figures often come from physics, engineering analysis, and laboratory experiments. As a result, they often are highly accurate and reliable. Even here, however, care must be taken in defining exactly what the figure means. Suppose that an F–15 firing a joint direct attack munition (JDAM) missile is accorded a 0.90 probability of destroying a ground bunker. Does this mean a 0.90 probability only if the JDAM actually hits the target and explodes properly? Or does it also account for the probability that the pilot might introduce the wrong GPS coordinates into the avionics system, or that the JDAM might malfunction on the path to the target? If these two variables are included, the probability of kill might drop from 0.90 to 0.70: a big difference. As a general rule, an analyst should include the full set of variables that could affect performance, but regardless, he or she should be aware of the variables being employed and use them consistently when endeavoring to compare the performance of different weapons and munitions.

Table 18–4. **Illustrative Impact of Improvement Programs on Battlefield Prospects**

	Probability of Success (percent)		
	Contingency A	Contingency B	Contingency C
Existing Capability Improvement Programs	50	50	50
500 new tanks	75	65	70
100 new attack helicopters	70	75	65
50 new fighter aircraft	65	70	75
Improved C⁴ISR systems	75	77	80
Mixed program	90	90	90

Even greater care must be taken when precise performance figures are being employed to judge the outcome of large-scale military operations with many weapons systems and large combat forces. Suppose that a U.S. Army armored brigade is accorded a 0.80 chance of destroying an enemy armored brigade in a meeting engagement. In all likelihood, this figure does not come from physics and engineering analysis. It might come from field exercises or dynamic combat simulations, which may produce correct answers, but which could be vulnerable to error if the conditions of the actual battle differ from those posited by the exercises and computers. It might come from professional military judgment, which is often correct, but sometimes can be wrong. It might come from past experience, but the conditions of the current battle may be different from past battles. For the operations researcher, the solution to such problems is not to discard these figures, but instead to gauge their reliability insofar as possible, and to employ sensitivity analysis to determine the conditions under which major conclusions could change if these figures change. Sometimes, sensitivity analysis will show that conclusions are highly robust: they do not change even if key figures prove significantly wrong. But when the conclusions are highly brittle—if the results change dramatically when the figures vary only slightly—they should be treated with caution and recognized for what they are: shaky.

Force Exchange Models: Mastering the Attrition Dynamic

Force exchange models are addressed in chapter 19 on nuclear forces and chapter 21 on conventional forces. An introductory overview is appropriate here. These models are used when critical defense issues, such as assessments of force balances, requirements, and program priorities, can be made only by studying how a war may unfold. They address the back-and-forth interaction of U.S. or allied forces with adversary forces during a lethal competition for supremacy on the battlefield. In addressing the time dimension of war, these models focus on such battlefield dynamics as how forces from both sides inflict attrition on each other and maneuver against each other from the start of a war until its end. They focus on details, seeking to determine how each individual part of the U.S. joint posture is likely to perform, in order to help determine how all of them can best be improved. They are highly quantitative, employing numbers to assess how U.S. forces are performing against explicit measures of effectiveness (MOEs) and criteria of evaluation, such as enemy targets destroyed, ground gained, cities captured, or U.S. casualties from one day to the next.

Force exchange models can be used to study air war, land war, naval war, or joint warfare. If they are properly configured with the right assumptions and data, these models can, in theory, predict the outcome of specific wars. But prediction is not their main purpose, and they should not be judged by their success in this arena. Any war can be significantly influenced by exogenous factors or events that lie outside such a model: the political designs and behaviors of participants is an obvious factor. The main purpose of force exchange models is to help assist policymakers to prepare U.S. and allied forces for war. This is the standard by which they should be judged.

Force exchange models range from simple to complex. A simple model can be a back-of-the-envelope construct that employs one or two equations. A spreadsheet model may employ more equations and typically is carried out on a few sheets of paper or with a simple computer program. Complex models vary greatly. They can take the form of human-interactive "board games" in which participants maneuver forces on a map of the battlefield, use simple algorithms to calculate attrition, and attempt to glean insights from the results. At their most elaborate and formal, they are sophisticated computer-based

Figure 18–4. **Force Exchange Models Address Interactive Dynamics of War**

U.S./ Allied Forces and Operations	⟷	Adversary Forces and Operations
Force Exchange Models: ■ monitor exchanges in terms of operations, fires, attrition, movement, and other key variables ■ track changes in force ratios and exchange ratios over a period of time, producing a dynamic sense of war ■ permit analysis of how U.S. forces can be strengthened and of how future threats can increase		

simulations that employ dozens of equations and process huge volumes of data. In a short span of time, such computer models can "fight" a war in 100 different versions, testing the impact of variations in multiple parameters along the way. None of these models is necessarily better than the others; the strength of a force exchange model is not measured by its elaborateness. What matters is its utility: whether it gets the job done by answering the policy questions at hand. Sometimes back-of-the-envelope models are more useful than computer simulations, sometimes less.[6]

Because they are dynamic, not static, force exchange models are good at monitoring how shifting force ratios beget shifting exchange ratios that, in turn, create new force ratios and new exchange ratios. Although they vary greatly in their size and composition, these models have another common feature: their mathematical equations allow them to monitor how forces on both sides are performing during combat from start to finish. Different models are equipped with different sets of equations depending upon their focus and purpose. Sometimes these are simple algebraic equations, or they can be quite complex, anchored in differential equations that chart the rate of change over time. The main thrust of most such equations, however, can be captured by considering a simple model (shown in figure 18–5) with one algebraic equation that addresses the competitive dynamic of mutual attrition.

Figure 18–5. **Simple Model of Force Exchange**

U.S./ Allied Forces and Operations	⟷	Adversary Forces and Operations
Two-Way Equation: $Nk_{P1} = N_{T0}(1 - Ps^n)$ ■ Nk is the number of U.S. forces suffering attrition durig Period 1 ($P1$) of combat. N is the initial number of U.S. soldiers at Time 0 ($T0$), before Period 1 begins. ■ Ps is the probability of survival for each U.S. force unit; n is the number of enemy units firing at each U.S. unit. ■ Nk for adversary forces is determined by using the equation to gauge how they are attrited by U.S. fires. ■ After each period of combat, number of survivors (Ns) on both sides can be determined by simultaneously applying the following equation to both: $Ns_{P1} = N_{N0} - Nk_{P1}$ ■ This equation is applied iteratively throughout each stage of combat, thereby generating a time-phased data base of surviving forces and losses on both sides at each stage of combat.		

This equation shows that if forces on both sides are equal in original size and quality (lethality and survivability), the result will be a symmetrical drawdown. That is, both sides will suffer attrition at the same size and rate as combat unfolds. Ultimately, they would both reach zero surviving forces at the same time, if they fought to the bitter end. This could be called a symmetrical stalemate battle. Table 18–5 shows a gradual drawdown, as each side loses 10 percent of its forces during each period of combat (a week, say, or a month). This might be the case in a conventional war. A nuclear war could unfold much faster because loss rates are higher (perhaps 30–50 percent per period), but the mathematics of the drawdown process would be the same. Neither side would emerge as a winner, because each would destroy the other.

Not all battles will be symmetrical and produce a stalemate. Indeed, the mathematics of this equation suggest that if either side has a usable advantage in size or fighting quality, it can parlay this advantage into a decisive victory in which it emerges with relatively few losses and the opponent is entirely destroyed. The reason is that its advantage can be used to gang up on the opponent, thereby creating an exchange rate dynamic unfavorable to the opponent. If the initial force ratio is 1.5:1 in favor of side A, for example, this can produce an asymmetrical exchange that results in a 2:1 advantage as the next phase of combat begins. As a result of the subsequent exchange, the force ratio then becomes 3:1 in favor of side A, and then 4:1, and then 8:1 until side B is totally destroyed while side A still has 70–80 percent of its forces intact. This cascading battle can be called an asymmetric victorious battle in which one side wins decisively and the other loses totally.

Table 18–5. **Symmetrical Stalemate Battle**

N = number of forces Nk = number killed	**U.S./Allied Forces**		**Adversary Forces**	
	Survivors	Losses	Survivors	Losses
N at $T0$	100		100	
Nk during $P1$		-10		-10
N at $T1$	90		90	
Nk during $P2$		- 9		-9
N at $T2$	81		81	
Nk during $P2$		-8		-8
N at End of Battle	0		0	

Figure 18–6, reflecting this equation, shows how the force balance can shift dramatically in side A's favor if it begins with an edge of 2:1 in either size or quality. Could such an explosive, cascading battle be real, or is it merely a theoretical construct? Massacres in such past battles as Custer's Last Stand—in which 250 cavalry troops were slaughtered by 1,500 Indians, with few losses to the Indians—suggest that total victory and crushing defeat can happen. Yet, as chapter 21 explains, contentious debates surround not only the conditions under which such explosive outcomes could occur, but also the mathematical equations that can be used to study them. The problem with any simple equation is that it leaves out exogenous factors. Better tactical skills, for example, can compensate for

disadvantages in size and firepower. As history shows, there are plenty of cases in which an outnumbered participant defeated its bigger rival; indeed, Custer himself won many such battles before the Little Bighorn. Yet most of these victories occurred because the smaller side had a big edge in fighting quality that enabled it to pursue winning tactics, and such an edge can be analyzed by well-conceived models. The lesson is that force exchange models and equations need to be calibrated thoughtfully to deal with unusual situations.

Figure 18–6. **Asymmetric Victorious Battle**

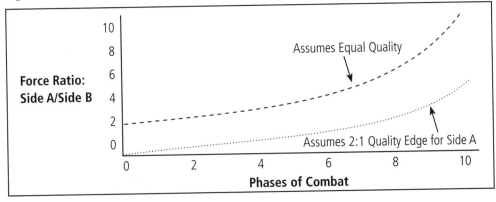

Analysts and historians will continue debating the conditions under which stalemates or victories—or outcomes somewhere in between—are likely to occur. Any of these outcomes is theoretically possible, because war is a highly complex, dynamic process of ebbs and flows when thousands of troops and weapons clash on the battlefield. Fortunately, force exchange models, while not perfect, provide valuable tools for studying this dynamic when they are properly configured and used competently. Without them, analysis of combat—attrition or other dynamics—would be reduced to words and arguments.

For U.S. and allied forces, the challenge is to become fully prepared so that they will be on the winning side of the competition. Knowing how to prepare against a determined, well-armed, skilled enemy is not easy. As chapters 19 and 21 show, force exchange models, with their emphasis on numbers, often have their greatest payoffs in helping guide how these preparations can be made and how programs can be assembled to pursue them. When force exchange models are used to study improvement programs, they can be employed in a nested hierarchy that examines combat at the tactical, operational, and theater levels. Their use of numerical MOEs can help gauge how alternative program elements compare to each other in producing battlefield impacts, and how composite programs compare to each other in aggregate cost-effectiveness.

Figure 18–7 portrays a major combat operation in a single war. Assuming that the U.S.-to-adversary force ratio is 1:1 at the start of combat, it shows how this force ratio changes as the war unfolds. At the bottom, the first curve displays an unchanging force ratio that reflects a stalemate battle. The second curve shows how the force ratio would move in modestly favorable directions in a hypothetical war pitting current U.S. forces against enemy forces. The third curve illustrates that a partly transformed U.S. force would have a significant impact. The fourth curve shows that a fully transformed force would have even greater impact. Whether such a major gain is really likely to come from transformation, only time will tell. The value of force exchange models is that they can help chart the path toward such a future while monitoring progress along the way.

Figure 18–7. **Impact of Defense Transformation on Combat Dynamics**

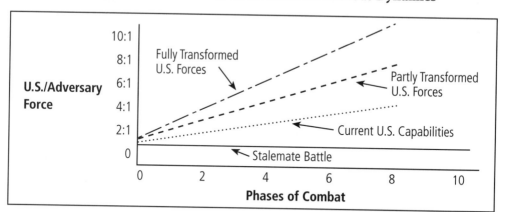

Multi-attribute Utility Analysis: Weighing Multiple Goals and Attributes

Multi-attribute utility analysis is a method for bringing intellectual order to complex situations in which multiple goals and their multiple attributes must be addressed at the same time. When these goals and attributes defy easy comparison, it can be hard for policymakers to judge how to act. Indeed, it may be difficult even to define the nature of the challenge. For example, a common goal of defense planning is to foster favorable military balances in key regions. Often, however, the military forces there are so different from each other that they cannot readily be compared. Similarly, other complex foreign situations cannot be assessed with enough clarity to make policy decisions about them, nor can the capacity of the United States to attain its political and strategic goals abroad be measured precisely. How can priorities and tradeoffs among these goals be assessed so that policies can be designed to bring about better achievement of them?

Multi-attribute utility analysis tries to help answer such thorny questions. It does not replace the need for human judgment in the face of uncertainty, but it helps discipline these judgments, and it displays their logical consequences. This method provides a technique for turning words into numbers, and then turning numbers into simple mathematical equations that can be used to assess foreign situations and U.S. goals for handling them. Initially, this method calls for giving goals and their attributes a numerical ranking on a common utility scale, perhaps from 0 to 100, which allows them to be compared to each other. Then, use of associated procedures makes it easier to appraise the degree to which these goals are being achieved, individually and collectively. It facilitates design of strategies for pursuing them, and permits a numbers-based comparison of how these strategies can be expected to perform.

Because this method often relies upon subjective judgments for key data inputs, it is subject to criticism that it lacks scientific precision and verifiability. But judgments can be accurate when they are based on knowledge and insight. When this method uses sound judgments, it can aid high-level decisionmaking by bringing simplifying order and clarity to otherwise indecipherable realities. In some cases, it is the only formal analytical method feasible, and it yields better results than no method at all. For this reason, it is a method worth knowing about and using when appropriate.[7]

Academic textbooks have been written on this method and its role in multiple-objective decisionmaking. Some private business firms use this method in their corporate planning, and it also occasionally appears in public-policy studies on domestic issues. Defense planning is an area where this method has been used in the past and seems likely to be used in the future. However, it seldom appears in foreign policy studies, although it seems well suited to the issues raised by them.

Within the Department of Defense, multi-attribute utility analysis first gained attention during the Cold War, when senior officials wanted a simple metric for comparing U.S. Army divisions with Soviet divisions in Central Europe. Each U.S. division was larger in manpower (with 16,000 troops, where a Soviet division would have 12,000), but this measure said little about weapons and associated fighting strength. A static metric that compared weapons was needed. Designing it was not easy: U.S. divisions contained many different types of weapons, and within each category, their weapons were different from Soviet weapons both in numbers and in quality. Multi-attribute utility analysis was employed to help solve the problem.

Analysts began by assigning category weights to each type of weapon in a U.S. armored division. These category weights were measured on a utility scale of 0 to 100. Perhaps tanks and artillery tubes were given scores of 100 points, mortars 35 points, and machine guns 5 points. Within each category, the number of weapons was multiplied by the category weight in order to determine an initial overall score for that category. To refine the score further, weapons were graded on a scale of 0 to 1.0 on the basis of how modern and how capable they were. Top-quality weapons were scored 1.0, and lesser-quality weapons were scored lower. When these quality indices were incorporated, the result was a final score for each category. The scores for each category were then totaled to generate a score for the entire armored division. Similar scores were totaled for other types of U.S. Army divisions, including mechanized, infantry, airborne, and air assault units.[8]

Table 18–6 illustrates how this method could be applied to an armored division. The scoring system was criticized by purists because of its reliance upon subjective judgments, and some disputed its use of category weights and quality indexes. What mattered more than its treatment of individual details, however, was the aggregate sense it gave of a U.S. Army division's combat power. The division's score was compared to a standard Soviet division, which scored about 20 percent less. This technique was then applied to the entire NATO and Warsaw Pact force postures. Comparisons showed that although U.S. divisions were stronger than their adversary counterparts, allied divisions were mostly not, and some were weaker. This was a sobering reminder that NATO could not fully rely upon its allegedly superior weapons quality to compensate for its sizable 2:1 disadvantage in numbers of divisions.

Next, modernization rates for both sides were examined by elevating the quality index score as new weapons arrived. Data showed that while the Warsaw Pact was modernizing faster than NATO during the 1970s, NATO would be catching up in the early 1980s. These forecasts were used to help evaluate programs for shoring up the force balance, such as additional U.S. reinforcements and allied reserve mobilization efforts.[9]

This was thus a technique not only for assessing the current military balance in Central Europe, but also for forecasting the future and designing NATO improvement plans. Critics questioned some aspects of this methodology, but policymakers were happy to have a management information tool that provided key insights that could not be gained from any other source. This methodology brought disciplined focus to the internal DOD debate over NATO priorities, and it helped enable DOD to explain its improvement plans to the Congress and American public. Multi-attribute utility analysis thus proved its worth during the Cold War.

Table 18–6. **Illustrative Multi-attribute Utility Analysis of U.S. Armored Division (circa 1980s)**

Types of Weapons	Determine Quality Index	Multiply times Number of Weapons	Multiply times Category Weight	Category Score
Tanks	1.0	270	100	27,000
Artillery tubes	.7	72	100	5,040
Multiple-launch rocket systems	1.0	12	100	1,200
Infantry fighting vehicles	1.0	216	50	10,800
Armored personnel carriers	.7	200	10	1,400
Mortars	.7	54	35	1,323
Attack helicopters	.8	36	70	2,016
Antitank weapons	.8	150	35	4,200
Machine guns	.7	200	5	700
Small arms	.9	2,500	1	2,250
Air defense systems	.8	36	35	1,008
			Total Score =	56,937

Today, comparisons of U.S. armaments with adversary armaments are infrequent: U.S. weapons are now so superior that static weighing and balancing is almost meaningless. A better way to gauge relative combat power is through dynamic simulations that take into account C⁴ISR systems, new doctrines, and operational skills as well as weapons and smart munitions. Yet different forms of multi-attribute utility analysis still have roles to play in other areas of defense management and planning where comparisons are needed, but incommensurable characteristics render them difficult.

For example, as chapter 20 explains, design of the future U.S. overseas military presence on a global basis is ripe for use of multi-attribute utility analysis. The reason is that a new presence must be shaped in order to advance multiple strategic goals that are not easily compared and that would respond to different types of policy actions. A few years ago, DOD took a step toward using this method to analyze overseas presence through its theater engagement plan (TEP) system. Although this system successfully articulated the multiple U.S. goals in each region, it was not developed to the point of being able to measure how different forms of overseas presence could contribute to pursuit of these goals. If the TEP system, or some other equivalent methodology, is used in the future, it will need to do so.

The case of overseas presence illuminates a larger trend in the analysis of U.S. national security strategy. In contrast to the Cold War, the main challenges facing the United States are not narrowly military, but instead political and strategic in a broad sense. Multi-attribute utility analysis can thus no longer be cast in such narrow terms as the military attributes of Army divisions. Instead, it must focus on the wide spectrum of political and strategic goals being pursued. It must help assess the degree to which these goals are being achieved under current strategies, and how they can be better achieved under new strategies.

While chapter 20 addresses the complex example of the U.S. overseas presence, a simpler example here helps illustrate how this methodology can be employed in new and useful ways. The example is the performance of U.S. national security strategy in a notional theater that faces a troubled future. The issue is how the United States can best respond to a menacing situation of deteriorating conditions and growing threats. Should it continue to pursue the current strategy, or should it adopt a different strategy? How can alternative strategies be compared in terms of performance?

Table 18–7 illustrates how multi-attribute utility analysis can help answer this question. It performs a four-step procedure to create an overall preference function, or utility function, that ranks options in terms of their overall ability to achieve goals. First, it lists five key strategic goals being pursued by the United States. Second, it assigns utility points to each of them to indicate their relative importance based on a total of 100 points. In this case, all goals are ranked equally with 20 points apiece, but in other cases, the goals might have varying levels of importance and would be given different scores. Third, the existing U.S. strategy is scored, both now and in the future; here, a steep slide in performance from 60 points to 40 points is shown. Fourth, three alternative, equal-cost strategies are scored. As table 18–7 shows, strategies A and B set stringent priorities among these five goals, while strategy C tries to strike a balance among all of them: strategy A aims mainly to enhance U.S. and alliance strengths (goals 1 and 2), and to preserve the current status quo for goal 3, while accepting a steep decline in goals 4 and 5. Strategy B accepts a future of deteriorating strengths and weakening deterrence. It tries to buffer the decline by preserving the status quo for goal 4 (fostering regional stability and integration) and goal 5 (defusing tensions and promoting arms control). Strategy C seeks to improve upon the current situation for goals 1, 2, and 3, while buffering against a steep decline in goals 4 and 5.

Table 18–7. **U.S. Strategic Goals in Endangered Region**

Step 1: List Strategic Goals	Step 2: Assign Utility Points	Step 3: Assess Performance of Existing Strategy		Step 4: Predict Performance of Alternative Strategies		
		Now	Future	A	B	C
1. Maintain U.S. influence and military preparedness	20	15	12	17	12	16
2. Preserve and strengthen multilateral alliances	20	12	9	15	9	13
3. Deter aggression and competitive rivalry	20	10	6	10	6	11
4. Foster regional stability and integration	20	12	7	7	12	10
5. Defuse tensions and promote arms control	20	11	6	6	11	10
Total Utility Points	**100**	**60**	**40**	**55**	**50**	**60**

These three alternative strategies thus differ significantly from the existing strategy and from each other in priorities and aims. The utility point totals shown in the table suggest that strategy C is the best, strategy A comes in second place, strategy B comes in third place, and the existing strategy finishes a distant last with a mere 40 utility points. Regardless of whether these forecasts are precisely accurate, the key value of the table lies in its ability to put forth numbers as the basis for comparison, enabling senior officials to evaluate the likely performance of these strategies in explicit terms based on performance measures and strategic outputs.

These numbers come from subjective human judgment. For strategic issues of this complexity, there is no scientific methodology for measuring the current situation, much less generating long-range forecasts with pinpoint accuracy. This methodology offers a technique for measuring things as accurately and precisely as possible. The technique is to create a hierarchical structure for each goal that is composed of subordinate objectives and sub-objectives. As this hierarchy becomes less abstract and more concrete, it will coincide more with ground-truth realities, and thus it will generate better measurements of performance. In the final analysis, nonetheless, this methodology is only as useful and reliable as the human judgments that go into it. But when these judgments are sound, this methodology can offer illuminating insights on complex situations and strategy tradeoffs.

A final point about multi-attribute utility analysis is that the optimal strategy is not necessarily the option that scores the most points in aggregate. The top point-getter could be the preferred strategy if U.S. policy is risk-neutral, but it may not be the best if U.S. policy is risk-accepting or risk-averse. Indeed, there are a number of decision strategies that could be adopted as a function of differing attitudes toward risk. A risk-accepting strategy would be to embrace the alternative that does the best job of pursuing the highest-priority goals and related outputs, regardless of whether lower-priority goals suffer. This can be called a maxi-max strategy (a term often used by specialists) because it tries to maximize the most important gains. A less-risky approach is a satisficing strategy, which selects the best alternative that performs acceptably well across the board, even though it might not offer top output in high-priority areas. This strategy may discard an option that fails to pass minimum thresholds for some goals, even if it offers stellar performance in other areas. A very risk-averse strategy, sometimes called maxi-min, may select the option that best avoids damaging setbacks or extremely weak performance in any area. It identifies the lowest-performing areas for each option, and then chooses the option offering highest outputs in these areas.

When multi-attribute utility analysis is employed, it must often account for these different decision strategies. Typically, such decision strategies are on the minds of senior officials who are conscious of risks, priorities, and tradeoffs. Sometimes senior officials will want to act cautiously; on other occasions, they will seek a balance between assertiveness and caution; on still others, they may place such a high priority on some goals that they are willing to go for broke on them even if it means abandoning others. The challenge for this methodology is to provide analyses that help these officials make their decisions as wisely as possible.

Decision Analysis: Evaluating Trees with Many Branches

Decision analysis is a method for analyzing policy and strategy choices when the outcome can be strongly affected by how events unfold during the implementation process. For example, the success of a strategy may be influenced by how the adversary tries to counteract it. It may be influenced by other events that cannot be controlled, such as weather or blind luck. It may be influenced by subsequent U.S. reactions to unpredictable twists of fate. Decision analysis provides a method for taking these possibilities into account in order to evaluate strategy options and their payoffs before they are put into practice.

Like many other operations research methods, decision analysis draws upon human judgments for key input data, and its results will be only as good as the quality of these judgments. Chapters 22 and 23 provide concrete examples of how decision analysis can be used to help guide battlefield campaign plans and weapons-development decisions. Here, the purpose is to illuminate the conceptual and theoretical properties of this valuable tool. While its mathematics are simple, its branching trees and computational procedures can be complex. However, application of this method to appropriate issues can yield fruitful results. Decision analysis is a quantitative method driven by a rigorous logic. One strength is that it provides a sense of how strategy actions might unfold along many different paths, with potential for surprising outcomes that might not otherwise be easily foreseeable. Another strength is that this method shows how payoffs are affected by a sequence of probabilities. In particular, it is useful for assessing the likelihood that high payoffs will actually transpire and measuring the prospects that other outcomes could occur.[10] Decision analysis can be valuable not only because of its eye-opening numerical forecasts, but also because it helps alert senior officials to the ebb and flow of events that may go right but could go wrong. When its numbers alert officials to danger, it can help caution them against the assumption that a predetermined game plan of unfolding success will necessarily prove true. It points toward flexible policies that can adjust to setbacks, and the need to prepare adaptive responses in advance. It also tends to favor cautious policies that are flexible and reliable over "go-for-gold" policies that may go bankrupt instead because they are vulnerable to events that cannot be controlled. Decision analysis thus can give rise to unglamorous conservatism when troublesome possibilities loom, but such conservative thinking can be wisdom.

Figure 18–8. **Simple Decision Tree**

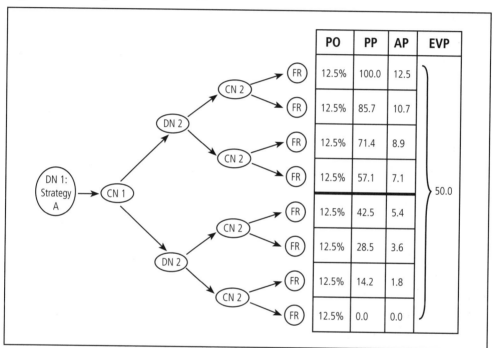

DN1 (Decision Node 1) is the U.S. strategy "A." CN1 (Chance Node 1) is the adversary reaction. DN2 is the U.S. reaction to the adversary's move. CN2 includes other exogenous events that subsequently unfold as the U.S. reaction is carried out. DN1 is a given. The remaining CNs and DNs are each assessed at a 50 percent chance of occurrence. FR is the Final Result. PO is the Probability of this FR Occurring, and PP is its Potential Payoff. AP is the resulting Actual Payoff. EVP is the Expected Value Payoff, or the sum total of all APs.

The conceptual foundation of this method is a decision tree that has numerous branches, nodes, probabilities, and payoffs. A simple diagram of such a tree for a single strategy is displayed in figure 18–8. The purpose of this tree is to provide a map showing how events could unfold once a strategy's actions have been launched. The tree displays a logical flow diagram to help decide how to implement the strategy in the face of uncertain events. As the figure shows, the tree includes a combination of chance nodes and decision nodes. Chance nodes show how external events, such as an adversary's reactions, can unfold in varying ways; each is assigned a probability of occurrence. A decision node indicates alternative ways in which the strategy could be adjusted to events flowing from chance nodes. The result of the interaction of chance nodes and decision nodes is a tree of multiple spreading branches, each of which produces a potentially unique outcome. The payoff for each branch is calculated by the technique of averaging out. That is, individual probabilities along the branch are multiplied in order to generate a combined probability of occurrence. This percentage value is then multiplied by the branch's potential payoff in order to determine its actual payoff. The actual payoffs for each branch are then added to determine the total payoff for the strategy in expected value terms. In order to gauge the likely payoff for each decision node along the way, a technique called folding back can be employed; it requires working backward to determine probabilities and payoffs for each node.

As the decision tree in figure 18–8 shows, strategy A could result in eight different final results, or branches at the end of limbs, determined by the interaction of just two chance nodes and one decision node during the implementation process. If 3 alternative U.S. strategies had been examined, the number of branches would grow to 24. If additional chance nodes and decision nodes had been examined, the number of branches would have increased dramatically. The main implication is that when multiple strategies are being examined in complex situations, decision trees can become quite large and complicated. In many real-life studies, trees that sprout 100 branches or more are common.

Even this example's small decision tree illuminates the value of the methodology and its strategic implications. Most important, this decision tree suggests that although the ideal goal of the U.S. strategy may be a perfect outcome of 100 points, realities encountered along the way may well drive the outcome downward to a middling expected value payoff of only 50 points. This, however, is an average payoff taking into account all possibilities. The wide spectrum of 8 possible results generates a range of payoffs that stretch from 100 points all the way down to 0. As shown in table 18–8, four broad categories of payoffs could emerge here, each with an equal probability of occurrence. The table suggests that although this strategy has a 25 percent chance of succeeding in major ways, it also has a 25 percent chance of yielding almost nothing. The greater likelihood of 50 percent is that this strategy will result in a payoff that is neither high nor low, but somewhere in the middle, between 29 and 71 points.

Given such a payoff matrix, is carrying out this strategy worth the costs? If the costs are considerable, the issue becomes a matter of even greater importance, and a tougher call.

Table 18–8. **Payoff Categories**

Category	Payoff Range	Probability of Occurrence (percent)
High payoff	100–86	25
Medium-high payoff	71–57	25
Low-medium payoff	43–29	25
Low payoff	14–0	25

Ultimately this issue must be resolved by policymakers who apply their own judgments. The decision tree contributes to their deliberations by showing that nothing can be guaranteed, that many things can happen along the way, and that the payoffs of the strategy will depend upon how events unfold: rather than accept the strategy at face value, policymakers need information about the obstacles, and they should take steps to ensure that the strategy will be implemented effectively. The decision tree also makes clear the risks of the strategy as well as the potential rewards, and the results that are most likely to transpire. This decision tree suggests that this strategy, with its middling payoffs and worrisome risks, may not be an attractive choice even if it offers a long shot at a big success. Senior officials might embrace it only if action were deemed necessary and affordable, and if no better alternative were available.

In addition to evaluating individual strategies, decision analysis can be employed to compare multiple strategies. The methodology calls for decision trees to be constructed for each strategy. The results can be illuminating not only about the strategies themselves, but also about the need to be aware of risk. Table 18–9 illustrates a new example, showing three different strategies with different payoff prospects and associated risks. Strategy A is a "go-for-gold" strategy that has a 50 percent chance of a high payoff but a 50 percent chance of a low payoff; it is a risky strategy. Strategy B is a "middling" strategy that has an equal chance of producing a high, medium, or low payoff; it is risk-neutral in the sense that it neither welcomes risks nor goes out of its way to avoid them. Strategy C is a "cautious" strategy that has a 66 percent chance of producing a medium payoff; it is risk-averse.

Table 18–9. **Alternative Strategies**

	Probability of Occurrence (percent)			Expected Value Payoff*	Attitude Toward Risk
	High Payoff	Medium Payoff	Low Payoff		
"Go for Gold" Strategy A	50	0	50	50	Risk-Taking
Middling Strategy B	33	33	33	50	Risk-Accepting
Cautious Strategy C	17	66	17	50	Risk-Averse

* Expected payoff represents sum total of payoffs in each category multiplied by probability of occurrence.

Which strategy is the best choice? Here, all of them have the same expected-value payoff of 50 points on a 100-point scale, so the choice boils down to attitudes toward risk. If the U.S. Government is willing to gamble, it may choose strategy A in hope of a big payoff, even though a low payoff is equally likely. If it is willing to accept some risk, it may opt for strategy B, preserving a 33 percent chance of a high payoff while lowering the risk of a low payoff to 33 percent. If it is inclined to caution, it may choose strategy C, further lowering the chance for a high payoff but also further decreasing the risk of a low payoff. Payoff matrices such as this show why senior officials often opt for unglamorous middling or even cautious strategies, even though as a result they are accused of lacking vision.

The problem with middling and cautious strategies is that they may not be sufficiently attractive in situations where a high payoff is needed. What can be done to enhance their prospects? Decision analysis offers two potential remedies. The first remedy is to gather additional information about the nature of adversary reactions and other unwelcome events in order to sharpen the strategy so as to lessen damaging impacts. The second remedy is to build options into the strategy to provide flexibility and adaptability in case of damaging events. Such options can enable the strategy to execute shifts of direction at the proper moments rather than plow deeper into trouble. Table 18–10 illustrates how these two remedies could shift the payoff matrix of a middling strategy upward, making a high payoff more likely.

Table 18–10. **Impact of Remedies**

	Probability of Occurrence (percent)			Expected Value Payoff*	Cost ($billions)
	High Payoff	Medium Payoff	Low Payoff		
Baseline middling strategy	33	33	33	50	$10
Additional information	40	50	10	62	$11
Flexible U-turns as well as additional information	75	20	5	78	$13

The problem with such remedies is that they are often expensive. In this example, the two remedies together provide a gain of 28 points at an added expense of $3 billion: a 56 percent gain in payoff at a 30 percent increase in costs. However, they elevate the chance of a high payoff from 33 percent to 75 percent, while reducing the risk of a low payoff from 33 percent to only 5 percent. In this example, the prospect of such gains may justify the added expense. But in other cases, the gains in payoffs might not be this large, and the costs could be greater, shifting the calculus against these remedies. Senior officials must make the final determination on a case-by-case basis.

Decision analysis has a great deal to contribute to the study of complex policy and strategy issues in which outcomes are affected by unfolding events as actions are being carried out. This method's usefulness for defense planning is well known with DOD, but it also has the potential to contribute to analysis of foreign policy and diplomacy. In today's world, many U.S. foreign policies and strategies are buffeted by overseas events. Developing advanced awareness of the consequences and implications could help produce refined approaches that tilt the odds toward success. In all likelihood, decision analysis will place a premium on strategies that have flexibility and adaptability for the same reasons that it endorses such characteristics in defense planning. Decision analysis has seldom been used to help guide foreign policy studies in any formal way, but it could be applied more often, sometimes with eye-opening results.

Game Theory: Choosing Optimal Strategies

Game theory is a formal, mathematical method for analyzing competitive situations in the form of chess or other games in which participants make moves against each other. Game theory can be used to predict the outcomes of such contests and to prescribe strategies for the contestants. When applied to national security, its main role is to develop U.S. strategies for use against adversaries. Game theory is not limited to analyzing contests of unmitigated rivalry. It can be used to study situations such as arms control negotiations in which participants pursue shared interests in ways aimed at profiting both sides. Nonetheless, the most-used model in defense policy is the two-person, zero-sum game in which one side profits at the expense of the other, and the sum total of gains and losses on both sides equals zero.[11]

This type of game theory has been addressed by numerous books. Its many specific formulations and mathematics can be complex. Its core concepts, however, are simple to describe. When game theory is used to craft strategies, it assumes that the decisionmaker (Blue) is faced with a rational opponent (Red) who is striving for victory. Game theory offers a way to find a Blue strategy that will yield the highest payoffs against Red's strategy. By providing a strategy anchored in mathematical rules, it tries to help Blue outfox Red. Its basic method is to create a table that displays payoffs in utility points for Blue and Red as a function of their interacting strategies. Table 18–11 shows a game in which each side has three potential strategies. Each cell of the matrix shows payoffs to Blue (Red's payoffs are the inverse value, so where the payoff is +5 for Blue, it is -5 for Red). At the right, the table shows the expected value payoff to Blue for each strategy averaged over Red's three possible strategies. At the bottom, it shows the expected value payoff to Blue for all nine cells of the matrix. The table thus presents Blue with a bird's-eye view of what its three available strategies can be expected to achieve, individually and collectively, to help answer the question of which of these three strategies is best for Blue.

Table 18–11. **Payoff Table for Game Theory (Utility Points for Blue)**

	Red Strategy D	Red Strategy E	Red Strategy F	Blue Payoff: Expected Value (total, averaged)
Blue Strategy A	0	-3	-7	-10/3 = -3.33
Blue Strategy B	5	2	0	7/3 = +2.33
Blue Strategy C	2	1	-4	-1/3 = -.33

Overall Expected Value -4/9 = -.44

The table shows that Blue cannot afford to choose its strategy at random. If Blue acts randomly and Red acts randomly, a game of multiple moves will produce a losing payoff of -0.44 for Blue. Moreover, Red will not act randomly once it sees Blue acting randomly, but will switch to strategy F full-time. As a result, Blue's payoff would be the sum total of the column under Red's strategy F: -11/3 = -3.67, which is an even a bigger loss for Blue than a purely random game. Blue can avert this problem by choosing a dominant strategy, which is a strategy whose payoffs always exceed the other two strategies. The table shows that strategy B is such a strategy: not only is its expected value highest, but for each of Red's strategies, B gives Blue a higher payoff than A or C. When Red sees Blue choose strategy B, Red will search for a dominant strategy of its own. In this case, strategy F is best for Red, not only because it is a dominant strategy for Red, but also because it minimizes Blue's payoff from its strategy B. Thus, this game will settle into a consistent pattern of Blue playing B and Red playing F, with a payoff of 0: a stalemate game in which neither side gains nor loses.

Often, however, zero-sum games do not generate dominant strategies. If so, the best course can be for both sides to adopt a risk-averse approach and to search for a "saddle point" solution to the game. One such approach is called maxi-min for Blue and mini-max for Red: that is, Blue tries to maximize its minimum payoff, while Red tries to minimize Blue's maximum payoff. Figure 18–9 illustrates a game in which the interaction of these two approaches produces a saddle point, which is a cell at which stability is reached. As the table shows, Blue can hope to win big with strategies A or C, but could also lose big. A risk-averse strategy would prevent Blue from losing big. Blue's maxi-min can be found by circling the minimum payoff for each strategy, and choosing the strategy that produces the maximum payoff for them. As shown on the table, B is Blue's maxi-min strategy. Similarly, Red's mini-max can be found by circling the maximum payoff to Blue from its three strategies, and selecting the strategy that minimizes this payoff. For Red, the best strategy is E. These two risk-averse approaches intersect at the middle cell, where strategy B for Blue meets strategy E for Red. This is the saddle point because the game will settle there. A stalemate of 0 points for both sides is the result.

Figure 18–9. **Saddle Point Game (Utility Points for Blue)**

Blue Strategies	Red Strategies			Risk-Averse Perspectives
	D	E	F	
A	15	-3	-5	Blue chooses B as maxi-min.
B	3	0	3	
C	-8	-3	10	Red chooses E as mini-max.
Saddle point occurs at intersection: Strategy B for Blue, E for Red.				

The conclusion that both sides should pursue a single risk-averse strategy applies only to games that produce a stable saddle point. But saddle points do not always occur. When they do not exist, the logic of game theory is that each side should pursue a mixed strategy based on a probabilistic assessment of payoffs. For Blue, the purpose of a mixed strategy is to deny Red the ability to deduce Blue's strategy; the same applies to Red's calculus. In a game of multiple moves, for example, Blue might select strategy A for 33 percent of the moves, strategy B for 33 percent, and strategy C for 33 percent. Red might distribute its moves in similar ways. Such equal distributions would produce an overall payoff that reflects the sum of the 9 cells, that is, 12 points divided by 9 cells, for a payoff of +1.33 to Blue.

However, an equal distribution is not necessarily the best strategy for both sides. Could either or both players anticipate performing better by adopting a different mixed strategy? Game theory provides a graphical procedure for answering this complex question. Consider an entirely new game and payoff table, as shown in table 18–12. Assume that Blue is following the maxi-min approach and Red is following the mini-max approach. Note that, although Blue does not possess a single dominant strategy, strategy B always dominates strategy C. As a result, strategy C can be eliminated because Blue will never choose it. Blue must craft a mixed strategy based on a combination of A and B.

Table 18–12. **Payoff Table for Game of Mixed Strategies**

	Red Strategy D	Red Strategy E	Red Strategy F	
Blue Strategy A	0	-4	4	Mixed Blue strategy will be combination of A and B
Blue Strategy B	10	8	-6	
Blue Strategy C	4	6	-8	Blue's Strategy C eliminated

Figure 18–10 shows how this mixed strategy can be chosen. The *y*-axis displays Blue's potential payoffs. The *x*-axis displays the probability that Blue will choose strategy A. The three lines represent payoffs to Blue arising from the three Red strategies of D, E, and F. Each line is generated by marking the payoff if Blue selects strategy A either 0 percent or 100 percent of the time, and then connecting the two points. Assuming Red is driven by mini-max, it will never select strategy D. Therefore Blue's strategy is determined by the intersection of E and F. This is Blue's maxi-min, because it maximizes Blue's minimum payoff if Red selects D, or F, or a combination of them. The figure indicates that Blue's mixed strategy should embrace strategy A about 65 percent of the time and strategy B about 35 percent of the time (indicated by where the center of the circle is on the horizontal axis). If Blue does so, the figure shows that Blue's overall payoff will be about +0.33 (by where the center of the circle is on the vertical axis).

An algebraic procedure can be employed to get the same result in more exact terms. It unfolds as follows: First, establish the equations that determine Blue's payoffs for Red's strategies E and F. Second, set them equal to each other in order to reflect their intersection point on the graph. Third, calculate the value for Blue's strategy A, and then the value for Blue's strategy B. Fourth, calculate the expected value payoff for the resulting mix of strategies A and B. As shown in the equation below, this procedure indicates that Blue should use strategy A at 64 percent frequency and strategy B at 36 percent frequency. The expected

Figure 18–10. **Graphical Solution for Game of Mixed Strategies**

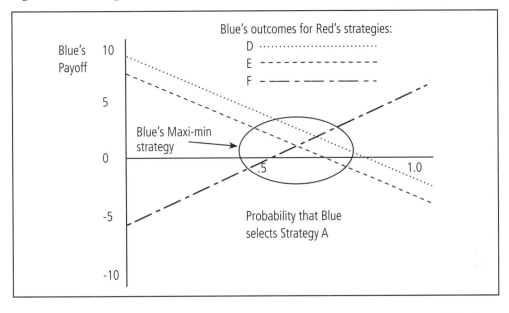

value payoff will be +0.37. Both results are essentially the same as those generated by figure 18–10. A similar algebraic procedure can be used to calculate a mixed strategy for Red of using its strategy E with 45 percent frequency and strategy F with 55 percent frequency.

For calculating Blue's mixed strategy and payoff:
Assume x_1 and x_2 are the probabilities of Blue selecting strategy A and B.
For E: $y = -4x_1 + 8x_2$. Since $x_2 = 1 - x_1$, the equation becomes $y = 8 - 12 x_1$
For F: $y = 4x_1 - 6x_2 = -6 + 10x_1$
Since the y values are the same for both equations at the intersection point,
$8 - 12x_1 = -6 + 10x_1$
Transposition yields the equation $22x_1 = 14$. Thus, $x_1 = 0.636$ and $x_2 = 0.364$
Payoff is determined by using the equation $y = 8 - 12x_1 = 0.37$.
For calculating Red's strategy if the goal is a Blue payoff of 0.37 or less:
Assume Blue's payoff is 0.37 and Red will never choose D.
Postulate y_2 and y_3 are the probabilities that Red will choose E and F.
Postulate that $y_2 (8 - 12 x_1) + y_3 (-6 + 10 x_1) = 0.37$
Solve for y_2 and y_3 by setting x_1 equal to 0 and 1.0
If $x_1 = 1.0$, then $8y_2 - 6y_3 = 0.368$. If $x_1 = 0$, then $-4y_2 + 4y_3 = 0.368$
Simultaneous solution of these two equations yields the two values for y:
   If Equation 1 is $8y_2 - 6y_3 = 0.368$
   and Equation 2 is $-4y_2 + 4y_3 = 0.368$
   Then, $y_2 = 0.45$ and $y_3 = 0.55$.

While such mathematics help establish game theory's credibility, its strategic concepts are more important for analysis of national security strategy. A main insight of game theory is that U.S. strategy always should be alert to the capacity of an adversary to forge a countervailing strategy of its own. An opponent's strategy may be tailored to take advantage of fault-lines in the U.S. strategy and thereby thwart it. The U.S. strategy, too, should be crafted to capitalize on the vulnerabilities of the enemy strategy in order to produce the best possible outcome. This observation may sound obvious, but history shows that it is not. When the United States has failed abroad, as in Vietnam, the reason has usually not been a lack of resources, but instead a failure to anticipate how the adversary's strategy could foil U.S. designs. U.S. successes have tended to be due to the ability to anticipate and countermand an adversary's strategy. This two-fold lesson is worth remembering, and game theory calls attention to the reasons why it remains important.

Another insight of game theory is that it produces cautionary advice about how strategies should be chosen. Like decision analysis, it often casts a skeptical light on the go-for-gold strategies that may run a serious risk of turning to dust. Game theory tends to favor unglamorous strategies that, although they do not promise gold, will not turn to dust and can be relied upon to steadily yield solid returns. To a degree, this viewpoint is a product of how these methods are constructed, but it also reflects difficult geostrategic realities. It does not mean that the United States should never go for gold; indeed, the United States won World War II and the Cold War by aiming high and not settling for a middling outcome. Nonetheless, the conservative advice that tends to come from these two methods suggests that when the United States is pursuing ambitious goals, it must have its plan and its resources ready, and it must know how to defeat a resistant adversary.

Game theory does not, however, generally offer detailed prescriptions about how U.S. strategies and programs should be constructed in specific situations. These tasks are the province of other operations research methods. Even so, a method that offers concepts, not details, can be valuable for reasons of its own. Interestingly, game theory contributed a great deal to the formulation of nuclear deterrence concepts several decades ago, but since then, its greatest impact often has been on charting a conceptual path toward arms control. In this arena, it has tended sometimes to favor sweeping arms reductions, but on other occasions it has shown the virtues of partial reductions that foster stability by reducing the vulnerability of both sides to surprise attacks. This positive stimulus to arms control may not have been predicted by the original architects of game theory, but it says something about the versatility of this valuable method.

Linear Programming: Pursuing Multiple Goals with Limited Resources

To many aspiring policy analysts, no operations research method sounds more alien and unapproachable than linear programming. The title of the method suggests a type of computer programming, but this is not the case. Computer programs can often help solve linear programming problems, but linear programming itself is a conceptual technique for thinking about complex policy issues, not a subdivision of the computer business. Some who are vaguely aware of linear programming might have a concern that its mathematical techniques are too exotic for untrained novices to master. This fear is understandable. Textbooks on the subject offer chapters on such topics as dynamic programming, integer programming, nonlinear programming, and stochastic programming, each of which is loaded with abstruse mathematics. However, the outer limits of this method do not have to be mastered for its basic features to be learned and applied to many real-world policy issues. A little time spent learning about linear programming can be fruitful and worth the effort.

Linear programming is basically a mathematical technique for analyzing how to invest scarce resources in several activities when multiple goals are being pursued or multiple constraints are being faced. It assists economic models of choice that are employed by systems analysts, and it can delve into details that these models cannot readily address. It can also produce data and analyses that help bring these models to life by expanding their capacity to handle complex procurement and acquisition decisions. For these reasons, linear programming is a method that systems analysts should know about, and it can sometimes augment strategic evaluations, too.[12]

Chapter 23 provides an example of how linear programming can be applied to real-world defense investment issues of today. Here, the purpose is to introduce its core concepts as well as its graphical and algebraic techniques. Linear programming bears close similarity to a mathematical technique that high-school algebra students learn: how to solve multiple equations simultaneously. Anybody who can recall this simple technique has made a start at grasping linear programming.

In order to set the stage for linear programming, consider first how the technique of solving simultaneous equations can be applied to solving defense policy issues. Suppose that two different missions must be performed sequentially, and that a program composed of two different assets must be created in order to perform them. For each mission, 100 utility performance points are needed from a combination of asset A and asset B, each of which performs differently in the two missions. Their different performance characteristics give rise to the two equations shown below. Simultaneous solution of them will yield the proper combination of A and B to be acquired. These two equations can be solved simultaneously through a simple two-step process:

Mission Equation 1: $5A + 2B = 100$
Mission Equation 2: $2A + 3B = 100$

Step 1: Eliminate one variable in order to determine the value of the other. This can be done by multiplying the top equation by 3 and the bottom equation by -2, and then adding the equations:

Equation 1: $15A + 6B = 300$
New Equation 2: $-4A - 6y = -200$
Solution: Since $11A = 100$, $A = 9.09$

Step 2: Use the value of A to find the value of B:

Original Equation 1: $5 (9.09) + 2B = 100$
$2B = 54.55$; $B = 27.28$

The same answer can be derived from a graphical technique. Figure 18–11 shows lines for equations 1 and 2. For each equation, the line can be drawn by first setting the A value equal to zero in order to calculate the B value, and then by reversing the procedure to determine the A value. As the figure shows, the two equations intersect at $A = 9.09$, $B = 27.28$, the point of simultaneous solution. Note also that these two equations create an indifference curve (explained in chapter 11), above which any output will meet the goals of the two missions, and below which any performance will not suffice.

Figure 18–11. **Graphical Solution of Simultaneous Equations**

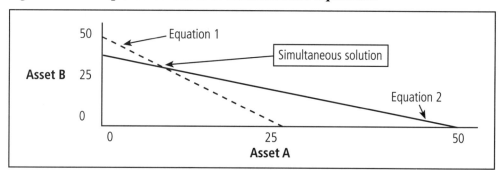

Linear programming employs techniques of simultaneous resolution, but instead of solving equalities, it solves inequalities. That is, it focuses on situations where the purpose of an activity is to match or exceed some goal, or not to go beyond a resource constraint. It employs constraint equations, objective functions, and the concept of feasible regions in order to carry out its search for solutions to minimization problems and maximization problems. Solutions to minimization problems seek to achieve fixed goals as inexpensively as possible, while the solutions to maximization problems seek to maximize the output of fixed resources. An example will illustrate how linear programming solves a minimization problem. Suppose that DOD must procure a posture of two types of fighter aircraft, A and B, in order to perform three different ground attack missions. These three missions do not all have to be performed on the same day, but the posture must be capable of performing the missions on succeeding days. It thus must have multi-mission flexibility. The principal MOE for measuring the posture's performance is tons of ordnance delivered per sortie. In addition, this posture must minimize costs for procurement and operations. Table 18–13 shows the minimum performance goals for each mission, along with the individual capacities of fighter A and fighter B.

Linear programming employs these data in order to generate three inequality constraint equations. Each of the equations dictates how an uncertain number of fighter A and fighter B must combine to match or exceed the relevant performance goal for each mission. Table 18–14 displays these three constraint equations. It also shows how many

Table 18–13. **Illustrative Fighter Capabilities and Performance Goals**

Missions	Aircraft Capability in Tons per Sortie		Performance Goals: Minimum Tons Delivered per Force Sortie
	A	B	
Close air support	12	6	1,500
Battlefield interdiction	9	7	1,275
Deep strike	5	7	1,125

aircraft of each type, if bought alone, could performance each mission. If only Fighter A is procured, 125 would be needed for the close air support mission, 142 would be needed for the battlefield interdiction mission, and 225 would be needed for the deep strike mission. If only fighter B is procured, the requirements would be for 250, 182, and 161 aircraft. The highest number required of each fighter would be where only that aircraft is bought: either 225 of fighter A or 250 of fighter B.

The problem is that if only one of these aircraft is bought, the costs will be high because of the large number required to perform the most demanding mission in each case. Assume that fighter A costs $50 million apiece and fighter B costs $40 million. If only fighter A is bought, a posture of 225 aircraft will cost $11.25 billion. If only fighter B is bought, a posture of 250 aircraft will cost $10 billion. Of the two aircraft, fighter B is the least-cost solution, but its expense is still high. The promise of a posture composed of a mixture of these two aircraft is that the total cost can be reduced. But what is the best mix, and how much would it cost? Linear programming introduces costs into the calculus by establishing an objective function, as shown below. In this case, the objective function says that in addition to performing the three missions, the posture must minimize its total cost.

Objective Function: Minimize (Cost) = 50A + 40B

Linear programming can solve this problem through a graphical technique. It does so by first employing the three constraint equations to draw three performance curves. Each curve is drawn by first determining the value for one variable if the other is zero, and then connecting the two points along the A and B axes. These three curves are displayed in figure 18–12. The manner in which these curves intersect establishes a feasibility range above an indifference curve. Whereas any force performance within this range is acceptable, any performance below it is unacceptable because it would violate one of the three constraint equations (in other words, the number of aircraft would be inadequate to perform one of the missions).

Normally, the list of potentially optimal solutions can be found by searching for corner points on the graph (a corner point occurs where the slope of the line bends sharply). In this case, only one corner point exists, but in other cases, two or three corner points might appear. Because all of them will offer options that are mission-effective, cost analysis must be employed to determine which of these options is least expensive. This is where the objective function enters the calculus. It is employed to generate a cost-exchange curve

Table 18–14. **Constraint Equations**

		Aircraft Needed of Each Type to Accomplish Missions	
		Aircraft A at $50 million each	Aircraft B at $40 million each
Equation 1	12 A + 6B ≥ 1500	125 (= $11.25 billion)	250 (= $10.0 billion)
Equation 2	9A + 7B ≥1275	142	182
Equation 3	5A + 7B ≥ 1125	225	161

Figure 18–12. **Initial Graphical Procedure**

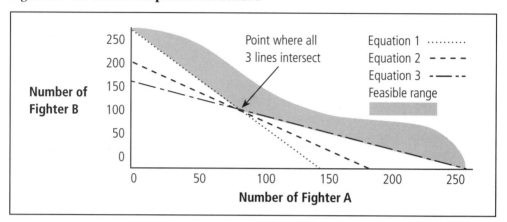

by displaying the mix of aircraft that can be purchased at any given budget level. A workable procedure is to start with a budget that will be significantly lower than the amount that is likely to be needed (here, for example, $5 billion), and then to draw lines at increasingly higher expenses until the cost-exchange curve touches one of the corner points. The result of this intersection is the optimal solution because it satisfies all three constraint equations as well as the objective function. In this case, figure 18–13 shows that the optimal posture will be about 64 of fighter A and 112 of fighter B. The cost of this posture will be $7.68 billion, or quite a bit less than the cost of buying only fighter A ($11.25 billion) or fighter B ($10 billion).

A more exact solution can be found by employing the algebraic technique called Simplex. This four-step technique provides for simultaneous solution of inequalities through an iterative process that moves from one corner point to the next. It employs such concepts as slack variables, pivot rows, and pivot columns in order to find an optimal solution based on proximity of corner points to the objective function. While space does not permit Simplex to be explained in detail, its procedures can be found in linear programming textbooks.[13] Standard computer programs contain Simplex and other computational techniques for solving linear programming problems.

Linear programming has a great deal to contribute to analysis of policy issues in which multiple activities must be blended together to pursue multiple goals in a resource-constrained setting. In order for this method to be used, quantitative estimates of performance characteristics, costs, goals, and mathematical relationships are needed. Linear programming can provide the cost-exchange curves and indifference curves that systems analysis requires in order to make judgments about the optimal composition of programs. A drawback of linear programming is that its techniques are often deemed too esoteric for the uninitiated to follow, much less to use. Behind the scenes, however, linear programming can be used by specialists to considerable advantage because it is often the only reliable method for making sense of otherwise overpowering complexities. It is especially useful when multifaceted programs must be not just approximately correct, but precisely correct.

Figure 18–13. **Final Graphical Procedure**

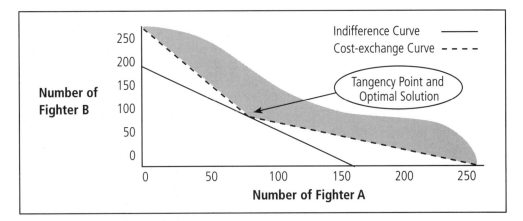

Operations Research Methods in Strategic Perspective

What applies to linear programming holds true for all seven of the operations re-search methods surveyed by this chapter. They come to the forefront when details must be examined, complexities must be studied, precise answers are needed, and data are available. Their mathematical equations can have great analytical power and can yield coun-terintuitive conclusions that would otherwise escape notice. These methods have their greatest usefulness when they can be joined together to shed light on perplexing policy problems. For example, decision analysis, game theory, and multi-attribute utility anal-ysis are natural partners for examining strategic policy choices. Force-exchange models, probability models, statistical models, and linear programming are natural partners for examining defense program issues.

Because of their Cold War heritage, many of these operations research methods are encrusted with barnacles from that conflict. They must be cleaned off and updated for the new era. This process is already under way, but additional progress is needed. An-other drawback is that while, as typically employed, these methods may shed considerable light on microscopic problems, they do not shed enough light on macroscopic prob-lems. A principal challenge now is to operate them as wide-angle lenses, not just mi-croscopes, so that they have something insightful to say about the strategic issues of the day. If they can be employed to meet this challenge, they can play an even greater role in analysis of national security policy and strategy.

Notes

[1] The Military Operations Research Society publishes two excellent journals on defense issues: *MOR Journal* and *Phalanx* (Alexandria, VA). Published quarterly, both journals offer articles that can be understood by non-specialists.

[2] An excellent textbook for operations research methods is Frederick S. Hillier and Gerald J. Lieberman, *Introduction to Operations Research*, 5th ed. (Stanford, CA: Holden-Day Inc., 2000). Since the Hillier and Lieberman book is heav-ily mathematical, new students may wish to begin with Edith Stokey and Richard Zeckhauser, *A Primer for Policy*

Analysis (New York: W.W. Norton and Company, 1978). This chapter draws upon both books for its treatment of methods. Many operations research methods require only knowledge of algebra; however, experience with differential calculus, integral calculus, and differential equations is helpful to learning the more advanced techniques.

[3] An introduction to descriptive statistics can be found in Hubert Blalock, *Social Statistics* (New York: McGraw Hill, 1979). See also William Mendenhall, *Introduction to Probability and Statistics* (Boston: Duxbury Press, 1983); and Ronald E. Walpole and Raymond H. Myers, *Probability and Statistics for Engineers and Scientists* (New York: Macmillan Company, 1972).

[4] For an introduction to regression analysis, see Ronald J. Wonnacott and Thomas H. Wonnacott, *Econometrics* (New York: John Wiley and Sons, Inc., 1970).

[5] See Bruce W. Morgan, *An Introduction to Bayesian Statistical Decision Processes* (Englewood Cliffs, NJ: Prentice-Hall, Inc., 1968).

[6] For examples of force-exchange models in various forms, see Paul K. Davis, *New Challenges for Defense Planning: Rethinking How Much Is Enough* (Santa Monica, CA: RAND, 1994).

[7] For an introduction to this method, see Ralph L. Keeney and Howard Raiffa, *Decisions with Multiple Objectives: Preferences and Value Tradeoffs* (New York: John Wiley and Sons, 1976).

[8] See Barry R. Posen, "Is NATO Decisively Outnumbered?" *International Security* 12, no. 4 (Spring 1988), 186–202. As Posen reports, this method was used during the Cold War to create an "Armored Division Equivalent" (ADE) index, which was then used to assign ADE scores to the entire NATO-Warsaw Pact military balance.

[9] Table 18–6 presumes that the category weights assigned to each weapon remain constant for all situations. In actual practice, situation scoring techniques were used during the Cold War. That is, one set of category weights was developed for combat in Central Europe, another set was developed for combat in Korea, and a third set was developed for combat in the Persian Gulf. Because terrain features differed in each case, category weights varied. As a result, for example, mechanized infantry weapons scored best (relative to the others) in Europe, armor scored best in the Persian Gulf, and infantry scored best in Korea.

[10] See Stokey and Zeckhauser, *A Primer for Policy Analysis*, chapter 12; Hillier and Lieberman, *Introduction to Operations Research*, chapter 15.

[11] For introductory mathematics of game theory, see Hillier and Lieberman, *Introduction to Operations Research*, chapter 8.

[12] See Hillier and Lieberman, *Introduction to Operations Research*; and Raymond A. Barnett and Michael R. Ziegler, *College Mathematics for Management, Life, and Social Sciences*, 3d ed. (San Francisco: Dellen, 1984).

[13] See, for example, Hillier and Lieberman.

Chapter 19
Designing Nuclear Forces and Missile Defenses

Analysis of nuclear forces is a good place to begin understanding how to apply operations research methods to defense resource allocation. Much of the original work using force exchange models and associated mathematics was in the arena of nuclear planning. Understanding nuclear force methods helps set the stage for grasping how operations research can be applied elsewhere. The mathematical models of nuclear force planning are mostly simpler than those of conventional force planning; typically they contain fewer variables, less complicated interactions, and fewer uncertainties. Becoming familiar with them helps establish a foundation for learning the more complex models and methods that come in succeeding chapters on conventional forces.

Moreover, nuclear issues are still an important part of U.S. defense policy and strategy. Addressing these issues and their policy options requires a grasp of associated operations research methods, and how best to combine them with strategic evaluation and systems analysis. Designing tomorrow's nuclear forces will require a clear sense of strategy, performance requirements, and budgetary realities. These key inputs to nuclear force planning can be crystallized and brought together only by applying operations research methods. The reason is that nuclear force issues, including the contentious topic of national missile defense, cannot be understood without mathematics, in the form of simple but powerful models of force exchanges. This has been the case since the early stages of the Cold War, and it remains true today.

The nuclear postures and strategies of the past are rapidly giving way to new departures in the early 21st century, and therefore operations research faces an agenda of change. During the Cold War, the United States and the Soviet Union both deployed large offensive nuclear postures while agreeing to ban ballistic missile defenses. Today, this equation is being reversed: offensive postures are being reduced and limited missile defenses are now sanctioned. In addition, proliferation means that sooner or later, a growing number of countries will acquire nuclear weapons, thus complicating force planning. New assumptions, frameworks, and calculations will be needed to reflect this future. Mastering this agenda is key to handling the challenging nuclear strategy and force posture issues ahead.

This chapter begins by briefly discussing the conceptual and mathematical foundations of nuclear force analysis. Next, it reviews the operations research tools and associated mathematical models that were employed during the Cold War to size and design U.S. offensive nuclear forces. Then it discusses the methods that were employed to analyze ballistic missile defenses and the need for nuclear arms control negotiations during the Cold War. With the historical stage thus set, this chapter turns toward the future. After briefly discussing how to analyze the downsizing of U.S. offensive forces, it concludes with a treatment of mathematical and statistical techniques for analyzing options for national missile defense, including prospects for mid-course intercept and boost-phase intercept. Along the way, this chapter's aim is not to pass judgment on past decisions or to prescribe for the future, but to help provide an introductory education in this field's mathematical models and to show how they can be applied to the nuclear issues ahead.

Conceptual and Mathematical Foundations of Nuclear Analysis

No field in defense policy has had more heated debates, ideology, and strategic theology than nuclear force planning. Thus, this policy arena cries out for rigorous thinking and tight logic, and mathematical models of the sort that operations research can provide. History shows that when impassioned arguments must be set aside and difficult decisions made, numbers often carry the day. Numbers that reflect cost figures, effectiveness parameters, and the interaction of forces dueling with each other are essential to sorting out the good from the bad and the ugly in nuclear force planning. They help determine what endeavors should not be pursued, what goals are feasible, and how money can best be invested to get maximum performance for funds spent. They can provide guideposts for comparing alternative options in situations that would otherwise be paralyzed by major uncertainties.

This is a core reason why the analysis of nuclear forces began relying heavily upon the mathematical models of operations research as far back as the late 1950s. Compared to conventional war, nuclear force operations were relatively simple, narrowly bounded, and clear. They mostly involved nuclear weapons shooting at each other and at other targets, rather than soldiers marching long distances, tanks maneuvering against each other for positional advantage, armies seizing and holding terrain, or forces toppling governments. As a result, they were susceptible to mathematical treatment by models that were both usable and credible. When operations researchers entered this policy arena, they were able to produce analyses that not only broke new conceptual ground, but also provided concrete answers to questions about strategic goals, force priorities, and spending patterns. Since then, operations research has contributed hugely to the lore of strategic concepts and calculations that shape today's common understanding of how preparations for nuclear deterrence can best be made.

From its earliest days, nuclear force analysis was anchored in game theory, which itself came to life in response to the nuclear balance of terror that began taking shape in the 1950s. The great advantage of game theory was that instead of portraying the United States and the Soviet Union in isolation from each other, it provided a formal framework for viewing their interactions as they built their nuclear force postures and strategies. It provided conceptual insights into the potential outcomes of various warfighting scenarios. Equally important, it helped provide mathematical insights about optimal strategy choices in situations where a competitor's countervailing actions could have a large impact on the likely consequences of each strategy option. Game theory showed that each side had a strong rationale for creating a survivable deterrent posture, lest it be vulnerable to a surprise first strike by the other. But game theory also showed that if both sides blindly sought nuclear domination over the other, the inevitable result would be an expensive arms race and an unstable nuclear balance that could trigger runaway escalation in a crisis. The reason was that, because neither side would allow itself to be dominated by the other, both sides would take whatever steps were necessary to checkmate the other.[1]

The matrix shown in table 19–1, drawn from game theory, helps illustrate this interaction. It shows the payoffs for both the United States and the Soviet Union from two different nuclear strategies: strategy A, a disarming first-strike strategy, and strategy B, a second-strike strategy. As the matrix shows, one side could hope for a dominating capability if it pursued strategy A while the other pursued strategy B. But because neither side could accept the risk of the other side having either the appearance or reality of such a dominating capability, the logical result would be that both sides would pursue first-strike strategies, creating a highly unstable relationship prone to rapid escalation. By contrast, both sides would find themselves adequately defended by second-strike postures aimed at deterring each other, thereby producing a stable nuclear balance at affordable cost.

Table 19–1. **Game Theory Matrix of Nuclear Strategies**

		Soviet Nuclear Strategies	
		Strategy A: First Strike Posture	Strategy B: Second Strike Posture
U.S. Nuclear Strategies	Strategy A: First Strike Posture	Neither side dominates; high risk of escalation	U.S. dominates; unstable balance
	Strategy B: Second Strike Posture	Soviet Union dominates; unstable balance	Stable balance at affordable cost

As a result, game theory helpfully advanced the idea that the two sides shared common interests in survival that gave them powerful incentives to moderate their competition not only to reduce the risk of nuclear holocaust to both, but also to avoid bankruptcy. It showed that managing the nuclear balance of terror was neither a zero-sum game nor an exercise in simplistic strategies aimed at winning in some triumphant sense. It called for nuclear strategies to be developed with care, wisdom, and a sense of restraint not normal for military planning. While it called for survivable force postures capable of multiple targeting options, it also laid the foundation for arms control accords aimed at ruling out acquisition of provocative, destabilizing weapons by both sides. It thereby showed how bitter strategic competitors in world politics could enhance their mutual security by cooperating in the realm of nuclear forces.

Having made this landmark conceptual contribution, however, game theory proved too abstract to handle the many detailed questions surrounding nuclear strategy, force postures, and budgets that rose to the fore as ICBMs began arriving in the early 1960s. It was here that operations research into the details of force exchanges began making its mark: it could provide the mathematical analyses that were needed to help guide decisions in these arenas. Over the years, operations researchers created an analytical tool-box centered on the "nuclear arsenal exchange model." Anchored in a set of mathematical equations and quantitative data that modeled the nuclear force exchange process, this model provided formal methodologies for appraising the performance of many different offensive and defensive weapons in a nuclear exchange. The nuclear arsenal exchange model (discussed further below) and other similar models set the stage for many mathematical analyses that were to have a major impact on U.S. nuclear decisions as the Cold War unfolded and that are still being used today.[2]

Virtually the entire rich heritage of nuclear ideas and concepts bequeathed by the Cold War grew directly from path-breaking analyses that employed operations research as well as systems analysis. This heritage includes such now-familiar concepts as assured destruction, damage limitation, counterforce and countervalue targeting, and graduated escalation. While many people employed these terms as common language during the debates of that period, few understood the extent to which they were anchored in mathematical modeling conducted by operations research analyses. Some critics charged that these analyses heavily contributed to the dangerous balance of terror that evolved. Other observers credited these analyses with helping defend the United States while avoiding the nuclear catastrophe that could so easily have happened. Regardless of how history appraises these judgments, these analyses and their nuclear concepts undeniably helped transform confused, emotion-charged policy debates into exercises in logic and reason. In the years ahead, operations research analysis has the potential to make similar contributions if it is conducted with comparable focus and expertise.

During the Cold War years, a main characteristic of nuclear analysis was its careful attention to a myriad of operational details. Because such details were important to the evaluation process, operations research scrutinized such key variables as alert rates, in-flight performance, survivability, communications, blast and yield parameters, and weapons effects against a variety of targets. As a result, operations research shed much light on the physics and engineering dimensions of nuclear forces. Another characteristic was its practice of thinking in terms of statistical probabilities rather than simplistic formulas of total success or total failure. By showing that a kill probability of 0.75 rather than 0.50 had significance, for example, it made clear that decisions for weapons systems needed to reflect a precise appraisal of how they would perform in nuclear war. A third characteristic was its focus on the dynamics of force interactions, as weapons on both sides dueled with each other in their efforts to perform their missions. For example, operations research showed how ICBMs with multiple warheads could be used to destroy enemy missile silos, and why defensive missiles would have trouble shooting down incoming ICBMs. This focus on force interactions led to creation of nuclear computer simulations capable of modeling a large-scale nuclear war and tracking its performance details from start to finish. The result was a growing capacity to provide mathematical interpretations of how nuclear war might be fought, and thus to make programmatic decisions with precise estimates of costs and effects.

A main legacy of operations research during the Cold War was that it debunked the idea of total victory in the nuclear competition, even while it outlined compelling reasons for building a strong deterrent posture anchored in second-strike retaliation. As a consequence, it helped bring stability to a competitive dynamic that might otherwise have erupted into war or bankrupted both sides. An added benefit is that operations research helped promote an insightful dialogue about the U.S.-Soviet nuclear balance by shifting attention away from such crude indicators as megatons and throw-weight, and toward such meaningful measures as the survivability and operational performance of the U.S. posture. Operations research made these contributions not through ideology and emotion, but through the irrefutable logic of mathematics. Along the way, operations research about nuclear war became a model of how to conduct serious defense analysis to shed light on choices of strategies and weapons systems. U.S. decisions to procure new nuclear weapons were often controversial for strategic reasons, but they normally withstood scrutiny on cost-effectiveness grounds, and they consumed only about 10 percent of the defense budget, leaving the sizable remainder for conventional forces.

Alongside this contribution, however, came a liability in the eyes of critics regarding the implications for offensive forces. Throughout the Cold War, nuclear operations research was excellent at analyzing offensive weapons in terms of their capacity to destroy enemy targets. But a wholly separate issue was whether and how the physical destruction of targets enhanced the capacity of the United States to achieve its overarching political goals in a nuclear encounter. In this realm, key questions arose. Did the capacity to destroy most of the Soviet Union's cities and industries, not just a portion of them, truly enhance deterrence in major ways? Did the capacity to engage in counterforce targeting duels—for example, ICBMs shooting at enemy ICBM silos—truly strengthen the Nation's ability to control and influence the escalation process? How many nuclear forces were enough to leave the United States prepared in strategic and political terms, while not stimulating an arms race?

Despite its capacity to analyze the dimensions of target destruction down to the third decimal point, operations research never, in the eyes of critics, provided satisfying answers to such key questions. As a result, it sometimes developed a reputation of not being able to see the forest for the trees. Some critics alleged that its preoccupation with targets created a proclivity for large nuclear inventories that bore little relationship to the political issues at stake. Such critics charged that, as a result, both the United States and the Soviet Union deployed offensive postures of 2,000 launchers or more, and over 10,000 warheads apiece, when deterrence presumably could have been maintained with far smaller forces. Defenders of the outcome countered by saying that these large offensive postures were, in fact, needed to safeguard against surprise attacks and to provide an adequate range of targeting options, and that the resulting nuclear balance was both stable and affordable.

While historians likely will be arguing about these issues for years, an enduring point is that in the future, nuclear analysis must be able to provide more than pinpoint estimates of warfighting scenarios. It must also be able to show how nuclear preparedness can contribute to achieving national goals in a world where bipolarity has fractured into fluid global politics. Such analysis will need to think in strategic terms, but it also will need to continue thinking in mathematical terms. Operations research will still have an important role to play even though nuclear forces, weapons, and budgets will be different from those of the past. Fortunately, many of the mathematical models inherited from the Cold War remain relevant to current issues if they are properly altered to reflect new realities. This is ample reason for understanding their origins, contents, and future possibilities.

Sizing the ICBM Force for the Cold War: Quality versus Quantity

Nuclear operations research sprang to life during the early 1960s, at a time when the United States was switching from a strategy of massive retaliation to one of flexible response. The effect of this new strategy was to downgrade nuclear weapons from their previous status as an all-purpose deterrent and warfighting instrument. Even so, sizable offensive forces were still needed for the new strategy: at a minimum, deterrence required that the United States have enough nuclear weapons to inflict massive destruction on Soviet urban areas. Operations research showed that this goal could be accomplished by a relatively modest force of a few hundred missiles and bombers. But U.S. strategy at the time was not limited to destroying cities. In its quest for flexibility and options, U.S. strategy also sought sufficient capabilities to strike a wider set of Soviet targets, including industrial infrastructure, nuclear forces, and conventional forces. This emphasis on "countervalue, counterforce, and countermilitary" targets seemed to require a sizable offensive nuclear posture. Since it came at a time when the United States was trying to limit spending on nuclear forces in order to fund a conventional military buildup, it raised the question of how many nuclear weapons were enough.

Initial attempts to answer this question focused on the thorny issue of determining how many ICBMs should be deployed. As of 1960, the U.S. nuclear posture was mainly composed of about 2,500 strategic bombers inherited from the 1950s. The new Minuteman ICBMs promised to provide assets for performing many of the strike missions of these bombers. The Kennedy administration was willing to purchase 1,000 ICBMs plus a sizable force of SLBMs to be launched from Polaris SSBN submarines. But senior military officers wanted several hundred additional ICBMs to fulfill their targeting plans. The result was an intense debate within the Pentagon. Operations research helped resolve this debate, not by creating an ironclad theory of total force needs, but by pointing out how efforts to improve the quality of the 1,000 ICBMs already funded would provide a better option for destroying enemy targets than increasing the quantity of ICBMs.[3]

Operations research was able to produce this insight by focusing on the full set of variables that determine the performance characteristics of ICBMs. It showed that steps to enhance their alert rates, their capacity to survive attack and then launch, their in-flight operations, their ability to penetrate enemy defenses, and their warhead detonation rates could greatly elevate their ability to deliver warheads. It also showed how equipping ICBMs with multiple independently targeted reentry vehicles (MIRVs), rather than one large warhead, could further enhance performance if the MIRV warheads were made accurate enough to destroy their targets. While table 19–2 shows illustrative, not actual, numbers, it reflects analyses conducted in the 1960s that illustrated how qualitative measures could produce greater capability, at lower cost, than adding 1,000 additional ICBMs. The core reason is the interaction of multiple factors that determine the operational performance of ICBMs. Because the improved ICBM possesses higher probabilities of successful performance in key areas, more of its warheads will actually reach their targets and detonate. Likewise, greater accuracy helps compensate for the reduced explosive power of the smaller warheads of the improved ICBM. The result is a capacity to destroy 1,062 targets at a cost of $8 billion, far more effective and less expensive than an unimproved force of 2,000 ICBMs that would cost $10 billion.

Table 19–2. **Impact of Qualitative Improvements on Missile Performance**

	Existing 1,000 ICBMs	2,000 ICBMs without Quality Improvements	1,000 ICBMs with Quality Improvements
Performance Variables (probability of success)			
Alert rate	.75	.75	.90
Launch rate	.75	.75	.90
In-flight performance	.80	.80	.90
Penetration rate	.80	.80	.90
Detonation rate	.80	.80	.90
Overall reliability*	.29	.29	.59
Cost-Effectiveness Measures			
Warhead yield	1 Megaton	1 Megaton	.330 Megatons
Warheads per missile	1	1	3
Total warheads	1,000	1,000	3,000
Warheads delivered **	290	580	1,770
Probability of kill per delivered warhead	.85	.85	.60
Targets destroyed ***	246	493	1,062
Cost	**$5 billion**	**$10 billion**	**$8 billion**

*Determined by multiplying the individual probabilities for each performance variable.
**Determined by multiplying total warheads by overall reliability.
***Determined by multiplying number of warheads delivered by the probability of kill per delivered warhead.

For reasons such as these, the Kennedy administration decided to deploy only 1,000 ICBMs and to focus on improving their quality. Ultimately, the ICBM force totaled 450 Minuteman II models, each with 1 large warhead, and 550 Minuteman IIIs, each with 3 MIRVed warheads. The military services came away satisfied because this approach provided them greater effectiveness than buying additional missiles. This case is important not only for historical reasons, but also because it is a model approach: improving the quality of existing forces can often make more sense than buying more forces. Higher quality is not always the preferred choice over more quantity—each case must be judged on its merits—but numbers are not the only consideration in determining force capabilities. Operational performance factors can spell the difference between a force that functions at a high level of proficiency and a force that functions at a low level. Analyzing the role of these factors can be key to determining how to strengthen not only nuclear forces, but conventional forces as well. Often the tradeoff between quality and quantity can be decided only by probing deeply into these operational details. Neither strategic evaluation nor systems analysis, nor any other methodology, can perform this task; only operations research can do so.

The idea that 1,000 upgraded missiles can perform much better than 2,000 unimproved missiles sounds counterintuitive. Its plausibility becomes clear, however, when the multiple factors that determine operational performance are taken into account along with their collective impact. The smaller upgraded missile force functions better because it performs with marginally higher proficiency in each of several performance variables. When these differences are totaled, the result is a big difference in reliability: 59 percent versus 29 percent. Additionally, each improved missile carries three MIRVed warheads rather than one big warhead. As a result, the smaller force delivers more warheads on target than does the force with twice as many ICBMs. Each of these smaller MIRVed warheads has a lower yield than the bigger warhead, but the difference is narrowed because it has greater accuracy; for many targets, accuracy is more important than yield. The combined result is that 1,062 targets are destroyed by the smaller ICBM force, over twice as many as the 493 targets destroyed by the larger force. Operations research was able to discover these differences because of its focus on performance variables and its ability to synthesize multiple data elements in order to generate a composite portrayal. It accomplished this task not by ultra-sophisticated mathematics, but by combining a grasp of operational details with simple statistics and probability models.

Choosing the Triad: The Virtues of Standing on Three Legs

Although the decision to deploy an ICBM force of 1,000 Minuteman missiles was important, it did not resolve the larger issue of the overall size and configuration of the entire nuclear offensive posture, which was composed of three legs: missiles, bombers, and submarines. To help address this issue, operations research and systems analysis developed a useful force-sizing construct called the assured destruction concept, which became famous in the defense community. The purpose of the concept was to determine how many megatons of nuclear power were needed to inflict "unacceptable damage" upon the Soviet Union by destroying its urban areas and industry. The core notion was that if such destruction were "assured" or unavoidable, the Soviet Union would be reliably deterred because it knew it would face hideous damage in an all-out nuclear war. The mathematics of the concept, which modeled damage only from immediate nuclear blast effects and not from long-term radiation, are displayed in table 19–3. As it shows, damage rises in relation to the amount of megatons delivered. At the level of 400 megatons, destruction totals 30 percent of population and 76 percent of industry. After this point, however, destruction rises much more slowly as additional megatons are added: little further damage to industry is recorded. The effect is to create a curve of diminishing marginal

Table 19–3. **Assured Destruction Calculus**

Delivered Megatons	Percent of Soviet Population Killed	Percent of Soviet Industry Destroyed
100	15	59
200	21	72
400	30	76
800	39	77
1,200	44	77

returns. After the "knee of the curve" is reached at 400 megatons, additional megatons would not provide additional damage commensurate with the cost of delivering them.[4]

Although the assured destruction curve provided a valuable metric for gauging the requirements of one mission, it did not provide an overall theory of total nuclear force needs. One reason is that because it measured only the megatons that must be detonated over targets, it did not gauge the number of megatons that the nuclear force must field in order to ensure delivery at the required level. The problem was that forces might be destroyed by enemy attacks before they arrived at their targets. The effect of taking this calculus into account was to elevate total force needs well above 400 megatons. For example, suppose that 200 bombers would be needed to drop 400 megatons. Suppose further that 30 percent of bombers would be destroyed by Soviet missile attacks before leaving their airbases, and that another 30 percent of the survivors would be destroyed by enemy air defenses as they entered Soviet airspace. Simple mathematics shows that 408 bombers would be needed to ensure that 200 bombers would arrive over their targets and drop their bombs:

If $x \, (.7) \, (.7) = 200$, then $x = 408$

Moreover, U.S. nuclear war plans called for the destruction of many targets other than cities and their associated industry. In particular, plans called for attacking Soviet conventional forces, including command and control sites, bases for ground forces, air forces, naval forces, logistic storage depots, and road and rail networks. This war plan created many targets that were dispersed over a wide area, and one or two warheads would be required for each to ensure that all would be destroyed. The effect of this enlarged target system was to elevate U.S. nuclear force requirements greatly, the more so when potential losses to U.S. forces from Soviet offensive and defensive attacks along the way were considered: four warheads, for example, might be needed to ensure that two arrived at their destination.

An additional force inflator was concern about catastrophic failure in one or two legs of the posture. Bombers had proven their reliability, but they were at risk because, despite their alert procedures, unexpected numbers might be destroyed on the ground by enemy missiles or lost enroute to air defenses. As for ICBMs and SLBMs, they had never been used in combat. Despite extensive quality assurance efforts, a plausible risk existed that significant numbers might be vulnerable to unanticipated technical flaws, such as failed electronics. The desire to provide insurance against such failures under-scored the value of the three-legged posture which became known as the triad. Beyond this, three legs provided operational synergy: for example, missiles could suppress ene-my air defenses, creating entry zones for bombers. Although bombers flew slower than missiles, they could be recalled in flight, and they could carry a variety of munitions for flexible targeting, leaving missiles available to be used for their optimal purposes, such as time-urgent targeting.

Confronted by these pressures and incentives, DOD force planners, supported by operations research, created the theory of the strategic triad. This theory held that the nuclear posture should permanently have three strong legs: ICBMs, SLBMs, and bombers. The effect was to quash any idea of retiring bombers in favor of missiles, or substituting SLBMs for ICBMs. The triad theory further held that each leg must have sufficient forces to survive an enemy attack and deliver an "assured destruction" level of damage on its own. When all of its calculations were added up, the triad theory held that a second-strike U.S. nuclear posture should be capable of delivering not just 400 megatons, but the equivalent of 1,200 megatons, because each leg must be capable of delivering 400 megatons by itself. These 1,200 megatons would provide sufficient nuclear warheads not only to destroy urban areas and industry, but also to attack other targets. Procurement of small warheads ultimately enabled the force posture to deploy about 10,000 warheads, about 50–60 percent of them aboard Polaris and Poseidon submarines, 20 percent aboard ICBMs, and the rest aboard bombers.[5]

By the early 1970s, the triad concept had become official U.S. military doctrine for nuclear war. Critics protested that it was overly conservative, that it unwisely elevated force requirements, and that its focus on multiple targeting options would stimulate an arms race with the Soviet Union. The triad doctrine, however, had advantages that offset these liabilities. It did not open the door, as feared by some, to a big U.S. nuclear buildup. Instead, it confirmed the nuclear posture that already existed. By this time, the United States had 350 B–52 strategic bombers, 1,000 ICBMs, and 656 SLBM missiles aboard 41 SSBN submarines. Because each leg of this triad already possessed a capacity to deliver the equivalent of 400 megatons or more, no additional forces were needed. A main effect of the triad doctrine was not to raise the ceiling and call for a further buildup, but instead to specify a floor below which each leg of the posture should not fall, thus ensuring that major cutbacks would not be taken in bombers, ICBMs, or SLBMs. Although critics com-plained that this stance damaged prospects for arms control negotiations, the triad doc-trine undeniably brought stability to nuclear planning while shaping a force posture that was survivable and capable of multiple targeting options because of its size and diversity.

The triad doctrine, by stabilizing each leg of the triad, enabled operations research to focus on just how each leg could be configured and improved for the future. The re-sult was a steady stream of analyses addressing how to make qualitative improvements in bombers, ICBMs, and SLBMs. The most important change was the MIRVing of 550 Minuteman III missiles and all 656 SLBM missiles, which greatly increased the number of deliverable warheads in the nuclear inventory. Additionally, the Poseidon submarine was procured to replace aging Polaris models. Initially these improvement efforts had limited horizons, both because nuclear budgets of the 1970s were tight, and because existing weapons systems were mostly still too new to need replacement anytime soon. This would change, however, as the 1970s gave way to the 1980s in an atmosphere of mounting Cold War tensions.

Modernizing the Triad: Countering the Soviet Missile Threat

The chief motive of U.S. force modernization of the 1980s was to counter the growing Soviet nuclear threat, which was eroding the credibility of U.S. nuclear strategy. In the 1960s, when many U.S. force-sizing decisions for nuclear forces were made, the Soviets fielded only a small offensive missile force. The situation began to change, however, when a big Soviet missile buildup gained momentum during the 1970s. The exact motive for this buildup was uncertain, but it unfolded in the context of a parallel modernization of Warsaw Pact conventional forces in Europe, and it seemed aimed at gaining the Soviets a form of exploitable strategic superiority over the United States and NATO. By 1980, the Soviets deployed a missile force of 1,400 ICBMs and 63 SSBN submarines carrying 942 SLBM missiles—enough to provide a 1.4:1 superiority over the United States in ballistic missiles. The nature of the Soviet ICBMs was equally worrying. Most were MIRVed, carrying numerous warheads. The Soviet posture included 308 SS–18 missiles, each of which carried 10 large MIRVed warheads. The effect was to equip the Soviet ICBM force with about 6,400 warheads, many of them high-yield. When Soviet missile tests showed growing accuracy, U.S. alarm grew that the Soviets were trying to acquire a capacity to destroy the Minuteman force in a disarming first strike.[6]

The question arose of how the United States should respond. Operations research helped answer this question by employing the arsenal exchange model. Originally developed in the 1960s to address offense and defense issues, discussed below, this model was reconfigured in the early 1980s to address the threat of a disarming Soviet first strike. This new version of the model posited a two-way interactive scenario in which the Soviets initiated a nuclear war by launching a disarming first strike aimed at suppressing all three legs of the U.S. triad. After absorbing this blow, the model portrayed a U.S. second-strike response aimed at the Soviet targets in U.S. war plans. The model, which came in versions of varying complexity, included sets of mathematical equations for analyzing both phases of this interaction. It thus allowed analysts to measure two critical outputs: the number of U.S. forces that would be destroyed or would survive a

Figure 19–1. **Conceptual Foundation of Arsenal Exchange Model for Disarming First-Strike Scenario**

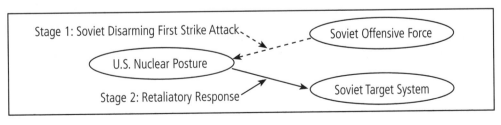

Soviet first strike, and the number of U.S. warheads that would thereafter arrive at their targets. By employing these equations and output variables, analysts could then compare how alternative modernization plans could increase the survivability of U.S. forces and their ability to destroy Soviet targets.

The first issue to be addressed by this model was whether the Soviet missile buildup in fact posed a serious threat to the survival of the U.S. Minuteman ICBM force. Close inspection of the operational details showed that there was enough of a threat to justify worry among U.S. planners, but that the buildup would not necessarily give the Soviets high confidence that a disarming first strike would actually succeed. The reason for this ambiguous conclusion lies in the complex statistics of nuclear force operations and performance parameters of missile strikes. The relevant statistics can be discerned by employing a simple mathematical equation for gauging the capacity of incoming enemy warheads to destroy hardened U.S. missile silos through nuclear blast and overpressure effects.

Equation: Total U.S. ICBMs killed = $n\,(1-Ps^n)$
Where:
n = total number of U.S. ICBMs (for example, 1,000);
Ps = the probability that a single silo will survive a strike by a single enemy warhead; and
n = the number of enemy warheads detonated over the silo.

Use of this equation shows that destruction of virtually the entire Minuteman force was theoretically possible. As a result of their ICBM buildup, the Soviets possessed ample warheads to allocate three warheads against each Minuteman silo. The large size of these warheads (perhaps one megaton) and their growing accuracy (they may have had the ability to land, on average, within one-eighth of a mile of the silo) suggested a high kill probability for each warhead (perhaps 0.70) and therefore a low probability of survival (Ps) for each Minuteman silo (here, 0.30). As the following calculus shows, if three enemy warheads were shot at a single silo, the statistical likelihood of the silo being destroyed would be, given those presumptions, 97 percent. If this prediction is generalized to the entire U.S. ICBM force of 1,000 Minutemen, the mathematical conclusion is that only 27 ICBMs will survive. This is, from the U.S. point of view, the virtual equivalent of a disarming first strike against the ICBM force.

Total U.S. ICBMs killed = $1,000\,(1 - 0.30^3)$
= 1,000 * (1 − 0.027)
= 1,000 * .973
= 973
U.S. ICBMs surviving = 1,000 − 973 = 27

Closer inspection, however, shows that this successful attack is predicated on the assumption that each incoming Soviet warhead would have a high single shot probability of kill (SSPK) of 0.70. While this SSPK was theoretically possible, it required Soviet missiles to show high operational reliability: about 90 percent of them would have to launch successfully, fly through the upper atmosphere, and arrive over the target field. Moreover, pinpoint accuracy was critical. Analysis of nuclear effects showed that in striking missile silos hardened to resist pressures of 3,000 pounds per square inch, accuracy is significantly more important than yield.[7]

As a result, the SSPK drops off markedly as accuracy declines. For example, if an enemy warhead needs an accuracy of one-eighth of a nautical mile to achieve an SSPK of 0.80, its SSPK will drop to about 0.50 if its accuracy degrades to one-fourth or one-half of a nautical mile. The potential combination of lessened reliability and degraded accuracy would undermine any Soviet expectation that a first strike would actually disarm the United States completely. Indeed, if reliability dropped to 0.80 and accuracy declined to one-fourth or one-half of a nautical mile, Soviet SSPK would decline to 0.40, and the Minuteman silo would have a 0.60 chance of surviving. As a result, a Soviet attack by 3,000 nuclear warheads would leave fully 216 Minutemen surviving, not 30: a big difference.

Total U.S. ICBMS killed = $1,000 * (1 - 0.60^3)$
= $1,000 * (1 - 0.216)$
= $1,000 (0.784) = 784$
U.S. ICBMs surviving = $1,000 - 784 = 216$

Because Soviet technology did not have a reputation for high reliability or pinpoint accuracy, simple mathematics suggested that the Soviets could not have confidence that they could wipe out nearly the entire Minuteman force in a single blow. But because such a scenario was theoretically possible, the United States could not afford to ignore it. Beyond this, the issue was broader than whether multiple Minuteman ICBMs would survive. The Soviet missile buildup also posed a threat to a significant portion of the U.S. bomber force and SLBM force. Up to one-half of U.S. bombers might be destroyed before they could escape their bases or else might be shot down by Soviet air defenses over the Soviet Union. Up to one-third of U.S. SLBMs might be destroyed because at any given time, their submarines were normally stationed in ports for normal repairs, rather than deployed at sea. As a result of losses in all three legs of the triad, only about 40 percent of total launchers would be available to carry out their missions.

The worrisome issue was not whether the United States would, after a Soviet first strike, still possess enough nuclear power to devastate Soviet cities. The surviving force would have ample megatons and warheads to accomplish this purpose. Rather, the issue was whether, apart from forces for counter-city missions, there would be enough warheads

Table 19–4. **U.S. Nuclear Forces Surviving a First Strike**

	Total U.S. Launchers	Potentially Destroyed in Soviet First Strike	Total Number Surviving Soviet First Strike
ICBMs	1,000	784–973	27–216
SLBMs	656	219	437
Bombers	315	158	158
Totals	1,971	1,161–1,350	622–811

and megatons to strike the many other targets in U.S. war plans. After losing 60 percent of U.S. launchers in a first strike, and setting aside 400 megatons for counter-city strikes, this would leave only about 400 launchers and as few as 1,200 warheads for counter-military strikes. In addition, the loss of virtually the entire Minuteman ICBM force could leave few missiles capable of swiftly and efficiently striking enemy hardened targets: neither the bombers nor the SLBMs were capable of performing such counterforce roles. Moreover, there was concern about what would happen if the bombers or submarines suffered some crippling technical or operational setback that removed them from the warfighting equation. Having lost its ICBM force and another leg of the triad, the United States might be left with a one-legged posture in a war for which it needs a triad.

All of these concerns added up to worry about the continued capacity of the nuclear posture to carry out U.S. nuclear strategy, with its emphasis on flexibility and options. Moreover, the Soviet Union was acquiring a reputation on the world political stage for surpassing the United States in nuclear power, and there was worry that the Soviet government might, as a result, feel free to commit aggression somewhere. An urgent need thus arose for the United States to embark upon a major modernization of its nuclear posture in order to offset this threat and restore its capacity to carry out the U.S. military strategy. But the critical question was exactly how this demanding agenda could be carried out with the funds that were available.

Answering the question became easier after 1981, when the Reagan administration greatly increased spending on nuclear forces. The annual budget for nuclear forces shot up from $12 billion in 1981 to $26 billion in 1985, and remained at that level until the Cold War ended. The effect was to fund vigorous modernization. Even so, all three legs of the triad needed modernizing, and competing options were available for each. For example, there was general agreement that the new MX ICBM should be procured and added to the Minuteman force. Bigger than the Minuteman, the MX carried 10 warheads with hard-target yield and accuracy. Adding 100 of these missiles promised to elevate the ICBM warhead total by 50 percent—from 2,000 to 3,000 warheads. But in order to survive a Soviet first strike, the MX required mobile basing. Three alternatives were available: a "race-track" system, road basing, and rail basing. Choosing the best option was anything but obvious, because complicated tradeoffs existed. Each option offered a different balance of survivability from attack, maintenance costs, operational readiness, and safety. Similar tradeoffs arose in deciding how to modernize the SLBM and bomber forces, where multiple competing options also had to be assessed.[8]

While the details are too complex to recount here, operations research played an important role in analyzing them and making sound recommendations. For all three legs of the triad, operations research employed mathematical equations, computer simulations, and quantitative data in order to assess the performance, costs, and tradeoffs of the various options. After prolonged studies and debates, a series of concrete decisions emerged. For the ICBM force, DOD decided to procure 100 MX missiles in the rail-mobile mode. For the SLBM force, it initiated procurement of 19 Trident submarines to replace the aging Poseidon. The Trident submarine carried 24 missiles, compared to 16 on the Poseidon. DOD also launched procurement of the D–5 missile for several Trident boats. A bigger missile than its predecessors, it had a capacity of 2.5 megatons, which permitted it to carry multiple warheads with the yield and accuracy to kill such hardened targets as ICBM missile silos. It also had a range of over 7,000 miles, allowing Trident submarines to remain farther away from Soviet waters and defenses. For the bomber force, DOD increased the readiness of its B–52 bombers and equipped many of them with accurate air-launched cruise missiles (ALCMs). A load of 20 ALCMs promised to turn each B–52 into a formidable weapons system that could deliver its ordnance from outside Soviet air defense networks. Equally important, DOD decided to buy not only 95 B–1 bombers, which had previously been rejected by the Carter administration, but also 20 stealthy B–2 bombers. With some old B–52s nearing retirement, the effect was to keep the bomber force at about 325 aircraft, but with a vastly better capacity to perform its missions.[9]

The effect of this triad-wide modernization program was profound. The U.S. nuclear posture remained at roughly 2,000 launchers while the number of warheads increased to 12,000 or more. At the same time, the posture's operational effectiveness greatly improved. The MX missile restored the ICBM posture's ability to survive a surprise attack and to play a big role in nuclear warfighting, including attacks against hardened targets. The Trident submarine and D–5 missile improved SLBM survivability and provided a seaborne missile for counterforce targeting. The bomber programs made these aircraft capable of surviving a first strike and penetrating thick enemy defenses with many ALCMs. In addition, improvements to communications, intelligence, and other systems enhanced C[4]ISR systems for nuclear warfighting, thereby further improving force effectiveness.

Critics complained that this modernization program was too expensive, unnecessarily provocative to the Soviet Union, and damaging to arms control negotiations. Whether these arguments were valid can be debated, but this program sent the Soviet Union a clear message during the 1980s that it could not hope to achieve nuclear supremacy over the United States. Perhaps the U.S. nuclear buildup played a role, along with other U.S. military programs, in influencing the Soviet Union to take the steps that resulted in an end to the Cold War in 1990. Regardless, the main purpose of this program was not merely to send political messages, but to strengthen the U.S. military's capacity to deter nuclear war, and to wage it if necessary. This program came at the cost of doubling the nuclear budget, but it elevated U.S. nuclear preparedness by a factor or two or more. It is likely to go down in history as one of the most successful defense modernization efforts ever undertaken by the United States, and reasonably cost-effective as well. Of the six major new weapons systems fielded, only one—the B–1 bomber—has in the years since then been seriously criticized as an underperformer. Operations research did not provide the main strategic motive for this program, but it helped shape the all-important details, and it consistently steered DOD toward wise choices. For this reason, operations research gets a share of the credit.

Why Missile Defenses Were Not Deployed: Mission Impossible

A remarkable feature of the Cold War is that, although the United States and the Soviet Union both deployed large offensive forces, neither of them deployed significant ballistic missile defenses. Such an outcome seems counterintuitive: many have questioned why two countries that were piling up missiles designed to destroy each other were at the same time doing little to protect themselves from each other's missiles. Why was this the case? Common lore holds that the two countries rejected ABM defense because it would have triggered a massive arms race and undermined prospects for arms control. While this explanation is partly true, ABM systems were not rejected because defense systems were deemed inherently evil and destabilizing. After all, both sides constantly maintained bomber defenses, and both sought ways to sink each other's SLBM submarines in a war. Moreover, a thin ABM system would not threaten the retaliatory deterrent of either side. The crucial reason was that the mission of full-scale, country-wide missile defense was too difficult to perform in operational terms, and it was also unaffordable. The technology of ABM defense did not allow either country to build a reliable shield over itself even had the large sums needed been devoted to this endeavor. Full-scale ABM defense was simply impossible for both sides, and this gave them an incentive to negotiate the ABM Treaty banning virtually all ABM systems.

This conclusion could not have been reached and widely accepted without the powerful mathematical insights provided by operations research. The origins lie in the famous DOD "Damage Limitation" study conducted in 1964. Commissioned by Secretary of Defense McNamara, this study was originally seen by many participants as a step toward a major ABM deployment. But when it emerged, it threw cold water on the enterprise. The study began by positing that both the United States and the Soviet Union would employ two strategic concepts to guide their nuclear planning: assured destruction and damage limitation. Assured destruction meant that each country would always possess a survivable second-strike posture that could retaliate against a first strike by inflicting massive destruction on the opponent's cities and urban areas, which would call for about 400 megatons of destruction by each side. Damage limitation meant that each side would erect defenses capable of preventing the other side from inflicting such destruction. The two concepts were arrayed against each other. The task of the damage limitation study was to determine whether and how the United States could use ABM defenses to limit damage to itself to an acceptable level in the face of a determined Soviet effort to preserve its capacity to inflict assured destruction.[10]

The study tackled this agenda by employing an early version of the nuclear arsenal exchange model. Addressing ABM defense as part of a larger nuclear war, the study focused on a scenario in which U.S. missile defenses tried to ward off a large Soviet missile attack aimed at American cities. The study used the arsenal exchange model to analyze the

Figure 19–2. **Arsenal Exchange Model for ABM Defense**

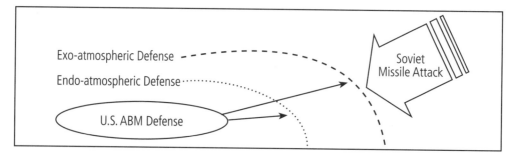

prospects of defeating this attack by employing various combinations of exo-atmospheric missile defenses such as the long-range Spartan missile and endo-atmospheric missiles such as the short-range Sprint missiles, backed by phased-array radars and modern command centers. It also considered the use of offensive U.S. missile strikes as part of this defensive mission. By analyzing the mathematics of this scenario, the study endeavored to determine the degree to which attacking Soviet missiles could be shot down, and the cost of deploying a sufficiently large ABM system to do so effectively.

This study by no means rejected missile defense as technically impossible; it noted that each Spartan and Sprint missile would have perhaps a 30 to 50 percent probability of shooting down an incoming missile. It further argued that a limited ABM system would stand a reasonable chance of defeating a limited attack by a few enemy missiles. But it also reached the landmark judgment that even a big ABM system would probably be overwhelmed if hundreds or thousands of enemy MIRVed warheads descended upon the United States at the same time. It showed that even if the United States fired 4 interceptors at each of 6,000 enemy warheads, as many as 400–1,500 warheads would nonetheless penetrate this ABM screen and inflict an assured destruction level of damage upon the United States. It further showed that the cost of such a large ABM system would be well beyond DOD's capacity to pay unless it stripped its conventional forces of their improvement programs. Table 19–5 provides data from official DOD documents of the period to illuminate this conclusion.[11]

Table 19–5. **Estimated Performance of an ABM System, Late 1960s**

Defense Program	10-Year Cost ($billions)	U.S. Fatalities (in millions)	
		After Soviet First Strike	**After Soviet Retaliation for U.S. First Strike**
No major defense system	0	130–135	90–105
Fallout shelters with no ABM	$3.4	110–115	80–85
Major ABM system	$22.5	80–95	25–40
Enlarged ("thick") ABM system	$30.1	50–80	20–80

On the table, funds for fallout shelters and improved bomber defenses are included in the two ABM options; they account for about 20 percent of the cost. As the table shows, "thick" ABM systems were believed able to protect millions of Americans: they would reduce fatalities from 130 million–135 million to as low as 50 million–80 million in the event of a Soviet first strike, or to 20 million–80 million in the event of Soviet retaliation after a U.S. first strike. But even losses near the low end, around 50 million people, would still be one-fourth of the entire U.S. population; moreover, this figure included only casualties due to immediate nuclear blasts, not those that would result from radiation and economic dislocation afterward. The cost—between $22.5 billion and $30.1 billion in 1960s dollars—was a prohibitive amount that would have doubled spending on nuclear forces. The basic message was that a thick ABM system was unaffordable, and even if it worked as advertised, the United States would still suffer unacceptable losses in a nuclear war. Damage could only be limited, not prevented, and vast destruction was unavoidable. The same judgment applied to the Soviet Union, which also would remain vulnerable to assured destruction even if it deployed a thick ABM system and launched a first strike.

What doomed thick ABM defense was the MIRVed warhead. Prior to the MIRV, ICBMs were armed with a single warhead. A Soviet ICBM force of 1,400 missiles could have been addressed by an ABM system capable of defending against 1,400 incoming warheads. MIRVing, however, greatly expanded the number of warheads carried by the ICBM force. Because Soviet ICBMs were big, they carried five or six MIRV warheads or more, creating a huge target system that would be arriving fast. Because ICBMs dispersed their MIRV warheads shortly after leaving the atmosphere, there was not enough time for long-range Spartan missiles to reach them before dispersal. As a result, a U.S. interceptor would be needed for each and every enemy nuclear warhead, not just for each missile. Moreover, MIRV warheads were independently targetable: as they flew through space, they separated from each other to a considerable distance, and they could be programmed to attack separate, widely spaced targets on the ground. Consequently, a single Spartan interceptor could not hope to destroy more than one of them, and Sprint missiles on the ground would have to defend many targets. The effect was to elevate ABM force requirements and budgets greatly, even if individual interceptors were reasonably effective.

Moreover, the damage limitation study showed that even if the United States deployed a big ABM system that threatened the enemy's assured destruction capability, the Soviet Union could react by further enlarging its missile forces. A competitive race between U.S. ABM defenses and Soviet offensive missiles would ensue. While the United States was not necessarily destined to lose this race, it would face adverse cost-exchange ratios of up to 4:1. If the Soviet Union's goal was to inflict only 40 million fatalities, it could offset an existing U.S. ABM system by spending $5 billion more on offensive missiles; in order to counter this Soviet increase, the United States would have to spend $20 billion more on ABM defense, as shown in table 19–6.

Table 19–6. **Cost-Exchange Ratios for ABM Defense**

Ratio of U.S. Spending on Thick ABM System to the Cost to the Soviets to Counter It	Level of U.S. Fatalities Needed to Assure Soviets that U.S. is Deterred from Attack
4:4	90 million
4:2	60 million
4:1	40 million

The study pointed out that such highly adverse cost-exchange ratios did not apply at modest levels of ABM defense which, while protecting against limited attacks, did not threaten either side's assured destruction capability. But they did apply at the high levels of ABM defense needed to establish an effective shield over U.S. soil aimed at reducing casualties to low levels in event of a full-scale nuclear war. The inevitable result would be a highly expensive arms race, fueled by endless offensive-defensive interactions, which the United States could not afford.

The study said that because ABM defense was feasible in a technological sense, a limited ABM might be affordable and effective. It thus left the door open to a thin ABM system configured to ward off small-scale attacks by a few Soviet missiles whose launch was accidental or unauthorized, or by an enemy such as China with a small nuclear posture. But it closed the door to a thick ABM system that could impair the Soviet Union's assured destruction capability. It closed the door not because it deemed missile defense improper, but because it viewed a thick ABM defense as too expensive, of questionable effectiveness, and easily countered by inexpensive measures that the Soviet Union could readily afford. The outcome of this judgment was a U.S. decision to begin deployment of a limited ABM system, but to abandon any plans for a thick ABM system until better technology became available. The thin ABM system, initially called Sentinel and later renamed Safeguard, was ultimately cancelled for reasons of operational ineffectiveness. In addition to deciding not to deploy a thick ABM system, the U.S. Government decided to initiate arms control negotiations with the Soviet Union aimed at getting bilateral agreement not to pursue thick ABM deployments.

Ultimately, these negotiations produced the ABM Treaty of 1972, which banned thick ABM systems but initially authorized thin systems. The ABM Treaty, when coupled with the Strategic Arms Limitation Talks (SALT) and the Strategic Arms Reduction Talks (START) that focused on limiting offensive forces, did much to advance the cause of arms control negotiations with the Soviet Union, and thus to help stabilize the Cold War. Contrary to common lore, however, the United States pursued an ABM Treaty not because it deemed a situation of mutual assured destruction (MAD) as desirable or even stable. The real reason was pragmatic: because full-scale ABM defense was impossible, the United States and the Soviet Union shared an incentive to prevent their nuclear competition from being channeled into this endless and unaffordable cycle. The ABM Treaty reflected this pragmatic calculus, not necessarily a decision to install MAD as a doctrinal centerpiece for managing nuclear tensions, nor to permanently forsake missile defense if new, better technologies were to arrive on the scene. In the view of the U.S. Government, according to Defense Secretary McNamara, MAD was a lamentable but irreversible situation to which accommodations must be made, not an outcome or strategy to be celebrated as a crowning achievement of wise arms control.

When the Reagan administration took power in 1981, it was determined to resurrect the idea of a thick ABM defense system capable of protecting the United States from a major Soviet missile attack. Indeed, President Reagan eventually put forth a vision of an entirely new nuclear balance in which the United States and the Soviet Union would have few offensive weapons pointed at each other, but both would have sizable missile defenses for guarding against attack. Accordingly, in 1983 the Reagan administration launched the well-funded Strategic Defense Initiative (SDI), often called "Star Wars."

SDI invested in RDT&E for new missile defense technologies to replace the outmoded Spartan and Sprint systems.[12]

During the course of the 1980s, the SDI investigated prospective space-based systems such as particle-beam weapons and "brilliant pebbles," a wide-area kinetic energy system. The idea that seemed to capture greatest interest was that of stationing a network of high-energy lasers in space that could be used to destroy enemy ICBMs as they rose from their launch pads. Technological problems were encountered, however, in designing lasers of the necessary high power, and of applying them effectively against a large number of fast-moving ICBMs in a short time. In addition, the cost of a satellite-based laser defense was prohibitive, at an estimated several hundred billion dollars for the large, globe-spanning system of laser-equipped satellites that would be necessary. Many satellites would have to be launched and maintained continuously in space in order to provide continuous coverage of the Soviet Union as the Earth rotated.

By the end of the Reagan administration, interest in a space-based system was fading. Focus returned to Earth-based defense missiles with kinetic energy weapons, rather than the nuclear warheads of Spartan and Sprint, to provide a limited missile defense system at affordable cost. Accordingly, RDT&E funds began to be invested in the C⁴ISR systems, communications technologies, advanced radars, and highly accurate defense missiles that such a posture would require. To disappointed SDI enthusiasts, the idea of a thin national missile defense (NMD) system sounded like old wine in new bottles that would not alter the "balance of terror" even if it could deal with limited strikes. However, the original verdict of operations research remained intact: thick missile defenses aimed at erecting an impenetrable shield over the United States remained beyond the state of art and would be neither effective nor affordable.

Analyzing Offense and Defense in the Early 21st Century

The years since the end of the Cold War have seen a major reversal in the nuclear balance inherited from that standoff. Offensive systems are now being reduced significantly, while limited national missile defenses are now being deployed by the United States. In both arenas, critical policy decisions will be needed in the coming years in order to make sure that the right types of forces are fielded. This new situation creates a need for a new kind of operations research that can help define reductions in the offensive arena and buildup in the defensive arena wisely.[13]

The changes that have already swept over U.S. offensive forces are profound. Whereas during the Cold War the United States deployed about 2,000 launchers from all 3 legs of the triad, today it deploys about 1,500. Meanwhile Russian launchers have been halved, from 2,400 to about 1,200. Further reductions will be brought about by the nuclear arms control agreements of recent years. Whereas the SALT agreements of the Cold War largely capped offensive systems but did not reduce them appreciably, the START I Treaty, signed in 1994 and implemented by 2001, started on the path toward major reductions by calling for limits on offensive postures on each side at about 6,500 warheads. The START II Treaty and the accompanying Moscow Treaty of 2002 will reduce the two sides to 1,750–2,250 missile warheads by 2007.

In addition to these numerical reductions, the United States and Russia have agreed to a major change in the operational configuration of their offensive forces. Essentially, both sides have agreed to remove MIRVed ICBMs that could be used for killing hard targets in large numbers. The effect is to stabilize the nuclear balance further by removing a potential incentive to first-strike attacks. The two sides are also moving away from the old model of actively targeting each other so as to be prepared for nuclear war at a moment's notice. The new purpose of their offensive nuclear postures is deterrence in a generic sense, not intimidation and coercion of each other. These major changes have been made possible, of course, because now that the Cold War has ended, the United States and Russia no longer regard each other as adversaries. The end of the NATO-Warsaw Pact confrontation has removed the old incentive to maintain large nuclear forces that could support conventional war plans in Europe. Likewise, the United States and Russia now see little purpose in large offensive missile forces that mostly counter each other without serving other political and strategic goals.

For the United States, the old triad doctrine has given way to what is called a "new triad" concept: offensive systems composed of nuclear and conventional weapons; defensive systems, both active and passive; and protection of homeland infrastructure and resources. The strategic forces budget, which previously consumed 9 percent of the DOD budget, is now down to 2.3 percent. The United States will continue to maintain an offensive force that has three legs—ICBMs, SLBMs, and bombers—but the size of each is being reduced appreciably in order to conform to new arms control limitations. By 2007, the U.S. force will be down to 500 Minuteman missiles that carry 1 warhead apiece, 14 Trident submarines with 24 D–5 missiles each carrying about 8 nuclear warheads, and about 100 B–52 and B–2 bombers, many armed with ALCMs. These reductions, coupled with the elimination of worry about a surprise enemy first-strike attack, greatly ease the problem of designing and affording future U.S. forces. But they do not eliminate the need to continue applying operations research to the challenges that lie ahead.

One challenge will be to determine whether, and to what degree, future arms control accords should aspire to reduce U.S. and Russian missile warhead levels below the currently planned level of 1,750–2,250. Some observers call for reductions to 1,000 warheads or even fewer, and for abandonment of the three-legged force posture in favor of two legs or even just one (perhaps only SLBMs). The presumed effect would be to make the nuclear balance even more stable and to further lessen the risks of war. The countervailing argument is that a three-legged posture of 1,750–2,250 warheads will still be needed for several reasons. One would be to ensure survivability against a surprise attack and to provide options other than targeting enemy cities. Another purpose would be to provide a hedge against other countries acquiring threatening nuclear postures, and to reassure allies of continued U.S. deterrence coverage over them. A third purpose would be to provide support for conventional operations. Bombers are already showing a capacity to perform dual nuclear and conventional roles, as are cruise missiles. In the future, long-range ballistic missiles might be used with highly accurate conventional warheads against individual targets, not large areas. Eventually the emergence of directed-energy weapons and other exotic technology may further alter the role of nuclear weapons and delivery systems. Until then, however, nuclear weapons mounted on the launchers of a three-legged posture will remain the basis of the U.S. strategic position.

Beyond these arguments over the future size and configuration of the offensive posture, the current U.S. nuclear weapons—Minuteman ICBMs, B–52 and B–2 bombers, and Trident submarines with D–5 missiles—are all aging and eventually will have to be replaced. Modernizing them will not be cheap in an era when the dominating emphasis will be on transformation of conventional forces, not of nuclear forces. Determining exactly how to replace aging systems will require a new form of operations research focused on the goals and missions of the future.

Arguments over the role of offensive weapons will continue, but the controversy over national missile defenses will dominate the debate over U.S. nuclear strategy in the years ahead. The goal of the current NMD effort is a thin defense against a limited attack by a rogue country, not defense against Russian missiles. DOD is also pursuing a robust set of theater missile defenses to defend forward-deployed troops and allies. All three services have programs under review, including the Army's PAC–3, the Air Force's air-launched systems, and Navy systems for defense at all altitudes. Some observers make the case that theater systems can make a bigger contribution to U.S. security than homeland defense missiles. A main reason is that future adversaries are likely to be more successful at deploying medium-range and intermediate-range missiles for their regions than at deploying ICBMs capable of reaching the United States. Nonetheless, adversaries such as North Korea may deploy a few ICBMs at some juncture; in addition, the risk of accidental or unauthorized launches from other nuclear powers will remain. As a consequence, the hot debate over national missile defense seems unlikely to cool any time soon.

After years of delay, the United States is now beginning to deploy a few missile interceptors in Alaska to provide an initial NMD capability. Meanwhile, it is pursuing RDT&E programs of about $9 billion annually in order to develop technologies for all forms of missile defense. The political atmosphere surrounding this effort includes intense debate over whether NMD systems should be deployed at all. Some participants claim that NMD systems are vitally important in a world of nuclear proliferation. Some claim that such threats are exaggerated, and that NMD systems will trigger a new arms race while being unaffordable and ineffective. Some quarrel over the type of NMD system to be deployed: mid-course interceptors (MCIs) stationed in the United States, or boost-phase interceptors (BPIs) stationed abroad near enemy launch sites. The result is a polarized debate between "either-or" choices.

Often missing in this debate is a pragmatic focus on the size, mix, performance goals, and costs of a future NMD system. Key choices will not boil down to "either-or" propositions. Instead, the decisions are likely to focus on how to shape an NMD program so that it is cost-effective. Key questions that will arise, if NMD is to be acquired in some form, include identifying what defense goals should be pursued, how many missiles should be deployed, what mixture of MCIs and BPIs would be best, how much money should be spent in order to provide adequate insurance at affordable cost, and what program and budget options are available. Operations research has the potential to contribute analyses of relevant issues and options that could help today's debates lead to constructive decisions, but in order to do so, operations research must employ its mathematical tools in new ways.

A good way to see how operations research could contribute is by combining back-of-the-envelope conceptual thinking with use of simple probability models of force interactions. In theory, the best way to shoot down enemy ICBMs during their flight is to employ space-based lasers, but despite ongoing RDT&E, this capability is unlikely to be available any time soon. National missile defense thus must be accomplished by Earth-based systems for the foreseeable future. Based on an updated version of the nuclear arsenal exchange model, figure 19–3 displays the key operational features of such an NMD defense. The flight path of enemy ICBMs will take about 30 minutes to pass through 3 stages. The first stage is boost phase, as the ICBM rises from its launch pad and passes through the Earth's atmosphere. This phase lasts only 4 or 5 minutes. The second stage is the mid-course phase of about 25 minutes, as the ICBM warhead separates from its missile and travels through space on its way to its target. The third stage of terminal re-entry lasts only a minute or so as the warhead re-enters the atmosphere and reaches the target. Interest in BPI systems for the first stage is growing, but today's NMD defenses focus largely on MCI systems for the second phase, while terminal defense is no longer being pursued. The guiding concept is to rely upon kinetic energy or "hit-to-kill" technology in which the warhead of an MCI directly collides with the incoming warhead, destroying it. The hope is that the combination of space-based radars for early warning, X–band radars for fire control, and accurate MCIs will provide a capacity to defeat an enemy threat of 20 ICBMs or so.

Figure 19–3. **Operational Features of National Missile Defense**

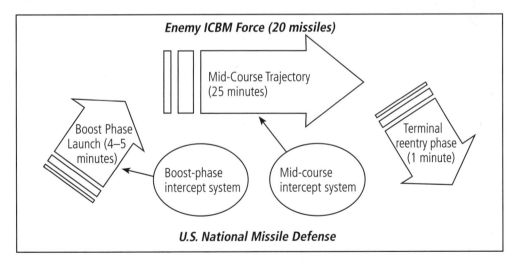

The figure suggests that the issue of whether an MCI system will work depends heavily upon the SSPK likely to be achieved by each MCI. Consideration of the mathematical extremes shows the sensitivities to this value. If the SSPK is zero, MCIs will not succeed regardless of the number of interceptors deployed. If the SSPK is nearly 1 (100 percent), 20 MCIs—1 for each ICBM, if each ICBM carries only 1 warhead—will have virtually 100 percent probability of destroying all 20 ICBMs. Based upon tests to date, which have been about one-half successful, the public literature suggests that with today's technology, an SSPK of 0.50 is a reasonable estimate. This figure is by no means the only number possible: in fall 2004, newspaper reports indicated that expert assessments varied, ranging from 0.25 to 0.75, with 0.50 as the midpoint. If 0.50 is taken as a basis for calculating, then an MCI force of 20 interceptors would shoot down only about 10 of the 20 enemy ICBMs, allowing the surviving 10 warheads to strike U.S. cities. Thus, a larger number of MCI warheads would be needed to defeat this threat. Use of a simple mathematical formula tells us how many.

Number Enemy ICBMs Killed = $n \left(1 - Ps^n\right)$
Where n = Total Enemy ICBMs (here, 20)
Ps = Probability of Survival (here, 0.50 since, SSPK = .50)
n = Number of MCI warheads that are independently shot at each ICBM.

Because of operational constraints, this equation assumes that "volley fires" (explained below) will be necessary, rather than a "shoot-look-shoot" strategy. A "shoot-look-shoot" strategy would elevate the effectiveness of an NMD force, reducing the number of interceptors required for any given level of effectiveness. For example, a defender who possessed 40 MCIs could initially allocate 20 of them to intercept the 20 incoming warheads. Assuming they destroyed 10 warheads, the defender could then employ 10 of the remaining 20 interceptors to attack the surviving 10 warheads. Assuming this destroyed 5 of them, the defender could then use 5 of the remaining 10 interceptors to attack the surviving 5 warheads; the defender can then send its last 5 interceptors against the remaining 2.5 incoming warheads. In this case, the MCI force could shoot down virtually all incoming warheads: 95 percent.

A "shoot-look-shoot" strategy, however, is infeasible today because the fast speed of incoming warheads likely does not provide the defender enough time to fire one round of interceptors, survey the new situation, and then fire one or more additional rounds. Instead, the defender must fire all of its interceptors at about the same time, with two allocated to each incoming warhead. Such "volley fires," as a result, destroy only 75 percent of the warheads, not 95 percent. Reliance on volley fires elevates the number of interceptors that must be deployed for any given defense goal.

By using this equation of volley fires, simple arithmetic generates the illustration in table 19–7 (in which the SSPK is still 50 percent or 0.5). As it shows, firing 2 missiles at each ICBM warhead would increase the NMD system's performance: instead of 10 ICBM warheads surviving, 5 survive. Additional interceptors are needed in order to reduce the number of surviving ICBMs close to zero. Because probability mechanics produce diminishing marginal returns, fully five interceptors must be fired at each ICBM warhead to reduce the number of expected survivors to less than one. Even then, one ICBM warhead could survive. Indeed, statistics dictate that a 100 percent perfect defense is impossible. Moreover, the hopeful forecast of destroying 19 ICBM warheads is sensitive to the assumption of a 0.50 SSPK for each MCI. If the SSPK were 0.30, or if only 50 interceptors could be fired instead of 100, 3 or 4 warheads would be likely to survive. The main message of this table thus is twofold: even a force of 100 MCI missiles would not provide an impenetrable shield against a threat of 20 ICBM warheads; however, such an NMD defense would greatly lessen the damage that could occur.

Table 19–7. Illustrative Capacity of Mid-Course Intercept System to Defeat Limited Attack of 20 Non-MIRVed ICBMs

MCIs Fired per Incoming ICBM	Total Number of MCIs Fired as Volley	Total Incoming ICBMs Destroyed (assuming 0.50 SSPK)	Total Incoming ICBM Warheads that Reach Their Targets
1	20	10	10
2	40	15	5
3	60	17.5	2.5
4	80	18.75	1.25
5	100	19.38	.62

Even though a 100 percent perfect defense is mathematically impossible, there is a big difference between losing 20 cities and losing just 1 or 2, or even 3 or 4. Hope for such a performance is a main motivator for an NMD system because it could help deter an enemy attack while providing mostly successful, even if not airtight, defense in the event of attack. Critics respond to this optimistic calculus, however, by pointing out that an MCI force of 100 interceptors could be foiled; an enemy need merely equip each ICBM with multiple warheads, or even with decoys. For example, an enemy force of 20 ICBMs with 3 warheads per missile would generate an enlarged system of 60 targets, rather than 20, for the MCI system to defend against. This is the case because mid-course intercept means that interceptors reach their targets well after the enemy disperses its MIRVed warheads. Enemy MIRVing or decoying thus greatly complicates MCI defense. But it does not make MCI defense impossible. Instead, it elevates the number of MCI missiles that must be deployed in order to have the confidence of shooting down virtually all of the larger enemy target system. Table 19–8 displays the mathematics of MCI defense against 60 enemy MIRVed warheads mounted atop 20 ICBMs.

As the table shows, MIRVing can restore an enemy's capacity to deliver nearly 20 nuclear warheads against U.S. targets even in the face of 100 MCIs. But the U.S. defense capacity could be restored by increasing the number of MCIs: doubling the force to 200 missiles would reduce the number of enemy warheads that get through from 18.8 to 6; tripling the MCI force would reduce the survivors to 1.9; and deploying 350 MCIs would reduce the number to only 1 survivor, or about the same as a situation of 100 MCI shooting at 20 enemy warheads on 20 non-MIRVed missiles. Such a large MCI deployment is technically feasible; the problem is its high cost. Illustratively, assume that the life-cycle cost of a system of 100 MCI missiles will be about $45 billion: $5 billion for further RDT&E; $20 billion for procuring the missiles, radars, and other assets; and $20 billion for operations over 15 years. If so, the cost of 350 interceptors would be fully $145 billion,

Table 19–8. **Illustrative Capacity of Mid-Course Intercept System to Defeat MIRVed ICBM Attack of 20 Missiles with 60 Warheads**

MCIs Fired per Incoming ICBM	Total Number of MCIs Fired as Volley	Total Incoming Warheads Destroyed (assuming 0.50 SSPK)	Total Incoming Warheads that Reach Their Targets
1.67	100	41.1	18.9
2.50	150	49.3	10.6
3.33	200	54.0	6.0
4.17	250	56.7	3.3
5.00	300	58.1	1.9
5.83	350	58.9	1.1

a large amount even by DOD standards. An MCI force of this size could require doubling of DOD's budget for nuclear forces, which would encroach upon conventional force transformation.[14]

It is here that boost-phase intercept systems enter the NMD calculus. A BPI system would be deployed overseas, near potential enemies. It could thus be used to shoot down enemy ICBMs during their launch phase, well before they could disperse their multiple MIRVed warheads. This advantage would greatly reduce the number of BPI missiles that must be deployed, and thereby reduce the cost. In theory, a BPI force of 100 interceptors in Asia could destroy virtually all of a North Korean force of 20 ICBMs. Coverage of the Middle East would require deployment of a second BPI cluster near that region. Even so, a BPI force of 200 missiles, large enough for both regions, could provide the same protection as an MCI force of 350 missiles. If life-cycle costs per interceptor were equal for each type of system, the BPI system could cost $85 billion, or $60 billion less than the $145 billion of the large MCI system.[15]

A closer look at operational realities, however, suggests a more complicated picture. Boost-phase intercept is a highly demanding mission. Because an enemy ICBM completes this phase in only 4 or 5 minutes, a super-fast BPI is needed to reach its target on time. Such an interceptor has not yet been developed. Even if an effective interceptor can be developed, command and control dynamics enter the operational equation. A period of only 4 or 5 minutes is not a great deal of time for a forward-deployed U.S. naval force or air force to receive authorization to fire and then to coordinate the firing of 5 missiles at each ICBM an adversary might launch. The risk is that constraints from the command and control process could result in a major NMD system failure if the United States were to rely solely upon BPIs to destroy the entire enemy ICBM force. This mission may be impossible, or at least an imprudent bet.

Fortunately, a less drastic option than a pure BPI defense is available. The option is to rely upon a combination of BPI and MCI missiles to perform the NMD mission. For example, the United States might deploy one BPI per enemy ICBM in each theater: most likely, one BPI could be fired at each ICBM even if time did not permit five to be fired. This limited BPI force could significantly degrade the number of ICBMs that would survive the launch process. The United States would deploy sufficient MCIs to destroy the remaining enemy ICBM warheads that escaped interception during the boost phase. Table 19–9 illustrates how such a combined NMD posture of 40 BPI missiles and 150 MCI missiles might perform, along with its costs. Against a threat of 20 non-MIRVed ICBMs, this force could use 20 BPIs and 50 MCIs in order to allow only 0.60 warheads to reach their targets, and it would still have a strategic reserve of 20 BPIs and 100 MCIs. Against a threat of 60 warheads from a single theater, this combined force could use 20 BPIs and all 150 MCIs in order to allow only 0.94 warheads to reach their targets. True, this force costs more than a posture of 100 MCIs, but it performs far better against a threat of 60 warheads. While its performance against this threat is similar to that of a posture of 350 MCIs, it costs significantly less: $86 billion versus $145 billion. Taking costs and effectiveness into account, this posture seems to be the best of the three alternatives.

Table 19–9. Performance of a Combined BPI/MCI System for NMD

Option	Number of Enemy Warheads that Survive NMD Defense (for Threats of 20 Warheads)	Number of Enemy Warheads that Survive NDM Defense (for Threats of 60 Warheads)	Illustrative Life-Cycle Cost
100 MCI missiles	.6	18.8	$45 billion
350 MCI missiles	.6	1.0	$145 billion
40 BPI and 150 MCI missiles	.6*	.94**	$86 billion

* 20 BPI and 100 MCI, leaving 20 BPI and 50 MCI in reserve.
** 20 BPI and 150 MCI, leaving 20 BPI in reserve. If an additional reserve of 50 BPI is sought, costs will rise to $106 billion.

Because these NMD mathematics are illustrative, they should not be taken literally. Actual performance and cost parameters might be different than assumed here. Yet these mathematics illustrate important policy themes that seem likely to hold true regardless of the actual numbers. The most important theme is that NMD is not an "either-or" proposition. Operations research shows that the United States does not have to choose between possessing an NMD defense and pursuing sensible arms control. Nor does the prospect of trying to defend itself from rogue nuclear powers mean it must bankrupt its defense budget. Instead, the United States can aspire to a viable and affordable NMD defense that is consistent with arms control and other foreign policy aims.

In building such an NMD defense, the United States can choose from a spectrum of options with varying costs and performance. Much depends upon its defense goals and the amount of money that it is willing to commit. An MCI posture of 50 missiles could provide defense against a small threat of 10 ICBMs and warheads at an illustrative cost of about $25 billion. If a future enemy were to field a larger force of 20 single-warhead ICBMs, an MCI posture of 100 missiles would provide a substantial defense, albeit not an airtight shield, at a cost of about $45 billion. If future threats were to grow to 60 warheads and decoys, a mixed force of 40 BPIs and 150 MCIs could provide equivalent assurance at a cost of about $86 billion. If BPI systems are not available, an all-MCI force of 350 interceptors would cost about $145 billion.

The viability of all NMD options depends greatly upon the technical performance of U.S. interceptor missiles, whether MCI or BPI models. SSPK is a hugely important variable in the NMD calculus: whereas an SSPK of 0.50 for MCI missiles makes missile defense a viable proposition, an SSPK of 0.25 would lessen the effectiveness of an NMD force while elevating costs considerably, from perhaps $86 billion to $162 billion–$210 billion. Conversely, an SSPK of 0.75 could lessen MCI requirements and costs from, perhaps, $86 billion to $66 billion. Continued RDT&E efforts aimed at achieving high SSPKs thus is vital to enhancing the performance and lowering costs of national missile defense.

Shooting down an enemy ICBM is technically possible, but because it is like hitting a fast-moving bullet with another bullet, it is a demanding task. Kinetic-energy "hit-to-kill" warheads make a direct hit absolutely essential: a near-miss achieves nothing. If high SSPKs cannot be achieved, use of a warhead that employs wide-area blast effects may become necessary. Ultimately, a mixture of warheads, including kinetic energy, conventional explosives, and low-yield nuclear weapons, may prove to be the best approach by providing a menu of defense options that can be tailored to the situation.

Another crucial technical issue is the performance of not only the interceptor, but also its back-up radars and C⁴ISR systems. The entire NMD system must orchestrate the successful firing of not just one interceptor, as on the test range, but of dozens or perhaps 100 to 200 interceptors. This is a tall order that requires the highest standards of systems engineering design and quality control. Performance in this area may be as important as the interceptor missiles, their warheads, and their costs. A space-based system of lasers or other directed energy weapons might improve upon today's cumbersome ground-based missiles and radars, but this breakthrough seems far in the distant future, and even then, its affordability might be questionable. Until then, a vigorous RDT&E effort on future missile defense technologies will be needed even as current systems are being fielded.

As matters now stand, the United States arguably needs a thin but effective NMD system, but nobody can offer an ironclad estimate of how large this force should be, how it should be composed, how much it would cost, and how well it could perform. As a result, the United States will be acting in the face of uncertainty about endstates, but it will know the basic direction to travel, and it can navigate the future by taking one step at a time and by making adjustments as better information becomes available. A flexible, multiyear program composed of further RDT&E and initial phased missile deployments makes sense. For example, the United States could deploy an initial batch of 50–75 MCI missiles and thereby gain protection against small-scale attacks and accidental or unauthorized ICBM launches. As this effort is unfolding, it can take stock of the emerging situation, including threats and the technical performance of its NMD system, and then make decisions about further deployments. Perhaps it will decide to halt deployments at 50–75 missiles if tests reveal their effectiveness to be high and threats to be low. Alternatively, it may decide to deploy more interceptors: perhaps as many as 150 MCIs and 40 BPIs or even more. Such decisions, however, can be made on a year-to-year basis, driven by funding requirements for procurement and by industrial production schedules. In this way, it can postpone decisions about the NMD endgame until it can be truly defined.

If a future of incremental steps and continued soul-searching lies ahead, operations research and its mathematics will have a great deal to contribute to the ongoing NMD debate. During the 1960s, the Damage Limitation Study employing these techniques transformed a heated theological debate about competing defense concepts into a reasoned dialogue about technological performance and cost-effectiveness. It showed that while a thick missile defense was a bad idea, a thin defense would make sense if it worked and was not inimical to arms control, a judgment that still holds true today. With the United States now starting to deploy a limited NMD system in a setting of vociferous debate, the time has arrived for such a dialogue again, and operations research may be able to help bring it about.

Seeing Offenses and Defenses in Strategic Perspective

Designing future nuclear offenses and defenses will require mathematical analysis, but it will require a sense of strategic perspective for the new era as well. During the Cold War, large offensive forces were needed to deter attack on the United States, but they also were needed to provide assurances of extended nuclear deterrence coverage over vulnerable allies. U.S. and allied conventional forces are now amply strong to deter and defend against non-nuclear attacks, lessening the need for nuclear reassurance in this respect. Nuclear proliferation into the hands of rogue powers, however, means that numerous allies will still need U.S. extended deterrence coverage. This is a good reason for keeping offensive nuclear forces sufficiently strong so that the intent and capability of the United States is never doubted, even by countries prone to misperception.

Because of the need to deter rogue powers, U.S. offensive nuclear forces will be targeted and employed in ways vastly different from the Cold War. Rather than flexible escalation and massive retaliation, the emphasis will be on limited options carried out by strategic forces capable of both nuclear and conventional responses. This argues for a force posture that can be used in a variety of ways. The need for flexibility and agility thus applies to both conventional and nuclear forces. Whereas the Cold War created a need for big nuclear warheads in order to destroy cities and other targets requiring major blast effects, future missions may require pinpoint attacks against small targets such as command centers, underground bunkers, industrial plants, and missile launchers. The precision accuracy of modern weapons will often permit the use of conventional warheads and special-effects weapons, or low-yield nuclear warheads designed to limit collateral damage. Growing numbers of strategic forces—not only bombers, but perhaps ballistic missiles as well—may therefore be armed with conventional warheads and specialized technologies rather than nuclear explosives. This may well contribute to the prevention of nuclear war and its consequences.

As for NMD defense, the United States was able to forsake missile defenses during the bipolar Cold War because it could safely rely upon the rational behavior of the Soviet Union as well as its capacity to maintain firm operational control over its force posture. This condition has, however, passed into history. The world is no longer bipolar, and in the coming years, additional countries will possess nuclear weapons and long-range delivery systems. Some of these countries will be led by rogue governments whose self-restraint and physical control over their nuclear forces cannot be taken for granted. Thus, the U.S. Government faces strong pressures to deploy limited national missile defenses, regardless of the debates surrounding their strategic effectiveness and costs.

A thin NMD will be needed not only to defend the U.S. homeland, but also to help strengthen the flexibility, determination, and credibility of the United States as it deals with a wide spectrum of potential overseas crises conducted under the shadow of WMD systems. A thin defense could also contribute to crisis stability by giving the United States other options besides preemptive disarming attacks in the event that intelligence data suggested that a rogue country was on the verge of deploying an ICBM. Also needed are thin theater defense systems that are networked with a U.S. NMD system to protect overseas allies—in Europe, Asia, and elsewhere—from missile threats that could reach them. An international regime of thin missile defenses could help strengthen integrative ties among peaceful countries, including Russia. It also could help dissuade rogues from acquiring expensive offensive missiles that would bring them few strategic fruits.

In today's world, there is nothing in a sound arms control philosophy that would keep the United States from protecting itself and its allies with a thin NMD from nuclear attacks or accidental launches. National missile defense remains controversial in some quarters for several reasons, including costs and doubts about its technical effectiveness. Yet many analysts judge that the United States cannot afford to be left vulnerable to a nuclear-armed rogue, with no missile system for even trying to defend itself, despite years of fruitless RDT&E on such a system. An NMD system should be made as operationally effective as possible, but even if an initial system is imperfect, proponents say, it will be far better than nothing. If so, the real issue is not whether to deploy an NMD system, but how best to do so in ways that are effective, affordable, and flexible enough to keep options open.

New-era strategic logic and the mathematics of operations research as employed here suggest that a future offensive force might be composed of a three-legged posture with 1,750–2,250 warheads, coupled with a combined NMD force in the vicinity of 40 BPI missiles and 150 MCIs, to defend against a MIRVed or decoyed enemy threat. This, of course, is not the only option that should be analyzed. Different threats, goals, priorities, budgets, and technologies could give rise to a different response. Alternative combinations of offense and defense can be imagined, and perhaps a better option can be found. The enduring point is more fundamental: the United States surmounted the great nuclear dangers of the Cold War largely because it applied serious thought and systematic analysis to its nuclear strategies, forces, and budgets. Operations research played a major role in this process. The ticket to a safer future lies in remembering this invaluable lesson and continuing to apply it.

Equally important, the United States cannot afford to focus narrowly on the issue of its nuclear posture and NMD systems in ways that leave it blind to other pressing requirements. While future adversaries plausibly may acquire nuclear-tipped ICBMs, the greater threat is that of terrorists employing WMD devices—nuclear, chemical, or biological—on U.S. soil. Clearly, the United States will need vigorous homeland defenses against this threat, including intelligence, law enforcement, border security, and consequence management. The challenge ahead is not to choose between NMD and homeland security, but instead to create a robust combination of them, both adequately funded.

Beyond this, the United States will need to pursue a strong effort to prevent nuclear proliferation abroad, especially into the hands of rogue governments or terrorists. Participation in such multilateral efforts as the Nuclear Non-Proliferation Treaty, the Missile Technology and Control Regime, the Wassenaar Agreement on Export Controls, and the International Atomic Energy Agency, as well as the Proliferation Security Initiative, can assist this cause. Diplomatic pressure and economic sanctions can help influence countries to refrain from seeking nuclear weapons and delivery systems, or selling them, or consorting with terrorists. In extreme cases, military intervention may prove necessary. Whether these instruments will prove adequate to the task is unknown, but it is clear that they will need to be employed vigorously and skillfully. The challenge facing operations research, systems analysis, and strategic evaluation is to contribute to this vital enterprise.

Notes

[1] For a historical account of nuclear studies and debates during the early and middle Cold War, see Fred Kaplan, *The Wizards of Armageddon* (New York: Simon and Schuster, 1983); Bernard Brodie, *Strategy in the Missile Age* (Princeton, NJ: Princeton University Press, 1965); and Lawrence Freedman, *The Evolution of Nuclear Strategy* (London: Macmillan, 1983).

[2] Much of the original nuclear force modeling was done at RAND during the 1950s. Pentagon expertise in this arena emerged during the 1960s under the impetus of Secretary of Defense Robert McNamara and his civilian advisers. Results of DOD analyses were regularly unveiled in annual reports to Congress by successive Secretaries of Defense during the 1960s, 1970s, and 1980s.

[3] A historical account is Alain Enthoven and K. Wayne Smith, *How Much Is Enough? Shaping the Defense Program, 1961–1969* (New York: Harper and Row, 1971), chapter 5.

[4] See testimony by Robert McNamara, Department of Defense Appropriations for 1969, Hearings Before a Subcommittee of the Committee on Appropriations, House of Representatives, 90th Congress, 2d sess., 49.

[5] The strategic triad theory first emerged in the McNamara era, and then was developed during the 1970s when James Schlesinger and Harold Brown served as Secretaries of Defense. For a discussion of programmatic issues during this period, see Alton Quanbeck and Barry M. Blechman, *Strategic Forces: Issues for the Mid-Seventies* (Washington, DC: Brookings, 1973).

[6] See U.S. Department of Defense, *Soviet Military Power: An Assessment of the Threat* (Washington, DC: Department of Defense, 1988). For analysis of nuclear targeting issues during this period, see Desmond Ball and Jeffrey Richelson, *Strategic Nuclear Targeting* (Ithaca, NY: Cornell University Press, 1986).

[7] A publicly available equation of kill probability for a nuclear warhead exploding over an ICBM silo is as follows:

$SSPK = 1 - e^{-1/2 x}$

Where $x = (y^{2/3}/H^{2/3}CEP^2 fH^{2/3})$

y = yield of ICBM warhead in megatons, H = hardness of missile silo in pounds per square inch of resistance to external pressure, CEP = average accuracy of ICBM warhead in nautical miles, and $fH^{2/3}$ is a constant of 0.170.

See Stockholm Paper No. 5, *Offensive Missiles* (Stockholm, Sweden: Stockholm International Peace Research Institute, 1974).

[8] For details of MX issues, see U.S. Congress, Office of Technology Assessment, *MX Missile Basing* (Washington, DC: Office of Technology Assessment, 1981).

[9] For details, see annual reports to Congress issued by Secretary of Defense Caspar Weinberger from 1982 to 1988 (Washington, DC: Department of Defense).

[10] For explanation of the assured destruction and damage limitation concepts, see Annual Reports to Congress issued by Secretary of Defense Robert McNamara during 1966–1968. For historical background on the damage limitation study, see Richard L. Kugler, *The Politics of Restraint: Robert McNamara and the Strategic Nuclear Forces 1963–1968*, Ph.D. dissertation, Massachusetts Institute of Technology, 1975.

[11] See Robert McNamara, annual reports to Congress, 1966–1968, Washington, DC.

[12] For details see annual reports to Congress issued by Secretary of Defense Caspar Weinberger during this period. For critical analysis, see Steven E. Miller and Stephen Van Evera, *The Star Wars Controversy: An International Security Reader* (Princeton, NJ: Princeton University Press, 1986).

[13] For discussion of new-era analytical and modeling issues, see Dean Wilkening, "Future U.S. and Russian Nuclear Forces: Applying Traditional Analysis Methods in an Era of Cooperation," in Paul Davis, *New Challenges for Defense Planning: Rethinking How Much Is Enough* (Santa Monica, CA: RAND, 1994); chapter 11; M. Elaine Bunn, "Strategic Nuclear Forces and National Missile Defense," in Michèle A. Flournoy, ed., *QDR 2001: Strategy-Driven Choices for America's Security* (Washington, DC: National Defense University Press, 2001), chapter 12; Peter A. Wilson and Richard D. Sokolsky, "Changing the Strategic Equation," in Hans Binnendijk, ed., *Transforming America's Military* (Washington, DC: National Defense University Press, 2002).

[14] In 2000, the Congressional Budget Office estimated that the Clinton administration's planned NMD system would cost $26 billion–$60 billion to build and operate over a 15-year period. See Congressional Budget Office, *Budgetary and Technical Implications of the Administration's Plan for National Missile Defense* (Washington, DC: Congressional Budget Office, April 2000).

[15] For analysis of the role of boost-phase intercept in national missile defense, see Hans Binnendijk and George Stewart, "Toward Missile Defenses from the Sea," *Defense Horizons* 14 (Washington, DC: Center for Technology and National Security Policy, National Defense University, June 2002). For analysis of BPI technical details, see *Report of the APS Study Group on Boost-Phase Intercept Systems for National Missile Defense* (Washington, DC: American Physical Society, 2003).

Chapter 20

Creating a New Overseas Military Presence

Reshaping the U.S. overseas military presence will be one of the main challenges facing U.S. foreign policy and national security strategy in the coming years. An era of change and transformation lies ahead because of fundamental shifts in both world affairs and U.S. global defense strategy. Configuring the future overseas presence so that it serves as a reliable servant of U.S. strategy, while helping propel world geopolitics toward stability and progress, is a difficult task for analysis and planning. In a complex and chaotic world, overseas presence will remain highly important in U.S. strategy, but in ways that differ from those of the past. Transformation of the U.S. overseas presence will be needed in order for defense transformation to succeed; in addition, the U.S. overseas presence must change in order to continue its vital role of empowering and magnifying other policy instruments, including political diplomacy and economic power. In the absence of a reconfigured overseas presence, neither defense transformation nor future national security policies abroad will pay their full strategic dividends. Indeed, both efforts could fall flat.

Successful change cannot be taken for granted. Crafting a new overseas presence will be hard, not only because the current model is becoming outdated, but also because a new model will not be a static construct. Instead of creating a new overseas presence that remains unchanged for many years, U.S. policy will need to be more dynamic. A new overseas military presence will, in most regions, change frequently as old strategic conditions give rise to new conditions, and as old goals and missions are replaced by new ones.

For the past 50 years and more, the continuity of a permanent peacetime presence of large U.S. forces on the soil of key allies and in nearby waters has been seen as a steadying influence in a world of danger and upheaval. This steadying function will still need to be performed, but the days are gone in which the United States could establish a particular force at a single location and expect it to remain unchanged for 10 or 20 years. In the future, a strong U.S. military presence will be needed at various places, but the size and mix of forces will fluctuate, and forces will be shifted back and forth among various regions, including all three key regions that host large U.S. forces today: Europe, Asia, and the greater Middle East. In keeping with the spirit of change now infusing overall U.S. defense strategy and transformation, tomorrow's overseas presence will need to be flexible, adaptable, and versatile.

A future of constant transformation will require a concerted effort to match means with ends. In its focus on means, U.S. policy will need to pay close attention to the types of military forces deployed abroad: their manpower levels, capabilities, activities, and missions. In its focus on ends, it will need to address how these military instruments can best be structured and employed in order to help achieve national goals abroad when these goals are challenged. In matching means with ends, U.S. policy will need a refined understanding of the relationship between military actions and strategic consequences so that it deploys the right forces that do the right things and thereby achieve the right political-military effects. This is where operations research, systems analysis, and strategic evaluation can make a strong contribution if they are blended to form a multidisciplinary analysis in the ways discussed below.

Contributions of Operations Research and Multidiscipline Analysis

Static continuity has, in the past, eased the task of force planning for overseas presence; dynamic change and uncertainty will make future planning far harder. Change requires original thinking in more than one dimension. The current task of creating a new, dynamic overseas presence is not only one of preparing for crises and wars and of transforming forces in response to new military doctrines and weapons. It also is one of determining how best to support peacetime political diplomacy. In the coming years, new force plans and strategic concepts will be needed, and they must reflect how the geography of overseas presence is changing. The extended period of anchoring the U.S. presence in large, permanent deployments in Central Europe and Northeast Asia for local border defense missions is ending. The new focus is on expeditionary missions along the southern arc of instability from the greater Middle East to the East Asian littoral in peace, crisis, and war. Military forces and bases in Europe and Asia, although still important, will increasingly function as regional hubs for projecting power along the southern arc, where there will be need for an expanded set of U.S. bases and facilities. Thus, today's mix of U.S. forces will need to change, providing more emphasis on naval forces, air forces, mobile ground forces, and rotating deployments from the United States, and placing less emphasis on permanently stationing large masses of heavy ground forces for local defense.

Creating a new overseas presence will require a multidisciplinary approach that includes use of strategic evaluation and systems analysis, along with contributions from operations research. Because of the importance of strategic evaluation and systems analysis, this chapter just as easily could have been placed in either of the other two sections of the book. It is placed here in order to illuminate the central role that operations research will need to play in focusing on military details and gauging the impact of future changes on the attainment of U.S. national security goals.

Provided strategic evaluation and systems analysis establish an overall framework for appraisal of issues and options, operations research is a good tool for examining the details of military force deployments, their multiple programs, and their activities, and for predicting how well various military means are likely to perform in pursuing multiple political ends. In order to make such a contribution, the methods of operations research, as applied to overseas presence, will need to develop new concepts, focal points, and measuring sticks. In particular, new measuring sticks will be needed to help gauge the relationship between new means and new ends: accurately calibrating this relationship will be both challenging and vital to shaping a new overseas presence that accomplishes its political and military purposes. With a new, dynamic theory of overseas presence anchored in quantitative analysis as well as abstract strategic formulas, operations research, in concert with other methods, can get the job done.

Chapter 20 begins by discussing the historical legacy of overseas presence during the Cold War, and then describes the new strategic departures for U.S. overseas presence that are already in progress. Next, it outlines why force planning must focus not only on overseas manpower levels, but also on the specifics of forces, programs, and operations. Then, it examines how one of the tools of operations research, the technique of multi-attribute utility analysis, can help guide future planning for overseas presence. The chapter concludes with an analytical discussion of U.S. presence options in Europe, Asia, the greater Middle East, and elsewhere in the southern arc of instability. This discussion suggests the policy challenges ahead and illustrates how operations research and other analytical methods can help advise how to handle them.

Historical Legacy of the Cold War

A discussion of the future can best begin by briefly noting how the U.S. overseas presence evolved during the Cold War in ways that still influence its composition today. Prior to World War II, the United States did not station large military forces overseas in peacetime. The only exception to this pattern was the presence of U.S. naval forces in Hawaii, coupled with a string of Pacific military bases stretching to the Philippines. After World War II, the United States began reverting to its prewar pattern by quickly withdrawing most forces that had been sent to defeat Germany in Europe and Japan in Asia. By the late 1940s, with disarmament in full swing, U.S. forces in Germany and Japan had been reduced to small constabulary forces for occupation duties, the global network of bases built during World War II was being disestablished, and the U.S. naval presence on the high seas was shrinking as well.

The outbreak of the Cold War produced an abrupt shift. Fearing a Soviet military attack in Europe, the Truman administration ordered a big rearmament effort and sent large combat forces to help guard exposed borders in Central Europe, including the newly formed Federal Republic of Germany. When war erupted on the Korean Peninsula in mid-1950, the Truman administration also rushed large forces there and to Japan, which became an important logistical foundation for waging the Korean War during 1950–1953. The Korean War finally ended in 1953 with an armistice, not a peace treaty. As a result, sizable U.S. forces had to remain there and in Japan to deter a further outbreak of war.

With the Cold War raging throughout the 1950s, the Eisenhower administration perpetuated this pattern of maintaining sizable U.S. ground and air forces in both Central Europe and Northeast Asia, coupled with large naval forces in both regions. During this period, tactical nuclear weapons were introduced into the U.S. military posture, but this increase in firepower was not accompanied by any reduction of overseas-stationed forces. When the Kennedy administration took power in early 1961, its new strategy of emphasizing conventional preparedness in order to reduce reliance upon nuclear deterrence further underscored the importance of keeping a large combat force abroad. During the Vietnam War, the buildup in Southeast Asia resulted in some forces being withdrawn from Europe and South Korea, but enough were left behind to maintain a viable conventional deterrent and defense posture.

The 1970s and 1980s saw overseas military presence retain its important role in U.S. national security strategy. Periodically, critics launched efforts to reduce forces in Europe and Korea, but their calls always were rejected on grounds that even partial withdrawals would weaken deterrence, worry allies, and have other damaging political effects. In the early 1970s, the Nixon administration fought off the Mansfield resolution, which would have pared U.S. forces in Europe. In the late 1970s, President Carter seriously considered removing most U.S. forces from South Korea, but backed away when his military commanders warned of an impending North Korean military buildup. During the 1980s, the Reagan administration modernized the still-existing presence of 330,000 troops in Europe and over 100,000 troops in Northeast Asia to help respond to the Soviet military buildup with countervailing U.S. power. In addition, it established U.S. Central Command, a new military command for operations in Southwest Asia, and began deploying naval forces there to help stabilize access to Persian Gulf oilfields during the Iran–Iraq war. Over these two decades, the only region that witnessed the withdrawal of U.S. forces was Southeast Asia. The presence of 500,000 U.S. troops in Vietnam in the late 1960s was reduced sharply in the early 1970s, ultimately reaching zero when South Vietnam fell to communist rule in 1975. The United States maintained a regional foothold in Southeast Asia through its air and naval bases in the Philippines, but growing nationalism there and disputes over payments to the Philippine government spelled the eventual elimination of these bases as well.

Throughout the course of the Cold War, until the late 1980s, the U.S. overseas military presence was employed to pursue multiple political and military goals. For the most part, nonetheless, the driving imperative was providing for border defense of allies, and the specific composition of forces was shaped by anticipated wartime requirements. This resulted in an overseas presence whose manpower was dominated by ground forces: for example, of the 330,000 troops in Europe, over two-thirds were U.S. Army personnel. Although naval forces periodically moved from one region to another for limited periods, most ground and air forces were viewed as stationary, for local defense purposes. Because they were treated as permanent vanguards of initial forward defense until reinforcements could arrive from CONUS, they were not configured as power-projection assets that could be swiftly deployed to distant places. For example, the four U.S. Army divisions stationed in southern Germany became synonymous with protection of the Fulda Gap, Cheb Gap, and Hof Corridor, not protection of northern Germany, much less distant missions in the Persian Gulf. Such stationary thinking, so different from today, was a deeply embedded imprint of the Cold War.

When the administration of President George H.W. Bush took power in early 1989, it inherited a Cold War that was rapidly ending. The fall of the Berlin Wall, the unification of Germany, the unraveling of the Warsaw Pact, the withdrawal of Soviet forces from Eastern Europe, and the collapse of the Soviet Union utterly transformed the security situation in Europe. A major reduction of U.S. forces became possible. Yet the Bush administration, wary of an uncertain future, wanted to avoid any premature or excessively large withdrawal that might weaken NATO, diminish U.S. influence, and encourage instability.

Accordingly, it reduced the U.S. presence only partially: from 330,000 to 150,000 troops that still included sizable ground, air, and naval components. In Northeast Asia, the end of the Cold War meant no amelioration of tensions on the Korean Peninsula or removal of other threats to regional stability. Accordingly, the administration decided to retain a peacetime presence there of about 100,000 troops, including nearly 40,000 troops in South Korea and an equal number in Japan and Okinawa. In the Persian Gulf, the victorious *Desert Storm* campaign of early 1991 pushed Iraqi forces out of Kuwait, but it did not end the Saddam Hussein regime or produce a stable Persian Gulf. Accordingly, the Bush administration left behind a presence of about 25,000 troops—mostly naval and air—after the big contingent that won the war had been withdrawn.

The 8 years of the Clinton administration, from 1993 to 2001, saw only modest changes to this global presence. The Clinton team pared the U.S. presence in Europe from 150,000 troops to 100,000, but this reduction was portrayed as a technical change rather than a strategic departure. The remaining presence was deemed adequate to meet new-era U.S. requirements and commitments to NATO and Europe. In Northeast Asia, the U.S. military presence remained virtually unchanged in a setting of mounting tensions with North Korea. In the Persian Gulf, continuing tensions with Saddam Hussein resulted in a steady presence of about 25,000 troops that were reinforced numerous times when airstrikes against Iraq became necessary.

The legacy of these 50 years—from 1950 to 2000—thus resulted in a large overseas military presence playing a role of continuing importance in U.S. national security strategy in Europe and Northeast Asia and, from the mid-1980s onward, in Southwest Asia as well. Overseas presence came to be viewed as necessary because it provided a powerful instrument for helping achieve prominent strategic goals in both wartime and peacetime. What also stands out is the extent to which continuity, rather than change, dominated U.S. strategic thinking in this period. This was the case not only because U.S. leaders valued overseas presence as an instrument for pursuing strategic goals, but also because many allied governments valued it as well. Public opinion in parts of Europe and Asia sometimes swung against the U.S. presence, but for the most part, governments supported it. Indeed, there were occasions in which the U.S. Government began to explore the idea of troop reductions or other major changes, only to back away because of fevered official protests from allies.

Contemporary Changes Under Way in Overseas Presence

The term *overseas presence* was adopted by the Clinton administration in 1993. Other terms commonly employed have been *forward defense, forward presence,* and *forward deployments.* All of these terms refer to U.S. military forces, assets, and activities stationed abroad during peacetime to help carry out national security strategy. Overseas presence works in partnership with military forces for power projection from the United States. While overseas presence has a mission of its own to perform, it also is intended to create the strategic conditions that enable forces based in the continental United States to deploy swiftly when crises and wars erupt. Overseas presence thus is one part of a larger strategic enterprise, and it should be judged in these terms.

When the George W. Bush administration took power in early 2001, it inherited an overseas presence of about 235,000 troops from all services. This global posture included about 100,000 troops in Europe, 100,000 in Asia, 25,000 in the Persian Gulf, and 10,000 elsewhere, including Latin America.[1] The principal military commands for these forces were U.S. European Command (USEUCOM), U.S. Pacific Command (USPACOM), U.S. Central Command (USCENTCOM), and U.S. Southern Command. However, this simple portrayal obscures complicated realities about the size and composition of U.S. forces stationed abroad. In Europe and nearby Mediterranean waters, the actual number was closer to 109,000 troops, and it periodically rose to 130,000 with naval deployments and commitments in the Balkans. About 65,000 of these troops were stationed in Central Europe (mostly in Germany), and most of the rest were based in the United Kingdom and Italy. The main military units comprised various headquarters and support staffs, two Army combat divisions with four heavy brigades in Germany and elements of an airborne brigade in Italy, two and one-third Air Force fighter wings plus other units at various bases, and the Navy's 6th Fleet in the Mediterranean Sea, which normally included a CVBG, an ARG, and other ships.[2]

In Asia, the number of U.S. forces varied somewhat from month to month, between 90,000 and 100,000, depending upon fluctuating naval deployments. This presence was represented by 37,000 personnel in South Korea, 38,000 in Japan and Okinawa, and 4,000 on Guam, plus naval forces at sea and small deployments elsewhere. The main military forces were the Army's 2d Division in South Korea, two and three-fifths Air Force fighter wings in South Korea and Japan, two-thirds of a Marine expeditionary force with ground and air forces in Okinawa, and a Navy CVBG and ARG on sea duty. Backing up this deployment in the western Pacific were about 32,000 personnel from all services in Hawaii, which were mostly assigned to reinforcement duties in the Asian region. In the Persian Gulf and Southwest Asia, USCENTCOM (based in Florida) commanded a small presence of 25,000 troops on shore and at sea. This presence included a CVBG and an ARG, plus an Air Force wing-equivalent, a Patriot missile defense unit, and small rotating Army forces in Saudi Arabia, Kuwait, and other Persian Gulf sheikdoms.

In the 1990s, this overseas presence remained mostly constant after the early days of the Clinton administration, when the European presence was reduced from 150,000 troops to 100,000. Three other changes were made during the decade. Several thousand U.S. troops were deployed to the Balkans after the Kosovo War and the Dayton Accord. Persian Gulf deployments periodically shot upward in response to fleeting crises. The goal of keeping three CVBGs and ARGs continually deployed overseas dropped, in practice, to an average of about two and one-half for each formation because of force shortages and maintenance needs. These fluctuations, however, were mostly minor and did not alter the overall pattern or the policy behind it. As of 2000, one might have been puzzled by how little overseas presence had changed during the years of post–Cold War global upheaval: while new missions were being performed, the forces and their regional deployments (aside from Europe) had changed little. The prevailing practice of continuity reflected reluctance to tinker with a good thing, coupled with a general belief that while larger forces were not needed, reduction to smaller forces might cause damaging ripple effects and unforeseeable events.

The first signs of impending change came when DOD issued its *Quadrennial Defense Review (QDR) Report* in late 2001.[3] It declared that, to contribute to the new U.S. defense strategy, the overseas military presence would play an important role in carrying out new strategic goals and political purposes, as well as new operational concepts for warfighting. As a consequence, the *QDR Report* said, overseas presence would be seen as an integrated global asset rather than as a set of disconnected regional postures with wholly separate rationales of their own. In addition, overseas presence would not just be an instrument of local forward defense in fixed locations, but would become a tool of power projection that would combine with CONUS reinforcements to provide a swift, flexible capacity to apply military power across all key regions.

The *QDR Report* called for design of regionally tailored forces in key theaters, and transformation efforts to strengthen their capabilities to deter aggression and to permit reallocation of CONUS-based forces that had been dedicated to reinforcement missions. In order to pursue these goals, the *QDR Report* instructed that the U.S. global military posture should take a number of steps. First, it should develop a basing system to provide greater flexibility for U.S. forces around the world, placing emphasis on additional bases and stations beyond Western Europe and Northeast Asia. Existing bases in Europe and Northeast Asia would be used as regional hubs for power projection elsewhere. Second, it should provide for temporary access to facilities in foreign countries to enable U.S. forces to conduct training and exercises where permanent ranges and bases did not exist. Third, it should redistribute forces and equipment based on regional deterrence requirements. Fourth, it should provide sufficient mobility, bases, debarkation points, and new logistical concepts to enable expeditionary operations in distant theaters against adversaries armed with WMD and other means to deny access to U.S. forces.

To help achieve these goals, the *QDR Report* announced several specific changes to overseas presence forces. It stated that the Navy should increase CVBG presence in the western Pacific and explore options for homeporting three or four more surface combatants and guided missile cruisers there. It further instructed the Navy to develop new concepts for maritime prepositioning, high-speed sealift, and new amphibious capabilities for the Marines. As part of this transition, it also called upon the Navy to shift some Marine prepositioned equipment from the Mediterranean toward the Indian Ocean and Arabian Gulf in order to become more responsive to Middle East contingencies, and to explore prospects for the Marine Corps to conduct training for littoral warfare in the western Pacific. The *QDR Report* instructed the Army to accelerate the forward stationing of interim brigade combat teams (for example, Stryker brigades) in Europe and explore options to enhance ground force capabilities in the Arabian Gulf. It called upon the Air Force to develop plans to increase contingency basing in the Pacific and Indian Oceans as well as the Persian Gulf. Finally, it instructed DOD to develop a new joint-presence policy to establish steady-state levels of ground, air, and naval presence in critical regions and to synchronize force deployments and cross-service trades in order to enhance the flexibility of forward-stationed forces while coordinating the readiness and operational tempo of all U.S. forces.

This strategic guidance was a harbinger of change for overseas presence, but it was written before the war on terrorism was launched in September 2001. Since then, major strategic changes have taken place that point toward further alterations. Several thousand U.S. troops have been deployed in Afghanistan to help guide stability and reconstruction, accompanied by additional periodic deployments to Central Asian countries. The invasion of and ongoing presence in Iraq radically altered the fundamentals of the U.S. presence in the Persian Gulf. What the future holds is uncertain, but U.S. forces may remain in Iraq for an extended period, even as the old focus on defending Gulf allies against an Iraqi attack gives way to a new strategic concept focused on regional stability supported by greater access to new operating locations in the Middle East and North Africa. Overall, a new U.S. military presence in the Middle East and the southern arc of instability seems likely to be different even from the changed model outlined in the *QDR Report* of 2001.

During 2001–2004, even as war was being waged in Afghanistan and Iraq, DOD engaged in a long-range study of its future global overseas presence. In fall 2004, DOD began publicly unveiling the results of this global basing study, which carry forth the departures of QDR 2001 with additional features. The core concept is to alter the future overseas presence significantly so as to reflect new-era strategic changes and requirements. While many details remain to be determined in the years ahead, the study envisioned three different types of bases and facilities for overseas forces: main operating bases (MOBs), forward operating locations (FOLs), and cooperative security locations (CSLs). Whereas MOBs will be hubs that house most U.S. forces that are permanently stationed abroad, FOLs will provide outer spokes that enable U.S. forces to quickly deploy to distant locations, and CSLs will provide facilities to work with both existing and new partners.

The study also articulated, in conceptual terms, new geographic patterns for reducing and redistributing U.S. forces stationed overseas. It proposes reducing the U.S. military presence in Europe from 109,000 troops to a permanent level of 50,000–65,000, to be enhanced by units temporarily deploying to Europe for training and exercises with allies. The main change is to come from withdrawal of the four heavy Army combat brigades, which will be replaced by at least a single Stryker brigade. Air Force units are also to be trimmed, but the exact number is unclear. Naval bases in the Mediterranean may be consolidated, as will the elaborate U.S. military command structure in Europe. The new, smaller U.S. military presence will not be anchored exclusively in Western Europe. Instead, it will begin using training, exercises, and temporary facilities to establish a growing presence in Eastern Europe and the Balkans in order to promote military cooperation with new friends and allies, and to provide springboards for projecting power outside Europe.

The DOD study also envisioned changes in Northeast Asia over a period of years. The U.S. military presence in South Korea will be changed by moving ground forces to new bases south of Seoul so they will be available for mobile counterattack missions should war occur. One of the two Army brigades in South Korea may eventually be withdrawn if circumstances permit. Some reductions and consolidations also will take place on Okinawa, even as new headquarters are opened on the Japanese mainland. Meanwhile, new bases and facilities will be created on Guam and in various places across Southeast

Asia to provide flexibility and options for deploying there. The need for these was manifested in early 2005 when a tsunami required a major U.S. humanitarian operation to assist Indonesia, Thailand, and other countries.

While the DOD study reflected considerable internal effort plus close consultations with allies, it was criticized by some outside observers, who especially faulted the idea of withdrawing substantial forces from Europe and Korea. Such criticisms suggest that the DOD plan will be subjected to careful scrutiny in the coming years. Like all long-range plans, it may be modified to one degree or another as it unfolds and if its underlying assumptions are altered. Even if its proposals are pursued, they will take years to carry out because new bases and deployment arrangements must be created. While the future has become even harder to predict, change will be a dominating feature of the future U.S. overseas presence. This is why analysis of this phenomenon is needed now. A new overseas presence cannot be crafted without coherent plans based on serious analysis. Overseas presence—not only its forces and other assets, but also its activities—must be shaped wisely, because its performance will depend on its makeup. The challenge facing operations research is to contribute to this analysis and planning.

Analysis of Means: Viewing Overseas Presence as a Defense Program

Overseas presence is a means to an end, not an end in itself. It is an instrument of policy whose reason for being derives from its capacity to help achieve national security goals in peace, crisis, and war. Its core purpose is to help bring about favorable strategic consequences that otherwise would not be fully achievable. Recognition of this elementary relationship between means and ends provides the foundation for analyzing overseas presence. Overseas presence must be scrutinized closely because it does not come in a prearranged package that can simply be placed in any region of choice. The specific composition of the U.S. overseas presence plays a major role in determining its performance; its internal details must be planned carefully with an eye on both costs and effectiveness.

Overseas presence can take a variety of different types of postures, ranging greatly in size and makeup. Moreover, it includes more than combat forces from each of the services; it also includes such assets as command staffs, support units, bases and facilities, other infrastructure, prepositioned stocks and materials, and security assistance to other nations (such as financial assistance in the form of grants, loans, and sales). The activities performed by the elements of the U.S. overseas presence also matter greatly in determining its effectiveness. Forward-stationed U.S. forces that focus solely on preparing for unilateral combat operations with reinforcements from CONUS would provide a different kind and level of effectiveness than if they train regularly with allied forces to promote military interoperability and close professional ties.

Because overseas presence includes so many diverse forces, assets, and activities, it should be viewed as a defense program and judged in terms of its ability to achieve its many goals. Its success at achieving its goals while making efficient use of its resources should not be taken for granted. Poor performance or failure is possible if an overseas presence program is not well constituted. Sometimes old assets and activities must be replaced by new ones in order for overseas presence to continue performing effectively in a new strategic situation.[4]

A good place to begin analyzing overseas presence as a defense program is to ask why the United States should continue deploying large military forces overseas now that, apart from Korea, the threat of major cross-border invasions of allies is fading. In an era where direct border defense is needed less than before, why not rely upon swift power projection from CONUS when crises and wars occur? Some analysts have argued in favor of such a "virtual presence," in which modern information networks provide intelligence and communications, and pledges of swift reinforcement take the place of deployed forces in U.S. treaties and alliance commitments. The virtual presence argument gained some adherents during the Clinton years, and although it has faded in response to the war on terrorism, it provides a benchmark against which to assess why a sizable overseas presence makes sense.

One reason is that modern information networks are not all-powerful. They can provide technical intelligence and communications, but whether they can give full situational awareness is another matter. They often cannot substitute for having "boots on the ground": trained military staffs and troops that can develop in-depth knowledge of a country or region. The success of the invasion of Iraq in 2003 owed a great deal to the fact that U.S. command staffs and forces had been present in the Persian Gulf for the previous 12 years, acquiring the necessary knowledge of details of weather, terrain, logistics, and the enemy.

Another reason for overseas presence is to enable U.S. forces to train and exercise with allied militaries to promote interoperability for combined operations. In theory, forces from CONUS can deploy overseas to conduct such training, but when extensive training must be conducted with multiple countries (as, for example, in NATO), the most economical and effective solution often is to station forces overseas permanently. An additional reason is to maintain U.S. political influence within alliances so that U.S. interests are safeguarded and U.S. authorities possess adequate flexibility to carry out their responsibilities for collective security. In alliances, each member tends to wield influence and authority commensurate with its contributions. Stationing large U.S. forces on the soil of allies is often the price that must be paid for having significant influence over common defense plans and programs. The considerable influence that the United States has long enjoyed within its European and Northeast Asian alliances is due in no small measure to the continuing presence of large U.S. forces in both regions.

Beyond this, a sizable U.S. military presence may be needed to help stabilize tense regional geopolitical affairs. The presence of American forces may reassure nervous allies about the credibility of U.S. commitments to their security. For example, the continuing presence of large U.S. forces in Germany and Japan has helped reinforce the decisions of those governments not to acquire nuclear weapons. Because reliability of commitments must be continuously demonstrated, allied governments are more persuaded by military forces than by paper treaties and information networks. Forward-stationed U.S. forces are exposed to the same dangers as allied countries, and their presence serves as a tripwire that virtually guarantees that the United States would respond in a crisis. Allies want reassurance on a daily basis that their trust in the United States is justified. Conversely, the United States is willing to make entangling commitments to allies only if it can keep military forces on-scene to influence planning and crisis responses. Overseas presence facilitates both U.S. commitments and allied trust in them.

For similar political reasons, the presence of large U.S. forces sends a signal of resolve that cannot be matched by diplomatic proclamations or by satellites in space and other manifestations of the information age. Literally showing the flag has the effect of impressing upon friends, foes, and neutrals that, even though the United States is located thousand of miles away, it must be reckoned with in local affairs. Adversaries are more likely to take U.S. deterrent and defense strategies seriously when large U.S. military forces are on the scene full-time rather than based on the other side of the world. It is no accident that over the past 50 years, aggression against a U.S. ally has never occurred in a situation where large U.S. forces were already present, but has occurred twice—Korea in 1950 and the Persian Gulf in 1990—where U.S. forces were not present. This experience helps underscore the continued importance of U.S. military presence not only to strengthen deterrence, but also to help stabilize otherwise volatile regional security affairs. U.S. force presence warns adversaries, reassures allies, and removes incentives for either to engage in provocative military actions. These are all important contributions to stability, arms control, and peace.

Finally, there continue to be potential warfighting reasons for the forward stationing of U.S. forces in today's world. This is especially true on the Korean Peninsula, where U.S. forces are needed on a daily basis to help safeguard against a surprise North Korean attack on South Korea. Elsewhere, the threat of surprise attack is less serious than during the Cold War, but in such sensitive areas as Northeast Asian waters and the Mediterranean Sea, the constant patrolling of U.S. naval warships and combat fighters helps guard important sea lines of communication. Their presence also helps protect allied borders from such new-era threats as long-range missiles and air bombardment, which are risks even when major ground invasions are no longer possible. Moreover, when crises occur, large U.S. forces cannot instantly deploy from CONUS and arrive immediately on the scene. Even tactical air forces take a few days to fly fighters and their supplies to distant hotspots, while ground and naval forces take considerably longer, sometimes weeks. The forward presence of joint U.S. forces provides valuable instruments for crisis management, escalation control, and quick response during the initial days of a flareup. It also greatly reduces the risk that reinforcing units would have to fight their way into a hot zone against strong access-denial efforts by enemies. For such tangible military reasons, senior U.S. officials commonly prefer a daily on-scene presence rather than relying upon reinforcement plans that could go awry in a crisis or could take too long to unfold.

The proposition that a credible U.S. military presence can have positive effects on a dangerous region, however, says nothing about its size and composition. Analytical standards are needed to make decisions in this arena. The natural temptation may be to specify an overall manpower level that seems appropriate, and then to delegate the task of allocating this manpower to military commanders. The rationale for this stance is that manpower level is often seen as a powerful signal of U.S. intent, and if sufficient manpower is made available, commanders presumably will have enough resources to perform their jobs if they choose wisely.

The problem with this simple approach is that manpower levels are not synonymous with strategic capability. A military force with a large number of troops may have unimpressive capabilities if it lacks the proper assets, while a smaller force with fewer troops might be far more successful if it is equipped with a proper blend of assets. Moreover, a fixation on manpower levels can result in irrational decisions driven by misplaced political perceptions. A long-established or symbolically appealing manpower level (for example, 100,000 troops in a single region) can acquire political meaning that is unrelated to its strategic requirements and performance. When the time comes to raise or lower this manpower level in response to changing conditions, allied governments, adversaries, and even U.S. diplomats may resist out of fear that U.S. commitments are being increased, decreased, or altered in unsettling ways. If this tendency is not countered through wise diplomacy that explains the reasons for change, the result can be a force posture that is perpetually defined in terms of its troop strength, and is frozen even when change is needed.

A manpower level, therefore, is best treated as a dependent, not an independent, variable. Planning should begin by first specifying the defense missions to be performed in order to achieve desired goals. Next, the forces, assets, and activities needed to perform these missions should be determined. Only after these tasks are accomplished should manpower levels be chosen. When the time comes for changes in forces and missions, manpower levels should be altered accordingly. Planning in this manner provides a safeguard against unwise decisions that fail to connect missions, forces, and manpower.

An example will help illustrate the need to make these connections. When the Clinton administration took power in 1993, some of its advisers wanted to reduce U.S. troop strength in Europe by half, from 150,000 troops to 75,000. Surface appearances suggested that this manpower level could accommodate the wishes of senior U.S. military commanders for a posture of four Army brigades, two or three Air Force fighter wings, and a Navy presence of a CVBG and an ARG. Closer inspection using operations research, however, showed a different reality. These combat formations could, indeed, be deployed within a ceiling of 75,000 troops, but command staffs, intelligence and communications units, logistic support units, bases, and facilities would add considerably to the total. For example, 5,000 support troops were needed for each Army combat brigade of 5,000; each fighter wing of 5,000 aircrew required an additional 3,000 aircrew in support roles; and 10,000 to 15,000 sailors were needed to operate naval bases in the Mediterranean for supporting carriers, amphibious ships, and other craft. When such details were totaled, they drove the manpower level up from 75,000 to 109,000 troops. The Clinton administration, quite sensibly, first determined missions and forces, and only then settled upon the manpower figure. As a result, enough forces and personnel were left in Europe to perform key missions. Had it clung to 75,000 troops as a benchmark, it would have been saddled with an ineffective presence, regardless of whether this number sounded good to outsiders.[5]

Viewing Forces and Capabilities in New-Era Terms

The idea that missions should determine forces and manpower has appeal to defense planners focused on maximizing performance, but as a practical matter, resource constraints and affordability enter the equation too. Therefore, determining how many forces to station abroad in future years will need to be conducted with a global perspective and limits on resources in mind. Crisis operations aside, today's normal overseas presence of 235,000 troops occupies about 17 percent of U.S. active-duty manpower. Although this percentage is not unduly high by historical standards—21 percent were deployed overseas in the 1980s—it affects service combat structures in disproportionate ways. The Army's deployment of 8 combat brigades is nearly one-fourth of its current total, compared to only 16 percent in the 1980s. The U.S. Air Force deploys nearly half of its 12 active wings (five and two-thirds fighter wings) overseas. The Navy's goal of deploying 3 CVBGs and 3 ARGs consumes 25 percent of its forces in both categories (as a practical matter, readiness constraints reduce average deployments to 2.5 CVBGs and 2.5 ARGs). All three services would prefer to reduce overseas deployments in order to husband their resources and to enhance readiness for major combat operations. Most likely, DOD will be able to maintain the current deployment level if necessary, but major increases in overseas presence would not be possible. Overseas presence thus will be limited to the forces already available or perhaps less. A global perspective is needed to ensure that these forces are distributed among the various regions in a manner that reflects their respective requirements and priorities.

In determining what forces should be deployed in each region, careful attention must be given to decisions about how best to achieve an optimal mix of combat units in light of new strategic conditions. For valid reasons, past experience has solidified the idea of stationing postures of ground, air, and naval assets in each of the three key theaters that are balanced in capabilities, although not necessarily manpower levels. For the past decade, as a result, the U.S. force presences in Europe and Asia have mirrored each other—about 100,000 troops, 4 or 5 ground brigades, 2 or 3 Air Force fighter wings, 1 CVBG, and 1 ARG—even though the strategic conditions in these theaters differ greatly. The Persian Gulf was different, but there the absence of large ground forces was due to regional political constraints rather than to U.S. strategic preferences. Although this approach worked in the past, new conditions are creating new and different requirements for forces and missions.

In the future, all three components—ground, naval, and air—will have important roles to play, but they will be different roles than in the past. The need for large, heavily armed, stationary ground forces is declining because classical border defense missions are fading in many places. Some ground forces will still be needed, but the requirement will often be for smaller, lighter, more mobile forces that can deploy rapidly to carry out expeditionary missions in distant locations far away from their home bases. The need for air and naval forces, by contrast, may remain constant or even increase. While threats from the ground are diminishing in many places, they are increasing in the air and at sea. Moreover, air forces have the advantage of being able to deploy quickly and cover large geographic spaces. Naval forces offer the advantage of being able to protect sealanes, whose importance has grown in response to globalization, and of being able to project power ashore into littoral areas. These are valuable capabilities along the southern arc of instability and other maritime zones. An additional important trend is the growing need for ballistic missile defenses in order to protect U.S. forces and allies. In the coming years, theater missile defense may become one of the most important missions of the U.S. overseas presence. Force deployments will need to reflect this change.

For these reasons, deployment of fixed combinations of joint forces in all key regions is not likely to be optimal; instead, future overseas presence will need to be tailored to the goals, missions, and conditions prevailing in each region. In some places, such as Korea and Iraq, ground forces may still need to predominate. In other places, such as other parts of Asia, air and naval forces may be the dominant components. In Europe and elsewhere, a balanced combination of joint forces may still be needed, but with different assets and capabilities. A single blueprint will no longer apply worldwide; the presence in each region will need to be tailored individually. As conditions within each region evolve, the U.S. presence will have to evolve too. What matters is whether U.S. forces for each region are capable of performing their missions and thereby achieving their strategic goals. Meeting this standard may require occasional changes in total force levels and reshuffling of the force mix.

Rotational practices seem likely to gain prominence in the role of ground forces overseas. In a rotational approach, CONUS-based forces periodically deploy overseas in order to conduct training, exercises, and visitations. The effect is to reduce the number of troops that must be permanently stationed overseas, to spread the responsibility for overseas missions among multiple CONUS units, and to reduce costs for overseas family housing and dependents. Rotational basing was not a regular practice during the Cold War, but it was used on some occasions: for example, Reforger in Europe, a program for dual-basing three brigades that were withdrawn in the late 1960s but returned regularly for exercises. While rotational basing has advantages, it imposes costs and upheavals of its own, so when overseas training requirements are high, the cheapest and most effective solution may be to station forces permanently. Nor is rotational basing viable where forces must guard against surprise attacks. Subject to these constraints, rotational basing may be increasingly used by the Army and Marines, especially for situations requiring visits to widely dispersed places.

For the Navy, the imperative seems to be moving in the opposite direction, toward more homeporting: permanently stationing U.S. naval vessels at foreign ports. This idea has appeal for operational and budgetary reasons. A vessel homeported abroad does not have to travel thousands of miles from CONUS to its duty station, nor does it have to make the long return journey to CONUS for maintenance and repairs after a duty cycle. The journey back and forth between ports and duty locations is shorter and quicker, so on-station time increases and operating costs decrease. Homeporting is already used in limited ways: for example, one U.S. carrier is homeported in Japan. Some analysts favor increased homeporting of surface combatants and submarines in order to minimize the Navy's need to enlarge its force structure in the coming years. The logic of operations research favors greater use of this approach when circumstances permit.

In addition to fresh thinking about force mixes, the designers of the future overseas presence will need to pay close attention to the other components of the enterprise, especially command staffs. An important issue will be whether the current structure of three separate combatant commands for Europe, Asia, and the greater Middle East should be retained. USPACOM has a unique focus on Asia, but USEUCOM and USCENTCOM share areas of responsibility in the Middle East, resulting sometimes in a confusing overlap: in order to launch some major combat operations, the two commands find themselves guiding separate forces that are part of the same strategic enterprise. In addition, USEUCOM-assigned forces are often assigned to USCENTCOM for Persian Gulf operations. This was the case during the Persian Gulf War of 1991, when USEUCOM's VII Corps helped lead the *Desert Storm* advance into Kuwait. In the war of 2003, USEUCOM's V Corps commanded the U.S. Army forces that invaded Iraq. Especially because of the growing strategic interaction between Europe and the Middle East, a case can be made for merging USEUCOM and USCENTCOM to form a single command for both regions. Regardless of whether this step is taken, commands must continue coordinating their efforts to ensure full coverage of the southern arc of instability, which spans all three commands.

The internal composition of each combatant command is another issue. Currently, each command has separate subcommands for each force component: ground, air, and naval. These subcommands are joint in theory, but in practice each is dominated by the relevant service: Army, Air Force, or Navy/Marines. The traditional arrangement has enabled the parent command to handle joint force operations and the component subcommands to manage resources. Defense transformation suggests a case for moving away from this stovepiping practice by creating better integrated joint command staffs that can better blend the operations and resources of all components. This could create opportunities for consolidating and trimming old-style regional command structures. At the same time, the increased scope and diversity of overseas presence missions requires that command staffs possess greater knowledge in many arenas, elevating the need for trained personnel and for sophisticated information networks. Making sure that wise decisions are made for command structures will be a major enterprise for analysis of future overseas presence in all regions.

Another big issue will be creating a better global network of bases, facilities, and infrastructure to facilitate new-era force operations. During the Cold War, bases and infrastructure naturally accompanied deployed forces, because defense planning focused on stationary protection of nearby borders. This meant that the forces could reside at their home bases and did not have to contemplate moving elsewhere. In the current era, however, conditions are different and rapidly changing. Some forces may still be stationed at home bases, but these bases will operate as central hubs for long-distance projection of those forces, as well as reinforcements. In order to carry out this power-projection mission, austere operating bases and associated infrastructure will be needed in outer areas, often in places that earlier would not have been considered as potential sites for operations. In all three key theaters, a looming challenge will be to build an adequate network of regional "hubs and spokes" that include outer bases and infrastructure; this endeavor is already being pursued by DOD. New bases, facilities, and infrastructure cannot be created overnight: they are expensive, and only limited funds are available each year.

Acquiring them requires sensitive, time-consuming negotiations with host countries. Over a period of years, however, major progress can be made through slow but steady efforts.

Prepositioning of weapons and stocks abroad is another important factor in the overseas presence calculus. The advantage of prepositioning is that it can greatly reduce the time needed to deploy forces to a crisis zone. Fully 85 percent of an Army division's weight can be prepositioned, as can Air Force munitions and stocks. As a result, strategic mobility can rely on aircraft that lift personnel rather than slower-moving ships necessary to carry bulky cargo. Prepositioning takes place both ashore and at sea. Each has advantages and tradeoffs: whereas ashore equipment is located near a potential crisis spot, afloat equipment can quickly be moved to different spots. After 25 years of efforts, DOD now has a sizable worldwide posture that includes equipment for 8 Army brigades (6 ashore and 2 at sea), 4 Marine brigades (3 at sea), and multiple Air Force airbase support sets in Europe, Korea, and Southwest Asia. Equipment for 5 of the 12 ground brigades is stationed in Europe, and for the other 7 in Southwest Asia and Asia. The *QDR Report* of 2001 calls for shifting some equipment sets from Europe to the other two regions. In the coming years, another issue will be whether additional brigade sites should be deployed, probably at sea. Currently, four Army and Marine division-equivalents have prepositioned equipment abroad. But this leaves seven CONUS-based divisions that must move by ships in a crisis. Prepositioning is not cheap: it entails commitment of sizable weapons inventories and high operating costs. Even so, prepositioning additional assets could enhance the capacity for rapid deployment and thereby help offset pressures for increased overseas stationing of the forces themselves.

Foreign military assistance is also an important part of overseas presence. The United States provides about $4 billion per year in foreign military financing aid, most of it to Israel and Egypt, and most in the form of loans for equipment purchases. In addition, the U.S. defense industry sells weapons and equipment on the open market at a rate of about $10 billion per year. Roughly $100 million is spent each year on grants, training, and education of foreign militaries, plus additional money for visits, exchanges, and other programs. These funds are regarded as critically important by regional combatant commands because they enhance outreach to foreign militaries, including potential new friends and partners. U.S. military commanders often complain that these high-leverage measures are chronically underfunded by DOD and the services. In the coming years, increased funding of these measures is likely to be warranted if the pace of U.S. military outreach efforts continues growing.

When the expenses for all of its forces and assets are added up, a reasonable estimate is that peacetime overseas presence costs $25 billion to $35 billion per year for the incremental cost of stationing forces overseas above the expense of basing the same forces in CONUS. This is an illustrative estimate; much depends upon the specifics of accounting. The cost would be even higher, except that Germany, Japan, and other allies provide financial offsets, reduce charges for bases and services, and contribute to U.S. research and development programs. Even so, some critics complain about the cost and urge withdrawals in order to save money. Withdrawing large forces from overseas locations would not, however, be a good way to reduce total expenses. The initial years would probably cost more, not less, due to the expense of moving forces back to CONUS and refurbishing bases for them. Major savings can be achieved only by disbanding withdrawn forces, but this step could weaken overall global strategy. Thus far, cost factors have not compelled any major force withdrawals in cases where powerful strategic requirements for the deployments existed. This pattern seems likely to continue, yet steps to trim costs make sense in situations where essential capabilities would not be sacrificed and where savings could be reinvested in other areas of overseas presence.

When all factors are added up, overseas presence is a strategic bargain. It is a high-leverage investment because of its contributions to global security and military preparedness. Absent an overseas presence, the United States would need to elevate its spending far more than $25 billion–$35 billion annually to gain comparable security. Yet overseas presence does cost as much or more than several other big programs in DOD's program budget. For this reason, a case can be made that overseas presence should not just be seen as a composite, integrated program of multiple related activities; it should also be treated this way at budget time. Perhaps overseas presence should become a separate, formal program in DOD'S budget. Better yet, a joint program budget document (that is, a POM) could be written on it. Measures such as these would help strengthen DOD's ability to see overseas presence as a whole, to ensure that adequate funds are committed to it, and to ensure that these funds are spent efficiently.

In the final analysis, the critical feature of overseas presence is not its costs, but the need to ensure its strategic effectiveness. It is becoming increasingly important because today's world is so complex, chaotic, and fluid. Overseas presence is counted upon to play a big role in shaping the international environment, and in making the difference between danger and progress. The strategic effectiveness of overseas presence is driven not only by the quantity of military forces and other assets stationed abroad, but also by their activities: the missions and tasks that they perform on a daily basis. These activities are growing and becoming more diversified. Today, overseas presence must do more than perform standard border defense and security missions; it must work closely with allies to promote interoperability and transformation, reach out to new partners through engagement efforts, and participate in the war on terrorism, along with a growing array of other missions including peacekeeping, stabilization, and reconstruction in places once viewed as lying outside the U.S. geostrategic perimeter.

The overseas presence is being called upon to carry out these growing activities at a time when its resources are not growing and may shrink. Whether a high operational tempo can be maintained with limited resources is to be seen. Regardless of future actions taken, the activities of overseas presence are a valuable resource that should be scrutinized carefully, with due regard for priorities. This can be a worthy job for operations research. Thus far, analytical attention has mostly been devoted to the big picture: the size and composition of the overseas presence program. The time has arrived to pay greater attention to the details of overseas presence, including its daily activities and strategic effects, which are discussed below.

Evaluating Ends: Using Multi-attribute Utility Analysis

A new overseas presence cannot be crafted effectively without a searching appraisal of how strategic ends can best be achieved on a global basis and in each key region. The task of analyzing the means-ends relationship would be easier if the purpose of overseas presence could be portrayed as one or two simple goals, such as "help shape the political terrain" and "be prepared for war." But such an approach is infeasible because, more than other types of defense planning, overseas presence is intended to help achieve multiple political and military goals, all of which must be taken into account in designing future deployments and priorities. In order to help guide future changes, intellectual order must be brought to the enterprise of gauging how new responses can best promote the multiple goals being pursued. The technique of multi-attribute utility analysis is well suited for such an effort.

A multi-attribute utility analysis of overseas presence begins by listing the full set of goals that must be taken into account in all three major regions of Europe, Asia, and the greater Middle East. Then, before it delves into quantitative techniques, it provides a simple verbal rating, based upon professional judgment, of how well the current overseas presence performs for each of these goals. Table 20–1 provides such a portrayal in illustrative terms. It lists two categories of goals: political and military, with five future goals within each category. While these goals may not cover the full spectrum, they are the ones listed in current U.S. policy documents as key aims. Other goals can be identified, but most are subsidiaries of these 10 parent goals. The table attaches rankings of high, medium, or low to suggest how well the current overseas presence in each region can be expected to achieve these goals during the next 5 to 10 years. These ratings provide a net assessment in verbal terms. They assess the effectiveness of overseas presence forces and activities in all three key regions when taken together with other U.S. instruments and prevailing strategic conditions there. Many of the low ratings do not indicate poor performance by overseas presence forces, but instead the sheer difficulty of doing better amidst inhospitable circumstances.

A criticism of such a table is that its ratings are based on human judgment, not scientific measurement. But in a strategic arena of such great complexity, virtually all evaluations must be based upon such judgments for the simple reason that scientific measurement is not feasible. The advantage of this table is that it assembles a large number of critical judgments—33 of them—into a single format where they can be stated and compared in similar terms and assessed for their overall strategic implications. Observers may debate whether the specific ratings of this table are correct, but to the extent they are correct in the aggregate, they suggest that the U.S. performance is best in Europe and lowest in the Middle East, with its performance in Asia falling in the middle. If the desired standard is a high score, even performance in Europe falls short, and both of the other two regions need major improvements, with the Middle East needing the most.

Multi-attribute utility analysis does not end here. While this table begins to bring some intellectual order to the subject, it has two significant deficiencies. First, it provides no basis for judging the importance of the 10 goals in relation to each other: overall performance evaluations could change if some goals were ranked higher than others. Nor does it define

Table 20–1. **Expected Strategic Performance of Current Overseas Presence (Verbal Model)**

	Major Regions		
	Europe	Middle East	Asia
Current Peacetime Troop Strength	109,000	25,000	100,000
Political Goals			
1. Maintain U.S. influence	High	Medium	High
2. Preserve and reform alliances and partnerships	Medium-High	Low-Medium	Medium
3. Promote regional stability and integration	Medium-High	Low-Medium	Medium
4. Dissuade geopolitical and military competition	Medium-High	Low-Medium	Medium
5. Help promote strategic stability and progress in adjoining regions	Low-Medium	Low	Low
Military Goals			
1. Deter aggression and war	High	Medium	Medium-High
2. Promote interoperability and transformation of allied forces	Low-Medium	Low	Low-Medium
3. Be prepared to carry out crisis actions and wartime operations	High	Medium	Medium-High
4. Be prepared to perform peacekeeping and stabilization and reconstruction missions	Medium	Low-Medium	Low-Medium
5. Prepare U.S. and allied force for operations in adjoining regions	Medium	Low	Low
Overall Performance	**Medium-High**	**Low-Medium**	**Medium**

exactly what is meant by the terms *high, medium,* or *low*; it leaves their interpretation to the beholder. The problem is that different people may define these terms in different ways. For example, one person may define a high score as demanding near perfection, and another may define it as requiring considerably less. Thus, this table provides fuzzy evaluations that are prone to misunderstanding or even flawed conclusions if used to forge policies and priorities. Something better is needed.

Multi-attribute utility analysis does provide a two-step technique that produces sharper judgments anchored in numbers, not words. First, it assigns numerical values to the goals; then, it assigns numerical scores to the standards of high, medium, and low performance.

Table 20–2 employs this two-step procedure to generate an illustrative appraisal of how overseas presence is performing in each region. It does so by first assuming that the 10 goals have a total value of 100 strategic "utility points" in each region, and that each goal is worth 10 points. Then, it employs a scale of 0–10 in order to gauge goal achievement in each area. A low performance is given a score of 0–3.3, depending upon judgment of where its performance lies. A medium performance receives 3.4–6.7 utility points, and a high performance receives 6.8–10 points. For an overall score in each region that reflects all 10 goals, low is 0–33 points, medium is 34–67 points, and high is 68–100 points.[6]

The result is a quantitative gauge of performance in all regions for each strategic goal. Overall strategic performance can be determined by adding up the totals for each region

Table 20–2. **Expected Strategic Performance of Current Overseas Presence (Utility Scores)**

Political Goals and Values	Possible Utility Points	Major Regions		
		Europe	Middle East	Asia
1. Maintain U.S. influence	10	9.0	6.0	8.0
2. Preserve and reform alliances and partnerships	10	7.5	3.8	5.6
3. Promote regional stability and integration	10	7.5	3.0	5.0
4. Dissuade geopolitical and military competition	10	7.5	3.0	6.0
5. Help promote strategic stability and progress in adjoining regions	10	5.0	1.0	3.0
Subtotal	50	36.5	16.8	27.6
Military Goals and Values				
1. Deter aggression and war	10	9.0	5.0	6.7
2. Promote interoperability and transformation of allied forces	10	5.0	2.0	3.0
3. Be prepared to carry out crisis actions and wartime operations	10	9.0	6.7	6.7
4. Be prepared to perform peacekeeping, stabilization and reconstruction missions	10	5.5	3.5	4.0
5. Prepare U.S. and allied forces for operations in adjoining regions	10	5.0	1.0	2.0
Subtotal	50	33.5	18.2	22.4
Overall Performance	**100**	**70.0 (High)**	**35.0 (Medium)**	**50.0 (Medium)**

and comparing them with each other. Once again, the criticism can be levied that these numbers are anchored in subjective judgments, not scientific measurements. But again, the central issue is not scientific precision, but whether these numbers do a better job of expressing human judgments than do fuzzy words. To the extent this is the case, this table and its numbers can contribute something worthwhile to the analysis.

When policymakers are first introduced to this quantitative technique, they often react with skepticism, but then they tend to warm to it. The reason is that it provides a useful way to collect, organize, and display the logical implications of many judgments and to show how they combine to produce aggregate assessments of goal achievement. It shows where some goals are being well achieved and others are not. It also focuses attention on the need to explain the underlying strategic reasons for the performance patterns that emerge. To the extent that this technique produces controversial numbers, they can be subjected to further analysis and refinement. The key issue is not the precision of the numbers, but their policy robustness. If the main policy priorities do not change as these numbers are varied within reasonable parameters, then the main strategic message communicated by these numbers can be relied upon as sound.

To the extent that the main message of table 20–2 seems robust and sensible, it derives not only from the numbers but from real-life trends in all three regions. The table suggests that overseas performance is being successful in Europe because, in combination with other trends, it is helping perpetuate NATO while unifying and stabilizing the continent in political terms. But comparable success is not being achieved at preparing Europe to play a strong contributing role in the Middle East, nor at preparing European militaries to operate with U.S. forces there. These are the reasons why the overall performance score for Europe falls toward the low end of the high category. In Asia, the overall performance score falls in the middle of the medium category because, although the region is at peace, its security system is not stable and it lacks multilateral defense structures in which the United States could exercise its influence. In the Middle East, the overall score is not quite in the low category, because the overthrow of the Saddam Hussein regime in Iraq has enhanced stability and security. But the score is at the low end of the medium category, and not higher, because the region is still prone to other instabilities and because multilateral security ties are virtually nonexistent.

This pattern—Europe receiving a higher score than the other two regions—suggests that perhaps overseas presence assets should be transferred from Europe to the Middle East and Asia to enhance strategic performance there. A limited transfer was proposed by the *QDR Report* of 2001 and the DOD global basing study of 2004. But how far should such a transfer be pursued: by a little, or a lot? Figure 20–1 is an elaboration of table 20–2; it helps illuminate this issue by showing performance curves for all three regions. It suggests that strategic performance in each region is affected by the size of overseas presence there. As troop levels rise, performance increases; as troop levels diminish, performance also diminishes. The key point is that the transfer of overseas-presence forces brings tradeoffs: strategic performance in the Middle East and Asia would be likely to improve if U.S. military assets now stationed in Europe were transferred there, but if U.S. troops were to leave Europe, performance there would be likely to drop by some amount. The question is whether the marginal gains in the Middle East and Asia would justify

Figure 20–1. **Strategic Performance Curves: Tradeoffs from Force Transfers**

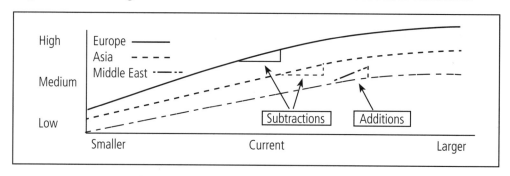

the opportunity cost of lower performance in Europe, such as less U.S. influence or less NATO preparedness. The answer is not obvious at first glance; much depends upon the exact nature of the gains and losses.

At a minimum, figure 20–1 suggests that the idea of transferring large military forces from Europe to the other two regions should be approached cautiously, with a careful eye on costs and tradeoffs as well as benefits. If the performance score in Europe were near 100, then a policy of transferring forces could be approached with equanimity. But all is not well there, especially in light of recent transatlantic frictions and the slow pace of NATO's progress toward defense transformation. Small force transfers might not have damaging consequences, but major transfers could exacerbate these problems. In addition, moving additional forces to the Middle East and Asia—assuming such a step is politically possible—might not automatically bring a rich harvest of strategic rewards. Much would depend upon the types of forces deployed, the missions performed by them, and how they were received by countries there.

The main implication is that the design of the future overseas presence should not be approached with a focus narrowly or solely on transferring forces from one theater to another. Improvements in all three regions are needed. Indeed, perhaps improvements to NATO's cohesion and military prowess might do as much, or more, to enhance U.S. goals in the Middle East than deploying more U.S. forces to that region. The challenge is to design a future overseas presence that strengthens performance across the board, with regard for the priorities and potentialities in each region. In an era of limited resources that must be allocated carefully to pursue a new global strategy, the best approach may be to reorganize the forces of each region while strengthening their support assets, activities, and missions to gain more strategic mileage. This focus on qualitative enhancements, along with well-conceived quantitative additions and subtractions, reflects the logic of operations research and of wise defense planning.

The multi-attribute utility analysis presented here, while only illustrative, indicates how such an approach could be focused. It suggests that efforts to upgrade the performance of remaining U.S. forces in Europe by altering their size and composition should focus on the elements where there is the most need for improvement: strengthening NATO's political unity, its military interoperability with U.S. forces, and its capacity to project military power to the Middle East. Parallel efforts in the Middle East should focus on strengthening regional stability and security while improving the capacity of friendly countries for multilateral cooperation with the United States. A similar approach should be followed in Asia, while broadening the U.S. focus beyond Northeast Asia to Southeast Asia. Such a global set of improvement priorities offers the promise of designing a new overseas presence focused not on change for its own sake, but on remedying deficiencies and upgrading strategic performance in critical areas.

A variety of options will need to be considered in determining how to pursue these strategic priorities. Multi-attribute utility analysis can contribute by providing quantitative techniques for comparing how such options perform. Table 20–3 illustrates this comparison with three options: preserving the current overseas presence; shifting a lot of forces from Europe to the Middle East and Asia, but not making quality improvements; or shifting some forces from Europe while making large quality improvements in all three regions. On this table, a global total of 300 strategic utility points is possible because performances in 3 regions are added together. The table suggests that option 3 is easily the best choice, while globally, option 2 might perform only 15 points better than option 1, a difference of only 10 percent. These exact numbers are not definitive, but if they are approximately correct, they say something important about basic strategic priorities ahead.

Table 20–3. **Performance of Overseas Presence Options (Strategic Utility Points)**

	Europe	Asia	Middle East	Global Total
Option 1: Current presence	70	35	50	155
Option 2: Major force transfers with no quality improvements	60	50	60	170
Option 3: Modest force transfers with major quality improvements	80	65	75	220

Exactly how can such capability improvements be achieved? For all regions, a careful appraisal of steps in multiple programmatic areas will be needed. Most often, changes to force size and mix, command structures, information networks, bases and infrastructure, prepositioning, military exercises, and security assistance will need to be blended together. The exact blend of improvements may differ from one region to the next. Careful planning will be needed. Multi-attribute utility analysis can contribute not only by tabulating overall scores for each option, but also by examining how the various programmatic components of each option contribute to the total score. Its capacity to probe into details while also aggregating them to determine the overall impact is one of its most useful features.

In projecting future performance, much depends upon the time frames for these scores. Table 20–3 deals with the near term and medium term, out to 5 or 10 years in the future: a normal horizon for defense planning. What about 20 years from now? While the distant future is impossible to predict, many observers judge that it may be considerably different not only from today, but from a decade from now as well. If U.S. efforts to promote democracy and stability in the Middle East are successful, this region may be less dangerous, and the need for a robust overseas presence less important. Conversely, Asia could be more dangerous if relations with China become adversarial. Consequently, a robust U.S. military presence in Asia may be more critical, and the situation may require a different type of presence, perhaps even more naval and air forces, along with missile defenses. Such prospects for major change are a key reason for adjusting analyses to evolving conditions, and for treating operations research and its multi-attribute utility functions in the same spirit.

Programmatic Priorities for Future Overseas Presence

In employing this framework of improvement priorities, the logic of operations research as employed here suggests a menu of specific measures for reorganizing and strengthening the U.S. overseas presence while making sensible use of limited transfers of forces. The task of portraying and evaluating these measures can begin with Europe; change there already is happening and the future can be seen with some clarity. For the near-to-mid term, a main challenge in Europe is to avoid acting impulsively, and to keep long-range U.S. interests and goals firmly in mind. Some Americans have urged major troop withdrawals from France and Germany in order to punish them for their positions in the debate over Iraq. The problem is that such withdrawals would also punish NATO as well as important U.S. interests. The United States would lose influence in Europe, NATO would weaken, and the prospect of gaining Europe's help in the Middle East would decline. Beyond this, it is doubtful whether the United States would want to continue providing extended nuclear deterrence coverage and other entangling commitments to an entire continent in a strained setting in which its influence is diminished. Full-scale troop withdrawals might make sense as part of an effort to dismantle NATO and tear up the Washington Treaty, but short of this drastic step, they are not a good way to punish wayward allies or to push them toward sensible reform and responsible conduct.

The better approach is to design a new U.S. presence in Europe that, while somewhat smaller than now, can help pursue such top priorities as leading NATO toward outward-looking security policies and transforming its military capabilities for new missions in distant areas. Rather than being anchored in Central Europe, a new joint posture would have a greater eastern and southern orientation: it should be configured for operations in such places as the Caucasus, Central Asia, and the Middle East. The U.S. presence must be capable of carrying out national military missions, and should also be tailored to help encourage alliance military transformation by working with the new NATO Response Force (NRF) and other important NATO forces. Such a strategic concept points toward an agenda of constructive changes that would foster potent joint forces having strategic influence, improved capabilities, and a multilateral orientation.

In the future, as the DOD study notes, the United States will no longer need to station 4 heavy Army brigades and 65,000 troops in Germany, as its borders are no longer endangered. But it will need to retain significant Army forces in Europe to provide viable power-projection options, to help encourage NATO defense transformation, and to work with NATO's new members from Eastern Europe. Perhaps a new Army force of two large brigade task forces would be appropriate. One brigade task force, composed of heavy units with new-era weapons and information networks, could be stationed in Germany and Poland. It would have the task of working with both long-time members and new allies to pursue transformation and interoperability for major combat operations. The other brigade task force could be stationed in Italy and the Balkans. Composed mostly of light forces with high mobility, its main purpose would be maintaining high operational readiness and interoperability for power projection into distant crisis zones. If necessary, the Army presence in Europe could be further reduced to only one brigade task force if backed by rotating units, but this would mean a loss of capability. If a single brigade is deployed, it should have a composite structure of heavy and light battalions in order to preserve interoperability with European forces and to provide assets capable of working with the NRF.

Deployed alongside this new Army presence should be appropriate Air Force and Navy forces, plus joint command centers and logistical infrastructure. A continued Air Force presence of two fighter wings and support assets makes sense. The Air Force should pursue interoperability and transformation with allies that are already well equipped and help provide air defense of Southern Europe, including the Mediterranean Sea and Turkey. The U.S. naval presence should continue to be centered on the 6th Fleet, which operates mainly in the Mediterranean. While maritime defense of NATO borders will continue to be one of its responsibilities, the 6th Fleet should work closely with European navies to support the NRF and other military reforms. Normal peacetime conditions would not necessarily require the full-time deployment of one CVBG and one ARG in or near European waters. But having one of these formations always on duty would be a good idea, both to show the U.S. flag and to provide viable crisis response options. To enhance the versatility of both formations, the ARG could be equipped with cruise missile ships, and the CVBG could be provided with a small force of Marines aboard amphibious craft. Small naval and air forces are also likely to be needed to help operate a theater missile defense system when it is deployed. Increased sea-based prepositioning of equipment and homeporting of more naval combatants in the Mediterranean may make sense.

Enough manpower would be needed to populate the combat forces plus new joint command centers and logistical support units. A reasonable first approximation is a posture of 60,000 to 70,000 troops from all services. Periodically this force would be supplemented by up to 10,000 troops that would temporarily rotate to Europe for training and exercises. A smaller posture of 30,000 to 50,000 troops can be imagined, but this would cut heavily into essential combat units and support assets. A posture of 60,000 to 70,000 troops would be smaller than the current force, but owing to its configuration, it would still be potent and effective. It could perform new-era U.S. and NATO missions, including power projection and defense against weapons of mass destruction. In particular, it would mean NATO could have two NRFs: one manned by U.S. forces and the other mostly manned by Europeans. These two forces could train and operate together, thereby expanding NATO's crisis response options. NATO's emerging military requirements may very well make this two-headed posture appropriate.

In Asia, the future U.S. force presence will be shaped largely by the situation on the Korean Peninsula. As long as North Korea remains a major menace, large U.S. forces will still be needed in South Korea and Japan. If tensions increase, even larger forces may be needed. But if the Korean situation were to cool down and reunification was pursued, major changes would be possible. In that event, the U.S. military alliances with South Korea and Japan could be reoriented to provide general region-wide security and defense. Today's presence of two Army brigades in South Korea and two Marine brigades on Okinawa could be reduced to one or two brigades that have regional missions. The withdrawn brigades could be returned to CONUS, but a better idea might be to station one or two of them at new bases in Southeast Asia, where they could work with new partners on behalf of collective security and multilateral defense cooperation.

This southern focus in Asia also applies to air and naval forces. An Air Force presence of 2.6 fighter wings, plus a Navy CVBG and an ARG, are still likely to be needed, but their peacetime missions would expand to include the entire East Asian littoral, including Southeast Asia. A new system of temporary operating locations for air and naval forces would be needed there, with hubs in Australia and perhaps the Philippines and a capacity to cover the strategic zone between the Philippines and Singapore while working cooperatively with Indonesia and Malaysia. Increased prepositioning of weapons and stocks is another priority. Homeporting of additional Navy surface combatants and submarines in Asia may become possible. Creation of theater missile defense units is also likely to be pursued. Taking all components into account, the new Asian overseas presence may be 80,000 to 90,000 troops supplemented by rotating forces. This force would be slightly smaller than the current posture of about 100,000 troops, but it would be designed to preserve U.S. political influence, provide a variety of response options, expand the zone of geographic coverage, and encourage collective, multilateral security across the East Asian and Pacific region.

In the Persian Gulf and Middle East, much will depend upon the situation in Iraq and larger political trends across the region. Prior to the invasion of Iraq, the normal U.S. presence of about 25,000 troops was subject to growing political pressures from Saudi Arabia for a lower profile and downsizing. The response was the shifting of U.S. forces to Kuwait and friendly Gulf sheikdoms. Now that the Saddam Hussein regime has been removed from Iraq, there may no longer be a need for a major U.S. reinforcement plan of multiple divisions, fighter wings, and naval combatants aimed at repelling a large invasion. A smaller reinforcement plan focused on swift entry and crisis response for a spectrum of new missions will probably suffice. Even after U.S. forces eventually withdraw from Iraq, some forces will be needed in the region to maintain influence, work with allies, bolster defense against WMD, and provide initial crisis response options. Such low-profile perennials as a fighter wing, a CVBG, an ARG, command centers, deployment bases, and increased prepositioning of equipment are the likely backbone of this posture. Deployment of one or two ground brigades might, however, also be advisable, with their location to be determined by prevailing political conditions.

Depending upon its size and composition, such a posture might be 25,000–40,000 troops supplemented by rotating forces. This would be as large as or larger than the previous peacetime presence but considerably smaller than the force in Iraq during 2005. Such a joint posture would be charged with the new mission of handling post-Saddam security affairs in the greater Middle East. Provided the region becomes more stable, this posture's main mission would not be solely to prepare for major wars, but to help pursue a new era of collective security, multilateralism, and democratization. Instead of focusing on Persian Gulf defense, it would have a larger geographic sweep and would be focused on fighting terrorism while promoting better multilateral ties with friendly countries in the Middle East and elsewhere along the southern arc. Such a mission would certainly be demanding, but if the new U.S. presence is equipped with the right assets and supported by robust military assistance programs plus rotational units from CONUS for training and exercises, it would have a good chance of getting the job done.

Table 20–4 displays illustrative manpower levels for a future overseas presence if these concepts were adopted. Global manpower levels remain similar to today, but there would be major changes in distribution among regions, force mix, missions, operations, and daily activities. The overall impact would be to create a new overseas presence that reflected strategic trends abroad and transformation imperatives at home. Such a presence would offer the promise of higher strategic effectiveness for tomorrow's world.

Table 20–4. **Illustrative Future U.S. Overseas Presence (Manpower)**

	Stationed Forces	Rotating Forces	Total Forces
Europe	60,000–70,000	10,000	70,000–80,000
Asia	80,000–90,000	10,000	90,000–100,000
Middle East	25,000–40,000	10,000	35,000–50,000
Total	165,000–200,000	30,000	195,000–230,000

These ideas for a redesigned, improved overseas presence are illustrations, not a fixed blueprint. In the final analysis, the size and composition of the future U.S. overseas presence in all three regions will depend upon emerging trends and will require study of many details and consideration of a wide spectrum of options. Moreover, any new global model would most likely be only temporary. Regardless of the issues that surface, they must be subjected to careful analysis of strategic matters and of military and programmatic matters as well. Indeed, careful attention to such details will be the key to mastering the relationship between means and ends in the coming era. Operations research provides a useful toolbox of methods that can be applied, provided they too change with the times by adopting new techniques for measuring the relationship between means and ends, and for scrutinizing the contents of complex programs.

Overseas presence is a classic case of the need for multidisciplinary analysis of future U.S. national security policies and defense strategies. Here, strategic evaluation is needed to gauge the political-military functions that overseas presence must perform on the world stage. Systems analysis is needed to understand the overseas presence as a global whole and as a composite program. Operations research is needed to address the military details and to assess the relationship between means and ends in formal terms. This topic has been covered in this section to highlight the role of operations research, but it easily could have been placed in either the section on strategic evaluation or the systems analysis section: the tools of operations research employed in this chapter are embedded in a larger context provided by strategic evaluation and systems analysis.

Similarly, many contemporary national security policy issues will, in one way or another, require the use of all three disciplines. Especially when this is the case, systems analysis and operations research should be seen not as separate disciplines, but as overlapping and mutually reinforcing. Systems analysis can provide the frame of reference, and operations research can provide the machinery for calculating the relationship between means and ends. Together these two disciplines can help bring strategic evaluation to life in ways that allow policymakers to gauge the advantages, liabilities, and tradeoffs of the options before them. Individually, these three methods may sometimes be unable to produce satisfactory answers, but together, they can often accomplish a great deal.

Notes

[1] See annual reports to Congress issued by Secretary of Defense William Cohen during the final years of the Clinton administration, 1997–2000.

[2] For details, see International Institute for Strategic Studies, *The Military Balance*, 2003–2004 (London: IISS, 2003).

[3] See Department of Defense, *QDR Report 2001* (Washington, DC: Department of Defense, 2001) for supporting analysis. For additional analysis, see Roger Cliff et al., "The Future of U.S. Overseas Presence," in Michèle Flournoy, ed., *QDR 2001: Strategy-Driven Choices for America's Security* (Washington, DC: National Defense University Press, 2001), chapter 9.

[4] For additional analysis, see Richard L. Kugler, *Changes Ahead: Future Directions for the U.S. Overseas Military Presence* (Santa Monica, CA: RAND, 1998); Kurt M. Campbell and Celeste Johnson Ward, "New Battle Stations?" *Foreign Affairs* 82, no. 5 (September/October 2003).

[5] For additional analysis, see Richard L. Kugler, *The Future U.S. Military Presence in Europe: Forces and Requirements for the Post–Cold War Era* (Santa Monica, CA: RAND, 1992).

[6] For an introduction to how to create a multi-attribute utility function, see Edith Stokey and Richard Zeckhauser, *A Primer for Policy Analysis* (New York: W.W. Norton, 1978). For a more detailed and mathematical analysis, see Ralph Keeney and Howard Raiffa, *Decisions With Multiple Objectives: Preferences and Value Tradeoffs* (New York: John Wiley and Sons, 1976).

Chapter 21
Analyzing Conventional Combat

Determining how best to improve U.S. conventional forces to enhance their capacity for wartime missions is one of the biggest and most expensive challenges facing defense planning. It requires both professional military judgment and concerted analysis. Strategic evaluation and systems analysis have important roles to play, but because mastery of details is critical, operations research is vital too. In this arena, operations research makes some use of static techniques, but its mainstay is a large set of dynamic force-exchange models and simulation tools that can loosely be grouped under the title of conventional combat models. Critics often accuse these models of various shortcomings, but when they are properly prepared and applied, their strengths are impressive. For this reason, combat modeling is a major activity in the defense world.

This chapter examines these models, what makes them tick, and how they can be used sensibly. The mathematical equations used here are relatively simple, but the same analytical principles apply to the most sophisticated equations on the books. This chapter begins by discussing the analytical foundations of combat models. It then examines the theater-wide attrition models of land combat that were popular during the Cold War, and how theater air and naval operations were modeled at that time. Next, it examines modeling of standoff strikes as it was done during the 1990s for rebuffing a hypothetical Iraqi invasion of Kuwait and Saudi Arabia. Finally, it discusses the future need for combat models that can help determine how to make quality improvements in U.S. forces for carrying out joint warfare in the early 21st century. This chapter paints a picture of both continuity and change: many fundamentals still apply, but they will need to be applied in new ways that reflect modern doctrine and operations.

Analytical Foundations of Combat Models

The role played by combat models is seldom trumpeted in official documents or even the academic literature, but the claims made for new weapons and programs often come from these models. Although few new weapons rest their entire justification on the analytical outputs of these models, almost no new weapon would be bought that failed to pass their tests. Many otherwise attractive ideas have fallen by the wayside because they failed to do so. These models thus function as gatekeepers: they help open the door to good ideas and close the door to bad ones. In the process, they often provide valuable insights on the gritty details of force operations, and they can aid policy judgments in other ways. These models can perform this important function effectively, however, only if they are well conceived and anchored in sound concepts, equations, and data. Getting these models right before they are used is an essential task facing operations research. Even then, their strengths and limits must be understood. They are best used and interpreted by people who see them for the mixture of science and art that they are.[1]

In appraising combat models and their usefulness, it is critical to remember that they are created by humans who rely upon judgments as well as hard evidence to determine their concepts, equations, and data. The results generated by combat models are normally the logical consequences of these human-derived inputs. As such, these results are often highly interesting because even the designers of the models could not have forecast them exactly or quickly. But this does not necessarily make these results accurate or true. Much depends upon whether the original inputs are sound. Their soundness cannot be verified by the combat model itself: it must come from elsewhere. For these reasons, combat models should be neither accepted unquestioningly nor neglected as always flawed or biased. Instead, they should be seen for what they are: human creations that come in varying degrees of accuracy, reliability, authenticity, and insight. Each model should be taken on its own merits.

Combat models can be understood even by people not schooled in advanced mathematics. Developing an understanding of them can best begin by noting that these models perform two key analytical functions. First, they provide a baseline assessment of how U.S. forces are likely to perform on the battlefield against enemy forces. They give a sense of which side is likely to win and which side is likely to lose in any given encounter. Second, they provide an appraisal of how U.S. forces can be improved to perform better in battle. They permit comparative judgments about alternative weapons and programs on a cost-effective basis. For example, they may show that more artillery and attack helicopters are a better choice than more tanks. Both functions—force assessment and resource allocation—are important, and both must be performed with sufficient accuracy and insight to allow for effective decisionmaking. Combat models should be judged by the standard of whether they facilitate wise decisions, rather than by the standard of pinpoint accuracy and airtight predictions.

Combat models that perform both of these functions can be arrayed along a spectrum of abstraction. Some are practically microscopic: they portray small-unit engagements such as two tanks or two ships firing at each other. Other models portray bigger force interactions, such as a division advancing on a brigade, an air squadron bombing an industrial site, or a naval task force firing cruise missiles at shore targets while warding off missile strikes. Still other models assess theater-wide interactions, such as a large joint force of multiple divisions, fighter wings, and CVBGs defending against an enemy country, or perhaps invading it. Applying a combination or nested hierarchy of these models is often the best way to address cases in which major decisions rest on a mixture of big issues and small details.[2]

Whether these models are used singly or in combination, they have a major feature in common: all of them provide quantitative output data on battlefield performance characteristics, such as the number of enemy tanks killed per day by a battalion of U.S. tanks. These data are generated by mathematical equations and input data. Sometimes a highly complex model will contain many such equations; often, however, just a few simple equations are the main drivers of results. Irrespective of the number and sophistication of the equations, they are all anchored in an analytical portrayal of the combat process. Coming to grips with this portrayal is key to understanding how and why the models operate as they do, for everything else—including the composition of their equations and how they handle data—flows from there.

Once this relationship among concepts, equations, and data is grasped, the procedures for understanding combat models become easy to follow. First, an interested observer should discern how a model conceptualizes or brings intellectual order to the combat process. Then, one should examine how the model uses its conceptualization to generate mathematical equations for describing and explaining the key features of force operations in the combat process. Next, one should identify the main data and assumptions about weapons performance (such as kill probabilities) that are fed into these equations to bring these models to life. Finally, one should examine how these concepts, equations, and data are brought together in the calculation stage to generate conclusions and recommendations.

The first step—understanding a model's conceptual features—is critical because they are the intellectual lenses that determine both what is perceived and how it is perceived. Getting this conceptualization right is critical to having a model that is capable of producing sound results. Figure 21–1 helps show why this is the case. It illustrates a tactical battle between five U.S. tanks and five enemy tanks, each of equal quality with a kill probability of 0.40. It suggests that this battle could take either of two different forms. Case 1 is a single big battle in which all five tanks on both sides engage each other at the same time, producing five separate one-on-one duels. Case 2 is a series of battles in which all five U.S. tanks first fight one enemy tank, and then fight another, and so on. The table shows two very different outcomes. In case 1, each side loses two tanks; this is a stalemate. In case 2, the U.S. force is victorious, destroying all five enemy tanks, losing two of its own.

Figure 21–1. **Small Unit Tank Duels**

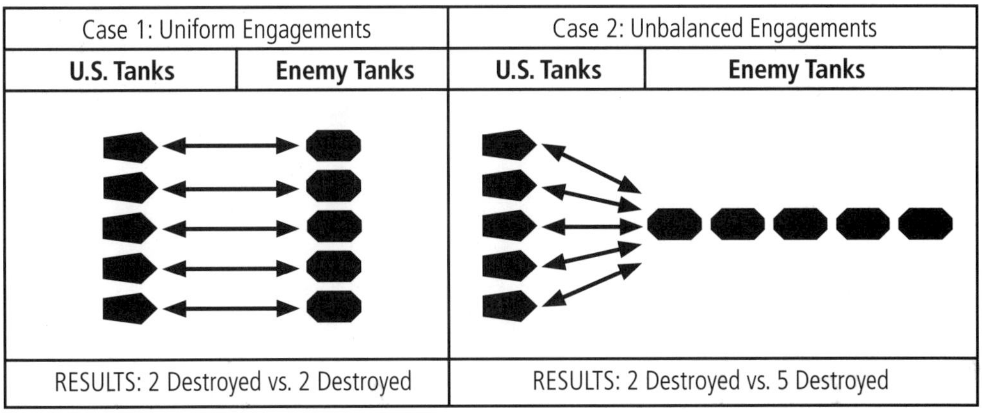

Case 1: Uniform Engagements		Case 2: Unbalanced Engagements	
U.S. Tanks	**Enemy Tanks**	**U.S. Tanks**	**Enemy Tanks**
RESULTS: 2 Destroyed vs. 2 Destroyed		RESULTS: 2 Destroyed vs. 5 Destroyed	

The reason for this difference between stalemate and victory is that in case 1, the two sides fight on equal terms, but in case 2, the U.S. tanks are able to gang up on the enemy and benefit from the advantage of superior maneuver and force concentration. In theory, both types of battles are physically possible. When a combat model is employed, it must be configured to portray the type of battle actually to be waged or prepared for. If two different models are available, the analyst should select the model that does the best job of assessing the specific battle being studied, not a different type of battle.

The basic point illustrated by this table is that a battle is determined not only by how many forces are employed, but also by how these forces engage each other in operational terms. This is the case for virtually all types of wars, large and small. Operational dynamics matter a great deal, because they govern force interactions and the results flowing from them. Good combat modeling requires accurately portraying these dynamics, and assessing a combat model requires discerning whether it does so. A model that gets these details right is likely to produce useful results if it is fed sound input data. A model that gets them wrong, however, will probably produce misleading results even if its input data are sound.

Once a model's concepts have been verified, its mathematical equations can be scrutinized. Trying to examine a computer model that contains dozens of complex equations can be difficult. Often such opaqueness becomes a reason to disqualify a model from serious decisionmaking, simply because its mathematical calculations cannot be understood, much less verified. But not all combat models are this complex, nor do all of them require computers. Such models come in three different types. Simple back-of-the-envelope models may have only a few variables and one or two algebraic equations. Spreadsheet models may have three or four such equations. Computer simulations may have many variables and equations, and may employ differential equations. Important defense studies often rely upon back-of-the-envelope models that can be easily scrutinized. Experienced defense analysts may rely upon spreadsheet models because their calculations can be verified and their results thus relied upon. Sometimes complex computer simulations are needed, but they can be boiled down to spreadsheet models or back-of-the-envelope models once their core properties are known. For these reasons, the mathematical equations of combat models need not be indecipherable, and they should not be feared by outsiders. Often, a modest amount of effort can uncover how they function and how they can be used.[3]

The mathematical equations of combat models are normally not deductively derived from irrefutable axioms or extracted from laboratory tests. Instead, they are created by analysts who are trying to portray the essential features of complex military phenomena. Because they reflect human judgments, these equations are approximations of reality, which may be in error even if guided by keen intelligence and the purest of intentions. Their accuracy is determined by the degree to which they are consistent with reality.

An algebraic equation is composed of elements such as variables, constants, coefficients, exponents, and such combinatorial rules as addition, subtraction, multiplication, and division. An example is the equation $y = 2ax + bx + c$. The manner in which these elements are chosen and put together determines what an equation says about military reality. The key to scrutinizing it lies in examining these elements to determine whether they seem to make sense. Such a reality check can help separate the wheat from the chaff, and further improve equations that are close to being on target.

A simple example, drawn from static indicators, will help illustrate why equations in dynamic combat models should be scrutinized in this way, not accepted at face value.

Consider equation 1, which purports to gauge the combat power of a tank. Through its coefficients, this equation says that firepower is three times as important as survivability, and that mobility is twice as important. Obviously this equation will favor a tank with a big gun and a powerful engine, even if it has only thin protective armor.

Equation 1: $P = 3F + 2M + S$
where P is combat power, F is firepower, M is mobility, and S is survivability.
Equation 2 provides a different appraisal because it sets the coefficient at 1 for
each variable.
Equation 2: $P = F + M + S$

The effect is to favor tanks whose armor is as substantial as their guns and their engines. Equation 3 carries forth equal coefficients but adds a fourth variable, reliability, which is determined by the tank's ability to operate for lengthy periods without breaking down and having to undergo repairs in a maintenance depot.[4]

Equation 3: $P = F + M + S + R$

Which of these equations best portrays tank performance? Tank designers may dispute the answer, but for most studies, equation 3 might be the safest bet because it includes more variables and it treats all of them as equally important. Each situation and equation must be judged on its own merits, but as a general rule, values that inflate performance or accelerate the pace of events—coefficients, exponents, and multiplication rules fall into this category—should be treated with caution.[5] Of course, the ultimate arbiter must be accuracy. The military world is not governed by linear relationships; some variables can be more important than others; inflators or deflators can provide valid insights about dynamic, non-linear phenomena. While few equations will be fully satisfactory, some are considerably more accurate than others. Key to knowing a good combat model is being able to distinguish between sound and unsound equations. If a model has questionable equations, they should be altered as necessary. Merely because they are embedded in an existing model does not make them untouchable.

After a model's equations have been surveyed, the final stage is to scrutinize its input data, such as its assumptions about fire rates, movement rates, sortie rates, kill probabilities, and the like. The central issue is whether a model's performance parameters are basically on target or wide of the mark. Have they been selected in order to provide an objective portrayal, or rather to bias the analysis in one direction or another? Often, there will be no scientific way to verify input data, but this does not mean that all input data are equally valid. If better data can be found, they should be used: time and effort are often required to build a good database. In determining what data and assumptions to employ, other studies can be surveyed to ascertain what judgments are commonly accepted: perhaps a missile is generally agreed to have a 0.50 SSPK, but not as high as 0.90 SSPK. Historical experience can be drawn upon, and the judgments of seasoned military officers can be used; so can common sense. Basically, input assumptions are more likely to be reliable when they pass these tests of reliability. When they fail them or otherwise seem odd, they should be questioned. Even in cases where there are no tests for reliability, the old standby is that of employing sensitivity analysis in order to show how performance varies as a function of different inputs. A good sensitivity analysis can help resolve many questions about data and assumptions.

These simple analytical procedures for scrutinizing concepts, equations, and data help provide a reliable approach for understanding today's world of combat models. Such procedures are regularly used by professional analysts to calibrate and apply existing models. They can also be used by novices who want to understand these models or to begin using them. Often newcomers will find back-of-the-envelope models and spreadsheet models more suited to their purposes than complex computer simulations. These simpler models are relatively easy to use and often foster more thinking and learning than do computer simulations, which may function as black boxes, grinding out reams of data while leaving the user uninformed about the reasons for the results.

The task of building new models employs the same procedures as scrutinizing old models, but it is a demanding art form that requires considerable original thinking. The need for new models arises when there has been a paradigm shift in how wars are likely to be fought.[6] At such a juncture, old models are unable to address new issues; if they are still used, they may prevent analysts from seeing new realities.

The proper solution often is not to tinker with existing models in the hope that they can be adjusted at the margins, but to create entirely new models that are anchored solidly in the precise military phenomena being studied. Creating new models is an exercise in fresh conceptualization. This begins by first determining the purpose of the model: the issues it is to address and the analytical products it is to produce. Then, a strong effort must be made to develop a clear and accurate picture of the military and operational situation being modeled, including its unique features. Only after this stage has been completed should the task of crafting mathematical equations and assembling data begin. Both of these steps must be taken with great care. The mathematical equations must faithfully reflect the military operation being studied. Quantitative date must be selected on the basis of accuracy and reliability. The model must be tested to determine whether it is performing effectively; if not, corrections must be made. Following these procedures will help ensure that the model, once completed, serves its purposes and can be used in studies. Needless to say, combat models are vulnerable to biased inputs that produce precooked solutions or otherwise confirm the designers' predilections. Avoiding this temptation is the best way to ensure that models not only produce accurate results but also acquire a reputation for credibility.

The early 21st century may well be a time of paradigm shift in combat modeling. Many of those who participate today in the design of forces and doctrines proclaim that these are truly revolutionary times. While many of today's models reflect the past, however, they also offer much for the new era. Over the past 10 years, a fair amount of innovation has occurred. Whether current models can handle such emerging phenomena as information networking, joint force employment, and new operational concepts may be questioned. To the extent that existing models fall short, they will lack the capacity to address issues that count even though they still appear sophisticated. Because substance matters far more than appearances, a future of change is mandated.

Theater-Wide Attrition Models from the Cold War: Land Combat

Theater-wide models of land combat that rely upon calculations of firepower and attrition have been a mainstay of the field for years. Most of today's models were created during the Cold War and therefore reflect its key military features. Today these models are sometimes criticized as being out of date. Becoming familiar with them is valuable, however, for several reasons. They show the origins of and foundations for contemporary mathematical modeling of conventional war. While modern wars are not solely driven by firepower and attrition—information networks and maneuver now play big roles—both factors still contribute importantly on the modern battlefield. Nor have Cold War military confrontations of big ground forces arrayed against each other become totally obsolete. There is still such a confrontation in Korea, and it is capable óf producing a violent war in which U.S. forces would participate.

Theater-wide attrition models appeared when computers first arrived on the scene with the software for conducting complex simulations, and the mounting NATO-Warsaw Pact military confrontation in Central Europe demanded insightful analyses. As of the late 1970s, static indicators had helped assess the evolving military balance there, but they had been taken about as far as they could go. Dynamic assessments were needed of how a war might unfold and how U.S. and allied forces could be improved to provide a more confident forward defense. NATO's forward defense was designed in a mostly linear way, with a frontal array of nine corps sectors lined up abreast on the inter-German border. Intelligence assessments suggested that an enemy attack might also be conducted in a mostly linear way, with enemy forces spread out across the entire front. If a linear war would be fought, theater-wide attrition models, which portrayed combat in terms of two giant pistons crashing against each other, were well suited to the task.

If linear force operations provided the conceptual framework for these models, where were their mathematical equations to come from? Lanchester equations provided the answer. These equations were first concocted at the time of World War I, when British analyst F.W. Lanchester was seeking to understand the mathematics of air-to-air dogfights as well as naval battles between British *Dreadnought* battleships and similar well-armed ships. Experience in that war had shown that even when a naval battle was fought between two similarly sized forces, seemingly minor disparities in numbers of ships, their gunnery, and their armor could spell a major difference in the outcome. For example, a clash pitting 10 *Dreadnoughts* from one side against 8 *Dreadnoughts* from the other side could result in the larger force totally destroying the smaller force with few losses. Why would the outcome be so unbalanced? Maneuver did not appear to be the answer: this result occurred even when the two forces lined up against each other in linear formations. Some other reason had to account for this unexpected dynamic.

Lanchester proposed that the answer lay in the physical properties and associated mathematics of such naval encounters. He reasoned that such battles created an unstable dynamic of accelerating effects that aided the side with the stronger forces and that progressively magnified its advantages. At the start of the battle, he observed, the force balance might be 10 *Dreadnoughts* for side A versus 8 *Dreadnoughts* for side B, a force ratio of 1.25:1 favoring side A. But the process of mutual firing and destruction would soon change this force ratio increasingly in favor of the side with the stronger forces. Because of the disparity in size and firepower, the first encounter might result in side A losing one ship and side B losing two ships. This uneven exchange ratio (2:1 in side A's favor) would, in turn, give rise to a new balance of nine ships for side A and six ships for side B, or a revised ratio of 1.50:1 in favor of side A, a greater margin of superiority than before.[7]

Owing to this enhanced superiority, the second stage of battle might result in an even more unbalanced exchange than the first stage. Side A might again lose one ship, but side B might lose three ships, because all of its ships were subjected to a greater volume of fires than during the first stage. The outcome of this 3:1 exchange might well be a new force balance of eight surviving *Dreadnoughts* for side A and only three *Dreadnoughts* for side B, or a 2.67:1 ratio in side A's favor. The third stage of the battle would therefore result in side A again losing one ship and side B losing all three of its remaining ships. As a result of this cascading dynamic in which force ratios and exchange ratios played upon each other in favor of the side with strongest forces, side A would emerge with 7 of its 10 ships intact and victorious over a side B that had been annihilated.

Table 21–1. **A *Dreadnought* Battle: How the Strongest Side Wins**

1st *Stage Force Ratio:* 10 ships for Side A vs. 8 for Side B, a ratio of 1.25:1.0.

1st Stage Exchange Ratio: Side A loses 1 & Side B loses 2 = 2:1 favors Side A

2d *Stage Force Ratio:* 9 for Side A vs. 6 for Side B = 1.5: 1.0 favors Side A

2d Stage Exchange Ratio: Side A loses 1 & Side B loses 3 = 3:1 favors Side A

3d *Stage Force Ratio:* 8 for Side A vs. 3 for Side B = 2.67: 1.0 favors Side A

3d Stage Exchange Ratio: Side A loses 1 & Side B loses remaining 2.67

Final Battle Results: 7 Side A survive, 0 Side B survive

	Stage 1	Stage 2	Stage 3	Final Result
Force Ratio	1.25:1	1.50:1	2.67:1	Infinity
Exchange Ratio	2:1	3:1	2.67: 1	n.a.

In order to encapsulate this startling dynamic in mathematical terms, Lanchester put forth two simple equations, called the Lanchester square equation and the Lanchester linear equation. They postulate that the force exchange process between two opponents is driven by the manner in which one side's mass (size) and lethality (capacity to generate firepower, and related characteristics) stack up against the mass and lethality of the other side. In essence, Lanchester's equations multiply lethality by mass to generate a quantitative measure of combat power. Lanchester square squares the value of mass on each side, while Lanchester linear does not do so. Each reflects the dynamics of different types of battles: Lanchester square portrays battles by direct fires, while Lanchester linear portrays battles by area fires. By adding the dimension of time, both equations treat mass as a variable, not a constant. As a result, the equations can show how mass on each side changes as casualties are absorbed during battle. From these two algebraic equations, differential equations can be generated in order to show the rate of change as a function of force interactions over a period of time.[8]

Lanchester Square Equation: $LD(MD_{t0}^2 - MD_{tn}^2) = LA(MA_{t0}^2 - MA_{tn}^2)$

Lanchester Linear Equation: $LD(MD_{t0} - MD_{tn}) = LA(MA_{t0} - MA_{tn})$

Where L is lethality, MD is mass of defender, MA is mass of attacker, $t0$ is the start of a battle, and tn is the end of the battle.

Of the two equations, Lanchester square is the most provocative. It confirms Lanchester's image of *Dreadnought* battles: if one side possesses an advantage in mass, it will win a decisive victory even if the two sides' ships have equal lethality. Likewise, it confirms that if the two sides have equal numbers, one side can win a decisive victory if it has an advantage in lethality. The core reason for decisive victory in both cases is the explosive interaction between force ratios and exchange ratios, which creates a spiraling dynamic that favors the stronger force more and more as the battle unfolds. The message for the British Navy was simple: when it fights sea battles, it should always strive to possess superior overall strength based on greater numbers, greater lethality, or both.

Although Lanchester square was originally developed to analyze naval warfare, it also can be applied to air battles and land battles. When applied to land warfare, an insightful feature of Lanchester square is its portrayal of war as a nonlinear process that affects the dynamics of offense and defense. By showing the big advantage for an attacking side that possesses larger forces, it illuminates how an outnumbered defender can encounter serious trouble even trying to survive on the battlefield, much less win. It shows that in situations of equal lethality, an attacker with a numerical advantage of 1.5:1 or 2:1 in force ratio will initially increase its advantage in steady ways through an exchange ratio process that also favors it in proportional terms. But once the force ratio rises to 2:1 or 3:1 or more, an explosive dynamic takes place because the exchange ratio soars upward in the attacker's favor. The reason is that the attacker is able to concentrate multiple weapons on each defender's weapon, and the defender possesses too few weapons to fire effectively at the attacker. As a result, the force ratio quickly grows to 5:1, then to 10:1 or more, ultimately resulting in the defender's annihilation.

Does Lanchester square reflect reality? Debates have raged on this question for years and the subject is clouded with competing arguments. What can be said is that Lanchester square seems logical if its key assumption—that tactical engagements reflect the overall force ratio—holds true. Indeed, similar results can be obtained by using a simple back-of-the-envelope model that employs kill probabilities as a function of fires to gauge reciprocal attrition. Table 21–2 uses an SSPK of 0.10 for force units on both sides; similar results hold true for other SSPKs. As the table shows, the exchange ratio favoring the attacker rises as the force ratio rises, producing an accelerating victory for the attacker even though the initial force disparity is only 2:1. This is because the initial exchange ratio is 1.9:1 against the defender, which produces a heightened force ratio disadvantage of 2.3:1. Events slide downhill for the weaker side as the battle unfolds. As the exchange ratio rises in favor of the attacker, the defender's disadvantage in force ratio grows to 2.8:1

and then to 4.8:1, which produces an elevated exchange ratio to the disadvantage of the defender of 3.9:1. From there, a highly unstable dynamic unfolds, resulting in the defender being annihilated and the defender emerging with nearly 80 percent of its force intact.

Table 21–2. **Interaction of Force Ratio and Exchange Ratio:**
Simple Model of Kill Probabilities

Stages of Battle	Initial Force Ratio: Advantage for Offense	*Resulting Exchange Ratio: Disadvantage for Defense
1	2.0:1	1.9:1
2	2.3:1	2.2:1
3	2.8:1	2.6:1
4	4.8:1	3.9:1
5	7.7:1	5.7:1
6	16.7:1	7.8:1

Surviving forces at end of battle: Offense: 79 percent; Defense: 1 percent
*SSPK of .10 is assumed.

A rejoinder to such arguments is that in order to win through this explosive attrition process, the attacker must fight as efficiently as the defender. In particular, the attacker must ensure that in each small-unit engagement, its local superiority matches the theater-wide superiority of 2:1. If the attacker fails to do so, its ability to dominate the attrition dynamic lessens. Even in the case where local force ratios are 1:1, however, the attacker's overall 2:1 edge in forces enables it to win the battle eventually. The main difference is that victory would take two or three times longer to achieve, and the attacker would emerge with perhaps only 50 percent of its forces intact, not 80 percent. Such mathematics, of course, do not guarantee an attacker victory. There are ample historical cases in which a military outnumbered by 2:1 or more has fought and emerged the winner.[9] But these are cases in which an outnumbered military enjoyed a big edge in quality, while the defender fought poorly or suffered from very bad luck. The key point about such mathematics is that they show that, all things being equal, the deck is stacked in favor of the side with the bigger and stronger forces.

To the extent that Lanchester square or some version of it reflects reality, a main effect is to throw cold water on the idea that an outnumbered defender can readily use favorable exchange ratios to wear down the offense. Before Lanchester equations were applied to analysis of Cold War ground confrontations, a classical theory held that a defender who faced a 2:1 disadvantage in mass could compensate by achieving favorable exchange ratios of 2:1, thereby creating a stalemate battle of parallel attrition rates in which both sides reach exhaustion at the same time. Lanchester square does not rule out this theory of fighting outnumbered if the defender has a big edge in lethality, but it shows that this can be very difficult to apply in practice. Indeed, it shows that the natural tendency is for the bigger attacker to increase its numerical advantage during the course of battle, and for the outnumbered defender to reach exhaustion long before the attacker absorbs so many losses that it cannot keep fighting.

A disadvantage of Lanchester square is that, when applied to land battle, it addresses only relative attrition and says nothing about the capacity of either side to seize and hold terrain, an important feature of many wars. When Lanchester square was applied to land warfare during the Cold War, analysts addressed this problem by positing a mathematical relationship between attrition dynamics and the speed at which a front line would move. They created a variable called "forward edge of the battle area (FEBA) movement rate" or "front line of troops (FLOT) movement rate," where FEBA and FLOT refer to the front line separating two warring armies. These analysts then adopted simple rules of thumb saying that movement rate would likely be slow in an attrition battle of stalemate and reciprocal losses, perhaps 2 to 5 kilometers per day, but it would pick up speed in a contest pitting a strong attacker against a weaker defender, perhaps 5 to 10 kilometers per day. Moreover, these rules of thumb, which reflected common sense and historical experience, suggested that the movement rate is nonlinear: an overpowered defender would find itself not only losing the attrition battle at an accelerating pace, but also losing ground at an accelerating pace, a double-whammy of defeat.[10]

When Lanchester square and its offshoots were incorporated into NATO computer models, they produced a frightening message. At the time—the early to middle 1970s—the Warsaw Pact enjoyed an edge over NATO in numbers of combat divisions and associated weapons of about 2:1 (90 Pact divisions to NATO's 45). If the two sides possessed equal lethality, the implication was that the Warsaw Pact could employ its superior numbers to grind NATO down and eventually annihilate it, while emerging with its forces significantly intact to occupy a conquered Western Europe afterward. Indeed, the Warsaw Pact seemed likely to conquer large amounts of territory during the war itself because, as its forces advanced, NATO's forces would be compelled to yield ground in order to protect themselves, trading space for time. Much uncertainty existed about the extent to which such depressing mathematics of attrition and movement would actually apply on the battlefield. But when computer models were equipped with prudent assumptions about how far and how fast NATO forces would be compelled to retreat, they typically showed Warsaw Pact forces advancing to the Rhine River and beyond.

If NATO could not hope to match the Warsaw Pact in numbers of ground forces, the question was how much of a lethality advantage was required to offset the opponent's numerical superiority. Specifically, what lethality advantage was needed to contain the attack in the forward areas while fighting a stalemate battle in which both sides lost forces by the same proportion? The answer put forth by Lanchester square was that NATO's lethality advantage would need to be fully the square of its disadvantage in force ratio. That is, if NATO trailed in mass by a ratio of 2:1, it must possess a lethality advantage of 4:1. Lanchester linear put forth a less demanding standard; it postulated that the lethality advantage must merely match the force ratio disadvantage. That is, NATO would need a 2:1 edge in lethality to offset a 2:1 disparity in force ratio. Careful analysis of ground combat showed that some battlefield operations such as tank duels conformed more neatly to Lanchester square, while other operations such as artillery fires conformed more to Lanchester linear.

NATO theater-level models were therefore typically equipped with a balanced combination of both equations. These models concluded that NATO would need a lethality advantage between 2:1 and 4:1, perhaps 3:1 or so, if it hoped to defend Central Europe.

The Warsaw Pact was then rapidly acquiring the modern weapons needed to wage a decisive linear attack. Sensing great danger, NATO responded by seeking to upgrade its own combat power in order to wage a forward defense that would be effective, at least in the initial stages. As outlined in chapters 11 and 12, NATO tried to increase its force size by fielding more European units and by accelerating U.S. reinforcement rates. Some progress was made, but not enough for NATO to be confident of its defense posture. Because the Warsaw Pact was enlarging its own weapons inventory, the numerical force balance would remain uncomfortably high. Accordingly, NATO turned to the task of improving its existing forces in qualitative terms in order to achieve a lethality advantage of 3:1 or better.

At first glance, the goal of achieving such a lethality advantage seemed daunting. Closer inspection, however, showed that because NATO would be fighting on the defense, it had some natural advantages. A defender could take advantage of prepared positions and preselected terrain, whereas an attacker would be advancing in the open and less able to coordinate its combined arms fires. This would enhance NATO's lethality and diminish the Warsaw Pact's lethality. NATO also possessed options for upgrading the firepower and survivability of its forces. It pursued them, for example, by configuring its air forces to aid ground forces, increasing its artillery fires and ammunition stocks, deploying large numbers of antitank guided missiles, and buying modern tanks and infantry fighting vehicles. NATO also strengthened the capacity of its air forces to contribute to the ground battle. The effect of these improvements was profound: by the early 1980s, theater modeling showed that NATO was steadily acquiring the capacity to contain an attack in the forward areas. In essence, it was using Lanchester equations to help determine how high lethality could compensate for low numbers.[11]

NATO's growing capacity to wage linear attrition war soon touched off a new stage in the contest for military supremacy in Central Europe. Sensing that a linear attack could be stalemated, the Warsaw Pact switched its offensive strategy. It adopted a new strategy

Figure 21–2. **Impact of NATO Force Improvements**
(Illustrative Results of Computer Simulations)

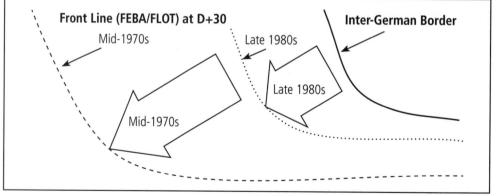

of concentrating its forces: it would aim to break through NATO's forward defenses at selected points, advance rapidly into the rear areas, and use fast maneuvers to defeat NATO's forces in detail. Because NATO was vulnerable to such a strategy of breakthrough and maneuver, it soon switched its own strategy away from linear defense toward nonlinear defense. Accompanying this switch in operational strategy were further improvements in force structures and weapons.

New theater models were created to help guide this transition. The technical features of the models were improved in several areas. For example, new models acquired a better capacity to model concentration and counter-concentration in battles at the operational and tactical levels. The effect was to portray theater-wide warfare as a collection of local battles in which local engaged force ratios might be different from the theater ratio. Similarly, progress was made in modeling such phenomena as battlefield force velocity, target acquisition and fire rates, prepared barriers, force density, terrain coverage, and flanking attacks.

Whereas old models had focused on theater defense in the aggregate, new models focused on the fighting qualities of each of NATO's nine forward corps. These models were still attrition-based and piston-driven, but they facilitated a focus on the details of how to strengthen each corps in ways uniquely tailored to the demands that would be made on it. Models that did a better job of analyzing maneuver in the forward corps battles were soon developed. One example was the FEBA expansion model, which assessed how NATO's front line would enlarge as advancing Warsaw Pact forces created bulges in it. Incorporating patterns characteristic of the 1944 Battle of the Bulge, this model sought to defend by positioning NATO ground forces on the shoulders of deepening enemy penetrations. It helped provide a time-phased theory of how NATO could employ force operations in order to prevent penetrations from becoming uncontrollable breakthroughs.[12]

Another example was the IDAHEX model, which was built to examine fluid maneuver battles in the rear areas. By placing hexes on a map rather than squares, it provided an analytic foundation for computer software that could maneuver ground forces in all directions on the battlefield. IDAHEX required that humans make decisions during each stage of combat about how to maneuver. While this feature lessened the capacity of the model to impose strict controls and verify procedures, it lent some operational reality to how war was portrayed. For example, it allowed for use of flanking attacks and envelopments, rather than modeling combat solely as a frontal encounter of "pistons." Its main contribution was to shed light on how maneuver could be used to gain positional advantage by fostering locally superior force ratios, and on how the dynamics of concentration and counter-concentration could shape big battles in the rear areas. In essence, it helped NATO see land warfare in the maneuver-oriented manner of Rommel and Patton.

These and other models by no means were solely responsible for NATO's shift to nonlinear defense, but they shed light on NATO's situation and priorities. Their analyses, professional military judgment, a new doctrine of operational art, and modern weapons together helped NATO craft programmatic responses that made intelligent use of the funds available. Figure 21–3 shows an example of how a maneuver-oriented defense, using blocking actions and flanking attacks, differs from a linear defense. The strategic result was NATO's growing confidence in its conventional defenses and the Warsaw Pact's declining confidence in its ability to carry out aggression. This successful outcome was a product of a strong NATO political and military response, but that response owed something to theater models that took Lanchester equations as their starting point.

Figure 21–3. **Non-Linear Options for Defeating Breakthrough Attacks**

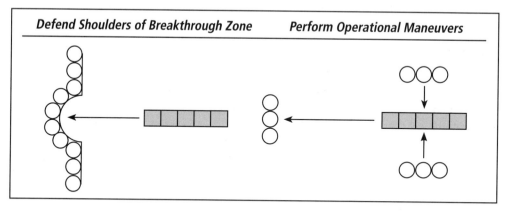

Theater-level models were not the only land warfare models employed during this period. A nested hierarchy of models was created that tied together force operations at multiple levels from top to bottom. The Army, for example, used a theater attrition model to gauge prospects for forward defense, another aggregate model to determine how to allocate manpower and supplies among its three corps in Central Europe, and a fine-grained model of tactical battles to determine how to equip its brigades and battalions with the appropriate mix of new weapons. An effect of such modeling was to make the debate over force requirements and resource allocation much more quantitative.

Historians will need to judge whether the decisions that emerged were well thought out, but the debate over them was animated by lots of numbers. A fair evaluation is that the defense community was enlightened by the enterprise. In retrospect, however, it can be said that the development of maneuver-oriented theater models was not carried far enough. While these models got the job done for NATO in Central Europe, they could also have been expanded to deal with nonlinear doctrines for waging war in other regions, such as the Middle East. There, old-style attrition models continued to hold sway and were hard-pressed to keep pace with new trends when focus later shifted from Central Europe to the Persian Gulf.

Theater-level models of land warfare will have a future if they show continuing progress in handling maneuver and other new-era military dynamics. Critics voice doubts about their suitability, but such models will be needed, because theater wars have not become extinct: the Iraq war of 2003 and the continuing standoff in Korea show this to be the case. Nor can attrition be neglected: it remains an ultimate determinant of the outcome of war. Because the Persian Gulf War of 1991 and Operation *Iraqi Freedom* of 2003 embodied offensive operations with fast maneuvers, they are sometimes cited as the death knell for theater modeling from the old school.[13] But while they mean that crude piston models portraying only frontal battles and face-to-face attrition are obsolete, they do not mean the end of theater models. Indeed, they suggest a strong role for models that can portray modern maneuver and related operations along with traditional attrition. The reason is that maneuver war is too complicated to be grasped by the human mind unaided. However, new-era theater models must be configured to handle the dynamics of information age warfare. For these models, a future of innovation is necessary.

Air and Naval Models in the Cold War: Analyzing Theater Campaigns

While land combat models played a big role in the Cold War, major progress was also made in building and using theater-wide models of air and naval warfare. Anchored in mathematical equations and data of their own, air models focused on the operational dynamics of a NATO-Warsaw Pact battle in the skies over Central Europe. Air forces were important to NATO alliance defense strategy because they were assigned the twin missions of defending alliance airspace and attacking Warsaw Pact ground forces as they advanced into Western Europe. Performing these missions would be a daunting task because the Warsaw Pact air threat was large, modern, and capable. The result was an intense modeling effort aimed at determining how best to employ NATO air forces and prepare them for future combat.

As figure 21–4 illustrates, theater models portrayed the air campaign as unfolding in three overlapping phases: first, rebuffing a big enemy air attack against NATO airbases, ground forces, and logistic infrastructure; second, seizing control over the battlefield and enemy airspace by shooting down enemy interceptors and suppressing other air defenses; and third, conducting strike attacks aimed at destroying enemy supplies, infrastructure, command systems, and ground forces. The models helped develop the theory that mastering these three phases was key to winning a war in Central Europe. In particular, the theory fostered recognition that the third phase of NATO's air campaign could not be performed successfully until the first two phases were carried out. To senior U.S. military commanders, this message was nothing new, but air models provided a quantitative

Figure 21–4. **Phases of NATO's Air Campaign**

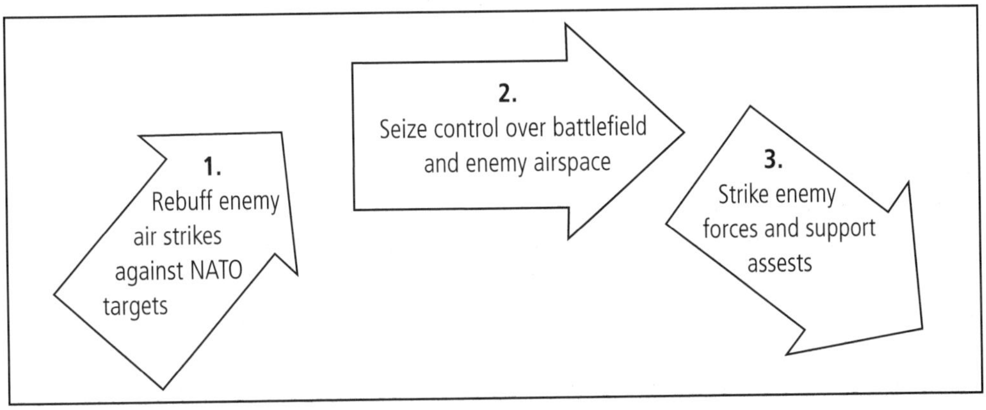

1.
Rebuff enemy air strikes against NATO targets

2.
Seize control over battlefield and enemy airspace

3.
Strike enemy forces and support assests

sense of how to evaluate this complex air campaign with aircraft and other assets that had to be shifted back and forth among three phases.

Theater air models employed a set of mathematical equations, along with associated algorithms and data, for each of the three phases. They had to portray a complex, constantly shifting air war of several thousand moving parts, but their subject was less difficult to handle than the huge accompanying ground war, which involved fully 200,000 weapons or more. Air warfare, moreover, was simpler to model because it was mainly an exercise in destroying selected targets rather than both inflicting massive attrition and occupying large amounts of ground. Air modeling, in addition, benefited from its ability to focus on a few key measures of effectiveness, including numbers of enemy aircraft and ground targets destroyed, and numbers of NATO aircraft surviving the encounter. This permitted allocation of NATO sorties among competing missions on the basis of measurable outputs. The result was a stream of studies that evaluated air strategies and targeting schemes in terms of quantitative results, a hallmark of good performance modeling.[14]

This modeling called attention to key priorities. One priority was to harden NATO airbases to reduce their vulnerability, and to equip them with sufficient stocks to generate high sortie surge rates. Another priority was to combine modern interceptors with Patriot surface-to-air missiles into an integrated air defense system. A third priority was to employ highly capable F–15 fighters to extract favorable exchange ratios in air-to-air duels, while using less sophisticated F–16s to bomb enemy airbases and SAM sites. Additional priorities were to buy large numbers of cruise missiles and other smart munitions to maximize destruction of enemy rear-area targets; acquire the C⁴ISR assets, avionics, and smart munitions needed to destroy enemy ground combat forces participating in the land battle; and develop a flexible air posture that could shift aircraft allocation strategies as the campaign unfolded, so that when one stage of the air campaign was successfully completed, aircraft could be concentrated to focus on the next stage. As a result of modeling, resources were channeled into programs for these priorities. Overall, therefore, air modeling had a positive impact and facilitated vigorous modernization; moreover, there was less contention over its accuracy and applicability than there was over ground modeling.

Naval modeling reflected a similar operational agenda and had a similar positive impact. As figure 21–5 illustrates, the U.S. and NATO naval campaign for a European war had three main components: first, seizing control of the North Atlantic sea lanes by suppressing Soviet submarine and air forces so that U.S. reinforcements could be sent to Central Europe; second, helping provide for the defense of Norway and southern region countries, including Turkey, and the Mediterranean Sea; and third, performing carrier power projection into the northern waters to destroy the Soviet Navy and apply pressure against the Soviet homeland. This three-pronged campaign required a mixture of simultaneous and sequential missions that could be carried out by multilateral operations led by the U.S. Navy.

Mathematical models were created to help address all three components and to develop approaches for building improved naval forces to carry them out. While the first two components were traditional NATO missions dating back years, the third component— carrier power projection— was new in the 1980s. During this decade, interest grew in a

Figure 21–5. **Components of NATO's Maritime Strategy**

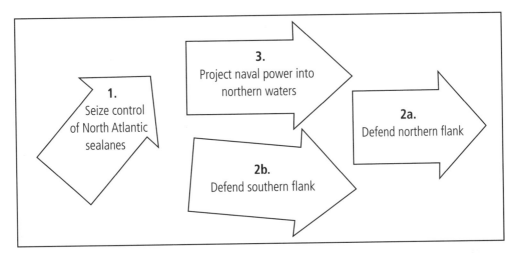

carrier power-projection campaign into northern waters, and controversy erupted over whether and how such a campaign could be successfully carried out. The survivability of U.S. CVBGs against enemy air, missile, and submarine attacks was an especially controversial issue. Accordingly, mathematical models were created in order to study this operation. As figure 21–6 illustrates, these models examined how layered U.S. Navy defenses could blunt the opponent's bomber and submarine attacks to make U.S. carriers less vulnerable.[15]

The air defense against Soviet/Warsaw Pact Backfire bombers and associated missiles was conducted by a combination of long-range F–14 fighters, medium-range Aegis missiles, short-range air defense missiles, local flares and decoys, and well-built carriers that could not be sunk by just a single hit. The antisubmarine defense was conducted by P–3 aircraft, attack submarines, destroyers and frigates armed with antisubmarine warfare weapons,

Figure 21–6. **Components of CVBG Defense**

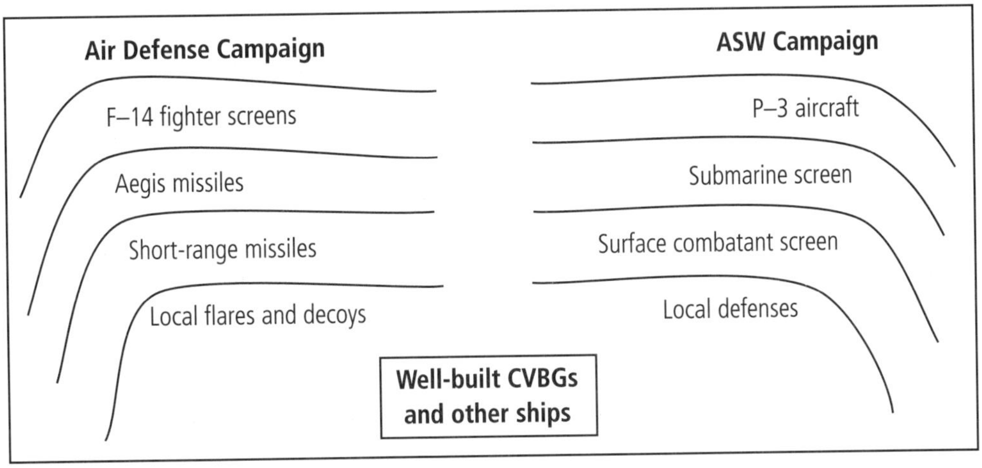

Air Defense Campaign	ASW Campaign
F–14 fighter screens	P–3 aircraft
Aegis missiles	Submarine screen
Short-range missiles	Surface combatant screen
Local flares and decoys	Local defenses

Well-built CVBGs and other ships

local defenses, and carriers designed to contain damage caused by torpedo hits. Mathematical models were created to assess all aspects of these two complex campaigns, and to determine how U.S. Navy defenses could be improved. Essentially, these models employed equations anchored in statistical probabilities that together would have a large cumulative effect. Illustratively, for example, F–14 interceptors might be able to shoot down only 30 percent of the bombers in a massed air attack. But Aegis missiles might be able to shoot down enough of the air-to-surface missiles launched by the surviving bombers to account for an additional 30 percent of the opponent's total bomber payload, while short-range defense missiles might be able to shoot down another 30 percent. Of the remaining 10 percent of the total bomber payload, many would be diverted by flares and decoys. As a result, only a few missiles would find their targets; however, nothing less than multiple hits could disable a carrier. The same logic of layered screens and cumulative probabilities applied to antisubmarine warfare. Mathematical models of these defensive screens provided assessments of how existing U.S. forces would perform and how they could be made better through a series of coordinated improvement measures in all layers. Once again, quantitative measures of outputs aided the process of debating and deciding about the alternatives.

These models helped lead to the conclusion that while the enemy could launch concerted attacks, Navy CVBGs could survive them with acceptable losses and then mount subsequent offensive attacks against critical maritime and land targets. They also helped show how the Atlantic sealanes and NATO's flanks could be guarded by naval forces working in concert with air and ground forces. The overall effect was to underscore the importance of NATO's naval forces in alliance defense strategy, to demonstrate the feasibility of new missions, and to support calls for a major modernization of U.S. naval forces. Like the air models, these naval models generally avoided the controversy that often surrounded models of land warfare. A reason for this acceptance was that compared to modeling of complex land dynamics, modeling of air and naval battles was easier to carry out: the forces and battles were smaller in size and simpler in scope.

Modeling Standoff Air Strikes in the 1990s

The collapse of the Soviet Union that ended the Cold War brought a huge upheaval to U.S. air and naval force operations. In essence, it meant that these operations would no longer be required to overpower major enemy threats in their domains before performing other missions. During the Cold War, the U.S. Air Force had faced the prospect of fighting a major air battle with the Soviet air force before devoting large numbers of its aircraft to attacking ground targets. Similarly, the Navy had faced a big sea battle with the Soviet navy before projecting its power ashore. After the Cold War, the new threats came from such hostile regional powers as Iraq and North Korea; while both countries had large ground forces, neither fielded significant air and naval forces. When the Persian Gulf War erupted in 1991, the Iraqi air force played no meaningful role in impeding U.S. force operations: most of its aircraft either stayed on the ground or fled to Iran. Those that entered air combat were quickly shot down. This war confirmed that weak air and naval threats would be a feature of the new strategic terrain.

The effect was to allow the Air Force and the Navy to reorient many of their forces to make major contributions to land warfare far sooner in a war. This change, in turn, opened the door to much more extensive joint force operations. The new questions were how the Air Force and Navy could best take advantage of the new situation by altering their forces, programs, and doctrines, and what the implications were for the standard practice of swiftly deploying large ground forces along with air and naval forces to wage major theater wars (MTWs).

During the 1990s, a main conceptual tool for answering these questions was analysis of the halt phase during an MTW in the Persian Gulf. The halt phase was a key part of a postulated scenario involving a new Iraqi invasion of Kuwait and Saudi Arabia. A U.S. fear was that in 1990 the Iraqis had learned a harsh lesson from stopping their advance at the Saudi border after conquering Kuwait. The halt had given the U.S. military 6 months to deploy a huge coalition force that then crushed the Iraqi force. In this new scenario, a rebuilt Iraqi army backed by modernized air defenses would not make the same mistake twice: this time, it might launch a surprise attack, rush through Kuwait, and pour deep into Saudi Arabia, striving to win the war rapidly in 2 to 3 weeks before sizable U.S. forces could arrive on the scene. In order to counter this hypothetical threat, DOD contemplated a three-phased campaign: first, an initial halt phase conducted by promptly available forces that aimed at stopping the Iraqi attack before Saudi Arabia had been conquered; then, a buildup phase in which large U.S. forces would converge on the scene; and finally, a counterattack phase in which these forces would destroy the Iraqi army, re-liberate Kuwait, and march on Baghdad.

Theater-level modeling of U.S. air and naval operations focused on how to use standoff strike assets in the initial halt phase. The need was obvious: in a fast-moving Iraqi surprise attack, only air and naval forces could deploy to the Persian Gulf in the few days that would be available. Ground forces could employ the two brigades of pre-positioned equipment sets deployed there, and some light infantry units could arrive by airlift, but sealift could not possibly deploy any additional heavy brigades in less than about 4 to 6 weeks. Air and naval forces must carry the load initially. At issue was whether they could do so successfully; large numbers of studies were conducted on this complex issue. A good example was a 1998 RAND study, which illuminated the new trends in theater modeling during the years before another war with Iraq erupted in 2003.[16]

The RAND study was a landmark in its attention to military details, its portrayal of new U.S. operations employing standoff airstrikes and information networks, and its use of simple mathematical equations with rich quantitative data. Its clarity made its audit trail of assumptions and calculations open to scrutiny, an admirable feature lacking in many studies. In some quarters, the study was controversial because it was thought to exaggerate the performance of airstrikes and underestimate the need for large ground forces. Events since then reveal that it did study a war that never occurred, rather than the war that actually was fought; instead of Iraq invading Kuwait, the United States invaded Iraq. But such criticisms aside, the study remains valuable because of its use of new-era theater war modeling as a methodology for force assessment and resource allocation in the information age.

Rather than rely upon old-style computer models that bury standoff airstrikes in a host of indecipherable equations and questionable assumptions about force operations, the RAND study applied a new methodology and procedure in sequential analytical stages. First, it identified the enemy threat in size and advance rates, and postulated a level of destruction to it, anchored in quantitative measures, that would compel its attack to stop. Next, it determined the U.S. military posture that would be available on D-day and shortly thereafter to contest the enemy attack. Rather than presuming that this U.S. defense would fail simply because large ground forces would be unavailable in traditional strength, it analyzed whether the task could be accomplished by sizable standoff airstrikes accompanied by a light screen of ground forces. Next, it calculated the number of standoff air sorties against enemy armored columns that would be available, taking into account the simultaneous need to perform other air missions. Then, it determined the number of enemy armored vehicles that could be destroyed if these sorties used smart munitions and modern information networks to locate and attack moving targets in near-real-time, accounting for how such smart munitions and networks could enhance performance compared to air operations without these capabilities. Next, it matched this estimated level of destruction with the performance standards needed to blunt the attack. Then, it subjected this baseline of best estimates to sensitivity analysis to determine whether its main conclusions were robust. Finally, it offered judgments and recommendations for U.S. defense strategy and force improvement priorities that reflected this quantitative appraisal.

The RAND study set the stage by carefully defining the military threat faced in this scenario. It postulated a rebuilt Iraqi army composed of 25 divisions, 12 of them heavy divisions equipped with a total of 9,600 armored vehicles (tanks, infantry fighting vehicles, and artillery). It further postulated that this invading force could advance in 2 columns, with vehicles spaced 50 meters apart, at a rate of 70 kilometers per day, and that its goal would be to advance 350 kilometers or more in 7 days, far enough to seize many Saudi oilfields north of Bahrain. The RAND study then surveyed the U.S. force that realistically would be available to contest this invasion. It identified an already-deployed force of 5 Air Force fighter squadrons, 1 Navy CVBG, and 2 prepositioned Army brigades with 24 attack helicopters and 250 Army Tactical Missile System (ATACM) missiles. Next, it added the U.S. reinforcements that could deploy within 12 days: 18 Air Force fighter squadrons and 50 B–1 bombers, 1 CVBG, 2 Marine air squadrons, and various support aircraft. The result was a summary portrayal of the force balance for this scenario: a large, fast-moving enemy ground force of 25 divisions would be opposed by a U.S. Air Force of about 10 fighter-wing-equivalents and other assets, and less than 1 division of ground troops.

The RAND study asked, simply, whether this joint air force could halt the Iraqi advance short of its goals and destroy many Iraqi ground forces. The study initiated its modeling by portraying a U.S. air strategy of multiple missions aimed at suppressing Iraqi air defenses, missile threats, and C⁴ISR assets before concentrating strikes against enemy armored columns. Its dynamic portrayal of this air strategy showed that about 350 sorties per day could be allocated to these missions. An average of about 175 sorties would be available per day for counter-armor strikes during the first 7 days; after that, the number would rise to 350 sorties per day as reinforcements arrived and aircraft were shifted to strikes against armored columns. At the peak of U.S. force buildup, sortie rates for strikes rose to 650 per day. Thus, after 2 weeks, ample sorties would be available for counter-armor missions, but during the critical first 7 days, only about 1,225 sorties could be flown. At first glance, this limited number seemed too small to halt the advance of an enemy armor force composed of 9,600 armored vehicles. But by closer inspection of the details, the RAND study shed a different light on the potential effectiveness of this air campaign.

If these air sorties carried old-style weapons and were not empowered by modern information networks, they might destroy only about 0.30–0.50 enemy armored vehicles per sortie. This weak performance would result in destruction of about 400–600 targets during the first week, or only 4–6 percent of the total enemy armored force: not nearly enough to slow its advance, much less seriously degrade its combat power. The RAND study argued, however, that this performance could be greatly enhanced if U.S. forces were equipped with smart munitions such as sensor-fused weapons, the sophisticated JSTARS command and control aircraft, and potent sensors and information networks. Such improvements would make U.S. air forces much better able to locate enemy targets from the air and destroy them in large batches.

The RAND study forecast a huge leap upward in the lethality of U.S. air sorties with these enablers. Based on results of weapons effects tests in the United States, it judged that B–1 bombers, with their large munitions loads, could destroy fully 12 armored vehicles per sortie. The study forecast lethality rates of 1.1–3.6 enemy vehicles per sortie for fighters, attack helicopters, and ATACMs. It acknowledged that such factors as increased vehicle spacing, delivery errors, inefficient fires, and operational degradation could diminish these results, but even so, it estimated that after 7 days, 3,000 enemy vehicles could be destroyed and that, after 12 days, the total could rise to 7,000, or nearly 75 percent of the enemy force. Moreover, the RAND study judged that the damage inflicted by this lethal air campaign would compel the enemy to halt its advance by Day 6 or 7, with Iraqi forces having advanced only 250 kilometers, or well short of their goal of 350 kilometers.

This RAND study was illuminating in more ways than one. It helped call attention to the risk of enemy surprise attacks and other asymmetric strategies. It cast a spotlight on the potential for growing contributions by air forces and standoff strikes in expeditionary warfare. It called for rapid air reinforcement plans as a foundation of halt-phase campaigns against access-denial threats. It called for modern air campaigns to be planned with attention to systems that included not only combat aircraft but also support aircraft, including JSTARS, AWACS, suppression of enemy air defenses aircraft, and other assets. It called for a major increase in procurement of smart munitions, including Skeet (a wide-area, dispensing anti-armor weapon with multiple small bombs) and others that had been in chronically short supply. Finally, it argued that it would take only a few F–22 fighters to sweep the skies clear of enemy aircraft, allowing other fighters to concentrate on ground attack. In all these areas, the RAND study was correct.

A lasting legacy of the RAND study and others like it is that they helped encourage the steady improvements during the 1990s of the capacity of U.S. forces to handle fresh scenarios in the Persian Gulf. In this sense, they passed muster by serving as aids to sound defense programming. Whether they provided a new general theory of warfighting, as some enthusiasts claimed, is another matter. Analyzing standoff strikes as the main response to this particular postulated halt-phase scenario made sense because they offered hope for success and because no other choice was realistically available. But this did not necessarily mean that the idea of using standoff strikes in a battlefield devoid of large ground forces would make sense for all halt phases, much less all phases of all wars in general.

When judged by the demanding standards of a general theory, the RAND study can be criticized for inflating the lethal effects of smart munitions, which were key to its judgment that airstrikes would kill 2 to 3 armored vehicles per sortie during the first week. Although these munitions score well on test ranges, in the real world of operational frictions their actual performance might be less impressive, as shown by historical experience with earlier "wonder-weapons." The RAND study focused on a geographic setting where airstrikes were almost sure to do well, with a bunched-up enemy advancing in a few long columns over straight roads on a flat desert in clear weather. Rugged terrain or bad weather might produce considerably less impressive results, as might dispersed enemy ground forces or effective air defenses. Beyond this, the RAND scenario itself helped stack the deck: it presumed that the Iraqis would have to travel a long distance before achieving their goals, and that U.S. forces could afford to yield 250 kilometers of terrain while bombing from the sky. If the Iraqis had chosen to advance only 100 kilometers by seizing just Kuwait, the need to defend that country would have denied U.S. forces the luxury of trading space for time, and standoff airstrikes would have had less time and opportunity to succeed.

A subsequent RAND study took these criticisms into account. Based upon a fine-grained operational appraisal, it argued that even in the Persian Gulf, a halt phase conducted almost entirely by standoff strikes could fail because of uncertainties about accurate targeting. Accordingly, it called for preparation of a modest but potent ground force of medium-weight mechanized units and light infantry with indirect-fire weapons for anti-armor missions. It proposed seabasing these ground forces so they would be available for rapid deployment within a few days.[17]

In determining the optimal balance of standoff targeting and ground defenses, the strategic environment is critical. While the Persian Gulf is ideal for standoff strikes, Korea presents a geographic and operational setting that is the opposite: with rugged terrain and an enemy poised only 25 kilometers from Seoul, rigid forward defense is essential. In this case, airstrikes would not likely be a cure-all, and large ground forces, perhaps 25 U.S. and ROK divisions or more, would still be needed to carry out the initial stages of a joint campaign. For conflicts that fall midway between these two extremes, a combination of air and ground forces would probably be needed, with the exact mix tailored to the situation.

The initial RAND study was right to identify airstrikes as an asset of growing importance, but the implication that ground forces would no longer be important in many wars was wrong. Operation *Iraqi Freedom* showed this to be the case. Yet the RAND study was unqualifiedly correct in one judgment in particular: it was on the mark when written, and remains so today, in rejecting old-style theater modeling and calling for a new type of modeling that takes into account the technologies and doctrines of the information age.

Future Combat Modeling: Charting Qualitative Improvements

Gauging the future of combat modeling involves assessing trends on both the demand side and the supply side. On the demand side, the need for combat models is likely to grow. The accelerating transformation of U.S. military forces means that a growing number of critical decisions about forces, operations, and programs will have to be made in the coming years. In many cases, alternatives will exist and the choices will not be obvious. These choices will require sophisticated analyses because warfare is becoming more complex, and cannot be seen as an exercise in mechanically applying fixed force packages organized in traditional, immutable ways. Such analyses of new-era warfare and forces will need to come from somewhere. While combat models will not be the only source of analysis, they will be indispensable. There is no substitute for them.

The question mark lies on the supply side: whether future combat models will be up to the task. Critics tend to underestimate their potential. Although changes in forces and warfare are profound, there is no reason why combat models cannot aspire to address them. If elaborate information networks can be created to operate modern forces, then sophisticated combat models can be designed to evaluate modern operations. Whether combat models will respond effectively is uncertain, but the agenda is clear enough. RAND's Joint Integrated Contingency Model is an example of an improved model for analyzing joint warfare, but as a complex model, it is not well attuned to the narrower issues that arise in force operations, such as the effects of standoff fires in bad terrain. Progress will need to be made on models to study these detailed issues that have major consequences for force design and resource allocation.

A main change taking place is that the U.S. military is now being called upon to carry out joint expeditionary wars, which typically are fought without the large, preestablished infrastructures created during the Cold War. Then, U.S. theater strategies were mainly defensive. Today, they are anchored in offensive operations intended to take the fight to the enemy and defeat it quickly and decisively, with few casualties to U.S. forces. The U.S. military is also developing new battlefield doctrines focused on operations that are joint, networked, simultaneous, dispersed, fast-tempo, and highly integrated. These modern doctrines and operations are no longer as platform-centric as before. Information networks and other assets are now emerging as equal partners of platforms. More fundamentally, modern warfare is becoming more knowledge-based: the combat capabilities of forces will be strongly affected by the knowledge that guides them. Future combat models will need to determine how these changes are being manifested and how to model them to provide meaningful analyses of issues and options facing U.S. plans, programs, and budgets.

Key contributors today include C[4]ISR systems, information networks, smart munitions, joint operations, and fluid maneuvers by forces based long distances apart. Future models will therefore need to be more analytically sophisticated than those of the Cold War, when battles were driven largely by highly congested combat forces and their platforms. New combat models will need to be anchored in new-era concepts and configured with new mathematical equations, data, and output metrics. Existing models will need to undergo major facelifts, and entirely new models will have to be created. Some of this innovation already is taking place, but more will be needed.[18]

The future will require both theater models and models capable of handling operations at the tactical level and by individual weapons. A nested hierarchy of such models will be necessary. These models must be able to address the key force assessment and resource-allocation issues at stake today and tomorrow. In particular, they will need to be capable of grappling with transformation priorities. The primary purpose of transformation is to strengthen the combat capabilities of U.S. forces not through quantitative increases, but through qualitative enhancements. Therefore, combat models will need to be skilled at analyzing the best approaches to improving force quality in the multiple different areas likely to be pursued. Among these areas are:

- new weapons and munitions
- support assets
- information networks
- joint operations
- effects-based operations.[19]

Qualitative improvements will be pursued, in part, by buying expensive new weapons systems. Combat models will need to help provide evaluations of their potential contributions to future missions, because promises of high effectiveness will be the main justification for their high costs. A case in point is the F–22 fighter. Its cost will be about double that of the F–15, the aircraft that it is replacing. Some analytical studies say that the F–22 will perform four times better than the F–15 in air-to-air duels, and that it will also perform much better in ground attack missions because of its stealthy characteristics. If so, these impressive performance features could justify its high costs. The same sorts of calculations will be needed for other new fighter aircraft and the bigger surface combatants now being developed by the Navy.

Quantitative estimates of weapon effectiveness come partly from field tests of individual weapons, but the effectiveness of large formations of them can truly be gauged only by examining how they operate in a setting of major combat operations. Short of actually fighting big wars, combat modeling is the only reliable way to generate such data on effectiveness. The challenge resides in configuring combat models to measure the types of effectiveness being sought and provided.

Although new weapons will be a major source of enhanced force quality, modern smart munitions will be an important contributor as well. Today's smart munitions have already greatly strengthened U.S. combat capabilities, and this trend will continue as improved versions of cruise missiles, GPS-guided bombs, multiple-target cluster munitions, and specialized munitions are acquired. A main feature of smart munitions has been their growing accuracy. The mathematical limits of accuracy will soon be reached, but even then, there will be technical opportunities to tailor improved munitions to specific target systems while reducing their secondary damage. Eventually, directed energy systems (such as high-energy lasers, high-powered microwaves, and electromagnetic launch guns) and other exotic technologies will be developed to the point of being procurable. As this transition occurs, combat modeling can help focus attention on the most cost-effective munitions and on making sure that enough of them are bought to meet requirements and avoid shortages.

Nuts-and-bolts contributors such as logistic support and related assets also play an important role. Table 21–3 helps illustrate their potential impact on tactical air operations. It suggests that the performance of a modern fighter wing could be enhanced by strengthening readiness in all of the categories listed because even though the impact of each of these enablers may be modest, together they can have a large cumulative impact. In this illustrative case, strengthening these assets could elevate the fighter wing's combat capability by about 23 percent even though each of the measures individually strengthens capacity by just 3 percent. The key point is that when these multiple effects are created, they have a combined impact. Something similar can apply to ground and naval forces.

Table 21–3. **Illustrative Combat Performance of Fighter Wing (Performance Metrics)**

	Capability of Unimproved Assets	Capability of Improved Assets
Enabling Assets		
1. Survivable airbases	1.0	1.03
2. Sortie rates	1.0	1.03
3. Munitions and fuels	1.0	1.03
4. Maintenance and repair	1.0	1.03
5. C^2, planning	1.0	1.03
6. Refueling aircraft	1.0	1.03
7. SEAD, search and rescue	1.0	1.03
Total Capability*	**1.0**	**1.23**

* Determined by multiplying the scores from each individual enabling asset, of which there are seven. Thus, 1.03 raised to the seventh power is 1.23. Multiplication is appropriate because each improved asset builds upon its predecessor, with accumulating effects.

The attraction of such enablers is that they often can be acquired at low expense, increasing the life-cycle cost of a fighter wing, division, or carrier strike group by perhaps 10 percent or less. Often a smaller force posture that possesses these enablers will perform better than a bigger posture that costs about the same but lacks them. Thus these enablers may often be highly cost-effective; however, they may be neglected when defense planners focuses mainly on high-profile platforms and munitions. Combat models can help call attention to investment opportunities in this arena, but only if they are configured to show how such enablers can contribute to new-era operations. As new theories and practices for these enablers emerge, combat models will need to evolve along with them.

The idea that information networking can improve force capability is simply common sense, and it is a guiding premise of U.S. transformation strategy. But exactly how it can contribute, and to what degree, is unclear. Thus far, studies on networking have been long on promises of enhanced communications and information flows, but short on concrete output metrics. Combat modeling can help provide such metrics by addressing the impact of force networking on how wars are fought. In general, networks can contribute by making force operations both more effective and more efficient. Effectiveness is easily measured by such traditional indicators as numbers of enemy targets destroyed. Information networks help increase effectiveness, for example, by providing data on the exact location of targets, thereby enabling forces to strike them precisely.

The importance of efficient operations, by contrast, is often overlooked, even though it too can be measured. Here, efficiency means the degree to which U.S. military operations focus on high-leverage battlefield missions rather than peripheral concerns. In past wars, a familiar shortcoming of battlefield strategy was the inefficient use of forces—for example, by allocating many airstrikes against low-value targets, or by dispatching ground forces to guard terrain features that are unlikely to be attacked by enemy forces. Wars have usually been won by the side most able to concentrate its forces at critical points, and are often lost by those who leave too many forces standing on the sidelines while the main battles are fought elsewhere. Inefficiency directly damages how military power is manifested on the battlefield. It is caused by lack of knowledge, in the well-known fog of war. A major promise of information networks is that they will provide increased knowledge of the battlefield, reducing waste of scarce military forces.

Similar ideas apply to joint force operations and effects-based operations. Both ideas make sense in conceptual terms and have vocal enthusiasts, yet concrete analyses of battlefield consequences and output metrics have typically been lacking. Joint operations are intended to enable the military services to operate side by side and to exchange assets and activities without degrading performance. But this is only a minimum standard and expectation; joint operations offer in addition the promise of synergy. They should help the services to magnify each other's performance so that the total effect is greater than the sum of its parts: the combat powers of the services are not merely added together, but multiplied by each other. Synergy could take place when, for example, ground forces compel the adversary's ground forces to mass in ways making them more vulnerable to airstrikes, or when airstrikes soften up opposing ground forces so as to make them more vulnerable to attack by U.S. ground forces. This idea makes sense in principle, but what it means in terms of requirements is uncertain. Does it allow for wars to be won with fewer forces? Does pursuing it mandate unique programs that would not otherwise be funded?

These intriguing questions merit answers, and combat models can help, but only if they accurately capture the full dimensions of how joint forces operate together and have impact on the battlefield. Joint operations cannot be modeled simply by adding up the attrition inflicted by each component: ground, air, and naval forces. Combat modeling of them must also examine how they affect maneuver, velocity, and synchronization of forces as well as the disruption inflicted upon enemy forces. Likewise, combat modeling must identify and take stock of the constraints on carrying out joint operations, which are quite demanding and not always exercised flawlessly. Occasions may arise in which ground forces perform better than air forces, or the reverse. Combat modeling will need to take such sensitivities into account.

Effects-based operations, too, is a concept in need of analysis. It implies that U.S. war planners should think in broader terms than merely inflicting attrition on enemy forces, but should in addition seek to apply U.S. forces in ways that fracture the operational cohesion and integrated combat power of the enemy. Maneuver is one means to this end: through the achievement of positional advantages for U.S. forces, it aspires to create favorable local ratios of engaged forces that are significantly greater than the overall theater-wide force ratio. Another aim is to destroy selected parts of the enemy's force structure in hope of causing widespread effects. For example, destruction of command centers and communication nodes could paralyze the enemy's whole posture. Denying the enemy opportunity to maneuver could prevent it from concentrating against U.S. forces and keep it from using its armor, infantry, and artillery in combined operations. Another effects-based operation would aim to cut off the enemy's logistic lifeline, denying its forces ammunition and supplies. Infliction of severe and rapid losses on selected enemy units, so as to damage morale across the entire enemy force, is another example. All of these concepts make sense in theory, but determining how to carry them out in actual combat situations is the job of war plans, while assessing their implications for requirements, programs, and budgets is a job for combat modeling.

A main promise of a transformation focused on these five areas of quality improvements—weapons, support assets, networks, joint doctrines, and effects-based operations—is that they can elevate future U.S. combat capabilities by a considerable amount. Perhaps each of them would have only a marginal impact, but when combined, their impact could be far greater. For example, if each of them were to improve force capability by only 10 to 20 percent, together they might produce a total gain of 50 to 100 percent. Moreover, they can produce this gain at an expense far lower than the cost of simply expanding the size of U.S. forces. Although these concepts are highly attractive in their promise and potential, they will be little more than hollow abstractions unless concrete programs bring them to life.

Identifying such programs and their relative priorities is the job of future combat models. During the Cold War, combat models rose to prominence not because of the whirring computers and the quantitative data that they produced, but because they were able to provide useful analyses for defense planning and programming. The same standard of practicality applies today, but it will be met only if today's combat models embrace change of the same scope and pace that is sweeping over modern military affairs.

In many quarters, skepticism about the future role of combat models stems from the wide differences between attrition models from the Cold War and today's military operations. But this gap already is being narrowed by modeling efforts at DOD, RAND, and other places. It is not as wide as the gap that existed when combat models first appeared in the Cold War. Today's computer technologies are far better and more adaptable. The gap then was mainly closed by innovative conceptual thinking, followed by creation of mathematical models and gathering of data; today's gap can be closed in the same manner. The key is talented analysts with creative minds, a grasp of the future, a nose for details, and an instinct for translating knowledge about new-era battles into useful policy advice for senior officials.

Notes

[1] A good example of a contemporary model is RAND's Joint Integrated Contingency Model, a computerized tool that allows for speedy analysis of multiple variables and parameters. Similar models are used by such organizations as the Office of Secretary of Defense (Program Analysis and Evaluation); the Joint Staff; the military services; and such think-tanks as the Institute for Defense Analyses.

[2] This chapter offers a general overview of the main analytical frameworks and issues governing combat modeling. It does not provide a catalogue of models that currently are being used or have been used in the past. There are too many models to list even the most important versions. Some years ago, for example, a major Pentagon study employed six different computer models to study a single issue; each provided a different angle of vision or coverage of different sub-issues. These models typically are designed to serve special purposes, and there is no single model that can address all issues satisfactorily. Each model should be judged on its role and contributions. When multiple different models are being used, ideally they should use similar concepts, data, and equations. Yet standardization can have the drawback of creating a conceptual straitjacket that induces neglect of important dynamics. The advantage of using models that work differently from each other is that they can sometimes generate new analytical insights that otherwise might go unnoticed.

[3] Spreadsheet models come in various forms, ranging from equations and data written on a few sheets of paper to relatively high-level personal computer models that analysts who are not programmers can use. The choice between spreadsheet models and computer simulations depends upon the level of investigation and detail needed. Computer simulations generally permit a more comprehensive investigation of complex issues, plus speedy examination of variations in multiple input variables. Spreadsheet models are appropriate for simpler issues and when multiple sensitivity analyses are not needed.

[4] Similar examples abound in dynamic modeling. For example, a ground brigade may be assigned a notional top score of 5.0 based on its armament, C^{4}ISR systems, and mobility rates, but this score may apply only to battles that allow it to employ its assets to maximum advantage. In other situations, it may score lower. For example, a brigade designed to perform defensive operations may perform less well in offensive operations, or vice versa. In both static and dynamic modeling, input performance data appropriate to the situation must be selected.

[5] While values that inflate and accelerate performance measures should be viewed with caution, the modern era is witnessing improvements that do, in fact, have inflationary and acceleration effects. Joint integration of air-ground fires, for example, may sometimes have synergistic multiplicative effects, not just linear additive effects. Each case must be judged on its individual merits rather than on the basis of some rigid rule.

[6] As Thomas Kuhn said, paradigm shifts occur in science when an existing theory is no longer adequate to explain key phenomena, and a new theory must be created. Paradigm shifts also occur in theories of warfare in response to new technologies and other changes. When new theories of warfighting emerge, new combat models and other tools are required to analyze them. See Thomas Kuhn, *The Structure of Scientific Revolutions*, 3^d ed. (Chicago: University of Chicago Press, 1996).

[7] In combat modeling, the force ratio is the ratio of forces between the two contestants before a particular stage of fighting begins. The exchange ratio is the ratio of losses to both sides during that stage of fighting. This exchange ratio gives rise to a new force ratio as the next stage of fighting begins. Here, both ratios use a denominator of 1.0 in order to provide a common basis for comparison. For an historical appraisal of World War I naval battles, see Robert K. Massie, *Castles of Steel: Britain, Germany, and the Winning of the Great War at Sea* (New York: Random House, 2003). Massie's study confirms the extent to which both British and German commanders heeded numbers and firepower in assessing the naval balance in the North Sea. The British navy outnumbered the German navy in *Dreadnoughts* and battle cruisers by about 1.6:1, and therefore the Germans tried to avoid a climactic battle pitting the two fleets against each other, as at Jutland in 1916, when the outnumbered German navy broke off contact (after initial success against British cruisers) rather than face the full British navy.

[8] For a technical analysis of Lanchester equations and related attrition modeling issues, see James G. Taylor, *Force-on-Force Attrition Modelling* (Arlington, VA: Military Applications Section, Operations Research Society of America, 1980). For a critique of Lanchester models, see Joshua Epstein, *The Calculus of Conventional War: Dynamic Analysis Without Lanchester Theory* (Washington, DC: Brookings, 1987).

[9] Many of General Lee's battles with the Union Army early in the Civil War—for example, Fredericksburg and Chancellorsville—are classic cases of an outnumbered defender defeating a larger attacker. The tables later turned only when the Union Army, under General Grant, greatly improved its fighting skill. Even then, the Union Army suffered great losses at the Wilderness, Spotsylvania Court House, and Cold Harbor as it drove toward Richmond and eventual victory.

[10] As combat models improved, their mathematics became more sophisticated than earlier versions that had relied on Lanchester equations in simplistic ways. Ultimately some models came to use many differential equations that portrayed different aspects of the combat process. They remained "Lanchesterian" in the sense of focusing on force interactions as a function of size and quality on both sides, but they were not, strictly speaking, Lanchester models. Perhaps "Lanchester Plus" is a good term for describing them.

[11] See Department of Defense, *NATO Center Region Military Balance Study: 1978–1984* (Washington, DC: Department of Defense, declassified 1985).

[12] For more detail, see Richard L. Kugler, *NATO's Future Conventional Defense Strategy in Central Europe: Theater Employment Doctrine for the Post–Cold War Era* (Santa Monica, CA: RAND, 1992).

[13] Some cite the Persian Gulf War of 1991 as showing that Lanchester-based theater models no longer apply, because they supposedly would have indicated that the side with the bigger forces—Iraq—would perform well in the land battle. In fact, the U.S.-led coalition of 17 divisions swept to victory over 40–45 Iraqi divisions in 100 hours. However, a properly configured theater model would have predicted this result. Lanchester models do not dictate that force size rules all battles. They merely say that when big disparities in size exist, qualitative differences must be highly potent to overpower them. This is exactly what happened in *Desert Storm*. This campaign was led by U.S. ground forces that fought far more effectively than did the Iraqi army. Something similar happened in Operation *Iraqi Freedom* of 2003. Once again, a smaller U.S. and British ground force used fast maneuver and support from air forces to shred a larger but static Iraqi defense. The decisive results of both campaigns were neither counterintuitive beyond the capacity of combat models to portray. Indeed, combat models were used to help prepare both campaigns.

[14] For an overview of air modeling in the context of joint operations, see Fred Frostic and Christopher J. Bowie, "Conventional Campaign Analysis of Major Regional Conflicts," in Paul Davis, *New Challenges for Defense Planning: Rethinking How Much Is Enough* (Santa Monica, CA: RAND, 1994). See also Christopher J. Bowie et al., *The New Calculus: Analyzing Airpower's Changing Role in Joint Theater Campaigns* (Santa Monica, CA: RAND, 1993).

[15] Naval modeling is performed, for example, by the Center for Naval Analyses, a Navy-funded think tank similar to RAND. For an appraisal of contemporary naval issues, see Sam J. Tangredi, ed., *Globalization and Maritime Power* (Washington, DC: National Defense University Press, 2002).

[16] David Ochmanek, Glenn Kent, and Ted Harshberger, *To Find and Not To Yield: How Advances in Information and Firepower Can Transform Theater Warfare* (Santa Monica, CA: RAND, 1998).

[17] Eugene Gritton et al., *Ground Forces for a Rapidly Employable Joint Task Force: First-Week Capabilities for Short-Warning Conflicts* (Santa Monica, CA: RAND, 2000).

[18] For an appraisal of exploratory modeling, see Paul Davis, "Exploratory Analysis and Implications for Modeling," in Stuart E. Johnson et al., *New Challenges and New Tools for Defense Decisionmaking* (Santa Monica, CA: RAND, 2003).

[19] *Effects-based operations* is a new-era concept referring to battlefield operations aimed at having a specific set of effects designed to unravel enemy forces, command structures, and warfighting capabilities. This chapter addresses combat modeling of effects-based operations, and chapter 22 examines it in its larger dimensions.

Chapter 22
Carrying Out Expeditionary Wars

U.S. defense strategy now mandates that U.S. military forces must be highly flexible in order to perform a wide spectrum of crisis interventions and expeditionary wars in the future, as outlined in chapter 12. Recent years have seen U.S. forces fight four expeditionary wars in different places and in widely varying circumstances; more of the same may be in the future. Deciding whether and how to intervene in crises and wars is the province of strategic evaluation, the realm of military professionals and their senior civilian leaders. Preparing for these contingencies in advance is where operations research can play a helpful role because of its focus on details and its ability to align means with ends.

No experienced participant would question the proposition that preparing U.S. forces in advance is crucial. Dwight Eisenhower was right when he said, "Plans are nothing, but planning is everything." He was a big proponent of planning during World War II, and the results speak for themselves. Today, crisis interventions and battlefield campaigns should not be mounted on the fly, without thinking about them beforehand or taking steps to be ready, come what may. Each individual contingency must be addressed on its own merits: there is no one-size-fits-all response. As combatant commands know, preparing plans for a demanding contingency is difficult and time-consuming. As they also know, the quality of their planning has a major bearing on whether success will be achieved on the battlefield and afterward. These days, although U.S. forces may be superior to their opponents, they are not so superior that the manner in which they are deployed and employed is inconsequential.

Contributions of Operations Research

The advantages of being well prepared are illustrated by the invasion of Iraq in 2003. Well before the war, U.S. defense officials took care to craft a battle plan and to assemble the joint posture of military forces needed to carry it out. The result was a swift victory with few U.S. and allied casualties. But after the battlefield win, the stabilization and reconstruction stage proved difficult. One reason for the difficulty was that detailed plans for the unexpected missions that arose in this stage had not been written in advance, and the U.S. forces immediately available for the missions were not well prepared for their particular demands.

No plans can fully anticipate what will transpire on the battlefield. In expeditionary war, each contingency is unique, having peculiar features capable of producing dynamics that are hard to foresee. Surprises are inevitable, as are changes in operations. But advance planning can help narrow the range of uncertainty, reduce the likelihood of crippling surprises, and ensure that U.S. military forces are equipped with the basic assets needed to respond effectively to whatever events may unfold. Operations research can help contribute to planning by performing three important functions. It can help identify the mobility assets that will be needed to deploy combat forces and support units to the region of operation on time; it can help craft a battlefield campaign for employing U.S. forces so that they can achieve their goals; and it can help configure U.S. forces so that they can respond flexibly when original campaign plans must be altered to deal with unexpected events.

This chapter deals with the role that operations research and its associated methods can play in performing these three functions. It sets the stage by discussing why future plans for crisis interventions and regional warfighting will need to be effects-based— that is, focused on the details of how force operations are intended to achieve specific military and political effects. Then it examines the role of mobility models in choosing how to deploy forces abroad. Next, it discusses how simulation models and similar techniques can help forge campaign plans that make use of modern doctrine to achieve specific military-political effects. Finally, it examines how the method of decision analysis can help analyze branches and sequels in campaign plans, and can help identify the forces required to shift directions at the moment of need.

Modern crisis interventions and expeditionary wars are almost always complicated and demanding affairs, not because their forces are necessarily large, but because their operations must be tailor-made and their mental gymnastics are difficult. One reason for difficulty is that expeditionary wars typically are mounted far from well-developed bases and infrastructure, thereby requiring forces to operate from austere settings. Another reason is that their complex circumstances demand an adroit blending of military and political responses in pursuit of multiple goals. Great expertise will be required to carry out expeditionary operations effectively without risking that U.S. forces will become bogged down or otherwise fail to achieve their purposes.

Effects-based planning provides a good tool for handling this challenge, but performing it requires a new kind of professional thinking, and a different kind of operations research. Theories of concrete effects are required to show how military actions can lead to the consequences being sought. As defense analyst Paul Davis said, effects-based planning creates a "grand challenge" to the analytical community.[1] Operations research and associated methods will need to change in order to meet this challenge.

The Need for Effects-Based Planning

The idea that plans should be prepared in advance for expeditionary wars and similar contingencies is hardly revolutionary. Indeed, crafting them is one of the main activities of the regional combatant commands, under the guidance of the Joint Staff. Specific contingencies normally cannot be anticipated years in advance, but this does not mean that nothing can be done to contemplate how they might unfold and what requirements they might pose for U.S. force operations. Typically, each combatant command prepares a set of operational plans, which guide deployment, and campaign plans, which cover battlefield force employment, to cover a spectrum of potential contingencies in its region. These generic plans provide a framework that can be used to craft tailored plans when a specific contingency occurs. When a contingency begins unfolding, normally a few months or weeks, sometimes just days, are available before force operations must commence. This period provides an opportunity to sharpen and modify existing plans. The planning process does not stop once a force operation begins; campaign plans are often adjusted as the operation unfolds and individual battles are waged.[2]

Both types of plans are prepared by regional combatant commands in response to guidance from the Secretary of Defense and the Chairman of the Joint Chiefs of Staff, who carefully review and coordinate the plans submitted by those commands. These plans, in turn, help inform the services of warfighting and operational requirements as they develop their programs and budgets. The intended result is the creation of forces and capabilities that can meet the needs of combatant commanders and their plans. Sometimes reality does not fully conform to this ideal, but the U.S. Department of Defense probably does a better job of ensuring a close linkage between its wartime plans and its force improvement programs than any other military in the world. Even so, ongoing efforts to maintain and strengthen this linkage will be needed.

Force plans for expeditionary wars include multiple elements, all of which must be meshed in a coordinated set of actions. These plans must cover how the forces and their logistic support assets are to be assembled, and how they are to deploy to the crisis zone. They must address how these forces are to operate once they arrive, and how they are to engage the enemy in operational and tactical terms. They also must address how the forces are to be used after battlefield victory is achieved, and how they are to withdraw when the operation is ended. Thus, plans must be sophisticated and comprehensive.

The need to prepare sound plans for expeditionary wars is one of the reasons behind recent efforts by DOD to upgrade joint staffs in the regional commands and to create joint task force headquarters that can deploy into a crisis zone. The existence of a sophisticated organizational process for such planning, however, is no guarantee that good plans will automatically be forthcoming. If contingency response plans are to be effective, they must be guided by coherent ideas and concepts. In particular, they must spell out the joint forces to be employed, the activities they are to perform, the consequences they are to produce, and the goals they are to attain. It is here that effects-based planning enters the equation, for it is a technique intended to bring greater intellectual coherence to the process.

The term effects-based planning originated in the Air Force but has since become a buzzword throughout the defense community. At first glance, the term sounds like a banal platitude with nothing new to offer: after all, virtually every military operation is conducted for the purpose of bringing about an effect of some sort, such as delivering a load of supplies to an overseas base, or destroying an airfield, or toppling an enemy government. However, the term has rich meaning related to its emerging role in defense planning for use of forces in expeditionary operations of military complexity and political subtlety.[3]

Effects-based planning is a product of a trio of new operational concepts. The Air Force term is *effects-based operations*, while the Navy offered *network-centric warfare*, and *rapid decisive operations* was coined by the Army. Initially, these three terms were seen by many as simply another stage of interservice bickering, but their capacity, together, to help articulate features of new-era expeditionary warfare soon became apparent.

Network-centric warfare helped specify how joint forces would be bonded by information networks to conduct combat operations. Rapid decisive operations was a term that helped portray how forces would operate: offensively, aggressively, and aiming for swift victory. Effects-based operations helped draw attention to what the forces try to achieve on the battlefield: positive effects that would mark successful performance of the mission and attainment of national goals. EBO, in particular, addressed the all-important issue of the relationship between means and ends, actions and consequences.

EBO gave rise to the term *effects-based planning*, which is planning of force operations with effects uppermost in mind. The core idea is that when the U.S. military sets out to prepare for a crisis or warfighting contingency, it should not start by defining the forces that will be available to it, and then determine how to employ them. Instead, it should begin by defining the strategic goals it is assigned to achieve and the political-military effects that must be brought about in order to achieve these goals. Then, it should determine what military missions, operations, and tasks must be performed in a coordinated fashion in order to produce these effects. Only after these steps are accomplished should it determine what forces will be used and how to tailor them so that they are capable of achieving the desired effects. Effects-based planning helps guard against the tendency to send similar packages of forces to all contingencies, by instead encouraging the tailoring of individual packages for each contingency.

In theory, effects-based planning is deductive planning from the top down, rather than from the bottom up. It uses ends to determine means, not means to determine ends. In reality, of course, actual planning is an iterative process. Means and ends are adjusted to each other through successive approximations. When the final plan emerges, there should be a coherent relationship between means and ends. The forces assigned to the operation should be capable of producing the desired effects, and producing these effects should result in achievement of the goals being sought. For example, two divisions and two fighter wings may be committed to an operation because these forces are needed to destroy an enemy force of five divisions, the prospect of which will compel the enemy government to withdraw its forces from territory being occupied, the ultimate goal of the U.S. operation. This is a simplified version of an effects-based plan: its means are intended to bring about a specific explicit end through specific effects.

Effects-based planning was embraced by Air Force officers who felt that past U.S. force operations had often focused too much on attrition of enemy forces rather than on larger political-military effects. The Vietnam War seemed to be an example of a war focused on attrition, without proper regard for the issue of how an enemy that was willing to absorb endless attrition was to be defeated. After Vietnam, the U.S. military paid greater attention to this larger issue in theory, but when the time came to make decisions about building and employing forces, attrition was often still the principal measure of merit. Realizing that new-era expeditionary wars would be fought and won through dynamics that went far beyond attrition, some Air Force officers set out to create a broader formula. The result was EBO and effects-based planning.

In principle, effects-based planning provides the building blocks for separate, unique strategies of warfighting for each contingency being mounted. It does so by trying to define the connecting link between actions and goals: the effects, or consequences, of actions that are expressly tailored to achieve specific goals being pursued. Effects-based planning is not abstract, but highly concrete and practical. It focuses on details. It demands "eyeball-to-eyeball contact" with reality. For example, it is not enough to say that an enemy division is to be destroyed; the question is exactly how many of that division's weapons must be put out of action. Destroying 50 percent of its weapons may require one type of force and operation, while destroying 90 percent might require another.

When expeditionary wars are launched, effects-based planning is typically concerned with more than one effect; it tends to think in terms of systems of effects. That is, it tries to define the multiple effects that must be achieved in order for a military operation to achieve its goals. It might, for example, call for the following six effects: push back the enemy's ground forces 100 kilometers from the front line; degrade its weapons inventories by 50 percent; liberate 3 cities; suppress the enemy's air defense system; paralyze the enemy government's communications network; and avoid damaging food and water supplies. Effects-based planning might call for such effects to be achieved either sequentially or simultaneously, but in either case in a choreographed fashion aimed at having a cascading impact. It will try to articulate a theory of how such a cascade of effects can bring about success. When its aim is battlefield victory, it will think in terms that are broader than attrition. In particular, it will focus on high-leverage effects aimed at fracturing the enemy's cohesion, stripping away its battlefield options, and eroding its morale. Its approach to creating military strategies might be called "old-school": guile and cunning combined with brute strength to produce decisive victories.

Equally important, effects-based planning is not restricted to a focus on military effects. It may often address political effects, the achievement of which is typically the goal of an expeditionary war. During the Kosovo war, for example, the main political effect being sought was to coerce the Milosevic government of Serbia into withdrawing its forces from Kosovo. The air operation mounted by NATO was intended to achieve this political outcome, not to bomb Serbia and its forces into oblivion. Whether it achieved this effect as neatly and swiftly as possible can be debated, but it does fall into the category of an effects-based plan with a political aim foremost. The wars in Afghanistan and Iraq were a blend of political and military effects. Militarily, U.S. forces aspired to defeat their opponents on the battlefield, but politically, they sought to remove hostile governments from power and to install stable, friendly governments afterward amidst receptive populations.[4]

In principle, effects-based planning can help guide the long-term transformation of the entire U.S. military posture. But it is not a typical tool of planning and programming for developing future forces so much as it is a tool for using existing forces in specific near-term contingencies. In a contingency, a military commander must draw upon the overall U.S. force posture to assemble the exact combination of joint forces that will be needed to perform the specified missions and achieve the desired goals. Typically, the commander is subject to resource constraints; like a professional football coach who must operate under a salary cap in building a team, a combatant commander will operate under a force cap, having access to only a portion of the forces in the overall posture. As a result, the commander must choose wisely, for he or she will be waging war with the forces thus assembled, and will win or lose on that basis. In choosing forces, the commander must mold modular assets into an effective package. Effects-based planning offers promise by focusing on exactly what is to be accomplished in military and political terms. Normally, a joint force that is designed with detailed effects in mind will be more likely to succeed.

To be comprehensive, effects-based planning must be applied to all three phases of a contingency: the deployment phase, the combat phase, and the post-combat phase. It must help specify how forces are to be sent overseas, how they are to be employed on the battlefield, and how they are to be used in shaping the postwar environment, including how enemy territory is to be occupied and, if this is a mission goal, how a new government is to be built. These three phases of planning can be complex and difficult; plans for all three must be interlocked, but they cannot be rigid. Instead, they must be flexible and adaptable, capable of responding to the ebb and flow of events. Effects-based planning is no magic wand or cure-all, but it can help tilt the odds toward success. It seems likely to be around for a long time because, if expeditionary wars have one thing in common, it is that each will require a uniquely tailored plan focused on specific effects.

Effects-based planning is aptly suited to the task of preparing for expeditionary wars on a case-by-case basis because of its ability to grapple with the ever-changing details of military operations. It is a natural partner of operations research, because both methods focus on details. But for operations research to be relevant, it must be able to address the specific effects being analyzed in each case; it must be able to go beyond attrition and other mechanical features of war that have been traditional features of its models. It must be able to analyze large systems of effects and how they combine to produce strategic outcomes. This is a challenge for a methodology that has traditionally been used to focus on a few effects, rather than gauge the interactions of many effects. Operations research must also be able to analyze such new-era operating concepts as speed, tempo, synchronization, pressure, and leverage—terms that physicists understand but that mathematical models and computer programs have not, to date, readily incorporated.

These are compelling reasons why operations research must show increased innovation and adaptability. It must address what must be measured, not just what can easily be measured. What operations research must avoid is being obsessive about minor issues and unhelpful on major issues. Being relevant to the major issues is truly a grand challenge for a method attuned to details. Further uses of operations research must work closely with strategic evaluation and systems analysis to support effects-based planning for the expeditionary wars ahead.

Planning the Deployment Process

Effects-based planning begins with assessing the capacity of U.S. military forces to deploy overseas in a crisis. When applied to individual contingencies, it focuses on determining how to get the right forces to the right place at the right time. In this arena, the "effect" is easy to measure: the timely arrival of joint forces that meet the needs of regional commands charged with carrying out the contingency response. What is difficult is getting the power-projection job done swiftly enough to meet force requirements that can build in a hurry.[5]

Mobility is not a subject that typically inspires the passions of those who are fascinated by combat, but knowledgeable defense planners know its importance for expeditionary wars. Distant wars cannot be won unless sufficient forces and logistic support assets are present at the scene to operate in the required scope and intensity or, in the words of Confederate cavalry officer Nathan Bedford Forrest, "get there fustest with the mostest." For many expeditionary wars and the crises that trigger them, time is at a premium and forces are needed quickly. The need for a swift response arises when an enemy commits aggression, but it also can hold true in a situation where the United States plans to attack an adversary and must move quickly for political-military reasons, such as in a preemptive war against an enemy armed with WMD.

Even when a concerted effort is made to move swiftly, the problem with most expeditionary wars is that they are waged at great distances from U.S. bases, perhaps 10,000 miles or more. Air forces and naval forces may be able to converge quickly, but large U.S. ground forces and other stocks are so weighty that deploying them to such distances can be difficult and time-consuming. The force buildup for *Desert Storm* in late 1990 took 6 months. The buildup for Operation *Iraqi Freedom* in 2003, which involved smaller forces, took 2 to 3 months and was not yet complete when the war began.

Providing an adequate time-phased buildup promises to be a continuing challenge. Most observers would agree that, while great strides have been made toward speeding force deployment, additional progress is needed. Public DOD documents reflect this theme; they talk, for example, in terms of being able to deploy a sizable ground force of several divisions plus commensurate air and naval forces within 30 days, but this is a statement of aspiration, not necessarily of current capabilities.[6] Meeting this demanding goal for all future contingencies will require not only strong mobility forces, but also considerable expertise at determining how to deploy forces with hundreds of moving parts.

Analyzing mobility is hard, but operations research provides analytical tools that can help. Mobility models are models equipped with the mathematical equations and data necessary to analyze the physical demands of moving forces abroad by air and sea. Although back-of-the-envelope models provide aggregate analysis, computer-based models are needed to handle the details of operational planning. Both types of models deal with tons of air cargo and millions of square feet of sea cargo to be deployed for each contingency. Once the models are equipped with data on delivery requirements, as determined by the regional combatant command, they can gauge the size and mix of mobility assets needed to meet the requirement on a time-phased basis. They can also be used to determine whether committed assets meet these requirements and to identify shortfalls. They thus can provide a scheme of supply and demand for contingencies, and they can be used to design improvement programs so that the military can do a better job of deploying forces at the size and rate required for future events.

The force deployment process is more complicated than merely cranking data through these models to determine how many mobility assets must be assembled to move a large force to a distant location in time to meet the desired delivery date. These models must be embedded in a larger organizational process that includes the Joint Staff, the combatant command, and Transportation Command. Planning by their staffs must address a myriad of details regarding the scheduling of the force-flow dynamic so that it unfolds speedily and efficiently. Typically, the force buildup process must take place in a phased, balanced manner. At each stage, combat forces must be accompanied by appropriate logistic support units and supplies. Some of these assets may arrive from prepositioned ships or depots stationed near the crisis zone; others may be delivered by airlift or by cargo ships that sail from CONUS. Orchestrating the time-phased arrival of these deliveries must take into account the possibility of bottleneck delays and breakdowns. For this reason, preparing an operations plan and its associated time-phased force deployment list can take months, and a great deal of staff analysis including the use of powerful computer models.

The force deployment process is time consuming even when sophisticated plans have been drawn up. The United States has built a sizable strategic mobility force over the past two decades, so it might seem that swift deployments should be relatively easy to carry out. These mobility forces are required to lift huge amounts of cargo, however, and many constraints impede the deployment process, slowing it down.

Currently, the Air Force possesses an active inventory of about 300 heavy cargo transports (C–5, C–17, KC–10, and C–141). It can also mobilize the equivalent of another 150 transports from the civil reserve air fleet. These aircraft can lift 40 to 100 tons each to long distances; thus, the entire force has a theoretical lift capacity of over 25,000 tons in a single sortie. Assuming one round-trip flight every 3 days, this air fleet should be able to lift 250,000 tons in 30 days. The Navy has a sea fleet of 60 cargo ships on active duty, and can draw upon a Ready Reserve Fleet of about 70 additional ships. On average, these ships can lift 10,000 to 20,000 tons apiece. DOD could also draw upon about 200 U.S.-flag commercial ships; if necessary, additional commercial ships could be mobilized as well. As an estimate, the DOD-owned cargo fleet can lift about 18 million square feet or about 1.4 million tons or more, and its ships are capable of sailing 10,000 miles in a month or less. These cargo ships include container ships, roll-on/roll-off (RO/RO) ships, large medium speed RO/RO ships, and other modern container-carrying vessels that are much more efficient than older ships carrying break-bulk cargoes.

Simple mathematics might therefore suggest that this combination of airlift and sealift, supplemented by prepositioned stocks, should be capable of delivering about 1.65 million tons of weapons, equipment, and supplies to a distant area such as the Persian Gulf in about one month. This was roughly the size and weight of the force actually deployed for Operation *Iraqi Freedom*. But that deployment took 2 or 3 months, and even then it was not complete on the day that war erupted. The reason for this big disparity between theory and reality is not incompetence or weak mobility forces. Surface appearances and simple mathematics overlook many constraints, including daily frictions that can transform a well-oiled mobility system into a creaky machine.

One constraint is that the combat forces may not be fully ready to deploy on the day that the movement order (C-day) is given. Unless preparatory steps have already been taken, even high-readiness forces can require a week or two to recall troops from other assignments, repair equipment, replenish stocks, perform administrative duties, and conduct final training. These forces must then travel to embarkation points such as airfields or ports. The process of loading them aboard trains and aircraft, traveling to the departure site, offloading them, and then loading onto aircraft or ships can take another several days. All of these preparatory steps can consume a month or more, even before the actual lifting process begins.

The time required to transport these forces overseas depends upon the number of air transports and cargo ships available for the contingency. Constraints are frequent at this stage. For example, the Air Force often cannot commit all of its active cargo transports because other normal missions must also be performed. Perhaps only one-half of these aircraft will actually be available; the number could be even less if readiness standards are not fully met. Taking care of necessary repairs and maintenance can take a few days. Likewise, the Navy can only draw upon those cargo ships not already employed in other missions. Repairs and maintenance, fueling, and assembling crews can take a few days or weeks. In theory, reserve ships can enlarge the available mobility force, but these ships typically can take longer to prepare than active forces. Air and sea assets can be prepared during the same period that combat forces are being prepared, but the need to prepare both combat forces and mobility forces contributes to the need to spend a month or more in this effort.

The lift process also encounters constraints. For example, some transport aircraft may have breakdowns as they shuttle back and forth between CONUS and the crisis location. Repairs can be made, but typically aircraft availability will decline as a deployment unfolds. After a month of surge flying, perhaps only 70 percent of the aircraft are still in the air, resulting in slowdowns in cargo delivery. In the best of circumstances, air deliveries are determined by daily sortie rates. At 4,000 tons per day, that is only 56,000 tons in 2 weeks; delivering 250,000 tons by air may easily take 9 weeks, not 4.

Other constraints apply to sea mobility. During the 3 or 4 weeks required to sail to a distant location, no ships are arriving at foreign ports, but then many ships may arrive at once. Typically, foreign ports cannot accommodate such a deluge of cargo ships; this was the case in Kuwait in early 2003. Limits on dock space, equipment, and workers mean that only a few ships can be offloaded at one time, and it may take more time to offload each ship than it would at a well-prepared U.S. port. As a result, a large convoy of ships may remain "parked" offshore for days to await their turn. Then, after they are offloaded, their equipment must be moved from docks to assembly areas. Wheeled or tracked vehicles can be driven to forward zones, but other equipment and supplies must be packed aboard cargo trucks and railroad trains. The process of moving 1 million tons or more to forward areas, which may be located a long distance from the ports, can take days, or even weeks if transport trucks and trains are in short supply.

Thus, a careful examination of details shows why the process of deploying large U.S. ground forces overseas could easily take 2 to 3 months, rather than the single month suggested by simple arithmetic. Indeed, 2 to 3 months is relatively speedy given the many frictions along the way. Today's capacity to move forces this fast owes much to the considerable progress that has been made in building mobility forces and expediting the movement process, but it still seems maddeningly slow when judged against the requirements of expeditionary wars.

Figure 22–1 shows an illustrative relation between demand and supply. It presumes that the regional command wants a ground presence of four divisions within a month of C-day. It displays a buildup rate driven by the interaction of prepositioned equipment, airlift, and sealift. This buildup, given real-life constraints, takes 3 months and does not reach completion until C-day+90. During the interim, the regional command has growing numbers of air forces and naval forces at its disposal; it is not entirely devoid of ground combat forces but, because most ground forces travel by sealift, they arrive slowly. The result is a lengthy period of deficiency that limits the operations that can be undertaken until the entire force arrives.

Figure 22–1. **Illustrative Ground Force Buildup Rate for an Expeditionary War**

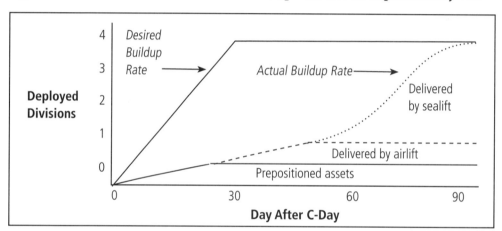

This does not mean that combatant commanders cannot start force operations until after fully 2 or 3 months have passed. Often, air and naval forces begin arriving within days of C-day, and they can be employed immediately. Some ground forces arrive during the first week or two, and they too can be committed to combat. Consequently a commander can start a rolling campaign early by using the forces at his disposal, and then gradually adding to the campaign as more forces arrive. Such a rolling campaign was used during Operation *Iraqi Freedom*, which began while some ground forces were still aboard cargo ships at sea. But a rolling campaign entails risks, and it is not always physically possible: for example, a campaign plan could require the presence of all forces to begin operations, not just some of them. Clearly, DOD should endeavor to improve upon its deployment capabilities by coming as close as possible to the 30-day goal.

What should be DOD's priorities for improving its mobility assets and force-deployment capabilities? This question can be answered by recalling that the current mobility force was sized to be able to handle two concurrent, short-warning MTWs by deploying virtually the entire active combat posture within 4 to 6 months or sooner. This two-war standard is likely to continue for mobility planning. Yet now that a surprise Iraq attack on Kuwait has been removed from the list of contingencies to worry about, the need for a faster two-MTW capability and a larger mobility force seems less likely to be a main motivator of future programs. Where bigger mobility forces may be needed is to help make the forces of allies more deployable; many future expeditionary wars will be multilateral operations in which forces from Europe and other regions will be fighting alongside U.S. forces. In order to deploy fast enough to be interoperable with U.S. forces, major improvements in allied mobility assets are necessary.

For the United States, the new motivator for mobility is likely to be the need to handle single contingencies that demand a faster, earlier response than available now. The likely goal will be to speed smaller force packages overseas more quickly, by closing the gap in capability during the first month or two of deployment. In response to this requirement, proposals are now surfacing to buy new transport aircraft that can lift 500 to 1,000 tons per sortie, and for more fast cargo ships or bigger ships. While both proposals have attractive features, they also raise questions.

Big air transports would be expensive, and even if they could carry 500 to 1,000 tons apiece, a large number would be needed to make a serious dent in the buildup deficiency during the first 30 days. Would a force of 100 to 150 such aircraft, at a cost of $20 billion to $30 billion, be cost-effective and affordable? Would faster and bigger cargo ships, which also are expensive, make a significant difference? Even if new ships could travel 50 percent faster than current ships, they would speed the deployment process by only a few days. The same applies to bigger ships that carry more cargo but still must travel 10,000 miles. Because such new ships would still be moving forces from CONUS, they would still be unable to deliver cargo in the first week or two of deployment. Here, again, the costs of this program may override its effectiveness.

A better answer may be increased reliance upon afloat prepositioning of Army and Marine equipment sets. The weapons for such sets could be drawn from existing stocks and therefore would not entail additional procurement expenses. Because the cargo ships could be low-tech, they would be more affordable than high-tech fast-lift options. By virtue of being stationed overseas, they could travel to most crisis locations in a few days. Additional prepositioning could be combined with other innovations, such as just-in-time logistics and slimmed Army support structures (as discussed in chapter 14), to close the gap between demand and supply in mobility forces at a price that DOD can afford to pay. Rotational policies could increase the readiness of on-call Army units, thereby lessening time lost in making last-minute preparations before deploying.

All of these options should be subjected to the careful scrutiny that operations research can provide. Perhaps analysis will show that a combination of some new air transports and ships, plus more prepositioning, slimmed logistics support, and readiness improvements, will provide the best overall program. Another consideration is that, barring a major change in DOD's strategic priorities, any improvement effort must come out of a program budget that will be allocated only about 4 percent of DOD's budget, or $20 billion per year. Competing procurement needs will prevent the mobility budget from rising rapidly in the future. Because existing air transports and ships will have to be replaced as they age, there will not be much room for major new investments. Strategic mobility will need to improve within the means available, and this will dictate an emphasis on affordable, high-leverage priorities rather than wholesale transformation.

Program investment options are, in any case, mostly solutions for the long term. In the meantime, DOD will need to work with the mobility assets that it currently has, employing them as effectively and efficiently as possible. Skillful mobility planning can produce improvements; while it cannot overcome the laws of physics, it can help reduce the frictions and constraints involved in moving forces. For example, it can help ensure that readiness of mobility forces is kept at high levels so that valuable time is not lost in repairing air transports and activating reserve cargo ships. It also can take steps to minimize the time needed to move combat forces to their debarkation points in CONUS. Further, it can ensure that foreign ports have the dock space, equipment, and workers needed to offload cargo ships faster, and that sufficient trucks and trains are available at arrival locations to move forces to forward locations. Practical steps such as these might reduce deployment times by 2 to 3 weeks or more, a meaningful amount when forces are needed urgently.

Skillful planning can also reduce the risk of major disruptions if mobility plans are changed on short notice. Such plans involve the intricate, sequential movements of many parts. If the plan is changed, the result can be great turmoil, causing additional delays in the movement schedule. The problem is that U.S. crisis response is often influenced by compelling political considerations that may conflict with existing mobility plans. For example, policymakers might want to delay force deployments in order to give diplomacy additional time to resolve the crisis; then, if diplomacy fails, they might ask for a speedy buildup in order to begin combat operations as soon as possible. This change could result in mobilization of more air transports than originally planned plus a shift to faster-moving cargo ships. These alterations, in turn, might result in the need to switch cargoes among carriers, to alter the schedule of force departures, and to change debarkation points. The result can be a ragged, prolonged deployment that leaves senior officials greatly frustrated by a deployment process that seems to have let them down.

Unfortunately, there is no certain solution to this problem. The need for fixed deployment schedules will always be in potential conflict with the need for political and diplomatic flexibility. But the problem can be lessened by deployment plans that incorporate multiple options, and by an organizational process that can produce new plans quickly. The need for flexible, adaptable plans is not new; it was recognized in the aftermath of *Desert Storm*, and some steps to improve performance were taken. Operation *Iraqi Freedom* suggested, however, that progress may not have been enough. Thus, further improvements are a high priority.

Operations research and its mathematical models can play a role in this endeavor when guided by effects-based planning for mobility. But high-level attention to the need for flexibility and efficiency is also needed to counter the natural inclination of bureaucracies to cling to the status quo. Better mobility planning cannot be undertaken at the moment of a crisis, but must be accomplished in the months and years beforehand.

In this arena, a future of innovation is mandated both for staff bureaucracies and for effects-based mobility models.

Forging Effects-Based Campaign Plans

Effects-based planning has its brightest prospects in the arena of contributing to the design of campaign plans that govern the choreographed execution of joint force operations to achieve the combatant command's goals. A campaign plan provides a framework within which individual battle plans can be developed and carried out. It also establishes a sequence for individual battles to follow, accumulating effects that result in ultimate victory. The U.S. military possesses a well-earned reputation for skill at this art, but campaign planning is becoming more complex in this era of expeditionary wars and new military doctrine. Because today's expeditionary wars depend on more than just brute-force firepower, skillful campaign planning must provide the extra margin of advantage during combat and afterward.[7]

The promise of effects-based planning is that, by focusing attention on concrete battlefield outcomes, it can strengthen campaign plans in high-leverage ways. Slogans such as "shock and awe" may have rhetorical appeal, but they must be backed by well-thought-out theories of how to apply military power in decisive ways. Military campaigns going back to the time of Caesar and before have attempted to inflict shock and awe on their opponents; in this sense, there is nothing new here. Such concepts are useful only if they provide meaningful guidance on how to execute U.S. force operations in specific, tailored ways that accelerate and magnify the process by which enemies are defeated. Such concepts must, therefore, be enlivened by effects-based planning.

Effects-based planning is especially needed for creating campaign plans anchored in joint operations. Even a land campaign fought entirely by ground forces should, of course, be guided by sound strategies and tactics, but planning a campaign by ground forces is considerably easier than planning a joint campaign in which ground, naval, and air forces all play crucial interacting roles. Joint campaigns must be integrated, coordinated, and balanced. Because each force component will play roles tailored to its unique talents, it will be pursuing battlefield effects of its own. The challenge is one of identifying these effects, combining them to create an overall campaign plan, and then tailoring joint force operations to carry out this plan in ways that produce the desired results. This is not simple, and it cannot be done by computers. It takes smart, knowledgeable, thoughtful work.

Recent experience underscores the premise that future campaign plans cannot be forged on the basis of one-size-fits-all. Peacekeeping missions aside, each recent U.S. expeditionary operation has been a unique creation, and each has differed greatly from the others. The 1988 invasion of Panama was conducted by a small force of about 25,000 ground troops, mostly led by airborne, air assault, and light infantry. In 1991, *Desert Storm* was conducted by a huge joint force of multiple divisions, fighter wings, and carrier battlegroups that carried out an offensive campaign of air bombardment followed by swift ground maneuvers. In 1993, the invasion of Haiti was carried out by small airborne forces similar to the Panama invasion, backed by naval assets. In 1999, the Kosovo war was waged by large air and naval forces; ground forces were entirely absent until Kosovo was occupied after fighting ceased. In 2001, the Afghanistan invasion was performed by joint air forces that employed spotters on the ground, with brigade-sized ground combat forces of 5,000 troops entering the war only later in spring 2002. The invasion of Iraq in 2003 marked a return to large-scale joint operations with about 250,000 total military personnel, but there, ground, air, and naval forces pursued new doctrines.

What these diverse expeditionary operations have in common is that they all sought decisive military effects in order to achieve specific political effects aimed at altering undesirable situations. All employed bold offensive military actions aimed at unraveling and defeating enemy forces quickly, avoiding prolonged, grueling attrition contests. But these military operations were also guided by concrete political goals for overturning the status quo. The goal in Panama was to overthrow the Manuel Noriega government. The goal in *Desert Storm* was to expel Iraqi forces from Kuwait. The goal in Haiti was to install a democratically elected government being kept out of office by an authoritarian regime trying to cling to power. The goal in Kosovo was to push Serbian forces out. The goal in Afghanistan was to topple the Taliban government, uproot al Qaeda, and install a democratic government that could rule a devastated country dominated by tribal chieftains. The goal in Iraq was to remove the Saddam Hussein dictatorship and install a democratic government to preside over an ethnically mixed population of Kurds, Sunnis, and Shiites.

Most of these political goals were achieved or are still being actively pursued. They required campaign plans aimed at fostering specific political-military effects. The same seems likely to hold true for future expeditionary wars. Many of them will involve serious military operations of varying size and scope, but political outcomes will be a dominating imperative. Their campaign plans will have in common that each seeks to employ combat operations in order to achieve military effects and goals that will be intended to attain, in turn, political effects and goals. Crafting campaign plans that seek specific military results in order to produce specific political consequences will be a demanding challenge for effects-based planning.

Mastering the causal relationship between expeditionary military operations and political results will not be easy because, as history shows, the line from military actions to political consequences is seldom straight. Clobbering an overmatched enemy military on the battlefield may be merely the first step toward the goal of creating a new, favorable political situation in a country or region. Often the latter phase is inherently harder and more prone to miscalculation. While the United States is amply endowed for the first step, it is less skilled and experienced at the vital second step.

To the extent that combat operations dominate future campaign plans, creating them will be a decidedly nontraditional enterprise. A core reason is that new doctrinal concepts are sweeping over the U.S. military. The old emphasis on linear operations, firepower, and attrition is being supplemented by such new concepts as information superiority, decision superiority, dispersed forces, distributed and networked forces, simultaneous operations, parallel and decentralized operations, adaptive operations, synchronization, precision targeting, positional maneuvers, continuous pressure, fast tempo, high-leverage applications, and cascading impacts. All of these concepts appear to be fine ideas that reflect information-age thinking, but if they are to be applied successfully to expeditionary warfare, they must be more than buzzwords. They must have concrete meaning and provide guidelines for force operations; they must be forged together to create sensible campaign plans.

While each of these doctrinal concepts could merit an individual treatise, here a brief discussion of a few will help illustrate why they must not simply be taken at face value and rubber-stamped into campaign plans. Take, for example, the concept of information superiority. Perhaps no modern-era concept has more prestige than this one. Yet unless some battlefield advantage can be extracted from it, information superiority is of no intrinsic value, and as an end in itself, it makes little sense. Indeed, a military that devotes excessive attention to acquiring and distributing information might damage itself if it becomes diverted from other important tasks. Information can be valuable if it produces knowledge superiority, but again, knowledge must be actionable if it is to be useful, for example, by permitting accurate targeting of air and artillery strikes so as to shift exchange rates in favor of U.S. forces. The key point is that superiority in information and knowledge should be seen as means to an end, not as ends in themselves.

A concept that has high inherent value, and that makes use of information and knowledge, is decision superiority: the capacity to make decisions faster and better than the enemy. Decision superiority can result in more effective operations, and can also enable U.S. forces to accelerate the pace and intensity of combat in ways that overwhelm the enemy's ability to respond. An enemy whose decisionmaking becomes paralyzed is likely to lose to U.S. forces that produce the accelerating speed of combat. Decision superiority, however, is not absolute, but relative: it depends partly upon the enemy's capacity to make decisions, which may vary a great deal from one enemy to the next. It also depends upon the situation; decision superiority may be highly important in fluid battles, but less important in static battles where infrequent changes are made in force dispositions and where crude strength determines results. While decision superiority should be a goal of campaign plans and force preparations, a sense of perspective should be kept about its relative magnitude and importance.

The concept of force networking should also be kept in perspective. Networking unquestionably makes military sense. History books are full of battles in which the lack of networking greatly inhibited operations. For example, the British Navy failed to score an annihilating victory over the German Navy at the Battle of Jutland in 1916 because its battleships, cruisers, and destroyers failed to communicate with each other about enemy dispositions and common tactics. But considerable progress has been made at force networking. The U.S. military during the Cold War was better networked than many people realize, and modern communications systems are now taking networking to a new stage. Networking can be invaluable in fighting naval and air battles where the speed of missiles makes nearly instantaneous reactions a necessity. For ground battles that unfold at slower speed, such networking may be important, but not the determining factor. In the final analysis, such battles are still won by trained soldiers putting weapons on target. The key point is that networking should be kept in perspective. It is an important goal, but it does not merit all-consuming preoccupation, nor is it a justification for hubris.

The concept of dispersed forces is also touted in many treatises about modern doctrine. The core idea is that U.S. forces should not be bunched closely together, as they often were during the Cold War. Instead, they should be spread out over the battlefield so that they have more room to maneuver freely, are less vulnerable to enemy fires, and are able to put pressure on the enemy from multiple directions. These notions, however, can be contrary to another key principle of war: concentration, which calls for forces to be massed at critical points on the battlefield rather than scattered. Armies that have succeeded in massing closely enough to conduct coordinated maneuvers often won big battles, and armies that dispersed their forces excessively have often been defeated in detail by enemies that did a better job of massing. Napoleon, for example, regularly lured his enemies into dispersing while he massed. Custer was massacred at the Little Big Horn because he dispersed his forces, allowing a concentrated enemy to pounce upon his small, fragmented columns of cavalry troops.

In today's world, air forces and naval forces can be widely dispersed because their fires can be quickly concentrated. Dispersal also offers them a way to split enemy defenses by compelling a focus on many avenues of attack. Ground forces, however, are less suited to dispersal because their fires and maneuvers cannot readily be concentrated. In the time that it takes them to concentrate, the enemy might have greater opportunity to counter-concentrate or otherwise prepare for battle. Nor are dispersed ground forces necessarily less easy to attack and destroy than massed forces: today, even a "massed" division is spread out along a wide frontage and is not vulnerable to fires directed at a few spots. Dispersed forces may be easier to destroy because, if they are too far apart to help each other, they can be defeated in detail. U.S. forces should be equally capable of concentrating or dispersing, and their choice of tactics should be dictated by an accurate reading of the situation at hand, not by rote formulas.

The same applies to simultaneous operations, which are now being touted as universally superior to sequential operations. Simultaneous operations can be advantageous because they increase the tempo of battle and the pressure placed on the enemy. Yet they also increase the pressure on U.S. forces and may result in forces being scattered in multiple directions, weakening operations if too few assets are allocated to each mission. Moreover, there can be situations in which sequential operations make sense because one mission must be achieved before a succeeding mission can be launched. For example, precursor airstrikes may soften up the enemy before ground strikes are launched. Sequential and simultaneous operations should both remain on the books, and each should be chosen on its merits, not because one has become fashionable in doctrine.

The interaction between precision fires and positional maneuvers also requires clear and orderly thinking. Both have their place on the modern battlefield, and each is capable of facilitating the other. The growing emphasis on precision fires by standoff weapons does not necessarily mean that maneuvers performed by ground forces can be neglected or dispensed with entirely. Fires are the main mechanism producing attrition, still a central element of combat. Precision fires are provided by both air and ground forces. Positional maneuvers shape the battlefield by fostering situations in which local U.S. forces have more firepower than local enemy forces. Such maneuvers commonly are performed by ground forces, but air forces may often be able to contribute greatly. Campaign plans should avoid rigid formulas, and instead seek the optimal combination of fires and maneuvers for the situation at hand.

This brief discussion helps illuminate why new doctrinal concepts should not be treated as dogma, nor slavishly followed in situations where traditional practices still make sense. Most campaign plans are likely to need to embody a blend of old and new doctrines. In this sense, new doctrinal concepts can make important contributions to campaign plans. Their impact will depend upon the enemy's mastery of modern doctrines. If the enemy is fighting out of its league, new concepts can help U.S. forces prevail quickly and easily. If the enemy is skilled, their impact may be less decisive, but still significant enough to give U.S. forces an important edge.

Several of these concepts offer the advantage of portraying war in dynamic, not static, terms. Such concepts as pressure, tempo, speed, and cascading impacts provide a sense of how combat can sometimes be an explosive process resulting in rapid victory. Likewise, such new concepts as synchronization, leverage, and disintegration aspire to fragment enemy forces and lift them off their hinges as battle unfolds. Some of these concepts have been on the lips of commanders since World War II or before, but regardless of whether or not they are truly new, they suggest ways to wage modern war that take advantage of emerging technologies.

Making best use of these concepts requires that effects-based planning provide a coherent theory of exactly how the enemy is to be defeated on the battlefield, with a framework for determining how to blend new doctrines and traditional attrition-oriented doctrines together. The goals of unraveling the enemy and fracturing its cohesion can be accomplished several ways. One stratagem is to attack the enemy with such blinding speed and power that its forces lose their morale and will to fight (as evidently occurred in Iraq in 2003). Another stratagem is to destroy the enemy's command and control architecture, thereby preventing its forces from communicating with each other. A third is to strip away the enemy's employment options, denying it the opportunity to defend in place, attack, retreat, move to a new location, or maneuver. The enemy's force posture might be broken apart by isolating units from each other to prevent them from operating together. Individual units might be neutralized by destroying key components such as tanks, artillery, or logistic support. Yet another stratagem is to hit enemy forces where they are weak and vulnerable, as by flanking attacks that avoid the enemy's strong points.

Such stratagems typically work best against an ill-prepared enemy that lacks the capacity and will to absorb reversals. They work less well against a well-prepared and determined enemy that is not about to collapse even if the fortunes of war turn against it. Such stratagems worked well against the Iraqi army, for example, but less well against the German Wehrmacht in World War II, a skilled army that simply had to be bludgeoned into submission. Even against strong opponents, however, these stratagems can complement well-prepared forces and traditional battle plans, if not substitute for them.

Such stratagems cannot be sprinkled lightly into a campaign plan, nor can they be chosen arbitrarily. They must be applied with the skill of a surgeon. Because one such stratagem normally will not succeed on its own, a system of them must be concocted. Their use must be carefully planned in individual battles and in the campaign plan as a whole. All of them require thorough evaluation of operational details.

Above all, they require effects-based planning that illuminates exactly how, when, and where they are meant to work. Provided such effects-based planning is accomplished, these stratagems offer potent approaches to use of modern doctrines by well-prepared forces to achieve decisive victory.

Operations research can contribute in many ways to the creation of campaign plans under the mantle of effects-based planning. It can do so, however, only with improved computer simulation models that can analyze individual campaign plans for modern expeditionary wars. Existing models that merely portray war as a crude attrition dynamic driven by weapons will no longer suffice. New models must be able to analyze not just forces and weapons, but also the roles played by modern doctrinal concepts. They must be able to gauge how these concepts elevate U.S. combat capabilities in specific situations against particular adversaries. They must be able to help commanders decide which operational concepts to employ when choices must be made between, for example, sequential and simultaneous attacks, or between concentration and dispersion. New models must be able to analyze battlefield effects in modern terms, showing how modern forces and doctrines can be used not only to bludgeon an opponent's forces, but also to fragment, dislocate, or paralyze them so that they cannot fight effectively. New models must be able to show how the cascading ascendancy of U.S. forces on the battlefield is intended to circumscribe the options of enemy leaders, pushing them toward the political actions sought by U.S. campaign plans.

All of this is a big but not impossible agenda for change. Careful study can develop estimates of how new-era doctrines enhance combat capabilities, how different operational concepts apply in various circumstances, and how battlefield effects take hold. These estimates often must be anchored in logical human judgments, not provable scientific facts, but they can be made more reliable by research. Provided that this agenda of change can be mastered, computer modeling and similar techniques can assist campaign plans by focusing on details and encouraging analytical thoroughness. They can help shape the process by which military actions are translated into causes and effects. They can provide a sense of numbers and quantification to a planning process that otherwise would be qualitative and subjective. They can help measure effects. They can help identify the size and combination of joint forces that must be assembled in order to carry out the campaign plan. They can help sort out, select, and prioritize individual battle plans. They can help determine the ways in which joint forces can be integrated to wage a succession of battles.

Operations research also can help provide a composite picture of how U.S. force capabilities stack up in relation to the requirements and demands of an emerging campaign. It can do so by combining its microscopic view of details to assemble a wide-angle appraisal of the overall campaign. Figure 22–2 provides an illustration of how this appraisal can be accomplished. The *y*-axis measures the total combat power generated by U.S. forces in a particular campaign. The shaded bar also shows how much combat power is needed to defeat the enemy in this campaign. The *x*-axis displays the size, readiness, and jointness of U.S. forces. The curves on the graph show three different measures of how combat power increases on the *y*-axis as a function of force size and strength on

Figure 22–2. **Impact of Modern Doctrine and Effects-Based Plans on Force Requirements in a Campaign**

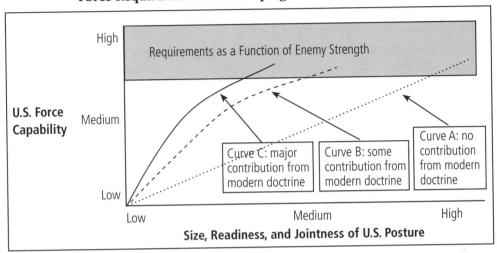

the *x*-axis. Curve A shows combat power without any contribution from modern doctrine that employs effects-based plans and battlefield stratagems. Curve B shows combat power that is modestly enhanced by these contributors. Curve C shows combat power that is enhanced in major ways.

This figure can facilitate judgments about the joint forces that should be committed, as a function of assumptions about the enemy's strength and the fighting prowess of U.S. forces. This graph is illustrative, not definitive, and any such graph is based on a host of assumptions; even so, such a graph can be useful when debates arise over how many U.S. forces should be committed to battle, as occurred when the campaign plan for Operation *Iraqi Freedom* was being designed. The graph's key point is that force needs for campaigns are a variable, not a constant. Much depends upon the estimated capacity of enemy forces to fight effectively. Much also depends upon the capacity of U.S. forces to take advantage of modern doctrine, effects-based plans, and battlefield stratagems.

On this graph, the perennial question of "How much is enough?" can be answered at a glance by assessing the enemy's strength and then determining which of the three curves applies to the coming campaign. Once the desired capability is located on the *y*-axis, the reader can find the associated point on the relevant curve, then look downward to the *x*-axis to gauge force needs for the campaign at hand. Such a chart must be used with common sense. Surface appearances might suggest that the quality coming from modern doctrine and other contributors can be relied upon to reduce the number of forces that might otherwise be needed. This might be the case in some wars, but it is not necessarily true for all wars. Quantity will often be needed to achieve the full benefits provided by the qualitative impact of these contributors. Even so, this figure helps provide valuable insights into a complex equation that might otherwise be indecipherable even to trained observers. It helps, at least, to highlight the judgments that must be made and the sensitivity of these judgments to alternative assumptions.

Campaign plans must include more than a theory of how to wage war: they also must include a reliable theory of how to win the peace afterward through occupation, stabilization, and reconstruction. As the U.S. experience in Iraq shows, this important phase of expeditionary war can require sizable forces. The capabilities demanded of them can be different from those needed to perform major combat operations; exactly which capabilities are needed will depend on the specific missions to be performed. The forces chosen should be determined by the effects desired and the goals sought. A force configured for light combat against guerrillas will be different from the force needed to rebuild destroyed bridges and powergrids. Normally, a combination of stabilization and reconstruction forces with a wide portfolio of capabilities will be needed. While this subject is too complex to address here, effects-based planning, supported by operations research, can help make the right choices so that the post-combat phase is as successful as the combat phase.

Shifting Operations: Branches, Sequels, and Adaptable Forces

Military history has many cases in which campaign plans anchored in a single concept of operations unfolded as expected and yielded victory. The invasion of Normandy in 1944 was such a case. Planned in detail months in advance and backed by imposing resources, it was carried out mostly as envisioned. U.S. and allied British forces established a strong foothold on the coast of France, which permitted a buildup and breakout that resulted in Europe's liberation. The Battle of Midway in 1942 was another example. This battle was based on a brilliantly conceived plan by the U.S. Navy to trap Japanese forces who were preparing to invade Midway Island. Key to the plan was keeping the Japanese in the dark about three U.S. aircraft carriers lurking north of Midway. As Japanese aircraft began to bomb Midway, warplanes from the U.S. carriers swooped down on the four enemy aircraft carriers that had launched them. This surprise attack sank all of the Japanese carriers, breaking the back of Japanese naval power in the Pacific and leaving the way clear for the island-hopping campaign that defeated Japan.[8]

Desert Storm of 1991 was another well-planned campaign that unfolded as envisioned. As envisioned by CENTCOM, it began with a sustained air bombardment of several weeks, and was followed by a brief, intense ground campaign that featured a frontal assault and a flanking attack that formed a classical "hammer and anvil" maneuver against the already battered Iraqi army. The result was a battlefield victory with few losses to U.S./allied forces that showcased the virtues of developing a sophisticated plan and carrying it out with a well-prepared force against an enemy incapable of adapting to such adversity.

But not all great battles and victories followed their scripts. Many featured eye-popping surprises, swift changes of fortune, and bizarre twists and turns that forced military commanders to grapple with unexpected situations, to improvise, and to use their forces in radically different ways than originally planned. The winner tended to be the side that did the best job of shifting directions effectively, while the loser was the side that clung stubbornly to a plan that had been overtaken by events.

A good example is the 1942 battle for Guadalcanal in the Solomon Islands. The original U.S. intent was to invade the Japanese-held island with a division of Marines, and then to provide reinforcements to secure it. The initial Marine landing was carried off successfully, but a few days later, the Navy suffered a catastrophic loss in local fighting with Japanese naval forces. This compelled the Navy to withdraw, leaving the Marines on Guadalcanal outnumbered by local Japanese forces and lacking reinforcements and supplies. Sensing that the Marines were vulnerable, the Japanese sent significant reinforcements to Guadalcanal and surrounding waters. The Marines had to dig in, ward off repeated attacks, and withstand continuous air and naval bombardment. Meanwhile, the Navy had to rebuild its depleted forces before re-entering the Solomon Island waters, where it fought repeated engagements with Japanese naval forces. The Marines held on, and the Navy, although initially outnumbered, ultimately prevailed. Months later, U.S. forces finally secured the island and surrounding waters, and completed a campaign that, while successful, bore little resemblance to the original plan.[9]

The 1944 battle of Leyte Gulf was another example. To support the invasion of the Philippines, the Navy sent a huge force of aircraft carriers and battleships that was easily large enough to crush a Japanese naval counterattack. But like all naval battles, the plan depended on the ability to concentrate the right forces at the right time in the right place, and the U.S. Navy campaign plan almost came unhinged. Admiral Halsey initially believed that there would be a Japanese carrier attack from the north and sent his main carriers and fast battleships there. But the attack from the north was a feint; the real attack came from the west, as big Japanese battleships sought to bombard U.S. forces ashore with lethal gunfire. Caught out of position with no big carriers, the local U.S. naval forces (those that not been lured north by the feint)—a motley collection of old battleships, escort carriers, cruisers, destroyers, and torpedo boats never designed to tangle with battleships—had to defend the troops ashore. Somehow, they drove the Japanese ships off. In the nearby Surigao Strait, the U.S. battleships still in the area managed to "cap the T" of the Japanese battleship column, inflicting major losses. Leyte Gulf ended in a big American victory, but only after a close call and speedy improvisation.

Recent expeditionary wars fought by U.S. forces have mostly been scripted exercises in military domination of overpowered enemies, but even here, improvisation has been necessary. Operation *Anaconda* of 2002 in Afghanistan was one example. Initially, U.S. commanders anticipated a minor battle that would be fought mostly by friendly Afghan troops. Light U.S. infantry forces were meant to prevent enemy fighters from escaping the Shahikot Valley, and U.S. air forces would play only modest support roles. But when friendly Afghan troops prematurely retreated and enemy opposition proved stronger than anticipated, U.S. ground troops found themselves in a hornets' nest and were compelled to call upon air attacks to save the day. The air forces had to switch quickly from interdiction to sustained close air support. The battle was ultimately won, but the operation bore little resemblance to the plan, and the necessary adaptations took several days.

Operation *Iraqi Freedom* showed noteworthy examples of tactical improvisation. The invasion of Iraq was originally launched by five and one-third U.S. and British divisions, but when fighting erupted, one U.S. mechanized division—fully one-fifth of the campaign plan's combat power—was still at sea in ships because Turkey would not let it come through from the north. The invasion plan had to be altered quickly to deal with the absence of the ground thrust from the north, which had been intended to accompany the primary invasion from the south. Air power helped make up the difference by pinning down Iraqi forces in the north so they could not move southward. The invasion from the south initially went well. However, after advancing close to Baghdad, the 3ᵈ Mechanized Division was compelled to halt temporarily by a sandstorm, enemy resistance, and lack of supplies. U.S. commanders adapted by using air power to bomb away the Iraqi resistance. They also withdrew a Marine division from its mission in the south and sent it on an advance northward toward Baghdad. In a few days, the Army and Marine divisions entered Baghdad at about the same time. DOD officials acknowledged that such shifts were a normal feature of campaign plans; had U.S. forces lacked this flexibility, the success might have taken much longer to achieve.

Recent experiences in Iraq show that unplanned changes of direction can also take place during the post-combat phase of stabilization and reconstruction. U.S. forces invading Iraq expected some tough challenges in the aftermath, but the type of trouble expected was different from that encountered. U.S. forces expected to find burning oilfields, destroyed bridges, and flows of refugees. None of these, in the event, occurred to any great degree. What did happen was breakdown of law and order, guerrilla attacks, looting and destruction of government services, collapse of electrical power systems, and disruptions in supplies of food and water. U.S. forces thus found themselves struggling to perform operations for which they were not prepared. Observers will debate whether these problems, and solutions to them, could have been fully anticipated by better planning. The point is that the challenges posed by stabilization and reconstruction are often hard to predict, and that regardless of how much planning is done, improvisation and adaptation will frequently be needed.

While the twists and turns of combat operations and occupation duties often cannot be foreseen, campaign plans must nonetheless prepare for them as well as possible. In other words, the campaign plan should not only put forth a script of how U.S. forces will operate if events transpire as desired or deemed most likely, but also provide guidelines on how U.S. force operations can be altered if events unfold differently, and how U.S. forces should be prepared in advance so that they can react as necessary. The goal should be a force posture that can execute not only the basic campaign plan but also diversions and digressions away from the plan. If potential diversions are anticipated and prepared for, the resulting force posture should be ready to handle anything encountered: it would be an adaptable force, capable of providing the flexibility, versatility, and agility necessary. This is, of course, an ideal model whose standards can be hard to meet in actual situations of great uncertainty and constraints on response options. But to the extent that this model can be approximated, it can help provide enhanced confidence and insurance even if basic campaign plans go awry.

One way to develop guidelines on how to plan for adaptability is a standard DOD methodology, the use of branches and sequels. In this technique, branches proliferate from the main campaign plan to show how actions can differ from the main script. Sequels spell out follow-up steps that can be taken if one or another branch is chosen. Each branch portrays a plausible but different situation from that postulated by the main plan: for example, if the enemy defends at location B instead of location A. It defines an appropriate U.S. military response to each such situation, as well as follow-on actions, such as, for example, a three-stage flanking maneuver rather than a linear attack. Together, these branches and sequels provide a system of potential response options that can be pursued in case the main campaign plan must be altered. This system of branches and sequels can be used to gauge the ability of the planned force to respond effectively and, if necessary, to determine what changes to the posture are needed to strengthen its flexibility and its capacity to perform new and different sets of operations. If the resulting posture is capable of performing the operations mandated by this system of branches and sequels, it will, at least in theory, be adequately prepared for a wide range of events.

The methodology of branches and sequels can be enhanced by effects-based analysis that illuminates what each branch and sequel of operations will produce in tangible terms. Operations research can contribute to such an approach. The branches and sequels methodology can draw upon decision analysis (discussed in chapter 18), whose decision trees provide conceptual paths of chance nodes and decision nodes, from which military branches and sequels can be designed and their potential effects measured. The methodology of branches and sequels can be made more formal and rigorous if decision analysis is applied to assist it.

Figure 22–3. Decision Tree Analysis of Campaign Plan Results Based upon Chance Variations

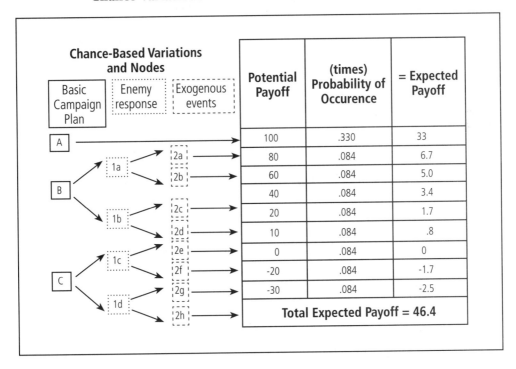

An example illustrates the role that decision analysis can play. Figure 22–3 displays various likely results of a campaign plan assuming no adjustments are made; that is, the plan is stubbornly followed regardless of how events unfold. The decision tree shows how this campaign plan could be affected by damaging twists and turns. The tree has three chance variations, each of which has a probability of occurrence of 33 percent. A is where events unfold as planned. B is where events take a modest turn for the worse. C is where events take a major turn for the worse. Variations B and C have two chance nodes: node 1 is the enemy's response, and node 2 is exogenous events such as weather and luck. For the enemy's response, events worsen for U.S. forces in the progression from 1a to 1d; for exogenous factors, events worsen from 2a to 2h.

The result is a tree with nine possible outcomes, ranging from very good to quite bad for U.S. forces. For each outcome, the tree shows the potential payoff, the probability of occurrence, and the expected payoff, which is the potential payoff multiplied by its probability of occurrence. The tree assumes a maximum payoff of 100 utility points. By recording how this potential payoff declines as a function of variations in enemy responses and exogenous factors, it shows the degree to which the results of this campaign plan can vary as a function of the situation encountered.

The decision tree makes five main contributions to evaluation of this particular campaign plan. First, it shows that although this campaign plan has the potential to score a perfect result (100 points), the likelihood of this result occurring is only 33 percent. Second, it shows how the likely payoff drops if events do not transpire in the manner contemplated by the campaign plan. If things go modestly worse (a 33 percent chance), the payoff drops from 100 points to somewhere between 80 and just 20 points, with an average of 50 points. If events take a major turn for the worse, the payoff plummets further, ranging from just 10 down to -30. Fourth, the figure shows that when the probabilities and payoffs of these chance nodes are summed up, the expected payoff of this campaign plan is only 46.4 points, or considerably less than 100 points. Fifth, the manner in which these 46.4 points are generated is noteworthy. Taking into account probabilities of occurrence, variation A provides an expected payoff of 33 points. Variation B provides a payoff of 16.8 points, and variation C, a loss of 3.4 points. Thus variation C is a ticket to trouble, and variation B, where events take a modest turn for the worse, is of significant concern unless the capacity to deal with it can be improved.

The main implication of this decision tree is that the campaign plan is likely to produce results that are only about one-half as impressive as the optimistic hopes that may have inspired it. Moreover, this campaign entails serious risks: there is about a 25 percent chance that U.S. forces could come away with nothing despite taking casualties, or could even suffer a serious reversal. This prospect compares to only a 33 percent chance of a total success. Such odds might not be worthwhile, especially when the dominant likelihood is that of a middling result. Conservative military planners might simply throw this plan into the trash. At a minimum, commanders and policymakers would have to make tough decisions about how much risk to take. If a military operation must be launched, the natural response would be to search for ways to strengthen this campaign plan's ability to react to unpleasant events.

The methodology of branches and sequels suggests approaches to salvaging this campaign plan by providing operational responses if events take a turn for the worse. Decision tree analysis offers a technique for quantifying how the payoffs could change as a function of operational choices if branches and sequels are built into the plan in ways producing an adaptable posture. Branches provide a capacity to alter battle plans quickly and effectively in order to react to new threats or opportunities, such as by altering how forces are committed and employed, or by using their weapons differently than originally planned. Sequels provide a capacity to follow initial successes with additional actions that magnify the positive effects, or that handle residual problems. Table 22–1 illustrates how adding branches and sequels can transform prospects. The prospects for a stellar performance if events go well have not been improved, but prospects if events go poorly have been elevated considerably, and the risks reduced. Overall prospects have been elevated from a middling performance of 46.4 points to a quite good performance of 73 points, without diminishing a 33 percent chance of a major (100 percent) success. The effect of reacting wisely to the battlefield options created by branches and sequels is to elevate this campaign plan to the status of a viable proposition.

Table 22–1. **Impact of Branches and Sequels**

Chance Variations	Expected Payoffs	
	Campaign Plan Without Branches and Sequels	Campaign Plan With Branches and Sequels
A	33.0	33.0
B	16.8	25.0
C	- 3.4	15.0
Total Expected Payoff	**46.4**	**73.0**

An interesting issue is whether the benefits provided by these branches and sequels is worth the cost of acquiring them. Such doubtless would be the case if the only cost is building a broader set of operational responses into the campaign plan while employing the same forces. But what if these branches and sequels can be acquired only by increasing the forces committed to the campaign plan by 20 percent, or by 50 percent? Perhaps a 20 percent increase would be judged a price worth paying, but a 50 percent increase might be judged unacceptable. Either judgment would have to be made by the commanders or civilian policymakers responsible for mounting the campaign.

This example illustrates how decision analysis, with its trees and numbers, can help crystallize the issues and options involving the development of flexibility and adaptability in campaign plans. This methodology helps formalize the thought process and attaches specific performance numbers to the options being addressed. One of its main impacts is to shed light on unanticipated situations, especially risks that might otherwise be neglected. It might show how a campaign plan might have to be radically changed rather than merely adjusted at the margins. Another impact is to underscore the importance of pursuing joint operations with a diverse set of military forces as the foundation of campaign plans, because diverse assets are more likely to provide a capacity to shift gears on short notice. Finally, decision analysis helps call attention to the value of being prepared for situations that might require bigger forces than otherwise would be committed to a campaign plan. In the future, the need for flexibility and adaptability, rather than the primary scripts laid down by the campaign plans themselves, may be a primary reason for committing large forces to campaign plans. If so, decision analysis can help provide analytical tools for making judgments about how many forces to commit to provide campaign plans with added insurance and increased confidence levels.

Similar to other operations research methods that address major combat issues, decision analysis requires numbers that are generated by judgment and experience rather than by mathematical logic or laboratory experiments. It does not necessarily provide the literal truth; the main issue is whether it helps get senior officials close enough to the truth to make wise decisions. If used sensibly, it has the potential to do so. Decision analysis with branches and sequels is not a stand-alone tool for campaign plans. It must be combined with effects-based planning and other standard methods. The combination can be powerful aids to designing campaign plans that have a central theme yet are flexible enough to overcome the risks of single-minded rigidity. These are especially useful tools when campaign plans face uncertainties about the situation, probabilities, performance, and risks. They are tools worth knowing, not because they make hard choices easy, but because they help make them possible.

The bottom line is that preparing for expeditionary wars is a demanding art and science because each war is unique. Concerted analysis is necessary if the proper preparations are to be made. The need for analysis applies to determining how to deploy U.S. forces, how to write campaign plans to guide their operations, and how to configure campaign plans with branches and sequels to provide adaptability. Effects-based analysis can contribute importantly to this endeavor. Operations research can help make effects-based planning better. Its methods of mobility modeling, battlefield computer simulations, and decision analysis can shed light on the difficult choices that must be made. But these methods must change with the times so that they can address current issues.

A larger point is that, while effects-based planning is a good idea, it is not necessarily a cure-all to the problems of preparing wisely and thoroughly for expeditionary wars. The conflicts in Afghanistan and Iraq show that these wars are typically messy and difficult, if not on the battlefield, then in the politics that precede them and follow them. Waging them requires great skill not only in modern doctrine, but also in the political uses of military power. For all its appeal, effects-based planning is nothing more than words on paper unless it is accompanied by expert analysis of exactly how military actions can be orchestrated to achieve their desired political and strategic consequences. Operations research can help provide concreteness and specificity, but it will be blind unless it is also accompanied by skillful strategic evaluation and systems analysis. Planning for expeditionary wars is truly an arena for multidisciplinary analysis, old-fashioned insight, and good judgment.

Notes

[1] Paul K. Davis, *Effects-Based Operations: A Grand Challenge for the Analytical Community* (Santa Monica, CA: RAND, 2001).

[2] Operations plans are typically the plans that provide for the time-phased deployment of joint forces overseas to a crisis location. They determine how, when, and in what sequence forces are to arrive in ways that meet the

commander's objectives. Campaign plans are those that determine how the forces are to be employed on the battlefield from the start of a war to the finish, and even afterward. For analysis of methodology, see Bruce Pirnie and Sam B. Gardiner, *An Objectives-Based Approach to Military Campaign Analysis* (Santa Monica, CA: RAND, 1996).

[3] See Davis; Edward Smith, *Effects-Based Operations: Applying Network Centric Warfare in Peace, Crisis, and War* (Washington, DC: Department of Defense, C⁴ISR Cooperative Research Program, 2002).

[4] See Wesley Clark, *Waging Modern War: Bosnia, Kosovo, and the Future of Combat* (New York: Public Affairs, 2001).

[5] For a discussion of mobility analysis, see David Kassing, "Strategic Mobility in the Post–Cold War Era," in Paul Davis, ed., *New Challenges for Defense Planning: Rethinking How Much Is Enough* (Santa Monica, CA: RAND, 1994), chapter 21.

[6] Of DOD's recent mobility studies, the two most widely known are the 1992 *Mobility Requirements Study* and the 1994 *Mobility Requirements Study*: Bottom-Up Review Update. See William Perry, *Annual Report to the President and Congress* (Washington, DC: Department of Defense, 1996).

[7] See Davis; Merrick E. Krause, "Decision Dominance: Exploiting Transformational Asymmetries," *Defense Horizons* 23 (Washington, DC: Center for Technology and National Security Policy, National Defense University, February, 2003).

[8] See David Eisenhower, *Eisenhower at War, 1943–1945* (New York: Random House, 1986).

[9] See John Costello, *The Pacific War 1941–1945* (New York: Quill, 1982).

Chapter 23

Forging Investment Strategies

Forging defense investment strategies for buying new weapons and other assets is a major arena for systems analysis and its economic models of choice. Operations research has an important role to play too; it often provides the technical data on costs and effectiveness that systems analysis needs to operate its models. Because of its focus on details, operations research can penetrate into the nooks and crannies of how weapons and programs perform in ways that systems analysis cannot. This chapter examines the important role of operations research and its mathematical techniques in analyzing investment strategy.

A Set of Methods

Several operations research methods can play helpful roles in this arena. This chapter sets the stage first by discussing cost analysis, the technical process by which operations research helps forecast costs of future weapons systems and programs. Then it shows how operations research methods can contribute to cost-effectiveness analysis of three key issues in determining investment strategy for conventional forces, by using combat models to analyze the need for joint improvements to air and ground forces for expeditionary warfare; linear programming to evaluate how best to craft procurement programs comprising multiple combat aircraft; and decision analysis to assess RDT&E strategies for developing new ground combat vehicles.

The chapter discusses some current investment issues, but the data, calculations, and conclusions are meant to be illustrative, not definitive. This chapter's aim is to identify the roles of operations research methods and to suggest broad directions for future investment strategies, not to offer recommendations about specific weapons or programs. It outlines a sizable set of thought-tools for assisting policymakers as they chart the course of future defense investments in force structuring, procurement, and research and development. If these tools are used properly, they can help bring intellectual order even to investment decisions of great complexity, and they can be a partner of systems analysis.

Cost Analysis: Forecasting Amidst a Thicket of Details

While cost analysis does not normally attract the attention of outside observers, insiders who participate in investment planning know its importance. Decisions about new weapons and programs are influenced by estimates of effectiveness, but also by forecasts of costs. Cost estimates can be make-or-break decisions about many weapons that otherwise pass muster on the basis of effectiveness. Cost analysis does not spring from a hard science of fixed procedures, and it may lack the firm data necessary to make airtight forecasts.

Partly for this reason, cost estimates often have attracted controversy and criticism. Recent decades have seen cases of new weapons that were chosen on the basis of fairly low costs but that, when they came rolling off the production lines years later, turned out to be much more expensive. Critics may charge that the original underestimate was deliberate, as part of a sales job, but more often, honest mistakes were made and costs were driven upward by unanticipated dynamics. Today, virtually all participants agree that costs must not be deliberately understated, but even with truthfulness, real-world events often reinforce the skeptical refrain, "Let the buyer beware." Use of good methods for cost analysis, however, can greatly reduce the vulnerability to error.

Accurate cost analysis of investments will be especially important in the years ahead when DOD's budgets for RDT&E and procurement are soaring because multiple acquisition programs are under way at the same time. Many of the current ambitious acquisition programs—in air forces, naval forces, ground forces, missile defense forces, C⁴ISR systems, space assets, and other areas—are pushing the technological state of the art toward new frontiers. The challenge is determining how to afford all of these programs as they come to fruition. Although DOD's procurement budgets are slated to grow to $100 billion–$120 billion annually by about 2011, the procurement programs under way by then will consume all of these funds and perhaps more. Accurate cost analyses are needed to guide the process by which multi-year expenditures stay within available budgets. If cost analyses overestimate costs, they could result in too few weapons being ordered, but if they underestimate, they could force cancellations and stretch-outs. These would damage the procurement effort and further magnify costs by necessitating inefficient production runs. The viability of DOD's accelerating procurement efforts will depend upon accurate forecasts of the costs of its many components.

To help avoid major mistakes, the Office of Secretary of Defense, the services, and other organizations operate full-time staffs that perform cost analysis. It is a big business, because cost estimates play a major role in shaping decisions about not only individual weapons systems, but also how entire acquisition budgets are put together. Cost analysis requires considerable expertise, and it cannot be done hurriedly. Crude estimates can be misleading and wide of the mark, underestimating costs or producing deceptive comparisons of candidate weapons. Yet precise accuracy is often hard to achieve because future costs can be difficult to predict. Accurately forecasting costs requires analytical skill of a sort that operations research can help provide.[1]

Fortunately, computer models can help generate cost forecasts. DOD employs them, as do Congressional staffs and think-tanks such as RAND. But like all computer models, they are only as good as the assumptions and data that go into them. When the need for a forecast of costs for a new weapons system or program arises, mechanically cranking up one of these models will not be enough. The better approach is first to craft a conceptual understanding of the issue and its particular dimensions, and then to configure the relevant computer program or mathematical model to produce the appropriate calculations. In the business of cost analysis, thinking should come first, and number-crunching afterward.

A simple example will illustrate why accurate forecasting of costs is often difficult. Suppose a homeowner wants to build a new house of 2,000 square feet. Because a standard house might be estimated to cost $150 per square foot, the homeowner projects a total expense of $300,000 for construction. But this square-foot estimate is based on a rule of thumb for an average new home; it does not take into account unanticipated increases in costs of the land, building materials and upgrades, the design features of the house, the amount of labor needed to construct it, and applicable codes. Departures from the norm may arise during the construction process and elevate costs upward, step by step. When the project is finished, the total bill could be, say, $350,000. The homeowner may complain of being fleeced by the contractor, but in this example the $50,000 overrun stems from real-life inflators that occurred during construction, not unfair profit-taking. The homeowner's real problem arose not with the final bill, but with his initial forecast, which underestimated the costs per square foot. The homeowner with a budget of $300,000 needed better information so he could order a house that cost only that much, either by limiting the size or by cutting back on features.

Forecasting costs for new weapons systems is vastly more complicated and imprecise than gauging costs for a new home. A key reason is that entirely new technologies are being developed that often push well beyond the existing state of the art. Another reason is that the cost per weapon will depend upon not only the hardware, but also the total number of weapons procured, the rate at which they are procured, and technological improvements both before production and afterward. A program to buy 500 new fighter aircraft might be forecast to cost anywhere between $50 billion and $75 billion at the time that the initial estimate is prepared. Uncertainties of this sort are often inevitable. But they still present difficulties for DOD officials, Congress, and the industries that are charged with building weapons that meet original cost standards.

The need to reduce uncertainty and avoid egregious errors is the special province of cost analysis. Experience shows that three factors can help produce reliable estimates. First, cost estimates should be comprehensive: they should include the full set of expenses that matter in the calculus of whether a weapon or program is to be acquired. Focusing solely on procurement, while ignoring costs for RDT&E and operations, might simplify the cost analysis, but it presents only a partial picture of the truth. Second, cost estimates should be thorough: they should not be based on crude algorithms or rules of thumb. They must be based on exhaustive, in-depth studies anchored in painstaking attention to the unique details of the weapon or program being appraised. Third, cost estimates should be comparable: they should use the same categories for tabulating costs when candidate weapons are competing against each other. If two weapons are being compared, both estimates should include costs for RDT&E and procurement, rather than only procurement costs for one weapon but both types of costs for the other. Because of its focus on details and its rigorous logic, operations research can help produce cost estimates that meet all three standards.

In the logic of operations research, cost analysis begins with a clear and consistent choice about the type of dollars; there is a big difference between constant dollars and current dollars in costing multi-year programs. Constant dollars measure future expenses in the value of today's dollar. They do not include tomorrow's inflation, which is factored into current dollar projections. An aircraft that costs $50 million today will cost the same 10 years from now in constant dollars, but its sticker price might be $65 million or more in "then-year" or current dollars, owing to inflation. As a general rule, constant dollars are a more reliable tool for forecasting because inflation is an unpredictable variable, not a constant. Constant dollars also remedy the problem of making long-range programs appear as if their costs are soaring sky-high when in fact the culprit is inflation, not a rise in real costs. Regardless of which type of calculation is employed, when two weapons are being compared, their cost estimates must employ the same dollar metric. Otherwise, one will appear more costly than the other even if their real expenses are equal.

Second, cost estimates must cover all of the expenses likely to be generated by a new weapon over its life cycle. Typically, costs of new weapons come from four elements: RDT&E, procurement, mid-life upgrades, and operations. Sometimes, estimates of investment spending include only RDT&E and procurement; the costs of mid-life upgrades and operations are often overlooked. Excluding them, however, can result in underestimates of costs, and it also can have a distorting effect on comparisons of candidate weapons. An example in table 23–1 illustrates why total life-cycle cost often is the best standard for comparison. Competing for procurement are aircraft A, a low-tech fighter, and aircraft B, a high-tech fighter. Aircraft A's procurement cost is $60 million per copy, considerably less that aircraft B's cost of $80 million per copy. If only initial investment costs (RDT&E and procurement) are considered, an aircraft A program of 500 fighters will be less expensive than the same number of aircraft B by a big margin: $40 billion versus $55 billion. But if mid-life upgrades and operating expenses for 15 years are considered, the two programs may cost the same because aircraft A has higher costs in these realms. Indeed, if operations over 25 years are considered—a typical lifespan of a modern fighter—aircraft B will cost less, at $98 billion, compared to $105 billion for aircraft A.

RDT&E costs are notoriously difficult to forecast accurately because the process is in a continual state of flux. As a new weapon passes through the RDT&E cycle, it moves

Table 23–1. **Illustrative Comparison of Life-Cycle Costs for New Fighter Aircraft ($, Constant)**

	Aircraft A (500 at $60 million each)	Aircraft B (500 at $80 million each)
RDT&E	$10 billion	$15 billion
Procurement	$30 billion	$40 billion
Initial Investment Costs	$40 billion	$55 billion
Operations (15 years)	$30 billion	$20 billion
Mid-Life Upgrades	$15 billion	$10 billion
15-Year Life-Cycle Costs	$85 billion	$85 billion
25-Year Life-Cycle Costs*	$105 billion	$98 billion

*Costs in years 16–25 presumed to be $2 billion/year for A, $1.3 billion/year for B.

from basic research to concept development, prototyping, and then to system development. Typically about 70 percent of the costs occur during prototyping and system development. These two stages often take years to complete and can be subject to prolonged delays if progress does not unfold smoothly. The effect of delays can be to elevate costs. The biggest delayer and cost escalator is often the tendency to revise the original design standard by adding new requirements and capabilities as the weapon is evolving. For major, high-tech weapons systems, RDT&E costs often comprise 20 to 33 percent of the total expense. Moreover, RDT&E does not stop once a weapon is being procured: for example, RDT&E for product improvements on the F–15 was still taking place 25 years after the first model entered service. The implication is that if cost estimates are to be accurate, they cannot rest upon initial design standards, but instead should take into account the potential elevation of these standards during RDT&E (even though this is very hard to predict). Cost estimates should, ideally, also take into account the possibility of RDT&E savings along the way. For example, when foreign countries agree to buy new U.S.-made weapons, they typically agree to pay a pro rata share of the RDT&E expense. If they buy these weapons in large numbers, this could cut U.S. RDT&E costs by perhaps one-half, but this offsetting money becomes available long after DOD has funded the original RDT&E expense. In any event, it is a variable in the cost equation, not a constant, and very hard to estimate; however, this does not reduce the importance of making it as accurate as possible.

Procurement costs include the costs not only for the weapon, but also for initial spares, testing equipment, and contractor maintenance. It might seem that procurement costs should be a fixed constant in the calculus: if the first aircraft coming off the assembly line costs $100 million, the last aircraft should cost the same. The reality is different. When many weapons are being produced, procurement costs typically fluctuate a great deal from start to finish of a program. Normally, per-unit procurement costs decline as production picks up. One reason is that start-up costs, such as buying equipment and creating assembly lines, must be paid before production can begin. As the size of the procurement program grows, these costs are amortized across more and more weapons, reducing the cost of each. Another reason for reduced per-unit costs is that, as production unfolds, the industry building the weapon benefits from economies of scale and a learning curve. The result is efficiency gains during assembly, which can gradually reduce per-unit costs by as much as one-third to one-half over the course of years.

By contrast, a decision to accelerate annual production rates can elevate per-unit costs if it results in the expense of opening additional assembly lines. Cost inflation also can occur, as initial models are replaced by improved models with expensive new components during a procurement cycle that can last many years. When the time arrives for major mid-life upgrades, per-unit costs can rise further. Because all of these price deflators and inflators are variables, there is no simple rule of thumb for predicting whether per-unit procurement costs will rise, shrink, or stay flat over a period of years. Cost analysis must consider each weapon on a case-by-case basis.

When should annual operating costs be included in a cost analysis? The argument against including them is that they are downstream costs that normally do not figure into the equation of whether a weapon should be acquired and in what quantities.

Moreover, some operating costs will be incurred regardless of whether the particular weapon is procured or not. If it is not procured, either a different new weapon will be acquired, or existing weapons will be kept in service, resulting in little difference in the total expense for operations. Yet there are situations in which inclusion of operating costs makes sense. This can be the case if operating costs dominate acquisition costs: not true for aircraft and ships, but often true for ground weapons. Inclusion of operating costs also makes sense when competing weapons have sufficient differences in this arena to affect decisions on which weapons to buy. When operating costs are to be included, they must be studied carefully. New weapons vary considerably in their operating costs. For example, some weapons cost a great deal more to repair and maintain than others.

Sunk costs may sometimes be included in an analysis. These are expenses that have already been paid at the time that a forecast is being prepared. For example, many RDT&E expenses may largely have been paid by the time procurement decisions approach and cost analysis shifts into high gear. Exclusion of sunk costs would have the effect of making a program seem less expensive in the aggregate than actually is the case, and creating such appearances does not square with the truthfulness imperative. Even so, there can be a good reason for excluding sunk costs. Because they already have been paid, they will not be a future drain on scarce discretionary funds, and they thus do not matter in the decisions that lie ahead.

Excluding sunk costs on the premise that only the future matters can help policy-makers resist the temptation to throw good money after bad, or to fund questionable programs just because they have already gobbled up a lot of money. Yet exclusion of sunk costs may skew the results when weapons are being compared as candidates for procurement. This can be the case, for example, if weapon A has already completed most of its RDT&E, while weapon B is earlier in the RDT&E process. In this event, weapon A gets a leg up in the competition that it does not deserve. Perhaps future budgetary considerations make such an award a desirable choice. But perhaps weapon A encountered steep cost rises during the RDT&E process, which may foretell similar increases during the procurement process. In this event, consideration of sunk costs could alert senior officials to lingering disadvantages of weapon A, although they must still be alert to the potential shortcomings of weapon B, which has yet to be tested by development. The bottom line is that while sunk costs often should be ignored, sometimes they should be taken into account, and this choice must be made thoughtfully, on a case-by-case basis.

Another issue that can merit consideration is cost streams. When a weapon is being developed and procured, the entire process often takes so many years that the time dimension can become a factor in the decision equation. Analysis of cost streams helps focus attention on the time dimension by charting the annual flow of costs on a year-by-year basis over the relevant period. The positive effects can be enhanced by comparing cost streams to benefit streams in order to determine how the ratio of costs and benefits stacks up on a yearly basis. The results can be illuminating, and they can affect how competing weapons are judged in relation to each other.

Take the earlier example of aircraft A and fighter B, whose programs for 500 aircraft yielded identical 15-year costs of $85 billion apiece. These two fighter programs have different cost streams. Whereas aircraft A costs less than aircraft B in the short term ($40 billion versus $55 billion), after these initial costs, A costs more in later years ($45 billion versus $30 billion). This big difference in cost streams could make aircraft A more attractive if near-term budgets are tight but long-term budgets will be bigger and more flexible. Benefit streams enter the equation in similar ways: if aircraft A is a low-tech aircraft, it might show off its operational strengths in the near term but fade in the long term as new threats appear, whereas weapon B's particular strengths may be less important in the near term but might become critical in the long term against major new threats.

The interaction of these differing cost and benefit streams can shed a different light on the tradeoffs at stake. As table 23–2 shows, aircraft A has a distinct edge over aircraft B in the near term because it costs less and performs nearly as well, so it has a higher "benefit-to-cost ratio" (B:C ratio), based on utility scores and life-cycle costs over 15 years. In the later term, however, aircraft B has the distinct edge: it costs less and performs substantially better, so it has a higher B:C ratio.

Table 23–2. **Comparing Cost Streams and Benefit Streams**

	Aircraft A	Aircraft B
Near-Term (first years)		
Costs (C)	$40 billion	$55 billion
Benefits (B)	675 utility points	750 utility points
B:C Ratio	16.9:1	13.6:1
Long-Term (later years)		
Costs	$45 billion	$30 billion
Benefits	525 utility points	675 utility points
B:C Ratio	11.7:1	22.5:1
Total Life-Cycle (near-term plus long-term, 15 years)		
Costs	$85 billion	$85 billion
Benefits	1,200 utility points	1,425 utility points
B:C Ratio	14.1:1	16.8:1

When the near-term and long-term factors (out to 15 years) are combined, aircraft B seems to be the better overall choice because, while it costs the same as aircraft A ($85 billion apiece), it yields a higher B:C ratio because of its edge in utility points (1,425 versus 1,200). However, this life-cycle appraisal is based on the assumption that the long term counts as much as the near term. It might not. If senior officials value near-term needs higher, are more fearful of near-term threats, or simply are not confident about long-term projections, they may favor aircraft A over aircraft B. Although aircraft A does not perform as well as aircraft B in the near term, it performs adequately, and its lower costs during this period allow for investments in other priorities. Higher costs might have to be paid in the long term ($45 billion or more), but to senior officials, the distant future may seem too hazy to worry about now. By then, new strategic conditions might emerge or new technologies might appear that render today's long-term forecasts irrelevant.

Such differences in attitudes toward cost streams and benefit streams over the course of time give rise to the issue of whether and to what degree the future should be given less weight than the present. In order to help address this thorny issue, the technique of discounting the future is sometimes employed in cost analysis and cost-benefit analysis. The premise is that, from today's standpoint, the present matters more than the future, or at least can be seen more clearly and predicted more accurately, so although the future should not be entirely ignored, it should be given less importance in the decision calculus than the present.[2]

Discounting performs this task by applying a discount rate to depreciate the future, normally 3 percent to 7 percent annually. Because the discount is compounded each year, the impact can be substantial. It can make the costs and benefits of year 7 appear to be only 60 to 80 percent as important as year 1, and year 15 only 35 to 65 percent as important. The effect can be to alter how weapons with different cost streams and benefit streams compare to each other. In the example cited above, this would diminish the value of aircraft B's edge in the long term, strengthening the case for aircraft A. Discounting should be employed when it could alter how two competing weapons are judged. A useful approach is to determine the discount rate at which the cost-benefit advantage swings from one weapon to another, and then to judge whether that rate is a sensible expression of the issues at hand.

Cost analysis is important not only for estimating future costs of weapons systems, but also for gauging the potential for costs to spiral upward, and identifying options to moderate this. It also is important for evaluating candidate weapons systems in comparative terms. Cost analysis is not easy, because a thicket of details must be considered and multiple calculations made. Operations research provides many of the techniques for making these calculations. Computer programs, properly configured, can make these calculations easier to accomplish, but they are not needed to gauge costs in roughly accurate ways. What matters is knowledge of the key variables and sensitivities, and access to basic cost data. With a little thinking, back-of-the-envelope models can be used to forecast costs in approximate but useful ways. The usefulness of such simple models means that cost analysis does not have to be an arcane exercise or a province left to specialists.

Charting Force Improvements for Expeditionary War: Combat Modeling

A big challenge facing U.S. defense plans is determining how best to strengthen air and ground combat forces for future expeditionary wars to quell threats. Some observers claim that U.S. forces are already so superior to opponents that further improvements are not needed. Others call for improvements, but urge that they be directed to air forces, leaving ground forces more or less as they are. Still others argue that strengthening ground forces is the greatest need, because air forces already enjoy supremacy. Often lost in the clamor is the argument for a joint approach that is aimed at making balanced improvements to both air and ground forces. Operations research can shed light on this contentious issue, without a high-tech computer model incorporating 50 complex mathematical equations. A simple, back-of-the-envelope combat model can crystallize the issues and tradeoffs, pointing toward broad answers that are approximately correct.

An example will help illuminate how such a combat model can be employed for this purpose. Postulate a combat situation in which 2 1/2 U.S. fighter wings, a heavy ground division, or some combination of these are assigned the mission of destroying 5 enemy divisions with 4,000 armored vehicles. The goal is to accomplish this mission as quickly as possible. Postulate also that currently both the air component and the ground component have similar life-cycle costs and that each, if operating on its own, is capable of destroying an average of 200 enemy armored vehicles per day in favorable conditions. This reasonably presumes about two kills per aircraft sortie available for this mission, and initially a 5 percent daily attrition rate inflicted by the ground division. Postulate also that if the fighter wings and the ground division are used together in a joint operation, the lethality of each component rises by 50 percent, to 300 targets destroyed per day. The reason is that the presence of ground forces enables air forces to attack enemy targets that are caught exposed in more vulnerable positions, and the presence of air forces has the same advantageous effect on ground force lethality. Using these data inputs, a simple combat model generates the results shown in table 23–3, under both favorable and unfavorable conditions in which lethality rates for each component are reduced by one-third. The table compares results from three different campaigns: air-only, ground-only, and a joint campaign of air and ground forces operating together.

Table 23–3. **Impact of Joint Operations on Performance by Current U.S. Forces**

	Days to Destroy 4,000 Enemy Armored Vehicles	
Current Capability	**Favorable Conditions**	**Unfavorable Conditions (lethality rates reduced by one-third)**
Air campaign only	20	30
Ground campaign only	20	30
Joint campaign	7	10

The table suggests that U.S. forces should be able to carry out this campaign successfully within 30 days regardless of the conditions or the nature of the campaign. The table also shows that there is a big difference between favorable and unfavorable conditions: the latter require campaigns that last 50 percent longer than the former (because the lethality rate is one-third lower). The chart also shows that this goal can be accomplished by either air forces or ground forces operating alone. Most important, however, the chart shows that when joint campaigns are possible, they offer major advantages because the lethality of both components is increased. Compared to single-component campaigns by either air or ground forces, they can produce victory in 7 to 10 days, as compared to 20 to 30 days if only one or only the other component is used. In the case of joint operations, success would have required a longer period of 10 to 15 days if the interactive effects of air and ground operations did not have mutually beneficial results. In addition to shortening the campaign, joint operations are likely to reduce U.S. casualties because, in destroying enemy forces at a faster rate, they give the enemy less time to fire at U.S. forces. This conclusion may seem obvious, but it often is missed in debates over whether one component or the other can win on its own. Joint campaigns are normally best because they more than double U.S. combat power and therefore produce victory faster at smaller losses.

Could the same results be achieved by doubling the air force while eliminating the ground force, or by doubling the ground force while eliminating the air force? Assuming the table's postulates are true, the answer is no. Whereas doubling the air forces or the ground force would increase lethality to 400 targets per day for each component, joint operations produce a lethality of 600 targets per day. The presence of U.S. ground forces compels the enemy to mass, thereby exposing it to U.S. air strikes. These air strikes, in turn, disrupt the enemy's ability to mount an organized defense, thereby making enemy armored vehicles more vulnerable to U.S. ground fires. Equally important, the table assumes that unfavorable conditions lessen lethality of both components by equal amounts. In reality, however, such conditions might affect only one component. For example, bad weather might damage air operations but not ground operations, or rugged terrain might degrade ground operations but not air operations. In many cases, joint force operations will provide insurance against unfavorable conditions by enabling at least one component to operate with full effectiveness. The key question is whether these postulates are accurate. While some observers might raise questions about the precise numbers used in table 23–3, the basic premise that air and ground operations have a synergistic impact on each other seems logical and squares with U.S. military doctrine.

If joint operations make sense with current forces, what are the implications for investment strategy? Should force improvements focus on upgrading just one component or both? These questions can be answered by using another back-of-the-envelope model. Postulate that $15 billion is available for force improvements. These funds could be spent entirely on air improvements (option 1) or ground improvements (option 2), or they could be divided equally among the two components (option 3). Suppose that if these funds were spent entirely on one component, they would enhance its lethality by 50 percent. If they were divided between the two components, they could enhance the lethality of each by 33 percent—not just 25 percent—because each component benefits from high returns to scale. As a result, total gain is 66 percent when both components are added together. Table 23–4 shows the implications. The metric of total days provides a summary portrayal of how the investment options perform if all three types of campaigns are fought sequentially.

The table shows that all three investment options promise to enhance U.S. combat capabilities significantly and would thereby speed victory in war. The table also shows that the joint investment option is the best overall performer because it upgrades the capabilities

Table 23–4. **Impact of Alternative Investment Strategies**

Current Capability:	Days to Destroy 4,000 Enemy Armored Vehicles	
	Favorable Conditions	Unfavorable Conditions
Total Days, 3 Campaigns	47	67
Option 1. Enhanced Air Capability		
Air campaign only	13.3	20
Ground campaign only	20	30
Joint campaign	6	9
Total days	39.3	59
Option 2. Enhanced Ground Capability		
Air campaign only	20	30
Ground campaign only	13.3	20
Joint campaign	6	9
Total days	39.3	59
Option 3. Enhanced Joint Capability		
Air campaign only	15	22.5
Ground campaign only	15	22.5
Joint campaign	5.6	8.4
Total days	35.6	53.4

of both air and ground forces. Under favorable conditions, option 3 produces a result of only 35.6 days for 3 campaigns, which is better than the 39.3 days for options 1 and 2. A similar pattern prevails for unfavorable conditions. Obviously these results are sensitive to input assumptions, but these assumptions seem logical when stock is taken of the advantages of investing in two components rather than only one. If anything, this table may underestimate the advantages of a joint investment strategy. Clearly an air investment strategy makes sense if the goal is solely to become better prepared for campaigns waged by air forces alone. Likewise, a ground investment strategy makes sense if the goal solely is to become better prepared for ground campaigns. But if the goal is to become better prepared for the wide spectrum of campaigns that might have to be fought, the joint investment strategy is the best choice. This is the case not only because such a strategy does the best job of inflicting attrition on enemy forces in a wide variety of situations, but also because it best enhances the flexibility and adaptability of U.S. forces and gains maximum mileage from investment dollars. An improved joint force would be better able to shift directions, adapt, and operate under varying conditions than a posture in which one component is improved, but not the other. Now that flexibility and adaptability are hallmarks of the new U.S. defense strategy, a joint investment strategy is the best way to achieve it.

As seen through the lenses of operations research, the enduring need for joint operations, flexibility, and adaptability casts a bright spotlight on another key issue that will help shape the future U.S. military. The issue is how best to strike a proper balance between air-delivered standoff fires and close-combat direct fires in preparing for ground combat. During the Cold War, the prevailing paradigm emphasized modest reliance upon standoff fires and major reliance upon direct fires in order to defeat well-armed opponents. The primary reason was that standoff fires could not be counted upon to destroy large numbers of enemy ground formations. As a result, emphasis had to be placed on close-combat direct fires by tanks, armored vehicles, and the like. As a consequence of new technologies and transformation, this old paradigm properly is now giving way to a new paradigm that assigns a growing role to air-delivered standoff fires. At issue is whether, and to what extent, this shift toward standoff fires can be accompanied by a trimming of traditional assets for close combat.

One theory carries this shift to its logical extreme. It would place primary reliance on standoff fires for destroying enemy ground combat forces on the battlefield. This mission would be pursued mainly by fighters and bombers delivering smart munitions, by attack helicopters, and by long-range ground-launched missiles and rockets. U.S. ground forces would therefore be stripped of their main battle tanks, infantry fighting vehicles, and the other armor that today provides most of their offensive punch. Instead, they would be equipped with a combination of light vehicles and C⁴ISR systems with which to keep the enemy at bay during the brief period that standoff strikes are sweeping serious opposition from the battlefield. Sizable ground forces might still be present, but they would be lightly armed, and their main role would be to clean up the detritus after standoff strikes have won the battles.

This theory is certainly visionary, but whether it is wise and whether it provides a sound foundation for future joint operations and the need for battlefield flexibility are other questions. The problem with this theory is the presumption that all future battles will be fought under conditions that enable it to work effectively; it is vulnerable to the fallacy of best-case planning. Unfavorable conditions need to be taken into account as well. The risk is that in such conditions, standoff strikes will fall short of their ideal. Ground combat could then be required not merely to ward off enemy attacks, but to take the fight to the enemy through powerful offensive maneuvers, direct fires, and shock action. Regardless of its C⁴ISR networks, a lightly equipped Army would not be able to carry out such traditional battlefield campaigns. For this reason, a better approach for gaining flexibility and adaptability would be to supplement the growing role of standoff fires by preserving an Army that can wage serious armored warfare.

Doubtless these insights about future joint forces derived from a back-of-the-envelope combat model could be sharpened by a sophisticated computer model with dozens of mathematical equations. But unless some new and different truths are discovered, the main message would not be altered. The reason is that while the simple model used here is short on frills, it gets the basics right, and this is a characteristic of a good model. The underlying point is that operations research has something valuable to contribute to the technical debate over whether and how to improve U.S. conventional forces for expeditionary war. It is not the only methodology that can be employed.

But it has the capacity to ask the right questions, to focus on gritty details, and to produce numerical results that reveal valuable insights about the issues and options at hand. For these reasons, it has a role to play, but only if it addresses the issues of the future, not those of the past.

Procuring New Combat Aircraft: Linear Programming

DOD is initiating a long-term program to upgrade its tactical air forces by buying six new aircraft for the Air Force, Navy, Marine Corps, and Army. Over 5,000 fighters and helicopters will be bought between 2006 and 2022 or later, at a cost of $300 billion or more. An important issue, already hotly debated, seems likely to remain controversial for many years: Assuming a modernization of this size and expense is necessary, what mix of aircraft should be acquired? How many of each type should be purchased? For example, the Air Force wants to buy about 280 F–22s and 2,850 F–35s. Is this the right number for both models, or can a better mix be imagined? The same question can be raised about all six new aircraft. Acquiring the right mix is important to ensure that available funds are used wisely and U.S. combat capabilities are increased optimally.

Decisions about force mix will need to be driven by numerous considerations. Among them are the operational needs of the services, budgetary feasibility, and the production capacities of industries that manufacture the aircraft. Cost-effectiveness analysis should also play an important role. Linear programming is a method that seems tailor-made for generating insights about the proper mix. In order to illuminate how linear programming can contribute, the example to be considered here will begin with a "minimization problem." It aims to determine the force mix that can best perform multiple different missions at a fixed cost. The aircraft types, mission requirements, performance data, and cost figures of this example are hypothetical, but they help illuminate many of the factors at work in today's real-life situations.[3]

In this example, the choice is between two new combat aircraft, A and B, for performing five different ground attack missions: close air support (CAS), battlefield interdiction (BI), deep strike (DS) against industrial targets, stealth strikes (SS) against critical command centers and air defense nodes, and deep-penetrating bombardment (DPB) of buried bunkers. Aircraft A is a high-tech stealth aircraft whose average life-cycle cost is estimated to be $200 million. Aircraft B is a lower-tech aircraft whose life-cycle cost is $160 million. Both carry advanced sensors, avionics, and smart munitions, and each is capable of performing all five missions, but with different degrees of effectiveness. A combatant commander may set performance requirements for each of the missions in terms of targets killed per day. The list is dominated by the first three missions—CAS, BI, and DS—but the other two, SS and DPB, pose significant requirements of their own. The challenge is to identify the least-cost combination of aircraft A and B that will be capable of performing all five missions at the necessary effectiveness. The key parameters are shown in table 23–5. Note that while aircraft A is superior in four of the missions (CAS, BI, DS, and SS), aircraft B is superior in DPB. As a result of their comparative advantages, a mix of them is likely to be the preferred choice over buying only one of them, as shown below.

Table 23–5. **Aircraft Capabilities and Performance Requirements**

Missions	Aircraft Capability (Targets Destroyed per Day)		Performance Requirements (Targets Destroyed per Day)
	Aircraft A	Aircraft B	
Close air support (CAS)	6.0	3.0	1,500
Battlefield interdiction (BI)	4.5	3.5	1,275
Deep strike (DS)	2.5	3.5	1,125
Stealth strikes (SS)	6.0	0.0	180
Deep penetrating bombardment (DPB)	0.0	6.0	240

These data can be used to derive the five constraint equations showing in table 23–6; these determine the combinations of aircraft needed to perform each mission. These equations show that if only A is procured, 450 aircraft will be needed in order to perform its most demanding mission, deep strike. If only B is procured, fully 500 will be needed for its most demanding mission, CAS. But buying 450 or 500 aircraft of a single type seems unnecessary where a mix could share duties emphasizing their comparative advantages. Beyond this, a single-model solution is ruled out because aircraft A cannot perform the DPB mission at all, and aircraft B cannot perform the SS mission. Thus, a mix of the 2 aircraft will clearly be needed, and the mix must include at least 30 of aircraft A and 40 of aircraft B to perform these missions at all. Ideally, the ultimate mix will entail fewer aircraft than prescribed by a single model solution of 450–500 aircraft, and it will cost less than the $80 billion to $90 billion needed for one of these options.

To determine what the optimal mix is, and what its price will be, costs must enter the calculus. Since aircraft A costs $200 million apiece and aircraft B costs $160 million, this yields a 5:4 ratio for costs. This ratio can be used to create the following objective function.

Table 23–6. **Constraint Equations**

Equations (Capability of A plus Capability of B must be equal to or greater than Performance Requirements [targets destroyed per day])		Aircraft Needed of Each Type to Accomplish Mission	
		Aircraft A	Aircraft B
Equation 1 CAS	$6.0A + 3.0B \geq 1,500$	250	500
Equation 2 BI	$4.5A + 3.5B \geq 1,275$	283	364
Equation 3 DS	$2.5A + 3.5B \geq 1,125$	450	321
Equation 4 SS	$6.0A + 0.0B \geq 180$	30	n.a.
Equation 5 DPB	$0.0A + 6.0B \geq 240$	n.a.	40

Then the problem becomes one of minimizing C while satisfying all five constraint inequalities.

Objective Function
Minimize Cost (C) = 5A + 4B

Figure 23–1 sets the stage for solving this problem. Notice that the vertical line drawn for equation 4 marks the limit for the smallest number of aircraft A that must be bought (30). Likewise, the horizontal line for equation 5 marks the smallest number of aircraft B that must be bought (40). Within these outer boundaries, the 5 equations intersect to establish a feasibility range with 3 corner points (which normally provide the optimal solution) that vary in mixes from about 60 of A and 350 of B (where equations 1 and 4 intersect) to about 350 of A and 60 of B (where equations 3 and 5 intersect). Somewhere within this range, along the associated indifference curve, is the optimal mix.

Figure 23–1. **Graphical Display of Constraint Equations: Two Aircraft Performing Multiple Missions**

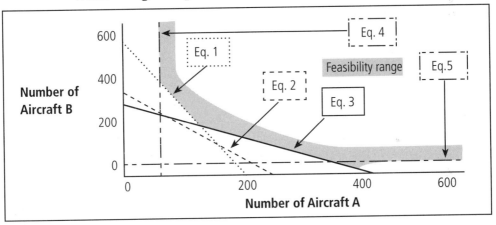

The optimal mix can be found by using the objective function to create a cost-exchange curve that touches one of the corner points, as shown in figure 23–2. The solution point is a mix of about 155 of aircraft A and 220 B of aircraft B, for a total of 375 aircraft. The logic of linear programming says that this posture is optimal because no cheaper effective alternative can be found. This posture would cost only $66.2 billion, considerably less than the $80 billion to $90 billion of the single-aircraft solutions.

A more exact solution could be determined by using the algebraic method called Simplex. But the approximate accuracy of this conclusion can be verified by entering its force mix into the constraint equations in order to determine whether their requirements are met. Only the first three equations need to be checked, because the final two requirements are clearly met. As table 23–7 shows, all three inequalities are satisfied. Thus, a force of 375 fighters composed of 155 aircraft A and 220 aircraft B will be able to perform all 5 ground attack missions at the effectiveness mandated. Of course, other force mixes with more aircraft could provide the same capability. What linear programming has accomplished

Figure 23–2. **Graphical Display of Solution: Optimal Mix of Two Aircraft**

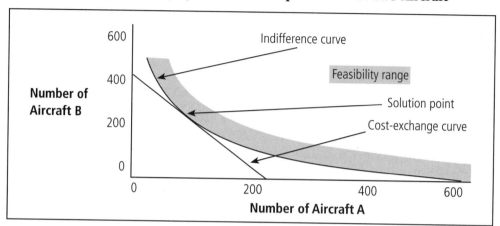

is to display the minimum, least-cost mix needed to get the job done. It has shown how $14 billion to $24 billion can be saved by purchasing an optimal blend of the two aircraft rather than only one or the other.

This optimal solution is the best force mix for performing the five missions at the lowest cost. The next question is whether the U.S. defense industry is physically capable of producing 155 of aircraft A and 220 of aircraft B in the required time. If the procurement effort is spread out over many years, industry would have ample time to add any necessary facilities. But if the production schedule is to begin soon and is to be compressed into a few years, industry must perform with the assets on hand, and this task might be more of a challenge. If industry is unable to produce the desired mix in the allotted time, perhaps it might be able to produce a different mix, but would this different mix be able to perform the missions while also being affordable? Such thorny questions about production capabilities often enter into the process of forging complex procurement programs.

Linear programming can help address such questions through use of a maximization problem. Whereas a minimization problem focuses on identifying an optimal solution at least cost, a maximization problem addresses how existing resources can be brought together in order to attain greatest productivity. In this case, it offers a procedure for gauging whether industry's assembly lines are capable of producing the optimal mix of 155 aircraft A and 220 aircraft B. Normally a maximization problem must be configured with

Table 23–7. **Algebraic Verification of Graphical Solution**

	Equation	=	Performance (number of targets destroyed per day)	Requirement (targets per day, from table 23–5)
Equation 1 CAS	6.0 (155) + 3.0 (220)	=	1,590	1,500
Equation 2 BI	4.5 (155) + 3.5 (220)	=	1,467	1,275
Equation 3 DS	2.5 (155) + 3.5 (220)	=	1,157	1,125

an objective function that defines the desired output. In this case, however, the objective function already exists in the form of the indifference curve identified above (shown in figure 23–2). Therefore, the task at hand is limited to determining whether existing industrial assets are capable of producing force mixes that fall on this indifference curve, preferably at its tangency point with the cost-exchange curve.

Examination of this issue begins by assembling data regarding the stages of the production process, the industrial resources on hand for each stage, and the assets required to produce aircraft A and B. Table 23–8 displays such data. The production process is shown in three sequential stages: manufacturing of subcomponent parts; assembly of subcomponent parts such as the engine and wings; and airframe assembly, in which the subcomponents are brought together to create a finished aircraft. The table shows that industry possesses assets for these three stages in varying degrees, and that each aircraft consumes these assets in varying degrees. At stage 1, for example, aircraft A consumes 0.40 units of industrial resources, and aircraft B consumes 0.60 units. The ability of industry to produce enough aircraft is determined by the interaction between demand and supply.

These data can be used to form three constraint equations that reflect resource consumption during the three stages of production. These three constraint equations can be placed on a graph, as shown in figure 23–3. The intersection of their three lines generates a production possibility curve, which defines the upper limits of industry's capacity to produce both types of aircraft at the same time. Below this curve is a feasibility range (located in the lower-left zone, because it is measuring maximum production capacity, not minimum mission requirements). It indicates that industry is capable of producing all

Table 23–8. **Industrial Assets and Production Requirements**

Production Stages	Production Requirements Per Aircraft (Units)		Total Industrial Resources (Units)	Equations	Maximum Production Capacity	
	Aircraft A	Aircraft B			Aircraft A	Aircraft B
Stage 1: Manufacture of component parts	.40	.60	200	Equation 1 $.40A + .60B \leq 200$	500	333
Stage 2: Assembly of component parts	.43	.37	150	Equation 2 $.43A + .38B \leq 150$	349	395
Stage 3: Airframe assembly	.33	.20	100	Equation 3 $.33A + .20B \leq 100$	303	500

Figure 23–3. **Production Possibility Curve: Industrial Capacity**

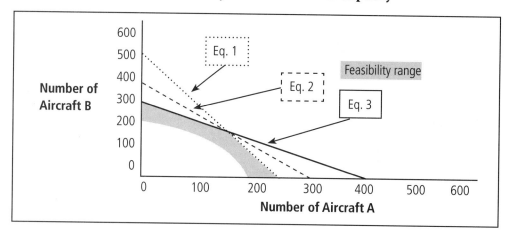

of the force mixes within this zone, but not any of the force mixes that lie outside it and beyond the curve.

Can this industrial capacity, as measured on the production possibility curve, produce the force mix mandated by the optimal solution of 155 aircraft A and 220 aircraft B? This question can be addressed by an additional graph shown as figure 23–4. The graph displays the production possibility curve along with the indifference curve and cost-exchange curve that were generated earlier. It shows that industry can, in fact, produce the required force mix, although there is little capacity to spare, nor is there room for industrial inefficiencies. The figure also makes clear that the single-model solution, 450 of aircraft A or 500 of aircraft B, would have to be ruled out simply because industry is not physically capable of producing it. Industry has the capacity to produce a mix of aircraft A and B mainly because these aircraft are being produced by two different firms, each of which has enough capacity to produce 200 to 250 aircraft on schedule, but neither of which could produce as many as 450 or 500 aircraft. By splitting the workload between these two firms, the mixed solution permits the required number of each aircraft to be produced on schedule.

Sometimes, however, industry is not capable of producing the best combination of weapons systems in the time allotted, and as a result, a less desirable mix must be chosen. This risk is a reason for endeavoring to ensure that sufficient lead-time is available for industry to assemble the physical assets needed to meet the government's requirements. A more basic point is that the defense investment process is more complicated than merely identifying the weapons desired by DOD and then placing orders for them; the physical capacity of industry to deliver on schedule must also be taken into account.

The task of defense planning is to match requirements with production capabilities. Linear programming can find a strong role in this arena. It helps call attention to the advantage of procuring several types of aircraft in order to capitalize on their comparative advantages. While pursuing multiple aircraft elevates RDT&E costs, it can lower life-cycle costs because fewer total aircraft must be bought. Put another way, it can make a smaller

Figure 23–4. **Gauging Industrial Capacity to Meet Production Requirements**

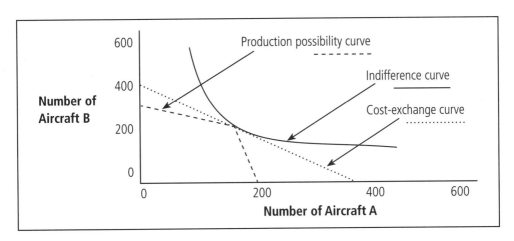

force perform as well as a larger force composed of only one type of aircraft. Even linear programming, however, cannot solve with precision the question of how to strike a sensible balance in procurement of six new combat aircraft. The right mix is highly dependent upon performance data in situations where such data may not be reliable, and where performance itself may be a variable, not a constant. Many additional factors, including the operational needs and budgetary priorities of the military services, must be taken into account. Even so, linear programming can be a useful conceptual tool for analyzing such procurement issues. Its main strength is that it can synthesize many different factors into a coherent whole, stretching the analyst's cognitive capacities and thus aiding judgment.

Developing New Ground Combat Vehicles: Decision Analysis

Whereas the Air Force and Navy face the challenge of shaping expensive procurement programs, their RDT&E efforts are mostly well along in the process toward fielding weapons systems. By contrast, the Army faces the more fundamental challenge of creating a viable RDT&E vision based on entirely new weapons systems. While they are still on the drawing boards, the Army hopes that they can be purchased in the foreseeable future and that they will operate effectively once fielded. Noting that the Army is trailing the Air Force and Navy in this arena, critics fear that it is on the wrong track with its ambitious and revolutionary RDT&E strategy. Their allegation is that the Army's Future Combat System (FCS) strategy, which is trying to create lightweight armored vehicles embedded in ultra-sophisticated C⁴ISR networks, will not only take too long to bear fruit, but also may fail to bear fruit at all.

Perhaps these critics overstate the dangers, but even so, the ambitious reach of the Army's FCS strategy is a legitimate concern. It is visionary, but it could also be a risky strategy with timelines and prospects that are genuinely uncertain. If the Army's FCS strategy were to be set aside, however, something better would have to be found to replace it. The extreme alternative is a cautious, incremental strategy aimed at upgrading existing armored vehicles and C⁴ISR systems in evolutionary ways. This risk-averse strategy would be almost certain to succeed, but its payoffs would be modest in a transformation era where big payoffs are demanded.

Can a third way or middle-ground RDT&E strategy for the Army be found, a strategy of moderate risks but meaningful ambitions? The Army itself is examining how the FCS strategy can be modified to lessen its risks and enhance its payoffs in the future. Such a moderate approach presumably would be more visionary than a cautious, evolutionary strategy, but less risky than the FCS strategy. It would be based on new armored vehicles that are significantly different from the current heavyweight norm. Acknowledging the state of the technological art, however, it would not leap ahead in a single bound into a futuristic realm of lightweight weapons that might lie beyond the capacity of scientists and engineers to produce any time soon. For example, it might aim for a new tank weighing 40 to 50 tons—lighter than the 70-ton Abrams tank, but heavier than the 15- to 20-ton tank envisioned by FCS advocates. Unlike the FCS model, this medium-weight tank would be tracked rather than wheeled, it would mount a large gun on a stable platform, and it would have stout armor plating capable of protecting against enemy fires. This strategy would pursue a similar approach to design of other weapons and C⁴ISR systems by focusing on significant but achievable goals, rather than revolutionary visions.

The operations research method of decision analysis cannot shape a moderate strategy. But decision trees and their visual display of probabilities can help bring intellectual order to the choice between the radical FCS strategy and the moderate strategy. The purpose of the analysis presented here is not to advocate any particular strategy, or to suggest that the Army has been wrong in the past or may be wrong in the future. (Indeed, the analysis concludes by recommending a new RDT&E strategy that combines the FCS strategy and the moderate strategy by using a larger budget to fund both in mutually reinforcing ways.) The purpose here is to show how the method of decision analysis can help illuminate the path ahead. The decision trees presented here are equipped with numbers that are chosen to help accomplish this pedagogical purpose. These numbers are also intended to reflect a sensible interpretation of reality. Whether they actually do reflect reality can be verified only by a wholly separate analysis of their contents.

The decision tree shown in figure 23–5 illustrates what these two strategies might produce in payoffs. It postulates that if the FCS strategy were to succeed fully, it would produce a potential payoff of 100 utility points, and that if the moderate strategy fully succeeds, it would produce a lesser payoff of only 75 points. It then employs chance nodes, one dealing with weapons and the other with RDT&E systems, to gauge the odds of each strategy succeeding and the payoffs if they fall short of success. Its conclusion is that the actual payoff of the moderate strategy would probably exceed that of the FCS strategy, 60 points to 50 points. The reason is that although the moderate strategy has a smaller potential payoff, its higher probability of success elevates its actual payoff above that of the FCS strategy.

This conclusion of a 60:50 advantage for the moderate strategy is based on the premise that its potential payoff is 75 points, or 25 points less than the FCS strategy. If the moderate strategy's potential payoff were elevated to 100 points, equal to the FCS strategy, its advantage in actual payoff rises to 80 points. If its potential payoff were further elevated to 125

Figure 23–5. **Decision Tree of Army RDT&E Strategies**

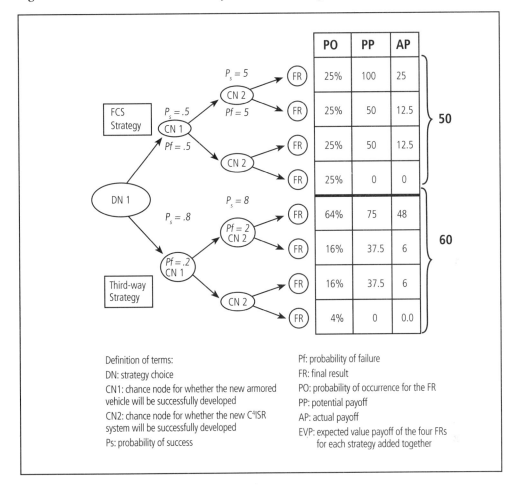

	PO	PP	AP
	25%	100	25
	25%	50	12.5
	25%	50	12.5
	25%	0	0
	64%	75	48
	16%	37.5	6
	16%	37.5	6
	4%	0	0.0

Definition of terms:
DN: strategy choice
CN1: chance node for whether the new armored vehicle will be successfully developed
CN2: chance node for whether the new C⁴ISR system will be successfully developed
Ps: probability of success

Pf: probability of failure
FR: final result
PO: probability of occurrence for the FR
PP: potential payoff
AP: actual payoff
EVP: expected value payoff of the four FRs for each strategy added together

points, actual payoff would grow to 100 points, or double the FCS strategy. Is such an elevation possible? While this seems uncertain, it is conceivable; it could happen if the moderate strategy opens the door to new, unanticipated technologies with concrete applications that are overlooked by a radical FCS strategy because of its ambitious horizons. Regardless of how potential payoffs are appraised, the FCS strategy suffers because of its high risks, and the moderate strategy benefits because of its lower risks.

Any conclusion will be sensitive to assumptions about probabilities and payoffs for both strategies. The core issue is not whether the conclusion is pinpoint accurate, but whether it is on target in strategic terms. If the moderate strategy can be expected to yield a better result than the FCS strategy because it is more likely to succeed, even though it embraces technology aspirations that are less revolutionary, it should be taken seriously. Moreover, the moderate strategy has three other attractive features: it would produce payoffs sooner, in the mid-term rather than the long term; it has a 64 percent chance of succeeding totally, compared to only 25 percent for the FCS strategy; and its downside risks are also lower, with only a 4 percent chance of failing totally, compared to a 25 percent chance for the FCS strategy. All of these considerations could make it the preferred strategy unless the Army is prepared to roll the dice about its future.

A key issue is whether either the FCS strategy or the moderate third-way strategy could be modified to become more flexible and adaptable. While both strategies are amenable to modification, the moderate strategy seems better in this regard because it is not self-contained. It could provide interim technological transfusions into the existing Army force posture and make a bridge to the distant future. By contrast, the FCS strategy is devoted to defining the distant future in radical new ways; thus, it is less able to provide mid-term benefits to the existing posture. In addition, the moderate strategy seems less brittle than the FCS strategy: it does not require that RDT&E programs for new weapons and new C^{4}ISR systems both succeed. If only one of these two programs bears fruit, the moderate strategy would still make a major contribution by introducing that program into the existing force. By contrast, the FCS strategy is very dependent upon the success of its lightweight vehicles. If these vehicles fail, its C^{4}ISR systems could still be introduced into the force, but if its C^{4}ISR systems fail, its vehicles would not be viable performers on the battlefield even if they themselves met their technical requirements.

A key difference between these two strategies is that they are anchored in different concepts of Army force operations on the future battlefield. The moderate strategy endeavors to preserve the Army as a force capable of armored operations, close combat, and offensive maneuvers, while also, like the FCS strategy, being capable of defensive operations or leaving it to airstrikes to bomb enemies into surrender or defeat. By contrast, the radical FCS strategy would eventually strip the Army of its heavy armor and associated counterattack options. It intends to rely mostly upon air-delivered fires to defeat the enemy. Until such fires succeed in battle, the Army would be mainly a defensive force, whose main job is to block enemy advances long enough for overhead fires to accomplish their purpose. While this changeover may make sense if air-delivered fires will always succeed, it makes little sense if these fires are potentially vulnerable to failure under unfavorable battlefield conditions. The moderate strategy preserves a wider spectrum of battlefield options. In addition, it seems more adaptable to the structural changes in Army brigades, divisions, and corps that may lie ahead. For example, the Army is in the process of reducing its brigades by one-third in size and equipment. Such a downsizing might make sense if the new brigade remains heavily armed with powerful tanks and other armored vehicles. But it can be questioned whether this smaller brigade would be able to fight effectively with a suite of light armored weapons. The same contradiction between lightening the Army's weapons and trimming its force structures applies to parallel schemes to reorganize divisions and corps. A downsized corps of 65,000 may be effective if it equipped with very capable tanks and other armored fighting vehicles, but less so if it is equipped with light vehicles that can only defend and not attack.

The operational drawbacks of lightweight FCS vehicles reflect their design criteria. In addition to their mobility and transportability due to their light weight, a main attraction is that their advanced C^{4}ISR systems will enable them to be fully networked at all echelons. They thus will have more real-time information available to them than current vehicles. Similar to the upgraded light armored vehicles assigned to Stryker brigades, however, many FCS vehicles may be wheeled, not tracked. If so, their wheels would enable them to travel fast along paved roads, but on rugged terrain they will be more likely to become bogged down than tracked vehicles. Their light weight also means that their protective armor will be thin, and thus far more vulnerable to rocket-propelled grenades and land-mines than are the Abrams tanks and Bradley infantry fighting vehicles (IFVs). They are also likely to be less well armed than the Abrams, which carries a 120–mm gun. FCS ar-mament plans, while not final, are likely to include a smaller gun, smaller missiles, and medium-caliber cannons. Each of these design features can be debated, but when they are added together, they yield a new vehicle that could encounter trouble fighting and surviving in armored warfare against well-equipped opponents. This will be the case until science produces new technologies beyond those now contemplated by the FCS strategy.

In its quest for lightweight weapons to increase the Army's mobility, therefore, the FCS strategy seems to suffer from a conceptual flaw. Apart from a few circumstances requiring equipment to be carried aboard C–130 aircraft, the Army does not need lighter weapons; what it needs is lighter forces. As chapter 14 explained, acquiring lightweight weapons will not solve the Army's problem of slow, ponderous overseas deployment, which is prin-cipally caused by its large logistic support tail. The solution to this problem is to trim logistic support, as is now feasible because of the reduced demands of expeditionary wars. Regardless of how the future logistic supply system is constructed, Army forces will need powerful weapons capable of counterattacks when they deploy abroad for these wars.

Lightweight weapons should be sought only if they still possess fully adequate per-formance capabilities for intense combat. Whereas the FCS strategy is willing to take risks in this critical area, the moderate strategy is not. This is a major difference be-tween them. The moderate strategy would aim for a new family of weapons based on foreseeable, achievable technologies. They might be lighter than now, but irrespective of their weight, they would possess the firepower, cross-country mobility, and surviv-ability needed to fight on the modern battlefield. They also would be anchored in cur-rently achievable C^4ISR systems, not futuristic designs that depend on extreme bandwidth and other characteristics that exceed anything now feasible. As they enter production in a few years, these weapons would gradually replace the Abrams tank, Bradley IFV, and Paladin artillery tube. They would increase the Army's capacity for close combat and armored warfare, not decrease it. Eventually these vehicles could be replaced by redesigned FCS systems that justified confidence that they would be potent warfighters.

For all these reasons, the moderate strategy may be preferable to the FCS strategy. Perhaps the Army will find a way to pursue both strategies at the same time: such ef-forts are apparently now under way. If so, the moderate strategy would be a practi-cal approach for the mid-term, while the FCS strategy functions as a vision for the dis-tant future. Such a dual-track approach would offer the advantage of strengthening the Army's capacity to upgrade its forces in the mid-term while allowing the FCS develop without rushing, and with a patient focus on distant achievements.

Such a parallel approach might initially be more expensive than pursuing either of these strategies alone, but it would not require a doubling of the Army's annual RDT&E budget of $14 billion. If the FCS program is relieved of its haste to meet near-term imperatives, both strategies could be funded with an annual RDT&E budget of about

$1billion to $2 billion more than now. In fact, over the long run, a dual-track approach might be cheaper, because the two strategies could support each other. Above all, this approach would be more effective than choosing one strategy over the other. It would spare the moderate strategy the dilemma of trying to be practical and visionary at the same time. It would enable the FCS strategy to gain information about the effectiveness of its programs before they are turned into expensive prototypes and development programs. It also would spare the Army the enormous cost of concocting a hurry-up moderate strategy overnight if the FCS strategy were to fail. Army RDT&E should be focused on both the mid-term and the long term. A dual-track approach that performs both functions might, in the final analysis, prove cheaper and more effective than one of these strategies trying to perform both functions at once.

If a dual-track approach is adopted, the Army would need to configure both strategy components to be adaptable as new technologies rise and fall. It would need to pursue spiral development, with new weapons hurried off the production run and introduced to the forces in limited numbers for real-life tests to guide additional improvements during later stages of RDT&E. Spiral development has risks of its own, but it seems far preferable to waiting for 20 years while new weapons systems march laboriously through the entire RDT&E process, to be introduced in large numbers only when they are approaching obsolescence. Spiral development makes especially good sense for the Army because otherwise it might lack new weapons for many years.

In any case, the Army will need a larger investment budget for both RDT&E and procurement. If more funds are forthcoming, the Army's options will broaden, allowing it to pursue better strategies for both RDT&E and procurement. Even with more funds, the moderate strategy may be preferable to the FCS strategy, not because it scores higher, but because its features are more promising: the decision analysis presented here has merely used illustrative numbers to record its advantages in numerical form. If it has done so accurately, it has served its purpose, reflecting the best traditions of operations research methods by helping illuminate alternative options for guiding RDT&E.

Operations Research and Systems Analysis Working Together

In this chapter, use of operations research methods has helped sketch a viable investment strategy for improving U.S. conventional forces in the coming years. This strategy rests on joint investments in order to enhance all force components in balanced ways on behalf of sound operational doctrines. It includes purchase of a balanced mix of new fighters to capitalize on their comparative advantages so that multiple missions can be performed at lowest cost. It also includes a future Army that remains well armed for intense combat while pursuing new, mobile weapons in the confidence that they will still possess the strength to fight effectively. This strategy is similar to that sketched in the portrayal of systems analysis methods in the middle section of this book. That these strategies are similar is no accident. They show the advantages of multidisciplinary thinking on parallel lines when it produces similar insights. But multidisciplinary thinking can also have advantageous effects when it produces different conclusions, because it compels a further stock-taking in order to determine the truth.

Operations research methods may seem complex, but they make valuable contributions to the analysis of defense investment strategies. Their advantage is an intense focus on details, and mathematical techniques with which to investigate issues and to assert conclusions with great precision. Their disadvantage is that they lack the capacity for abstract generalization and cross-cutting appraisals provided by systems analysis. Thus, operations research methods normally should not be used on their own when complex program budget issues are at stake. When systems analysis and operations research are teamed to analyze defense issues from multidisciplinary perspectives, they can make a great pair.

In addition, strategic evaluation can make a contribution by providing an overarching framework of goals and policies that stem from national security strategy and defense strategy. This framework can help establish the basic parameters within which systems analysis can be conducted. Systems analysis, in turn, can help establish the basic parameters within which operations research can be carried out. In order for operations research to work effectively, appropriate methods must be selected for the issues at hand. Combat modeling, linear programming, and decision analysis have been the techniques illuminated here, but the field of operations research offers others as well. Regardless of the techniques selected, a careful cost analysis must be conducted, and the same applies to the selection of numbers for performance data based on weapons effects. Accurate cost data and performance data are vital. In cases where basic accuracy cannot be guaranteed, sensitivity analysis should be carried out to illuminate the options and provide a frame of reference for making decisions.

Sometimes a single operations research method can be adequate for the task at hand. But often, better results will be attained if multiple methods are applied to the same problem. For example, combat models, linear programming, and decision analysis could all be applied to the same issue. When their results point toward similar conclusions, analysts and senior officials can have greater confidence about the implications for decisions. When the results point toward different conclusions, they can help illuminate the tradeoffs, sensitivities, and judgments that must be made. Either way, the defense community comes away better informed.

It is imperative to remember that the results of operations research should not always be accepted at face value. Its techniques can generate impressive graphs and mathematical equations that have the appearance of great sophistication and even hard science at work. But these graphs and equations are all based on quantitative input data—specific numbers—that come from outside sources. Are these numbers themselves accurate? How reliable are they? Do they represent the results of considerable research and clear thinking, or only researchers' best estimates made in the face of considerable uncertainty, or even just somebody's policy agenda? These are questions that should be answered before an operations research analysis is accepted. Normally a discriminating eye and common sense can help identify good numbers and ferret out bad numbers. The trick is to apply human reasoning to operations research, rather than let operations research substitute for reasoning.

When operations research is done well and its results are valid, it can provide a strong foundation of judgments about details, upon which a superstructure of systems analyses and strategic evaluations can be built. In this way, these three methods can work together, building intellectual capital from the top down and the bottom up. When this is the case, these three methods are working at their best, and the national security community is well served.

Notes

[1] For a technical analysis of methodologies for defense cost analysis, see Gene H. Fisher, *Cost Considerations in Systems Analysis* (Santa Monica, CA: RAND, 1970).

[2] For a discussion of discounting, see Edith Stokey and Richard Zeckhauser, *A Primer for Policy Analysis* (New York: Norton, 1978), chap. 10.

[3] When applied to procurement issues, a major conceptual contribution of linear programming is that it tends to endorse the idea of a mixed program composed of several weapons rather than a program composed of only one weapon. The advantage of acquiring only one weapon is that it limits RDT&E costs: where three weapons may cost $30 billion to develop, a single weapon may cost only $10 billion. But typically, a single weapon cannot perform multiple missions with equal proficiency. Acquiring three different weapons allows each mission to be performed with weapons that are optimally designed for the purpose. When large numbers of weapons are bought, a mixed program can result in a requirement for fewer total weapons, thus offsetting the high RDT&E costs of developing several weapons.

Chapter 24
Conclusions

The main goal of this book has been to introduce readers to methods of analysis in national security affairs, and to motivate them to learn more about these methods and how to use them. They are accessible, not arcane. They are relevant and powerful. They do not always provide answers to questions, but they can illuminate options, and when they do so, they perform their function. They can be used by government officials, scholars, and think-tank researchers. They also can be used by the average citizen who is seeking to understand national security policy in today's world, and to develop an independent capacity to think for himself or herself.

Another goal of this book has been to make clear the need for multidisciplinary thinking and updated methods for evaluation of U.S. national security policies in this era of great complexity and rapid change. Each of the three classes of analytical methods surveyed here—strategic evaluation, systems analysis, and operations research—has its own strengths and specific applications. Each can help improve policy analysis, while their power and relevance are far greater when they are combined. Even together, however, they will serve their purposes only if their users can master the new challenges that the 21st century brings.

Multidisciplinary analysis is crucial; neither the global challenges facing the United States nor the U.S. strategic responses to them can be stovepiped into separate categories any longer. U.S. foreign policy cannot be seen apart from defense strategy, nor can defense strategy be analyzed apart from the details of budget and force structure. As never before, these different dimensions of national security policy must be fused together to give policymakers a picture of the whole, not just of component parts.

Along the way, this book's application of analytical methods has sketched a vision of a future U.S. national security strategy for a dangerous world in an era of accelerating globalization. This vision calls for a strategy that is global in scope, while responding to each region's unique dynamics, by using U.S. power wisely and multilaterally. It calls for a blend of military strength, political diplomacy, and economic instruments to lay a foundation of peaceful security affairs so that democracy and economic progress can take root in troubled regions. It calls for a defense strategy attuned to this national security strategy, backed by a transformed force posture that is technologically sophisticated and that provides flexibility and adaptability. It calls for a defense budget and programs that allocate resources wisely in order to field such a transformed military.

To be sure, this is the author's vision, and, to the author, it makes sense because it is a logical byproduct of applying these analytical methods. Others may disagree. They may have different visions of their own, and be able to marshal credible analyses to support them. Regardless of one's vision, the central point is that visions should be developed by means of analysis. The analytical methods presented in this book provide tools for creating visions, and for the accompanying tasks of appraising how to handle an uncertain future in light of America's values, goals, resources, and priorities.

Regardless of how any particular vision is appraised, multidisciplinary thinking and analysis will be key to shaping future national security strategy and its constituent parts so that they stand the tests of time. The analytical methods of this field cannot remain locked in past practices, past glories, and past idiosyncrasies. Updating them is not merely a matter of tinkering with their measuring sticks, equations, and data, but of recalibrating their conceptual lenses. If these methods do not take account of new-era realities, they will not be able to produce useful analysis, regardless of their technical sophistication. The work of updating these methods has begun, but additional progress is needed.

Meeting this challenge is the responsibility of the U.S. Government, think tanks, consulting firms, and universities that conduct research and teaching in this arena. It is, ultimately, the responsibility of the professionals who practice in this field. In the past, perhaps, they could afford to remain in three separate intellectual camps, each laboring in its own vineyard while knowing little about the other. That time has passed. For the entire analytical community, newcomers and old hands alike, pursuing multidisciplinary analysis with new methods for a new era is both the challenge and the opportunity.

Reforming Each Discipline

Of the three disciplines, strategic evaluation is the most in need of strengthening of its core methodologies. It is responsible for analyzing the most complex issues of U.S. national security strategy, including fundamental decisions about how the United States faces the world. Judged in relation to its immense responsibilities, strategic evaluation relies upon a collection of relatively unsophisticated methods: essentially, clear conceptual thinking supported by logical reasoning. Thinking and reasoning are powerful tools, but no business or corporate leader would be prudent to rely solely upon them for tough decisions. A prudent leader would demand, in addition, hard data, accurate measurements of effectiveness, explicit criteria of evaluation, and searching appraisals of the options and tradeoffs. Ideally, these inputs would be quickly available from trained staffs that have the necessary information and tools at hand. While this practice is common for business firms that face tough competitive markets, it is less common in the field of strategic evaluation of U.S. foreign policy, at least in the community that writes popular books on this subject.

Among the relatively rare examples of useful strategic evaluations are two recent books by Kenneth Pollack. In his 2002 book, *The Threatening Storm: The Case for Invading Iraq*, Pollack examined U.S. policy for handling Iraq and the Saddam Hussein regime; he concluded by urging invasion of Iraq. In his 2004 book, *The Persian Puzzle: The Conflict Between Iran and America*, Pollack examined U.S. policy for handling Iran, its quest for nuclear weapons, and its behavior in the Middle East; there, he concluded by urging a diplomatic approach toward Iran. What unites these books is that, in both cases, he presented a lengthy historical treatment of U.S. policy toward those countries, identified a spectrum of policy options, and subjected these options, both their costs and their benefits, to critical scrutiny. Readers may agree or disagree, but they doubtless came away better educated for having read these books, and better able to reach their own conclusions.[1]

Such analysis is far from common in this field. While many books analyze the international problems facing the United States, far too few thoroughly analyze and compare the policy choices. Most simply advocate a favored policy or strategy, on the presumption that it alone makes sense. Whether this is as true for internal U.S. Government studies as for public literature is for senior officials to decide, but no experienced participant would question the conclusion that sustained excellence has always been needed, and will continue being needed.

A better literature using strategic evaluation and its new-era methods is badly needed. Such a literature could profit by drawing upon the insights of systems analysis and operations research, whose economic curves and mathematical models often have much to contribute to foreign policy choices. Both already have an imposing array of technical methodologies at their disposal, but in this era of interconnected policies and systemic thinking, they too will need to broaden their viewpoints, acting as wide-angle lenses and not just microscopes. In addition, core methods will have to be modified and updated so that they can analyze the issues of tomorrow. Creating new techniques for systems analysis and operations research is anything but easy because it requires reformulation of conceptual frameworks, analytical procedures, mathematical equations, and data. As this volume has suggested, a challenging agenda of change confronts all three of these disciplines.

Institutional Reforms

A call for better analytical methods cannot focus solely on an improved academic literature and better policy studies by the U.S. Government; institutional reforms are also needed. Improvements are needed in how policy analysis for national security affairs is taught at major universities. Some already do well: the Massachusetts Institute of Technology, Harvard, and the Pardee Graduate School at RAND are examples of PhD programs that endeavor to teach methods of policy analysis in national security from a multidisciplinary perspective. But there are few other similar programs. More often, this subject is taught only at the masters level; students are given a solid grounding in the methods of political science and international relations, but not comparable training in managerial economics or policy-relevant mathematics. More PhD and master of arts programs are needed that are truly multidisciplinary. Such graduate-level programs could foster original research on methods of policy analysis from both theoretical and applied perspectives.

What applies to the academic community also applies to the U.S. Government. A professional school for national security policy analysts at the National Defense University, for example, could train both military officers and civilians in this field's multiple disciplines at the graduate level. Similar steps aimed at upgrading policy analysis could be pursued in the service academies and in other DOD schools. Within the policy bureaucracies of the executive branch, recent efforts to strengthen the process of interagency analysis and coordination should be continued. The need for better intelligence about global trends has been widely recognized, but equally acute, if not more so, is the need for expert policy analysis of how to grapple with these trends, in the State Department, other executive agencies, and Congressional staffs alike.

The Department of Defense is commonly regarded as a hotbed of analytical expertise, but while this appraisal applies to its handling of weapons systems and budgets, the imperative need for improved skills also holds true for its ability to handle the crucial interplay among force posture, defense strategy, and national security policy. In this arena, DOD's organizational structure has become a maze of different and often competing staffs assigned mainly to the Office of Secretary of Defense and the Joint Staff. Doubtless they include many talented people, but it is not clear that they are able to produce sophisticated strategic planning and policy analysis consistently. A common complaint of participants is that they spend so much time processing paperwork and coordinating with each other that they have little time to think and analyze. Another common complaint is the difficulty regularly encountered by the Office of the Secretary of Defense in blending the analytical work of its Undersecretary for Policy with the Office of Program Analysis and Evaluation, the Joint Staff, and the combatant commands. Something better is needed: an organizational structure and process that produce rich new ideas. Producing such ideas is how and why the Pentagon helped play such a major role in winning the Cold War. It needs to do so again. Recently the Pentagon altered its strategic planning process to provide more time and scope to conduct searching analysis and evaluation. Whether this effort will succeed is to be seen, but clearly it is moving in the right direction. If additional reforms are needed, they should be pursued—a judgment that applies not only to the Department of Defense, but to other departments and agencies as well.

For all their importance, organizational reforms can set the stage, but they cannot substitute for brainpower: it is needed for decisions on U.S. national security policy to be made wisely. Analysis is key to developing brainpower, and methods are key to producing good analysis. Methods, in turn, must be up-to-date, relevant, and useful. This simple formula is a good one to remember as the United States confronts the prospect of a complex, unruly world in the years ahead.

Note

[1] Kenneth M. Pollack, *The Threatening Storm: The Case for Invading Iraq* (New York: Random House, 2002), and *The Persian Puzzle: The Conflict Between Iran and America* (New York: Random House, 2004).

Postscript

Quadrennial Defense Review 2006

D OD's long-anticipated *Quadrennial Defense Review* 2006 was published in February 2006, too late to be integrated into this book's chapters. Accordingly, this epilogue briefly summarizes *QDR* 2006 and assesses its implications for defense planning as well as for the analytical methods discussed in this book. As its authors acknowledge, *QDR* 2006 did not launch a new beginning for U.S. defense policy and strategy. Rather, it carries forth the strategic premises established in *QDR* 2001 by the George W. Bush administration and updates them to reflect experiences since then, including the wars in Afghanistan and Iraq and the paths taken by U.S. defense transformation. *QDR* 2006 thus is best seen as an evolutionary document that reflects a mixture of continuity and change, that strikes a balance between near-term imperatives and long-term requirements, and that strives to integrate strategy, goals, and budgetary limits. In the process of handling this complex agenda, *QDR* 2006 launched a number of departures in policies, plans, and programs that seem likely to affect U.S. national security strategy in the coming years—a departure that probably will be praised by some observers and criticized by others.

Fighting the Long War

QDR 2006 focuses on the challenge of "fighting the long war" in the coming years. By "long war," it means the diverse and long-enduring military actions taking place in Iraq, Afghanistan, and other places where U.S. forces are fighting terrorists and other new-era adversaries, many of which are not the regular military forces of nation-states. In both Iraq and Afghanistan, *QDR* 2006 points out, the major phase of combat operations has ended successfully, but stability operations aimed at suppressing insurgents and terrorists continue, as do efforts to build effective governments and military forces. In addition to fighting adversaries in these distant places, U.S. military forces are being called upon to perform other missions on a global basis. One example is providing help to governments in Africa and elsewhere to build military establishments capable of maintaining order and quelling terrorism. Other examples include the humanitarian relief efforts in response to the tsunami of 2004 and the Pakistani earthquake of 2005. Yet another example is the U.S. military's efforts to help the government of Colombia suppress drug usage, terrorism, and violence within its borders.

Beyond this, the long war has compelled DOD to become more involved in homeland defense through such steps as creating the U.S. Northern Command and working with other Federal agencies to be prepared for such contingencies as biological attacks and WMD use. According to *QDR* 2006, the long war has greatly increased the pressure on the U.S. military to perform more missions at higher operational tempos than was the case 5 years ago. Yet the report also observes that this experience has taught valuable lessons in such areas as building better partnerships with other U.S. agencies and foreign governments, taking early preventive measures to prepare local problems from becoming larger events, enhancing the flexibility and freedom of action of U.S. forces, and taking steps to increase the costs facing adversaries. *QDR* 2006 offers no blueprint of when and how the long war will end, but it implies that U.S. military forces are becoming better able to wage it effectively. The report thus strikes a guarded but upbeat note about prospects ahead.

Operationalizing the Strategy

QDR 2006 analyzes at length how DOD can best pursue the multiple components of its diverse national defense strategy over the coming years. It acknowledges that although the United States possesses many advantages over opponents in traditional forms of warfare, it now faces a widened spectrum of potential challenges, including not only traditional challenges, but also irregular challenges (terrorism, insurgency, and guerrilla warfare), catastrophic challenges (WMD use on U.S. soil), and disruptive challenges (efforts to damage U.S. space systems or information networks). To prepare for such challenges, *QDR* 2006 calls upon DOD to address four priority areas:

- defeating terrorist networks
- defending the homeland in depth
- shaping the choices of countries at strategic crossroads
- preventing hostile states and nonstate actors from acquiring or using WMD.

The report says that efforts to defeat terrorist networks include U.S. combat operations, but also encompass many other activities, including cooperating with foreign governments and militaries, and winning the battle of ideas and ideologies. This endeavor requires a cluster of capabilities, including human intelligence, persistent surveillance, special operations forces, cultural awareness, prompt global strike capabilities to attack fleeting enemy targets, and the capacity to communicate human actions effectively while rapidly countering enemy propaganda. In all of these areas, *QDR* 2006 calls for efforts to strengthen U.S. allied capabilities against terrorist networks.

QDR 2006 indicates that whereas threats to the U.S. homeland traditionally were posed by the nuclear missiles of hostile states (for example, the Soviet Union), today's threats are also posed by terrorists that can attack through a variety of measures, from incidents similar to September 11, to use of chemical, biological, and nuclear weapons. The report calls for military capabilities for the direct defense of the United States, including air, missile, and maritime defenses, and for close DOD cooperation with other government agencies in dealing with natural disasters such as Hurricane Katrina.

In addressing the goal of shaping the choices of countries at strategic crossroads, *QDR* 2006 highlights countries in the Middle East, Latin America, and other developing regions that are struggling with whether to create democratic governments and market economies. It suggests the need for strong U.S. efforts, supported by U.S. military programs, to help these countries achieve democracy and capitalism. *QDR* 2006 also calls for strong U.S. efforts to build partnership relations with Russia and India, both of which are major powers in geostrategic transition. Even greater attention is devoted to China because of its size, fast economic growth, importance to the Asian security system, and potential capacity to compete with the United States militarily. *QDR 2006* states that U.S. policy is focused on encouraging China to play a constructive and peaceful role in the Asia-Pacific region, to become a partner in addressing common security challenges, and to pursue economic growth and political liberalization in its internal affairs. Nonetheless, *QDR 2006* also notes the extent to which China is increasing its defense budget, modernizing its military forces, and developing capabilities that could be used against Taiwan or across the Asia region. As a result, the United States must maintain strong forces in Asia, preserve and develop partnership relationships with key friends and allies, and improve its military capabilities in important areas, such as communications, intelligence, missile defenses, and long-range strike assets.

QDR 2006 emphasizes the importance of preventing WMD acquisition or use. North Korea and Iran are singled out as countries in pursuit of nuclear systems, but in future years, other countries as well as terrorist groups could fall into this category. In response, *QDR 2006* calls for strong preventive measures, such as the Proliferation Security Initiative, which creates multilateral efforts aimed at tracking and interdicting the supply of nuclear materials. It also advocates U.S. capacity to respond to WMD proliferation if preventive efforts fail; although the United States will use peaceful and cooperative measures whenever possible, it must be capable of employing military forces against WMD systems when necessary. This mission, according to the report, requires the ability to locate, characterize, disable/destroy, and secure potential targets, an ability made possible by several important military capabilities, including intelligence and surveillance systems, interdiction capabilities, SOF forces, and other strike assets needed to render WMD sites safe and secure.

In reacting to the four priorities, *QDR 2006* imposes a change to the "1-4-2-1" force-sizing construct that DOD had adopted after *QDR 2001*. This construct stated that U.S. military forces should be sized to defend the U.S. homeland, carry out normal U.S. military activities in the 4 regions of Europe, the Middle East, the Asian littoral, and Northeast Asia, carry out 2 nearly simultaneous major combat operations (for example, wars against Iraq and North Korea), and occupy 1 defeated power. By contrast, *QDR 2006* adopted a new threefold construct of:

- providing for homeland defense
- prevailing in the war on terror and conducting irregular (asymmetric) warfare, including steady-state and surge operations
- remaining capable of conducting and winning two nearly simultaneous conventional campaigns, or one campaign if U.S. forces are already engaged in a large-scale, long-duration irregular campaign.

The main impact of this new construct is to call attention to the important roles now being played by U.S. military operations against terrorism and for other irregular purposes. This formulation clearly is intended to be global, rather than linked to specific regions. Yet it clearly calls attention to the Middle East and adjoining regions as main focal points of future U.S. military actions. A noteworthy feature of the new construct is that it retains the long-standing formula of possessing sufficient forces to wage two concurrent regional wars. This judgment is one reason why *QDR* 2006 concluded that the existing U.S. military posture will remain adequate for the years ahead; neither major force additions nor subtractions are desirable.

Reorienting Capabilities and Forces

Although *QDR* 2006 envisions no major changes in the size or basic composition of current U.S. military forces, it calls for improvements and reorientations in a number of capability portfolios (the diverse assets from different services that together provide a portfolio of capabilities in a specific area of operations):

- joint ground forces
- special operations
- joint air forces
- joint maritime forces
- tailored deterrence assets and new triad
- capabilities for combating WMD
- joint mobility assets
- ISR and space capabilities
- network-centric assets
- joint command and control.

In *QDR* 2006, concrete decisions about plans and programs for all force components stem from this emphasis on building improved capability portfolios in specific areas. For ground forces, the recommendation is made that the Army rebalance its posture by creating 42 active combat brigades and 28 National Guard combat brigades, plus 75 active support brigades and 136 Guard/Reserve support brigades. For SOF assets, *QDR* 2006 calls for major increases, including a one-third increase in SOF battalions, additional psychological operations and civil affairs units, creation of a Marine Corps Special Operations Command, increased SEAL units, and other enhancements. For joint air assets, the report prescribes development of a new land-based, penetrating capability by 2018, modernization of existing bombers to support global strike operations, development of a carrier-based unmanned strike aircraft, doubling of UAV coverage by acquiring more Predators and Global Hawks, extension of F–22 production, and a restructuring of Air Force wings to emphasize long-range strike capabilities. For joint maritime capabilities, *QDR* 2006 suggests a larger fleet that includes 11 carrier strike groups, accelerated procurement of littoral combat ships, procurement of 8 maritime pre-position force ships, an improved riverine capability, and return to steady-state production rate of 2 attack submarines per year.

A variety of additional programmatic decisions also flow from *QDR* 2006. Examples are to:

- develop a capability to deliver precision-guided conventional warheads using Trident SLBMs

- expand the number of U.S. forces capable of participating in WMD elimination missions

- continue the acquisition of new wide-bodied cargo aircraft to increase U.S. strategic mobility capabilities

- develop new technologies in order to improve ISR capabilities

- acquire new communications systems to strengthen the global information grid

- activate additional standing joint force headquarters and develop better adaptive planning capabilities

- strengthen the DOD capacity to make use of Reserve Component forces for homeland defense, natural disasters, and civil support missions

- begin reorganizing the DOD budget into joint capability areas

- improve joint training, transform the National Defense University into a National Security University, and broaden U.S. military language and cultural skills.

Achieving Unity of Effort

QDR 2006 moves toward further developing DOD ability to work within the interagency team of the U.S. Government and to cooperate closely with friends and allies abroad. It declares that the realities of globalization, complex information networks, and new missions make improvements in these areas imperative. The days are gone when individual governmental agencies could operate as stovepipes, separate from other agencies and governments. Twenty-first-century missions require a unity of effort not achieved before.

To achieve greater interagency cooperation, *QDR* 2006 recommends creation of National Planning Guidance to direct the development of both military and nonmilitary plans and institutional capabilities. In field operations where multiple instruments are employed, it urges greater collaboration between military combatant commanders and civilian chiefs of mission. *QDR* 2006 devotes special attention to the task of carrying out stabilization and reconstruction efforts in such countries as Iraq and Afghanistan, noting that in 2005, DOD issued guidance to place stability operations on par with combat operations by the U.S. military. It calls for efforts by the State Department and other governmental agencies to strengthen their capabilities for stabilization and reconstruction missions, and for improved interagency coordination at all levels, from Washington to local offices in the field.

Finally, *QDR* 2006 emphasizes the need to work closely with international allies and partners in the coming years—especially with NATO and European countries, many of which possess assets and capabilities that could assist U.S. military forces in future operations ranging from combat interventions to stabilization and reconstruction missions. The report praises NATO for such recent steps as creating the NATO Response Force and Allied Transformation Command, accepting leadership of the International Security Assistance Force in Afghanistan, and establishing the NATO Training Mission in Iraq. In addition to supporting further improvements to European combat forces, creation of a NATO stabilization and reconstruction capability and a European constabulary force is recommended.

The effect was to make clear DOD willingness to work closely with capable friends and allies as new, challenging missions in the long war occur.

Appraising *QDR* 2006

Supporters of the report are likely to praise it for several reasons. They likely will say that it does a good job of portraying how DOD is endeavoring to wage the war on terrorism on a daily basis while also transforming itself over the long haul. They also are likely to credit *QDR* 2006 for putting forth a useful list of tangible ideas for improving U.S. military forces, capabilities, and operations, for attaching greater importance to stabilization and reconstruction missions, and for paying more attention to relationships with allies. Critics may say that *QDR* 2006 fails to address how DOD intends to face a growing procurement challenge because future acquisition budgets may not be large enough to fund the many new ground, air, and naval weapons sought by the services. Critics also are likely to fault the report for failing to cancel or scale back any new weapons systems, for not doing enough to stem the rising costs for operations and maintenance budgets, and for raising insufficient challenges to Service-sponsored force structures and weapon designs.

Regardless of how these positive and negative reactions are appraised, *QDR* 2006 tabled important updates and departures while carrying forth many of the basic geostrategic premises, foreign policies, and defense strategies of its predecessor. This is hardly surprising since both documents were written by the Bush administration, which perceived considerable strategic continuity between the years that these two documents were written, and was using *QDR* 2006 mainly to update its predecessor. As history shows, major departures in U.S. national strategy tend to occur only when new administrations enter office, rather than when they reach their halfway points. To the extent that the past is prologue, another full-scale review of this subject will await the next Presidential election in 2008. Until then, one conclusion is beyond dispute. The world will remain a highly complex place, and U.S. national security policies will need to continue being guided by wise judgments and careful calculations. As a result, the analytical methods portrayed by this book will remain relevant, and perhaps in demand as well.

Selected Bibliography

Albert, David S. et al. *Network Centric Warfare: Developing and Leveraging Information Superiority.* Washington, DC: CCRP Publishing Series, Department of Defense, 1999.

Almond, Gabriel et al. *Strong Religion: The Rise of Fundamentalisms Around the World.* Chicago: University of Chicago Press, 2003.

American Physical Society. "Report of the APS Study Group on Boost-Phase Intercept Systems for National Missile Defense: Scientific and Technical Issues." Washington, DC: American Physical Society, 2003.

Art, Robert J. *A Grand Strategy for America.* Ithaca, NY: Cornell University Press, 2003.

Asmus, Ronald D. *Opening NATO's Door: How the Alliance Remade Itself for a New Era.* New York: Columbia University Press, 2002.

Aspin, Les. *Report of the Bottom Up Review.* Washington, DC: Department of Defense, 1993.

Bacevich, Andrew J., ed. *The Imperial Tense.* Chicago: Ivan R. Dee, 2003.

Baker, James, with Thomas DeFrank. *The Politics of Diplomacy: Revolution, War, and Peace, 1989–1992.* New York: Putnam, 1995.

Bardach, Eugene. *A Practical Guide to Policy Analysis: The Eightfold Path to More Effective Problem Solving.* New York: Chatham House Publishers, 2000.

Barnet, Raymond A., and Michael R. Ziegler. *College Mathematics for Management, Life, and Social Sciences.* 3^d ed. San Francisco: Dellen, 1984.

Barnett, Thomas P.M. *The Pentagon's New Map: War and Peace in the Twenty-first Century.* New York: Putnam, 2004.

Battilega, John A., and Judith Grange, eds. *The Military Applications of Modeling.* Wright-Patterson Air Force Base, OH: U.S. Air Force Institute of Technology Press, 1984.

Behn, Robert D., and James W. Vaupel. *Quick Analysis for Busy Decision Makers.* New York: Basic Books, 1982.

Bellamy, Christopher. *The Evolution of Modern Land Warfare: Theory and Practice.* London: Routledge, 1990.

Betts, Richard K. *Surprise Attack.* Washington, DC: Brookings, 1982.

Biddle, Stephen. *Military Power: Explaining Victory and Defeat in Modern Battle.* Princeton, NJ: Princeton University Press, 2004.

Binnendijk, Hans, and Stuart Johnson. *Transforming for Stabilization and Reconstruction Operations.* Washington, DC: Center for Technology and National Security Policy, National Defense University, November 2003.

Binnendijk, Hans, and Richard Kugler. "Sound Vision, Unfinished Business: The Quadrennial Defense Review Report 2001." *The Fletcher Forum of World Affairs* 26, no. 1 (Winter/Spring 2002).

———. "Transforming European Forces." *Survival* 44, no. 3 (Autumn 2002).

Binnendijk, Hans, and George Stewart. "Toward Missile Defenses from the Sea." *Defense Horizons* 14. Washington, DC: Center for Technology and National Security Policy, National Defense University, June 2002.

Binnendijk, Hans, ed. *Transforming America's Military.* Washington, DC: National Defense University Press, 2002.

Bjorkman, Tom. *Russia's Road to Deeper Democracy.* Washington, DC: Brookings, 2003.

Blackwill, Robert D., and Michael Stürmer, eds. *Allies Divided: Transatlantic Policies for the Greater Middle East.* Cambridge, MA: MIT Press, 1997.

Blalock, Hubert, Jr. *Conceptualization and Measurement in the Social Sciences.* New York: Sage Publications, 1982.

———. *Social Statistics.* 2^d ed. New York: McGraw-Hill, 1979.

————, ed. *Causal Models in the Social Sciences.* 2^d ed. New York: Aldine De Gruyter, 1985.

Bowie, Christopher et al. *The New Calculus: Analyzing Airpower's Changing Role in Joint Theater Campaigns.* Santa Monica, CA: RAND, 1993.

Bracken, Jerome et al. *Warfare Modeling.* Alexandria, VA: Military Operations Research Society, 1995.

Brainard, Lael et al. *The Other War: Global Poverty and the Millennium Challenge Account.* Washington, DC: Brookings, 2003.

Brodie, Bernard. *Strategy in the Missile Age.* Princeton, NJ: Princeton University Press, 1965.

Brown, Seyom. *The Illusion of Control: Force and Foreign Policy in the Twenty-first Century.* Washington, DC: Brookings, 2003.

Brzezinski, Zbigniew. *The Grand Chessboard: American Foreign Policy and Its Geostrategic Imperatives.* New York: Basic Books, 1997.

————. *Out of Control: Global Turmoil on the Eve of the 21st Century.* New York: Charles Scribner's Sons, 1993.

Bush, George W. *Economic Report of the President.* Washington, DC: The White House, 2003.

————. *The National Security Strategy of the United States of America.* Washington, DC: The White House, 2002.

Calder, Kent E. *Pacific Defense: Arms, Energy, and America's Future in Asia.* New York: William Morrow, 1996.

Clark, Wesley K. *Waging Modern War: Bosnia, Kosovo, and the Future of Combat.* New York: Public Affairs, 2001.

Clinton, William J. *A National Security Strategy for a Global Age.* Washington, DC: The White House, 2000.

Cohen, Bernard I. *Revolution in Science.* London: Belknap Press, 1985.

Cohen, William. *Report of the Quadrennial Defense Review.* Washington, DC: Department of Defense, 1997.

Congressional Budget Office. Testimony to Committee on the Budget, U.S. House of Representatives, "Long-Term Implications of Current Defense Plans." Washington, DC: Congressional Budget Office, 2003.

————. *Transforming the Navy's Surface Combatant Force.* Washington, DC: Congressional Budget Office, 2003.

————. *The Effects of Aging on the Costs of Operating and Maintaining Military Equipment.* Washington, DC: Congressional Budget Office, 2001.

————. Testimony to Senate Armed Services Committee, "Modernizing Tactical Aircraft." Washington, DC: Congressional Budget Office, 1999.

————. *Increasing the Mission Capability of the Attack Submarine Force.* Washington, DC: Congressional Budget Office, 2002.

Cooper, Robert. *The Breaking of Nations: Order and Chaos in the Twenty-first Century.* London: Atlantic Books, 2003.

Cordesman, Anthony H. *The Iraq War: Strategy, Tactics, and Military Lessons.* Washington, DC: Center for Strategic and International Studies, 2003.

Costello, John. *The Pacific War 1941–1945.* New York: Quill, 1982.

Daalder, Ivo H., and James M. Lindsay. *America Unbound: The Bush Revolution in Foreign Policy.* Washington, DC: Brookings, 2003.

Dallas, Gregor. *1918: War and Peace.* Woodstock, NY: The Overlook Press, 2001.

Davis, Paul K. *Analytic Architecture for Capabilities-Based Planning, Mission-Systems Analysis, and Transformation.* Santa Monica, CA: RAND, 2002.

————. *Effects-Based Operations: A Grand Challenge for the Analytical Community.* Santa Monica, CA: RAND, 2001.

————, ed. *New Challenges for Defense Planning: Rethinking How Much Is Enough.* Santa Monica, CA: RAND, 1994.

Davis, Paul K. et al. *Measuring Interdiction Capabilities in the Presence of Anti-Access Strategies.* Santa Monica, CA: RAND, 2002.

Davis, Paul K., David Gompert, and Richard Kugler. *Adaptiveness in National Defense: The Basis of a New Framework*. Santa Monica, CA: RAND, 1996.

Deitchman, Seymour J. *Military Power and the Advance of Technology: General Purpose Military Forces for the 1980s and Beyond*. Boulder, CO: Westview Press, 1983.

Denoon, David B.H. *Real Reciprocity: Balancing U.S. Economic and Security Policy in the Pacific Basin*. New York: Council on Foreign Relations, 1993.

Deptula, David A. *Effects-Based Operations: Change in the Nature of Warfare*. Washington, DC: Aerospace Education Foundation, 2001.

Eisenhower, David. *Eisenhower At War, 1943–1945*. New York: Random House, 1986.

Enthoven, Alain, and K. Wayne Smith. *How Much is Enough? Shaping the Defense Program 1961–1969*. New York: Harper and Row, 1971.

Epstein, Joshua M. *The Calculus of Conventional War: Dynamic Analysis Without Lanchester Theory*. Washington, DC: Brookings, 1987.

——. *Strategy and Force Planning: The Case of the Persian Gulf*. Washington, DC: Brookings, 1987.

Erickson, John et al. *Soviet Ground Forces: An Operational Assessment*. Boulder, CO: Westview Press, 1986.

Fisher, Gene H. *Cost Considerations in Systems Analysis*. Santa Monica, CA: RAND, 1970.

Flanagan, Stephen J. et al. *Challenges of the Global Century: Report of the Project on Globalization and National Security*. Washington, DC: National Defense University Press, 2001.

Flournoy, Michèle A., ed. *QDR 2001: Strategy-Driven Choices for America's Security*. Washington, DC: National Defense University Press, 2001.

Fox, J. Ronald. *The Defense Management Challenge: Weapons Acquisition*. Cambridge, MA: Harvard University Business School Press, 1988.

Franks, Tommy. *American Soldier*. New York: Regan Books, 2004.

Freedman, Lawrence. *The Evolution of Nuclear Strategy*. London: Macmillan, 1983.

Freund, John H. *Mathematical Statistics*. Englewood Cliffs, NJ: Prentice Hall, 1962.

Friedman, Lee S. *Microeconomic Policy Choices*. New York: McGraw-Hill, 1984.

Friedman, Norman. *Terrorism, Afghanistan, and America's New Way of Life*. Annapolis, MD: United States Naval Institute Press, 2003.

Friedman, Thomas L. *The Lexus and the Olive Tree: Understanding Globalization*. New York: Farrar, Strauss, and Giroux, 1999.

Fukuyama, Francis. *The End of History and the Last Man*. New York: Avon Books, 1992.

Gansler, Jacques S. *Affording Defense*. Cambridge, MA: The MIT Press, 1989.

Garten, Jeffrey E. *A Cold Peace: America, Japan, Germany, and the Struggle for Supremacy*. New York: Times Books, 1993.

Gell-Mann, Murray. *The Quark and the Jaguar: Adventures in the Simple and the Complex*. New York: W.H. Freeman, 1994.

General Accounting Office. *NATO-Warsaw Pact: U.S. and Soviet Perspectives of the Conventional Force Balance*. Washington, DC: General Accounting Office/NSIAD-89–23A, 1988.

Gilpin, Robert. *The Challenge of Global Capitalism: The World Economy in the 21st Century*. Princeton, NJ: Princeton University Press, 2000.

——. *The Political Economy of International Relations*. Princeton, NJ: Princeton University Press, 1987.

Glasstone, Samuel, and Philip J. Dolan, eds. *The Effects of Nuclear Weapons*. 3d ed. Washington, DC: U.S. Department of Defense, 1977.

Goldgeier, James M., and Michael McFaul. *Power and Purpose: U.S. Policy Toward Russia After the Cold War*. Washington, DC: Brookings, 2003.

Gompert, David C. et al. *Mind the Gap: Promoting a Transatlantic Revolution in Military Affairs*. Washington, DC: National Defense University Press, 1999.

Grayson, George W. *Strange Bedfellows: NATO Marches East*. New York: University Press of America, 1999.

Greenfield, Liah. *Nationalism: Five Roads to Modernity*. Cambridge, MA: Harvard University Press, 1992.

Gritton, Eugene et al. *Ground Forces for a Rapidly Employable Joint Task Force: First-Week Capabilities for Short-Warning Conflicts*. Santa Monica, CA: RAND, 2000.

Halper, Stefan, and Jonathan Clarke. *America Alone: The Neoconservatives and the Global Order*. Cambridge, UK: Cambridge University Press, 2004.

Hamilton, Daniel S., ed. *Transatlantic Transformations: Equipping NATO for the 21st Century*. Washington, DC: Center for Transatlantic Relations, Johns Hopkins University, 2004.

Held, David et al. *Global Transformations: Politics, Economics, and Culture*. Stanford, CA: Stanford University Press, 1999.

Hillestad, Richard et al. *Modeling for Campaign Analysis: Lessons for the Next Generation of Models*. Santa Monica, CA: RAND, 1996.

Hillier, Frederick, and Gerald Lieberman. *Introduction to Operations Research*. 7th ed. New York: McGraw-Hill, 2002.

Hitch, Charles J. *Decision-Making for Defense*. Berkeley: University of California Press, 1967.

———, and Roland N. McKean. *The Economics of Defense in the Nuclear Age*. Cambridge, MA: Harvard University Press, 1963.

Hughes, Wayne P., Jr., ed. *Military Modeling for Decision Making*. Alexandria, VA: Military Operations Research Society, 1997.

Holbrooke, Richard. *To End a War*. New York: Random House, 1998.

Huntington, Samuel P. *The Clash of Civilizations and the Remaking of World Order*. New York: Simon and Schuster, 1996.

———. *The Third Wave: Democratization in the Late Twentieth Century*. Norman, OK: University of Oklahoma Press, 1993.

International Institute for Strategic Studies. *The Military Balance, 2003–2004*. London: International Institute for Strategic Studies, 2003.

International Monetary Fund. *World Economic Outlook*. Washington, DC: International Monetary Fund, 1999.

Jackson, Paul et al. *Jane's All the World's Aircraft: 2003–2004*. Surrey, UK: Jane's Information Group Ltd., Sentinel House, 2003.

Johnson, Stuart et al. *New Challenges, New Tools for Defense Decisionmaking*. Santa Monica, CA: RAND, 2003.

Kaplan, Fred. *The Wizards of Armageddon*. New York: Simon and Schuster, 1983.

Kaplan, Robert D. *The Coming Anarchy: Shattering the Dreams of the Post–Cold War*. New York: Vintage Books, 2000.

Kaufmann, William W. *The McNamara Strategy*. New York: Harper and Row, 1964.

———. *Defense in the 1980s*. Washington, DC: Brookings, 1981.

———. *The 1986 Defense Budget*. Washington, DC: Brookings, 1985.

———. *A Reasonable Defense*. Washington, DC: Brookings, 1986.

———. *Glasnost, Perestroika, and U.S. Defense Spending*. Washington, DC: Brookings, 1990.

Keeney, Ralph, and Howard Raiffa. *Decisions with Multiple Objectives: Preferences and Value Tradeoffs*. New York: John Wiley and Sons, 1976.

Kegley, Charles W., Jr., and Gregory Raymond. *A Multipolar Peace? Great-Power Politics in the Twenty-first Century*. New York: St. Martin's Press, 1994.

Kennedy, Paul. *Preparing for the Twenty-first Century*. New York: Random House, 1993.

Keohane, Robert O., ed. *Neorealism and Its Critics*. New York: Columbia University Press, 1986.

Khalilzad, Zalmay et al. *Strategic Appraisal 1997: Strategy and Defense Planning for the 21ˢᵗ Century*. Santa Monica, CA: RAND, 1997.

Kitcher, Philip. *The Advancement of Science: Science Without Legend, Objectivity Without Illusions*. New York: Oxford University Press, 1993.

Kissinger, Henry. *Diplomacy*. New York: Simon and Schuster, 1994.

———. *Does American Need a Foreign Policy? Toward a Diplomacy for the 21ˢᵗ Century*. New York: Simon and Schuster, 2001.

———. *Years of Upheaval*. Boston: Little, Brown, 1982.

Krugman, Paul, and Maurice Obstfeld. *International Economics: Theory and Policy*. 4ᵗʰ ed. Reading, MA: Addison-Wesley, 1997.

Kugler, Richard L. *Changes Ahead: Future Directions for the U.S. Overseas Military Presence*. Santa Monica, CA: RAND, 1998.

———. *Commitment to Purpose: How Alliance Partnership Won the Cold War*. Santa Monica, CA: RAND, 1993.

———. *Toward a Dangerous World: U.S. National Security Strategy for the Coming Turbulence*. Santa Monica, CA: RAND, 1995.

———. *NATO's Future Conventional Defense Strategy in Central Europe: Theater Employment Doctrine for the Post–Cold War Era*. Santa Monica, CA: RAND, 1992.

———, and Ellen L. Frost. *The Global Century: Globalization and National Security*, vols. I and II . Washington, DC: National Defense University Press, 2001.

Kuhn, Thomas S. *The Structure of Scientific Revolutions*. 2ᵈ ed. Chicago: University of Chicago Press, 1970.

Lambeth, Benjamin S. *NATO's Air War for Kosovo*. Santa Monica, CA: RAND, 2001.

Lawrence, Richard D., and Jeffrey Record. *U.S. Force Structure in NATO: An Alternative*. Washington, DC: Brookings, 1974.

Lewis, Bernard. *The Middle East: A Brief History of the Last 2,000 Years*. New York: Touchstone, 1995.

Lo, Bobo. *Vladimir Putin and the Evolution of Russian Foreign Policy*. London: Oxford University Press, 2003.

Macgregor, Douglas A. *Breaking the Phalanx: A New Design for Landpower in the 21ˢᵗ Century*. Westport, CT, and London: Praeger, 1997.

———. *Transformation Under Fire: Revolutionizing How America Fights*. Westport, CT, and London: Praeger, 2003.

Macrae, Duncan, Jr., and Dale Whittington. *Expert Advice for Policy Choice: Analysis and Discourse*. Washington, DC: Georgetown University Press, 1997.

Mako, William P. *U.S. Ground Forces and the Defense of Central Europe*. Washington, DC: Brookings, 1983.

Mansfield, Edwin. *Micro-Economics: Theory and Application*. 5ᵗʰ ed. New York: W.W. Norton, 1985.

Massie, Robert K. *Castles of Steel: Britain, Germany, and the Winning of the Great War at Sea*. New York: Random House, 2003.

McCarthy, James. *Transformation Study Report, Executive Summary: Transforming Military Operational Capabilities*. Washington, DC: Department of Defense, 2001.

McKercher, B.J.C., and Michael Hennsey. *The Operational Art: Development in the Theories of War*. New York: Praeger, 1966.

McPherson, James M. *The Battle Cry of Freedom*. New York: Oxford University Press, 1988.

Mead, Walter. *Power, Terror, Peace and War: America's Grand Strategy in a World at Risk*. New York: Alfred A. Knopf, 2004.

Mearsheimer, John J. "Numbers, Strategy, and the European Balance." *International Security* 12, no. 1 (Spring 1988).

————. *The Tragedy of Great Power Politics*. New York: W.W. Norton, 2001.

Mendenhall, William. *Introduction to Probability and Statistics*. Boston: Duxbury Press, 1983.

Metz, Steven et al. *Revising the Two MTW Force Shaping Paradigm*. Carlisle, PA: Strategic Studies Institute, U.S. Army War College, 2001.

Missile Defense Agency. *Fiscal Year 2004/2005 Biennial Budget Estimates Submission*. Washington, DC: Department of Defense, 2003.

Moore, Barrington, Jr. *Social Origins of Dictatorship and Democracy: Lord and Peasant in the Making of the Modern World*. Boston: Beacon Press, 1966.

Morgan, Bruce. *An Introduction to Bayesian Statistical Decision Processes*. Englewood Cliffs, NJ: Prentice-Hall, 1968.

Motz, Lloyd, and Jefferson Hane Weaver. *The Story of Physics*. New York: Avon Books, 1989.

Murray, Williamson, and Robert H. Scales. *The Iraq War: A Military History*. Cambridge, MA: Harvard University Press, 2003.

Ochmanek, David et al. *To Find and Not To Yield: How Advances in Information and Firepower Can Transform Theater Warfare*. Santa Monica, CA: RAND, 1998.

O'Hanlon, Michael, and Mike Mochizuki. *Crisis on the Korean Peninsula: How to Deal with a Nuclear North Korea*. New York: McGraw-Hill, 2003.

O'Hanlon, Michael. "A Flawed Masterpiece." *Foreign Affairs* 81, no. 3 (May/June 2002).

————. *Defense Planning for the Late 1990s: Beyond the Desert Storm Framework*. Washington, DC: Brookings, 1995.

————. *Technological Change and the Future of Warfare*. Washington, DC: Brookings, 2000.

Osgood, Robert E. *NATO: The Entangling Alliance*. Chicago: The University of Chicago Press, 1962.

Pirnie, Bruce, and Sam B. Gardiner. *An Objectives-Based Approach to Military Campaign Analysis*. Santa Monica, CA: RAND, 1996.

Pollack, Jonathan D., and Young Koo Cha. *A New Alliance for the Next Century: The Future of U.S.-Korean Cooperation*. Santa Monica, CA: RAND, 1995.

Pollack, Kenneth M. *The Persian Puzzle: The Conflict Between Iran and America*. New York: Random House, 2004.

————. *The Threatening Storm: The Case for Invading Iraq*. New York: Random House, 2002.

Posen, Barry R. "Is NATO Decisively Outnumbered?" *International Security* 12, no. 1 (Spring 1988).

Quade, E.S., and W.L. Boucher, eds. *Systems Analysis and Policy Planning: Applications in Defense*. Chicago: American Elsevier Publishing Company, 1968.

Quanbeck, Alton, and Barry M. Blechman. *Strategic Forces: Issues for the Mid-Seventies*. Washington, DC: Brookings, 1973.

Quandt, William B. *Peace Process: American Diplomacy and the Arab-Israeli Conflict Since 1967*. Washington, DC: Brookings, 2000.

Quinlan, Joseph. "The U.S. Trade Deficit: A Dangerous Obsession," *Foreign Affairs* 83, no. 1 (May/June 2002).

Radelet, Steven. "Bush and Foreign Aid." *Foreign Affairs* 82, no. 5 (September/October 2003).

Riggs, James L. *Economic Decision Models for Engineers and Managers*. New York: McGraw-Hill, 1968.

Rumsfeld, Donald. *Report of the Quadrennial Defense Review*. Washington, DC: Department of Defense, 2001.

————. "Transforming the Military." *Foreign Affairs* 83, no. 1 (May/June 2002).

Simon, Jeffrey. *NATO-Warsaw Pact Force Mobilization*. Washington, DC: National Defense University Press, 1988.

Simpkin, Richard. *Race to the Swift: Thoughts on Twenty-first Century Warfare*. London: Brassey's Defence Publishers, 1983.

Slocombe, Walter B. et al. *Missile Defense in Asia.* Washington, DC: The Atlantic Council of the United States, June 2003.

Smith, Edward. *Effects-Based Operations: Applying Network Centric Warfare in Peace, Crisis, and War.* Washington, DC: CCRP Publishing Series, Department of Defense, 2002.

Sokolsky, Richard D. et al. *The United States and the Persian Gulf: Reshaping Security Strategy for the Post-Containment Era.* Washington, DC: National Defense University Press, 2003.

Spinney, Franklin C. *Defense Facts of Life: The Plans/Reality Mismatch.* Boulder, CO: Westview Press, 1985.

Stokey, Edith, and Richard Zeckhauser. *A Primer for Policy Analysis.* New York: W.W. Norton, 1978.

Tangredi, Sam J. et al. *Globalization and Maritime Power.* Washington, DC: National Defense University Press, 2002.

Taylor, James G. *Force-on-Force Attrition Modeling.* Arlington, VA: Military Applications Section, Operations Research Society of America, 1980.

Thomson, David. *Europe Since Napoleon.* New York: Alfred A. Knopf, 1964.

Thurow, Lester. *Head to Head: The Coming Economic Battle Among Japan, Europe, and America.* New York: William Morrow, 1992.

Tow, William T. *Asian-Pacific Strategic Relations: Seeking Convergent Security.* New York: Cambridge University Press, 2003.

Tuchman, Barbara. *The Proud Tower.* New York: Bantam Books, 1967.

U.S. Department of Commerce. International Trade Statistics, 2003.

U.S. Department of Defense. *Joint Operations Concepts.* Washington, DC: U.S. Government Printing Office, 2003.

———. *Joint Vision: 2020.* Washington, DC: U.S. Government Printing Office, 2003.

———. Department of Defense Budget for Fiscal Year 2005: Financial Summary Tables, Part One: Operations Programs; RDT&E Programs; Procurement Programs; Program Acquisition Costs by Weapon Systems. Washington, DC: U.S. Government Printing Office, February 2004.

———. *Soviet Military Power: An Assessment of the Threat.* Washington, DC: Government Printing Office, 1988.

———. Office of the Undersecretary of Defense (Comptroller). National Defense Budget Estimates for FY2004. Washington, DC: Department of Defense, 2003.

———. *Department of Defense Budget for Fiscal Year 2005: Procurement Programs.* Washington, DC: Department of Defense, 2004.

———. Office of Force Transformation. *Military Transformation: A Strategic Approach.* Washington, DC: Department of Defense, 2003.

———. Department of the Air Force. *Air Force Transformation Flight Plan.* Washington, DC: Defense of Defense, 2003.

———. Department of the Army. *Army Force Transformation.* Washington, DC: Department of the Army, 2003.

———. Department of the Navy. *Navy Force Transformation.* Washington, DC: Department of the Navy, 2003.

Van de Walle, Nicolas. *Economic Globalization and Political Stability in Developing Countries.* New York: Rockefeller Brothers Fund, 1998.

Van Evera, Stephen. *Guide to Methods for Students of Political Science.* Ithaca, NY: Cornell University Press, 1997.

Volker, Paul A., and Toyoo Gyohten. *Changing Fortunes: The World's Money and the Threat to American Leadership.* New York: Times Books, 1992.

Von Manstein, Erich. *Lost Victories.* Novato, CA: Presidio Press, 1984.

Von Mellenthin, F.W. *Panzer Battles.* London: Futura, 1979.

Waldrop, M. Mitchell. *Complexity: The Emerging Science at the Edge of Order and Chaos.* New York: Touchstone, 1992.

Wartofsky, Marx W. *Conceptual Foundations of Scientific Thought: An Introduction to the Philosophy of Science.* London: Macmillan, 1968.

Weiner, David L., and Aidan R. Vining. *Policy Analysis: Concepts and Practice.* Upper Saddle River, NJ: Prentice Hall, 1999.

Williams, Michael D. *Acquisition for the 21ˢᵗ Century: The F–22 Development Program.* Washington, DC: National Defense University Press, 1999.

Wolf, Charles et al. *Fault Lines in China's Economic Terrain.* Santa Monica, CA: RAND, 2003.

Wolfe, Thomas W. *Soviet Power and Europe, 1945–1970.* Baltimore, MD: Johns Hopkins University Press, 1970.

Wonnacott, Ronald J., and Thomas H. Wonnacott. *Econometrics.* New York: John H. Wiley and Sons, 1969.

World Bank. *World Development Indicators 2000.* Washington, DC: World Bank, 2000.

———. *World Development Report 2004.* Washington, DC: World Bank, 2004.

World Economic Forum. *The Global Competitiveness Report: 2002–2003.* London: Oxford University Press, 2003.

Yergin, Daniel, and Joseph Stanislaw. *The Commanding Heights: The Battle Between Government and the Marketplace that is Remaking the Modern World.* New York: Touchstone, 1998.

Yost, David S. *NATO Transformed: The Alliance's New Roles in International Security.* Washington, DC: United States Institute of Peace, 1998.

Index

About the Author

Richard L. Kugler is a professional policy analyst and a practitioner and teacher of this book's analytical methods. Currently, he is Distinguished Research Professor in the Center for Technology and National Security Policy at the National Defense University. He advises senior leaders of the Department of Defense and other U.S. Government agencies on national security strategy and defense plans. He is also an adjunct professor of international affairs at Georgetown University, where he teaches graduate courses on defense analysis.

Dr. Kugler holds a PhD from the Massachusetts Institute of Technology, where he studied political science, defense economics, and operations research. He has been a member of the Federal Senior Executive Service since 1981 and is a recipient of multiple decorations and awards for his government service. An original architect of NATO enlargement and the NATO Response Force, he has contributed to many innovations in U.S. national security strategy and defense planning.

Dr. Kugler entered Federal service as an Air Force officer during 1968–1972, including a combat tour in Vietnam. During 1975–1984, he was an analyst and senior executive in the Office of Secretary of Defense (Program Analysis and Evaluation), where he was Director of the European Forces Division. During 1984–1988, he was Director of the Defense Department's Strategic Concepts Development Center, and a statutory adviser to the Secretary of Defense and the Chairman of the Joint Chiefs of Staff. From 1979 to 1988, he also taught defense analysis at George Washington University. During 1988–1997, he was a research leader at RAND and taught defense analysis at the RAND Graduate School. He has been at the National Defense University since 1997.

Dr. Kugler is author of 15 books on U.S. national security strategy and defense policy, plus many articles in *Foreign Affairs*, *Survival*, and other journals. He is also the author of many studies within the U.S. Government. His books include *Commitment to Purpose: How Alliance Partnership Won the Cold War*, *Toward a Dangerous World: U.S. National Security Strategy for the Coming Turbulence*, *Enlarging NATO: The Russia Factor*, and (with Ellen Frost) *The Global Century: Globalization and National Security* (two volumes). He lives in Fairfax, Virginia, with his wife, Sharon A. Stapleton.